TCP/IP

Primer Plus

Heather Osterloh

201 West 103rd St., Indianapolis, Indiana, 46290 USA

TCP/IP Primer Plus

International Standard Book Number: 0-672-32208-0

Library of Congress Catalog Card Number: 2001093492

Printed in the United States of America

First Printing: September 2001

04   03   02   4   3   2

Trademarks

Warning and Disclaimer

ASSOCIATE PUBLISHER
Jeff Koch

ACQUISITIONS EDITOR
Katie Purdum

DEVELOPMENT EDITOR
Mark Renfrow

MANAGING EDITOR
Matt Purcell

PROJECT EDITOR
Christina Smith
Emily Morgan

COPY EDITOR
Rachel Lopez

INDEXER
Sandra Henselmeier

PROOFREADER
Kelly Thompson
Plan-it Publishing

TECHNICAL EDITOR
Michelle Truman

TEAM COORDINATOR
Vicki Harding

INTERIOR DESIGNER
Gary Adair

COVER DESIGNER
Alan Clements

PAGE LAYOUT
Michelle Mitchell

CONTENTS AT A GLANCE

INTRODUTION   **1**

CHAPTER 1   Overview of Industry Models and Standards 3

CHAPTER 2   IP Addressing 33

CHAPTER 3   Network Layer/Internet Protocols 61

CHAPTER 4   Address Resolution 89

CHAPTER 5   IP Routing 125

CHAPTER 6   Routing Protocols 137

CHAPTER 7   Transport/Host-to-Host Layer 203

CHAPTER 8   Transmission Control Protocol (TCP) 211

CHAPTER 9   User Datagram Protocol (UDP) 241

CHAPTER 10   Upper-layer Protocols 249

CHAPTER 11   Telnet 257

CHAPTER 12   File Transfer Protocol (FTP) 269

CHAPTER 13   Simple Mail Transfer Protocol (SMTP) 287

CHAPTER 14   Name Resolution 299

CHAPTER 15   HyperText Transfer Protocol (HTTP) 321

CHAPTER 16   Trivial File Transfer Protocol (TFTP) 335

CHAPTER 17   Simple Network Management Protocol (SNMP) 345

CHAPTER 18   Open Network Computing Protocols 353

APPENDIX A   Request for Comments (RFCs) 371

APPENDIX B   Abbreviations and Acronyms 423

APPENDIX C   TCP/UDP Port Numbers 431

APPENDIX D   Glossary 433

APPENDIX E   Answers 465

INDEX   **481**

TABLE OF CONTENTS

INTRODUCTION 1

CHAPTER 1: Overview of Industry Models and Standards 3
Overview of the OSI Reference Model 3
Overview of the Department of Defense Model 5
Benefits of the OSI's Layered Design 6
Layer Functions Clarified 6
Well-defined Framework for Vendors 7
Reduced Networking Complexity 7
Promotes Specialization 7
General Description of OSI Layers 7
Application Layer 9
Presentation Layer 10
Session Layer 10
Transport Layer 11
Network Layer 12
Data Link Layer 12
Physical Layer 13
Data Link Architecture and Topologies 14
Ethernet and IEEE 802.3 14
Slow Ethernet 21
Fast Ethernet 21
Gigabit Ethernet 22
Token-Ring and IEEE 802.5 22
FDDI and ANSI X3T9.5 25
Wide Area Networking (WAN) Technologies 25
WAN Encapsulation Protocols 29
Request For Comments (RFCs) 30
Internet Versus intranet 31
Groups Responsible for Internet Technology 31
Summary 31
Review Questions 32

CHAPTER 2: IP Addressing 33
Understanding Binary to Decimal Conversion 33
IP Addressing 35
Address Classes 35
Network and Subnet Masks 40
Subnetting and Examples 44
Network Address Translation (NAT) 55

Static 57
Dynamic 57
Summary 58
Review Questions 58

CHAPTER 3: Network Layer/Internet Protocols .61
IP 61
IP Header 62
ICMP 73
ICMP Header and Message Formats 75
Codes 75
Checksum 76
ICMP Message Types 77
Ping: Echo Request and Reply—Types 8 and 0 77
Destination Unreachable—Type 3 78
Source Quench—Type 4 82
Redirect—Type 5 83
Router Advertisement and Solicitation—Types
9 and 10 84
Time Exceeded—Type 11 84
Parameter Problem—Type 12 85
Timestamp Request and Reply—Types 13 and 14 86
Information Request and Reply—Types 15 and 16 86
Address Mask Request and Reply—Types 17 and 18 86
Summary 86
Review Questions 87

CHAPTER 4: Address Resolution 89
ARP 91
ARP Operation 91
ARP Cache Mechanisms 94
Proxy ARP 95
Proxy ARP Operation 95
ARP Header 96
Hardware Type 97
Protocol Type 98
Length of Hardware Address 98
Length of Protocol Address 98
Opcode 99
Sender's Hardware Address 99
Sender's Protocol Address 99
Target Hardware Address 99
Target Protocol Address 99

RARP 99
RARP Operation 100
    ARP Versus RARP Operation 101
    Disadvantages of RARP 102
RARP Header 103
    Hardware 103
    Protocol Type 103
    Length of Hardware Address 103
    Length of Protocol Address 103
    Opcode 103
    Sender's Hardware Address 104
    Sender's Protocol Address 104
    Target Hardware Address 104
    Target Protocol Address 104
BOOTP 104
    BOOTP header 105
    BOOTP Request and Reply 109
DHCP (Dynamic Host Configuration Protocol) 110
    Allocating Configuration Information 111
    DHCP Messages 111
    DHCP Message Exchanges 112
    DHCP Header 119
Summary 122
Review Questions 123

CHAPTER 5: IP Routing 125
IP Routing Basics 125
    Directly Connected Interface 126
    Static Routing 126
    Default Routing 127
    Dynamic Routing 128
Routing Protocols and Best Path 129
    Distance Vector Routing Protocols 129
    Link State Routing Protocols 131
    Hybrid Routing Protocols 133
Summary 134
Review Questions 134

CHAPTER 6: Routing Protocols 137
Introduction to Routing Protocols .137
RIP 138
    RIPv1 139
    The RIPv1 Header and Fields 142

Disadvantages of RIPv1 144
RIP Timers 147
RIP and Demand Circuits 148
RIPv2 150
OSPF 152
OSPF Characteristics 154
OSPF Databases 155
OSPF Operation 156
The LSA Header 160
OSPF Router States 162
OSPF Router Types 167
OSPF Operation Over Various Data Link Architectures 167
Area Types 170
Standard OSPF Fields 173
Additional Headers 175
IGRP 181
IGRP Networks 182
EIGRP 184
EIGRP Operation 184
EIGRP Packet Types 187
BGP 187
IGPs Versus EGPs 188
BGP Routers 189
BGP Operation 190
The BGP Header and Fields 191
Path Attributes 194
BGPv3 Versus BGPv4 198
Summary 199
Review Questions 200
CHAPTER 7: Transport/Host-to-Host Layer 203
Transport Layer Protocols 203
Connection-Oriented Protocols 204
Connectionless Protocols 206
Connectionless Versus Connection-oriented Protocols 206
Ports and Sockets 207
Summary 209
Review Questions 209
CHAPTER 8: Transmission Control Protocol (TCP) 211
Introduction to TCP 211
TCP Header 212
Source Port 213
Destination Port 213

Sequence Number 214

Acknowledgement Number 214

Data Offset 215

Reserved 216

Control Flags—6 Bits 216

Window 217

Checksum—2 Bytes 217

Urgent Pointer 217

TCP Options—Variable Length 217

Fundamentals of TCP Operation 218

Connection Setup and Teardown 219

Multiplexing 219

Data Transfer 220

Flow Control 221

Reliability 221

Precedence and Security 222

Connection-oriented Characteristics 223

Session Setup 223

Session Teardown 227

Sequencing and Acknowledgements .230

Keepalives 234

Flow Control 234

TCP Ports 237

Summary 238

Review Questions 238

CHAPTER 9: User Datagram Protocol (UDP) 241

UDP Operation 242

UDP Applications 243

UDP Ports 244

UDP Header 244

Source Port 245

Destination Port 245

Length Field 245

Checksum 246

Summary 247

Review Questions 247

CHAPTER 10: Upper-layer Protocols 249

Introduction to Upper-layer Protocols .249

Application Layer 251

World Wide Web and HTTP (Hypertext Transfer Protocol) 251

E-mail and SMTP (Simple Mail Transfer Protocol) 252

Telnet (Telecommunications Network) 252
File Transfer 253
Presentation Layer 253
Session Layer 254
NetBIOS (Network Basic Input Output System) 254
NFS (Network File System) and ONC Protocols 255
Summary 255
Review Questions 255

CHAPTER 11: Telnet 257
Remote Access 257
Basic Services 259
Network Virtual Terminal 259
Telnet Commands 261
Telnet Options 264
Summary 267
Review Questions 268

CHAPTER 12: File Transfer Protocol (FTP) 269
Introduction to File Transfer 269
FTP Session 270
Data Representation 274
FTP Data Types 275
FTP Data Structures 277
FTP Transmission Modes 278
FTP Commands 278
FTP Replies 281
FTP Operation and Examples 282
Anonymous FTP 284
Summary 284
Review Questions 285

CHAPTER 13: Simple Mail Transfer Protocol (SMTP) 287
X.400 Naming Model 289
Message Transfer Agents (MTAs) 290
SMTP Format 291
SMTP Commands 292
SMTP Replies 293
MIME 295
Summary 296
Review Questions 297

CHAPTER 14: Name Resolution 299

    Why Do We Need Name Resolution? 299

        Namespace 300

    DNS Delegation of Authority 301

        Internet Domain Names 304

    Queries and Mappings 305

    Caching 305

    Domain Server Message Format 306

        Identifier (ID) 306

        QR 306

        Opcode 306

        Flags 307

        Rcode 307

        Answers and Questions Headers 309

        Domain Name Types 310

    DNS Examples 310

    NetBios 313

        NetBIOS Over TCP/IP 314

        Node Types 315

        WINS (Windows Internet Name Server) 317

        NetBIOS Examples 317

        Summary 319

        Review Questions 319

CHAPTER 15: Hypertext Transfer Protocol (HTTP) 321

    HTTP and the World Wide Web 321

    HTTP Features 322

    HTTP Components 322

    HTTP Sessions 324

    HTTP Message Format 325

        Generic Start Line 326

        General Header 326

        Message Headers (Request, Response, or Entity) 328

        Empty line (CRLF) 330

        Message Body 330

    HTTP Response Messages, Status, and Error Codes 330

    HTTP Error Messages 332

    Summary 333

    Review Questions 334

CHAPTER 16: Trivial File Transfer Protocol (TFTP) .335

Introduction to File Transfer Protocols 335

TFTP Packet Types 336

RRQ and WRQ Packets 337

Data Packets 338

ACK Packet 338

Error Packets 339

TFTP Operation 340

TFTP Extensions 342

OACK Packet 343

Summary 343

Review Questions 343

CHAPTER 17: SNMP (Simple Network Management Protocol) 345

Introduction to Network Management 345

SNMP 346

SNMP Managers 347

SNMP Agents 347

Proxy 348

SNMP Message Format 348

Version 349

Community Name 349

SNMP Protocol Data Units (PDUs) 350

Summary 351

Review Questions 352

CHAPTER 18: Open Network Computing Protocols 353

Introduction to Open Network Computing Protocols 353

NFS Features 354

NFS Operation 356

NFS Client 357

NFS Server 358

XDR 359

RPC 360

Call Message 361

Reply Message 366

NFS Examples 367

Summary 369

Questions 369

APPENDIX A: RFCs Organized by Chapter 371

Chapter 1: Overview of Industry Models and Standards 371

Chapter 2: IP Addressing 371

Chapter 3: Network Layer/Internet Protocols 371
Chapter 4: Address Resolution 374
Chapter 5: IP Routing 375
Chapter 6: Routing Protocols 382
Chapter 7: Transport/Host-to-Host Layer 389
Chapter 8: Transmission Control Protocol (TCP) 389
Chapter 9: User Datagram Protocol (UDP) 391
Chapter 11: Telnet 391
Chapter 12: File Transfer Protocol (FTP) 396
Chapter 13: Simple Mail Transfer Protocol (SMTP) 398
Chapter 14: Name Resolution 410
Chapter 15: Hypertext Transfer Protocol (HTTP) 414
Chapter 16: Trivial File Transfer Protocol (TFTP) 415
Chapter 17: Simple Network Management Protocol (SNMP) 416
Chapter 18: Open Network Computing Protocols 421

APPENDIX B: Abbreviations and Acronyms 423
A 423
B 423
C 424
D 424
E 425
F 425
G–H 425
I 426
J–L 426
M 427
N 427
O 428
P 428
Q 428
R 429
S 429
T 430
U 430
V 430
W 430
X–Z 430

APPENDIX C: TCP/UDP Port Numbers 431

APPENDIX D: Glossary 433
Numeric 433
A 434

B 435
C 437
D 439
E 442
F 443
G 445
H 445
I 446
J–K 447
L 447
M 448
N 450
O 451
P 451
Q 454
R 454
S 456
T 460
U 462
V 462
W 463
X–Y 464
Z 464
APPENDIX E: Answers 465
Chapter 1 465
Chapter 2 465
Chapter 3 466
Chapter 4 467
Chapter 5 467
Chapter 6 468
Chapter 7 471
Chapter 8 471
Chapter 9 472
Chapter 10 473
Chapter 11 473
Chapter 12 474
Chapter 13 475
Chapter 14 476
Chapter 15 477
Chapter 16 477

Chapter 17 478
Chapter 18 479
INDEX 481

ABOUT THE AUTHOR

Heather Osterloh has earned industry recognition as a Cisco Certified Network Associate (CCNA), Cisco Certified Network Professional (CCNP), Cisco Certified Design Associate (CCDA), Cisco Certified Design Professional (CCDP), Network Associate Sniffer trainer, Certified Network Expert (CNX) for Ethernet and Token Ring, Novell CNI/ECNE, Microsoft Certified Systems Engineer (MCSE) and Microsoft Certified Trainer (MCT). She also holds her Cisco Certified Internetworking Expert (CCIE), written portion and is currently waiting to take the practical lab exam.

Having spent the last 15 years training and consulting worldwide, Heather is an acknowledged leader in the networking industry. Author of one book, *CCNA 2.0 Prep Kit 640-507 Routing and Switching,* and of several popular Microsoft, Cisco, and Novell video series geared towards the busy professional, Heather continues to produce material that helps educate people about the world of networking.

Heather also has lectured at the University of California, Berkeley; NetuCon's NetWare User Conference in San Jose; and the University of Puerto Rico; and was president of IT Academy, LLC for three years.

Heather lives in Northern California with her husband Kirk and her dogs, Cocoa and Kato.

DEDICATION

In memory of my grandfather and grandmother, Anthony and Nina.

ACKNOWLEDGMENTS

For a project of this magnitude, there are many people to thank:

First, Sams Publishing for giving me this opportunity to write this book. And all the people at Sams that made this book happen, especially William Brown, Mark Renfrow, Christina Smith, Rachel Bell, Kitty Jarrett, and Michelle Truman, all of whom went beyond the call of duty to support me.

My amazing team, Jason Burita and Christine Sepiol, who managed to keep me focused and polished my chicken scratches into manageable text.

The team at IT Academy, Heidi, Beverly, and Bryce—without their additional support and sacrifices, this project would not have been possible.

Laura Chappell, who first inspired me by introducing me to the world of network certification.

To all my students, who continue to challenge me in class and inspire me to write the best possible book.

To my parents, Rita and Karl, who have always been supportive and behind me 100 percent.

My dogs, Cocoa and Kato, who jumped up on my laptop while I wrote, forcing me to take a much needed break and providing a little comic relief.

And most important, my husband Kirk, for having patience with me during the panic attacks, stressful deadlines, and lack of sleep that went into completing this book. His constant support endears my heart and makes me realize that I can accomplish anything. Thanks honey.

TELL US WHAT YOU THINK!

As the reader of this book, *you* are our most important critic and commentator. We value your opinion and want to know what we're doing right, what we could do better, what areas you'd like to see us publish in, and any other words of wisdom you're willing to pass our way.

As an Associate Publisher for Sams Publishing, I welcome your comments. You can fax, e-mail, or write me directly to let me know what you did or didn't like about this book—as well as what we can do to make our books stronger.

Please note that I cannot help you with technical problems related to the topic of this book, and that due to the high volume of mail I receive, I might not be able to reply to every message.

When you write, please be sure to include this book's title and author's name, as well as your name and phone or fax number. I will carefully review your comments and share them with the author and editors who worked on the book.

Fax: 317-581-4770

E-mail: feedback@samspublishing.com

Mail: Jeff Koch
          Associate Publisher
          Sams Publishing
          201 West 103rd Street
          Indianapolis, IN 46290 USA

INTRODUCTION

Franz Kafka once wrote, "A book must be the axe for the frozen sea inside of us." This book will help you break through the ice, enabling you to understand the world of TCP/IP without being as obscure as a Kafka quote. After all, it is not rocket science—just a few routers, keyboards, PCs and protocols that make everything work…or in some cases, not work. In this book we give you enough information to understand what works and what doesn't, and hopefully remove the mystery from networking.

This book unfolds in a logical order, starting with background on the OSI and DoD models, focusing on the Data Link and Physical layers. The book then proceeds up the OSI model and discusses the various TCP/IP protocols that reside at those layers. At the end you should have a solid foundational knowledge of all the major protocols that reside in the TCP/IP suite. However, you also can use the book in a nonlinear manner, because it references chapters where other protocols or ideas are covered.

Throughout the book, we have tried to involve the reader as much as possible. Often books discuss TCP/IP as theory or as if no human is involved in internetworking. As you are aware, this is simply not the case. It is you who configures the router or types an e-mail to your coworker. It is for this reason that we often use "you," the user and reader, in an active manner; we feel involving you helps you learn.

We also have included many screen shots. In the text, we will refer to these screen shots as "a screen capture as seen through a Sniffer" or "Sniffer Network Analyzer." A Sniffer screen shot merely captures frames (network traffic) in a way that is readable and understandable to you. In short, a Sniffer is a networking troubleshooting tool. However, for this book's purposes, it provides us with a window to what occurs in the internetwork—what a protocol is doing.

Often the Sniffer screen shots will show a particular frame; this frame will be highlighted. The output, or what is contained below the frame portion of the screen capture, details the header information. From this header information, you can gather various information, from IP addresses, to Opcodes, to what protocol it is. In addition, these screen shots often will be paired with clinical diagrams of headers. The clinical diagrams portray the protocols in a way that is defined by an RFC (Request for Comment); however, a screen shot details a protocol in a more realistic manner. We feel that showing both gives you broader, more realistic hands-on experience.

In this book, you also will see RFC references (and then a number; for example, RFC 1583). RFCs are generally dry, factual documentation and specifications of TCP/IP protocols. Rather than merely repeating what an RFC says, we reference it and then use a more exciting and accessible language to describe it. However, we have provided you with a list of RFCs by chapter in Appendix A if you want to research the various RFCs. RFCs can be found free on the Web; the full details are contained within this book.

Hopefully, we have given you enough background to aid you in reading this book. However, if you have any additional questions regarding the book, please feel free to contact Heather Osterloh by e-mail at `heather@itacademy.com`. She will gladly answer any of your questions as promptly as possible.

CHAPTER 1

OVERVIEW OF INDUSTRY MODELS AND STANDARDS

You will learn about the following in this chapter:

- The OSI model
- The DoD model
- Seven-layer Architecture
- Network Architecture and Topologies
- Wide Area Network Technologies
- Request For Comments

Overview of the OSI Reference Model

In the early days of networking only proprietary systems and protocols existed. Operating systems developed by large companies, such as IBM's SNA and Digital Equipment Corporation's DECNet, included proprietary protocol suites. These operating systems and their corresponding protocols primarily facilitated mini- and mainframe network communication; however, these companies made no provisions for interconnection or to allow for communication with outside systems. When IBM developed SNA and Digital Equipment Corporation developed DECNet, no one anticipated the prevalence of the mixed computing environments that exist today; thus only systems using compatible protocols and operating systems could communicate with each other and exchange data.

As you can imagine, these different proprietary systems had a hard time communicating with each other, if they were able to at all. It soon became necessary to create some type of protocol translation to enable companies to communicate and share information with one another. The Department of Defense (DoD) developed an intercommunication model in the early 1970s, which became the source model for the TCP/IP protocol suite.

However, this model has been largely replaced with the OSI Reference Model released in the early 1980s. The OSI Reference Model consists of a seven-layer architecture that defines the different networking functions that occur at each layer (see Figure 1.1). Later in this chapter you will find a further discussion of the DoD model and how it maps to the OSI model. We refer to both models throughout the book when describing the purpose and function of each protocol within the TCP/IP suite.

FIGURE 1.1
The OSI Reference Model defines the seven layers and their functions.

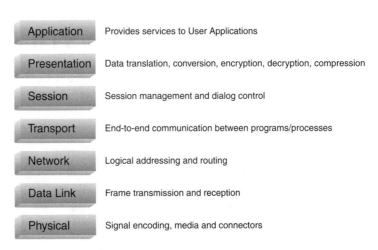

OSI Model and Functions

Application — Provides services to User Applications

Presentation — Data translation, conversion, encryption, decryption, compression

Session — Session management and dialog control

Transport — End-to-end communication between programs/processes

Network — Logical addressing and routing

Data Link — Frame transmission and reception

Physical — Signal encoding, media and connectors

The OSI Reference Model enables both similar and dissimilar systems to communicate seamlessly by providing an architectural framework for vendors and manufacturers to follow when designing their hardware, protocols, and operating system environments. This provides engineers and developers with standard specifications for system intercommunication. It also provides for the use of different protocols in different network architectures and lower-layered media types. Although seamless communication is not always achieved, the OSI Reference Model considers it the primary goal.

Before the OSI model, the protocols in existence did not lend themselves easily to interconnectivity. In most cases retrofitting these protocols would be infeasible. As such, most protocols and hardware currently implemented by vendors and manufacturers conform to the guidelines of the OSI model. The smooth, swift exchange of data and seamless interconnectivity required in today's mixed computing environments depends on manufacturers and vendors adhering to a standardized reference model.

The OSI model is a *conceptual* framework. It consists of a series of standards defining what should happen and how to package data so it can go out on the wire to a remote host. The logical layers of the model do not specifically define what needs to be performed at each layer; they simply define which functions reside at each respective layer. How the functionality occurs at each layer depends on the vendor or the manufacturer that creates or implements the hardware or the protocols. Individual manufacturers have the liberty of interpreting and deciding how closely they wish to adhere to the specifications for a given layer. The end results do not always create seamless compatibility between dissimilar devices; however, this framework and model provides the best resource available for this compatibility.

The OSI model consists of the following seven (from top to bottom):

- Application

- Presentation

- Session

- Transport

- Network

- Data Link

- Physical

Overall, each layer has distinct functions that must occur within it to prepare data to go out on the wire to communicate with a remote station. The vendor can determine the specifics within the general functions; that is, the manufacturer or developer defines how those specifics work, so vendors need to concern themselves with only their part of the puzzle. As long as an organization or vendor follows the guidelines laid out by the ISO for a developer's particular layer, the result is a product that can easily integrate with other products that follow the model.

Keep in mind that you use the OSI only when you package data for transmission to connect to a remote host, similar or dissimilar (in other words, one using the same protocols and same operating system that you are—or are not). The OSI Reference Model is not used when accessing data locally on a system. For example, to access file and print services, you would simply access as usual a local computer's hard drive and open a local application. In a situation such as this, no user intervention is required to access the data. However, if you want to perform that same function on a remote host you must somehow send a message to the other device to access files or a printer, and have that device respond to you by transferring the data.

To redirect the request of accessing a file or print services, you need a redirector. The redirector redirects this request to the remote host for processing. The remote host prepares the request for transmission across the internetwork by adding header and control information so the destination knows what to do with the data and how to respond.

Overview of the Department of Defense Model

The history of the DoD model began long before the OSI model, which has since superseded it. Beginning in 1973 the Department of Defense Advanced Research Projects Agency (DARPA) began a program to formulate technologies that could interlink various kinds of packet networks. This research was called the "Internetting Project" and, as you might surmise from the name, resulted in today's Internet.

The model developed by DARPA as an initial standard by which the core Internet protocols would conform became known as the DoD model. This four-layer model consists of the following (from top to bottom):

- The Process layer

- The Host-to-host layer

- The Internet layer

- The Network Access layer

As shown in Figure 1.2, the DoD model maps roughly to the OSI model from top to bottom.

FIGURE 1.2
The DoD model consists of four distinct layers.

DOD Model

Benefits of the OSI's Layered Design

The layered design of the OSI Reference Model provides benefits for manufacturers and software developers, and for those who offer support and troubleshooting, such as network engineers. The OSI model's benefits can be broken down as follows:

- Makes general functions of each layer clear.

- Provides a well-defined framework for vendors to use in writing applications and developing hardware.

- Reduces complexity of networking by compartmentalizing model functions.

- Promotes interoperability between dissimilar networks and protocols.

- Simplifies troubleshooting by reducing the focus for locating network complications.

- Accelerates evolution in the industry by facilitating specialization.

Layer Functions Clarified

By narrowing the scope of a layer's responsibility, the OSI model eases the development and support burdens that manufacturers and network engineers address in their work. Additionally, the minimized responsibility of each layer eliminates the need to reinvent the boundaries of a product or protocol for a desired use. By having the layers clarified, vendors can develop products that work specifically for one layer; not seven. This enables them to specialize in certain areas and reduces the complexity of the network.

Well-defined Framework for Vendors

Vendors can write their specifications to one layer or multiple layers. A layered approach removes much of the complexity and allows vendors to focus on and specialize in only their particular layer of the OSI model. This also makes for better interoperability between systems and creates an open environment that allows multiple protocols to coexist. For example, a vendor that creates a Network Interface Card (NIC) can simply work with the Data Link layer of the OSI model.

The modular design of the OSI enables vendors to produce specialized products. Because they don't need to address all functions from top to bottom they can focus on a particular layer and function of the OSI model. This makes it easier for vendors to write and release hardware or software. Additionally, despite the variation among vendors in adherence to each layer's conceptual guidelines, the very existence of a standardized model increases both the current level of interoperability between systems and the likelihood that future protocols and products will coexist harmoniously on the same network.

Reduced Networking Complexity

The layered approach also allows the network engineer to apply a divide-and-conquer approach to troubleshooting. Once you know what should happen at each layer, you can identify which function does not work properly based on which layer is not performing its functions. The protocol or piece of hardware should function according to the specifications defined at that layer.

Perhaps more important, the model offers seven smaller pieces to work with rather than forcing us to focus on the whole structure to locate problems. If a particular layer does not function properly you can use that model to isolate and compartmentalize the problem, which makes troubleshooting much easier. Overall, network operations function as simpler pieces rather than a single, more complicated entity.

Promotes Specialization

Finally, the use of a widely accepted, industry-wide set of guidelines for networking inspires even faster and more reliable programs and protocols. Knowing they can compete at any layer of the OSI Reference Model to improve on the specifications and performance, vendors push efficiency to the utmost limits. When vendors can focus on meeting the specific standards of only one layer, they are able to specialize in manufacturing products that meet the specific needs of the consumer; for example, a router (Layer 3) for the small office or home office.

General Description of OSI Layers

When you get ready to send data (this could mean anything from an e-mail message to a request to read a file from a remote host), that request needs to be packaged and redirected. The sending system must follow these steps, which are based on the specific functions of the OSI Reference Model:

1. Apply addressing to it

2. Associate protocols with it

3. Modulate it

4. Send it out on the wire

When a system prepares data to be sent out on the wire, a redirector first captures the message, puts its header and control information on it, and sends it down to the next layer. Lower layers in the OSI model provide upper-layer support services. These can include reliable transport services, routing services, and addressing services. The message could be as simple as "Hi" from one user to another; these services still apply.

Each layer in the OSI model helps provide header and control information so that a peer layer in the remote host can remove that header and control information and know what to do with it. Each layer has a distinct role in preparing data to be sent out on the wire to communicate with a peer remote host (see Figure 1.3). All of the steps inherent to these roles appear transparent to the user.

FIGURE 1.3
Each layer of the OSI model adds header and control information used by the corresponding layer at the receiving host.

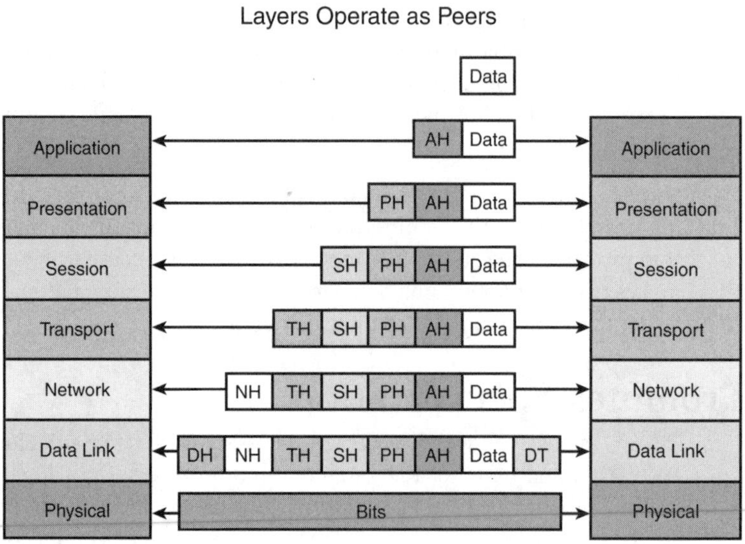

Layers Operate as Peers

When the computer passes data from one layer to the next, each layer adds header or control information to it as the data makes its way down to the Physical layer and the actual physical media (such as the wire or network cable). Each layer simply treats everything handed down as generic upper-layer data. This process is similar to an envelope being placed inside another envelope at each layer.

For example, the Application layer provides header and control information to the peer Application layer at the remote host location. It then passes this header and control information, along with the data down the Presentation layer. The Presentation layer reads the upper layer's information as data. The Presentation layer disregards both the header and control information, and the data of the upper (Application) layer. The Presentation layer adds header and control information for the peer Presentation level at the remote host. In other words, each lower layer (in this case the Presentation layer) ignores the upper layer's control and header information or data. It views it only as data, which it disregards. Each layer only uses its peer layer's control and header information and data at the remote host. Each subsequent layer adds its own header and control information and sends the data down to the next level.

Once the data reaches the Data Link level, the system runs an algorithm called a cyclical redundancy check (CRC) or a frame check sequence (FCS). It then adds the CRC as a trailer to the end of the information to guarantee that the bits being sent match the bits the end host receives. The term *frame* refers to the logical grouping of information that data undergoes at the Data Link layer. From there the data goes out on the wire as electrical or light signals—1s and 0s—and the intended remote host receives the data (see Figure 1.4).

FIGURE 1.4

The receiving host removes headers and trailers before sending it up to the next layer.

Headers and Trailers

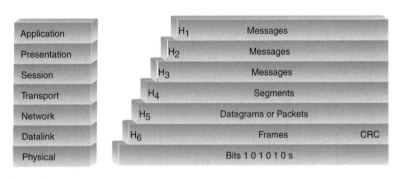

Upon reception, this process is reversed. Each layer removes its header information and passes it up to the next layer, exposing that layer's header and control information and data until it arrives at the Application layer, which strips off its own header and control information and passes the data up. This happens with every single frame that goes out on the wire. Each layer must attach header and control information so the peer layer can identify the upper layer that should receive it next.

Application Layer

The top layer of the OSI model can confuse people because they think it refers to user "applications" such as Word, Excel, PowerPoint, and so on. The Application layer does not refer to the software applications themselves, but rather a window that enables you to provide data access from one application to another across a network, and a window to the OSI Reference Model to prepare your data to be packaged and sent out on the wire.

The Application layer enables user applications to send data across the network. It simply affords access to the lower layers, or provides a window to the OSI model. Remember the Application layer's job is to provide an interface to your protocol stack. Unlike the other OSI layers, this layer does not provide services to any of those other layers; rather it provides access for Application layer services only.

Some of the Application layer services include:

- Applications with network and internetwork services

- File and print services

- E-mail

- Web access and HTTP

- Telnet access on a remote host

- File Transfer Protocol (FTP)

We will discuss all of the preceding processes and more within this book.

Presentation Layer

The Presentation layer provides a common data format across different platforms. It is responsible for the following services:

- Data conversion and translation

- Compression/decompression

- Encryption/decryption

An example of a true Presentation layer protocol is eXternal Data Representation (XDR). Sun MicroSystems uses this protocol in its client/server-based Network File System (NFS) implementation. NFS uses XDR to provide platform independence. XDR actually is incorporated into the programming code. We will discuss NFS and XDR in Chapter 18, "Open Network Computing Protocols."

Session Layer

The Session layer manages and sets up sessions. A session consists of a dialog between Presentation layers on two or more systems. This layer also handles the requests for different services between systems and manages the responses to those requests between systems. It also controls the dialog between two applications on different hosts and manages data streams.

The efficiency of dialog control between hosts in the Session layer depends on whether the communication mode is *half-duplex* or *full-duplex*. In a half-duplex configuration, only one device can communicate or transmit at a time while all others wait in standby mode for their turns. Each side must wait until the other process has finished sending and then respond with a separate acknowledgement. A full-duplex communication can send and receive at the same time; therefore it is more efficient than half-duplex communication. Full duplexing accomplishes its efficiency by piggybacking, or including data within the same frame.

An example of a Session layer protocol that you might know is the Network Basic Input Output System (NetBIOS). NetBIOS sets up a session between two Windows NT or Windows 95 machines. NetBIOS, a true Session layer protocol used by Microsoft, provides name services and session management between two devices using simple naming.

The Session layer also includes Remote Procedure Call (RPC), developed by Sun, which allows clients to make requests for remote execution. The requests are sent to a remote host for processing and a response, which enables communication between two hosts across a network. NFS uses RPC to send calls and get responses at the session layer, and uses XDR at the presentation layer.

Transport Layer

The Transport layer generally is thought to provide guaranteed reliable delivery of data only between two communicating processes or programs running on remote hosts. However, this holds true only if the vendor decides to implement Transmission Control Protocol (TCP) rather than its less-reliable counterpart User Datagram Protocol (UDP). We will discuss TCP in Chapter 8, "Transmission Control Protocol (TCP)" and UDP in Chapter 9, "User Datagram Protocol (UDP)."

The Transport layer does the following:

- Controls end-to-end communication between two processes running on different hosts.

- Provides connection-oriented or connectionless services to upper layers.

- Uses client- and server-port addresses to identify processes running within a host.

- Segments data for upper-layer applications.

The Transport layer has the task of identifying which processes are communicating on each host and providing either connection-oriented services and reliable transport, or speed of delivery. It manages the data flow and deals with flow control if it's a connection-oriented session. Both Transmission Control Protocol (TCP) and User Datagram Protocol (UDP) reside at the Transport layer.

The Transport layer has the task of segmenting the data (messages) handed down by upper-layer applications. It handles addressing with *ports,* also referred to as *sockets,* addresses that identify which upper-layer program or process is communicating on a particular device. To govern the tracking and management of various segments, the Transport layer uses port numbers for each application.

Socket Pairing

When you have end-to-end communication between hosts that involves source and destination IP addresses and ports (also called sockets), the industry refers to this as a socket pair.

The Transport layer can provide both connection-oriented and connectionless service to an upper-layer protocol. However, whether connection-oriented or connectionless, the Transport layer deals with ports or process addresses. Client-based and server-based addresses such as TCP or UDP ports are used to identify the process that is running within a host. We will discuss the Transport layer in more detail in Chapter 7, "Transport/Host-to-Host Layer."

Network Layer

The Network layer primarily assigns logical source and destination addresses and determines the best path for routing data between networks. The Network layer covers the following:

- End-to-end communication between two hosts

- Logical addressing

- Packet delivery

- Routing

Network layer protocols deal with *logical addressing,* which is distinguished from the Physical layer Media Access Control (MAC) address associated with a network card. Unlike physical addresses, vendors do not burn in logical addresses (addresses that are permanently assigned). Instead, an administrator assigns them either manually or dynamically. We will discuss logical Network layer addresses in Chapters 4–6, "Address Resolution," "IP Routing," and "Routing Protocols," respectively.

To achieve the best routing of data, Network layer devices such as routers utilize *packet switching.* In this process the router identifies the logical destination Network layer address of traffic received in one interface; then sends it out on a different interface to its destination.

The following protocols exist at the Network layer:

- **RARP, ARP, BootP, DHCP**—Protocols that perform address resolution or configuration

- **ICMP**—Diagnostic and control protocol

- **RIP, IGRP, EIGRP, OSPF and BGP**—Routing protocols

Data Link Layer

The OSI Data Link layer's main responsibilities include frame transmission and reception, and physical addressing. The Data Link layer adds both a header at the front and a four-byte trailer at the end of each frame prior to transmission, thereby forming a *frame* around the data. The term *packet framing* refers to the formation of such frame sequences. Only the Data Link layer adds a trailer to the data.

The Data Link layer has the following characteristics and duties:

- Controls access to the medium.

- Adds source and destination hardware addresses.

- Prepares frames for transmission by converting data packets to frames.

- Assumes the function of sending and receiving data over the wire.

- Calculates CRC or FCS.

- Bridges and switches function at this level.

Layer 2 Addresses

Manufacturers burn in Data Link addresses or MAC addresses on each Network Card. Manufacturers define the numbering sequences when they produce the cards. Each address is six bytes in length, as mandated by the IEEE. The first three bytes refer specifically to a vendor; the vendor uniquely assigns the last three bytes. Devices that function at the Data Link layer must have the ability to identify those addresses.

The Data Link layer adds source and destination MAC addresses to the header to identify both the NIC (Network Interface Card) address of the device that sent the frame, and the local device that should receive the frame. Every MAC address has to have a unique address throughout the entire network. Layer 2 devices use the destination address to decide whether to forward information.

Sending devices perform a Cyclic Redundancy Check (CRC) or Frame Check Sequence (FCS) algorithm before transmission. The industry uses the terms CRC and FCS interchangeably. The devices at the Data Link layer add this CRC or FCS as a trailer to the end of the data handed down from the Network layer framing the bits. This is why we call them "frames" at the Data Link layer. CRC or FCS does not guarantee delivery of data. It merely verifies that the transmitted bits match the received bits at the receiving host. Receiving hosts use the same algorithm to identify whether the frame remained undamaged during transit. If the CRC or FCS does not match, the receiving host simply tosses the frame without notifying the sending station. Stations never pass data up to the next layer unless the frame is good. The sending devices have the responsibility of retransmitting damaged frames.

Physical Layer

The Physical layer deals with 1s and 0s—bits that make up the frame. *Bits* are encoded as electrical or light pulses. This layer also deals with electrical and mechanical characteristics, signal encoding, and voltage levels. Generally speaking, the Physical layer involves tangible items; that is, physical items that you can touch, such as cabling and repeaters. The Physical layer includes the following:

- Electrical and mechanical characteristics

- Signal encoding

- 1s and 0s

- Physical connector specifications

Data Link Architecture and Topologies

The term *application* means the literal use of the standards in the form of network architecture and specifications for the major topologies. Those standards include IEEE and ANSI specifications for:

- Ethernet
- Fast Ethernet
- Gigabit Ethernet
- Token-Ring
- FDDI

The standards also include the frame types and channel access methods for IEEE and ANSI. The following sections provide a general discussion of these technologies as a refresher.

Ethernet and IEEE 802.3

We start with the most popular Data Link architecture, Ethernet technologies, as defined by IEEE within the 802.3 specification. The Xerox Corporation usually receives credit for inventing Ethernet; however, Xerox actually acquired the original technology (then known as Aloha Net) in the 1970s from the University of Hawaii. Xerox then joined DEC and Intel to develop the earliest Ethernet standard, called Version 1, which was released in 1980. The three companies released a follow-up standard, Ethernet Version 2, in 1982.

In the mid-1980s the IEEE 802 committee adopted Ethernet as the 802.3 standard. All current and future development on Ethernet technologies ostensibly builds on this base standard. Since its inception, Ethernet has become the most popular LAN standard used throughout the world.

It is important to note that Ethernet is not the same as the IEEE 802.3 implementations and the terms should not be used interchangeably (although sometimes they are). Whereas Xerox, DEC, and Intel developed Version 1 and Version 2 with somewhat similar parameters, the IEEE committee added several standard expanded capabilities not shared with its predecessors. Table 1.1 provides an overview of the similarities and differences between the three implementations.

TABLE 1.1   Ethernet Versions 1, 2, and IEEE 802.3

Version 1	Version 2	IEEE 802.3
Data Link layer architecture	Includes Ethernet_II to detect and disable faulty frame (the *defacto* industry frame to carry IP traffic over Ethernet LANs)	Adds jabber control (or jabber inhibit) transceivers

TABLE 1.1   Continued

Version 1	Version 2	IEEE 802.3
Delivered data at 10Mbps as linear bus topology	Delivers data at 10Mbps as linear bus topology	Expands physical topology support to star configurations
Could use only thick coaxial media	Can use only thick coaxial media	Adds media types such as thin coaxial, fiber, and twisted pair
Used unbalanced signaling with ground as reference point (susceptible to noise and EMI)	Uses balanced signaling	1995 enhancements provide 100Mbps transfer rates (802.3u)
Did not support Signal Quality Error (SQE) (also known as heartbeat), so more difficult to detect collisions	Adds SQE	Supports SQE but is necessary with only external transceivers
Incompatible with Version 2	Incompatible with Version 1	Incompatible with Version 1

Version 1 of the Ethernet specification uses the presence or absence of voltage to represent data, known as **unbalanced signaling**. This type of transmission makes transmissions highly susceptible to outside interference. Figure 1.5 shows an example of unbalanced signaling.

FIGURE 1.5
Unbalanced signaling varies voltage levels between 0 (referenced by ground) and +5 volts to represent data.

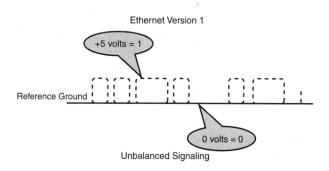

Ethernet Version 2 improved the signaling method by implementing **balanced** signaling, which represents data through positive and negative voltage changes using 0 or ground as a common reference point (see Figure 1.6). This approach diminishes the effects of interference on transmissions, which improves signal quality.

FIGURE 1.6
Balanced signal improves signal quality by using a common reference point and uses positive and negative voltage levels to represent data.

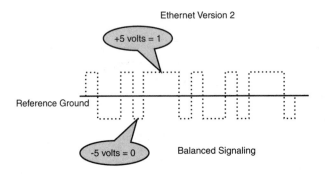

The IEEE 802.3 specification defines the general operation, components, and distance limitations of Ethernet. They are as follows:

- Defines all Data Link and Physical layer components, functions, channel access methods, and operations.

- Provides vendors with rules for implementing or developing Ethernet 802.3 LAN technologies.

- Is based on the IEEE standard known as 10Base5, which all other 802.3 standards follow with minor variations.

The IEEE 802.3 standard defines a 10Mbps broadcast-based linear network architecture using a contention channel access method known as CSMA/CD (*Carrier Sense Multiple Access with Collision Detection*), which is discussed in the next section.

Channel Access Method

Various channel access methods exist today; the one that is implemented depends on the network architecture. Ethernet uses a contention-based channel access method. *Channel access methods* describe the rules used by devices that dictate how

- The communication medium is accessed.

- Frames are transmitted.

- The channel is released for use by other devices.

Devices using the CSMA/CD channel access method

- Contend for the right to transmit.

- Can successfully transmit only one at a time.

- Must wait for channel availability to transmit a frame when other devices are using the channel (half-duplex operation).

When devices transmit simultaneously on the same channel, signal collisions occur and frames become corrupted. This contention-based access is called *Carrier Sense Multiple Access with*

Collision Detection (*CSMA/CD*). Because Ethernet uses silence as the indication to transmit, devices perform a carrier sense to detect that silence. If no frequency exists on the wire, they can access the channel and begin transmission at once. After transmission, devices release the channel and wait at least 9.6μ (microseconds) before attempting to access the channel again, thereby giving other transceivers a chance to transmit their frames.

Collisions

Collisions are just that—collisions. In a baseband network, no more than one signal should occupy the channel at any one time. The result of more than one signal traversing the wire simultaneously is a collision, which impedes successful transmission. During transmissions a transceiver (transmitter/receiver) encodes the signal on the medium and listens for collisions. If one occurs, the transceiver's internal collision detection circuitry notifies the network adapter card by sending a signal, causing the adapter to abort its transmission. It is the responsibility of the transmitting device to detect and retransmit frames when collisions occur.

Collisions are a fact of life with Ethernet; however, excessive collisions or late collisions are cause for concern. Overloading a segment with too many devices causes excessive collisions. When you have too many devices attached to a segment and each one is contending for the channel, the chance of collisions increases due to sheer volume.

The 802.3 specification defines *late collisions* as those occurring any time after the 64th byte in a frame. Exceeding the maximum distance limitations of the media (known as *propagation delay* or *hardware failure*) can cause late collisions. You should never consider late collisions a part of normal Ethernet operation.

Ethernet Frames

There are four different frame types within the realm of Ethernet standards, each designed with a different purpose by a different entity. The four frame types are as follows:

- Ethernet_II (DIX)
- Ethernet_802.3 (Novell proprietary)
- IEEE 802.3
- IEEE 802.3 SNAP (SubNetwork Access Protocol)

DEC, Intel, and Xerox developed the original Ethernet frame known as Ethernet_II (also called *DIX*). Novell developed its own proprietary frame (Ethernet_802.3) exclusively for IPX/SPX traffic. The IEEE developed and named the last two frames. Despite specific companies naming the frame types, the industry and IEEE have different names for the frames. The various names seem to stem largely from companies, not the IEEE, which incorporate or develop the frames into their own architectures and languages. For example, Cisco refers to the Ethernet_II frame as ARPA. Table 1.2 shows the four Ethernet frame types and compares the naming conventions used by the IEEE and industry; Table 1.3 contains information specific to each frame type.

TABLE 1.2   Ethernet Name Mapping

IEEE	Industry
N/A	Ethernet_II (DIX)
N/A	Ethernet_802.3
802.3	Ethernet_802.2
802.3 SNAP	Ethernet_SNAP

TABLE 1.3   Ethernet Frame Types

Ethernet_II -(DIX)	Ethernet_802.3	Ethernet_802.2	Ethernet_SNAP
Designed to carry IP traffic	Designed to carry IP/SPX traffic	Contains LLC headers using DSAP and SSAP addresses to identify upper-layer protocols	Contains LLC headers using DSAP and SSAP addresses to identify upper-layer protocols
Uses two-byte registered Ether-type values to identify protocols; for example, 0800=IP	Limited to carrying only IPX protocol	Uses registered SAP addresses; for example, E0=IPX	Specifies special SAP address of AA to indicate SNAP header follows with two-byte Ether type
	Most common frame type in use today; was de facto frame type for IPX networks prior to Ethernet 802.2		Adds a five-byte SNAP header after the LLC header to identify the protocol

All four frame types can coexist in a single network but are not compatible. When stations configured with dissimilar encapsulation types want to exchange information they must communicate through a router that supports both types. The router performs the conversion between the hosts. Conversion adds unnecessary overhead and delays to the network, so it's best to select and use only one frame type for your network. Table 1.4 shows the primary and secondary characteristics of Ethernet frames.

TABLE 1.4   Comparing Ethernet Frame Types

Primary Characteristics	Secondary Characteristics
Adds a 14-byte header before transmission.	First 12 bytes consist of 6-byte destination MAC address and 6-byte source (sender) MAC address followed by a 2-byte field defining either the length of the datagram or protocol type.
Includes a 4-byte trailer (CRC or FCS) before transmission.	Added by sender and compared by receiver to guarantee frame was undamaged.
Sends a 64-bit preamble before transmission of each frame to achieve synchronization.	Includes 7 bytes of alternating 1s and 0s; last 2 bits of 8th byte alert stations that data follows.
Minimum frame size allowed is 64 bytes (frames of fewer than 64 bytes must be padded); maximum is 1518 bytes.	Includes 14-byte data link header, 4-byte trailer and up to 15 bytes of upper-layer protocols and data.

Figures 1.7–1.10 illustrate each type of frame. Compare both functional representations and actual appearances of the frames. Note that all these frames have the same basic characteristics. All begin with a 6-byte destination MAC address followed by a 6-byte source address. In addition, all end with a 4-byte CRC field.

FIGURE 1.7

The Ethernet_II frame is the only frame that includes a 2-byte Ethertype value following the source address used to identify the protocol being carried within the frame.

Ethernet_II

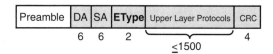

Preamble = 64 Bits for Syncronization;
         7 bytes of 1010 1010, 8th byte is 1010 1011

DA = Destination Address

SA = Source Address

Type = 2 Bytes Registered Protocol Value (for example, 0800 = IP)

Data = Upper Layer Protocols, Data and Padding

CRC = Frame Check Sequence

FIGURE 1.8
Ethernet_802.3 frames always follow the length field with an IPX header that includes a 2-byte null checksum of FFFF.

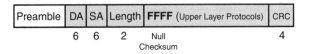

Ethernet_802.3

| Preamble | DA | SA | Length | **FFFF** (Upper Layer Protocols) | CRC |

6   6   2   Null Checksum   4

Preamble = Synchronization

DA = Destination Address

SA = Source Address

Length = Amount of Data contained within the Frame
Must be ≤**1500** Decimal or **05DC** Hex

FFFF = 2 Byte Null Checksum; IPX Header

Data = Upper Layer Protocols, Data and Padding

CRC = Frame Check Sequence

FIGURE 1.9
The IEEE's 802.3 frame, known industry wide as Ethernet_802.2, includes the 802.2 header with DSAP (destination SAP) and SSAP (source SAP) addresses for protocol identification.

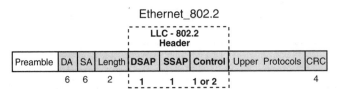

Ethernet_802.2

LLC - 802.2 Header

| Preamble | DA | SA | Length | **DSAP** | **SSAP** | **Control** | Upper Protocols | CRC |

6   6   2   1   1   1 or 2   4

Preamble = Synchronization; 7 Byte Preamble, 1 Byte SFD

DA = Destination Address

SA = Source Address

Length = Amount of Data ≤**1500** Decimal or **05DC** Hex

DSAP = Destination Service Access Point

SSAP = Source Service Access Point

Control = Connectionless or Connection-Oriented LLC

Data = Upper Layer Protocols, Data and Padding

CRC = Frame Check Sequence

FIGURE 1.10
The IEEE's 802.3 SNAP frame, known within the industry as Ethernet_SNAP, adds a 5-byte extension header to the 802.2 header. This header includes a 3-byte vendor code followed by a 2-byte Ether-type identifying the protocol being carried.

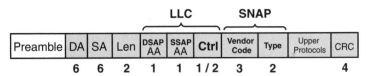

Ethernet_SNAP

LLC   SNAP

| Preamble | DA | SA | Len | DSAP AA | SSAP AA | **Ctrl** | Vendor Code | Type | Upper Protocols | CRC |

6   6   2   1   1   1 / 2   3   2   4

Preamble = Synchronization; 7 Byte Preamble, 1 Byte SFD

DA = Destination Address

SA = Source Address

Length = Amount of Data <**1500** Decimal or **05DC** Hex

DSAP = Destination Service Access Point

SSAP = Source Service Access Point

Control = Connectionless or Connection-Oriented LLC

SNAP = 3 Byte Vendor Code followed by 2 Byte EType

Data = Upper Layer Protocols, Data and Padding

CRC = Frame Check Sequence

Figure 1.11 provides a quick reference comparison of the four frame types discussed previously.

FIGURE 1.11
Use the Frame Type Quick Reference to quickly identify the differences between each frame.

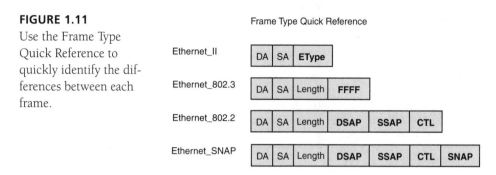

Frame Type Quick Reference

Slow Ethernet

Slow (10Mbps) Ethernet has been the mainstay of LAN networks since it came out in the mid-1980s. In the sense that the early days of networking were somewhat chaotic, with vendors making strictly proprietary products and the rules that governed them, it is interesting to follow the development toward official industry standards and recent improvements in them. Despite the emergence of standards-defining bodies to provide clear rules for implementing technologies (such as 802.3), desire to exceed limitations drives the industry to ignore many of those rules.

Slow Ethernet specifications include the following:

- **10Base5**—Transmission takes place at 10Mbps using thick coaxial cable on a linear bus.

- **10Base2**—Transmission takes place at 10Mbps using thin coaxial cable on a linear bus.

- **10BaseT**—Transmits 10Mbps over twisted pairs in a physical star configuration.

Fast Ethernet

Fast Ethernet has exactly the same base standards as Slow Ethernet. The difference lies in the additional 10 clauses of the IEEE 802.3u addendum, released in 1995. These clauses define the standard for three different 100Mbps implementations known generally as 100BaseX. Table 1.5 illustrates a comparison between the Slow and Fast Ethernet configurations.

TABLE 1.5 Fast Versus Slow Ethernet Comparison

	Fast	Slow
CSMA/CD channel access	X	X
Same min/max frame sizes	X	X
Supports same frame types	X	X

TABLE 1.5   Continued

	Fast	Slow
Supports cat 3, 4, and 5	X	X
Supports fiber	X	X
Supports physical star	X	X
Full-duplex/half-duplex	X	X
Coaxial bus topology support		X
Manchester signal encoding		X
100BaseX hardware required	X	
Component and timing changes	X	

100BaseX Standards

All three 100BaseX standards define 100Mb baseband technologies over twisted pair or fiber. Distance and limitations vary within each standard based on Physical layer characteristics. There are three types of 100BaseX standards:

- **100BaseTX** —Defines 100Mbps over a minimum Category 5 UTP, implementing the same two pairs as 10Mbps Ethernet.

- **100BaseFX**—Defines 100Mbps transfers over fiber-optic media.

- **100BaseT4**—Uses four unshielded twisted pairs for transmission; three pairs for transmission and reception and one pair for collision detection.

Gigabit Ethernet

The Gigabit Ethernet (GE) standard enables transmission speeds of up to 1000Mbps using Category 5 UTP cabling. The task force specification is the IEEE 802.3z, which uses 802.3 Ethernet frame formats, and the CSMA/CD access method. Note that the continuing use of the 802.3 standard supports backward compatibility with the 100BaseT and 10BaseT technologies.

Token-Ring and IEEE 802.5

Although IBM usually is considered to be the founder of the Token-Ring LAN standard, Dr. Olaf Solderblum in Sweden actually patented it in 1967. IBM obtained the technology from Dr. Solderblum, and with the assistance of Texas Instruments, developed the chipset technology and guidelines. IBM released the technology to the IEEE, whose 802.5 subcommittee developed and released the 4Mbps Token-Ring standard in 1985. The IEEE 802.5 specification defines the MAC sublayer and the Physical layer specification, using the 802.2 specification at the LLC layer for protocol identification. In 1989 the IEEE released an enhancement to the 802.5 standard that defines 16Mbps Token-Ring operations.

Token-Ring uses a unidirectional transmission, with each device always receiving from its upstream neighbor and sending to its downstream neighbor. It utilizes token-passing ring topology that passes frames with no collision risk because only one device can transmit at a time. However, devices can access the medium and transmit upon reception of a free token, which is a 3-byte signal that propagates around the ring.

Token-Ring exhibits these important characteristics:

- All devices connect serially, transmitting a signal in one direction.

- Each device's transmit pair connects through to its downstream neighbor's receive pair.

- Signal transmission is unidirectional.

- Each device directly connects in a physical star formation through central hubs known as *Multi-Station Access Units* (MSAUs) (see Figure 1.12). The MSAU's objective is to keep the ring functional by electrically bypassing a non-functional device or port when end devices are either turned off or fail.

FIGURE 1.12
Token-Ring operation.

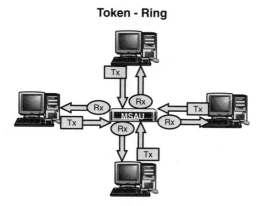

Token - Ring

- Each device's network card operates as a fully functional unidirectional repeater, completely regenerating the signal and bit repeating it on.

- Operates at either 4Mbps or 16Mbps, but not both, as determined by the configuration of the network card.

- All devices must agree on the speed of the ring.

Bit Repeating

The industry uses the term "bit repeating" to describe the amplification and regeneration of a received signal that is repeated out all other interfaces.

Channel Access Method

Token-Ring devices access the channel using a token-passing method. When a device has information to transmit, it waits for a free token, a 3-byte frame that traverses the ring and provides access to the medium. When it receives a token it can convert it to a frame.

Stations send their frames around the ring hoping to find the destination host. All other devices on the ring check the destination address of the frame to determine whether it is for them; then they bit repeat the signal on. Each network interface card acts as a repeater, amplifying, retiming, and bit repeating the signal. The responsibility of stripping its frame and releasing a new token belongs to the sending device.

Token-Ring Frames

The two types of Token-Ring frames are token and data/command. Figure 1.13 shows an example of a token frame. In Figure 1.13, stations identify the signal as a free token by looking at the status of the token bit within the AC field. If the bit contains a 0 in the AC field, it is a token frame. SDs and EDs simply mark the beginning and end of a frame. Figure 1.14 shows an example of a Token Ring frame used to transmit data and commands. Note that the MAC/LLC field following the SA (source address field) indicates whether the frame is a command (MAC) or data frame (LLC).

FIGURE 1.13
A 3-byte signal circles the ring providing attached devices with access to the channel.

Token Frame

SD = Start Delimiter

AC = Access Control byte indicates whether
this is a Token or Data/Command frame

ED = End Delimiter

FIGURE 1.14
The structure of a Token-Ring frame with field descriptions.

Token-Ring Frame

SD	AC	FC	DA	SA	MAC or LLC	RIF	Upper Layer Data	FCS	ED	FS

SD = Start Delimiter for frame
AC = Access Control byte indicates whether this is a Token or Data/Command frame
FC = Frame Control indicates whether frame is a Data (LLC) or Command (MAC) frame
DA = Destination Address
SA = Source Address
MAC or LLC = MAC frames carry MAC data. LLC frames contain 802.2 header for
protocol identification
RIF = Route Information Field, only exists when Source Route Bridging is being used
Upper Layer Data = Headers for upper layer protocols and User Data
FCS = Frame Check Sequence, similar to CRC
ED = End Delimiter for frame
FD = Frame Status byte used to identify whether recieving device recognized and copied
a frame

FDDI and ANSI X3T9.5

Fiber Distributed Data Interface (FDDI) is a type of media access defined by the American National Standards Institute (ANSI) X3T9.5 specification. Although FDDI also uses a MAC addressing scheme, it differs from Ethernet and Token-Ring. The difference is that instead of referring to the MAC address in terms of a 6-byte address (like other topologies), FDDI uses 4-bit symbols to refer to the MAC addresses.

FDDI incorporates token passing in a dual-ring physical topology, which provides a self-healing redundancy. If there is a problem with the primary ring, the secondary ring serves as a backup. If a break occurs, it reroutes the data from the primary ring to the secondary ring at two or more locations. This is known as a *ring wrap.*

FDDI once was a favorite standard for network backbones because it enables transmission speeds of up to 100Mbps and, unlike copper, is immune to EMI and RFI. In fact, fiber-optic cabling has many advantages over conventional copper cable, including the following:

- Speed at which data can travel

- Signal distance achieved before attenuation

- Immunity to EMI and RFI

- Redundancy in having counter-rotating rings

Note

Note that FDDI once was a favorite standard for backbones; however, most places have replaced FDDI with the cheaper Fast or Gigabit Ethernet.

Channel Access Method

FDDI uses a token access method for transmission of packets. FDDI communications access the physical medium (the ring) through the token being passed around the ring. When a node wants to transmit, it simply grabs a token, sends its transmission, and then releases a new token on the ring. Note that unlike with Token-Ring, which allows only one token to circulate at a time, FDDI allows multiple tokens to circulate at any given time.

Note

Although Token Ring vendors did implement something called *early token release* to allow for multiple transmissions on the ring at a time, only one token is allowed.

Wide Area Networking (WAN) Technologies

WAN (Wide Area Network) technologies use transmission facilities provided by common carriers, such as service providers or telephone companies, to provide a data path to networks covering a broad geographical area. WAN technologies operate at the lowest two levels of the OSI model—the Physical and Data Link layers (see Figure 1.15).

FIGURE 1.15

Mapping the OSI model to WAN protocols.

OSI WAN Protocols

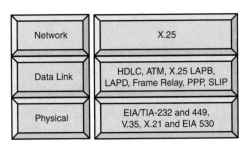

WAN connection types enable companies to connect to remote sites to extend their networks. Most companies that have remote sites over a large geographical area require some sort of WAN connection type. Which connection type they choose depends on a company's specific needs. Three WAN connection types can be used to transfer data across a service provider's network:

- **Leased (dedicated) line**—The leased line, also known as a point-to-point or dedicated line, employs a synchronous serial connection through a service provider.

- **Circuit-switched**—Circuit-switched has a dedicated circuit path and employs an asynchronous serial connection through a telephone company.

- **Packet-switched**—Packet-switched uses a synchronous serial connection through a service provider.

Table 1.6 explains the three connection types.

TABLE 1.6 WAN Connection Types, Layer One

Connection Type	Description
Leased Line (also known as point-to-point or dedicated)	Provides a single, existing WAN communications path through a service provider network, from a customer to a remote network. Service providers reserve the connection and bandwidth for a client's private use. Guarantees bandwidth is available. Has the drawback of being expensive because connection is always active even if it's unused. Employed over synchronous serial connections up to E3 speeds, 45Mbps. Supports PPP, SLIP, and HDLC Data Link encapsulations.

TABLE 1.6   Continued

Connection Type	Description
Circuit-switching	Dedicated circuit or path is built on the fly for each session and must exist between sender and receiver for the duration of the transmission. Commonly used in environments that require only minimal or infrequent WAN usage. Used to provide asynchronous serial connections over standard telephone lines or ISDN connections. Supports PPP, SLIP, and HDLC encapsulations.
Packet-switching	WAN switching method. Network devices share common point-to-point links to deliver packets from a source to a destination across a service provider's network. Establishes temporary virtual circuits (VCs) to provide an end-to-end connection between source and destination. Switching devices establish the virtual circuit and use multiplexing devices to provide customers with shared access to the circuit. Less expensive because the circuit is not dedicated. Employed over a serial connection with speeds ranging from 56Kbps to E3. Supports X.25, ATM, and Frame Relay encapsulation.

Figures 1.16, 1.17, and 1.18 show the different WAN connection types. A leased line, known as a *dedicated line,* provides a single existing WAN communication path through a service provider network, from a customer to a remote network (see Figure 1.16). Figure 1.17 shows a path being built on the fly for a WAN circuit-switched connection. Figure 1.18 shows an example of packet-switching.

FIGURE 1.16

Leased lines tend to be expensive because the connection remains active even when not in use.

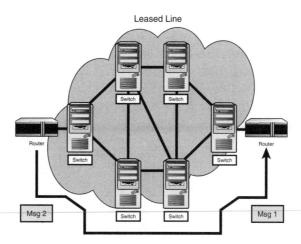

FIGURE 1.17
Circuit-switching requires
that a connection be set
up and torn down for
each session between the
sender and receiver.

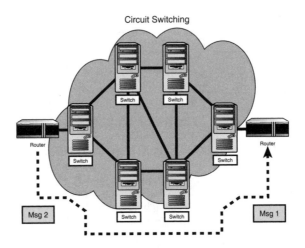

FIGURE 1.18
Packet-switching relays
packets from node to
node, occupying the
channel only for the
duration of transmission.

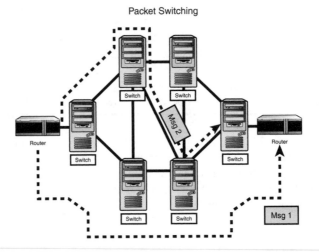

Service providers and telephone companies provide most of the WAN connections today. You
can use routers to access servers providing circuit-switched dial-up connections through standard analog modems or dial-on-demand routing (DDR) over analog or ISDN lines. You can
configure dedicated leased line connections through CSU/DSUs to support consistently high
volumes of traffic over synchronous serial connections. Packet-switched connections, such as
X.25, ATM, and Frame Relay, require that Multiplexer/Demultiplexer (MUX/DEMUX) devices
be used to provide devices with shared access to the same circuit. You can use any of these
methods to deliver data across a service provider's network to remote sites all around the
world.

WAN Encapsulation Protocols

WAN encapsulation is a way of wrapping a packet to enable it to traverse a mesh of distance-separated networks. The Internet is based on many different types of WAN connections, including dedicated and non-dedicated. On each WAN connection, local LAN data must encapsulate into frames before crossing the WAN link. You need to know the proper protocol to configure the appropriate Data Link layer encapsulation type. The protocol depends on the WAN technology being used; your service provider should provide you with the specific configuration information to connect to their network successfully.

Several options can provide an interface to a service provider's network. These options are all variations of the High-Level Data Link Control (HDLC) protocol—the widely used standard introduced by the ISO, which was patterned after IBM's Synchronous Data Link Control (SDLC) protocol. These protocols operate at the Data Link layer of the OSI model, providing Data Link layer connection-oriented and connectionless services to upper-layer applications and user data across the WAN.

Most WAN protocols come from descendents of HDLC. Vendors have several implementations of HDLC, and not all are compatible. For instance, Cisco has its own proprietary HDLC implementation, which is incompatible with other HDLC protocols. IBM's SDLC protocol, used in its Systems Network Architecture (SNA), is very similar in functionality and provides connection-oriented, reliable delivery between IBM minis, mainframes, and their clients. Other protocols, such as X.25's LAPB, ISDN's LAPD, and even LLC2, are all subsets of HDLC. Table 1.7 shows the primary WAN encapsulation protocols.

TABLE 1.7   Primary WAN Encapsulation Protocols

Protocol Type	Description
Frame Relay Two encapsulation types: • Frame relay (Cisco's encapsulation) • Frame relay IETF (RFC 1490 standard encapsulation)	Establishes multiple virtual logical paths or virtual circuits. Operates at the Data Link and Physical layers. More efficient than X.25 because it does not establish connections and does not employ error correction or recovery. Assumes most networks are physically reliable and have low error rates. Relies on upper-layer protocols for error detection and recovery. Frame relay supports congestion control.
ISDN (Integrated Services Digital Network)	Uses existing telephone lines to transmit data, voice, and other source traffic. Uses two types of channels: D and B. D channel carries signaling and control information. B carries data. There are two main types of ISDN services: BRI (Basic Rate ISDN) and PRI (Primary Rate IDSN). BRI supports total bit rate of 144Kbps, and PRI supports 1.544Mbps (in the U.S., Canada, and Japan) or 2.048Mbps (in Europe).

TABLE 1.7 Continued

Protocol Type	Description
X.25 LAPB (Link Access Procedure, Balanced) encapsulation for signaling channel	LAPB is the Data Link layer protocol in the X.25 protocol stack. Derived from HDLC, it is a connection-oriented protocol that provides error detection and recovery at layer two. Extremely reliable but slow because of the high overhead involved in connection maintenance. Good to use if your WAN link is prone to error. It has generally been replaced by Frame Relay and other WAN standards.
HDLC (High-Level Data Link Control)	Connection-oriented protocol at the Data Link layer introduced by ISO. Does not support data compression or authentication. ISO's HDLC can't identify the type of protocols being carried inside HDLC encapsulation. Therefore, only one protocol can be carried over HDLC at a time. Vendor implementations vary.
PPP (Point-to-Point)	Provides a communications path from the customer over an established WAN asynchronous connection, and a synchronous connection over a carrier network to a remote network. Supports multiple protocols, such as IP, IPX, and AppleTalk. Supports data compression authentication, error detection, and multilinking.
Serial Line Internet Protocol (SLIP)	Older protocol supporting point-to-point serial connections using TCP/IP. Replaced by PPP.
Asynchronous Transfer Mode (ATM)	International standard for cell-based switching and multiplexing technology. Supports multiple service types (voice, video, and data) through fixed-length (53-byte) cells. Fixed-length cells reduce processing overhead and transit delay. Supports high-speed transmissions over copper or fiber lines with data rates ranging from 1.544Mbps (T1 service) up to 622Mbps (OC-12).

Request For Comments (RFCs)

No one owns the TCP/IP technologies, nor can one obtain information in the form of documentation, policies, protocols, and standards from a vendor. However, you can find this type of documentation online at no charge in the form of Request for Comments (RFCs). Although vendors do publish documentation on the implementation of these technologies, RFCs provide the base standards, describing protocol functions, rules, and methods of implementation; vendors interpret these standards.

RFCs provide documentation in the form of a series of technical reports written by committees, individuals, and corporations for the development of various protocols, policies, implementations, and so on. The RFCs appear in chronological order; revised RFCs supersede earlier documents and are assigned new numbers. We recommended that you be careful to obtain the latest RFC when researching.

RFCs vary from technical documentation of a protocol to suggestions for changes to proposals for new protocols and can range from dry and academic to humorous in tone. In this book, we refer to RFCs as a reference. We also provide a categorized list of RFCs in Appendix A, "RFCs Organized by Chapter." You can access RFC through the Web at `http://www.faqs.org/rfcs/`.

Internet Versus intranet

You might have heard the saying "All cognacs are brandies but not all brandies are cognacs." The same analogy holds true of the *Internet* and *intranet*. Although the uppercase *Internet* is an *intranet*, an *intranet* is not the *Internet*. The lowercase *intranet* means multiple networks (within a company) connected together and communicating internally with a cohesive governing body (algorithm). The uppercase *Internet* allows numerous people (hosts) from different organizations around the world with no controlling body to talk to each other using TCP/IP. Just as a brandy is not as grand as a Cognac (but similar in design), so is the lesser *intranet* to the grander *Internet*.

Groups Responsible for Internet Technology

The industry is in a constant state of change, and it seems new protocols and standards appear out of thin air. However, the following four groups govern Internet technologies:

- **The *Internet Society* (*ISOC*)**—A non-profit organization that promotes interest in the Internet. Host organization of the IAB (Internet Architecture Board).

- **The *Internet Architecture Board* (*IAB*)**—Small group of international volunteers that set policies for the quality of Internet (TCP/IP) standards. Falls under the ISOC.

- **The *Internet Engineering Task Force* (*IETF*)**—A small standards-oriented group divided into specific areas of TCP/IP and the global Internet. Each area has an independent manager and working groups.

- **The *Internet Research Task Force* (*IRTF*)**—A group that works on research projects related to the TCP/IP and the Internet.

Summary

The OSI Reference Model was created to enable both similar and dissimilar systems to communicate seamlessly by providing an architectural framework for vendors and manufacturers. It consists of seven layers: Application, Presentation, Session, Transport, Network, Data Link and Physical.

The OSI model benefits manufacturers and software developers, and network engineers who offer support and troubleshooting. By compartmentalizing each layer's function, it narrows the scope of each layer's responsibilities. This eases the development and support burdens that manufacturers and network engineers face.

Review Questions

1. What is the reason for the importance of the OSI model and why was it created?

2. Which layer of the OSI model manages the communication dialog (full or half duplex) between services?

3. Which layer provides error handling and flow control as well as guaranteed delivery?

4. At which layer of the OSI model does switching occur?

5. At which layer of the OSI model do IP and ICMP function?

6. Name the four layers of the DoD model.

7. What are two functions of the Data link MAC Layer?

8. Name the Transport layer protocol that is connectionless?

IP ADDRESSING

Understanding Binary to Decimal Conversion

Before you can understand the derivation of IP addresses you must have a basic understanding of decimal and binary numbering, and how to convert from one to the other. For those unfamiliar with binary and decimal numbers, the base-10 numbering system is referred to as the decimal numbering system. Decimal numbering consists of the numbers 0,1,2,3,4,5,6,7,8, and 9. This comprises the 10 unique digits of 0 through 9.

Computers use the binary numbering system, which consists of only two unique numbers 0 (zero) and 1 (one). Computers recognize only the uncharged 0 and charged 1. Unlike decimal numbering, binary numbering uses powers of 2 rather than powers of 10 (see Figure 2.1).

To understand binary numbers we convert them to the decimal numbering system. A byte (also called an *octet*), which measures storage and memory, is composed of 8 bit positions, with a maximum value of 255. Binary numbering uses powers of 2 for each bit position. As shown in Figure 2.2, moving from right to left, beginning with the number 1 and moving to 2, each position is equivalent to the value squared of the previous position. The last position on the left is equal to 128. To convert a number from binary to decimal, assign the decimal value to each corresponding bit position; then add them together. Remember that the computer recognizes only the number in the on position, represented by 1. The highest possible total is 255 if all bits are in the on position (128+64+32+16+8+4+2+1). That is, 128+32+8+4=172 or in binary numbers, 10101100.

To convert 172 to its binary equivalent, place a 1 under the bits (turning them on) until the total equals 172. Use Figure 2.3 and the number 176 as an example. In binary, 176 is represented by placing a 1 under the 128 at the far left. Again, 128 is the largest number within our numbers (to the power of 2) in our byte (8 bits). As 128 is the largest number, you build upon it for any numbers larger than 128.

FIGURE 2.1

The binary numbering system uses the base-2, not base-10 system.

Binary (Base-2)

- The Binary Number System uses 2 values to represent numbers
- 0 and 1

8 Bits=1Byte

1011 0100

FIGURE 2.2

The number 1 indicates that the bit is in the on position.

Binary to Decimal Conversion

$2^7 \longleftarrow \hspace{2cm} 2^0$

128	64	32	16	8	4	2	1
X	X	X	X	X	X	X	X
1	0	1	0	1	1	0	0

128 + 32 + 8 + 4 = 172

If you place a number 1 (on position) under the 64, the sum (64+128) adds up greater than the value of 176, so you place a zero (off position) under the number. If you add all the numbers, except 32, it totals less than 176; so place a 1 under the number 32 for a total of 160. You need a sum of 16 to reach 176, which means you place a 1 under the 16, giving you a total of 176. You then place zeros under the remaining numbers. Your binary number is 10110000.

FIGURE 2.3

The 1s represent the numbers the computer recognizes.

Decimal to Binary Conversion

176

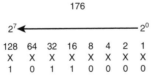

$2^7 \longleftarrow \hspace{2cm} 2^0$

128	64	32	16	8	4	2	1
X	X	X	X	X	X	X	X
1	0	1	1	0	0	0	0

IP Addressing

In Chapter 1, "Overview of Industry Models and Standards," we discussed Data Link layer two (MAC) addressing, and how those addresses uniquely identify devices on a network. We now move up one layer in the OSI model to the Network layer. As you recall, the Network layer controls routing and the decision of where to route traffic. Those routing decisions stem from information in the 4-octet, or 32-bit destination IP address. The parameters for a unique 32-bit value to define both the network and host portions with a 2-level addressing hierarchy appeared in the 1985 publication *Request for Comment (RFC) 950*. Its purpose is to logically divide the IP address into at least 2 parts, identifying the network and device, such as a router, and maybe even a third part that describes a subnetwork within the network. A subnet is an extension of the IP addressing scheme and we will discuss subnetting later in this chapter.

The hierarchy differentiates the network address and subnetwork within the network from the node address. A node address uniquely identifies an individual device on a given subnet or network, and that network is assigned to a company identifying the major network as a whole. Think of the logical network assigned to an organization as a city, the subnet as a street within the city, and each unique logical host portion of the address as a specific house.

For example, if someone asks where you live, you might respond with "San Francisco" and leave it at that. The general term "San Francisco" gives someone a reference point for where that city is located and the path to get there. However, it says nothing about how to specifically find you once he or she gets to San Francisco. Because thousands of streets (subnets) and houses (hosts) exist within San Francisco, this person would require more specific information if he or she actually tried to find you. In this analogy, the network and subnet portions of the address are what the router uses to identify which city and street receives the routed traffic. Once a datagram reaches the street (subnet), it can easily find the house (host) because each house (host) has a unique address on that street (subnet).

Address Classes

When the Internet community developed an addressing scheme it divided the 32-bit or 4-byte addresses into classes based on predicted use. They defined these addresses as *classful* because they clearly differentiate the classes in predefined boundaries. There are five major classes of network addresses: Classes A, B, C, D, and E. You obtain these registered Internet addresses through ARIN (American Registry for Internet Numbers), which assigns them based on your network size or class. The ARIN organization makes these assignments to individual companies and Internet service providers based on the size of network defined by the class type.

The Internet community originally defined the classes to address networks of varying sizes designated by their high-order bits, and with specific ranges. Table 2.1 exhibits this information for Classes A, B, and C.

TABLE 2.1 Attributes of Class A, Class B, and Class C Addresses

Attributes	Class A (Slash /8)	Class B (Slash /16)	Class C (Slash /24)
Size	Meant to define the relatively few networks such as government, university, military, and research facilities in which a vast number of hosts exist.	Encompasses large numbers of networks with equally large numbers of hosts, as in medium-sized companies.	Intended to tackle the needs of small networks by providing a very large number of network addresses with a minimal number of hosts per network.
Bit Designations	Begin with zero (0) as their first bit.	Begin with 10 as their first two bits.	Begin with 110 as their first three bits.
Value Range	1-126	128-191	192-223
Assigned Network Bytes	1 Byte	2 Bytes	3 Bytes
Available Host Bytes	3 Bytes	2 Bytes	1 Byte
Number of Networks	126	16,384	2,097,152
Number of Hosts	16,777,214	65,534	254

Classes D and E addresses have special uses and are not assigned to mainstream networks. Class A network 127 is reserved as a loopback address (127.0.0.1) used for testing purposes.

To further explain the designation of bits, the first 7 bits within the first byte of a Class A address (the first bit is a zero) define the network address, or NetID. You can use the last 24 bits (3 bytes) to define multiple subnetworks and uniquely identify hosts within the network if the network has been subdivided. If you have not subdivided the network, the remaining bits within the last three bytes define hosts.

Class B addresses begin with a starting 2-bit value of 10 within the first byte and use the remaining 14 bits within the first and second bytes as the NetID. You can use the second 2 bytes to define additional subnetworks (if you have subdivided the network) or hosts. Following this pattern, Class C addresses use the first 21 bits (within the first three bytes) and begin with a value of 110, which identifies the NetID. You can use the last byte to define subnetworks and hosts on these subnetworks. Figure 2.4 shows the structures of Classes A, B, C, D, and E addresses.

FIGURE 2.4

Note that only A, B, and C are for public use.

IP Adress Classes

Class Type	First Byte Range	Default Mask
Class A	1 to 126	255.0.0.0
Class B	128 to 191	255.255.0.0
Class C	192 to 223	255.255.255.0
Class D	224 to 247	Used for Multicast Broadcasts
Class E	248 to 254	Reserved

127.0.0.1 is Loopback Address

Figure 2.5 shows the class addresses in bits. Note that Class A has 7 bits for network and 24 bits for hosts; Class B has 14 bits for network and 16 bits for hosts; Class C has 21 bits for network and 24 bits for hosts.

FIGURE 2.5

Note that the number of hosts and networks you have available depends on what address class you have: A, B, or C.

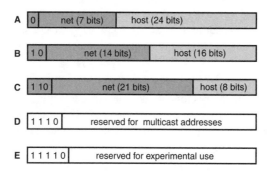

5 Classes of Addresses

Each of the preceding address classes define major classful boundaries. You can further subdivide these address classes to allow for subnetworks within a single network rather than many hosts on one network. This subdivision requires that you allocate the leftover bits—anything not assigned by ARIN—to subnets and hosts.

We discuss the topic of subnetting later in this chapter. For now let's keep it simple: Assume the assigned network has not been subnetted and all leftover bits are host bits only. This is a representation of classful addressing, in which only the major class-based network address defines the network.

Class A

Class A networks, or Slash 8 (8-bit registered addresses) begin with the first (high order) bit of zero, followed by another 7 bits that define the network number, and 24 variable bits that can define host addresses for that network. Slash 8 describes the total number of bits within the subnet mask that indicate the network portion of the address. RFC 950 puts networks in this class within the range of 1 through 126. The limitation for the maximum number of networks uses this algorithm: 2^7-2. To understand it, remember that the leading bit of 0 occupies the first bit. You must subtract 2 because a 0 in the first byte or network portion is not a legal network address. Additionally, the value 255 is reserved as a broadcast address.

As you will soon discover, 126 networks is not a large number. However, your tradeoff is a large number of possible hosts resulting from the last three bytes. More specifically, the formula to determine the maximum number of hosts with a Class A address is $2^{24}-2$, which equals a total of 16,777,214 hosts per network. Again, you subtract 2 because an address of all 1s with this 24-bit range indicates a broadcast to all hosts on the network, and an address of all 0s simply designates the network and is not a valid host address. Those in Class A have an address range of 1.xxx.xxx.xxx through 126.xxx.xxx.xxx.

You must consider one more address as a Class A address: 127. However, this particular address is a loopback address and cannot be used as a standard network address. You typically would use IP address 127.0.0.1 to verify that a device's internal IP configuration functions properly by pinging this address. Although technically we consider this address a Class A because of its special use, ARIN would not give it out as a network address.

Class B

Class B, or Slash 16, networks follow the same basic formula as described above in that the first 14 bits, with the first 2 bytes, are assigned by ARIN as the network ID. Slash 16 describes the total number of bits within the subnet mask that indicate the network portion of the address. This leaves the second 2 bytes available for the host ID. The first two high order bits within the first byte of a Class B address always equal 10. The maximum number of networks is 2^{14}, which equals 16,384 networks. With 16 bits left over for hosts, you can assign a total of $2^{16}-2$, or 65,534 hosts per network. Those in Class B have an address range value of 128.0.xxx.xxx through 191.255.xxx.xxx.

Class C

Class C, or Slash 24, networks have the value 110 for their first 3 high order bit designations. Slash 24 describes the total number of bits within the subnet mask that indicate the network portion of the address. Following the same basic formula, you can get 2^{21}, equaling 2,097,152 networks, with a total of 2^8-2, or 254, hosts per network. You can easily identify Class C addresses if the value within the first byte falls in the range of 192 to 223.

Classes D and E

As previously noted, the public cannot use Classes D and E. ARIN reserves Class D addresses for multicast addresses, and it is not for use by individual hosts on a network. The Class D address range is between 224 to 239. ARIN has reserved the Class E address for future use. Its address range falls between 240 and 247.

Reserved Addresses

Reserved addresses can be used for a variety of special purposes. These specific addresses and ranges, which remain reserved and have restricted uses, include

- **255.255.255.255**   An entire IP address set to all ones, such as this one, signifies a network-wide message sent to all nodes and all networks. Used for broadcast purposes.

- **0.0.0.0**   An IP address set to all zeros represents an unknown network or host, and typically is used to define a default gateway of last resort.

- **127.0.0.1**   This is a special Class A address used for internal loopback testing. It designates the local node and will not generate any network traffic.

Although IP address 255.255.255.255 is considered a network-wide flooded broadcast, routers do not forward this type of broadcast. Routers isolate broadcasts to subnets. To broadcast to all hosts on a subnet or network, set all host bits to ones. For example, to send a broadcast to all hosts on a Class B network 131.107.0.0 with a standard mask of 255.255.0.0, you would specify the destination address as 131.107.255.255.

Reserved addresses also include private networks. RFC 1918 defines private networks as the following:

- 10.0.0.0-10.255.255.255

- 172.16.0.0-172.31.255.255

- 192.168.0.0-192.168.255.255.

You cannot use the nonregistered private addresses on the Internet. However, companies commonly use them internally within a company's network.

Many companies use the 10.x.x.x private network because it offers internal addressing flexibility. With 3 bytes available for subnetworks and hosts, it provides more than enough bits to handle any company's IP addressing needs. With registered IP addresses becoming scarce, it is common to use inside private addressing schemes with address translation mechanisms allowing one or two outside registered addresses to be used for Internet access.

Translation between inside private addresses and outside registered addresses is defined as NAT (network address translation). Typically, a gateway (router) or firewall connecting a company's network to the outside world or Internet, where private addresses are not allowed, is responsible for the NAT process. We discuss NAT in further detail later in this chapter.

Network and Subnet Masks

You might wonder, "What are subnet masks, and why do we need them?" The simple answer is that they are address indicators that end hosts and routers use to determine whether to *shout* or *route* traffic to forward datagrams to a destination host. You might ask, "What do *shouting* and *routing* mean?" The short answer is that if a sending end host knows a destination host resides on the same *local* segment, it can shout a local Address Resolution Protocol (ARP) broadcast to resolve the logical Network layer IP address to a MAC address. Conversely, if the sending host knows the receiver resides on a *remote* subnet or network, the sender has to route the frame by sending it to a local gateway router. A sending host uses its local mask to determine whether to shout or route. We will discuss address resolution and the ARP protocol in more detail in Chapter 4, "Address Resolution."

Each of the three classful network types comes with a corresponding default classful subnet mask. As previously mentioned, Class A addresses use a default mask of 255.0.0.0 or Slash 8 (/8). Class B addresses use a default mask of 255.255.0.0 or Slash 16 (/16). In this case, notice that the first 16 bits have been masked off by turning on each of the 8 bits within each of the bytes. If you add up the value of all the bits within each octet, you come up with a maximum value of 255. The last 16 bits remain unused (and not defined for network purposes), thus all are 0s and remain available for subnets and hosts.

Class C addresses have a default mask of 255.255.255.0 or Slash 24 (/24), indicating that the first 3 bytes of this address definitely are part of the network. This leaves the last 8 bits unmasked and available for subnets and hosts. For example, host 166.3.22.1 (note the Class B address) wants to establish a connection to a remote Telnet server 151.10.5.2 (another Class B address). It's important to understand that sending hosts have absolutely no idea where the destination host really resides. That is, the IP address of the destination host alone does not tell the sender where or how get to that host, or even if it resides on the local segment.

For the sending host to determine whether the destination host resides on the same local segment, the sender compares the sending host's subnet mask to the destination host's IP address. If the sender finds that the receiving host resides on the local subnet it knows that it can shout (send) a local ARP to resolve this logical address to a MAC address.

The source host must determine whether the destination host resides on the same subnet by performing *bitwise ANDing,* which compares the destination host's IP address to the sending host's subnet mask. Until it conducts bitwise ANDing the source host has no idea whether this host is local or remote. (We will discuss bitwise ANDing later in this chapter.) If the sender determines that the host does not reside on the local segment (remote), it knows that sending a local ARP will not reach the remote host. The sending host now knows it must route the frame by sending it to a local gateway router. To get the datagram to the router for forwarding, this host must know the MAC address of the local gateway. Hopefully this host has already used this gateway before and still has this information in cache. If not, the sending host must send a local ARP to resolve the gateway's IP address to a MAC address before it sends datagrams for forwarding (see Figure 2.6).

FIGURE 2.6

Depending on whether the destination resides locally or remotely determines how the router goes about resolving the address.

Can I Shout?
Or do I Route?

Source IP Address is: 166.3.22.1

Destination Host: 151.10.5.2

Source Host MASK: 255.255.0.0

It is important to note that an improperly configured subnet mask could cause an end host to shout (send out a local ARP broadcast for the end host) when it should route, (send out a local ARP broadcast for the gateway) and vice versa. For example, let's say Host A and Host B reside on the same physical segment. The user on Host A (IP address 155.10.1.1) types in Telnet and the IP address, wanting to connect to Host B (IP address 155.10.2.2). However, Host A cannot determine that Host B is on the same segment until it compares its address to Host A's mask.

Both hosts have Class B addresses, meaning the first 2 bytes are the network address, which is 155.10.0.0, and should have a mask of 255.255.0.0. However, Host A's mask is incorrectly configured as 255.255.255.0. This causes Host A to think the first 3 bytes are the network address. When Host A compares this mask to Host B's IP address, it assumes Host B is remote because its address appears to be 155.10.2.0. This causes Host A to route (send out a local ARP broadcast for the gateway) and forward datagrams to the gateway destined for Host B instead of shout (send out a local ARP broadcast for the end host and forward datagrams directly to Host B).

If Host A had the proper subnet mask, it would have found that Host B was on the same local subnet and simply sent a local ARP broadcast to resolve Host B's IP address to a MAC address. It then would forward datagrams to that host without help from a gateway. Because Host A has bad information it makes a poor choice, sending what should be a local frame to the gateway instead.

Assuming the gateway is properly configured, it performs the same IP address to subnet mask comparison, determines that Host B resides on the local subnet, and retransmits the frame back out the same interface on which it received it. The gateway also sends an ICMP (Internet Control Message Protocol) redirect message to Host A notifying it that there is a better way to send this frame. (We discuss ICMP messages in more detail in Chapter 3, "Network Layer/Internet Protocols"; and ARP and RARP in Chapter 4.) However, this does not resolve the problem of a misconfigured mask on Host A. The best way to resolve this problem is to fix the subnet mask on Host A; otherwise Host A will continue to send local frames to the gateway when they could be sent directly to local hosts on this segment.

Bitwise ANDing

Bitwise ANDing compares the destination host's IP address (see Figures 2.7 and 2.8) to the sending host's subnet mask, a process that is governed by a set of rules. Before beginning the process of ANDing, you must convert these addresses to their binary forms so you can understand how the comparison occurs. Bitwise ANDing has the following rules:

- If both values are one, the result is one.

- If one of the values is zero, and the other is one, the result is zero.

- If both of the values are zero, the result is zero.

FIGURE 2.7

Note that during Bitwise ANDing the number remains one only if both values are one.

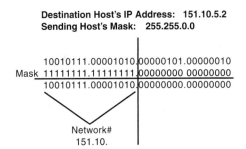

Using Figure 2.7 as an example, determine whether the destination host resides on the same local subnet as the sending host. To determine this:

1. Compare the destination host's IP address with the sending host's subnet mask. The destination host's IP address is 151.10.5.2; the sender's mask is 255.255.0.0.

2. Convert the IP address and subnet mask to binary.

3. Draw a line vertically to separate the masked area (which represents the network address) from the unmasked area (which represents the host portion).

4. Consider any values within the IP address falling within the masked portion on the left to be part of the network. In this example, the first two bytes have been masked off and represent the network (151.10) or 151.10.0.0.

5. Any values to the right of the vertical line represent the host address with the last two bytes being 5.2. Remember routers only care about the network and subnet in terms of routing traffic to a destination.

Using Figure 2.8 as an example, determine whether the sending host resides on the same subnet as the destination host. To determine this:

1. Compare the IP address of the destination host with the subnet mask of the sending host.

2. With an IP address of 166.3.22.1 and a standard Class B mask of 255.255.0.0, convert both the IP address and mask to their binary equivalents to identify which part of this address represents the network or subnet.

3. Draw a line vertically to separate the masked area (which represents the network address) from the unmasked area (which represents the host portion).

4. Consider any values within the IP address falling within the masked portion on the left to be part of the network. In this example, the first two bytes have been masked off and represent the network (166.3).

5. Any values to the right of the vertical line represent the host address with the last two bytes being 22.1.

FIGURE 2.8

To compare the subnet mask of the sending host and the IP address of the destination host, convert the decimal value into binary.

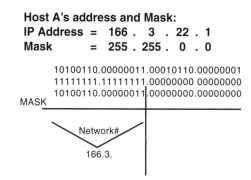

Host A's address and Mask:
IP Address = 166 . 3 . 22 . 1
Mask   = 255 . 255 . 0 . 0

10100110.00000011.00010110.00000001
11111111.11111111.00000000 00000000
MASK 10100110.00000011.00000000.00000000

Network#
166.3.

Note that host 5.2 does not reside on the same subnet with host 22.1 on subnet 166.3, listed in Figure 2.7. As a result, Host A sends the frame to its gateway instead of directly to Host B. The router then forwards the frame onto the adjacent segment to Host B (see Figure 2.9).

FIGURE 2.9

Host A has been configured with the wrong mask and should be sending datagrams to Host B, which is local.

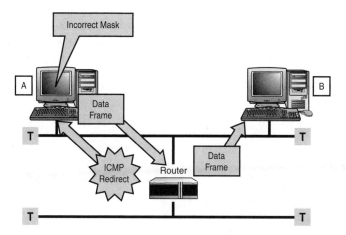

Misdirected Frames

Subnetting and Examples

Let's say you have a TCP/IP network and ARIN or your ISP (Internet service provider) has assigned your IP network address and default classful mask. When you look at the four bytes of an IP address, the first byte determines the class. If you have a network address of 130.57.0.0 with the default mask of 255.255.0.0, you have a Class B address with a network capable of supporting more than 65,000 hosts. You probably won't need a network with more than 65,000 hosts; instead you'll want to subdivide your network into smaller, more manageable pieces called subnets connected through gateways.

Subnetting is breaking up larger networks into smaller networks. Take the example of a pie. If you are given a whole pie, chances are you will not want to eat it all. Instead, you slice the pie into pieces and use what you need. Just like the pie you slice, you can borrow bits from the host side and add them to the network side, which creates a subnet. You need to keep four things to keep in mind if you want to evenly break up a larger network:

- How many subnets are presently required for the organization?

- How many additional subnets will need to be provided for in the future?

- What is the number of hosts in the network's largest subnet?

- What is the anticipated size of the largest future subnet on the network?

To understand the process of breaking up a network, consider breaking up a 130.57.0.0 network address with the default network mask of 255.255.0.0. If you want to subnet the network you borrow from the host bits and add them to the network side. For example, let's say you need 254 subnetworks within your network. To achieve this you would need to borrow 8 of the host bits and use them for subnets within network 130.57.x.0 (x represents the 8-bit byte you are borrowing). This changes your mask of 255.255.0.0 to a subnet mask of 255.255.255.0.

In Figure 2.10 the network 130.57.0.0 has been broken up into several subnetworks by borrowing all 8 bits within the third byte and masking them off. From there, you need to identify the network IDs for each new subnet such as 130.57.1. Now instead of one network, you have a total of 254 usable subnets. You can continue to borrow bits to increase the number of subnets and decrease the number of hosts. Although this example shows only 2 subnets, network 130.57.0.0 now can support a total of 254 subnets, providing for future growth. With 1 byte left over for hosts, each of these subnets could support up to 254 hosts.

When you vary the length of the default network mask beyond the default classful boundary, it is referred to as VLSM (variable length subnet mask). Some routing protocols do not understand VLSMs and thus have difficulty routing datagrams destined to subnets that they cannot discover. We discuss routing in Chapter 5, "IP Routing" and routing protocols in Chapter 6, "Routing Protocols."

FIGURE 2.10

Subnetting a Class B network.

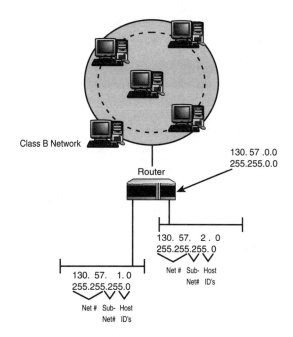

To figure out how many bits you need to borrow, you first need to know how many subnets are needed within your network. For this example, let's say you need 13 additional subnets for a Class C network address of 192.3.1.0 with a default mask of 255.255.255.0. To calculate the number of bits required for a specific number of subnets use the chart in Figure 2.11.

To determine the number of bits to borrow:

1. Start from the right.

2. Cover bits with a your hand or a piece of paper until you reach a value that is at least 2 greater than the number of subnets you need.

FIGURE 2.11

Use this chart to determine how many bits are required for subnets and hosts.

IP Calculation Chart

65536	.	32768	16384	8192	4096	2048	1024	512	256	.	128	64	32	16	8	4	2	1
X	.	X	X	X	X	X	X	X	X	.	X	X	X	X	X	X	X	X

3. Take that number and subtract 2 (subtracting 2 from the number eliminates 2 bit values that are all 1s and all 0s, which are invalid).

4. The resulting value represents the number of subnets you get if you borrow the bits you covered.

For instance, for 13 subnets:

1. Cover the following bits from right to left 4, 2, and 1.

2. You should see a value of 8 in the next bit position.

3. Subtract 2 from 8, which equals 6; with 3 bits you do not get enough subnets.

4. Cover one more bit so you have covered 4 bits total.

5. Look at the next value, 16 (this is at least two greater than the 13 subnets you need).

6. Subtract 2 from 16, which equals 14.

7. You now have enough for the required 13 subnets (see Figure 2.12).

You can use the same calculation chart and method to calculate the number of bits necessary for hosts. Note that when you have a finite number of bits to be shared between subnets and hosts, bits you use for one cannot be used for the other. For example, if you have 16 bits available and you borrow 7 bits for subnets, you have only 11 bits for hosts. If you borrow 12 bits for subnets you have only 4 bits for hosts. It's simple math. You can use the chart to determine how many subnets you will get with 7 or 12 bits and how many hosts you will get with 11 or 4 bits using the earlier method.

FIGURE 2.12

In this example you need to borrow 4 bits.

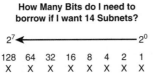

How Many Bits do I need to borrow if I want 14 Subnets?

$2^7 \longleftarrow \longrightarrow 2^0$

128	64	32	16	8	4	2	1
X	X	X	X	X	X	X	X
				1	1	1	1

8 + 4 + 2 + 1 = 15

15 - 1 = 14 Subnets

Now that you have determined you need 4 bits to have 13 subnets, you need to extend the network mask to include the subnets; that is, the 4 subnetted bits (subnet mask). You know the default classful mask for network 192.3.1.0 is 24 bits in length or 255.255.255.0, so you leave these bits alone. To determine the subnet mask:

1. Start from the leftmost bit within the last byte (the 25th bit, and so forth).

2. Count from left to right 4 bit positions.

3. Add up the bit values of the four bit positions you counted off: 128+64+32+16=240 (see Figure 2.13).

4. The subnet mask for 14 subnets equals 240. The standard Class C network mask changes to include subnets within the last octet, making your new network and subnet mask 255.255.255.240. You now have 14 usable subnet addresses with 4 bits left over for hosts on each of the subnets.

FIGURE 2.13

To figure the subnet mask, add up the masked bits to calculate the mask value.

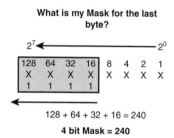

You also need to identify the available subnet range within the 240 subnet mask. There are two ways to calculate the subnet range; one is to list all the possible combinations of subnetted bits as in the following:

1. List all bit combinations with the 4 bits reserved for subnet addresses.

2. Add the charged bits for each unique bit combination that falls within the subnet masked portion. Again, remember to throw out the combinations of all 1s and all 0s.

3. Place 1s and 0s under the different combinations of high order values (see Figure 2.14).

4. Add up the different combinations.

5. You should have 16, 32, 48, 64, 80, 96, 112, 128, 144, 160, 176, 192, 208, and 224, respectively. These 14 numbers represent your subnetwork addresses (see Figure 2.14).

The other way to calculate the subnet range is as follows:

1. Use the lowest value in the masked range (16, start of range) as your base value. This represents the first valid subnet. You can figure all other subnets with this base value.

2. Continue to add 16 (the difference between each range) to these numbers until you reach the highest value below the mask. These numbers create your subnet range.

3. For example, add 16 to 16 (32). Add 16 to 32 (48). Your next subnet range should equal 64.

FIGURE 2.14

This subnet range. Remember that all 0s and all 1s are illegal.

What is the Subnet Range?

	240							
	128	64	32	16	8	4	2	1
	X	X	X	X	X	X	X	X
0	0	0	0	0				
16	0	0	0	1				
32	0	0	1	0				
48	0	0	1	1				
64	0	1	0	0				
80	0	1	0	1				
96	0	1	1	0				
112	0	1	1	1				
128	1	0	0	0				
144	1	0	0	1				
160	1	0	1	0				
176	1	0	1	1				
192	1	1	0	0				
208	1	1	0	1				
224	1	1	1	0				
240	1	1	1	1				

You now must figure the number of hosts per subnet. Different classes and a different number of bits borrowed affect the number of hosts per subnet. Because you borrowed 4 of the 8 bits within the last byte for subnets, you have only 4 bits left over for host assignment. You already know the calculation for 4 bits; it is the same calculation you did for subnets. To figure the number of hosts per subnet (host range):

1. Start from the low order bit and move to the left. Cover the 4 bits you have left to use for hosts.

2. Look at the next uncovered value (16).

3. Subtract 2 to find out how many hosts you get with the remaining four bits. Of course you already know the answer to this question because you did the math for subnets (16–2=14 hosts per subnet).

4. For valid host IDs on each subnet, add 1 to each starting subnet range (for example, 16+1) and subtract 2 from the next value in the subnet range (for example, 32–2).

5. Continue this process for each subnet range to get the values of the valid hosts for each subnet.

6. You should have 17–30, 33–46, 49–62, 65–78, 81–94, 97–110, 113–126, 129–142, 145–158, 161–174, 177–190, 193–206, 209–222 and 225–238 as your valid ID ranges (see Figure 2.15).

Note that the broadcast value for each subnet is 1 less than the next valid subnet value. For example, the broadcast address for subnet 16 would be 31 (32–1, as 32 is the next subnet).

FIGURE 2.15

This figure shows the valid ID ranges.

Valid Host and Broadcast Addresses

	240									Host Range			Broadcast
	128	64	32	16		8	4	2	1				
	X	X	X	X		X	X	X	X				
0	0	0	0	0						Host Range			Broadcast
16	0	0	0	1		17	-		30				31
32	0	0	1	0		33	-		46				47
48	0	0	1	1		49	-		62				63
64	0	1	0	0		65	-		78				79
80	0	1	0	1		81	-		94				95
96	0	1	1	0		97	-		110				111
112	0	1	1	1		113	-		126				127
128	1	0	0	0		129	-		142				143
144	1	0	0	1		145	-		158				159
160	1	0	1	0		161	-		174				175
176	1	0	1	1		177	-		190				191
192	1	1	0	0		193	-		206				207
208	1	1	0	1		209	-		222				223
224	1	1	1	0		225	-		238				239
240	1	1	1	1									

As previously mentioned, class type affects the number of host bits available for borrowing. The good news is the calculation procedure does not. Let's take a look at a Class B address. For a Class B address with a standard 16-bit network mask (255.255.0.0) with an additional 4 subnetted bits, you can see that you have 12 host bits available to borrow. We already did the math on 4 bits. We know that 4 bits will get you 14 (subnets or hosts), depending on what you are using the bits for.

With that information we know how many bits we need to extend the Class B default mask: 4 additional bits to include the subnets. That changes the mask to 255.255.240.0. We have extended the mask to include 4 bits within the third byte as subnetted bits. This means we have 12 bits left over within the third and fourth bytes to assign hosts. Use the calculation chart to find out how many hosts we will get per subnet with 12 bits. Cover all 12 bits with a piece of paper and look at the next uncovered value, which should be 4096. Subtract 2 (4096–2= 4094) to determine the number of hosts per subnet (see Figure 2.16).

Earlier you learned how to derive the subnet range from a Class C network with 4 subnet masked bits. With 4 subnetted bits you get this subnet range: 16, 32, 48, 64, 80, 96, 112, 128, 144, 160, 176, 192, 208, and 224, respectively. These 14 numbers represent your subnetwork addresses. Now that you know the subnet range, you identify the valid host IDs and broadcast address on each subnet. This is where you deviate from the previous method. With a Class C example, as previously used, you had only 8 bits to worry about; now you have 16 bits to deal with.

FIGURE 2.16

The Class B network 130.100.0.0 has been further divided into subnets by masking off four of the host bits within the third byte (240).

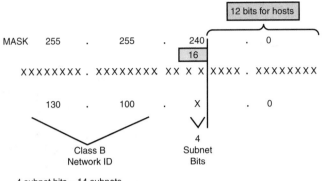

4 subnet bits = 14 subnets
12 host bits = 4094 hosts per subnet

With a Class B network, when you cross over an 8-bit boundary, such as this example (network 130.100.0.0 255.255.240.0 mask, representing the 4 subnetted bits in the third byte) in which the host bits straddle the third and fourth bytes, calculating the host ranges gets a little more complex. The best method of tackling this is to use binary. To calculate the host range:

1. Take the first subnet within network 130.100.16.0 (the lowest subnet within the mask) and convert it to binary.

2. Start with the lowest possible value within the host ID bits. This gives you the first valid host within the subnet.

3. Identify the highest possible value (which represents the broadcast for the subnet). By doing this you can easily back into the highest valid host range within the subnet (which is always one less than the broadcast).

4. When you cross over an octet boundary, you add the values in each octet separately. Remember to add only the charged bits within each byte.

3rd byte								.	4th byte							
4bit mask 240																
128	64	32	16	8	4	2	1	.	128	64	32	16	8	4	2	1
0	0	0	1	0	0	0	0	.	0	0	0	0	0	0	0	1

5. To identify the first valid host address on subnet 16, place 0s in all host bit positions except the rightmost bit, which is a 1. This represents the lowest possible host value available within this subnet. Remember you cannot have all 0s in the host portion (invalid host ID).

6. Take each byte separately and add the charged bits within the byte. The third byte contains only 1 charged bit, 16; therefore, the value within that byte equals 16.

7. The fourth byte contains only the last byte charged bit, which is a value of 1. Your first valid host IP address for subnet 16 on network 130.100 would be 130.100.16.1 (see Figure 2.17).

FIGURE 2.17

This figure shows how to calculate the first valid host for each subnet.

What is the First Valid Host for each Subnet?

240																	
Sub nets	128 X	64 X	32 X	16 X	8 X	4 X	2 X	1 X	•128 • X	64 X	32 X	16 X	8 X	4 X	2 X	1 X	First Valid Host
16	0	0	0	1	0	0	0	0	• 0	0	0	0	0	0	0	1	16.1
32	0	0	1	0	0	0	0	0	• 0	0	0	0	0	0	0	1	32.1
48	0	0	1	1	0	0	0	0	• 0	0	0	0	0	0	0	1	48.1
64	0	1	0	0	0	0	0	0	• 0	0	0	0	0	0	0	1	64.1
80	0	1	0	1	0	0	0	0	• 0	0	0	0	0	0	0	1	80.1
96	0	1	1	0	0	0	0	0	• 0	0	0	0	0	0	0	1	96.1
112	0	1	1	1	0	0	0	0	• 0	0	0	0	0	0	0	1	112.1
128	1	0	0	0	0	0	0	0	• 0	0	0	0	0	0	0	1	128.1
144	1	0	0	1	0	0	0	0	• 0	0	0	0	0	0	0	1	144.1
160	1	0	1	0	0	0	0	0	• 0	0	0	0	0	0	0	1	160.1
176	1	0	1	1	0	0	0	0	• 0	0	0	0	0	0	0	1	176.1
192	1	1	0	0	0	0	0	0	• 0	0	0	0	0	0	0	1	192.1
208	1	1	0	1	0	0	0	0	• 0	0	0	0	0	0	0	1	208.1
224	1	1	1	0	0	0	0	0	• 0	0	0	0	0	0	0	1	224.1

Now go to the opposite extreme to derive the broadcast address. Change all 12 host bits to 1s; then add the charged bits within the third and fourth bytes separately (see Figure 2.18).

3rd byte 4th byte

4bit mask 240

128   64 32 16 | 8   4   2   1   .   128 64 32 16 8   4   2   1

  0   0   0   1 | 1   1   1   1   .   1   1   1   1   1   1   1   1

Broadcast 130.100.31.255—You get this by adding all charged bits within the third byte; then the fourth byte. You have 16+8+4+2+1=31 in the third byte. From here you can easily determine that highest possible valid host ID, which is always one less than the broadcast address for the subnet. To determine this, just change the rightmost bit to a 0; then add them up again. You have 130.100.31.254 as your last valid host range (see Figure 2.19).

3rd byte 4th byte

4bit mask 240

128   64 32 16 | 8   4   2   1   .   128 64 32 16 8   4   2   1

  0   0   0   1 | 1   1   1   1   .   1   1   1   1   1   1   1   0

FIGURE 2.18

The broadcast address is indicated by all 1s in the hosts' bits.

What is Broacast address for each subnet?

240

Sub nets	128	64	32	16	8	4	2	1	.	128	64	32	16	8	4	2	1	Subnet Broadcast
	X	X	X	X	X	X	X	X	.	X	X	X	X	X	X	X	X	
16	0	0	0	1	1	1	1	1	.	1	1	1	1	1	1	1	1	31.255
32	0	0	1	0	1	1	1	1	.	1	1	1	1	1	1	1	1	47.255
48	0	0	1	1	1	1	1	1	.	1	1	1	1	1	1	1	1	65.255
64	0	1	0	0	1	1	1	1	.	1	1	1	1	1	1	1	1	79.255
80	0	1	0	1	1	1	1	1	.	1	1	1	1	1	1	1	1	95.255
96	0	1	1	0	1	1	1	1	.	1	1	1	1	1	1	1	1	111.255
112	0	1	1	1	1	1	1	1	.	1	1	1	1	1	1	1	1	127.255
128	1	0	0	0	1	1	1	1	.	1	1	1	1	1	1	1	1	143.255
144	1	0	0	1	1	1	1	1	.	1	1	1	1	1	1	1	1	159.255
160	1	0	1	0	1	1	1	1	.	1	1	1	1	1	1	1	1	175.255
176	1	0	1	1	1	1	1	1	.	1	1	1	1	1	1	1	1	191.255
192	1	1	0	0	1	1	1	1	.	1	1	1	1	1	1	1	1	207.255
208	1	1	0	1	1	1	1	1	.	1	1	1	1	1	1	1	1	223.255
224	1	1	1	0	1	1	1	1	.	1	1	1	1	1	1	1	1	239.255

FIGURE 2.19

As you can see, the last valid host within a subnet is always 1 less than the broadcast, indicated by a value of 0 in the right-most (value of 1) bit position.

What is the Last Valid Host for each Subnet?

240

Sub nets	128	64	32	16	8	4	2	1	.	128	64	32	16	8	4	2	1	Last Valid Host
	X	X	X	X	X	X	X	X	.	X	X	X	X	X	X	X	X	
16	0	0	0	1	1	1	1	1	.	1	1	1	1	1	1	0		31.254
32	0	0	1	0	1	1	1	1	.	1	1	1	1	1	1	0		47.254
48	0	0	1	1	1	1	1	1	.	1	1	1	1	1	1	0		65.254
64	0	1	0	0	1	1	1	1	.	1	1	1	1	1	1	0		79.254
80	0	1	0	1	1	1	1	1	.	1	1	1	1	1	1	0		95.254
96	0	1	1	0	1	1	1	1	.	1	1	1	1	1	1	0		111.254
112	0	1	1	1	1	1	1	1	.	1	1	1	1	1	1	0		127.254
128	1	0	0	0	1	1	1	1	.	1	1	1	1	1	1	0		143.254
144	1	0	0	1	1	1	1	1	.	1	1	1	1	1	1	0		159.254
160	1	0	1	0	1	1	1	1	.	1	1	1	1	1	1	0		175.254
176	1	0	1	1	1	1	1	1	.	1	1	1	1	1	1	0		191.254
192	1	1	0	0	1	1	1	1	.	1	1	1	1	1	1	0		207.254
208	1	1	0	1	1	1	1	1	.	1	1	1	1	1	1	0		223.254
224	1	1	1	0	1	1	1	1	.	1	1	1	1	1	1	0		239.254

Supernetting, Summarization, Aggregation, and CIDR

The networking industry throws around the terms supernetting, route summarization, route aggregation and CIDR (class interdomain routing) on a regular basis as if they were completely different technologies. However, these terms do not merit a distinction as separate technologies. In reality they all describe a method of reducing route update traffic and routing tables by condensing a group of contiguous IP addresses into a single address representative of the entire group.

Whichever term you decide to use, it enables routers to advertise a subset of routes reducing the number of route updates that need to be sent and reducing the size of route tables. I'm most comfortable with the term "summarization," so I'll use it throughout this section and book in describing the process.

Even though summarization might seem like a foreign concept, believe it or not you're already implementing it in your network. If you have a network that has been assigned a registered IP address to connect to the Internet, the address ARIN or your upstream service provider assigned to you represents the summarization of your company's network to everyone on the Internet.

The ARIN organization through its classful addressing scheme deliberately defined Class A, B, and C addresses which, if defined with one summarized address and assigned to a company, represent the company and all of the internal subnets. Of course you could advertise to the entire world all of your internal subnets through the Internet; however, I do not advise this for two reasons: It's an obvious security issue, and it's not necessary.

You do not need to do this because to get to your network and its subnets, other routers within the Internet need to know only how to get to your major unique classful network assigned by ARIN. Once traffic destined for network reaches your local gateway, this gateway and the gateway's internal to your company's networks take care of the rest. Consider the additional route update traffic that would be required to advertise all of your routes, and the resources it would take for all routers on the Internet to keep track of all networks and subnets for every network in existence. This is why summarization is so important.

You also can implement summarization within your company's routing infrastructure to reduce the amount of route update traffic and routing table sizes. Typically you perform summarization on routers connecting to a company's core, where link congestion and bandwidth capacity are important issues. By summarizing multiple IP addresses into a single address before this information is sent into the core you can reduce update traffic, conserving precious bandwidth.

CIDR

The industry tends to use the term "CIDR" to describe route summarization performed on contiguous Class C addresses. This type of summarization typically is done by ISPs or service providers, which have been assigned a group of contiguous Class C addresses—which they in turn have given to their downstream clients.

ISPs and Service Providers

Most of the time the terms *ISP* and *service provider* can be used interchangeably. However, the term *ISP* describes a company that provides Internet service (thus, the name Internet Service Provider) and only Internet service. A service provider can provide Internet service (an ISP) as well as other services that an ISP does not provide, such as Frame Relay and WAN connections.

The provider knows the Class C address of each client representing its network. The ISP can advertise each of the Class C network addresses out to the Internet or a subset of them. It might summarize several of these addresses into a single address to reduce the route information it passes to other gateways on the Internet.

Summarization of a group of addresses can be performed only when the addresses being summarized are contiguous and can be summarized only on a power of 2 boundary. Let's take the following IP addressing example and perform summarization: You have a Class B network address assigned to your organization (130.100.0.0, default mask 255.255.0.0) with many internal subnets. Look at a subset of these subnets for simplicity. You have x number of IP addresses that are contiguous; instead of advertising each of these separately, you want to group them and advertise the summarized route.

You would

1. Convert the IP addresses in question to binary (see Table 2.2).

2. Move from left to right.

3. Look for the longest binary match (or common bit pattern) within each address; this represents the IP address for summarization.

TABLE 2.2   Route Summarization

IP Address	Mask	Binary Representation							
		128	64	32	16	8	4	2	1
130.100.16.0	255.255.255.0	0	0	0	1	0	0	0	0
130.100.17.0	255.255.255.0	0	0	0	1	0	0	0	1
130.100.18.0	255.255.255.0	0	0	0	1	0	0	1	0
130.100.19.0	255.255.255.0	0	0	0	1	0	0	1	1
130.100.20.0	255.255.255.0	0	0	0	1	0	1	0	0
130.100.21.0	255.255.255.0	0	0	0	1	0	1	0	1
130.100.22.0	255.255.255.0	0	0	0	1	0	1	1	0
130.100.23.0	255.255.255.0	0	0	0	1	0	1	1	1
130.100.24.0	255.255.255.0	0	0	0	1	1	0	0	0
130.100.25.0	255.255.255.0	0	0	0	1	1	0	0	1
130.100.26.0	255.255.255.0	0	0	0	1	1	0	1	0
130.100.27.0	255.255.255.0	0	0	0	1	1	0	1	1
130.100.28.0	255.255.255.0	0	0	0	1	1	1	0	0

TABLE 2.2   Continued

IP Address	Mask	Binary Representation							
---	---	128	64	32	16	8	4	2	1
130.100.29.0	255.255.255.0	0	0	0	1	1	1	0	1
130.100.30.0	255.255.255.0	0	0	0	1	1	1	1	0
130.100.31.0	255.255.255.0	0	0	0	1	1	1	1	1

You really don't need to do a binary conversion to determine whether they match because each address starts with 130.100, so the binary match would be identical. In this case only the third byte is in question. Now that you have the list of binary values for each subnet, it's clear that all of these subnets have the first 4 bits in common, in addition to the 16 bits within the first and second bytes. This means you can summarize all of these subnets with a single IP address of 130.100.16.0 using a 20-bit mask (16 networks bits plus 4 subnet bits) or 255.255.240.0 or /20.

Remember the point of summarization is to reduce route updates. You might have recognized that subsets within this group all contain further matches. However, only those addresses that match exactly can be summarized and only to the longest match. You could group the subset of matches and summarize them separately; however, you would need to advertise that group separately. Because all 16 of the previously mentioned networks have 4 common bits you can group and summarize all 16 of them with a single address. Summarizing a subset proves less efficient and unnecessary.

Implementing Route Summarization

The implementation of route summarization within your network requires configuration of routers, which is vendor specific and beyond the scope of this book.

Network Address Translation (NAT)

The term *network address translation* describes the process of translating nonregistered (private) IP addresses (listed earlier in this chapter) to a single registered valid IP address or range of addresses to be used when communicating with hosts on the Internet. Remember that ARIN is responsible for assigning registered IP addresses to organizations for use on the Internet. However, the 32-bit addressing scheme it developed way back when cannot support the millions of Internet hosts in existence today.

To address the issue of dwindling IP addresses and the exponential growth of Internet hosts, new IP addressing solutions became necessary. The networking industry proposed one solution—to change the current IP addressing scheme, increasing the number of Network layer bits from 32 to 128, making more addresses available. The industry has discussed this new addressing scheme, referred to as

- IPNG (NG stands for "next generation," which I assume was named by some Trekkies out there in the virtual galaxy).

- IPv6 (v6 meaning version 6).

The current version of IP is version 4. Although the industry has debated IPv6 regularly, this option has been largely ignored because it would require everyone participating on the Internet to redesign their addressing schemes. In addition, adjustments would have to be made to current routing protocols, and so on, to effectively implement it. Meanwhile, other solutions have emerged that enable us to continue using the existing addressing structure of IPv4, such as NAT.

An administrator must enable and configure a router with the NAT service (specific configuration is beyond the scope of this book). Routers supporting NAT basically convert inside private addresses, such as 10.x.x.x to a registered outside IP address, when a host within the private network attempts to communicate with a host on the Internet. NAT has three types of implementation:

- Static (see Figure 2.20)

- Dynamic (see Figure 2.21)

- Combination of static and dynamic

FIGURE 2.20

This shows a one-to-one (static) mapping of the inside to the outside address.

Static Mappings

NAT Table	
Inside Private	Outside Registered
10.1.1.2	36.1.2.3
10.1.1.3	36.1.2.4

FIGURE 2.21

This shows multiple private addresses mapping to the same outside registered address using different port numbers (dynamic).

Dynamic Mappings

Inside Private	Outside Registered:	Client Port
10.1.1.2	36.1.2.3	1004
10.1.1.3	36.1.2.3	6002

Static

Think of static NATs as one-to-one network translations—each inside address is mapped to a different outside address. Administrators must manually create the static mapping on the router performing the translation. With this type of NAT you must have as many outside addresses as inside, which makes NAT seem useless.

Dynamic

Think of dynamic NATs as many-to-one or many-to-a-couple network translations—multiple inside addresses mapped to a single outside address or small pool of addresses. Administrators typically define a small pool of registered addresses to be used when translating any inside address. Because a single IP address or small pool of addresses is used to translate all inside addresses, an administrator must implement a method of uniquely identifying each inside host.

To uniquely identify each inside host, even though they map to the same outside address, the source host's Transport layer port (identifying the process or program) is appended to the outside address. The industry uses this type of NAT the most. With this type of NAT, you need only one or a couple of outside addresses, making the most efficient use of the registered addresses.

Routers performing NAT maintain mapping tables to keep track of the mapped addresses. When an inside host wants to send a datagram to a host outside the private address, it sends the datagram to the gateway for forwarding. The router maps the inside address to a registered outside address using one of the methods previously mentioned and forwards the datagram. It then holds the mapping in memory for later use (see Figure 2.22).

FIGURE 2.22

This figure shows the router holding the mapping for the private addresses to the same outside address in memory.

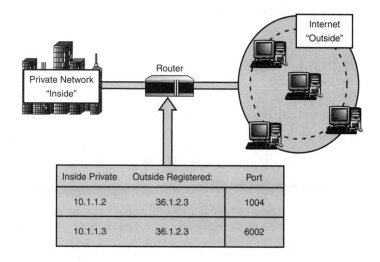

Inside Private	Outside Registered:	Port
10.1.1.2	36.1.2.3	1004
10.1.1.3	36.1.2.3	6002

Once the router has mapped the inside address to an outside address, it uses this address within the IP header of the datagram, indicating the source or sending host. The destination host does not know that the sending host's address is actually a translated address, nor does it care. When the destination host responds to the source host, the router remaps the outside address to the inside address and delivers it to the original host. Because translation is transparent, you can effectively hide your inside network hosts and infrastructure from the outside world and still allow them to communicate.

Summary

The base-10 numbering system, known as decimal numbering, consists of the numbers 0, 1, 2, 3, 4, 5, 6, 7, 8, and 9. Computers use the binary, or base-2 numbering system. To understand binary numbers, we convert them to the decimal.

The Network layer controls routing and where to route traffic. These decisions stem from the 4-octet, or 32-bit, IP address. The network address represents a company's network and subnetwork (a major network) and a node address represents a specific device on that network.

There are five major address classes: A, B, C, D, and E. The public uses only Classes A, B and C.

Subnet masks help routers and end hosts determine how to route datagrams. If the destination host resides on the same local segment, it can send an ARP broadcast to resolve the logical Network layer IP address to a MAC address. If the destination is remote, it routes the datagram to a local gateway router.

The process of comparing the destination host's IP address to the sending host's subnet mask is called bitwise ANDing.

Summarization enables routers to advertise a subset of routes. This reduces the size of the routing tables and the number of route updates that need to be sent.

Review Questions

1. What are the various IP address classes and their ranges?

2. What purpose do subnet masks serve?

3. What is the difference between the network address and the node address?

4. What are the restricted addresses and for what are they used?

5. How many bits in a Class C address are used to define the network number?

6. With a network address of 193.1.1.0 and a subnet mask of 255.255.255.240, how many subnetworks are available and how many hosts per subnet?

7. If you have an IP address of 193.1.1.32 and a /28 subnet address, what would the subnet mask be?

8. What is the correct number of subnets and hosts available on a Class B network with a subnet mask of 255.255.254.0?

9. On a Class C network, how many bits would you need to borrow if you needed 19 hosts?

10. On a Class B network, how many bits would you need to borrow if you needed 1000 hosts?

11. What is the decimal equivalent of the binary 10110111?

12. What is the binary equivalent of a subnet mask of 201?

CHAPTER 3

NETWORK LAYER/INTERNET PROTOCOLS

You will learn about the following in this chapter:

- IP operation, fields and functions
- Fragmentation and reassembly of datagrams
- ICMP messages and meanings

IP

IP (Internet Protocol) does most of the work in the TCP/IP protocol suite. All protocols and applications within the TCP/IP suite run on top of IP and utilize it for logical Network layer addressing and transmission of datagrams between internet hosts. IP maps to the Internet layer of the DoD and to the Network layer of the OSI models. ICMP (Internet Control Message Protocol) is considered an integral part of IP and uses IP for its datagram delivery; we will discuss ICMP later in this chapter. Figure 3.1 shows how IP maps to the DoD and OSI models.

How Do I Buy a Ticket on the IP Train?

The phrase "runs on top of" might sound as if an application or protocol is buying a ticket to ride on an IP train. This term is not restricted to IP. In reality, it is industry jargon used to describe any upper-layer protocol or application coming down the OSI model and utilizes another lower-layer protocol's features (in this case IP at the Network layer).

IP provides an unreliable, connectionless datagram delivery service, which means that IP does not guarantee that an IP datagram successfully reaches its destination; rather it provides best effort of delivery, which means it sends it out and hopes it gets there. IP simply adds logical source and destination network layer addresses and delivers the datagram relying on other layers to guarantee it gets to its destination. If there is a problem with delivery, IP relies on ICMP to send messages when it encounters an error. When IP encounters an error in delivery, it simply trashes the datagram, causing an ICMP message to be sent to the source host detailing what kind of delivery problem occurred. IP relies on upper layers to provide reliability; for example, TCP (which will be discussed in more detail in Chapter 8, "Transmission Control Protocol (TCP)").

FIGURE 3.1
IP provides logical addressing and connectionless delivery of datagrams for all protocols within the TCP/IP suite.

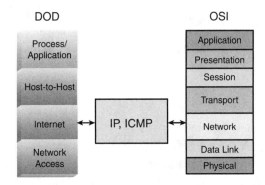

The Internet Protocol's primary function is logical network layer addressing of hosts and delivery of information in the form of datagrams between hosts. IP addressing is discussed in detail in Chapter 2, "IP Addressing." IP also performs other important functions such as fragmentation and reassembly, which are necessary when datagrams are too large to be sent by a source host and must be broken up into smaller datagrams. Because IP is connectionless it does not require a connection between hosts. It does not sequence, acknowledge, or control the flow of data between hosts. IP treats each datagram as a separate entity; it merely addresses the datagram and sends it out, hoping it reaches the destination.

IP receives a stream of data from UDP or TCP, breaks up this information into chunks, and addresses and packages each piece as a datagram, which then can be sent to a destination host across the network. Routers and routing protocols determine the path selection between a source and destination, which we discuss in more detail in Chapters 5, "IP Routing" and 6, "Routing Protocols."

RFC 791

RFC 791 defines IP, and its fields and functionality. In this chapter we will look at an IP header and its fields and examine the other protocols that reside on the Internet layer. We will discuss IP routing in Chapters 5 and 6.

IP Header

Figure 3.2 shows the format of an IP datagram as defined by RFC 791. An IP header contains a minimum of 20 bytes, unless options are present. Figure 3.3 shows an IP header as seen through a Sniffer protocol analyzer. We will describe each field after the figures.

FIGURE 3.2

The Internet Protocol header provides for identification of logical source and destination network addresses.

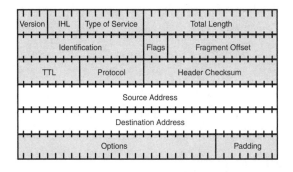

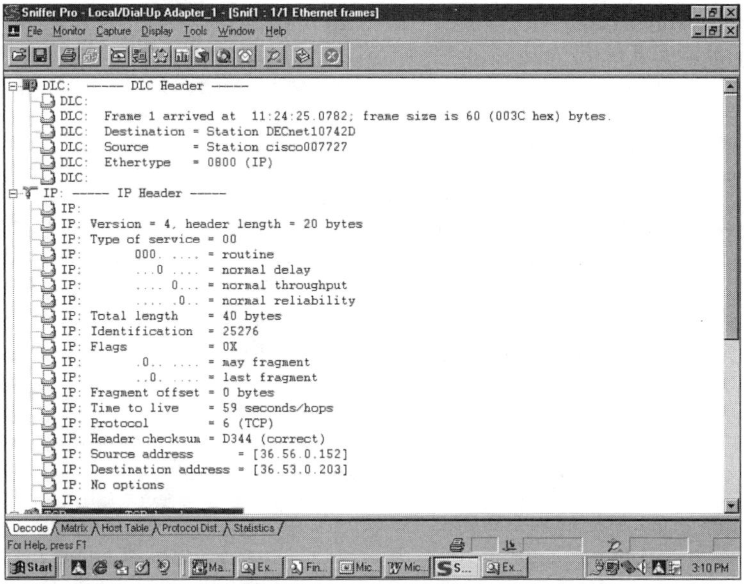

FIGURE 3.3

Note the Ethertype value contained within the DLC (Data Link Control) header states that protocol type 0x0800 or IP is the protocol being carried within this frame.

Take a look at the IP header in Figure 3.3. The first field is the version type, which should always be version 4, the official standard. This is followed by the header length, indicating the size of the IP header as 20 bytes. Type of service (ToS) values follow. Most often the ToS value, as in this case, will have a value of zero because ToS is seldom used. However, this trend is changing as ToS becomes more understood and more vendors implement it successfully in their products. New applications capable of setting these bits to influence a router's routing of datagrams are emerging. This allows them to request from routers a certain level of ToS service for transmitted data.

The total length of the datagram is 40 bytes, which includes the IP header and data being carried within the frame. The IP ID value given to this datagram is 25276. Note that in the Flags field the datagram can be fragmented if necessary, and that this is the last fragment. Because the fragment offset has a value of zero, we can deduce that this is the first, last, and only fragment within the stream.

The TTL value currently is set to 59 seconds, which is the amount of time left for this datagram to live on the internetwork. The next protocol being carried within the frame is TCP. IP uses the checksum value to identify frame damage. The sending host's logical IP address is 36.56.0.152 and the destination host's address is 36.53.0.203.

Version

The value within the 4-bit version field identifies the version of IP being implemented. This value will always be version 4. It is the most current and popular version of IP.

Internet Header Length

The 4-bit header length field identifies the size of the IP header in 32-bit words. All IP headers must have a minimum of 20 bytes in size unless additional options are implemented and specified within the option field, which we will discuss later in the "Type of Service" section of this chapter.

Type of Service

The ToS bits (8 total bits) within the IP header can influence the path datagrams take when being forwarded by routers from source to destination. ToS bits allow upper applications and processes to indicate the type of quality or service they require from a router. Until recently, the use of the ToS bits has been nonexistent. However, many companies now implement them to facilitate more intelligent path selection. If ToS has not been implemented, this field will have a value of zero. Because the use of ToS is uncommon, zero is an expected value. RFC's 1340 and 1349 describe the specific use and functions of these bits. The following explains the various ToS bits.

Bits 0–2: Precedence Bits

Bits 0–2, known as precedence bits, when used in the following combinations mean different things, and typically only the government uses these implementations to define the importance of a datagram. This value uses the options field within the IP header, discussed later in this chapter, to further describe the type of precedence requested. The precedence value typically describes the type of security levels requested defined by the Defense Intelligence Agency. Table 3.1 describes the various precedence bits set.

TABLE 3.1   Bits 0–2 = Precedence

Bit Position	Description
000	Routine information
001	Priority information
010	Immediate delivery
011	Flash

TABLE 3.1   Continued

Bit Position	Description
100	Flash override
101	Critical information
110	Internetwork control
111	Network control

Until recently most applications did not support or use precedence bits. However, they comply with governmental network implementations, which require multilevel security functions. No further discussion of these bits will follow. Precedence is described in further detail in Chapter 8. The organization that chooses to implement these bit must specifically define the precedence bits, and their use and meanings.

The next three ToS bits are the most commonly used for influencing traffic patterns.

Bit 3

Bit 3 can have one of two values:

- 0 = Normal delay
- 1 = Low delay

Delay is based on the end-to-end propagation delay of data transmitted over a link. When multiple paths exist to a destination, an application can direct routers en route to select the path with the least delay—a faster path.

Bit 4

Bit 4 can have one of two values:

- 0 = Normal throughput
- 1 = High throughput

When an application requires a path to a destination that offers high throughput rates, it sets the throughput bit to 1. Routers forward traffic along paths that support the highest possible data rate, measured as the bandwidth capacity of a link between source and destination.

Bit 5

Bit 5 can have one of two values:

- 0 = Normal reliability
- 1 = High reliability

Routers measure a link's reliability by the number of errors encountered and lost datagrams it experiences when forwarding or receiving across an interface. If multiple paths exist and one appears to be more reliable than the other, a router forwards traffic for applications, setting the reliability bit to 1 across this interface. Critical applications that cannot tolerate data loss may request this type of service.

Bits 6 and 7 (Reserved)

Bits 6 and 7 are reserved and not currently used.

Upper-layer applications or processes can request for routers to deliver their data along paths that meet their service requirements. For ToS delivery to work all routers and routing protocols within the path from source to destination must understand, and be configured to forward datagrams based on the ToS designation. Not all routing protocols understand these bits. The following routing protocols understand ToS:

- OSPF

- EIGRP

- IGRP

- BGP

The following protocols do not understand ToS:

- RIP v1

- RIP v2

Although a routing protocol might have the capability to understand and act upon these bits, it still requires configuration. If someone has not configured the router to support ToS, it simply ignores this information and forwards the datagram the best it can. Let's look at an example of how ToS works. When an application requests datagrams to be sent through a low delay path, it sets bit 3 to a value of 1. Routers along the path attempt to send datagrams across links offering faster transmissions, such as 100Mb Ethernet versus slower WAN links. Keep in mind that delay is measured by the round-trip propagation delay across the link. Therefore, a link with a lower delay would be the preferred path.

High throughput translates to high-capacity links, which have the capability to carry larger amounts of data in a shorter time frame. This is useful for large file transfers. Routers measure the capacity of a link in terms of bandwidth, which is the transfer rate in bits across the interface. For example, an Ethernet 100Mbps link carries 100 million bits per second, which is faster than a 10Mbps (10 million bit per second) interface. If reliability is the objective, such as the case in an application performing critical processes or requiring security, an application can request a more reliable transmission path by setting bit 5 to a value of 1. This might be a transaction-based processing application, which requires access to a company's fault-tolerant backbone.

It is very important to understand that by setting these bits, you change the way routers route traffic. Without a thorough understanding of the types of protocols, applications, traffic flows and protocol timers within your network, this manipulation could have catastrophic results. It is imperative that you baseline your network thoroughly before attempting to implement them. When properly used, they can dramatically increase the performance of your network and network applications.

Total Length

The 2-byte total length field within the IP header defines the length in bytes of the entire IP datagram. This value includes the IP header and data being carried within the datagram.

Identification

The sender gives each IP datagram an ID value prior to transmission, which is found in the 2-byte identification field. This ID uniquely identifies a datagram or stream of datagrams. The destination host uses this ID to reassemble the datagrams received. When a source host's IP process receives a large stream of contiguous data from UDP or TCP for datagram packaging, it breaks up this stream (fragmentation) when it receives a packet that is too large for the transmission medium. IP then assigns all datagrams belonging to the stream the same ID.

When transmitted from source to destination, datagrams can take different paths with widely varying characteristics, causing them to arrive out of order. The destination host uses this ID to recognize that all the datagrams belong to a stream. It then reassembles them in the correct order based on the fragment offset value, which we will explain later in this section.

Flags

Bit 0 = Reserved. Must be a value of zero.

Bit 1 = Can have one of two values:

- 0 = May Fragment

- 1 = Don't Fragment

The 3-bit flags field is used on hosts and gateways for fragmentation purposes. If a host or a gateway supports fragmentation, it can break a stream of data into smaller pieces before transmission. If it does not support fragmentation (the don't-fragment bit is set), the host or gateway cannot fragment the stream. Typically, the sending host has the responsibility of performing fragmentation. The destination host reassembles the datagrams into the original stream before passing it up to the upper layer (TCP or UDP) for processing. However, this is not always the case.

When a source host sends a datagram that reaches a segment and is too large to be forwarded, the gateway performs the fragmentation, breaking the datagram into smaller units acceptable for the media. Having intervening gateways perform fragmentation of datagrams in transit is not a good idea. Routers forced to perform this function require additional resources and add unnecessary overhead and latency to the delivery of the datagram. Because different underlying network architectures support varying frame sizes, find out what the lowest value MTU (Maximum Transmission Unit) size is for your network and configure your hosts and gateways to support it. For example, Ethernet has a maximum frame size of 1518 bytes, whereas Token-Ring frames might range from 4,500 bytes to 17,800 bytes.

The DF bit has another use. Some implementations use the DF bit to dynamically discover the MTU size of the network end to end. If this bit is enabled, when an end host attempts to send a datagram that is larger than the next segment along the transmission path, the intervening router will not forward the frame. Instead, the router drops the datagram and kicks back to the source host an ICMP message indicating the datagram is too large and has exceeded the maximum segment size. The host then can use this information to resize its next datagram. This process will continue until the sending host has discovered the proper size to send, allowing intervening routers to simply forward datagrams without performing fragmentation en route to its destination.

Bit 3 = Can have one of two values:

- 0 = Last Fragment
- 1 = More Fragments

The Last or More Fragments bit indicates whether this is the last datagram within a stream or more datagrams are to follow. If there is only one datagram this bit will be zero, indicating that this is the first and the last, meaning it is the only one. When a destination host receives a datagram, it notes the ID value and checks whether this bit is a one or zero, indicating that this is the last datagram or more are expected. If it expects more, this host holds the datagrams in memory until all others with the same ID arrive and the stream is reassembled and passed up to the appropriate upper-layer protocol for processing. By matching the IDs and referencing the last or more bit, the host knows when to stop expecting future datagrams within this stream and when to start reassembling them.

Fragment Offset

The sending host uses the 13-bit fragment offset value to identify the position of the datagram with the stream being sent—the order in which this datagram belongs when more than one is sent with the same IP identification. The sending host always assigns the first datagram with an offset value of zero. It assigns the second, third, or more datagrams with a number based on the MTU size. The receiver uses the fragment offset value to put the datagrams within the same stream back together upon reception or detect that one is missing within the stream.

For example, if a sending host has three datagrams to send that belong to a stream, it goes through this process:

1. Assigns each of these datagrams the same ID.

2. Sets the More Fragments bit to a one on the first two datagrams to indicate that these are not the only datagrams in this stream and that more are to follow.

3. Sets the Last Fragment bit on the final datagram in the stream.

4. Each datagrams offset bears an offset value identifying where this datagram belongs in the stream.

Figure 3.4 shows an example of a sending host and a receiving host using the fragment offset value to determine in what order datagrams belong. In Figure 3.4 Station A wants to communicate with Station B and sends a single datagram containing 1500 bytes of information on the wire. Note that the local segment attached to segment A can accept a maximum transmission unit (MTU) size of 1,518 bytes, which is sufficient to support this frame size. The datagram makes it through Router 1, which forwards it on to Router 2 as is. Note that the segment between Router 1 and 2 also accepts an MTU of 1,518.

In Figure 3.4 the WAN segment between Routers 2 and 3 will not accept a segment larger than 512 bytes, so Router 2 must break up the original datagram sent by Host A to fit this datagram on the wire; this is called fragmentation. There now are three datagrams forwarded across this link to Router 3 and ultimately to their final destination, Host B. Once these datagrams reach Host B, this host performs the reassembly prior to sending them up to the upper-layer process. Host B (the receiving host) uses the IP identification field, Last and More Fragments bit, and the fragment offset to piece the datagram back together.

FIGURE 3.4

In this figure, Host A sends a 512-byte datagram, which is too large for the WAN. Router 2 breaks up the datagram (fragments) into smaller chunks, forwarding them. The destination host is responsible for reassembly.

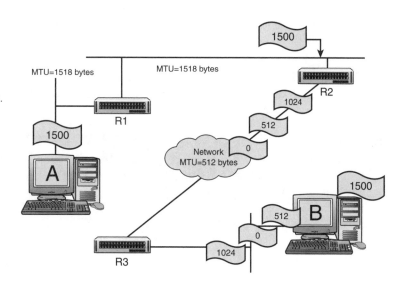

Fragmentation and Reassembly

Using Figure 3.4 as an example, the receiving host expects to find and reassemble the datagrams in the following order:

1. The first datagram in a stream always has an offset value of zero, indicating the first one in the stream.

2. The second datagram has an offset value of 512.

3. The third datagram has an offset value of 1024.

The receiver stores datagrams in its memory buffer waiting for messages within the stream to arrive. However, it does not always receive the datagrams in order. For example, if the second datagram arrives first with offset 512, the receiver knows to expect several others because

- The sending host has set More Fragments bit in the second datagram.

- This is not the Last Fragment.

- The receiver has not received a datagram with the same ID containing fragment offset zero, which indicates the beginning.

Because it has received a datagram with the More Fragments bit set and has not received a datagram with a Last Fragment bit set, it knows to expect more datagrams. Once the receiver gets all the fragments within the stream, it can put them in the correct order and pass them up to the upper-layer application for processing.

Figures 3.5, 3.6, and 3.7 depict another example of fragmentation and reassembly as seen through a Sniffer. Figure 3.5 details the first datagram within the stream; Figure 3.6 details the second datagram within the stream and Figure 3.7 details the last datagram within the stream. In Figure 3.5 notice that in frame 1 (highlighted in the detail pane), the IP ID value of this frame (frame 1) and all other frames (frames 2–5) shown in the summary pane bear the same value of 2052, shown as "continuation of indent=2052." This means that frames 1–5 all belong to stream 2052.

Note that the sending host has set the More Fragments bit within the first frame, indicating the this datagram has more fragments or datagrams within this stream. In other words, this is not the last datagram. Also note that the sending host set the fragment offset to zero, indicating the first fragment in series 2502.

FIGURE 3.5

The More fragments bit is set indicating more datagrams will follow. The fragment offset set to zero indicates this is the first datagram within the stream.

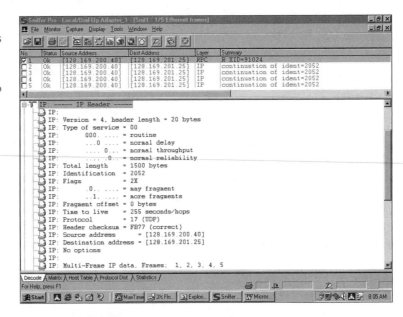

Figure 3.6 shows the second fragment in stream 2502. Note that the More Fragments bit is set, indicating that more datagrams follow this one. Note that the fragment offset is 1480, which

indicates this is not the first datagram (because it is not zero). Because the last fragment bit is not set, we know it is not the last but somewhere in the middle (in this case second). The destination host uses this information to put the fragments in the stream in the right order when it receives all the fragments within the stream.

FIGURE 3.6

The fragment offset is used by the receiving host to reassemble datagrams.

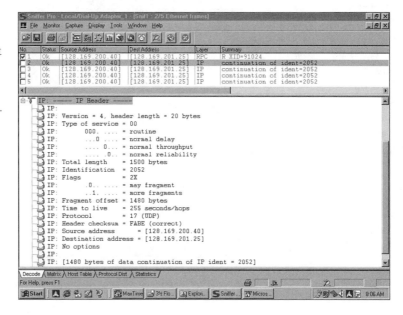

Figure 3.7 skips fragment 3 and shows the final fragment in the stream. Note that this fragment belongs to the stream because it has the identification value of 2502 like all the other fragments. We know this is the last fragment because Last Fragment is set. The fragment offset of 7400 is higher than the previous fragments so the destination host knows this is the last fragment and starts at the offset.

Time To Live

All devices processing a datagram decrement the 1-byte TTL value, which is measured in seconds. This value has two main purposes:

- To define the maximum time a datagram may live on the Internet prior to being discarded.

- To ensure that undeliverable datagrams also are discarded.

Before routers existed on the Internet, to ultimately remove a lost datagram from the network it was necessary to recognize and limit the time it traversed the network. The TTL timer was used for this purpose. It remains today and is used for various purposes, such as tracing a route to a destination host or network, which we will discuss later in this chapter. Basically, whenever a device such as a gateway processes a datagram, it must decrement this value by at least one before forwarding it. Each TTL value indicates a value of one second, which is more time than it should take for a router to process a datagram. This value can typically be equated to a hop count indicating the datagram has passed through *x* number of routers by determining how many TTL units this value has been decremented.

FIGURE 3.7

Note the Last fragment bit is set indicating to the receiver that this is the last datagram within the stream.

A network administrator can configure the starting TTL value but this value cannot exceed 255 (seconds). The general rule is that a device may not forward a datagram with a TTL value of 1 or less. If a datagram has lived on the wire for 255 seconds and has not reached its ultimate destination, it has lived too long on the network and should be removed. When this occurs, the device that the TTL expired on sends an ICMP message back to the source indicating that the datagram TTL time has exceeded. We will discuss ICMP messages later in this chapter.

Protocol

The 1-byte protocol field contains a value that specifies the next protocol expected within the datagram. This value will contain one of two values:

- 06 (TCP)
- 17 (UDP)

IP uses these values to identify to which upper-layer protocol to hand the information when it receives it.

Header Checksum

Because IP is a connectionless protocol, it does not implement any type of error correction mechanism, such as sequencing and acknowledgments. IP simply sends datagrams out, addresses them, and hopes they reach their destination. Therefore, IP uses a simple checksum, contained in this 2-byte field, to verify the integrity of the IP header and the data being carried to ensure that nothing has happened to the bits while in transit between source and destination hosts. Intervening devices must recalculate and verify this checksum value along the way because some of the fields within the IP header change while in transit (for example, time to live). If at any point in time a device deems this value invalid due to damage, it trashes the datagram without sending a message to the source. IP relies on upper-layer protocols to detect the loss of a datagram and recover from it (retransmit).

Source Address

The sending host places its logical Network layer (IP address) address within this 4-byte field for identification purposes.

Destination Address

This 4-bit field identifies the recipient's logical network layer address. This logical 32-bit IP address identifies the destination network and host.

Options

Hosts or gateways can implement optional parameters; when used, this variable-length field defines them here. However, options do not have to exist within a datagram; if implemented, all hosts and gateways must recognize and support their implementation. This could include the use of a security option as specified within by the precedence value used in the ToS field.

Padding

IP uses this variable-length field only when an IP header does not end on a 32-bit boundary. Because the IP header is expressed in 32-bit words, padding is used to ensure that this happens.

ICMP

End hosts and gateways (routers) use the Internet Control Message Protocol (ICMP), defined by RFC 792, as a control, messaging, and diagnostic protocol. ICMP exists at the Network layer of the OSI and Internet layer of the DoD models. (See Figure 3.1 to view where ICMP falls within the DoD and OSI models.) Although ICMP resides at the same layer as IP, ICMP is considered an integral part of the IP protocol. As such, it utilizes the services of IP for its delivery of messages. Figure 3.8 shows an ICMP echo message encapsulated within an IP datagram.

There are many types of ICMP messages; the ICMP echo request probably is the most common. You can use the echo request as a diagnostic tool to check connectivity between end hosts. We discuss all ICMP types in more detail later in the chapter. Note the ICMP protocol type in the IP equals one (ICMP).

Echo Request and Reply

The term *echo request and reply* describes messages you can use to test network connectivity. You can do this by using the Ping utility. The Ping program uses these ICMP echo request and reply messages. An echo request is like you shouting to a network, "Hello, are you there?" What bounces back, be it negative or positive (connectivity or no connectivity), is the echo reply. Just as with an echo, you always receive a reply.

FIGURE 3.8

The ICMP echo message is used to verify network layer communications between hosts.

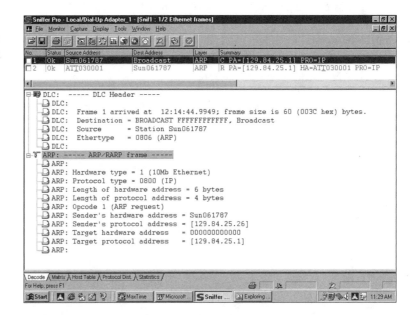

Destination hosts and gateways on occasion need to inform a source host of delivery problems, test connectivity to that host, ask for transmission to slow down, and so on. ICMP has a total of 15 different messages identified by the value contained within its type field used to inform a source host. These messages allow a source host to learn and recover from some (not all) of the problems that can occur on an internetwork. Although these messages inform a host of problems, ICMP does not guarantee a solution to these problems. Like IP, ICMP is a connectionless protocol. Hosts or gateways can send unsolicited ICMP control or diagnostic messages. ICMP uses many types of messages for different purposes.

You might have used the familiar Ping utility (ICMP message types 0 and 8). Ping allows a user to send a sonar-like ping from one host to another to verify connectivity. The Ping utility utilizes the services of ICMP messages to perform this task. When a user executes the Ping command specifying a remote host's name or address, the host receives a series of ICMP messages, known as *echo requests*. The receiving host in turn responds to each of these messages using the ICMP Echo Reply message type 0. We discuss Ping and the other various message types and their purposes later in this chapter.

ICMP Header and Message Formats

IP identifies ICMP messages contained within an IP datagram with protocol type 1. Figure 3.9 shows the general format of an ICMP echo message. The first four bytes (1-byte type field, 1-byte code field, and 2-byte checksum) have the same format for all message types. All other fields and information contained within the ICMP header vary depending on the message type being sent. We describe the various types, codes, and the checksum later in this chapter.

Hosts and gateways use ICMP as a messaging, control, and diagnostic protocol to alert a host of problems or test connectivity. Note the protocol value contained within the IP header is 1, indicating this is an ICMP message. To determine the type of ICMP message, look in the ICMP header at the type field. Once you determine the type of ICMP message, you can use the code field to further identify the purpose of the message. The type field identifies the particular ICMP messages. Some ICMP messages use different values in the code field to further specify the error condition. The checksum field covers the entire ICMP message.

FIGURE 3.9

ICMP messages have a registered value of 1. The type field within the ICMP header identifies the type of ICMP message being sent.

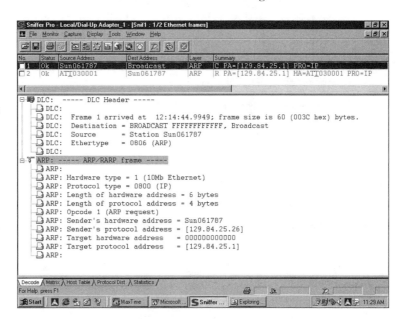

Codes

Many of the type fields contain more specific information about the error condition identified by a code value. ICMP messages have two types of codes:

- Query
- Error

Queries contain no additional information because they merely ask for information and will show a value of 0 in the code field. ICMP uses the following queries:

- Type 0 = Echo Reply

- Type 8 = Echo Request

- Type 9 = Router Advertisement

- Type 10 = Router Solicitation

- Type 13 = Timestamp Request

- Type 14 = Timestamp Reply

- Type 15 = Information Request (obsolete)

- Type 16 = Information Reply (obsolete)

- Type 17 = Address Mask Request

- Type 18 = Address Mask Reply

Error messages give specific information and will have varying values that further describe conditions. Error messages always include a copy of the offending IP header and up to 8 bytes of the data that caused the host or gateway to send the error message. The source host uses this information to identify and fix the problem reported via the ICMP error message. ICMP uses the following error messages:

- Type 3 = Destination Unreachable

- Type 4 = Source Quench

- Type 5 = Redirect

- Type 11 = Time Exceeded

- Type 12 = Parameter Problems

Table 3.1 lists all of the ICMP codes along with the ICMP message types. We will discuss error codes and the various ICMP message types to which they pertain later.

Checksum

The checksum verifies the validity of the ICMP header. The sending host performs the initial checksum calculation and places the results in this field. The receiving host performs the same calculations to assure that it does not receive data damaged in transit. If the checksum values do not match, it trashes the datagram.

Identifier

The user on the source host can set this optional value to match sent echo requests with received replies.

Sequence Number

The user on the source host can set this optional value to match sent echo requests with received replies.

ICMP Message Types

The type field identifies the type of the message sent by the host or gateway. Many of the type fields contain more specific information about the error condition. Table 3.2 lists the ICMP message types.

TABLE 3.2   ICMP Message Types

Type	Description ICMP Message Types
0	Echo Reply (Ping Reply, used with Type 8, Ping Request)
3	Destination Unreachable
4	Source Quench
5	Redirect
8	Echo Request (Ping Request, used with Type 0, Ping Reply)
9	Router Advertisement (Used with Type 9)
10	Router Solicitation (Used with Type 10)
11	Time Exceeded
12	Parameter Problem
13	Timestamp Request (Used with Type 14)
14	Timestamp Reply (Used with Type 13)
15	Information Request (obsolete) (Used with Type 16)
16	Information Reply (obsolete) (Used with Type 15)
17	Address Mask Request (Used with Type 17)
18	Address Mask Reply (Used with Type 18)

Because each of the ICMP message headers vary depending on which one is sent, we will discuss each type separately, identifying the corresponding code fields, if applicable.

Ping: Echo Request and Reply—Types 8 and 0

We discuss the ICMP Echo Request Type 8 and Echo Reply Type 0 because ICMP uses these messages in tandem. Remote hosts use these two message types to test connectivity. As previously mentioned, the user executes the Ping utility, initiating the generation of ICMP echo requests with the expectation that the destination host sends a corresponding echo reply. Upon successful receipt of the replies to the echo requests, the messages do the following:

- Indicate a successful test.

- Assume that a valid communication path between the hosts exists.

- Assume the end host works through the Network layer.

Figure 3.10 shows an example of an echo request; Figure 3.11 shows an example of an echo reply. In Frame 1 host 36.53.0.202 sends an echo request to test the connectivity with host 36.21.0.1. Note the detail pane indicates a type 8 value stating this is an echo request. The ID value of 52743 and the sequence number of 57098 are optionally included to provide a reasonable match with the echo reply. In Frame 2 host 36.53.0.202 returns the echo reply to host 36.21.0.1. The type code 0 indicates this is a reply and the previous ID and sequence number values used in the echo request frame match.

FIGURE 3.10

This is an example of an echo request and reply generated as a result of the Ping Utility.

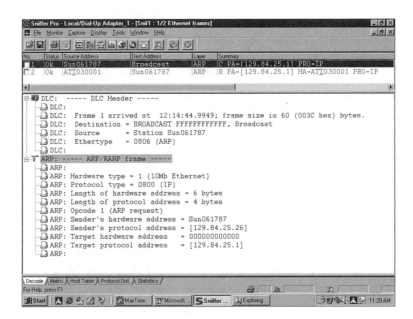

Destination Unreachable—Type 3

ICMP Type 3 message Destination Unreachable alerts a source host of delivery problems encountered while trying to reach the destination. Note that a destination host sends only code types 2 and 3; a router can send all codes. Destination Unreachable uses several code values to further describe the function of the ICMP message being sent. Each code type describes a different delivery problem encountered, as shown here:

FIGURE 3.11

This is an ICMP echo reply message sent in response to a previously received echo request.

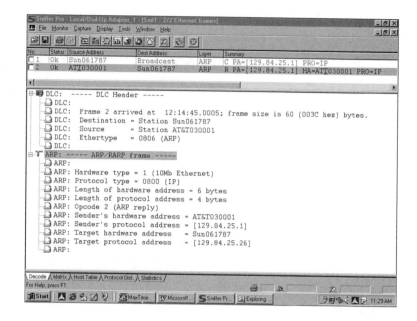

0 = Network Unreachable

This message indicates that the router cannot find the destination network (does not exist or has failed) or has no route to this network. In other words, the router cannot deliver or forward an IP datagram to the destination network. This could be the result of a network that is beyond the maximum distance limitation for the routing protocol in use and is therefore considered unreachable (too far). When a client attempts to connect to a host on a network that is unreachable, a gateway generates this message to alert the source host of the problem. You can think of this message as the gateway saying to the sending host, "The street you are trying to locate is not found or is too far to reach."

1 = Host Unreachable

The host unreachable message alerts the sending host that the destination host requested cannot be found. This could happen because this host has been turned off or does not exist. You can think of this message as the gateway saying to the sending host, "I found the street you were looking for, but the house you are trying to find is not there."

2 = Protocol Unreachable

Protocol unreachable indicates that the Transport layer protocol (UDP or TCP) is not available. The destination host or an intervening gateway might send this message. You can think of this message as saying, "The transport layer protocol you are attempting to communicate with is not active on this host."

3 = Port Unreachable

A port unreachable message indicates that the process or application the source host is attempting to establish a connection with is not active on the destination host. Typically this type of message is sent when an application has not been started or has failed on this host. The destination host or an intervening gateway might send this message. You can think of this message as saying, "The process or application you are attempting to communicate with is not active on this host," or, "I found the street, I found the house, the lights were on, but no one was home."

Figure 3.12 shows a request being sent from a BOOTP client looking for a BOOTP server. Figure 3.13 shows an example of an ICMP destination port unreachable message generated because the router or gateway could not find the BOOTP server, or the server was unavailable. We discuss BOOTP in Chapter 4, "Address Resolution," and UDP in Chapter 9, "User Datagram Protocol (UDP)."

FIGURE 3.12

In frame one, highlighted in the summary pane and show in the detail pane, we see a BOOTP client, "UDP port=68," sending a broadcast to all hosts using UDP port 67, which identifies a BOOTP Server process requesting an IP address.

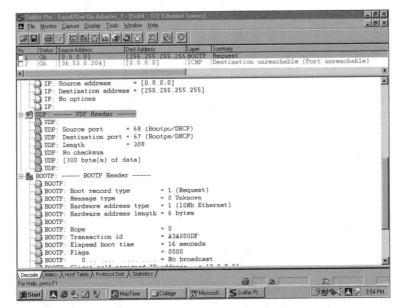

In Figure 3.13 note that the gateway has added a copy of the offending IP header within the ICMP header that caused the error from frame one. By including a copy of the offending IP header, the source might be able to use this information to correct the problem that resulted in this ICMP message being sent.

4 = Fragmentation is needed, but don't-fragment bit set

This message occurs when a router receives a datagram that requires fragmentation, but the originator has the DF (don't-fragment) flag turned on. We discussed fragmentation earlier in the chapter. If you recall, the sending host generally has the responsibility of fragmentation. The receiver has the responsibility of reassembly.

However, when a router cannot forward a datagram because it is too big, if allowed the router might fragment the datagram further before transmitting it to an attached segment. If the originator has the DF bit set, this will not happen and the router will trash the datagram. It then generates a message to alert the sender of this action by sending a Type 3, Code 4 message. The fragmentation bit also can determine the maximum packet size or MTU that hosts can transmit end to end along the communication path.

FIGURE 3.13

In frame two, highlighted in the summary pane and shown in the detail pane, we see an ICMP message being sent by a gateway (36.53.0.204) stating the previous request failed because the port request (68) is not active and therefore unreachable. As you can see in the detail pane, immediately following the IP header is the ICMP header.

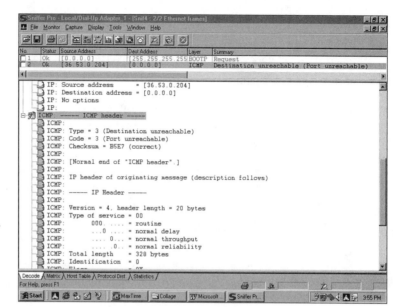

Hosts can use the ICMP messages sent by routers to resize datagrams, dynamically adjusting to the needs of the network. This allows the host to determine the smallest MTU path to a destination.

5 = Source Route Failed

The message occurs if a router encounters a next hop in the source route that does not reside on a directly connected network.

6 = Destination Network Unknown

This message occurs when a router receives an IP datagram that it cannot deliver or forward to a particular network because it is unknown.

7 = Destination Host Unknown

This message occurs when a router receives an IP datagram that it cannot deliver or forward to a particular host because it is unknown.

8 = Source Host Isolated (obsolete)

9 = Destination Network Administratively Prohibited

This message occurs when a router receives an IP datagram that it cannot deliver or forward to a particular network because it is not allowed. Access to this network has been prohibited.

10 = Destination Host Administratively Prohibited

This message occurs when a router receives an IP datagram that it cannot deliver or forward to a particular host because it is not allowed. Access to this host has been prohibited.

11 = Network Unreachable for ToS

This message occurs when a router receives an IP datagram that it cannot deliver or forward to a particular network because the ToS requested is not available.

12 = Host Unreachable for ToS

This message occurs when a router receives an IP datagram that it cannot deliver or forward to a particular host because the ToS requested is not available.

13 = Communication Administratively Prohibited by Filtering

This message occurs when a router receives an IP datagram that it cannot deliver or forward to a particular host because it is not allowed. An administratively configured filter has prohibited access to this process or application.

14 = Host Precedence Violation

This message occurs when a router receives an IP datagram that it cannot deliver or forward to a particular host because the precedence level requested does not match, and is not accepted or is invalid. This could be a source host attempting to access a high security host without the necessary security clearance values.

15 = Precedence Cutoff in Effect

This message rarely occurs. However, you will receive this message when a packet is dropped by the cutoff function.

Precedence Handling For All Routers

Routers must accept and route incoming traffic of all precedence levels normally, unless you have configured it to do otherwise. If you want to learn more about precedence and Destination Unreachable messages 14 and 15, please refer to RFC 1812, 5.3.3.3, "Precedence Handling for All Routers."

Source Quench—Type 4

A receiving host generates this message when it cannot process datagrams at the speed requested due to a lack of memory or internal resources. This message serves as a simple flow control mechanism that a receiving host can utilize to alert a sender to slow down its transmission of data. When the source host receives this message, it must pass this information on to the upper-layer process, such as TCP, which then must control the flow of the application's datastream. A router generates this message when, in the process of forwarding datagrams, it has run low on buffers and cannot queue the datagram for delivery.

Redirect—Type 5

A router sends a redirect error to the sender of an IP datagram when the sender should have sent the datagram to a different router or directly to an end host (if the end host is local). The message assists the sending host to direct a misdirected datagram to a gateway or host. This alert does not guarantee proper delivery; the sending host has to correct the problem if possible.

Only gateways generate redirect messages to inform source hosts of misguided datagrams. Note that a gateway receiving a misdirected frame does not trash the offending datagram if it can forward it. The gateway forwards the frame, sends an alert message to the source, and hopes the source host will properly direct future frames to the designated host or gateway indicated in the message. ICMP redirect messages alert source hosts when a datagram has been misdirected and should be resent. Four redirect error codes can occur:

1. 0 = Redirect for Network

2. 1 = Redirect for Host

3. 2 = Redirect for Type-of-Service and Network

4. 3 = Redirect for Type-of-Service and Host

Figure 3.14 shows an example of a ICMP redirect message. In this example, a gateway (36.53.0.1) alerts host (36.53.0.174) that it should be sending future datagrams to the following gateway internet address (36.53.2.2). This alert message also includes a copy of the offending IP header for the source host's inspection.

FIGURE 3.14

ICMP redirect messages are sent by gateways to hosts alerting them of messages that have been misdirected.

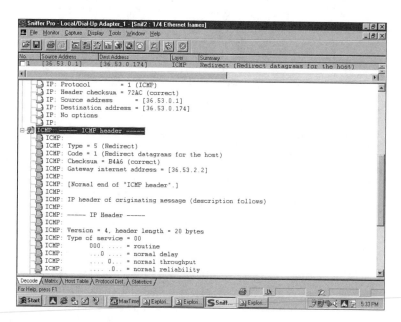

Router Advertisement and Solicitation—Types 9 and 10

Rather than initializing a routing table with static routes specified in configuration files, you can use the router ICMP advertisement and solicitation messages. After bootstrapping, a host can transmit a broadcast or multicast a solicitation message to which a router or routers responds with a router advertisement. This allows communicating hosts to learn of available routes dynamically and update their routing tables. We will discuss routing in more detail in Chapters 5 and 6.

Time Exceeded—Type 11

The time exceeded message occurs when a router receives a datagram with a TTL (Time To Live) of 0 or 1. IP uses the TTL field to prevent infinite routing loops. A router cannot forward a datagram that has a TTL of 0 or 1. Instead, it trashes the datagram and sends a time exceeded message. Two different time exceeded error codes can occur:

1. 0 = Time-To-Live Equals 0 During Transit

2. 1 = Time-To-Live Equals 0 During Reassembly

Note that a router cannot forward a datagram with a TTL of 0 or 1 both during transit or reassembly.

As previously mentioned in the IP section of this chapter, the TTL timer is measured in seconds and originally was used before the existence of routers to guarantee that a datagram did not live on the Internet forever. Each gateway processing a datagram reduces this value by at least one if it takes longer to process and forward the datagram. When this value expires, the gateway trashes the datagram and sends a message back to the sender notifying the host of the situation.

The traceroute utility also uses the TTL value to discover the path or route to a destination host or network. Upon execution of the traceroute command, the initial ICMP message is sent out with a TTL value of 1 set in the IP header. You can use the traceroute program to determine, or rather trace, the path to a destination. Traceroute accomplishes this by sending a sequence of datagrams with the TTL set to 1, 2, and so on. It then uses the ICMP Time Exceeded messages like a trail of breadcrumbs to trace the routers along the path. We will provide you with examples later in this section.

As you might recall from earlier in this chapter, when a router receives a datagram with a TTL of zero, it trashes the datagram and returns an ICMP time exceeded message to the source. This message allows the host to learn of the first router in the path to the destination. Figure 3.15 shows an ICMP message generated as a result of a TTL expiration.

As shown in the figure, ICMP message type 11 alerts a source host of a TTL expiration. Code 0 identifies the reason for the expiration as time to live being exceeded while the datagram was in transit. This message also includes a copy of the original datagram header that caused the error to assist the source host in correcting the problem. Within the offending header contained within the ICMP message, you can see that the "TTL value = 0 seconds/hops," which is why the original datagram was trashed.

FIGURE 3.15

The ICMP time exceeded message is sent when the TTL timer expires.

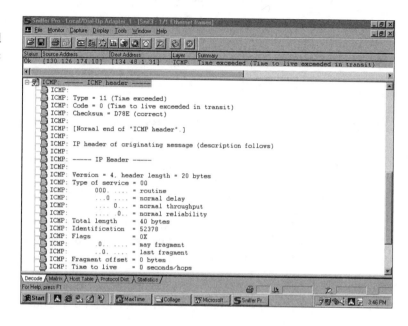

Now the source host sends a new ICMP trace with a TTL value of 2, which allows this datagram to be forwarded by the first router (which decrements the value by one) and reaches the next router in the path with a TTL of one. This router must trash the frame and send back an ICMP time exceeded. This process continues until the path to the destination network or host is fully discovered or deemed unreachable. As you can see, traceroute is another useful troubleshooting tool, typically used in conjunction with other utilities such as the Ping utility to test connectivity between two hosts.

Tip

Both the Ping and traceroute utilities can help you when troubleshooting.

Parameter Problem—Type 12

The parameter problem message indicates that a host or gateway received and could not interpret an invalid or misunderstood parameter. A host or gateway also can send this message when no other ICMP message covering the problem can be used to alert the sending host. In this respect, it is a *catchall message*. In most cases this message indicates some type of implementation error occurred, perhaps because of vendor incompatibility issues. A host or gateway will not send this message unless it trashes the datagram containing the parameter problem.

Two parameter problem error messages can occur:

1. **0 = IP Header Bad (catchall error0)**

    A host or gateway sends this error to indicate a general implementation error of an unspecific nature.

2. **1 = Required Option Missing**

    The host or gateway expected a specific option, but the sender did not send it.

Timestamp Request and Reply—Types 13 and 14

Timestamp request and reply messages work in tandem. You have the option of using timestamps. When used, a timestamp request permits a system to query another for the current time. It expects a recommended value returned to be the number of milliseconds since midnight, Coordinated Universal Time. This message provides millisecond resolution, considered a beneficial feature when compared to other means of obtaining time from another host who provides resolution in seconds. The two systems compare the three timestamps and use RTT to adjust the sender's or receiver's time if necessary. Note that most systems set the transmit and receive time as the same value.

The process for time resolution goes as follows:

1. The requestor stamps the originate time and sends the query.

2. The replying system stamps the receive time when it receives the query.

3. The replying system stamps the transmit time when it sends the reply to the query.

Information Request and Reply—Types 15 and 16

Although ICMP messages list information request and reply as a potential ICMP message type, they actually do not occur; thus they are obsolete. A host can request information such as to what network it was attached.

Address Mask Request and Reply—Types 17 and 18

Address mask request and reply messages work in tandem. Although we rarely use this message today, its original design supported the function of dynamically obtaining a subnet mask. Hosts can use the ICMP address mask request to acquire subnet masks during bootstrap from a remote host. However, problems can occur when using ICMP to receive a mask if a host gives an incorrect mask from an external source. If the external source does not give a response, the source host must assume a classful mask (that the network is not subnetted).

Summary

IP is the workhorse of the Network layer within the TCP/IP suite. All protocols and applications utilize IP for logical Network layer addressing and transmission of datagrams between internet hosts. IP provides an unreliable, connectionless datagram delivery service and uses ICMP to send messages when it encounters an error.

End host and routers use ICMP as a control, messaging, and diagnostic tool. ICMP utilizes IP to deliver its messages and is considered an integral part of IP. ICMP messages notify a host of problems. Although ICMP does not offer a solution to these problems, it can provide enough information for a source host to solve some of the problems that might occur in the internetwork. The most popular ICMP message is the echo request and reply. Utilizing the Ping utility, these messages allow you to test connectivity between end hosts.

Review Questions

1. Which Network layer protocol is responsible for fragmentation and reassembly of datagrams?

2. A user would like to test connectivity between two remote hosts, so the user executes Ping. Which two ICMP message types are used to accomplish this test?

3. What does IP do when it receives data from UDP or TCP?

4. How many minimum bytes are there in an IP header and what fields are contained within that header?

5. What are the ToS bits within the IP header used for?

6. What two field values does the destination host use to ensure that it reassembles datagrams in the correct order?

7. What type of ICMP message is Destination Unreachable, and what does it mean if you receive a Destination Unreachable ICMP message?

8. What does a 0 (zero) error code mean when you have a type 3, Destination Unreachable ICMP message?

9. What does a 4 error code mean when you have a type 3, Destination Unreachable ICMP message?

10. What type of ICMP message is Time Exceeded and what does it mean if you receive a Time Exceeded ICMP message?

CHAPTER 4

ADDRESS RESOLUTION

You will learn about the following in this chapter:

- Address Resolution Protocol

- Reverse Address Resolution Protocol

- BOOTP

- Dynamic Host Configuration Protocol

Because of the complexity of the various layers and the various addresses that reside at those layers, there must be a method to resolve differences between computer addressing schemes. Address resolution assumes that role and enables end devices to dynamically discover a local hardware address for delivery of data to a remote host, or retrieve logical IP addresses and configuration parameters necessary to participate on the network. Without some type of resolution method, remote hosts could not communicate. In the IP world address resolution converts a protocol address into a corresponding physical address or vice versa; for example, converting an IP address into an Ethernet address. There are four methods of address resolution:

- ARP (Address Resolution Protocol)

- RARP (Reverse Address Resolution Protocol)

- BOOTP (Bootstrap Protocol)

- DHCP (Dynamic Host Configuration Protocol)

Figure 4.1 shows how these protocols map to the DoD and OSI models.

Of the four protocols that perform address resolution, ARP is the only one that resolves Network layer addresses to hardware addresses. The RARP, BOOTP, and DHCP protocols allow an end device to dynamically resolve its hardware address to a logical Network layer address. Figure 4.2 shows an example of ARP resolution. Figure 4.3 shows an example of RARP, BOOTP, and DHCP resolution. We will discuss these protocols in more detail later in this chapter.

FIGURE 4.1

Note that ARP and RARP utilize IP at the Network layer, and DHCP and BOOTP run on top of UDP at the Transport layer.

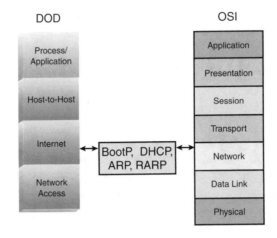

FIGURE 4.2

ARP resolves logical Network layer addresses to a local hardware address.

FIGURE 4.3

RARP, BOOTP, and DHCP protocols resolve an end device's hardware address to a logical Network layer address. These protocols perform the opposite function of ARP.

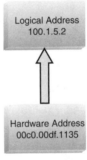

ARP

When you attempt to initiate a session with a remote host's application, you can use either the name of the remote host or the logical Network layer address. For example, if you utilize the remote host's name and request a Telnet session by typing **Telnet TelnetServ** (name of the remote server), this name would need to be resolved to a logical Network layer IP address and then resolved to a Data Link layer hardware address. If you attempt the session using the logical Network layer address, you do not need to perform the name resolution portion. However, the remote host still needs to resolve its logical Network layer IP address to a hardware address for proper delivery. ARP (Address Resolution Protocol), defined in RFC 826, performs this last address resolution dynamically.

The initial design of the ARP protocol supported the resolution of logical Network layer addresses into 48-bit (6-byte) Ethernet hardware addresses. Since then, it has evolved to support resolution for other types of networks. RFC826 documents these changes.

Upper-layer applications and processes need the ARP protocol to dynamically resolve Network layer addresses for proper data delivery. Without this dynamic protocol you would have to resolve them manually by creating a static table on each host mapping the logical IP addresses of all internet hosts to their local hardware address or the address of a local gateway. This would prove impractical because there are many different types of logical Network layer addresses, and they vary in size. For example, they could be IP addresses (32 bits) or Xerox (8 bits). Rather than manually identifying and mapping these addresses to the lower layer, 48-bit address, ARP performs this process automatically. Although the ARP protocol can resolve various types of logical Network addresses to hardware addresses, we will focus only on the resolution of IP addresses in this chapter.

ARP Operation

Before any communication can occur between remote hosts, the sender must obtain a local address for delivery. If the source and destination hosts exist on the same segment, this local address will be the hardware address of the ultimate destination. If the source and destination hosts do not reside on the same local segment (hosts separated by a router or multiple routers), the sender uses the router's (gateway's) local address for delivery, forwarding the datagram to the remote host.

To obtain the local hardware address, the sending host first checks its local ARP cache table for a previously learned address. Each host maintains a local ARP table in memory containing static (manually entered) or dynamic learned address information. A host can learn the address information in the following ways:

- Through an administrator mapping a logical Network layer to a hardware address (statically).

- Dynamically through ARP.

However the host learns, it stores the address information in its local ARP table. If an address pair exists in the table, the source host can simply use this information without going through the process of using ARP to resolve the address. If the address pair does not exist, which might be the case if the host has just initialized and has an empty ARP cache, the sending host uses ARP to resolve the destination host's Network layer address to a local hardware address. Once the sending host resolves the Network layer address and determines a local address, it places this information in the local host's ARP cache for later use. Storing this information in cache eliminates the need for this host to perform this resolution in the near future when connecting to the same host.

ARP is broadcast based. This means that when a sending host wants to resolve a remote host's Network layer address, it sends a broadcast out to all hosts on the local segment. Routers do not forward broadcasts; therefore, broadcasts remain localized to the sending host's segment. Note that routers will forward a broadcast if a helper address has been configured (for BOOTP and DHCP) or if you have IP directed-broadcast enabled; however, please remember that routers do not inherently forward broadcasts.

As we discussed in the previous chapter, the sending host determines whether the destination resides on the sending host's local segment by comparing the destination host's IP address to the sending host's local subnet mask. If after performing this task the sending host finds the destination host resides on the same subnet, the sending host knows that it can *shout* (send a local ARP broadcast to resolve the destination host's hardware address). However, if the sending host finds that the destination host does not reside on the same subnet, it must *route*, which means the sending host sends a local broadcast to resolve the local gateway's IP address to a hardware address for forwarding. Once the sending host determines whether it can shout or route, it sends a local query to resolve the destination host or local gateway's IP address to a hardware address.

The sending host asks in its ARP broadcast, "Does anyone recognize the Network layer address x.x.x.x?" (The *x*'s in this case would represent the 32-bit IP address of the destination host or local gateway). The sending host expects one of two things to happen:

- The destination host responds to this query
- The local gateway that forwards this datagram responds

Figure 4.4 shows a sending host sending an ARP broadcast to resolve a local host's hardware address. In this figure, Host A wants to communicate with Host B, which is on the local segment. Host A simply sends an ARP broadcast on the local segment querying whether anyone recognizes the address 100.0.0.2. Host B responds to this request with its local address. If a sending host finds that a destination host resides on the same subnet, it sends a local ARP broadcast to resolve the destination host's hardware address.

If a sending host finds that a destination host does not reside on the same subnet, it sends a local ARP broadcast to resolve the local gateway's hardware address, which forwards the datagram to the remote host. Figure 4.5 shows a host sending an ARP broadcast resolving a local gateway's IP address to a local hardware address for delivery to a remote host. In this figure, Host A wants to communicate with Host B, which is not on the same network. Host A sends an ARP broadcast on the local segment to resolve the local gateway address to the hardware address. End hosts must be configured with the IP address of a local gateway to communicate beyond their local segment.

FIGURE 4.4

In this case, Host A simply "shouts" out an ARP broadcast on the local segment.

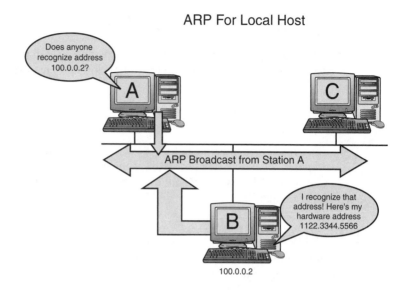

FIGURE 4.5

In this case, Host A needs to "route."

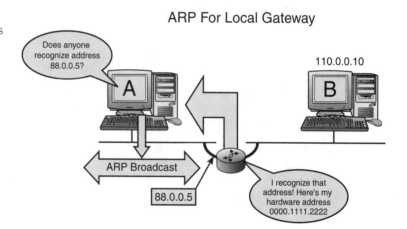

Basically the destination host or the local gateway responds, "I recognize that address and here is my hardware address." The sending host then has enough information to forward the datagram to the end host or the gateway en route to this host. With this information the sending host now can address a datagram properly, reflecting the logical Network layer address of the ultimate destination and the hardware address of the local host or gateway responsible for delivering the datagram.

If the sending host sends the datagram to a gateway for delivery, the gateway determines how to forward the datagram to the remote host. The gateway that has this responsibility goes through the following process to determine how to forward the datagram:

1. If the destination host resides on a segment local to this gateway, the gateway checks its local ARP cache for a previously cached entry.

2. If no entry exists for the destination host, the router sends an ARP request querying all devices on that segment to learn the destination host's hardware address for delivery.

3. If the destination host does not reside on a segment local to this gateway, the gateway uses ARP to learn the hardware address of another local gateway it can use to forward the datagram to the destination host.

4. This process continues along the delivery path until a gateway connected to the same subnet as the destination host receives the frame and uses a previously cached hardware address or performs a local ARP, resolving the Network layer address to the local address of the ultimate host.

ARP Cache Mechanisms

Depending on the implementation, hosts can use one or more control mechanisms to remove old or invalid entries from the ARP table. These mechanisms ensure valid entries exist in the table. For example, if a local host changes its Ethernet address (someone replaces the network interface card), it needs a new mapping. The control mechanisms are discussed in the following sections.

Timeout

Each host has a configurable ARP cache timer that controls how long it retains a dynamically learned entry. Configuration of this timer varies based on the operating system used. When a host adds an entry to the ARP table, it sets the timer value. When the timer expires, it considers the entry obsolete and flushes the entry from cache.

If this host attempts to contact the other host using the address it flushed, it sends a new ARP query, causing a new entry to be added to the table. Each time a host uses an entry within its cache, the timer resets for that entry. This means if this host communicates on a regular basis with a remote host, the entry will remain in the ARP cache.

Unicast Poll

A directed datagram using the mapping information previously learned and cached polls a host periodically. If the remote host does not send an ARP reply in response to the polls, the sending host considers the entry for this remote host invalid and removes it from the table. If the remote host responds, the sending host considers the entry valid and keeps it in the table.

Link Layer or Higher Layer Advice

If the Link layer or a high-layer protocol detects a delivery problem, that protocol sends notification of this problem to the active ARP process within the host. Upon notification, ARP considers the entry for the remote host invalid and removes it from the table.

Proxy ARP

Proxy ARP enables another device, such as a gateway, to respond to ARP requests on behalf of a remote host for address resolution purposes. The router acts as the actual destination host (a proxy agent). In reality, the intended destination host lies on the other side of the proxy agent on another network. This fools the sender, allowing the gateway to relay datagrams from it to other hosts transparently. Sometimes it is necessary to enable Proxy ARP; for example, if a network administrator misconfigured network hosts or wanted to connect multiple segments through a router, yet simulate a single subnet. An administrator can enable Proxy ARP on networks through configuration options in hosts or gateways where desired.

Proxy ARP allows transparent communication to occur between remote hosts even with misconfigured hosts. In this respect Proxy ARP acts as a bandage that masks an underlying problem within the network's addressing scheme. Enabling Proxy ARP does not provide an ultimate solution to this problem. Following a hierarchical addressing scheme and configuring hosts and gateways properly serves as the only true solution.

Proxy ARP Operation

The best way to understand how Proxy ARP works is to look at an example. In Figure 4.6 the sending host and the destination host reside on different subnets (Host A resides on 172.15.1.0 and Host B resides on 172.15.2.0). Note that the gateway between them is configured for Proxy ARP. The gateway has the capability to respond to local ARP requests on behalf of remote hosts. When a gateway enabled for Proxy ARP does so, it responds with its own hardware address. Host A, misconfigured with an incorrect subnet mask (255.255.0.0), believes that Host B resides on the same network. Because of this, Host A believes that it can shout (send a local ARP broadcast to resolve Host B's IP address to hardware address) when in fact, Host A actually should route (send a local ARP broadcast to resolve the gateway's IP address to hardware address for delivery.)

FIGURE 4.6
Proxy ARP allows a router to answer ARP requests for a host on another network.

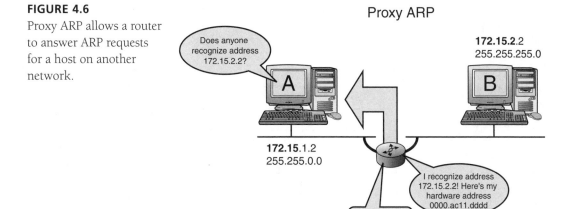

Take a look at Figure 4.6 and walk through the steps of what occurs during a Proxy ARP request:

1. Host A, 172.15.1.2, on network 172.15.1.0 and Host B, 172.15.2.2, on remote network 172.15.2.0 want to communicate. A router configured for Proxy ARP separates Host A and the remote network, Host B.

2. An administrator has configured Host A with a standard Class B subnet mask of 255.255.0.0. This is a problem because the network (172.15.0.0) actually is further subnetted and instead should have a standard Class C mask of 255.255.255.0. Host A attempts to determine whether to send a local ARP request to station B (shout) or the gateway (route) by taking the destination host's IP address and comparing it to Host A's mask.

3. Because Host A's mask states that the values within the first and second byte are network, it appears to Host A that they both reside on the same network 172.15.0.0, which is not the case. Because of this incorrect information Host A decides to send a local ARP broadcast (shout) out on this segment to resolve Host B's Network layer address to a hardware address.

4. Because Host B does not reside on this local segment it does not hear this broadcast; thus it does not respond. Normally this local ARP would fail. However, with the local gateway configured as an ARP Proxy Agent, this is not the case.

5. The gateway (router) configured for Proxy ARP picks up this ARP request and responds on behalf of Host B, replying with its own hardware address. This allows Host A to transparently communicate with Host B even though Host A is misconfigured.

ARP Header

An ARP header contains 28 bytes. Figure 4.7 takes a look at the format of an ARP header. Figure 4.8 takes a look at the fields and functions within an ARP header as seen through the Detail pane of a Sniffer protocol analyzer. Figure 4.9 shows an ARP request and reply used to resolve an IP address to an Ethernet hardware address. The descriptions for each field follow the figures.

FIGURE 4.7
Note that ARP and RARP use the same header format.

HARDWARE TYPE		PROTOCOL TYPE	
HLEN	PLEN	OPERATION	
SENDER HA (octets 0-3)			
SENDER HA (octets 4-5)		SENDER IP (octets 0-1)	
SENDER IP (octets 2-3)		TARGET HA (octets 0-1)	
TARGET HA (octets 2-5)			
TARGET IP (octets 0-3)			

Notice in Figure 4.8 that ARP protocol type is indicated in the Data Link Control header as Ethertype 0806. The destination hardware address has all Fs in the field, indicating that this request is being broadcast to all devices on this local segment. The Opcode value of 1 indicates that this is an ARP request as opposed to an ARP reply (OpCode 2). The sending host identified as Sun061787 (hardware address) and 129.84.25.26 (IP Address) queries to resolve a 4-byte IP protocol (Ethertype hex 0x0800) target address 129.84.25.1 to a 6-byte Ethernet hardware address. Note that the target hardware address has all zeros, indicating it is unknown.

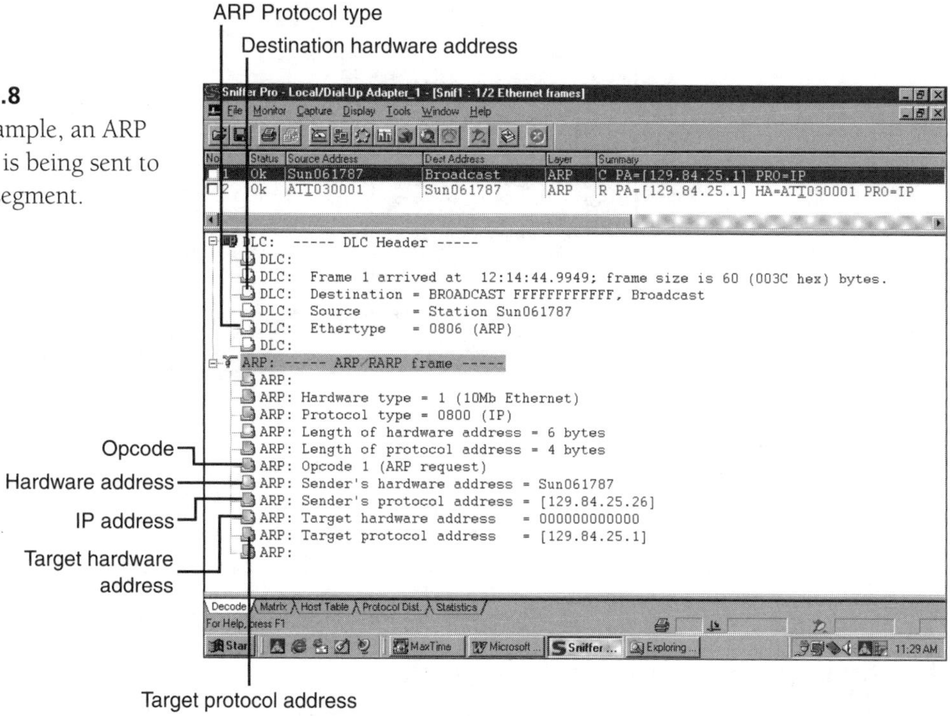

FIGURE 4.8

In this example, an ARP broadcast is being sent to the local segment.

The sending host Sun061787 sends a broadcast to all hosts on the local segment in Frame 1 asking whether they recognize the PA (Protocol Address) 129.84.25.1 PRO (Protocol Type being resolved) as IP. In frame two, Host 129.84.25.1 sends the ARP response stating its HA (Hardware Address) is ATT030001.

Hardware Type

This 2-byte field identifies the hardware type resolved as Ethernet, Token-Ring, or some other network type. ARP uses this field in conjunction with the protocol type field during ARP requests and replies to indicate which protocol is being resolved and to what hardware address.

FIGURE 4.9

Note the response (frame two) to the broadcast in frame one.

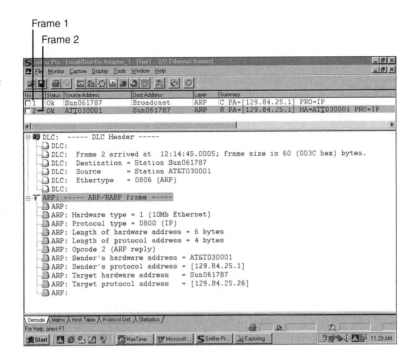

Protocol Type

The 2-byte protocol type field identifies the Network layer protocol type. This value makes ARP capable of resolving various Network layer protocol addresses. For example, IP has the well-known 2-byte registered protocol type of 0x0800 (hexadecimal) and IPX has the registered protocol type 0x8137.

Length of Hardware Address

This 1-byte field specifies the length in bytes of the hardware address ARP expects as a result of address resolution. This value varies depending on the hardware type, indicated in the hardware type field. For example, if the hardware type field indicates Ethernet (shown as a value of 1), which uses a 48-bit or 6-byte hardware address, the field will have a value of 6.

Length of Protocol Address

The length of the protocol address is the protocol size. The 1-byte protocol length field specifies the length in bytes of the Network layer protocol address being resolved. Because ARP can resolve logical Network layer addresses for multiple protocols, it needs the protocol value defined. For example, if the protocol type field specifies IP (0x0800), the field expects a 4-byte value, indicating a 32-bit address.

Opcode

The two-byte Opcode (operation code) field specifies the type of operation occurring:

1. ARP request (value of 1)

2. ARP reply (value of 2)

3. RARP request (value of 3)

4. RARP reply (value of 4)

ARP needs this field because the frame format used by both ARP and RARP include the same fields. Therefore they look the same. The Opcode value identifies the purpose of the frame. The frame clearly states whether an ARP or RARP request or reply has occurred. You also can distinguish an ARP frame from an RARP frame by checking the Ethertype value identified within the DLC header. ARP has a protocol type of 0806, whereas RARP has a protocol type of 8035. We discuss the RARP protocol later in this chapter.

Sender's Hardware Address

The sending host places its hardware address within this field for identification purposes. The sender's hardware address field is 6 bytes.

Sender's Protocol Address

The sending host places its logical Network layer (IP address) address within this field for identification purposes. The sender's protocol address field is 4 bytes.

Target Hardware Address

This 6-byte field identifies the destination host's hardware address if known or all zeros if unknown. When a host tries to resolve a target host's Network layer protocol address to a hardware address, this field will have all zeros as its value, indicating an unknown value.

Target Protocol Address

This 4-byte field identifies the Network layer protocol (IP) address of the destination host. When a host sends an ARP request, this field shows the logical address of the host being resolved.

RARP

RFC 903 defines the RARP protocol, which was designed to perform dynamic resolution of a host's hardware address into a logical Network layer protocol address. RARP has the opposite function of the previously discussed ARP protocol. In fact ARP and RARP use the same header format and fields. Because they both use the same fields, we will not cover them again. Please refer to the ARP header if you want more information. Another way to tell ARP from RARP is the protocol type; RARP is identified within the DLC header as Ethertype 8035, whereas ARP is type 0806.

The RARP protocol was initially developed to enable diskless clients to dynamically retrieve a logical address from a remote host. Because diskless clients have no permanent area to store this information, they require a remote RARP server to store the hardware address and its corresponding Network layer address mapping in a static table. A network administrator must create this static mapping table on the RARP server for every client on a subnetwork and update it each time a host's hardware address or Network layer address changes.

Like the ARP protocol, the RARP protocol is broadcast based. This means internet gateways (routers) do not forward these datagrams. Because of this limitation, at least one RARP server needs to be located on each local subnet to service RARP client requests. Multiple RARP servers on a local subnet provide redundancy, eliminating a single point of failure. The requirement to have at least one RARP server per segment means there must be many RARP servers throughout a network to service the needs of diskless hosts or any host requiring dynamic logical address assignment. In addition, the administrator must update and maintain the static table regularly, which adds a lot of management overhead to a network.

RARP Operation

Before a host can communicate on any network, RARP requires certain configuration information. Diskless hosts or any host lacking this information must obtain it from somewhere. When a host initializes, if a host has not been previously configured with this information or has no place to store it, it can request the assignment of a logical Network layer protocol address from a remote host running the RARP process. The code RARP needs to initialize and complete the bootstrap operation for a client is small enough to fit in PROM (Programmable Read Only Memory) on the local host.

To obtain a logical protocol address:

1. The sending host transmits a local RARP broadcast.

2. The host states its known hardware address and requests assignment of a logical protocol address from any RARP server receiving this request.

3. RARP servers on the local segment receive this request and check their RARP database for an entry mapping the sending host's hardware address to a logical protocol address.

4. If this pair exists in the table, the RARP server sends a directed datagram to the source host providing the requested information.

5. If the address pair does not exist, which might be the case if no hardware address mapping exists in the RARP server's table, the server does not respond.

6. If the client does not receive a response from a RARP server it abandons the effort to obtain this information and does not initialize itself successfully as a participant on the network.

7. Once this process resolves a hardware address and determines a protocol address, it places this information in the local host's memory. Its memory is maintained until the next boot.

ARP Versus RARP Operation

As you might recall, when we discussed the operation of the ARP protocol, we stated that you could think of a host sending an ARP query as "Does anyone recognize the network layer address x.x.x.x?" (The x's in this case would represent the 32-bit IP address of the destination host). Look at Figures 4.8 and 4.9 for examples of an ARP query.

However, when a RARP sends a query, you can think of it as "I know my hardware address; here it is. Can you tell me what my network layer address (x.x.x.x) is?" Figures 4.10 and 4.11 show examples of a RARP request and RARP reply exchange.

FIGURE 4.10.

In frame one, highlighted within the Summary pane and shown in the detail pane below, you can see the various fields of a RARP header. Note that the RARP protocol is Ethertype 8035.

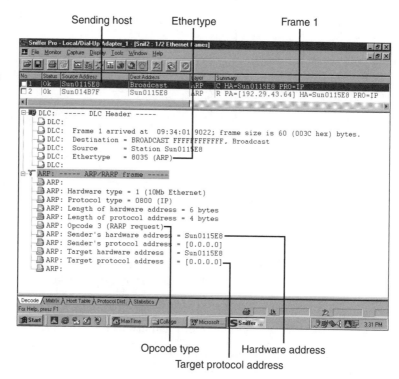

In Figure 4.10 Sun0115E8 sends the RARP request as a broadcast. Note that Opcode is type 3, indicating a request, not a reply. Also note the sending host knows and identifies its hardware address, but does not know its logical Network layer address; therefore, it uses all zeros in that field (0.0.0.0). The sending host does not know the hardware or IP address of the RARP server, nor does it need to because it sends this frame out as a Data Link layer broadcast and any RARP server on the segment will pick it up.

Keep in mind the purpose of this frame is to resolve its hardware address to a logical protocol address. Therefore, the target hardware address indicated within the RARP header for resolution is its own hardware address, and the target protocol address stated within the RARP header also is all zeros. Notice in Figure 4.11 that in the response frame the RARP reply has an Opcode value of 4. Note also that this frame is not a broadcast, but a directed datagram sent by the RARP server Sun014B7F (192.29.43.51) to host Sun0115E8 assigning it an IP address of 192.29.43.64.

FIGURE 4.11
RARP does the opposite of ARP; it resolves a hardware address to an IP address.

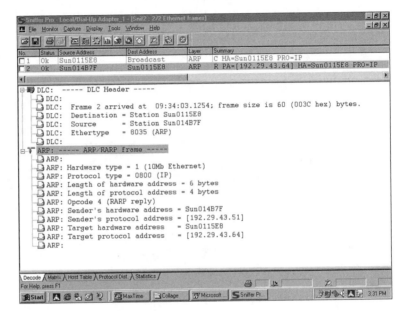

Disadvantages of RARP

Other, more robust protocols such as BOOTP and DHCP have replaced RARP; we will discuss this later in this chapter. RARP has two major disadvantages:

- Routers cannot forward requests and replies.

- An administrator must create and maintain a static mapping table.

Because routers cannot forward requests and replies, RARP servers must exist throughout the internetwork (at least one per segment). This drastically affects the cost and implementation of RARP.

Because RARP requires a static mapping table, an administrator must manually build and maintain the mapping table on a regular basis. This proves impractical when thousands of hosts exist or if changes frequently occur in your network. Each time a host moves, an administrator must update this information on the RARP servers. If a host has moved to a segment and the local RARP server has not received this client's mapping information, or the administrator has input the mapping information incorrectly, the client will fail to connect to the network.

RARP Header

The RARP header looks nearly identical to an ARP header. The only difference appears in the frame type field in the RARP packet format (attached to the RARP header), indicating 0x8035 for an ARP request or reply. In addition, the Opcode field has a value of 3 for a RARP request and 4 for a RARP reply. Like an ARP header, the RARP header contains 28 bytes. We will take a look at the fields and functions within an RARP header. Refer to Figure 4.7 for an example of a RARP/ARP header.

Hardware

This two-byte field identifies the hardware type being resolved as Ethernet, Token-Ring, or some other network type. RARP uses this field in conjunction with the protocol type field during RARP request, asking the protocol address to correspond with the hardware address. If the RARP process resolves an Ethernet hardware address, this field will have a value of one.

Protocol Type

This two-byte field identifies the Network layer protocol type. This value makes RARP capable of resolving a hardware address to various logical protocol addresses. For example, if the RARP process resolves the protocol type IP, this field will have the value of the well-known registered protocol type for IP 0x0800.

Length of Hardware Address

This 1-byte field specifies the length in bytes of the hardware address that RARP resolves. This value varies depending on the hardware type indicated in the hardware type field. For example, if the hardware type is Ethernet (shown as a value of 1), which uses 48-bit or 6-byte hardware addresses, the hardware address field will have a value of 6.

Length of Protocol Address

This 1-byte field specifies the length in bytes of the Network layer protocol address that RARP expects as a result of address resolution. Because RARP can resolve a hardware address to various logical Network layer addresses for multiple protocols, it needs this value defined. For example, if the protocol type field specifies IP (0x0800), it will expect the length of protocol address field to be 4 bytes or 32 bits.

Opcode

This two-byte field specifies the type of operation occurring:

1. ARP request (value of 1)

2. ARP reply (value of 2)

3. RARP request (value of 3)

4. RARP reply (value of 4)

RARP needs this field to differentiate between a RARP request and RARP reply.

Sender's Hardware Address

The sending host places its hardware address within this field for identification purposes. This field has 6 bytes.

Sender's Protocol Address

The sending host places its logical Network layer address within this field for identification purposes. This field has 4 bytes. If this field has a protocol address value of all zeros, the RARP client has performed its initial request broadcast to all RARP servers. All zeros indicate the sending host does not know this address.

Target Hardware Address

This 6-byte field identifies the destination host's hardware address. In a RARP request this value has the sender's hardware address. In a RARP reply this value has the hardware address of the RARP client.

Target Protocol Address

This 4-byte field identifies the network layer protocol address of the destination host (target). A RARP request sends this value as all zeros (unknown) because by sending this request, RARP attempts to learn this address. In a RARP reply this value has the logical address assigned to the RARP client by the RARP server.

BOOTP

You already know why we need address resolution; you also are familiar with the operation of the ARP and RARP protocols, and their fields and functions. As you might recall from this chapter, both are broadcast based and are used to resolve addresses for hosts. ARP resolves a host's logical to hardware address; RARP resolves the hardware to logical address. Remember that as broadcasts these datagrams do not pass through routers.

The evolution of the BOOTP (Boot Parameter) protocol was intended as the next protocol to replace RARP. Defined within RFC 951, BOOTP initially was intended (like RARP) to be used by diskless clients requesting IP address information from a remote server. In addition to retrieving address information, a diskless host also could request a remote boot file from a TFTP server or some other remote boot server for initialization purposes.

Like RARP, upon initialization BOOTP clients address all hosts running the BOOTP server process (this can be a host or a gateway), requesting IP address configuration information. All BOOTP servers maintain a local static configuration table mapping hardware addresses to valid IP addresses used to fulfill client requests. The network administrator must manually update and maintain this table.

Unlike ARP and RARP, which sit at the Network layer and actually use the services of IP for the delivery of their requests and responses, BOOTP utilizes the services of UDP and IP for delivery. The UDP port value 68 identifies a client, and the value 67 identifies a server port. TCP and UDP ports are discussed in detail in Chapter 7, "Transport/Host-to-Host Layer," and Chapter 8, "Transmission Control Protocol (TCP)," respectively. Also, unlike ARP/RARP, routers can forward BOOTP requests and responses. This allows BOOTP servers to be strategically placed throughout the internetwork without requiring a BOOTP server on each and every network segment.

You have three options when configuring a BOOTP server:

1. Configure routers (gateways) on the internetwork to forward BOOTP client, and server requests and responses by enabling UDP ports 67 and 68.

2. Configure a gateway or local host as a BOOTP server by configuring a local static mapping table and enabling the BOOTP process.

3. Configure a device, such as a local host or a gateway, as a BOOTP proxy agent for the local segment.

This first option is not a good idea because if you simply open up these ports on your router, BOOTP broadcast frames are forwarded. It negates the main purpose of having a router in the first place—to cut down on this type of traffic.

With the second option, the BOOTP requests do not have to be forwarded beyond the local gateway. However, this option does add overhead to what perhaps is an already overburdened gateway. Use this option for a local host running the BOOTP server process, offloading this process and its overhead from a gateway, which should be used only for datagram forwarding.

The third option enables a local host or a gateway to intercept local BOOTP broadcasts and repackage them as directed datagrams, sending them directly to a BOOTP server or servers located on another segment. On behalf of the requesting host the agent sends the request as a unicast datagram or directed broadcast (subnet broadcast). This enables an administrator to control broadcast traffic on the internetwork yet still provides remote IP configuration to hosts needing it.

BOOTP header

A BOOTP Header and a DHCP header use the exact same format. Figure 4.12 shows the format of a BOOTP header; Figure 4.13 shows a BOOTP header as seen through a Sniffer. Note that within the Sniffer, the Opcode field is referred to as "boot record type." The Sniffer also refers to the second field as "elapsed boot time," the unused field as "flags," the client IP address field as "client self-assigned IP address," and your IP address field as "client IP address." In addition, the Sniffer lists the unused field, referred to as "flags," which will always contain a value of zero (0000). This field also states "no broadcast," which is not true. This should just be ignored.

FIGURE 4.12
Notice that a BOOTP header contains 300 bytes. Both BOOTP and DHCP use the exact same header format.

Op	Htype	Hlen	Hops
Transaction ID			
Seconds		Unused	
Client IP Address			
Your IP Address			
Server IP Address			
Gateway IP Address			
Client Hardware Address (16 octets)			
Server Host Name (64 octets)			
Boot File Name (128 octets)			
Vendor-Specific Area (64 octets)			

FIGURE 4.13
Remember that BOOTP and DHCP use the same header format.

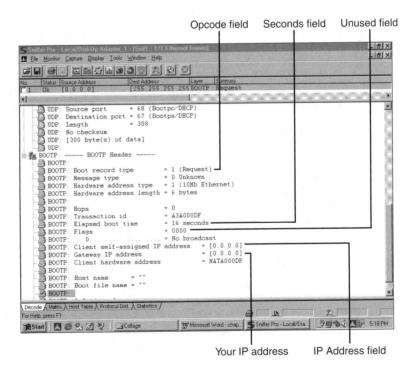

Opcode field   Seconds field   Unused field

Your IP address   IP Address field

Op—Operation Code

This 1-byte field specifies the type of BOOTP datagram being sent. There are two types of Operation codes:

- Opcode 1 = BOOTP Request (sent by clients)
- Operation Code 2 = BOOTP Reply (sent by servers)

Htype—Hardware Type

This 1-byte field identifies the hardware type resolved as Ethernet, Token-Ring, or some other network type. For example, Ethernet has a hardware type value of one (1), thus BOOTP expects an address of 6 bytes or 48 bits in length.

Hlen—Hardware Length

This 1-byte field specifies the length in bytes of the hardware address that BOOTP expects as a result of address resolution. This value varies depending on the hardware type, indicated in the hardware type field.

Hops

This 1-byte optional field indicates that a client is retrieving remote boot information across a router or routers. This indicates the number of hops this datagram has taken. The client initially sets this value to zero. Gateways increment this value by one each time they forward a BOOTP request.

Transaction ID

Although BOOTP is connectionless it implements a transaction ID value. This allows a client to match its request with a server response. The client randomly chooses the transaction ID value. The transaction ID field has 4 bytes.

Seconds

Each BOOTP client sets this timer value upon initialization and notes the time a request goes out, measuring how much time has passed since the client booted up and is still expecting its configuration from a BOOTP server. If a BOOTP client does not receive a response within a certain amount of time, it attempts to retransmit its request, hoping for a response from a BOOTP server. Each BOOTP client process implements some type of timer mechanism that controls how long a client will wait and how long it will wait between requests before it retransmits. These values vary based on vendor implementations. If these timers expire the device times out, fails to initialize itself, and cannot participate on the network. The seconds field has 2 bytes.

Unused

The BOOTP does not use this 2-byte field.

Client IP Address

Upon the first client boot, this field's value will contain all zeros. If the client is diskless this field will always have a value of zero, because the client has no place to store previously used parameters. If the client is not diskless and has stored this information, this field will have the original IP address assigned by the BOOTP server, which the client has stored and would like to reuse.

Your IP Address

In a BOOTP request sent by a client the following situations apply:

- If the previous field (client IP address) contains all zeros, this field will not appear. This indicates that this client has never received an address from a BOOTP server.

- If the client knows its IP address and would like to continue to use this address, this field will contain the same value (the original IP address assigned by the server).

In the BOOTP response, this value will have the IP address assigned by the BOOTP server to this client.

Server IP Address

If the client does not know the address of the server, this field will contain all zeros and not appear within the analyzer output screen. A field of all zeros occurs when a client has initialized for the first time or if this is a diskless client without a storage area. If the client has stored this information from a previous boot, this field has the IP address of the BOOTP server to which this message is being sent. If this is a BOOTP reply, this field has the IP address of the BOOTP server that responded to the request.

Gateway IP Address

When a new host sends its initial request, this field should contain all zeros. If the BOOTP client knows it must forward this request through a local gateway and knows the address of the gateway or relay agent, it adds this information. If the client does not know this information (perhaps it is its first boot), it broadcasts the request and the gateway or relay agent forwarding this datagram adds its IP address. If the BOOTP client has previously received its configuration from a remote BOOTP server and has stored this information, this field will contain the IP address of the gateway or relay agent it used previously.

Client Hardware Address

This field identifies the BOOTP client's hardware address. For example, if the BOOTP client has an Ethernet hardware address, this field will contain the 6-byte or 48-bit unique address burned into the Network Interface Card (NIC). This field can have up to 16 bytes.

Server Host Name

This optional value identifies the BOOTP server by name. The value specifies that a particular BOOTP server can respond. If this value is left blank, any server can respond. The field can have up to 64 bytes.

Boot File Name

This optional value identifies the name of a boot file that the BOOTP client can request from the BOOTP server to retrieve configuration information carrying remote initialization parameters for the host. When the server responds, it identifies the full path of the boot file. If the client leaves this field unspecified (blank), the server attempts to download a default boot file for the client. If no default file exists and this field is blank, the server returns only basic parameters to the client, such as IP address and gateway address, but no boot file. This field can have up to 128 bytes.

Vender Specific

This field contains a list of specific options the client is requesting or is being assigned. Specific parameters vary based on vendor implementation.

BOOTP Request and Reply

Take a look at a BOOTP client and server exchange. Figure 4.14 shows a BOOTP client request being broadcast to all BOOTP servers on the local segment. Notice the UDP port values are 67 for BOOTP, which is the server, and 68 for the client. Within the summary pane you can see that the client does not know its IP address (0.0.0.0) and is broadcasting this request to all hosts (255.255.255.255). Within the detail pane the only address this host knows is its hardware address (NATA000DF).

FIGURE 4.14

Both a BOOTP request and reply use the same header format. You can tell which type of exchange it is by looking at the Opcode value, 1 for request and 2 for reply. In this case, it is a request. If this was a reply, the server would be giving the client an IP address.

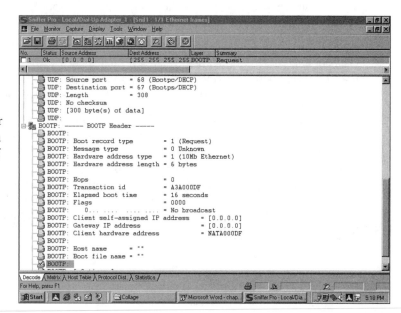

DHCP (Dynamic Host Configuration Protocol)

Just as the name implies, DHCP (Dynamic Host Configuration Protocol) is a dynamic protocol that provides devices such as hosts or gateways with IP configuration parameters. These parameters include logical IP address, gateway address, DNS (Domain Name Service) addresses, and many more. RFC 2131 defines DHCP and is the official standard in the industry today, replacing previous protocols such as RARP and BOOTP.

As you might recall RARP was the first protocol within the Internet Protocol suite to provide this type of service and has three major disadvantages, which DHCP tried to eliminate:

* It uses a static addressing table, which means an administrator must manually create and maintain the tables.

* It uses broadcasts for facilitating the requests and replies.

* Because routers cannot forward RARP broadcasts, a RARP server has to be located on every subnet throughout the internetwork to service client needs.

BOOTP, which replaced RARP, also implemented a static table mapping MAC (hardware) addresses to logical network layer addresses. However, routers can forward BOOTP requests and unlike RARP, responses can be forwarded across routers to remote BOOTP servers; therefore do not require BOOTP servers on each segment. DHCP, actually an extension of BOOTP, uses the exact same UDP port values (port 67 = DHCP server and port 68 = DHCP client). It also uses an identical header format for its request and response messages as BOOTP, with one exception: The "Vendor Specific" field has been renamed "Options" and has a variable length.

Like BOOTP, routers can forward DHCP. DHCP and BOOTP have one main difference—DHCP does not limit itself to using a static mapping table; hence its dynamic nature. You can configure DHCP with static mappings of hardware addresses to logical IP addresses. This typically is the case when a specific IP address must always be given to a host or gateway.

However, unlike RARP or BOOTP, DHCP can maintain a pool of IP addresses (also known as a scope or range) that is available for dynamic assignment to hosts or gateways. This enables hosts to be mobile and still obtain IP address and configuration necessary to participate on a segment when they initialize. A host or gateway can serve as a DHCP server maintaining the address pool and configuration as necessary. A network administrator defines a scope with a valid range of IP addresses and lease times, and configures additional information to be assigned to end devices as requested. These parameters might include the following:

* The IP address of a gateway to be assigned to an end host so it may communicate beyond its local segment.

* IP addresses for DNS servers.

* IP addresses for WINS servers.

Allocating Configuration Information

DHCP is client/server based. Clients send requests and servers send configuration parameters in response. DHCP supports three methods of allocating configuration information:

- **Automatic**—Automatic allocation is the permanent allocation of configuration information, such as IP address to a client.

- **Dynamic**—Dynamic allocation allows a DHCP server to provide a client with configuration information to be used for a specific period of time (limited use), typically identified by a lease value. This is the most common method of allocation. Dynamic allocation is ideal when you have mobile clients on a group of devices who must share a pool of addresses. This allocation method works by reclaiming unused addresses and reassigning them to new hosts as needed. This allows for more efficient use of the address pool.

- **Manual**—The manual allocation method, just as its name implies, requires an administrator to manually assign an IP address to a device.

When you implement and design the network, you can choose a single method or a combination of automatic, dynamic, or manual. The method you choose depends on the implementation. Some implementations use one or a combination of the above methods to facilitate address and configuration allocation.

DHCP Messages

DHCP clients and servers exchange the following DHCP message types:

- Discover

- Offer

- Request

- ACK

- NAK

- Decline

- Release

- Inform

Table 4.1 gives a description of the different DHCP client and server messages types.

TABLE 4.1   DHCP Client and Server Message Types

Message Type	Description
Discover	DHCP clients send the discover message upon the initial boot as a local broadcast to DHCP servers.
Offer	DHCP servers send the offer message in response to a client's discover message. This message includes the set of configuration parameters being offered by the DHCP server sending the offer. More than one server can respond to a client's request, each with its own offer.
Request	Sent by clients in the following instances: • Acknowledging and accepting receipt of a previous offer. If the client receives multiple offers from several DHCP servers, acceptance of a specific server's offer implies rejection of all others. • Sent by a client to renew the use of parameters previously allocated and currently in use by this device. • Request by client to extend the lease of previously assigned IP address.
ACK	Acknowledgment sent by servers confirming the client's acceptance of this server's offer and providing the client with IP address and configuration parameters.
NAK	Negative acknowledgement sent by servers indicating that configuration parameters previously requested by a client are invalid or unacceptable.
Decline	Sent by clients to notify servers that another host or gateway is already using the allocated IP address.
Release	Sent by clients to notify servers that the client no longer requires the previously assigned IP address and configuration parameters, which releases the server. This allows the server to re-allocate this information to another host or gateway requesting configuration.
Inform	Sent by clients that have been manually configured with an IP address, but require additional parameters stored on a DHCP server.

DHCP Message Exchanges

Four general message exchanges occur between DHCP clients and servers to facilitate the configuration of a new client.

Client broadcasts a DHCP discover message to locate servers. All servers respond to the discover with a DHCP offer message. If you have multiple DHCP servers capable of responding, they all respond to a client discover message with a DHCP offer message.

The client selects a server and requests configuration by sending a DHCP request message. The client can include a wish list of parameters it would like to receive. The client then must choose which offer it would like to accept by sending a DHCP request bearing a specific server's IP address. The acceptance of this server's offer automatically implies the rejection of all others. In the request the client can ask for specific configuration parameters it would like to receive.

The selected server responds with a DHCP ACK including the configuration information requested. The server then must provide all the requested parameters or a partial set of them. The server does so by including this information with a DHCP Acknowledgement message. The address assigned to the client must be valid for the subnet the host resides on. If the server cannot fulfill the client's request for specific parameters or the client requests invalid parameters, the server responds with a DHCP NAK (negative acknowledgement).

Once the client receives the configuration information, it performs one final function: It verifies that this IP address is not being used by some other host on the network by generating an ARP request with the given IP address as the target. It hopes that this request will go unanswered; in other words, that no other host on the network claims to recognize this IP address. If a host does recognize this address, this address is already in use and is unavailable to this host. If this occurs the host sends a DHCP decline message to the server and restarts the configuration process. If the ARP goes unanswered, meaning the address is not in use by another host, the client keeps the IP address. At this point it has completed the client initialization process. The client now has enough configuration information to participate on the network.

Figures 4.15, 4.16, 4.17, 4.18, and 14.9 show the four-phase message exchange between client and server. In Figure 4.15, we see in Frame 1 a DHCP client with an unassigned IP address of 0.0.0.0 broadcasting (255.255.255.255) a discover message to locate a DHCP server. In Frame 2 (161.69.97.200), a DHCP server replies by broadcasting an offer message. In Frame 3 the client accepts the previous offer and requests an IP address and configuration parameters by broadcasting a request message. In the Frame 4, the last frame, the server confirms the request and assigns the parameters to the client in a broadcast acknowledgement.

As you can see, these frames are all sent by broadcast, not unicast. That is because the client does not have an IP address yet and is unable to accept any other type of datagram. Once the client has been configured, future exchanges will use unicast datagrams.

In Figure 4.16 the address being resolved is a 6-byte Ethernet hardware address. A gateway or agent has not forwarded this datagram, so the hop count is zero. The client uses the transaction ID (87C6A131) to match this with the corresponding reply from a server. The client booted 768 seconds ago. The flag options indicate that this request was sent as a broadcast. Note that all logical addresses such as client, server, and gateway (or relay agent) are zeros because this client has not learned this information. However the client does know its hardware address and reports it as NwkGn1093F5E; it attempts to resolve this hardware address.

FIGURE 4.15
In this example we see the four-frame exchange that occurs between a DHCP client and server when a new client comes online.

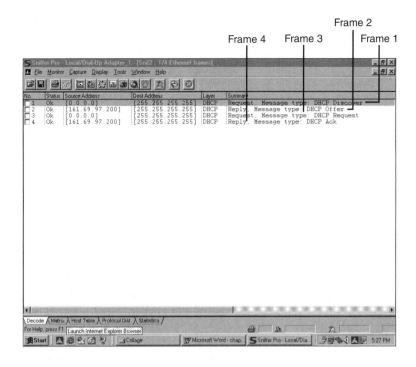

FIGURE 4.16
Note that this is an Opcode 1 (shown in the Sniffer output as "boot record type"), indicating that this is a request, message type "discover."

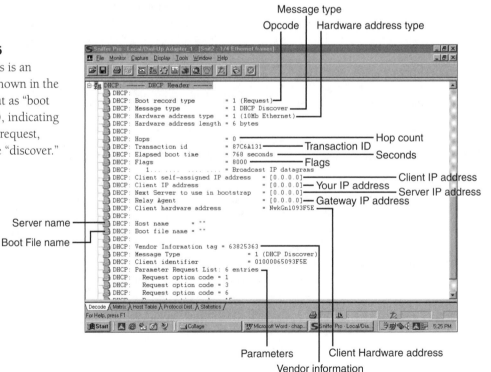

The client has not specified the DHCP server name or boot file. The client has specified options it would like to receive within the "vendor information" field. Beneath the vendor information field it lists requested options identified by values. These represent the "wish list" configuration parameters the client would like to receive from the DHCP server. To learn which option codes represent what parameters, please refer to the DHCP options RFC.

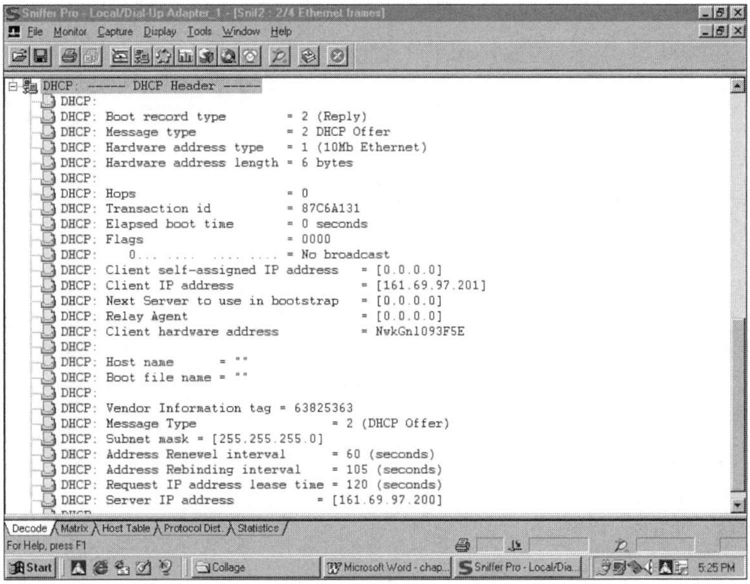

FIGURE 4.17

Note Opcode field contains a value of 2, indicating a DHCP reply, message type 2, a DHCP offer. This is the response from the server.

In Figure 4.17 note the transaction ID matches the one previously used by the client in Figure 4.16. Also note the IP address offered to the client (161.69.97.201). Look at the parameter below the "vendor information tag" field to see what parameters are being offered to this host. As you can see, the server has given the client a subnet mask of 255.255.255.0, a T1 (60 second or one half the lease) and T2 (105 seconds) timer for lease renewal and the lease value itself, 120 seconds. The server also has identified itself (161.69.97.200), which the client uses in future renewal requests.

In Figure 4.18 the Opcode field contains a value of 1 with a message type of 3, indicating a DHCP request. The client has accepted the DHCP server's previous offer message and accepts the offered parameters. Note the transaction ID matches the ID used in the discover and offer datagrams. This means it is part of the same four-phase process.

In Figure 4.19 the Opcode field contains a value of 2 (a reply message) with a message type of 5, indicating a DHCP acknowledgement (ACK). The server completes the four-phase exchange by sending this final datagram. In this datagram the server confirms the client's acceptance of its offer and is not allocating the parameters to the client previously listed in the offer message.

FIGURE 4.18
This figure shows a DHCP request.

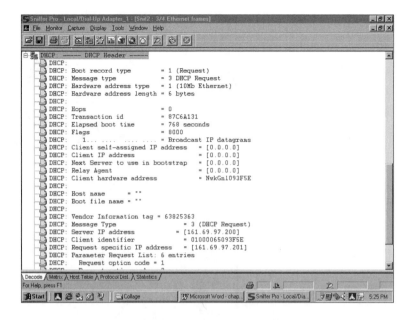

FIGURE 4.19
This figure shows a DHCP acknowledgement.

The specific parameters a host requests vary based on implementation. If the client is diskless, it performs this process upon each boot; if the client is not diskless, this occurs only upon the initial boot up or if its lease has expired. If the client is not diskless, this is not its first boot, and it has stored the previously learned parameters after completing the four message exchange. If a client has a lease that has almost expired, the following two message exchanges occur upon each boot:

1. The client sends a DHCP request message to the original server that provided it with its configuration to request the continued use of the configuration parameters.

2. The server responds with a DHCP ACK confirming the request and renewing the lease. If the server does not respond in time or is unavailable, and the lease expires, the client releases its IP address and configuration parameters and immediately ceases to participate on the network.

Figures 4.20, 4.21, and 4.22 show the two-phase process between client and server to renew its lease. In Figure 4.20 DHCP client 161.69.97.201 sends a DHCP request to DHCP server 161.69.97.200, asking to renew its lease of the previously assigned IP address and configuration parameters. Notice this exchange is not broadcast-based because the client already has an IP address and therefore has the capability of sending and receiving directed datagrams.

FIGURE 4.20

In the response frame (DHCP acknowledgement), the server renews the lease.

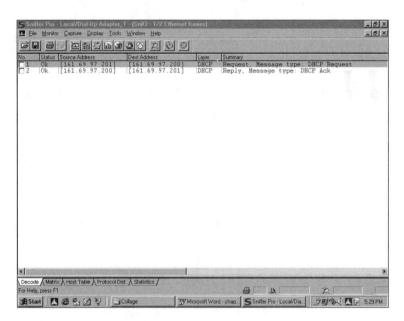

Note in Figure 4.21 the Opcode field contains a value of 1, message type 3, indicating a DHCP request. In the first part of this message exchange, the DHCP client sends a request to the DHCP server, asking the server to renew its lease. In Figure 4.22 the Opcode field contains a value of 2 (reply) with a message type of 5, indicating a DHCP acknowledgement. In this second part and final part of the message exchange, the DHCP server sends an ACK (responding to the client's request) to renew the client's lease.

FIGURE 4.21
Note that the DHCP client wants the server to renew its lease.

FIGURE 4.22
The DHCP server acknowledges the client's request.

If a client no longer requires the IP address to be assigned, it sends a DHCP release message to the DHCP server, which previously assigned this address notifying it that it can return this address to the pool. This message exchange makes this address available to other clients. Although an administrator might have already configured clients with an IP address, some clients need specific parameters from a DHCP server to function on this subnet. When this occurs, the client sends a DHCP inform message on the local segment requesting additional configuration parameters. DHCP servers with valid configuration parameters for this host respond with a DHCP ACK message including this information. When the client receives a response, it adopts the use of the parameters given and initialization is complete.

Lease Duration

The administrator can configure the lease duration, measured in seconds, on the DHCP server. The lease value varies based on implementation. Static mappings on the DHCP server have unlimited lease values, as the mapping of hardware address to IP address is hardcoded and never changes unless manually modified. This permanently reserves a specific address for a client.

Dynamic assignment of addresses usually includes a lease time, which governs how long a client may keep an IP address. If a client remains consistently active, the server continues to renew this lease for the client's use. However, if the lease expires because the client cannot contact a DHCP server, the client ceases using this IP address and cannot participate on the network. If this happens, the client must start the four-phase allocation process again, obtaining a new IP address from a DHCP server.

Two-timer values configured on DHCP servers control lease expiration and extensions: T1 and T2. The T1 value typically has a 0.5 * lease value; it dictates when the client will attempt to contact the DHCP server to renew its lease. If left at the default value, this means the client starts trying when the lease is half over (a 0.5 * lease value). When this occurs, the client sends a DHCP request to renew in hope that the server responds and reassigns the IP address to the client. If the client's attempts to renew its lease go unanswered and it reaches the T2 timer (the lease is 87.5% over), the client, in a desperate attempt to maintain its participation as a network client, starts sending its DHCP requests out as broadcasts to any DHCP server in hope that they renew the lease. T2 value typically has a 0.875 * lease value. Of course, an administrator can change either value.

DHCP Header

A DHCP header looks and functions in almost the same manner as a BOOTP header. A DHCP header has one major difference from the BOOTP header: The "Vendor Specific" field contained in the BOOTP header has been renamed "Options" and has a variable length. Figure 4.23 shows the format of a DHCP header.

Op—Operation Code 1 Byte

This field specifies the type of DHCP datagram being sent. There are two types of Operation codes:

- Opcode 1 = DHCP Request (sent by clients)
- Operation Code 2 = DHCP Reply (sent by servers)

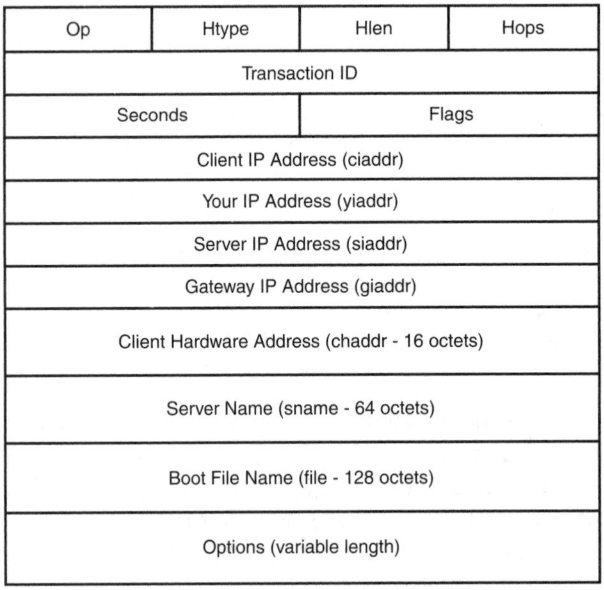

FIGURE 4.23
Note that a DHCP header
and a BOOTP header use
the same formats.

Op	Htype	Hlen	Hops
Transaction ID			
Seconds		Flags	
Client IP Address (ciaddr)			
Your IP Address (yiaddr)			
Server IP Address (siaddr)			
Gateway IP Address (giaddr)			
Client Hardware Address (chaddr - 16 octets)			
Server Name (sname - 64 octets)			
Boot File Name (file - 128 octets)			
Options (variable length)			

Htype—Hardware Type 1 Byte

This field identifies the hardware type resolved as Ethernet, Token-Ring, or some other network type. For example, Ethernet has a hardware type value of one (1), thus DHCP expects an address of 6 bytes or 48 bits in length.

Hlen—Hardware Length 1 Byte

This field specifies the length in bytes of the hardware address that DHCP expects as a result of address resolution. This value varies depending on the hardware type, which is indicated in the hardware type field.

Hops—1 Byte

This optional field indicates that a client is retrieving remote boot information across a router or routers. This indicates the number of hops this datagram has taken. The client initially sets this value to zero. Gateways or relay agents increase this value by one each time it forwards a DHCP request.

Transaction Id (XID)—4 Bytes

Although DHCP is connectionless, it implements a transaction ID value, which allows a client to match its request with a server response. The client randomly chooses the transaction value.

Seconds—2 Bytes

DHCP clients set this timer value upon initialization and note the time when a request goes out, measuring how much time has passed since the client has booted up and is still expecting its configuration from a DHCP server. If a DHCP client does not receive a response within a certain amount of time, it attempts to retransmit its request, hoping for a response from a DHCP server. Each DHCP client process implements some type of timer mechanism that controls how long a client will wait and how long it will wait between requests before it retransmits. These values vary based on vendor implementation. If these timers expire, the device times out, fails to initialize itself, and cannot participate on the network.

Flags—2 Bytes

The Flags field specifies whether the datagram was sent as a broadcast or unicast frame.

Client IP Address—4 Bytes

Upon the first client boot, this field's value will contain all zeros. If the client is diskless, this field will always have a value of zero because this client has no place to store previously used parameters. If the client is not diskless and has stored this information, this field has the original IP address assigned by the DHCP server, which the client has stored and would like to reuse.

Your IP address—4 Bytes

In a DHCP request sent by a client the following situations apply:

- If the previous field (client IP address) contains all zeros, this field also will contain zeros.

- If the client knows its client IP address and would like to continue use of this address, this value will contain the same value (the original IP address assigned by the server).

In the DHCP response, this value will have the IP address assigned by the DHCP server to this client.

Server IP Address—4 Bytes

If the client does not know the address of the server, this field will contain all zeros. A field of all zeros occurs when a client has initialized for the first time or this is a diskless client without a storage area. If the client has stored this information from a previous boot, this field has the IP address of the DHCP server to which this message is being sent. If this is a DHCP reply, this field has the IP address of the DHCP server that responded to the request.

Gateway IP Address—4 Bytes

When a new host sends its initial request, this field should contain all zeros. If a local gateway or relay agent must forward the request to locate a remote DHCP server, the gateway or agent forwarding this datagram adds its IP address. If the DHCP client has previously received its configuration from a remote DHCP server and has stored this information, this field will contain the IP address of the gateway or relay agent it used previously.

Client Hardware Address—Up to 16 Bytes

This field identifies the DHCP client's hardware address. For example, if the DHCP client has an Ethernet hardware address, this field will contain 6-byte or 48-bit unique address burned into the Network Interface Card (NIC).

Server Host Name—Up to 64 Bytes

This optional value identifies the DHCP server by name. This value specifies that a particular DHCP server can respond. If this value is left blank any server can respond.

Boot File Name—Up to 128 Bytes

This optional value identifies the name of a boot file that the DHCP client may request from the DHCP server to retrieve configuration information carrying remote initialization parameters for the host.

When the server responds, it identifies the full path of the boot file. If the client leaves this field unspecified (blank), the server attempts to download a default boot file for the client. If no default file exists and this field is blank, the server only returns basic parameters to the client, such as IP address and gateway address; but no boot file.

Options—Variable Length

This field contains a list of parameters requested by the client or granted by the server.

Summary

Four types of protocols are used for address resolution: ARP, RARP, BOOTP and DHCP. ARP dynamically resolves a remote host's logical Network layer IP address to a hardware address for proper delivery. Upper-layer applications and processes need the ARP protocol to dynamically resolve Network layer addresses for proper data delivery.

RARP dynamically resolves a host's hardware address into a logical Network layer protocol address. RARP has the opposite function of ARP, although both are broadcast based and use the same header format and fields. RARP has two major disadvantages: Routers cannot forward requests and replies and an administrator must create and maintain a static mapping table regularly. Both ARP and RARP utilize IP for their delivery of requests and replies. BOOTP evolved to replace RARP and provides the same type of address resolution utilizing UDP—not IP—for delivery of requests and replies. Routers can forward BOOTP requests and responses, allowing BOOTP servers to be strategically placed throughout the internetwork without requiring a BOOTP server on each and every network segment. However, BOOTP still requires manual updates by an administrator.

DHCP, evolved to replace both RARP and BOOTP, is named by the industry as the official standard. DHCP stops the disadvantages of RARP and BOOTP by maintaining a pool of IP addresses, known as a *scope* or *range* that is available for dynamic assignment to hosts or gateways. DHCP uses nearly the identical header format as BOOTP and the same UDP ports—67 and 68.

Review Questions

1. What type of address resolution does ARP perform and how does ARP go about resolving this type of address resolution?

2. RARP performs what type of address resolution and how does RARP go about resolving this type of address resolution?

3. What protocol did BOOTP evolve to replace and what are the differences between the two protocols?

4. What are the major differences between DHCP and BOOTP?

5. What are the different ARP cache mechanisms?

6. What is Proxy ARP?

7. What does the Opcode field specify in a ARP or RARP header?

8. What is the difference between shouting and routing?

9. Name the different DHCP messages types.

10. Name the DHCP message types that accomplish the initial four-phase configuration process between client and server.

CHAPTER 5

IP ROUTING

You will learn about the following in this chapter:

- Basic Routing Principles
- Static Routing
- Default Routing
- Dynamic Routing
- Distance Vector Protocols
- Link State Protocols

IP Routing Basics

The purpose of routing is to forward user datagrams beyond the local segment across an inter-network to the destination. When hosts do not reside on the same local segment, routers must get involved in the forwarding process.

The local host determines whether the destination host it wishes to communicate with resides on its local segment. The local host achieves this by comparing the destination host's IP address to the sending host's local mask. If the destination host is remote (not on the sending host's local segment), the local host directs the datagram to the local gateway for forwarding.

To properly deliver its datagram the sending host relies on any number of unknown gateways between itself and the ultimate destination. If multiple routes exist, hopefully the datagram takes the fastest, shortest path possible. This is where routing methods come in. Routers use several methods to route datagrams between source and destination. Typically, routers use a combination of the following routing methods to build a router's route table:

- Directly connected interface
- Static
- Default
- Dynamic

Directly Connected Interface

Directly connected interfaces are routes that are local to the router; that is, the router has an interface directly connected to the destination network to which it wants to forward a datagram. Directly connected routes are always the best method of routing because the router knows the route to this network firsthand and does not rely on some other means to learn this route, such as static or dynamic routing protocols.

Static Routing

Static routes are routes to destination hosts or networks that an administrator has manually entered into the router's route table. Static routes define a specific gateway or interface to use when forwarding traffic to a particular destination. Because this type of route has a static nature, it is not capable of adjusting to changes in the network. If the defined gateway or interface fails or becomes unavailable, the route to the destination fails.

This type of routing method has the advantage of eliminating all traffic related to routing updates. Static routing tends to be ideal where the link is temporary or bandwidth is an issue, so you want to use this method for dial-up networks or point-to-point WAN links. You can implement static routes in conjunction with other routing methods to provide routes to destinations across dial backup links when primary links implementing dynamic routing protocols have failed. Also, static routes are preferable when there are few to no topology changes in the network and when a remote site has only one exit point from the network.

Note

Remember with static routing, you must manually configure each route into the router's route table. This includes any topology changes in the network.

You would not want to design an entire network with only this method because you would have to enter each route manually, which is highly impractical. In addition, if a link or a router within the internetwork fails, you would have to enter a new route. Meanwhile routers obviously cannot forward traffic to that destination because the original path has become invalid. Static routing can have extremely high overhead in intense administrative hours spent getting the network up and keeping it going.

Static routes work better with small to very small networks with perhaps as few as 10–15 links total; even then, dynamic routes offer so much more versatility.

Note

Increasingly companies are using static routes for exits at every remote site they have (sometimes up to 20,000 remote locations). Usually these companies have a core-distribution-access model with the distribution layer running OSPF and BGP and the access layer running all static routes. The primary reason companies do this is that the remote sites have only one way to go and don't require a dynamic protocol.

Remember that static routing has the following characteristics:

- Advantage of eliminating all traffic related to routing updates

- Ideal for point-to-point WAN links or dial-up networks

- Can use as backup when primary link fails

- Impractical to have entire network static

- Has disadvantage of extreme administrative overhead

- Better to implement on small networks

Default Routing

Every IP host needs to have a default route either manually configured or dynamically learned. Default routes provide end hosts a way out of their local subnet and provide gateways with a last resort if there is no other route in the gateway's route table.

Although capable, end hosts do not usually maintain their own local route tables; they rely on local gateways to forward traffic to remote hosts. For an end host to communicate hosts beyond its local segment, an administrator at least must configure it with an IP address of a gateway (known as the *default gateway*). Depending on the vendor implementation, you can configure end hosts to send datagrams to an alternate gateway if the first one on the list becomes unavailable. If an end host does not have a default gateway configured, it limits this host to communicating to hosts on its local segment only.

Routers use default routing as a last resort. Gateways inspect received datagrams to identify the logical Network layer address of the ultimate destination. If a static or dynamic route exists within the gateway's route table, it forwards the datagram.

If the destination remains unknown; that is, no method of routing has resulted in a learned route, it forces the gateway to use a default route. Typically, administrators implement default routes on point-to-point or dial-up connections, linking a company's network to the outside world.

You can implement dynamic or static routes within the company's network to facilitate learning of local link route information. You then can use a default route to direct all traffic outside your network regardless of destination. This is a good method because there are about 105,000 routes on the Internet and it would overwhelm gateways if they had to learn and maintain each one of these routes. By implementing a default route the gateway simply directs all traffic to unknown destinations through the default path, typically serviced by an ISP.

Dynamic Routing

There are many different types of dynamic IP routing protocols:

- Distance Vector (RIPv1, RIPv2 and IGRP)

- Link State (OSPF)

- Hybrid (EIGRP)

Dynamic routing has the main advantage of automatically detecting and adjusting around failed links or routers, reducing the overhead involved with building and maintaining route information. Dynamic routing protocols fall into one of two main categories:

- IGPs (Interior Gateway Protocols)

- EGPs (Exterior Gateway Protocols)

IGPs propagate network reachability and routing information within an (interior) autonomous system. EGPs allow a router in one autonomous system to advertise network reachability information to a router in another (exterior) autonomous system.

IGP (Interior Gateway Protocols)

Designed for implementation within a company's internetwork of Autonomous System infrastructure, IGPs allow routers to build and maintain route information pertaining to local subnets and networks. Consider the following as IGPs:

- RIPv1 and v2 (Routing Information Protocol)

- IGRP (Interior Gateway Routing Protocol)

- EIGRP (Enhanced Interior Gateway Routing Protocol)—Cisco proprietary

- OSPF (Open Shortest Path First)

A single company can run multiple IGP routing protocols within its internetwork. In general, IGPs work best in small- or medium-sized networks, although some might support large networks. We will discuss each one of these protocols in more detail in Chapter 6, "Routing Protocols."

EGP (Exterior Gateway Protocols)

Designed for use between Autonomous Systems, EGP routing protocols (for example, BGP) connect different companies' networks together. Typically, EGP protocols do not concern themselves with the IGP protocols running within the AS. They typically see the entire AS as a single entity. The prolific BGP does most of the routing work for the Internet, handling AS routes interconnecting thousands of autonomous systems. We will discuss BGP in more detail in Chapter 6.

Routing Protocols and Best Path

No matter what type of routing protocol, once a router has determined what it believes to be the best path to the destination, it installs this route into its route table to forward datagrams. When a router receives a datagram, it inspects the destination IP address within the IP header to determine where this datagram is going. It checks its local route table to see whether it has a route to this destination. If it has a route, it identifies which local interface it will use to transmit this datagram en route to its destination. It also identifies the IP address of the next hop gateway in the path to the destination.

If the router does not have a specific route in its route table, it uses the default route. If the default route does not exist, it trashes the datagram and generates an ICMP message to the source host stating the requested destination network, or host, is unreachable.

Distance Vector Routing Protocols

Distance vector routing protocols, such as RIP v1, v2, and IGRP, judge best path based on one value–distance (measured in hops). These protocols utilize the distance vector algorithm: RIPv1 and v2, and IGRP. Typically, these routing protocols support only broadcasts, although RIP v2 does support multicasts.

These broadcasts are sent out periodically based on timers. When a distance vector router comes on line, it sends a request to all other routers on the segment asking them to send their entire route tables. Thereafter, each router broadcasts its entire route table when its update timer has expired, whether a change has occurred or not. This adds unnecessary traffic to the network without adding any new information.

When a router receives update information, it adds one hop to the previously advertised route and updates its local route table. It then waits for its update timer to expire before passing this information to all other routers and all other interfaces except the one on which it was received. Because timers control the propagation of route information, rather than triggered by an event, such as a failed link, it takes time for all routers to learn, adjust, and agree on changes in the network (known as convergence).

Distance vector protocols have the following characteristics:

- Broadcast
- Classful routing, with the exception of RIPv2 (updates do not include the subnet mask)
- Timers control updates
- The entire table is always sent regardless of a change
- Subject to routing loops
- Best used in small to medium networks
- Maximum distance defines the diameter of the network
- Uses hops as its sole metric

If a router learns that a link is unavailable, it might not immediately notify its neighbors, with-holding this information until its timer goes off. This opens the possibility for routing loops to occur and delays the detection and correction. Because of this, distance vector implementations must employ several loop avoidance mechanisms to minimize the routing loops and their adverse effects.

When there are multiple active paths to a destination, a routing loop can occur. If there are misconfigured routers within the internetwork, the routers might pass bad route information to a neighbor router, causing the receiving router to reinstate a dead route.

In addition, a router can learn that a route is down, and although ready to notify other routers, it must wait for its timer to expire before doing so. Because of this, another router could receive an update from a router that this route is good. In turn, the router believes this information and reinstates the route in its table.

What both routers might not know is that they think the path to the route is through each other (which causes routing loops). This happens because when distance vector routing protocols advertise route information, they include only the destination route and how far it is (in hops) from the advertising router. These updates do not include the subnet mask (except RIP v2) and the gateway or path this router is using to forward traffic to this network. To avoid routing loops, you can employ several methods, as discussed in the following sections.

Split Horizon

The *split horizon* rule states that a gateway must not advertise route information it received through an interface back out the same interface. It can only advertise routes learned in one direction—out all interfaces other than the one through which it was received. This prevents feedback from occurring.

You can think of split horizon as the old grape vine game you played as a kid, in which some-one tells you a secret and you pass it on to the next person in line and so on. After being told a secret, you would not tell the secret to the same person who just told you the secret because they already know it. The same applies to a gateway. With split horizon, a gateway will not tell a secret (send route updates) to the same person (interface) from whom it learned the secret. It will send the information only to others (interfaces) who don't yet know that information.

Poison Reverse

Poison reverse allows a router to basically break the split horizon rule by advertising information it learned from an interface out the same interface. However, the routes learned through this interface would be advertised back out this interface with a hop count one greater than the maximum value allowed, or infinity value (RIP 16 hops, IGRP 256 hops). Routers with better metrics to this route simply ignore this, keeping their current route to this network in their route tables.

Count to Infinity (Maximum Hop Count) and Hold Down

Distance vector routing protocols determine the best path based on distance to each destination. Each protocol defines a maximum distance supported to a destination. Distance vector protocols measure distance in hops with RIP having a maximum distance of 15 hops and IGRP, 255. Routers consider routes further than the maximum and do not forward datagrams to routes beyond the maximum hop distance.

Routers exchanging route information advertise the destination network or host and the distance to that network. Routers receive this information, update their tables, and add another hop to the route (considering it one hop farther than the advertised route they received).

Using RIP as an example, when route information propagates from one router to another, each router increments this value (hop count) until a router receives an advertisement with a hop count of 15. Adding a hop count to an advertisement with a value of 15 exceeds the maximum distance value, making the destination unreachable at 16 hops or more. This router then would advertise it with an infinity hop count in its next advertisement.

The router trashes any datagrams destined for this network that it considers unreachable (exceeds maximum hop count). By keeping infinity low this enables routers to deal with routing loops within the internetwork and discard endlessly looping datagrams. If there is a loop in the network and routers keep feeding each other bad routes, the count to infinity allows the detection of this bad information, eventually killing the route to this destination.

A router begins a count to infinity when it receives a route advertisement from a neighbor router stating that it can reach a network. In this example, this router (Router A) knows a destination route is dead. It prepares to advertise this information to its neighbors when it receives a route advertisement (from Router B) stating that it can reach that destination network with a hop count of 4.

However, Router A's path to the dead network was through Router B. Router A does not know that Router B thinks it can get to this network through Router A (perhaps split horizon is disabled). The receiving router (Router A) does not know the path Router B will use to reach this network; it knows only that the sending router (Router B) thinks it can get to this network. Router A has no choice but to treat the route information as reliable and adds the route to its table, adding a hop count (5) to the route.

Unfortunately, these routers do not have the proper configuration, so Router A readvertises the route back out the same interface, stating that it can reach this destination in 5 hops. The original sending router receives it and assumes if this router advertises that it can reach this network within 5 hops, it can reach it in 6 hops (incrementing the hop count by one). This continues with each router updating its information, adding hops until they exceed the maximum hop count. Once they exceed the maximum hop, they kill the route.

Meanwhile the datagrams these routers forwarded to the destination network (which they couldn't actually get to) loop back and forth between these routers until it exceeds the maximum hop count. At this time one of the routers trashes the datagram and sends an ICMP destination unreachable message back to the source host.

Link State Routing Protocols

Unlike distance vector protocols, which judge best path on distance, link state protocols can make more intelligent route decisions using one or a combination of metrics describing the state of the link, including

- Bandwidth

- Delay

- Reliability

- Load

- MTU

OSPF, considered a link state routing protocol, is capable of supporting route decisions based on these parameters, although typically it defaults to implementing only one of them—bandwidth.

Routing protocols that understand these metrics use this information to derive the lowest-cost path to a destination when multiple paths exist. These metrics actually appear within the IP header portion of a datagram; routing protocols supporting them can make use of this information. We described each metric in Chapter 3, "Network Layer/Internet Protocols."

Link state protocols exhibit the following characteristics:

- Multicast

- Triggered updates sent only when changes occur and include only the change

- Classless routing (updates include the subnet mask)

- Capable of ToS or QoS through bandwidth, delay, reliability, load, and MTU

- Best used in medium to large implementations

- Large amount of CPU time, memory, and resources to build and maintain route information

Link state protocols do not use periodic timers to send updates. After the initial exchange of route information when they first come online, routers send only triggered updates (an event has occurred that changed the topology). In these triggered updates, the router sends only the changes, reducing the amount of update traffic generated. Routers send these updates through multicasts—not broadcasts—which reduces the amount of processing needed by all hosts on the local segment. Only devices belonging to the multicast group fully process the datagram.

Link state protocols support classless routing (VLSMs) through the inclusion of the subnet mask within the route advertisement. By including the mask with the destination route being described, receivers can tell whether the destination address reflects a subnet or network.

Other routing protocols, known as *classful routing protocols* (RIPv1 and IGRP), do not support VLSMs (*classless routing*); thus they do not include the mask in their advertisements. These protocols can assume only that a classful A, B, or C IP address is being used based on the value contained within the first byte because they have no other information to go by. Classful routing protocols do not include the subnet mask within their advertisements. This means receivers cannot tell whether a destination address has been subnetted; therefore they apply a classful default mask to derive the network portion of the address.

Hybrid Routing Protocols

Cisco Systems developed its own proprietary routing protocol, known as EIGRP (Enhanced Interior Gateway Routing Protocol). Cisco extended the IGRP distance vector protocol by adding link state characteristics to EIGRP. For this reason, Cisco classifies EIGRP as a hybrid.

EIGRP has the capability of making more intelligent routing decisions than distance vector routing protocols. It uses one or a combination of the same metrics utilized by link state protocols to determine best path selection:

- Bandwidth

- Delay

- Reliability

- Load

- MTU

EIGRP, although capable of supporting all of the previously listed ToS and QoS parameters, defaults to bandwidth and delay. It uses this information to derive the lowest-cost path to a destination when multiple paths exist. EIGRP shares many of link state's characteristics:

- Multicast

- Triggered updates only sent when changes occur and only includes those changes

- Class routing (updates include subnet mask)

- Capable of ToS or QoS

- Best used in medium to large networks

- Supports multiple protocols: IP, IPX, and AppleTalk

EGRIP's one unique characteristic is that it can maintain route information for three different protocol suites: IP, IPX, and AppleTalk. All other protocols mentioned in this chapter can maintain route information for only one.

When a company's network includes more than one major protocol suite, they must implement multiple routing protocols to maintain routes for each. If a company has IP, IPX, and AppleTalk implemented, it would require three different routing protocols. Each routing protocol would generate route update traffic, adding a lot of overhead to a network. EIGRP solves this problem by enabling you to implement a single routing protocol to keep track of all the routes, drastically reducing the traffic on the network by offering features such as triggered and incremental updates.

EIGRP, like link state protocols, do not use periodic timers to send updates—only events trigger updates. Even then, it sends only the changes, reducing the amount of update traffic. EIGRP uses multicasts, not broadcasts, for its updates and supports classless routing (VLSMs) through the inclusion of the subnet mask within the route advertisement.

Summary

Routing forwards user datagrams beyond the local segment across an internetwork to the destination. When hosts do not reside on the same local segment, routers get involved in the forwarding process. Routers use directly connected interfaces, static routing, dynamic routing, default routing, or a combination to build route tables.

Directly connected interfaces are the best method of routing because the router directly knows the route information. Static routing requires an administrator to manually configure and maintain the network. Every IP host needs to have a default route. Default routes provide end hosts a way out of their local subnets and gateways with a gateway of last resort. Dynamic routing automatically learns changes in topology and reduces the amount of time spent building and maintaining a network.

Dynamic routing protocols fall into one of two categories: IGPs (Interior Gateway Protocols) or EGPs (Exterior Gateway Protocols). IGPs include RIPv1 and v2, IGRP, EIGRP, and OSPF. EGPs include BGP. IGPs allow interior autonomous systems to propagate routing information; EGPs allow exterior (another company's) autonomous systems to propagate routing information.

Distance vector protocols use one metric to choose the best path, with the distance measured in hops. Distance vector protocols tend to have routing loop problems. You can use the following methods to prevent routing loops: split horizon, poison reverse, count to infinity, and holddown. Link state protocols can make more intelligent routing decisions and base best path on a variety of metrics.

Review Questions

1. What routing methods do routers use to build their routing tables?

2. What are the characteristics of static routing?

3. What are the characteristics of dynamic routing?

4. When would you want to use static routing and when would you want to use dynamic routing?

5. What does default routing provide?

6. What are the two main categories that dynamic routing protocols fall under and what is the difference between the two?

7. What five protocols are considered to be IGPs?

8. What are the characteristics of distance vector protocols?

9. What one metric does distance vector use and how does it vary between protocols?

10. What routing loop remedies for distance vector protocols can you employ?

11. How does split horizon work when enabled?

12. What five metrics are used by link state protocols to determine the best path?

13. What are some of the characteristics of link state protocols?

CHAPTER 6

ROUTING PROTOCOLS

You will learn about the following in this chapter:

- RIP (RIPv1 and RIPv2)
- OSPF
- BGP
- IGRP
- EIGRP

Introduction to Routing Protocols

Routing protocols enable routers to dynamically learn paths to destination hosts and networks. This dynamic learning allows routers to adapt to changes in the network. Without some type of routing mechanism to learn about new or failed segments, routers could not forward datagrams.

The purpose for every routing protocol, regardless of the type, is the same: to forward datagrams to their destinations. When a router receives a datagram, it identifies the destination network or host. It then uses this information and checks its local routing table to determine whether it has a known path to the destination. The path in the routing table identifies the local outbound interface that the router should use, as well as the next-hop router address to reach the destination.

In Chapter 5, "IP Routing," you learned about static and dynamic routing mechanisms. In this chapter, we will discuss the various dynamic routing protocols and how they work. Dynamic routing protocols enable Layer 3 devices, known as internetwork gateways or routers, to make intelligent and dynamic path selections. We will start with the IGPs (interior gateway protocols) used within a company's autonomous system and finish with BGP (Border Gateway Protocol), an EGP (exterior gateway protocol) that controls routing between autonomous systems.

RIP

Two versions of RIP (Routing Information Protocol) exist: version 1 (RIPv1) and version 2 (RIPv2). Both versions of RIP were originally designed around Xerox's XNS and the routeD program that is integrated into the Berkeley implementation of Unix.

> **Note**
>
> Two Requests for Comments (RFCs) define RIP: RFC 1058 defines RIPv1 and RFC 2453 defines RIPv2.

RIP can run on end hosts or gateways. Although it runs on top of UDP (User Datagram Protocol) and IP (Internet Protocol), using UDP port 520, it functions as a Network layer protocol. RIP functions as an IGP, providing route determination within an autonomous system. RIP works best when implemented on small-sized networks because of its limitations, which we will discuss later in this chapter.

> **Note**
>
> An autonomous systems (AS) is a collection of networks that share a common routing protocol under a common administration.

RIP exhibits the following characteristics:

- It is broadcast based.
- It is an IGP.
- It works best on small-sized networks.
- It is a Distance-vector routing protocol.

As a Distance-vector routing protocol, RIP implements the Bellman-Ford (also referred to as Ford-Fulkerson) algorithm to determine best path selection. RIP determines best path selection to a destination based on the shortest distance, measured in hops, between the source and destination. Although many other routing protocols today are capable of more intelligent and efficient route selection, RIPv1, second only to OSPF, remains one of the most popular protocols.

As previously mentioned, two versions of RIP exist, RIPv1 and RIPv2. We will begin with a full discussion of RIPv1 and then discuss the differences between the two versions. RIPv1 is the most widely used routing protocol in the world today because of its simplicity. RIPv1 has the advantage of being easy to understand and implement. Although RIPv1 and RIPv2 have similarities, RIPv2 has added extensions that overcome some of the limitations of RIPv1. We will discuss RIPv2 later in this chapter.

RIPv1

End hosts or gateways implement RIP to keep track of routes to destinations, such as hosts, networks, subnets, and default routes. End hosts or gateways learn routes to destinations via route updates that devices exchange dynamically on the local segment via periodic broadcasts.

All devices that are running RIP listen on UDP port 520 and transmit from the same UDP port. On broadcast-based networks, such as Ethernet or Token-Ring, all devices receive these datagrams, but only devices listening on UDP port 520 process these datagrams. On WAN (wide area network) links, such as point-to-point links that do not support broadcasts, you must specifically identify and configure neighbors (that is, gateways) with each other's IP addresses in order for exchanges to occur.

RIP-enabled devices maintain local route databases (known as routing tables) that list all locally connected networks as well as networks that are both statically and dynamically learned via RIP neighbors. Initially this list only includes entries for local or directly connected networks, but after exchanging route updates with its neighbors, a router modifies the routing table to include remote routes learned from its neighbors. The routing table includes the following information:

- The IP address of the destination host, network, subnet, or default route (0.0.0.0).

- The IP address of the next-hop router en route to the destination.

- The metric (or cost) value, expressed as an integer between 1 to 15 hops that defines how far the network is from the device.

- The local interface that the host uses to forward the datagram to the destination and others.

Each RIP host listens to updates and builds its database by adding one entry for each destination learned.

Gateways advertise their entire routing table via broadcasts sent every 30 seconds. Each gateway maintains its own clocking mechanism, which controls when it sends updates. The gateway includes all known routes in its updates, in addition to the distance, in hops, to each destination. A gateway can include up to 25 entries in each update. If it has more than 25 entries, it must send further updates to send the remainder of the entries.

Note

Although hosts support RIP, you typically only find RIP enabled on gateways.

The broadcast nature of RIP, and the fact that one update may not be enough to advertise all routes, adds additional network overhead and traffic. Furthermore, gateways broadcast their entire table every 30 seconds, regardless of whether any of the route information has changed. When a gateway receives this update, it takes the following steps:

1. It adds all unknown routes to its routing table and increments the hop count value by one.

2. It replaces previous routes with routes that have lower metrics, where applicable.

3. It removes failed or unreachable routes.

4. It prepares to advertise this information to its neighbors on adjacent segments.

Similar to how you might call friends on your cell phone to tell them about traffic conditions (such as which routes are available and how far away the route is), a router advertises what routes are available to destinations. When a gateway advertises a route, it states the IP address of the destination and the distance in hops. Receivers listen to these advertisements, learn from them, and incorporate the information into their local routing tables. When gateways incorporate a route in their routing table, they always increment the distance (that is, hop) value by one, indicating that the destination learned lies one more hop away from this gateway than the gateway from which it learned the route. After it includes this information in its routing table, the gateway advertises the routes contained within its routing table to all other neighbors connected to local segments and point-to-point links, advertising all the routes that it knows about.

Path Selection

RIP uses distance as the base metric to determine the best route—the shorter the distance, the better the route. When multiple routes exist to a destination, a router running RIP chooses the route that has the shortest distance (measured in hops) as the best route and installs it in the routing table; it then uses the information to forward future datagrams.

RIP's simplistic approach to path selection doesn't always choose the best route to a destination. For example, say two routes to a destination exist:

- One of the paths is four hops away and consists of three 100 Mbps Ethernet links and one T1 WAN link.

- The other path is three hops away and consists of two 100 Mbps Ethernet links and a 19.2 Kbps WAN link (see Figure 6.1).

Because RIP uses strictly distance to determine the best path, it chooses the path with three hops instead of the best path—the four-hop route that has a higher end-to-end overall transfer rate. If both paths had three hops, RIP would only consider the fact that both paths have the same hop count. In this case, RIP would try to load balance across these two paths, sending datagrams along both links. In this situation, due to the unequal transfer rates across the links, datagrams sent across the 19.2 Kbps link (the upper path) would slow the transmission process between remote hosts and might even cause connections to timeout and fail.

FIGURE 6.1

The path with the smallest number of hops is not always the best path. In this case, the best path is the four-hop route, which has a better overall transfer rate than the route with three hops.

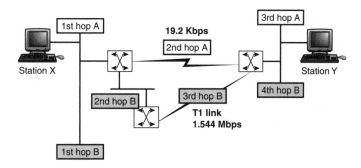

Problems with Least Hops
- Which route do you want your data to take (Path A or Path B)?

Unlike Link-state routing protocols, RIP does not take into consideration factors other than hop count, such as the following:

- Bandwidth capacity of a link

- Reliability

- Load

- Delay

- MTU (maximum transmission unit)

RIP makes decisions based on a limited amount of data—distance—and this can pose a problem. Think about your commute to work. You might have a shorter commute (in terms of distance) if you take the surface roads. However, you might be able to take a longer route on the freeway and get to your destination more quickly (considering bandwidth, or the capacity of link). But there might be an accident on the freeway, and it might take four times as long to get to your destination. RIP doesn't concern itself with any data other than distance when determining the best path.

Both versions of RIP have a maximum distance limitation of 15 hops, which equals the number of gateways a datagram can traverse. RIP considers a destination of 16 or more hops away too far, or unreachable. If a datagram traverses 15 gateways, the 16th gateway discards the datagram and returns an ICMP (Internet Control Message Protocol) message "destination unreachable" to the sender. (ICMP messages are discussed in Chapter 3, "Network Layer/Internet Protocols.")

The RIPv1 Header and Fields

RIP uses two different message types:

- Routing information messages

- Messages that are used to request information

Both message types use the same general header format: They have a fixed header, followed by a list of network (IP address) and distance (metric) pairs. The length of a RIP header depends on the number of network and distance pairs within the datagram. However, RIP datagrams cannot exceed a maximum size of 512 bytes or a maximum of 25 route entries. Maximum size (512 bytes) does not include the Data Link, IP, or UDP headers. Figure 6.2 shows the format of a RIPv1 message.

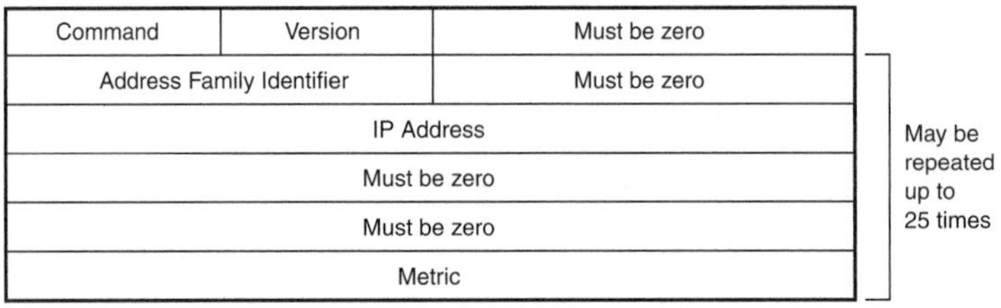

FIGURE 6.2

In a RIPv1 message, a sequence of pairs appears after the general 32-bit header. Each pair has a network IP address and an integer that indicates the distance, in hops, to that network.

Command	Version	Must be zero	
Address Family Identifier		Must be zero	May be repeated up to 25 times
IP Address			
Must be zero			
Must be zero			
Metric			

The route and distance information fields repeat, depending on the number of routes being advertised, for example, if a gateway advertises five routes, two unused and metric fields repeat five times, one for each advertised route. The RIP datagram can carry up to 25 route entries within each datagram.

The following sections describe the RIPv2 header fields.

Command

The 1-byte command field identifies the intended purpose of the frame (for example, a RIP request versus a response). Eight commands exist, and the one used depends on the kind of RIP message sent. Table 6.1 describes the commands and their meanings.

TABLE 6.1   RIP's Command Messages

Command	Meaning
1	A request that a host or gateway sends upon initialization (or after the local routing table has been cleared), requesting that all neighbors respond with their routing information.

TABLE 6.1 Continued

Command	Meaning
2	A response that provides route information and is sent by a host or a gateway in response to a RIP request. Or a regular periodic update sent every 30 seconds, advertising a host's or gateway's routes to its neighbors.
3	An obsolete command that turns on trace mode.
4	An obsolete command that turns off trace mode.
5	A command that is reserved for Sun Microsystems internal use.
9	An update request that is used with demand circuits.
10	An update response that is used with demand circuits.
11	An update acknowledgement that is used with demand circuits.

Version

The 1-byte version field identifies the RIP version as 1 or 2. RIP hosts and gateways must agree on which version type to use.

RIPv1 devices do not support the extensions implemented by RIPv2 (that is, VLSM [variable-length subnet masks], authentication, or multicasting), so if both RIPv1 and RIPv2 exist on a network, there may be interoperability problems.

However, RIPv2 hosts or gateways support the RIPv1 specifications, and in a mixed environment, they use the fields and values recognized by the lowest common denominator (RIPv1) to exchange route information with RIPv1 devices.

You can configure RIPv2 routers to support RIPv1 or RIPv2 on a per-interface basis. If one interface connects to a segment where both RIPv1 and RIPv2 devices exist, you must configure for RIPv1 support on that interface. If another interface connects to a segment where only RIPv2 devices exist, you can configure for RIPv2.

Although RIPv1 and RIPv2 have almost identical features, the RIPv2 extensions not supported by RIPv1 make the two versions incompatible.

Unused

RIPv1 has several 2-byte fields (the Unused field) that it does not use. These fields always contain zeros and repeat depending on how many routes the datagram carries.

Address Family Identifier

Although RIP technically may support various Network layer protocols, the 2-byte address family identifier field only contains the value 2, which represents IP.

IP Address

The 4-byte IP address field identifies the address of the destination host, network, or subnet, or the default being advertised by the router.

Metric

The 4-byte metric field identifies the cost in hops, representing the distance to reach the destination network from the host or gateway that is advertising the route. The field should have a value between 1 and 15. If the field contains a value of 16, RIP considers the advertised route unreachable, due to a network link or gateway failure.

Figure 6.3 shows an example of a RIP advertisement sent from a gateway.

FIGURE 6.3

A message containing a series of route pairs (IP address and distance metric) appears after the Address Family Identifier field.

```
IP: Protocol         = 17 (UDP)
IP: Header checksum = A3AC (correct)
IP: Source address      = [128.104.170.17]
IP: Destination address = [128.104.0.0]
IP: No options
IP:
UDP: ----- UDP Header -----
UDP:
UDP: Source port      = 520 (Route)
UDP: Destination port = 520 (Route)
UDP: Length           = 32
UDP: Checksum         = CE4F (correct)
UDP: [24 byte(s) of data]
UDP:
RIP: ----- RIP Header -----
RIP:
RIP: Command = 2 (Response)
RIP: Version = 1
RIP: Unused  = 0
RIP:
RIP: Routing data frame 1
RIP:     Address family identifier = 2 (IP)
RIP:     IP Address  = [128.104.0.0]
RIP:     Metric      = 1
RIP:
```

Disadvantages of RIPv1

Despite being one of the most popular protocols in use today, RIP has the following disadvantages:

- It is broadcast based.

- It sends the entire table, even when no changes occur.

- Slow convergence due to periodic timers.

- It has a maximum distance limitation of 15 hops.

- It is prone to routing loops.

- It is a classful routing protocol and therefore does not support VLSM.

Because RIPv1 is broadcast based, each gateway broadcasts its entire table every 30 seconds, even when no changes occur and there is no new or viable information. This adds unnecessary traffic to the network. Other routing protocols, such as Link-state routing protocols, use multicast advertisements and send updates only when a change has occurred on the network. The timer-based control slows convergence and the response to problems, such as routing loops.

When a gateway learns of a change in the network, such as the addition of a new link or notification of a failed link, it goes through the following process:

1. The receiving gateway incorporates the new information into its table and increments the hop count by one. This indicates that the gateway resides one hop further than the gateway from which it learned the route.

2. If the gateway learns of a failure, it updates the entry with a hop count of 16 and gets ready to remove the route.

3. The gateway waits for its periodic timer to expire before advertising, causing the gateway to send out this information with its regular updates.

If the network has many gateways and segments, new information can take a while to reach all gateways throughout the network. In the meantime, the gateways operate with outdated and incorrect information. In addition, the maximum distance between any two communicating devices on an internetwork is 15 hops, which limits the diameter of the network and makes RIP an unacceptable routing protocol for medium to large networks. Routers cannot forward datagrams that have traversed or been forwarded through more than 15 gateways. When a router receives a datagram that has traversed more than 15 hops, it sends an ICMP "destination unreachable" message back to the sender, alerting it of the problem.

RIP, like other Distance-vector routing protocols, is prone to routing loops, as described in Chapter 5. RIP implementations usually use a combination of routing loop prevention mechanisms, including the following:

- **Count to infinity**—Distance-vector protocols limit the distance (in hops) that a datagram can traverse. If a route loop exists within the topology, the router automatically discards the datagram when it exceeds the maximum hop count (in this case 15), stopping the count to infinity (see Figure 6.4).

- **Holddown**—Keeps a route in the route table even though it has been marked unreachable or possibly down. While in a holddown state, the network does not consider any further updates. When the router figures out the status of the route, it either flushes (that is, discards) the route or reinstates it.

- **Split horizon**—Remember from Chapter 5 that split horizon dictates that a gateway or RIP-enabled host cannot advertise route information out the same interface from which the information came (see Figure 6.5).

- **Poison reverse**—Poison reverse allows gateways to break the split-horizon rule, by advertising information learned from an interface out the same interface from which it learned the information. It advertises the routes with an infinity hop value, indicating that the route is unreachable, and it thus poisons the route. Routers that have a route with a better metric (that is, hop count) to the network ignore the "destination unreachable" update (see Figure 6.6).

Implementations vary based on vendor support and your specific configuration of RIP in the network.

FIGURE 6.4
Distance-vector protocols consider only the distance when choosing the best path for a datagram.

Counting to Infinity
• Each time a packet passes through a router, the hop count increases.

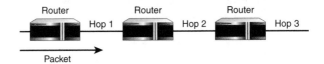

• Maximum Hop Count
(RIP = 15 Hops)

FIGURE 6.5
The middle router learns about networks 12.0.0.0 and 14.0.0.0 from the interface on the right and can only propagate this information out the opposite interface. It learns about networks 11.0.0.0 and 15.0.0.0 from the interface on the left and can only propagate this information out the opposite interface.

Split Horizon
• Routing information learned from an interface is never advertised back out that same interface.

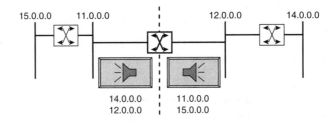

FIGURE 6.6
Poison reverse allows a router to break the split-horizon rule.

Poison Reverse
• Routers use a metric of 16 for all network advertisements learned from that interface.
• The middle router will advertise out interface 1 that network 12.0.0.0 and 14.0.0.0 have a metric of 16.

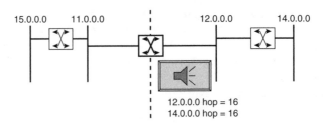

RIPv1, which is a classful routing protocol, recognizes only classful IP addresses, such as Class A, B, or C addresses. It does not understand subnets and cannot identify subnets within a network because route advertisements do not include the subnet mask. Because route advertisements do not include the subnet mask of the destination being advertised, receiving gateways can only assume the default mask based on the address class being advertised. For example, in Figure 6.7, Routers A and B are RIPv1 routers. Router A advertises the classful network without including the subnet masks to Router B. Without the subnet mask information, Router B (which is not directly connected to the remote subnets being advertised) can only assume that this route is a Class B destination with a default mask of 255.255.0.0. Therefore, Router B thinks there are no subnets. This is incorrect, but without the correct mask, Router B cannot make any other conclusion.

FIGURE 6.7
Classful routing protocols, such as RIPv1, do not understand subnetting, which requires the use of VLSMs.

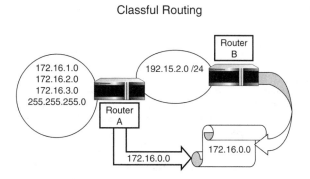

Classful Routing

- "Classful" Networks (RIP1 and IGRP)
- Router A sends a classful update without a mask.
- Router B does not learn about the subnets.

RIP Timers

RIP uses three timers to control routing updates: the periodic update timer, the invalid timer, and the holddown timer.

RIP sends a periodic update every 30 seconds. It broadcasts its entire routing table, regardless of whether any change has occurred.

RIP uses its invalid timer every 180 seconds. If a gateway does not receive a route advertisement that relates to a route in its routing table within 180 seconds, it considers the route invalid and marks it as such.

RIP uses its holddown timer every 180 seconds. After a router marks a route as invalid because it detects a link failure or receives a lack of updates, the gateway starts the holddown timer. This suspends the reception of updates relating to this route until the timer expires. During the holddown period, the gateway does not listen to any advertisements from other gateways to reinstate the route. When the timer expires, the gateway either flushes (that is, discards) or reinstates the route. If it does not receive an advertisement from another gateway stating that the route is valid, the gateway discards it. If the gateway receives an advertisement from another gateway stating that the route is valid, it reinstates it.

Controlling Route Update Traffic

Some RIP implementations enable an administrator to control the amount of RIP update traffic generated on a network. Implementations vary, so you should consult your vendor for specific application and configuration parameters. You can do the following to control RIP update traffic:

- **Adjust the RIP timers**—You can adjust RIP timers on RIP-enabled devices; for example, you can adjust the periodic update timer from 30 seconds to a greater value. Increasing the interval between updates cuts down on the amount of broadcast traffic on a network, but it slows convergence times. If you increase the interval, broadcast traffic increases, but convergence times are reduced.

Note
It is extremely important to note that all RIP-enabled hosts and gateways must agree on timer values for convergence to occur. On nonbroadcast networks, such as point-to-point or multipoint WAN links, each gateway must know the IP address of all other gateways with which that gateway will exchange RIP updates.

- **Configure gateways on a broadcast network by using neighbor statements**— Although this is seldom practiced, you can configure gateways on a broadcast network, such as Ethernet or Token-Ring, with neighbor statements, which causes the gateways to exchange updates as directed datagrams instead of broadcasts. However, this means that if the network adds or removes a gateway, you have to manually change these statements to facilitate route information exchange.

- **Configure route update filters**—Probably the most common and effective way of mini-mizing route update traffic is to configure route update filters on RIP-enabled devices to filter inbound or outbound updates on an interface. Filters typically consist of permit or deny statements that allow or disallow route information from being received or propa-gated. Because each RIP datagram can include only a maximum of 25 routes, a gateway with 27 routes to advertise must send two RIP broadcasts. If you could filter 2 of the 27 routes, you could effectively cut the number of broadcasts in half. Implementation of fil-ters is vendor specific.

RIP and Demand Circuits

RIP uses demand circuits, or WAN links (such as ISDN or X.25 links), to provide bandwidth by establishing a link between remote sites when it needs to forward data, and it terminates the link when it no longer needs the transfer data. Demand circuits are ideal when low-volume or infrequent data transfers occur between remote sites or as backup links in case of primary link failure.

Because demand circuits activate only when needed and terminate when not needed, they conserve resources and reduce costs. However, the temporary nature of demand links does not work well with dynamic routing protocols. If a link goes down, gateways cannot exchange periodic updates, which means they lose their routing information. Without this information, routers cannot exchange data between sites.

Typically to create demand circuits, an administrator enters permanent routing table entries by using static or default routing as the type of routing method. When the link initializes, gateways immediately know how to route data. This method adds no extra broadcast or multicast route advertisement traffic to the link.

Modifications to RIP make the use of dynamic protocols possible on these demand circuits. RFC 2091 defines this modification, called *triggered updates*, which enables RIP to support dynamic routing over demand links. *Triggered* means that an event, not a timer, triggers the router to send an update.

Gateways also use triggered updates. As mentioned earlier in this chapter, the use of neighbor configuration on each gateway connected to the link supports route update exchange. By specifying each gateway's neighbor, RIP can send directed route updates to the gateway at the other end of the link without broadcasting. With demand links, the following events trigger RIP gateways to send updates:

- **A gateway initializes and requests route update information**—The entire routing table is exchanged.

- **A change occurs in the network**—Only changes in the network are sent.

- **Link status transitions from up to down state or vice versa**—These transitions may be the result of a gateway powering up due to demand.

Some vendor implementations also include mechanisms that allow remote gateways connected to demand circuits to permanently or semipermanently store route information learned while the circuit is up. For example, Cisco implements Snapshot routing. As the name implies, gateways connected to the link take a snapshot of the routing table after they exchange route information. They then use this snapshot of the network to route traffic, maintaining this information statically while the link remains down. This enables routers to learn about remote networks and routes to those networks. Snapshots enable routers to keep information, even when links are unavailable.

Demand Circuit Packet Types

Triggered update supported across demand circuits requires the use of three additional RIP packet types and an extended 4-byte update header. Both RIPv1 and RIPv2 support all three packet types and the extended 4-byte header.

Figure 6.8 shows the header format of the three additional RIP packet types that support triggered updates across demand circuits. Table 6.2 explains the three packets types.

FIGURE 6.8
Demand circuit packet
types extend the RIP
header by 4 bytes.

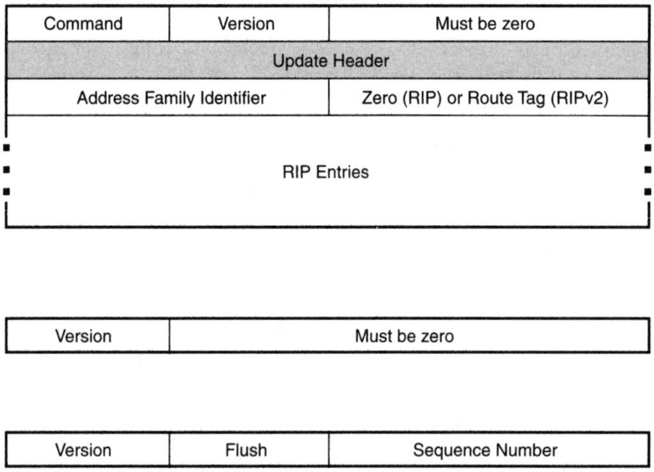

Command	Version	Must be zero
Update Header		
Address Family Identifier		Zero (RIP) or Route Tag (RIPv2)
RIP Entries		

Version	Must be zero

Version	Flush	Sequence Number

TABLE 6.2   Demand Circuit Packet Types

Packet Type	Description
9 (request)	Sent by gateways to request update information
10 (response)	Sent in response to a request; includes either the entire routing table or changed routes, depending on the initial request
11 (acknowledgement)	Sent to acknowledge receipt of update information contained within a response datagram

Unlike in the connectionless LAN-based broadcasts, sequencing and acknowledgements help track demand circuit route exchanges. All RIP responses (type 10 packets) carry sequence numbers. Each response increments these sequence numbers by one. Gateways receiving these responses must acknowledge receipt of route information carried within the response datagram by sending an acknowledgement that has a matching sequence number. Gateways assume that unacknowledged datagrams are lost and that the sender will retransmit them.

RIPv2

RFC 2453 defines the RIPv2 specification as an extension to the original specification of RIPv1 (RFC 1058). RIPv1 and RIPv2 perform similarly.

Designed to address some of the limitations of RIPv1, RIPv2 includes some enhanced features to support authentication and subnetting capability. Although some companies rarely use RIPv2, other companies have moved to RIPv2 where they need RIP (for example, with a PIX firewall), but they use RIPv2 because they also need VLSM support. Other routing protocols, such as Link-state routing protocols, have been developed to address RIPv1's limitations and offer much better route selection criteria, reduced bandwidth consumption, and faster convergence than RIPv2.

RIPv1 Versus RIPv2

Table 6.3 compares RIPv1 and RIPv2.

TABLE 6.3   RIPv1 Versus RIPv2

RIPv1	RIPv2
Broadcast only	Broadcast or multicast
No authentication	Authentication
Classful routing	Classless routing
Distance-vector protocol	Distance-vector protocol
Uses hops as the metric	Uses hops as the metric
Maximum distance = 15	Maximum distance = 15
IGP	IGP

Figure 6.9 shows the format of the RIPv2 header.

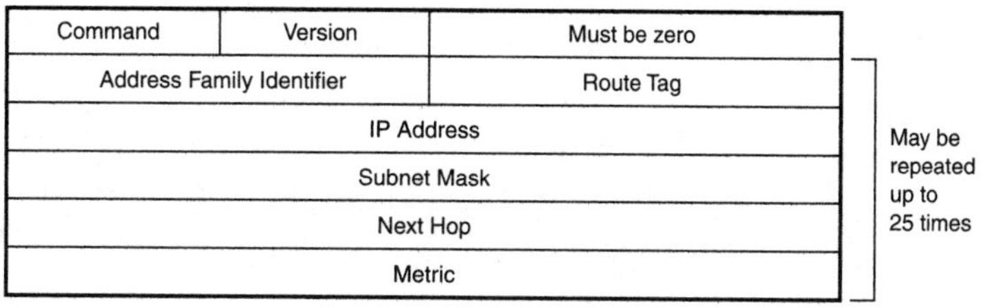

FIGURE 6.9

The RIPv2 header contains a subnet mask and a Next Hop field, which are zeros in the RIPv1 header.

Command	Version	Must be zero	
Address Family Identifier		Route Tag	
IP Address			May be
Subnet Mask			repeated
Next Hop			up to
Metric			25 times

RIPv2 gateways exchange route information with each other by using multicast rather than broadcast advertisements, using the address 224.0.0.9. When RIPv1 and RIPv2 routers exist in the same network, support for broadcast capability allows for interaction.

Unlike RIPv1, which does not support any type of authentication, RIPv2 allows assignment of a plain-text password, which enables low-level security to be implemented between gateways that exchange information.

Figure 6.10 shows the format of an authenticated RIPv2 packet. If authentication information is included in the RIPv2 packet, the maximum number of entries is reduced to 24. Note that the Address Family Identifier field changes to FFFFH, and the Route Tag field identifies the authentication type.

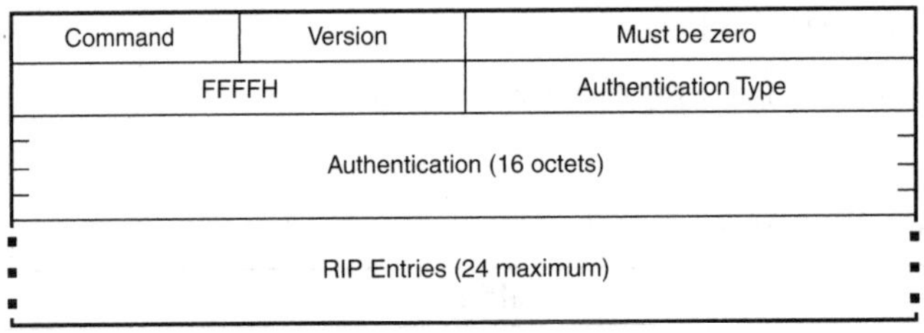

FIGURE 6.10
RIPv2 supports authenti-
cation, but RIPv1 does
not.

Command	Version	Must be zero
FFFFH		Authentication Type
Authentication (16 octets)		
RIP Entries (24 maximum)		

Including subnet mask information within route advertisements allows for classless routing. When a RIPv2 router advertises its route information to neighbors, it includes not only the networks it knows about but the subnet mask of each network. With this information, the receiving gateway can determine whether the network has been subnetted.

RIPv2 does not limit itself, as RIPv1 does, to the recognition of classful addresses. VLSM support allows a classful address and its subsequent subnets to easily be determined and advertised.

RIPv2 Compatibility with RIPv1

RIPv2 is considered to be backward compatible with RIPv1 gateways. However, for RIPv1 and RIPv2 gateways to exchange information, they must use the lowest common denominator, which means they must be broadcast only, have no authentication, and use classful addressing only. This, of course, negates the benefits of RIPv2.

If you have RIPv1 and RIPv2 implemented on the same subnet, RIPv2 devices must adhere to RIPv1 standards and limitations. If, on another interface, one of these RIPv2 devices connects to a subnet that has RIPv2 peers, it can use RIPv2 on that interface. Configuration of RIPv1/RIPv2 support varies, depending on vendor specifications, but typically you configure on a per-interface basis.

OSPF

As mentioned in Chapter 5, OSPF (Open Shortest Path First) uses a Link-state Algorithm (LSA), and therefore, it makes more intelligent path selection than Distance-vector routing protocols. When making routing decisions, OSPF, like all Link-state routing protocols, considers any or all of the following:

- Link capacity (bandwidth)
- Delay
- Reliability
- Load
- MTU

Note

Although two versions of OSPF exist—version 1 and version 2—we will discuss version 2 only because version 1 is considered obsolete.

In addition, OSPF offers several advantages over Distance-vector routing protocols, including the following:

- It is able to configure hierarchical (instead of flat) routing domains by dividing an autonomous system into multiple areas. This isolates changes, routes update traffic to different areas, and reduces overhead involved with routing table recalculations.

- It is able to adapt quickly to internetwork changes with triggered updates.

- It sends only changes, not the entire table.

- It supports large networks.

- It supports load balancing of traffic over redundant equal- and unequal-cost paths.

- It authenticates routing table information exchanges.

- It supports VLSMs.

- It uses multicasts rather than broadcasts.

Designed as an IGP, OSPF can support medium to large networks within a single autonomous system. An OSPF autonomous system, within the context of this discussion, refers to single or multiple OSPF areas and the routers within these areas that are used within an organization's internetwork.

THE IETF (Internet Engineering Task Force) originally developed OSPF (defined in RFC 1247 and replaced by RFC 1583), which only supports the routing of IP datagrams, identified by IP type 89.

OSPF makes routing decisions based on the logical Network layer address of the destination and ToS (Type of Service) bits within the IP header, which offers Quality of Service (QoS) routing to upper-layer applications and services as needed. OSPF routers detect route failures and adapt quickly to changes in the network. When a router detects a link failure, it triggers an update that is flooded to all routers within the OSPF area to notify them of the failure. In contrast, Distance-vector routing protocols, wait for their periodic timers to expire before sending updates. When a problem occurs, an OSPF router immediately generates a multicast advertisement and floods it out all OSPF ports, notifying all routers within its area of the downed link. All routers compute route changes in parallel, which speeds convergence times.

We will discuss the operation of OSPF as it relates to a single area, and then move on to a more complex autonomous system that involves multiple areas in a hierarchical structure.

OSPF Characteristics

OSPF is characterized by the following:

- **Multicast**—224.0.0.5 for all OSPF routers and 224.0.0.6 for designated router (DR)/backup designated router (BDR).

- **Fast convergence**—Routers immediately flood updates when a change occurs, and they compute calculations in parallel.

- **Triggered updates**—Routers send changes immediately, without waiting for a periodic timer.

- **Classless routing**—OSPF supports VLSMs.

- **ToS or QoS**—OSPF routers can forward datagrams to a destination, based on the level of service required by the application.

- **Authentication**—Routers can use password protection, which enables them to exchange information only with authorized routers.

- **Equal- and unequal-cost routes**—Routers can forward datagrams across redundant equal- and unequal-cost paths to a destination to balance the load of traffic.

- **Areas**—OSPF can be implemented in a single area or divided into multiple areas. Subdividing an autonomous system into areas reduces the amount of update traffic. (Link-state database and SPF calculation are discussed later in this chapter.)

OSPF supports VLSMs through the inclusion of subnet masks within updates. OSPF routers not only advertise the destination network or host, but they include the subnet mask, allowing the receiver to identify subnetted networks.

OSPF supports IP ToS through the recognition of the bits set within the IP header that enable OSPF routers to forward datagrams to a destination based on the level or class of service required by the application. OSPF support for IP ToS is vendor specific. OSPF primarily relies on the following complex metrics for best path selection:

- Bandwidth

- Delay

- Reliability

- Load

- MTU

Although OSPF routers can support any or all of these, unless specifically configured to do so, routers typically default to bandwidth only. You can modify any of the metric values to identify the cost parameter by which a router determines the best path—the lower the cost, the better the route. Administrators may configure different cost values on different interfaces of a router. If multiple paths exist to a destination with different metrics, lower-cost paths are placed in the routing table as the preferred route. When IP ToS is in use with redundant paths that offer different types of service, routers place multiple routes within the routing table—one for each ToS. When multiple paths exist and have the same cost, routers can use both routes to forward datagrams; this is referred to as *load balancing*.

OSPF Databases

All OSPF routers maintain and build three separate databases:

- Adjacency database (neighbor table)
- Link-state database (topology map)
- Forwarding database (routing table)

Adjacency Database

For an OSPF router to exchange and learn about routes, it first forms an adjacency with its directly connected neighbors on the local segment. If it does not form this relationship, it cannot participate in OSPF routing.

For an OSPF router to form an adjacency when it first comes online, it goes through the following steps:

1. It transmits Hello packets out on the local wire to identify itself to its neighbors.

2. Receiving OSPF routers add the new router to their adjacency databases and respond to the Hello packet with their own Hello packet, to identify themselves.

All neighbors should know about each other and have theoretically formed a neighbor relationship. This is a very simplistic view of the process because it assumes that all required parameters within the Hello packet match and that the neighbors agree on them. If this is not the case, the neighbors will not form an adjacency. We will discuss the Hello packet and other packets types later in this chapter.

Link-state Database

When OSPF routers know with which routers to exchange information, they can build a Link-state, which is a complete map of the internetwork topology of the OSPF area, to identify every network and subnet and the path to each. From this database each router creates a tree structure identifying itself as the root connected to each destination through the shortest path.

Forwarding Database

A forwarding database, or routing table, uses the link-state database to form its database. When each router has a complete topology map, it can run the SPF algorithm to determine the best route to each known destination. It then places these routes in its local routing table so that it can forward data.

OSPF Operation

OSPF can support various Data Link layer architectures, such as LAN and WAN connections. How adjacencies and database exchanges take place depends on the architecture over which OSPF runs. For the purposes of this section, we focus on LAN-based (broadcast) architectures. We describe other architectures later in this chapter.

Let's start by discussing OSPF operation within a single area. When only a single area exists, the OSPF autonomous system and area are one in the same. All routers within an OSPF area maintain a copy of the same Link-state database (see Figure 6.11). When multiple areas exist, routers connected to all the areas maintain separate databases for each area.

FIGURE 6.11
In a single-area OSPF implementation, all routers within the area maintain three databases: a topology map, a neighbor table, and a routing table.

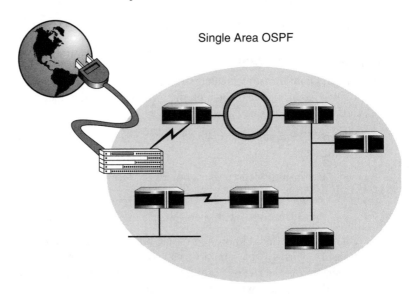

Single Area OSPF

OSPF has six different Link-state advertisements (LSAs), grouped into three categories:

- Intra-area advertisement
- Inter-area advertisement
- External advertisement

Each of these categories describes the type of advertisement and where its propagation occurs. Table 6.4 describes the six different packet types.

TABLE 6.4 LSA Types

Link-state Type	Advertisement Name (Type)	Description
1	Router link (intra-area)	Describes the router's directly connected network and the state of the interfaces
2	Network link (intra-area)	Identifies all routers that are connected to the local network
3	Summary link (inter-area)	Summarizes the routers' subarea to a network outside the area
4	Summary link (inter-area)	Summarizes routes to external non-OSPF networks outside the autonomous system
5	Autonomous system external link (external)	Describes a route to a destination in another autonomous system
7	Autonomous system external link (external)	Carries route information through a stub network

Intra-Area Advertisement

Routers send intra-area advertisements within an area. These advertisements only propagate within the area of origination, and they describe local router links and networks within an area. Routers flood Type 1 (originated by all routers) and Type 2 (originated by DRs only) advertisements throughout a single area only.

There are two types of intra-area LSAs:

- Type 1 (router link)
- Type 2 (network link)

Routers send Type 1 advertisements to the destination multicast address 224.0.0.6 (DR and BDR multicast group address). These advertisements describe their directly connected networks and the state of the interfaces connected to these networks.

On LANs (broadcast networks), the DR sends a Type 2 advertisement to the destination address 224.0.0.5, the multicast group address for all OSPF routers. These advertisements identify all routers connected to the local network.

Figure 6.12 shows an example of a Type 1 intra-area LSA and Figure 6.13 shows an example of a Type 2 intra-area LSA.

FIGURE 6.12
All routers send LSA Type 1 intra-area LSAs to the destination multicast address 224.0.0.6.

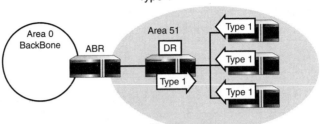

Link State Advertisements
Type 1

Router Link Advertisements: "O" (OSPF)
• Sent by all routers using 224.0.0.6

FIGURE 6.13
Only the DR sends LSA Type 2 intra-area LSAs to all routers on the same segment.

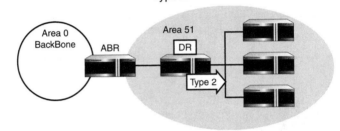

Link State Advertisements
Type 2

Network Advertisements: "O" (OSPF)
• Sent by DR only using 224.0.0.5

Inter-Area Advertisement

ABRs (area border routers) send inter-area advertisements between directly connected OSPF areas. Typically, ABRs connect subareas to the backbone (Area 0), the main transit area for all inter-area traffic. These advertisements summarize the routes within an OSPF subarea. ABRs send these advertisements into Area 0, where other ABRs learn and then propagate the new inter-area information to their own areas.

There are two types of inter-area LSAs:

- Type 3 (summary link)
- Type 4 (summary link)

ABR routers also send summary link advertisements to summarize their sub-area into Area 0 (backbone). ABRs also use these advertisements to advertise summarized routes from other subareas learned through Area 0 into their own subareas.

ABRs send Type 4 LSAs to identify ASBRs (autonomous system boundary routers) that provide access to external non-OSPF networks outside their autonomous systems.

Figure 6.14 shows examples of Type 3 and Type 4 inter-area advertisements.

FIGURE 6.14
ABRs send LSA Type 3 and 4 inter-area summary advertisements.

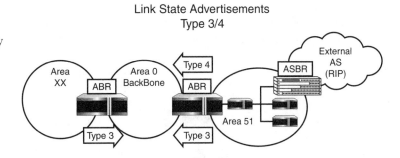

Link State Advertisements
Type 3/4

Summary Advertisements: "IA" Inter-Area
• Type 3: Sent by ABRs into Area 0
  summarizing their local area
• Type 4: Used to identify route to ASBRs

External Advertisement

Only ASBRs send external advertisements. These advertisements propagate throughout the entire OSPF autonomous system, except for stub areas, which are described later in this chapter. These advertisements describe external non-OSPF routes that are outside the autonomous system. An example of an external route would be a RIP route that is being injected (that is, redistributed) into OSPF to be advertised within the autonomous system. Because RIP is not OSPF, OSPF considers this information foreign and advertises it as such. (External route injection is beyond the scope of this book and its configuration varies based on vendor implementation. In this book we will simply refer to an external route as any route that OSPF cannot natively learn.)

There are two types of external LSAs:

• Type 5 (external link)

• Type 7 (external link)

Only ASBRs that are running more than one routing protocol—such as OSPF and RIP, IGRP, EIGRP, and static routing—send Type 5 LSAs. An administrator can configure OSPF ASBRs to inject non-OSPF routes into the OSPF environment. The Type 5 LSAs allow foreign routes to be advertised throughout the autonomous system, making them known to all other OSPF areas and routers.

Only ASBRs connected to an NSSA (not so stubby area, described later in this chapter) and routers connected to a stub network that are running more than one routing protocol (such as

OSPF and RIP, IGRP, EIGRP, static routing, and so on) can send a Type 7 LSA. You can config-ure OSPF ASBRs to accept non-OSPF routes and inject them into the OSPF NSSA environment as Type 7 LSAs, which are used to carry the route information through the stub network. An ABR connected to Area 0 converts a Type 7 LSA to Type 5 before passing this information into the backbone.

Figure 6.15 shows an example of a Type 5 external advertisement, and Figure 6.16 shows and example of a Type 7 external advertisement.

FIGURE 6.15
ASBR routers send Type 5 LSAs to advertise external non-OSPF routes.

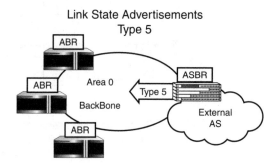

FIGURE 6.16
Similar to Type 5 adver-tisements, ASBRs use Type 7 advertisements to send external route updates describing non-OSPF routes through an NSSA area to reach Area 0.

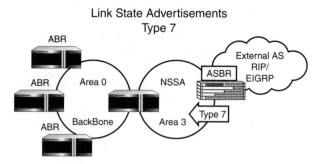

The LSA Header

A database description packet can include one or more LSAs. Each LSA header, which is 20 bytes long, has the same format and contains the same fields. Figure 6.17 shows the format of an OSPF LSA header.

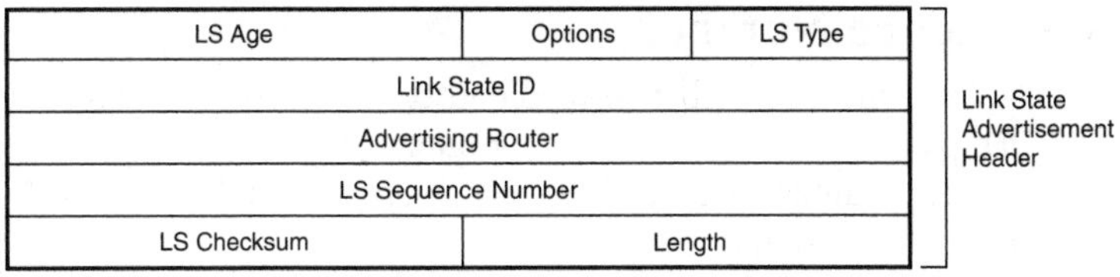

FIGURE 6.17

An OSPF LSA header contains 20 bytes.

LS Age	Options	LS Type	
Link State ID			Link State
Advertising Router			Advertisement
LS Sequence Number			Header
LS Checksum		Length	

The following sections describe the OSPF LSA header fields.

LS Age

The LS age field contains a value that is measured in seconds and indicates the time that has passed since the originating router sent the LSA.

Options

The options field contains the same option values described in the Hello packet. We discuss Hello packets later in the OSPF section of this chapter.

LS Type

The LS type field defines the type of LSA being sent as either intra-area (Type 1 or 2), inter-area (Type 3 or 4), or external (Type 5 or 7).

Link-state ID

The value in the Link-state ID field identifies either the IP address of the originating router (LSA Type 1 and 4) or IP address of the network being advertised (LSA Type 2, 3, 5, or 7). This varies based on LSA type. Table 6.5 shows the Link-state IDs that exist.

TABLE 6.5   Link-state IDs

ID Value	Description
1	Slave router ID
2	DR
3	IP address of the destination network being advertised
4	ASBR router ID
5	IP address of the destination network being advertised

Advertising Router

The advertising router field identifies the router that originated the advertisement.

LS Sequence Number

The LS sequence number field guarantees the delivery and receipt of database description (DD) packets. Each time an OSPF router sends an advertisement, the originator includes a sequence number that identifies the advertisement. We discuss DD packets in more detail in the "OSPF" section of this chapter.

LS Checksum

The LS checksum field verifies that the contents of the OSPF DD packet have not been damaged in transit.

Length

The length field contains the length of the OSPF datagram, in bytes.

OSPF Router States

As discussed earlier in this chapter, a router must form an adjacency (that is, become a neighbor) before it can exchange route information with neighbors. OSPF routers go through the following states, from beginning to end:

1. Down

2. Init

3. Two-way

4. Exstart

5. Exchange

6. Loading

7. Full

You can easily remember the first and the last states. *Down* means OSPF is either not enabled on this router or the interface has been reset. In other words, this router cannot currently participate, or it is not currently participating, in route information exchange. In the Full state, the routing table has converged and the router can actively route datagrams. Routers must pass through all other states to get to Full. The following sections describe the states in detail.

The Init State

A router identifies itself to all its neighbors when you enable OSPF on an interface. It does this by generating a multicast Hello datagram, announcing itself and its parameters. At this point no adjacency between neighbors exists. Figure 6.18 shows an example of the Init state.

FIGURE 6.18
In the Init state, a router initiates the adjacency process with its neighbors.

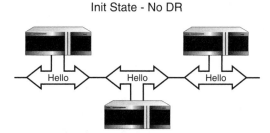

Init State - No DR

• Routers send "Hello" messages to establish adjacencies with neighbor routers.

In the Init state, no DR or BDR router exists because the DR and BDR election process has not yet taken place. The router passes through this state when an administrator initially enables OSPF or resets an interface. In this state, routers transmit Hello messages, announcing their presence to all other routers on the network. All routers send this advertisement to all OSPF routers on the same segment. Routers attached to the same subnet receive this Hello message and thereby learn of their new neighbor and can incorporate them into their adjacency databases.

The Two-way State

After a router receives response Hellos from the other local routers, adjacencies begin to form. Each router learns who its neighbors are and adds them to its local adjacency database. Adjacencies only form if the following Hello fields match:

- Area ID
- Hello and Dead timers
- Authentication
- Stub ID

If any of these values do not match, neighbor routers will not form an adjacency and thus cannot exchange route information. (These are only a portion of the Hello parameters. We will discuss all Hello parameters in more detail later in this chapter.) Figure 6.19 shows OSPF routers using Hello messages to form an adjacency database.

At this point each router on the local segment knows its neighbors and has established a bidirectional (that is, two-way) relationship (see Figure 6.20). The Two-Way state assumes that routers have received and exchanged the initial Hello messages and incorporated them into their adjacency tables. OSPF routers transmit Hello messages every 10 seconds to maintain neighbor relationships with local routers.

FIGURE 6.19
Routers use OSPF Hello messages to build the adjacency database.

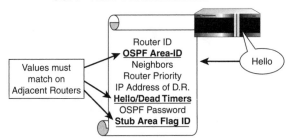

OSPF "Hello" Announcements

Router ID
OSPF Area-ID
Neighbors
Router Priority
IP Address of D.R.
Hello/Dead Timers
OSPF Password
Stub Area Flag ID

Values must match on Adjacent Routers

Hello

Note: If an authentication password is assigned, this too must match!

FIGURE 6.20
In the two-way state, routers on the same network have achieved a bidirectional relationship.

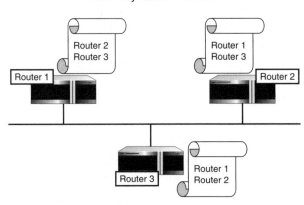

Two-Way State - No DR

Router 2
Router 3

Router 1
Router 3

Router 1

Router 2

Router 3

Router 1
Router 2

• Each router adds all other routers to their Database.

The Exstart State

After the Init and Two-Way states finish, all routers on the segment have enough information to elect a DR and a BDR. Each broadcast network (that is, LAN) elects a DR and BDR for each segment. The routers use two parameters, priority ID and router ID, within the Hello fields for electing a DR and BDR.

The routers consider the priority ID first and the router ID second. The routers elect the router with the highest priority ID as the DR and the router with second-highest priority ID as the BDR. If all routers have the same priority ID, the router with the highest router ID becomes the DR and the router with the second-highest becomes the BDR. You can modify both of these parameters to manipulate the DR and BDR selection.

The DR and BDR become the focal point of the segment. The DR and BDR have the following responsibilities:

- Collect all route advertisements from the local routers

- Build the Link-state database

- Disseminate this information to all other routers on the same segment (DR only; BDR is on standby to do so if the DR cannot)

All other routers become slaves to the DR and BDR, which are masters. The DR and BDR become the recipients of all router advertisements. Both the DR and BDR belong to the multicast group 224.0.0.6, to which all routers address their advertisements. When the DR and BDR exist, they both receive and process the local Type 1 router advertisements from all other routers on the segment. However, only the DR has the responsibility for distributing this information to the local routers, addressing them to the destination multicast group 224.0.0.5. The BDR remains in standby mode until the DR cannot disseminate this information. At that time, the BDR becomes the DR. If the DR fails, the BDR takes over, and if the original DR returns, it does not supersede the current router performing the DR role.

Electing a DR for each segment reduces the number of adjacencies necessary throughout the internetwork, limiting the processing of OSPF multicast traffic that needs to be done by all routers (see Figure 6.21).

FIGURE 6.21

Think of the Exstart state as the state routers must pass through prior to *star*ting their route information *e*xchange.

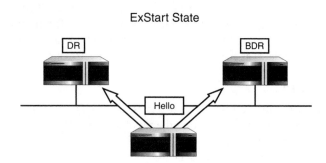

ExStart State

- All Routers send LSAs to the DR and BDR using multicast 224.0.0.6.

The Exchange State

As the name implies, during the Exchange state, all slave routers exchange route information with the DR and BDR. All slave routers transmit their route information to the DR/BDR address 224.0.0.6. Both the DR and BDR assimilate the database changes. However, only the DR manages the synchronization and dissemination of this information. The DR (master) transmits learned route information to all slave routers on the segment on multicast address 224.0.0.5 (see Figure 6.22).

FIGURE 6.22
The Exchange state
allows routers to
exchange their route
information.

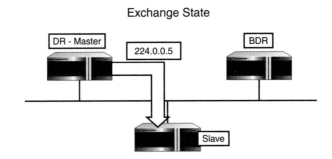

If any of the previous states fail, a topology map will not be built at this point. The first time a router enters this state, it has an empty Link-state database; therefore, it receives all route information to build the database. After that, routers send only updates to show topology changes. However, OSPF routers send all their route information every 30 minutes just to make sure that all OSPF routers have the current topology.

The Loading State

The router enters the Loading state only when it receives conflicting information with the DR during the Exchange state. If the information received differs from the currently held topology map, a router may enter the Loading state to send a Link-state request for more specific information to complete the map. If it finds no discrepancies, it skips this state.

The Full State

A router reaches the Full state after it passes through all the other states. In this final state the router builds the routing table from the topology map. The router derives and installs the best routes to destinations in the forwarding database by running the SPF algorithm on all routes identified within the Link-state database.

Routers only transition through all these states when an administrator first enables OSPF and the routers have not actively participated in OSPF. After a router has reached the Full state, it only transitions through one of three states:

- Exchange
- Loading
- Full

If something changes, the router generates a triggered update, and the exchange starts. If the router receives conflicting information after receiving an update, it enters the Loading state. In the Loading state, the router requests more information from the DR. After it receives the necessary information, it runs the SPF algorithm on the LS database, convergence occurs, and routing begins.

OSPF Router Types

OSPF defines different roles that routers assume based on their placement within the autonomous system. Remember that an autonomous system functions as a group of routers exchanging information via a common routing protocol (in this case, OSPF). A router can assume multiple roles at the same time. OSPF has four router types (see Figure 6.23):

- **Internal**—An internal router has all its attached interfaces contained within a single OSPF area. This type of router does not run any other routing protocol.

- **Backbone**—A backbone router has at least one interface connected to Area 0. A router that has all interfaces within Area 0 functions as an internal backbone router.

- **ABR**—An ABR sits on the border of two OSPF areas. These routers connect to multiple areas, typically a subarea to Area 0. ABRs connecting to Area 0 also function as backbone routers. ABRs maintain multiple Link-state databases, one for each area to which they connect.

- **ASBR**—An ASBR sits on the boundary of two autonomous systems that run OSPF and some other routing protocol (any routing protocol besides OSPF), such as RIP. You can configure ASBRs to advertise non-OSPF routes into the OSPF autonomous system, to disseminate this external route information to all other areas within the autonomous system.

FIGURE 6.23
A router's placement within an OSPF network determines its type.

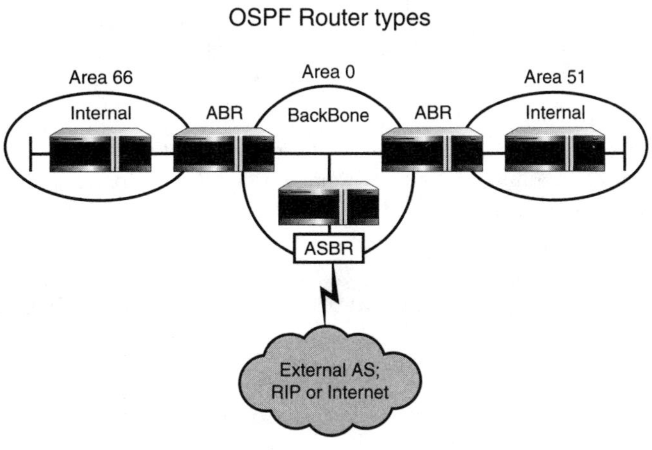

OSPF Router types

OSPF Operation Over Various Data Link Architectures

As mentioned earlier, OSPF functions over various network types. However functionality differs based on the type of network it runs over. OSPF supports broadcast-based architectures as well as point-to-point and NBMA (nonbroadcast multiaccess) networks.

Broadcast

The broadcast-based LAN networks (Ethernet, Token-Ring, and FDDI) support broadcast and multicast traffic, allowing for the dynamic discovery of neighbors, election of DR and BDR, and route information exchanges (see Figure 6.24).

FIGURE 6.24
Each broadcast multi-access network has one DR and one BDR. Because these types of networks support broadcast and multicast traffic by default, neighbor relationships and DRs/BDRs are created automatically.

Neighbor Relationships on
Broadcast Multi-Access Networks:

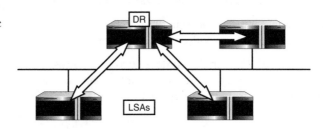

Point-to-Point

A point-to-point, or dedicated leased-line, connection consists of two routers connected at each end of the link. In this environment, an administrator needs to manually configure a router with the IP address of its neighbor. This facilitates the ability to form an adjacency across the link and exchange route information. Because only two routers exist, there is no need to have a DR or BDR controlling the creation and synchronization of the Link-state database (see Figure 6.25).

FIGURE 6.25
Point-to-point WAN links do not have a DR or BDR because a dedicated leased-lined connection has only two routers, one at each end of the link.

Neighbor Relationships on
Point to Point Serial Connections:

No DR or BDR election is required since
there are only two devices on the link.

NBMA

NBMA (nonbroadcast multiaccess) networks consist of two or more routers communicating over a nonbroadcast network, such as X.25 or Frame Relay. Because NBMA does not support broadcasts, you need to manually configure each router with the IP address of all other neighbor routers in order for adjacencies to form. After you manually configure the routers with this information, they can elect a DR and BDR and exchange route information without the use of broadcasts.

If the underlying architecture supports broadcasts, then you need to manually configure neighbor information. If it does, then everything having to do with neighbor discovery, DR/BDR election, and route information exchange happens automatically (see Figure 6.26).

FIGURE 6.26

NBMA networks do not support broadcast.

Neighbor Relationships
Non-Broadcast Multi-Access Networks

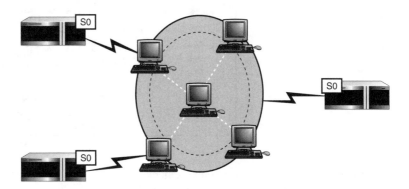

Multiple Areas

You can implement OSPF in a single area for a small- to medium-size internetwork; however, most medium-size to large OSPF internetworks subdivide the autonomous system into smaller, more manageable subareas.

A single-area implementation has one big disadvantage: As the number of networks and routers grows, so does the size of the Link-state database. When the Link-state database grows, it requires routers within a single area to keep track of changes to any router or network state change within that area. Storing and maintaining a large database requires a lot of memory and CPU time for all routers involved. Whenever a link within the area becomes unavailable or available, all routers within the area must recalculate the SPF algorithm for all routes within the database.

When you divide an autonomous system into multiple areas, you reduce the amount of route update traffic by isolating it to each area and reducing the overall size of the routing table. Routers maintain databases only for areas they directly connect to, and this isolates intra-area route update traffic to the area where it originated. State changes affecting routes in one area do not require routers in other areas to recalculate. Because routers do not have to recalculate their routing tables when the status of a route in another area changes, this dramatically reduces the number of SPF calculations a router performs.

You can break up an autonomous system any way you like, but typically design follows geography, with each physical location representing a subarea. When you use multiple-area design, the Area 0 (that is, backbone area) must exist as a major transit area for all inter-area traffic (see Figure 6.27). Just as all roads lead to Rome, all routes must lead to and through Area 0.

FIGURE 6.27

When multiple areas exist in an OSPF implementation, the entire OSPF routing domain is referred to as the OSPF autonomous system. All multiple subareas must connect to the main backbone transit area, known as Area 0.

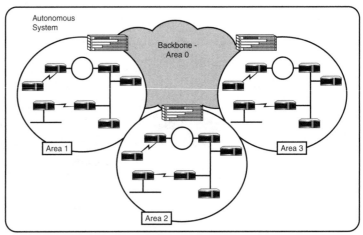

AS with Multiple Areas

Routers within an area may only exchange information with routers in their same area. In Figure 6.27, there are three subareas—1, 2, and 3—all physically connected to Area 0 through ABRs, which summarize and advertise routes into the core, which in turn advertises the other areas' route information into their own areas.

Area Types

Within a multiple-area environment, each area type defines the type of LSAs that it will accept and which router types will generate these LSAs. OSPF has three main area types:

- Backbone area (Area 0)
- Standard area
- Two stub areas (that is, standard stub and NSSA)

Virtual links are not an area; however, virtual links provide a logical link between two areas through another.

Area 0

The backbone is the glue for all other areas. In addition to all intra-area advertisements that propagate within its own area, all inter-area summaries (sent by ABRs) and external autonomous system routes (sent by ASBRs) traverse this area en route to subareas. This area can accept all OSPF LSAs; therefore, it accepts all LSA Types 1–5 LSAs.

The Standard Area

The standard area functions as a subarea of Area 0. This area accepts intra-area Type 1 and 2 LSAs and inter-area summarized routes, Type 3 and 4, from other subareas sent by the ABR connecting this area to the backbone. In addition, this area accepts external autonomous system routes advertised by an ASBR connected to the area (Type 5). You can have standard areas physically connected to Area 0 through multiple gateways, to provide redundant paths to and through the core.

Stub Areas

A *stub area* has only one way in and one way out—that is, a single connection to Area 0. You typically do not need to have OSPF updates sent across this link, especially if you have a slow WAN link or dial-up connection. Most often in this situation, you would use a default route to identify the path to networks outside a stub area. Configuring a default, or static, route eliminates update traffic on the link, conserving precious bandwidth. RFC 1583 defines two types of stub areas:

- Standard Stub

- NSSA

(Cisco Systems also has a proprietary stub area known as totally stubby, which we do not discuss in this book.) Stub areas have the following general restrictions:

- Area 0 and ASBRs cannot be part of a stub area.

- An administrator must configure all routers connected to or within a stub area or an NSSA network as stub routers.

Standard Stub Area

Although stub areas cut down on the OSPF advertisements sent into the area by implementing a default router, the standard stub area accepts intra- and inter-area routes (that is, LSAs of Type 1, 2, 3, and 4). This area does not accept any external route advertisements (Type 5 or 7) by ASBRs.

NSSA

NSSAs accept only intra-area (that is, Type 1 and 2) because without intra-area advertisements there would be no point to running a routing protocol if it could not at least learn routes within its own area. The NSSA does not accept external route advertisements (that is, Type 5 LSAs) by ASBRs. However, the name *not so stubby area* indicates that it allows something else into this area: It allows external routes to be carried through it en route to Area 0 as a LSA Type 7 generated by an ASBR.

ABRs convert Type 7 external routes to Type 5 before advertising them into the core (see Figure 6.28).

FIGURE 6.28
NSSAs carry external routes through into Area 0.

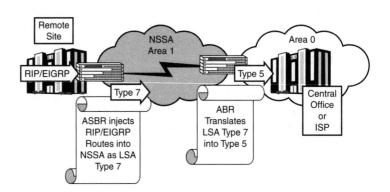

In Figure 6.27, the NSSA (Area 1) directly connects to Area 0 via an ABR and to another non-OSPF routing domain (that is, autonomous system) via an ASBR. The ASBR connected to the non-OSPF routing domain runs the RIP, EIGRP, and OSPF protocols. The non-OSPF route information needs to be redistributed into the OSPF network at the ASBR. This causes the router to generate a type 7 LSAs into the NSSA. When these external LSAs get to the ABR connecting the NSSA to Area 0, these advertisements convert to regular external Type 5 LSAs and propagate throughout the rest of the OSPF autonomous system areas.

Virtual Links

Virtual links provide a logical path to Area 0 through a subarea, connecting either a new subarea to the backbone when a physical connection is impossible or when multiple Area 0s exist but are physically separate (for example, when two companies with existing OSPF implementations have merged). In either case, virtual links utilize a standard area as a transit path connecting the subarea to Area 0 or two backbones together.

In Figure 6.29, a new OSPF area was added, but no way existed to connect it to the core. Area 3, used as the transit area, provides a virtual path to the core. In Figure 6.30, two departments with existing OSPF multiple-area implementations have merged. Both OSPF Area 0s need a link through a virtual path via a transit area, in this case, Area 51.

FIGURE 6.29
Virtual links are logical paths through subareas, connecting another area to Area 0.

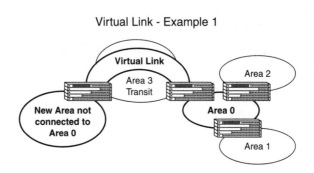

Virtual links create a logical path to Area 0.

FIGURE 6.30

Area 0 is the backbone.

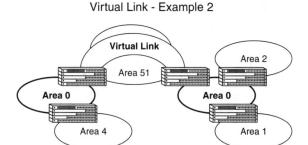

Virtual Link - Example 2

- Create a link between two backbones after merging networks.

> **Note**
>
> You must manually configure virtual links on border routers. Configuration varies depending on vendor implementations and is beyond the scope of this book.

Standard OSPF Fields

All five OSPF packet types (described later, in the section "The Packet Type Field") have the same common fields within the 24-octet OSPF header (see Figure 6.31). One of these five packet types performs protocol operations. The OSPF header fields are described in the following sections.

FIGURE 6.31

The five OSPF packet types use the same standard header.

Version	Type	Packet Length	
Router ID			OSPF Packet Header
Area ID			
Checksum		AuType	
Authentication			
Hello, Database Description, Link State Request, Link State Update, or Link State Acknowledgement Header plus data			

We will discuss the various packet types and look at their headers later in this chapter.

Version Number

The 8-bit version number field identifies the OSPF version number. Currently, OSPF uses RIPv2.

Packet Type

The 8-bit packet type field identifies the OSPF packet type. Table 6.6 lists the five different packet types and their protocol functions.

TABLE 6.6   OSPF Packet Types

Packet Number	Packet Type	Description
1	Hello	Establishes and maintains adjacencies
2	Database description	Summarizes database content
3	Link-state request	Requests specific route information or a complete update (that is, a database download)
4	Link-state update	Sends route information in response to a request (that is, a database update)
5	Link-state acknowledgement	Acknowledges receipt of route information

A further discussion of the header format for various packet types appears later in this chapter.

Packet Length

The 16-bit packet length field identifies the length, in bytes, of the OSPF datagram, including the header and contents.

Router ID

The 32-bit router ID field contains a unique value that identifies the router that originally sent the OSPF packet. OSPF uses this value for DR and BDR selection. An administrator can manually configure the router ID, or it can be configured dynamically.

Area ID

The 32-bit area ID field identifies the area that the OSPF datagram came from. Area 0 always has an area ID of 0.0.0.0. This value varies for subareas, and an administrator can optionally configure the value to follow the subnet number of the subarea.

Checksum

The 16-bit checksum field verifies that the contents of the OSPF packet remain intact during transit. The Checksum field excludes the Authentication field when checking the integrity of the content of an OSPF packet.

Authentication Type and Authentication

OSPF routers optionally support simple password authentication. When configured to do so, routers form adjacencies with only routers that share the same authentication password. Together these two fields validate the packet. The Authentication Type field contains 16 bits and the Authentication field contains 32 bits.

Additional Headers

Every OSPF header contains an additional header that contains specific routing information about one of five packet types found after the common fields in an OSPF header:

- Hello packet (Type 1)

- Database Description packet (Type 2)

- Link-state Request packet (Type 3)

- Link-state Update packet (Type 4)

- Link-state Acknowledgement packet (Type 5)

We discuss these packets and their headers in the following sections.

Hello Packets

Hello datagrams are OSPF Type 1 packets. Hello packets establish and maintain adjacencies. Figure 6.32 shows the basic format of a Hello packet. Figure 6.33 shows a Hello packet as seen through a Sniffer.

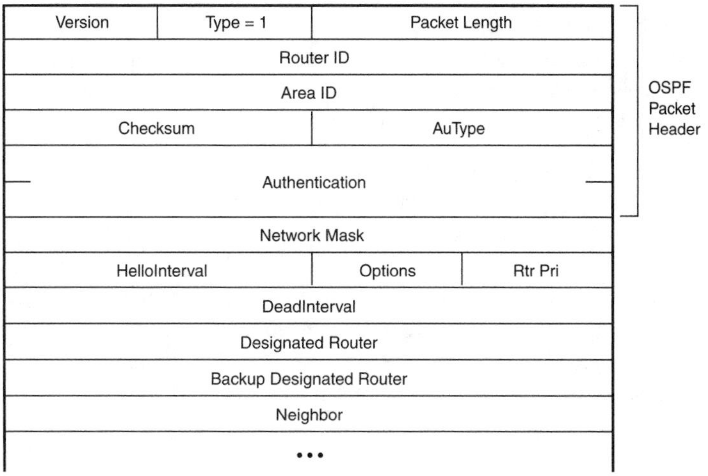

FIGURE 6.32
OSPF Hello packet fields include Network Mask, Hello Interval, Options, Routing Priority, Dead Interval, Designated Router, Backup Designated Router and Neighbor.

FIGURE 6.33
Only OSPF gateways with matching area IDs, authentication password, stub configuration, and Hello and Dead intervals will process information and form an adjacency.

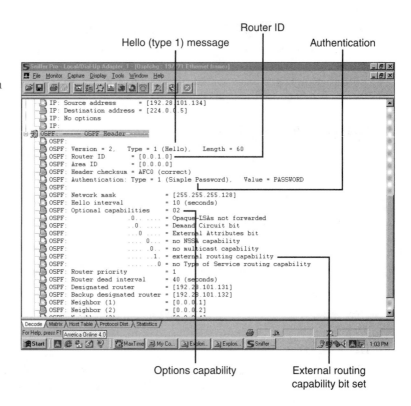

In Figure 6.33, router 150.3.233.25 uniquely identifies itself with its router ID, which is used for BDR and DR selection. Remember that the router with the highest priority or router ID becomes the DR, and the next highest becomes the BDR. The area ID specifies the OSPF area from which the advertisement originated. If you implement authentication, which is optional, only gateways sharing the same password can form adjacencies.

In Figure 6.33, the header lists the subnet mask for the gateway (255.255.255.0), along with the options it supports. A value of 1 in the Options Capability section of the header indicates that it supports that particular option. In this case, this router has the External Routing Capability bit set, as shown in the header. This indicates that this gateway supports non-OSPF advertisements and either an ASBR or a router within an area that supports external routes passing through it exists. In addition, this router identifies the IP address of the DR as 150.3.233.249 and announces itself as the BDR. Finally, this router lists the neighbors it knows of (in this case there is only one, 1.0.0.5).

The Hello packet fields are described in detail in the following sections.

The Network Mask Field

The network mask field identifies the local interface subnet mask.

The Options Field

The options field specifies the OSPF capabilities that the router supports. All routers cannot support options. If they do not support the options, the router either rejects or ignores the options. The following two options are defined:

- **T bit**—This bit is used to indicate that this OSPF router can support ToS/QoS routing. ToS-capable routers indicate the level of ToS by setting this bit to a value greater than zero. A T bit set to zero indicates that the router does not have the capability to perform ToS routing. Routers enabled for ToS build multiple shortest-path trees, with themselves as the root: one for ToS-enabled routes that avoids non-ToS routers, and one for non-ToS routes (see Figure 6.33).

- **E bit**—Routers with this bit set can process external non-OSPF route information. Stub area routers do not support external route updates and therefore do not set or recognize the use of this bit. ASBR routers always have the E bit enabled (see Figure 6.33).

Table 6.7 describes these two options. Vendors may implement other option bits in the future.

The Hello Interval Field

The Hello interval controls how often the router transmits Hello datagrams. This value varies depending on the Data Link layer topology over which OSPF is running. On a broadcast network, routers send Hello packets out every 10 seconds. On a nonbroadcast network, by default, routers sends Hello packets out every 30 seconds.

The Router Priority Field

OSPF routers use the router priority ID exclusively for electing a DR and BDR for each segment. The router that has the highest priority ID becomes the DR. The DR controls the collection, synchronization, and dissemination of route information for the segment.

The router that has the next-highest priority ID becomes the BDR. The BDR only collects and builds the Link-state database. It remains in standby mode until the DR fails. If this occurs, the BDR automatically promotes itself to DR for the segment, and the OSPF router then elects a new BDR.

The default value for this parameter depends on the vendor implementation.

If all routers have the same router priority value (that is, an administrator has not configured the default value higher on any gateway than on others), the router ID determines the DR and BDR for the segment.

The Dead Interval Field

The dead interval detects a failed neighbor. By default, a router considers a neighbor dead when it does not hear from a neighbor router (that is, no Hello packets are received) within four Hello intervals.

The Dead interval has a value four times (in seconds) that of the Hello packet value. This value varies, depending on the Data Link layer topology over which OSPF is running. On a broadcast network, routers send out Hello packets every 10 seconds, which makes the Dead interval

40 seconds. On a nonbroadcast network, by default, routers send out hellos every 30 seconds, which makes the Dead interval 120 seconds.

The Designated Router Field

The designated router field lists the IP address of the DR, if it is known by this router. If the router does not know the IP address of the DR, this value appears as 0.0.0.0.

The Backup Designated Router Field

The backup designated router field lists the IP address of the BDR if it is known by this router. If the router does not know the IP address of the BDR, this value appears as 0.0.0.0.

The Neighbor Field

The neighbor field lists the router IDs of all neighbor routers that this router has learned about through local Hello packets.

OSPF Database Description Packets

Data Description packets (Type 2) convey data needed to initialize the topographical databases of adjacent devices. Figure 6.34 shows the format of the Database Description packet.

FIGURE 6.34
OSPF Database Description packet fields include Interface MTU, Options, and Sequence Number, as well as an LSA header.

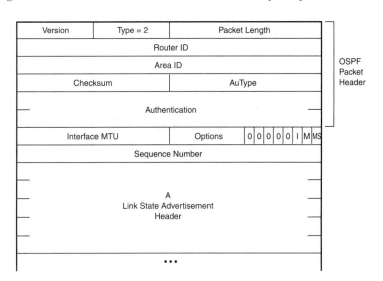

The Options Field

The options field describes the OSPF capabilities supported by the router. Although this field exists in other OSPF packet types, the bits mean different things, depending on the packet type in use. There are three bits within this field (see Table 6.7).

TABLE 6.7   Database Description Packet Options

Option	Description
I (Init)	When set, the I bit indicates that this is the first OSPF database description packet transmitted.
M (More)	When set, the M bit indicates that more of the Database Description packet should follow. If the M bit has a value of zero, it indicates the last packet.
MS (Master/Slave)	The MS bit identifies whether the transmitting router is a master (DR) or slave (all other routers): • MS = 1 (router is master) • MS = 0 (router is slave)

The Sequence Number Field

The sender sequences all database description packets, and the receiver acknowledges each packet. The initial value of the Sequence Number field is uniquely chosen when the first DD packet is sent (Init bit = 1); thereafter, it is sequentially incremented.

The Link-state Advertisement Header Field

A router can include one or more LSAs within a Database Description packet. The specific fields are described earlier in this section.

Link-state Request Packets

OSPF Link-state Request packets (Type 3) get current route information or database downloads from a specific neighbor router. Figure 6.35 shows the format of a Link-state Request packet.

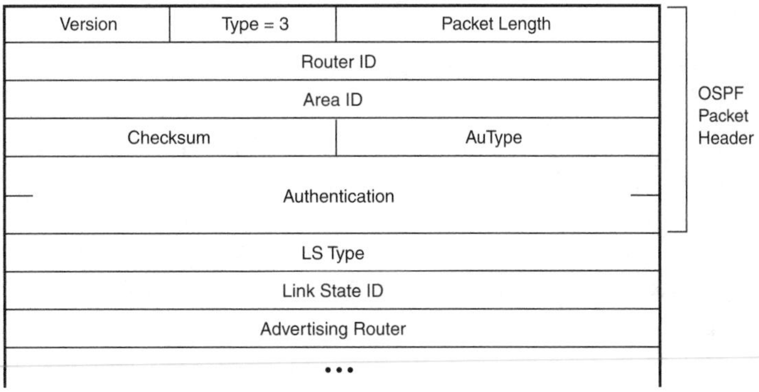

FIGURE 6.35
OSPF Link-state Request packet fields include Link-state Type, Link-state ID, and Advertising Router.

The Link-state Type Field

The Link-state type field identifies the LSA.

The Link-state ID Field

The Link-state ID field further describes the LSA. It assigns the LSA a unique identification that is used by other routers.

The Advertising Router Field

The advertising router field identifies the router that originally sent the LSA.

Link-state Update Packets

OSPF Link-state update packets (Type 4) route information sent in response to a request (that is, a database update). These packets contain information about the condition of various links within an internetwork. A single Link-state Update packet can include several LSAs (described earlier in this section). Figure 6.36 shows the format of a Link-state update packet.

FIGURE 6.36
OSPF Link-state update packet fields include Number of Advertisements and Link-state advertisements.

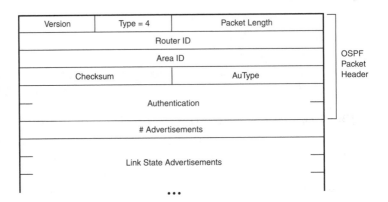

The Number of Advertisements Field

The number of advertisements field identifies the number of LSAs included in the update packet.

The Link-state Advertisement Field

The Link-state advertisement field makes up the bulk of the Link-state update packet. This field contains a list of LSAs. Each Link-state advertisement field has a common header, followed by one of six LSAs. A complete list of LSAs and description of fields appears earlier in this chapter.

The Link-state Acknowledgement Packet

The Link-state acknowledgement packet (Type 5) acknowledges the receipt of route information. This packet has a similar format to the database description packet and includes a list of LSA headers. Figure 6.37 shows the format of a Link-state acknowledgement packet.

FIGURE 6.37
OSPF LSA packet verifies the database information that it received.

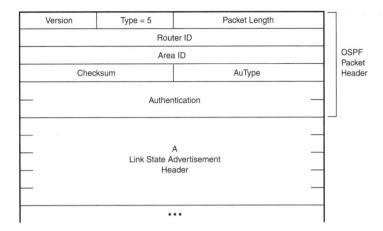

IGRP

The Distance-vector routing protocol IGRP enables gateways to build their routing tables by exchanging information with adjacent gateways (that is, *neighbors*). The routing information contains a summary about the rest of the network, which helps IGRP make decisions about the best path choice. Unlike RIP, which bases its path choice on hops only, IGRP (despite being considered a Distance-vector protocol) can use a combination of metrics when making route decisions. With IGRP, you can adjust several values to meet the specific needs of your network:

- **Delay**—Measures the speed of the link, in units of 10 microseconds
- **Bandwidth**—Reflects the data transfer rate across the link, from 1200bps to 10Gbps
- **Reliability**—Represents fractions of 255 (that is, 255 = 100%)
- **Load**—Represents the saturation of the link, in a fraction of 255 (that is, 0 equals no load, 255 equals a fully loaded link)

Table 6.8 describes the function of each of the cost metrics.

TABLE 6.8 IGRP Metric Components

Metric	Function
Delay Time	Represents the amount of time it takes a signal to propagate end to end. Additional delay occurs with a loaded network; however, the channel occupancy figure accounts for load.
Bandwidth	Represents the bandwidth, in Kbps, of the slowest link in the path.

TABLE 6.8   Continued

Metric	Function
Load	Calculates a channel occupancy over time to indicate how much bandwidth is currently in use.
Reliability	Displays the current error rate. Measures the percentage of packets that arrive at the destination undamaged.

Because IGRP can use a variety of metrics when making route decisions, it provides a variety of features:

- It supports larger networks than RIP because it can specify a maximum hop count of 255.

- It can perform load balancing for traffic when parallel routes exist.

- It supports complex metrics.

Because IGRP considers a variety of metric components, it calculates a single *composite metric* for the path. The composite metric combines the weighted values of the various metric components into a single number, which represents the best cost. IGRP then selects the best route, based on the smallest composite metric, or cost.

Although IGRP keeps track of two additional pieces of information—the hop count and MTU (that is, the maximum packet size that can travel along the entire path without fragmentation)—it does not use this information in the cost calculation. Although IGRP can combine and pass on several cost values, by default it uses only the bandwidth and delay values.

If you want to affect path selection, you can change either of these values. The bandwidth value has a higher priority, and routers refer to bandwidth when calculating routing algorithms. However, this value has no effect on the amount of data a particular link can support. On the other hand, it does directly affect path selection, so you need to make sure that you accurately define a bandwidth value to reflect actual data rates across a link. If a value is incorrect, routers might select bad paths for forwarding based on that incorrect value.

IGRP Networks

An IGRP network defines a single routing domain that is identified by an autonomous system number. Generally, a single company manages and controls each autonomous system, and each autonomous system is considered separate from the others.

When you have routers configured with IGRP, all routers share the same autonomous system number (which is assigned by an administrator) to exchange route information. In this usage, the term *autonomous system* describes the IGRP routing domain and all routers within this domain. Although a company may run other IGP routing protocols within its autonomous system, this autonomous system number defines only the IGRP routing domain within the larger autonomous system.

For example, if a large enterprise network spanned multiple continents with many routers and links, you would break up this network into multiple autonomous systems. These autonomous system segments would route update traffic based on clear domains. Routers in the same domain share the same network information and adjust to changes within their domain as they occur. However, route changes in other domains would not affect these routers.

Defining boundaries reduces the amount of update traffic within a domain, making more efficient use of network bandwidth by keeping intradomain updates off critical backbone segments and slower WAN links. It also makes remote failures transparent to other domains. For example, if a route fails in Japan, the failure would not affect routers in San Francisco.

Network Stability

IGRP uses many techniques to ensure stability in the network. Similar to RIP, IGRP uses periodic broadcasts and triggered updates on nonbroadcast networks, holddowns, split horizon, poison reverse, and an infinity value of 256 to prevent routing loops. Considered a classful routing protocol, IGRP does not support subnetting.

In addition, IGRP uses multipath routing to provide network stability. *Multipath routing* provides additional flexibility because it enables you to split traffic across redundant links with similar or almost similar metrics, which provides load balancing. Multipath routing also contains an automatic switchover to a second link if one link goes down.

IGRP Timers

IGRP includes several control timers that dictate IGRP's general operation (see Table 6.9). These timers control route propagation and expiration. Although the timers have default settings, you can set different time constants.

TABLE 6.9   IGRP Timers

Timer	Function/Default Setting
Update	Defines interval between route updates. The default is every 90 seconds.
Invalid	Specifies how long a router should wait in the absence of a routing update message before declaring that route invalid. The default is every 270 seconds (three times the Update timer).
Holddown	Specifies the holddown period for an unreachable destination. The router does not accept updates for the same destination during the holddown period. The default is every 280 seconds (three times the Update timer plus 10 seconds).
Flush	Indicates how much time should pass before a failed route is removed from the routing table. The default is every 630 seconds (seven times the Update timer).

Load Balancing and Load Sharing

IGRP can send traffic across redundant paths, splitting the traffic stream across equal- or non-equal-cost links, referred to as *load balancing*. This enables you to maximize the use of the bandwidth to a destination site. If you do not configure unequal-cost load balancing, IGRP balances traffic across equal-cost paths only. However, IGRP does not support VLSM.

EIGRP

Cisco's proprietary routing protocol Enhanced Interior Gateway Routing Protocol (EIGRP) combines the advantages of Link-state routing protocols with the advantages of Distance-vector protocols. Because EIGRP combines the advantages of both protocols, it is considered a *balanced hybrid protocol*.

The following are some of the characteristics of EIGRP:

- It provides faster convergence because it sends partial updates immediately.
- It supports VLSMs and includes subnet masks in updates.
- It supports multiple protocols, including IP, IPX, and AppleTalk.
- It keeps backup paths in routing tables.
- It supports IP ToS.
- It uses cost-based metrics, similar to IGRP.
- It maintains backup paths when multiple routes exist.
- It is both multicast and unicast.

EIGRP Operation

After an EIGRP router goes through its initial startup, it receives and copies routing tables from its neighbors. When the router detects changes, it sends only partial updates to neighbor routers. This decreases bandwidth use, which results in better efficiency and performance.

EIGRP offers a single-routing-protocol solution by supporting multiprotocol networks. This gives companies an advantage if they use multiple protocols, such as IPX, IP, and AppleTalk. Otherwise they would need a separate routing protocol for each, which means a greatly increased amount of update traffic to learn and maintain routes. The only disadvantage to EIGRP is that it requires you to use only Cisco routers, unless the third-party vendor's router supports it.

EIGRP keeps a highly detailed topology map (that is, the topology database) and uses the Diffusing Update Algorithm (DUAL) to calculate changes and avoid routing loops. It prevents routing loops by referring to copies of neighboring routing tables and using the detailed topology map.

Because of the absence of routing loops and the use of triggered updates, EIGRP networks converge very quickly. In addition, EIGRP transmits the subnet mask for each route entry, enabling it to support VLSMs, which makes it a classless routing protocol.

EIGRP defines its routing domain (which includes all EIGRP-enabled routers and the networks within the domain) with an autonomous system number, similar to IGRP. Only EIGRP routers that share the same autonomous system number can exchange information because they are considered part of the same domain. EIGRP autonomous systems that have different autonomous system numbers cannot exchange information. An administrator arbitrarily assigns the autonomous system number by enabling and configuring EIGRP on the first router within the domain. After the autonomous system number is assigned, all other routers within the autonomous system must share the same value.

EIGRP routers within the same autonomous system must first discover their neighbor routers (that is, routers directly connected to the same local segment or WAN link). By identifying their neighbors, routers can detect unavailable neighbor routers, thereby detecting failures in the network. This allows them to quickly respond to failures and adjust their path selection.

The exchange of Hello packets controls the process of discovery. Neighbor routers discover all other local routers by building and maintaining a neighbor, or adjacency, table that lists all routers it has learned about. After routers build neighbor tables, they can begin to exchange route information with their neighbors.

Although EIGRP is not connection oriented, it does attempt to guarantee the delivery and receipt of update information by using sequencing information within the EIGRP header portion of the datagram. Receivers must acknowledge the receipt of route information. If the receiver sends no acknowledgement, the sender retransmits the route update. The sending device keeps track of the revision or sequence numbers previously sent, to ensure that all acknowledged updates are accounted for.

Successor and Feasible Routes

EIGRP can maintain multiple routes within the routing table for a single destination. The best route (that is, the route with the lowest-cost path, based on bandwidth and delay by default) is referred to as the *successor*, and the second (or backup) route is referred to as the *feasible successor*.

EIGRP routers learn successor and feasible successor routes by running DUAL against the topology map that is built based on the neighbor discovery process. EIGRP routers first discover their neighbors, and then they exchange update information to build their topology map. After they have a map of the network, they run the DUAL algorithm against all routes to destinations identified within the map in order to build the local routing table, which lists the following information:

- Successor and feasible successor routes

- The local interface

- The next-hop router address for forwarding traffic to the destination

By keeping a backup path in the routing table, EIGRP routers can quickly promote the feasible successor to successor when the successor becomes unavailable. This allows the router to continue routing traffic to that destination. Meanwhile, the router can actively query its neighbors for a new feasible successor to use. This allows EIGRP routers to quickly detect and adjust around failed paths.

EIGRP keeps a separate copy of each of the previously mentioned tables for each major protocol suite for which it performs routing—such as IP, IPX, and AppleTalk—by running separate routing processes for each routing protocol. So if you have all three of these protocols on your network (see Figure 6.38), EIGRP routers have three separate adjacency and topology maps in addition to routing tables. In this case, the router has nine databases—three for each protocol—in addition to the neighbor database, the topology database, and the routing table. A lot of resources and overhead are required to maintain these additional maps and tables. Normally, three different routing protocols—IPX, RIP, and AppleTalk's RTMP—would need to be run on each of the routers within the internetwork with each routing protocol separately keeping track of route protocol information. This adds substantial broadcast and multicast traffic for each routing protocol implemented.

FIGURE 6.38

All EIGRP routers within the same autonomous system must maintain three separate databases for each protocol family for which they route.

EIGRP Tables

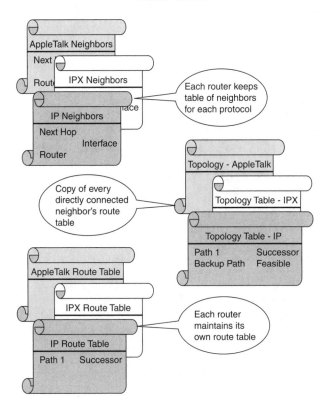

EIGRP Packet Types

EIGRP exchanges five different packets so that routers can communicate with other routers about the state of their autonomous systems. EIGRP uses the following five packet types:

- **Hello/ACKs**—Sent as multicast advertisements, IGRP routers use Hello packets to build the adjacency table. Some Hello messages do not contain data, known as an acknowledgements (ACKs), and are always sent as unicast datagrams.

- **Updates**—Routers send update packets to exchange route information. They use the information gained in this exchange to build a topology map of the internetwork. Updates always include sequencing numbers. Router sends update packets as either multicast or unicast datagrams.

- **Queries**—Routers send query packets to all neighbors when they have no successor or feasible successor route available or when they need to choose a new one. Routers send query packets as a multicast or unicast datagram, depending on whether the query goes to all neighbors (multicast) or to a specific neighbor (unicast).

- **Replies**—Routers send reply packets in response to a previous query from a neighbor. Routers always send replies as unicast datagrams.

- **Requests**—A router may send a request packet to all neighbors when it first comes online, requesting a complete list of all destinations in order to build its routing table. Or it might send a request for specific information to a particular neighbor. Depending on the request type, a router can send this message as a multicast or unicast datagram.

BGP

The protocols described thus far in this chapter (that is, IGPs) use frequent updates and routing methods for propagating traffic, which makes them incapable of handling a very large environment. In addition, a company generally uses IGPs within a single autonomous system or company internetwork. The explosion of the Internet created a need for BGP, an EGP that provides loop-free interdomain routing and is a robust, stringent, rules-based routing protocol.

RFC 1771 defines BGP version 4 (BGPv4), the current version of BGP, as an inter-autonomous system routing protocol. The Internet uses BGP as its primary protocol, to support the transit of traffic across the great superhighway. The enhancements to version 4—VLSM and Classless Interdomain Routing (CIDR; that is, supernetting)—have allowed BGPv4 to handle the exponential growth of the Internet.

Most companies connecting to the Internet do not need or use BGP. If an organization has only one gateway (that is, a single exit point) connecting the internetwork to the outside world, it can usually put in a default route. This allows all traffic destined to unknown networks to be forwarded through the default path, serviced by the upstream provider's gateways, and the upstream provider participates in the BGP network. Implementing a default route means there is no routing update traffic overhead or resources necessary on the gateway to store and maintain all routes within the Internet.

BGP should be implemented in the following situations:

- If you have multiple exit points connecting to a single ISP (for load sharing)

- If you have multiple paths to different ISPs and would like to dictate how traffic is forwarded across these links

- If your routing policy or methods are different or go beyond the simplistic use of a default route (that is, you need intelligent path selection and specific criteria)

- If your network's infrastructure is used as a transit area for other organizations' traffic

IGPs Versus EGPs

BGP routers learn and maintain information about all destination networks within the Internet and about the path through the autonomous systems to get to these networks. When traffic reaches the ultimate destination network, IGP protocols (that is, RIP, IGRP, EIGRP, and OSPF) take care of the local route forwarding within the autonomous system.

As an EGP, BGP connects independent autonomous systems together. Autonomous system numbers, which are assigned by ARIN, define BGP routing domains. The autonomous system number assigned to an organization represents a major hop (that is, transit area) within the Internet. Each autonomous system may have many IGPs running within it, but the number and types of these dynamic protocols is irrelevant and transparent to BGP. Although you can use BGP as an IGP, you use BGP almost exclusively as an EGP.

The Internet today consists of many transit areas. Different organizations control these transit areas, with no one organization governing the lot of them. The Internet's vastness and lack of governing created a need for a robust, stringent rules-based routing protocol such as BGP.

Currently, more than 105,000 routes exist on the Internet. Each BGP router within the Internet must learn and maintain path information and perform intelligent path selection to facilitate the forwarding of datagrams throughout the Internet, not to mention the resources (such as memory and CPU time) necessary to maintain this information. With so many routes, transit areas, and multiple paths throughout this internetworking maze, BGP has to have the ability to detect and correct problems (for example, downed networks, routing loops).

Sources for Current Internet Routing Table Numbers

You can use the following sources to find information on the current Internet routing tables today:

- `http://antc.uoregon.edu/route-views/dynamics`
- `http://www.mcvax.org/~jhma/routing/bgp-hist.html`
- `http://www.apnic.net/stats/bgp/TOTAL/totalann.html`

Because BGP has to have the ability to detect and correct network problems, it can eliminate routing loops. You can implement BGP version 4 in one of two ways:

- **Full mesh**—A *full-mesh* topology requires separate logical TCP connections between all BGP routers within the same autonomous system, allowing gateways to quickly determine whether a loop exists and prune it.

- **Partial mesh**—A *partial mesh* topology does not require all routers to maintain logical connections with one another. This reduces the number of TCP connections, but it opens up the possibility of routing loops.

To aid in reliability, BGP has one characteristic unlike any other routing protocol: It uses TCP to provide connection-oriented, reliable transport of its update traffic. All IGP protocols are connectionless—that is, they do not require a logical connection to pass information to other gateways. IGP protocols typically send updates as either broadcasts or multicasts, although a few send them as unicasts. Whatever the method, they do this over connectionless protocols, such as IP and UDP.

BGP guarantees reliable delivery of data, running on top of a logical TCP session, which sequences and acknowledges each exchange between BGP peers. BGP uses TCP port 179. Unlike previous versions of BGP, BGPv4 supports classless routing by including subnet masks within routing updates when describing destinations (referred to as *network reachability information*). Also, unlike earlier versions of BGP, BGPv4 supports route summarization (that is, the aggregation of multiple IP addresses into a single route advertisement).

BGP Routers

Routers placed in different areas of a BGP network have different names. In a BGP network four different types of routers exist:

- **BGP speaker routers**—These are BGP routers.

- **Peer or neighbor routers**—These are routers that connect to a common segment.

- **Internal peer routers**—These routers are peers within the same autonomous system.

- **External peer routers**—These routers are BGP neighbors from different autonomous systems.

For example, if Autonomous System 100 consists of three gateways in a full-mesh topology, each of these routers would have a TCP connection with each other and would form an internal BGP (IBGP) relationship with its neighbors in the same autonomous system. The gateway connecting Autonomous System 100 to another autonomous system—for example, Autonomous System 200—would form an external BGP (EBGP) relationship with the gateway from the other autonomous system. The type of relationship a neighbor has with its peer—internal or external—defines the rules for exchange (see Figure 6.39).

All BGP routers have some type of peer relationships with other routers. The type of peer relationship depends on whether the routers reside within the same autonomous system. Two routers connecting different autonomous systems are external peers, and routers within the same autonomous system are internal peers.

Routers that belong to the same autonomous system are called IBGPs. IBGP neighbors cannot advertise route information beyond their local peers, or neighbors.

FIGURE 6.39
Rules for exchange vary, depending on what type of relationship a router has with its peer.

Multiple BGP Connections to One ISP

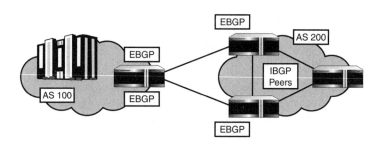

Routers that belong to different autonomous systems are called EBGPs. EBGP neighbors may propagate route information learned to all other neighbors on all other interfaces.

BGP Operation

When you enable BGP on a gateway, you assign it an autonomous system number based on the autonomous system to which it belongs. In addition, you configure the BGP speaker with the addresses of all its peers. When this speaker comes online, it must establish TCP connections with all its peers (both internal and external) in order to facilitate the exchange of BGP information. When BGP peer routers establish a TCP session, peers may exchange the BGP reachability information that builds their routing tables. BGP uses this information to create a loop-free map of the autonomous systems.

After the initial exchange of the entire table, peers exchange changes only. TCP tracks all exchanges by sequencing and acknowledging. TCP uses keepalives to maintain connections between BGP peers when these peers do not actively exchange data. BGP generates a notification message when it encounters an error, causing the TCP session to terminate between peers. If the TCP session fails, BGP fails.

BGP routers do not store routing information within the same routing table as they store IGP learned routes. BGP routers, depending on the vendor implementation, may maintain up to three additional routing tables or combine them into one. However, no matter the number of tables they maintain, each BGP speaker needs to distinguish the following:

- Route information received (that is, updates)
- Route information to be advertised
- The local BGP routing table

BGP speakers advise peers of changes to destination routes through the exchange of updates. If a route becomes unavailable, a speaker advertises within the update sent to its neighbors that it plans to withdraw a route from service, so its neighbors should remove the route from their table.

If the BGP speaker has a better path available to a destination, it advertises the new path and its attributes. Receivers then replace the old route with the new one.

Unlike all IGPs, BGP does not use metrics, such as hop, delay, bandwidth, reliability, load, or MTU, in its path selection. Rather, BGP uses *path attributes* in a hierarchical fashion to facilitate best path selection to a destination. (We will discuss BGP attributes in detail later in this chapter.)

The BGP Header and Fields

All BGP datagrams begin with a common 19-byte header. Figure 6.40 shows the format of a common BGP header.

Marker

The marker field is up to 16 bytes in length. This field identifies the beginning of an open request between peers and BGP authentication implementation.

FIGURE 6.40
All BGP datagrams have the same header.

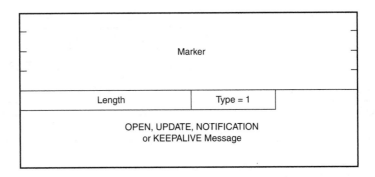

Length

The 2-byte length field identifies the length, in bytes, of the BGP datagram plus the header.

Type

The 1-byte type field identifies the type of BGP message that a router sent. BGP routers can send four different types of messages:

- Open
- Update
- Notification
- Keepalive

The type of message that appears in this field affects the rest of the BGP header. The types of message formats are described in the following sections.

Open Messages

BBP routers send an open message immediately after establishing the TCP port 179 peer connection. This first BGP message initiates a BGP peer relationship between internal or external peers. Figure 6.41 shows the BGP open message format.

FIGURE 6.41

The BGP open message includes six fields: Version, My Autonomous System, Hold Time, BGP Identifier, Optional Parameters Length, and Optional Parameters.

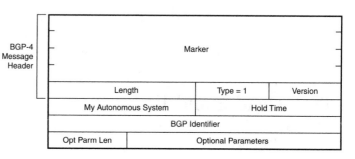

The Open message adds six fields to the BGP header. Table 6.10 describes them.

TABLE 6.10   BGP Open Message Fields

Field	Bits	Description
Version	8	Displays the version of BGP (currently version 4).
My Autonomous System	16	Displays the autonomous system number of the sender.
Hold Time	16	Controls the timer between keepalives and update messages.
BGP Identifier	32	Uniquely identifies the BGP speaker (that is, sender).
Optional Parameters Length	8	Identifies the length of any optional parameters that might exist, such as authentication information. If no parameters exist, this field contains a zero. If parameters are present, this value identifies the size in bytes of the expected optional parameter field that follows.
Optional parameters	Variable	Lists the implemented optional parameters, such as authentication.

Update Messages

Update messages (Type 1) contain network reachability information. Peers exchange updates with peers to learn and maintain routes. Figure 6.42 shows the BGP Update message format.

The Update message (Type 2) adds five fields to the BGP header. Table 6.11 describes them.

TABLE 6.11   BGP Update Message Fields

Field	Bits	Description
Unfeasible Routes Length	16	Specifies withdrawn routes. If no routes are being withdrawn, this value is zero. If routes are being withdrawn from service, this indicates the size, in bytes, of the withdrawn routes' field.
Withdrawn Routes	Variable	Lists all routes withdrawn from service.
Total Path Attribute Length	16	Identifies the total length, in bytes, of the Path Attributes field, included within this message.
Path Attributes	Variable	Defines the advertised attributes. This field contains two main categories of attributes: well known and optional. Path attributes are discussed later in this chapter.
Network Layer Reachability Information	Variable	Lists all destinations that the router advertises.

FIGURE 6.42

BGP Update messages have five additional fields: Unfeasible Routes Length, Withdrawn Routes, Total Path Attributes, Path Attributes, and Network Layer Reachability Information.

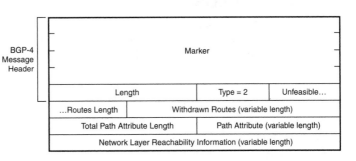

Notification Messages

Notification messages (Type 3) occur when BGP routers encounter an error. When a router sends a notification, BGP fails and the peers tear down the TCP connection they had established. Figure 6.43 shows the notification message format.

The Notification message adds three fields to the BGP header. Table 6.12 describes them.

FIGURE 6.43

The BGP Notification message has an additional three fields: Error Code, Error Subcode, and Data.

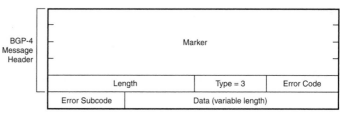

TABLE 6.12   BGP Notification Message Fields

Fields	Bits	Description
Error Code	8	Displays the type(s) of error(s) that have occurred.
Error Subcode	8	Gives more specific information about the type of error that occurred.
Data	Variable	Diagnoses the reason for the notification. This value is dependent on the contents of the other two fields (Error Code and Error Subcode). See RFC 1771 for specific values.

Keepalive Messages

In response to the initial Open message, Keepalive messages confirm the establishment of the peer connection, whether it is internal or external. After the routers establish peer relationships, neighbors continue to exchange keepalives to maintain the connection to determine reachability between peers. Figure 6.44 shows the keepalive message format.

FIGURE 6.44

Keepalive messages consist of the BGP message header only, without any additional information. This allows the BGP connection to remain open between peers.

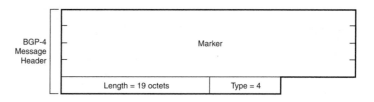

Path Attributes

Routers use path attributes to describe a destination route's reachability and to determine the best path. BGP speakers parse these attributes in order, giving a higher precedence to attributes in ascending order. You can adjust these parameters (that is, path attributes), which gives BGP its flexibility. BGP path attributes have four categories, as described in Table 6.13.

TABLE 6.13 Path Attribute Categories

Category	Description
Well-known mandatory	All vendor implementation must recognize well-known attributes, and they are included in all updates. The BGP speaker must fully process these attributes.
Well-known discretionary	These attributes may or may not be present in an update. If they are present, all vendor implementation must recognize them, and BGP speakers must fully process them.
Optional transitive	If a BGP speaker receives this attribute, it passes it. The receiver does not have to recognize an optional attribute.
Optional nontransitive	The receiver does not have to recognize or process this optional attribute. A BGP speaker does not pass this attribute to its neighbors.

BGP update messages advertise path attributes within BGP update messages identified by type codes. Table 6.14 shows the path attributes defined within RFC 1771.

TABLE 6.14 BGP Path Attributes

Type Code	Attribute	Description
1—Origin	Well-known mandatory	Identifies the origin of the route (that is, how the route was learned and placed into the routing table by the reporting router). The following origin types exist: • IGP—Learned via network reachability, which is internal to the originating router's autonomous system • EGP—Learned via EGP • Incomplete—Learned from an unknown source
2—AS_path	Well-known mandatory	Lists the autonomous systems that describe the path to this destination. For example, a destination such as 192.15.2.0 may have an autonomous system path of 100 to 300 to 800, which means it takes three autonomous system hops to get to this network. When autonomous system routers (that is,

TABLE 6.14   Continued

Type Code	Attribute	Description
		EBGP peers) pass route information between autonomous system routers, the router forwarding the update to the new autonomous system adds its autonomous system to the path. This allows BGP speakers to identify the autonomous system path that the route has traversed through the Internet.
3—Next_Hop	Well-known mandatory	Identifies the IP address of the next-hop router or border gateway used to reach the destination.
4—Multi-Exit-Disc (see Figure 6.45)	Optional nontransitive	Allows an autonomous system's routers to influence the routing decisions of another autonomous system's routers. When multiple exit points exist, connecting two autonomous systems together, routers from one of the autonomous systems may advertise different Multi-Exit-Disc (MED) values to the external neighbor router in the other autonomous system. The lower the MED value, the better the path. By advertising one path with a lower MED value, routers will prefer one of the paths over the other. This is the only attribute that provides this function.
5—Local Pref (see Figure 6.46)	Well-known discretionary	Only routers within a single autonomous system use this, and it is not propagated to other autonomous systems. When multiple paths exist to route traffic outside this autonomous system, routers within an autonomous system may set the local preference value higher for one path, indicating the preferred route. Internal routers then

TABLE 6.14   Continued

Type Code	Attribute	Description
		forward traffic based on this information, choosing the path with the highest preference.
6—Atomic_Aggregate	Well-known discretionary	This value is set only after route summarization configuration. When a system administrator configures route summarization, the router where the summarization originated sets this attribute. It is included in advertisements, advising other BGP routers that the advertised route represents a less specific summary of other routes that are not identified within the update.
7—Aggregator	Optional transitive	This value is set only when the atomic aggregate is set. Identifies the autonomous system and router where route summarization originated.

FIGURE 6.45

The MED attribute influences routing decisions between autonomous systems. For example, if an ISP maintains multiple connecting paths between itself and a downstream autonomous system, the ISP may configure its routers with different MED values to influence the path the downstream router uses to send traffic.

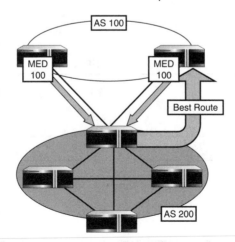

MED-Multi Exit Descriptor

BGPv3 Versus BGPv4

BGPv3 (RFC 1267) and BGPv4 cannot work together. However, you can configure routers to support BGPv3 or BGPv4 on a per-interface basis to operate in a mixed environment. Table 6.15 is a quick reference to the difference between BGPv3 and BGPv4.

FIGURE 6.46

The Local Preference attribute propagates only within an autonomous system and designates a preferred path to a destination when multiple paths exist. In this case, autonomous system 300 has multiple outbound paths connecting through autonomous system 100 and autonomous system 200. The router chooses the path with the highest local preference as its outbound path. In this case, it chooses the leftmost router with a local preference of 200.

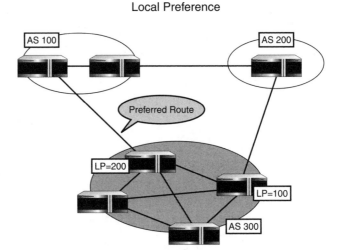

Local Preference

TABLE 6.15 BGPv3 and BGPv4

Characteristic	BGPv3	BGPv4
Supports VLSM (that is, classless routing). Includes subnet masks within updates.	No	Yes
Supports summarization.	No	Yes
Full or partial mesh.	Full mesh	Both
Supports Local Preference, Atomic_Aggregate, and Aggregator attributes.	No	Yes

Summary

Routing protocols allow routers to dynamically learn paths to destinations and to adjust to changes in network topology. Whether you use BGP or RIP, the purpose for every protocol is the same: to forward datagrams to their destination.

RIP is a Distance-vector protocol. Like all other Distance-vector protocols, it uses the metric distance (measured in hops) to determine best path selection. RIP is broadcast based, it is an IGP, it works best on small-sized networks, and it uses a Distance-vector algorithm. Two versions of RIP exist: RIPv1 and RIPv2.

OSPF uses a Link-state algorithm and makes more intelligent decisions regarding path selection than RIP. OSPF, like all other Link-state routing protocols, considers any or all of the following metrics: link capacity (bandwidth), delay, reliability, load, and MTU. OSPF provides several advantages over Distance-vector protocols; however, RIP still remains the most popular protocol in use today, primarily because of its simplicity.

The Distance-vector protocol IGRP allows gateways to build their routing table by exchanging information with adjacent gateways (that is, neighbors), similar to OSPF. Unlike RIP, which is also a Distance-vector protocol, IGRP uses a variety of metrics to determine best path selection. This is called a composite metric. IGRP considers the metrics bandwidth, delay, reliability, and load, which allows it to provide support to large networks, and handle load balancing.

Considered a hybrid protocol, EIGRP combines the advantages of Link-state routing protocols and Distance-vector protocols. RIP, OSPF, IGRP, and EIGRP are all IGPs.

With the explosion of the Internet, the public needed a robust, stringent, rules-based protocol that had enough flexibility to handle the ever-changing Internet. BGP proved to be the answer. BGP, which is an EGP, bases path selection on path attributes. The enhancements to BGPv4—support for VLSMs, route aggregation, and CIDR—have enabled it to become the primary protocol for the Internet.

To keep track of the various protocols and their specific characteristics, Table 6.16 is a summarizes the routing protocols discussed in this chapter.

TABLE 16.16 Routing Protocols Summary

Characteristic	RIPv1	RIPv2	OSPF	IGRP	EIGRP	BGP
Classification	Distance-vector	Distance-vector	Link-state	Distance-vector	Hybrid	Path-vector
Number of hops	15	15	N/A	100–255	N/A	N/A
Number of seconds between periodic updates	30	30	Triggered	90	Triggered	N/A
Broadcast	Yes	Yes	Multicast	Yes	Multicast	No

TABLE 16.16   Continued

Characteristic	RIPv1	RIPv2	OSPF	IGRP	EIGRP	BGP
Entire table sent	Yes	Yes	Only changes	Yes	Only changes	Only changes
VLSM	Classful	Classless	Classless	Classful	Classless	Classless
Primary metric	Hops	Hops	Bandwidth	Bandwidth and delay	Bandwidth and delay	Path attribute
ToS/QoS	No	No	Yes	Yes	Yes	Yes
Type of connection	UDP	UDP	UDP	UDP	UDP	TCP

Review Questions

1. What kind of routing protocol is RIP considered to be?

2. Name some of RIP's characteristics.

3. What metric does RIP uses to determine best path selection?

4. How often does RIP send its broadcasts, and what does it send in these broadcasts?

5. How many entries can RIP send in its broadcasts?

6. With RIPv1, how many hops can a datagram traverse if the destination is considered unreachable?

7. What three features does RIPv2 support that RIPv1 does not?

8. Why is RIPv2 virtually obsolete?

9. What are some of the disadvantages of RIPv1?

10. What various mechanisms does RIP use to avoid routing loops?

11. What timers does RIP use?

12. What kind of routing protocol is OSPF is considered to be?

13. What metrics does OSPF consider when making routing decisions?

14. What advantages does OSPF have over RIP?

15. What are some of the characteristics of OSPF?

16. What three databases do OSPF routers maintain and build?

17. What is an OSPF adjacency database?

18. What is an OSPF Link-state database?

19. What is an OSPF forwarding database?

20. What is an OSPF LSA?

21. What is the difference between an OSPF inter-area advertisement and an intra-area advertisement?

22. What are the six OSPF router states?

23. What are the four OSPF router types?

24. What is the OSPF backbone area type?

25. What are the five OSPF packet types?

26. What is the function of an OSPF Hello packet?

27. What is the function of an OSPF Database Description packet?

28. What different metrics does IGRP use to make routing decisions?

29. What is the maximum hop count for IGRP? Why is it significant that IGRP has a larger hop count than RIP?

30. What are the various IGRP timers and what are their functions?

31. What are some of the characteristics of EIGRP?

32. What type of protocol is EIGRP?

33. What are some of the advantages and disadvantages of the fact that EIGRP offers multi-protocol support?

34. What is the difference between EIGRP successor and feasible successor routes?

35. What are the five different EIGRP packet types? Briefly describe each.

36. What is the difference between IGPs and EGPs?

37. What enhancements to BGPv4 allowed it to become the primary protocol used by the Internet?

38. In what situations would you want to implement BGP?

39. What is the difference between a BGP partial-mesh and a BGP full-mesh topology?

40. What are the four types of BGP routers?

41. Each BGP speaker, no matter what table it maintains, needs to distinguish what things?

42. On top of what protocol does BGP run?

43. What are the four different BGP message types?

44. When is a BGP Open message sent, and what is its function?

45. What is a BGP Notification message used for?

46. What metric does BGP use to determine the best path to a destination?

47. Into what four categories do BGP path attributes fall?

48. In BGP, what is meant by *local preference*?

49. What are some of the differences between BGPv3 and BGPv4?

CHAPTER 7

TRANSPORT/HOST-TO-HOST LAYER

You will learn about the following in this chapter:

- Connection-oriented Protocols
- Connectionless Protocols

Transport Layer Protocols

Communication systems do not use a single protocol to handle all transmission tasks; most transmission tasks require a series of protocols that work together within a protocol suite. The Transport layer or Host-to-Host layer provides a reliable flow of data between two processes running on remote hosts. The protocols that reside on this layer take messages (data streams) from upper-layer applications and processes and convert them into segments to be sent down to the Network or Internet layer for packaging as datagrams.

We will discuss the two Transport or Host-to-Host layer protocols, known as UDP (User Datagram Protocol) and TCP (Transmission Control Protocol), within the TCP/IP protocol suite, in Chapters 8, "Transmission Control Protocol (TCP)," and 9, "User Datagram Protocol (UDP)." We limit our discussion in this chapter to the function and services provided by the Transport or Host-to-Host protocols. The type of service provided depends on the Transport layer chosen. UDP (connectionless) provides fast, unreliable delivery of segments between remote processes. TCP, which is connection-oriented, provides the sequencing of data to ensure reliable delivery from two hosts. All protocols fall into one of two categories: connectionless and connection-oriented.

Vendors can choose whether upper-layer applications utilize UDP or TCP. If vendors want speed, they choose UDP, as it offers fast, best effort delivery of datagrams. If speed is less important than reliability, they implement TCP, as it offers slower, guaranteed delivery. Simply put, the choice comes down to speed versus reliability. Figure 7.1 shows how the TCP/IP protocol suite maps to the DoD (Department of Defense) and OSI Reference Model.

UDP offers fast, unreliable delivery of messages between applications running on remote hosts. Considered a simple protocol, UDP provides this fast service by merely sending packets from one host to the other, relying on upper-layer or application protocols to provide reliability. However, UDP has a major drawback: It offers no guarantee that the datagrams it sends actually arrive at the other end.

FIGURE 7.1
Notice that TCP and UDP
map to the Transport
layer of the OSI model
and to the Host-to-Host
layer of the DoD model.

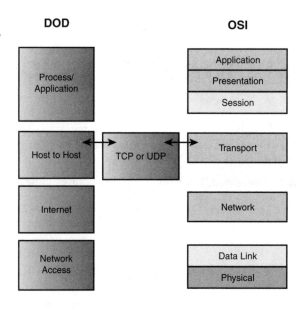

TCP offers slower but guaranteed delivery of data. It provides this service by controlling the flow and size of the datagrams being sent so the Network or Internet layer can handle the transmission. It then goes through a series of acknowledgements and sequencing to guarantee each segment reaches the destination. Because of all the checks and balances that TCP goes through during delivery, it can provide a reliable but slower flow of data, which means the application layer does not have to concern itself with guaranteeing delivery, as with UDP.

The Transport layer or Host-to-Host layer provides the following services:

- Controls end-to-end communication between two processes running on different hosts

- Provides connection-oriented or connectionless services to upper layers

- Uses client and server port address to identify processes running within a host

- Segments data for upper-layer applications

Connection-Oriented Protocols

TCP is the only connection-oriented protocol that resides within TCP/IP suite at the Transport layer. Vendors decide what applications will utilize TCP as its Transport layer protocol depending on whether they require its features. Whether connection-oriented protocols reside on the Transport layer or another layer, they always exhibit the same six characteristics:

- **Session setup**—Establishes a virtual circuit between two communicating processes running on end systems (see Figure 7.2).

- **Acknowledgements**—Notifies the sending device that it has received the data.

- **Sequencing**—Keeps track of the order of datagrams.

- **Flow control**—Controls the speed of incoming data. Hosts can tell other hosts to speed up or slow down the transmission of data.

- **Keepalives**—Maintains a connection during times when no data transmission occurs.

- **Session teardown**—Occurs when either end system requests to terminate the virtual connection (see Figure 7.3).

A connection-oriented session setup always starts from the lower layers and goes to the upper layers of the OSI model. TCP is the primary connection-oriented protocol within the TCP/IP suite. This means whenever an application runs over TCP, TCP sets up the virtual connection before any meaningful data transmission occurs. Once the lower layers have established a session with the upper layers, data transfer can occur over this connection between communication applications. TCP uses a three-frame exchange to set up the session. We will discuss this in more detail in Chapter 8.

FIGURE 7.2

Any application that utilizes TCP as its Transport protocol must establish a connection before it can transmit data.

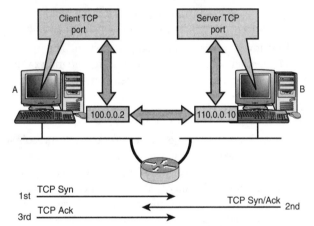

Session Setup

FIGURE 7.3

Exiting an application causes a TCP teardown to begin.

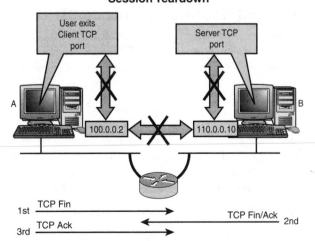

Session Teardown

To ensure that a host does not lose data during transmission, connection-oriented protocols exchange sequencing and acknowledgements. The way protocols sequence each frame varies with each protocol. Some sequence frame by frame; some sequence each byte within the frame. Whatever the method, the purpose remains the same: to detect lost data or frames, and if lost, recover them by retransmitting the data.

When hosts remain idle (not exchanging data), they still need to maintain the virtual connection by using *keepalives*. Keepalives are small messages sent between two machines to ensure connectivity. They enable the virtual connection to be maintained while the host's process remains idle. Keepalives do not carry upper-layer data and hosts send them only to maintain idle connections.

Sometimes a host can send too much data at once and overflow a receiving host's buffers. A receiving host using a connection-oriented protocol can utilize the flow control mechanism to control the flow of data. By using the flow control mechanism, a receiving host can tell a sending host to speed up or slow down the amount of data sent, thus regulating the amount of traffic. Flow control methods vary depending on the protocol used.

TCP implements flow control through a sliding window mechanism. The sliding window mechanism enables TCP to dynamically adjust its window size when needed to alert the sending host to slow down transmission or stop altogether. The upper layers tear down the virtual connection when either side sends a request for termination of the session. We will discuss TCP's use of all six characteristics in more detail in Chapter 8.

Connectionless Protocols

Regardless of what layer they reside on, connectionless protocols send data but do not check whether the receiving host actually receives the data or not. Connectionless protocols rely on other protocols to ensure that the sent data gets to the receiver and recovers lost data. These protocols do not have the reliability that their connection-oriented counterparts do, but they provide something that connection-oriented protocols can't offer—speed and minimal overhead. UDP is considered a Connectionless protocol. We will discuss the UDP protocol in more detail in Chapter 9.

Connectionless Versus Connection-oriented Protocols

Before implementing a particular protocol vendors ask themselves the age-old networking question: speed or reliability and overhead? Connectionless protocols prove faster and more efficient because they do not have the overhead from sequencing and acknowledging each frame or byte; for example, in a connection-oriented session setup. Additionally, connectionless protocols don't have to maintain idle connections with keepalives, which create more overhead.

When vendors want fast delivery, they choose connectionless protocols; when they need reliability more than speed, they choose connection-oriented protocols. For example, if a vendor writes a printing application, he or she typically would use a connection-oriented protocol. Users want to be sure—not hope—their print jobs go through.

Table 7.1 compares the two protocols.

TABLE 7.1   Connection-oriented and Connectionless Protocols

Protocol	Attribute
Connectionless	No session setup
	No session teardown
	No acknowledgements
	No sequencing
	No flow control
	No keepalives
	Best effort of delivery
	Fast delivery of data
	Little overhead
	No recovery or retransmission
Connection-oriented	Session setup
	Session teardown
	Acknowledgements
	Sequencing
	Flow control
	Keepalives
	Reliable, guaranteed delivery
	Slower delivery of data
	Tons of overhead
	Error recovery
	Retransmission of data

Ports and Sockets

The Transport layer, whether using connection-oriented (TCP) or connectionless (UDP) proto-cols, processes addresses and uses ports, also referred to as sockets to identify the process run-ning on the host. The Transport layer handles source and destination addressing of ports, addresses that identify which upper-layer protocol or process wants to communicate on a par-ticular device. This layer uses client-based and server-based addresses, such as TCP and UDP ports, to identify the process running within a host.

As previously mentioned, the Transport layer is responsible for segmenting the data stream handed down by the upper-layer applications. To govern, track, and manage these segments, the Transport layer utilizes port numbers for each application. Remember that a vendor can either implement connectionless or connection-oriented protocols at this layer, which means that depending on the protocol implemented, the data may or may not have guaranteed deliv-ery. This confuses some people because they think the Transport layer provides only guaran-teed reliable delivery of data. Just remember that the delivery is not always guaranteed.

For example, if a user wants to open a client Telnet connection with a remote Telnet server, that session opens up a unique port, which is a variable or made-up port. The connection uses this port to reach a Telnet server. Client ports are chosen randomly whereas server ports have an assigned port value, typically known as *well-known ports*. When you connect to the host or server, you typically connect to a well-known port; in this case Telnet, which uses well-known port 23 (see Figure 7.4). Table 7.2 shows the different port categories.

FIGURE 7.4
In this case, Telnet always uses TCP port 23.

Client and Server Ports

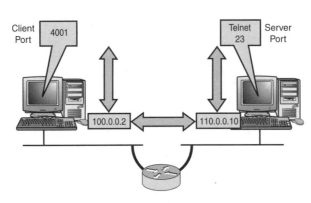

Client Range = 1024-65,536
Server Range = 1-1023

TABLE 7.2   Port Categories

Port Category	Range and Description
Well-known server ports	0-255 Defines well-known programs used in the industry that have become the official standard for addressing such programs.
Less well-known server ports	256-1023 Reserved ports that vendors can implement on an as-needed basis.
Client	1024-65536 Variable (or ethereal) ports made up on-the-fly each time a client process begins and opens a new port.

In Figure 7.4 the client IP address and port 4001, or variable port made up on-the-fly, and the destination host's IP address and well-known Telnet server port 23 make up what is known as a socket pair. A socket pair is an end-to-end connection between two hosts (source and destination) that uses both (or pairs up) their respective IP addresses and their ports. The client and server ports clearly identify the process communicating on each box. By linking the sending host's address and port to the destination host's address and port, TCP or UDP can manage the communication between these hosts and their processes, and distinguish them from other virtual connections to the same hosts.

Note
Remember that the Transport layer deals with sockets or port addresses. Socket pairing describes an end-to-end connection of two hosts, source and destination, which include both their IP addresses and ports.

Within the TCP/IP suite, TCP and UDP ports identify the process or program running within a host. TCP, or the connection-oriented protocol, then maintains the connection-oriented process. Using a connectionless protocol such as UDP, you would simply pass data unreliably, hoping it gets to its destination, and rely on upper-layer protocols to maintain the connection.

Summary

The Transport layer or Host-to-Host layer controls end-to-end communication between two processes running on different hosts and provides connection-oriented or connectionless services to upper layers. It also uses client and server port address to identify processes running within a host and segments data for upper-layer applications.

Within in the TCP/IP suite, two vastly different protocols reside on this layer, UDP (connectionless) and TCP (connection-oriented). All protocols fall into two categories: connectionless and connection-oriented.

Connection-oriented protocols provide guaranteed reliable delivery of data between two end systems. Connectionless protocols offer fast, unreliable delivery of messages between applications running on remote hosts.

Connection-oriented protocols will always exhibit the same six characteristics: session setup, acknowledgements, sequencing, flow control, keepalives, and session teardown.

The Transport layer handles addressing with ports and sockets, addresses that identify which upper-layer protocol or process wants to communicate on a particular device. A client port, which is a variable port; a server port, which is an assigned port; and the source and destination IP addresses of two hosts with end-to-end communication make up a socket pair.

Review Questions

1. What four services does the Transport or Host-to-Host layer provide?

2. What do all connection-oriented protocols exhibit?

3. What are well-known ports and what is their range?

4. What are less-known ports and what is their range?

5. What are client ports and what is their range?

6. Describe socket pairing.

7. Compare and contrast the two Transport or Host-to-Host layer protocols that reside in the TCP/IP protocol suite.

8. What is flow control?

9. What choice do vendors have to make when implementing a particular Transport layer protocol?

10. What protocol utilizes acknowledgements and sequencing and what functions do acknowledgements and sequencing have?

CHAPTER 8

TRANSMISSION CONTROL
PROTOCOL (TCP)

You will learn about the following in this chapter:

- TCP Header and Fields

- TCP Operation

- Connection Setup and Teardown

- Sequencing and
  Acknowledgements

Introduction to TCP

Originally, Vinton Cerf and Robert Kahn designed TCP to provide reliable data transmission between remote hosts communicating over a packet-switched network. Before the invention of TCP, data transmission over packet-switched network infrastructures proved somewhat unreliable. The quality of delivery (or lack of reliability), different media types, and the potential for congestion to impede data delivery made it necessary for a connection-oriented protocol to provide end-to-end reliable services to processes and applications communicating between remote hosts. The DoD (Department of Defense) adopted TCP as its primary protocol for reliable delivery of information over the ARPA network. Since its invention, TCP has become a standard protocol for the Internet, providing guaranteed delivery of data between hosts.

TCP maps to the Host-to-Host layer within the DoD and Transport layer of the OSI model. Only TCP and UDP function at these layers. Vendors can implement TCP when they need guaranteed delivery of data or use UDP when they require speed more than guaranteed delivery. Figure 8.1 shows how TCP maps to the OSI and DoD reference models.

FIGURE 8.1

TCP guarantees the delivery of data at the Host-to-Host or Network layer.

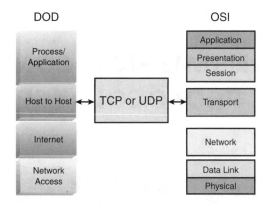

TCP Header

Now that you understand the general functions and implementations of connection-oriented TCP let's explore the fields within the TCP header futher. Figure 8.2 gives an example of a TCP header as defined in RFC 793. Figure 8.3 shows a tangible TCP header as it actually appears during implementation. The TCP header specifies the source and destination ports, sequencing and acknowledgement (ACK) values, and TCP flags used by a host to identify how to process the information. A description of each item contained in the TCP header will appear following the figures.

FIGURE 8.2

This figure shows the format of a TCP header. A TCP header normally contains 20 bytes unless options are being used. Note that a header can contain no options or data.

Source Port							Destination Port
Sequence Number							
Acknowledgement Number							
Offset	Reserved	U	A	P	R	S	F	Window
Checksum							Urgent Pointer
Options + Padding							
Data							

FIGURE 8.3

Note that in this particular TCP header no options are being used and the reserved bits and urgent pointer fields are not present.

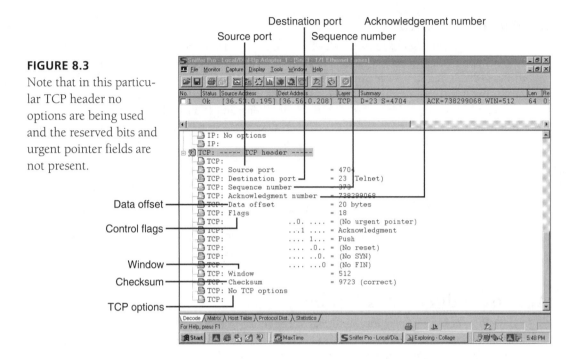

Source Port

The 2-byte source port field identifies the sending host's communicating process (socket). An example of this is a client port 1024–65,535 or server port 1–1023. Because TCP supports bidirectional communication, the value in this field depends on from which direction the communication comes. If the client initiates the request, the port falls within the client range. If a server responds to the client request, the port falls within the server range.

Destination Port

The two-byte destination port identifies the receiving host's communicating process (socket). The port that appears in this field depends on who is communicating with whom: client to server or server to client.

Note

Remember that each TCP segment has a source and destination port number. These port numbers identify the sending and receiving devices. These two values, along with the source and destination IP addresses in the IP header, make a socket pair. A socket pair indicates the two end points that uniquely identify each TCP connection in an internet.

Sequence Number

TCP uses sequencing to keep track of each byte of data. Every octet of data sent over a TCP connection has a sequence number. An algorithm calculates the initial sequence number, which is included in the synchronization frame during session setup and is contained within the 4-byte sequence number field. This sequence number identifies the first byte within each datagram being sent. Think of the sequence number being expressed as "I am now sending data starting with this number." If the receiver does not acknowledge (ACK) the data sent, the sender assumes the data is lost and retransmits it.

Note

Note that TCP does not sequence every byte of data, but guarantees delivery of each byte by sequencing each octet. It merely acknowledges (ACKs) the particular sequence number within each packet being sent. TCP also utilizes windowing to control the transmission of datagrams. We discuss acknowledgements (ACKs) and windowing later in this chapter.

Acknowledgement Number

The 4-byte acknowledgement number field contains the value that identifies the next sequence value the host expects to receive from the other side. The ACK number should equal the other side's previously sent sequence number plus the length value. The receiver implies that it received all the data sent up to that point. This is called an *implied acknowledgement*. The receiver can acknowledge receipt of multiple frames with a single acknowledgement (ACK). This process operates more efficiently than individually acknowledging each frame and its payload of bytes.

Remember that the window size determines the maximum number of bytes a sending host can transmit. The sending host can send multiple frames if the receiver has a window size large enough to accept them. When the receiver meets the window size, it stops and waits for permission (acknowledgement) from the receiver before sending more. To calculate the acknowledgement, add the first frame within this burst's sequence number to the total of all subsequent frame length fields; for example,

- A sending host sends 5 frames.

- The sequence number of the first frame within this stream has a sequence number of 10.

- Each frame contains 10 bytes of data.

The receiving host acknowledges this with a value of 60 (starting sequence number 10 + 50 (5 frames multiplied by the total length in bytes). The receiving host then acknowledges the receipt of all 50 bytes of data and expects the 60th byte from the sending host. You can think of the acknowledgement as stating, "Next I expect to receive…"

Figure 8.4 shows an output screen taken from a Sniffer of a file transfer between hosts and how the calculation works for this particular example. Note the starting sequence number,

number of frames sent, amount of data in each frame, and the acknowledged value. To calculate the acknowledgement, add the starting sequence number to the number of frames, multiplied by their length in bytes.

FIGURE 8.4

Note that the Sniffer output details information from frame two, which is highlighted.

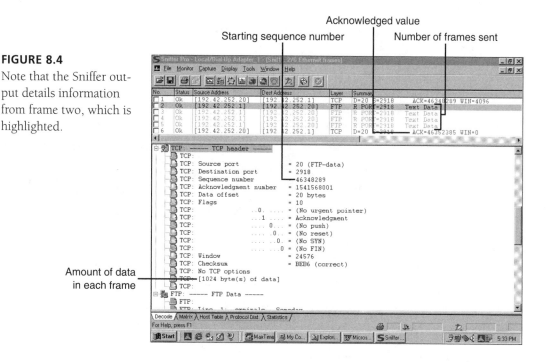

In the first frame shown in the top pane of the Sniffer summary screen, you can see that two FTP hosts (client 192.42.252.20, FTP port 2918, and FTP server 192.42.252.1, port 20) already have a functioning TCP session. In this frame the server now expects the client to now send data beginning with sequence number 46348289, indicated by the ACK value in this frame.

Notice that the next four frames sent by the client carry FTP data. Look in the detail pane. As expected, the starting sequence number is 46348289, and the total amount of FTP data contained within each of these four frames is 1024 bytes (indicated at the end of the TCP header).

Apply the formula and check the math (starting sequence number plus the number of frames sent multiplied by the amount of data in each frame). If the starting sequence number is 46348289 (frame 2) and the client sends four frames with a length of 1024 bytes (frames 2–5), the server expects 46352385 as the next sequence number. You can verify the formula with the acknowledgement value sent by the server. It appears in the last frame (frame 6) as 46352385.

Data Offset

The 4-bit data offset field indicates where the start of upper-layer data that follows the TCP header begins. Because the length of a TCP header can vary in size when it has certain options present, data offset is necessary. TCP uses it to accurately predict where the first byte of upper-layer data is to be expected within the frame.

Reserved

The six-bit reserved field is reserved for future use and is always represented by zeros.

Control Flags—6 Bits

The 6-bit control flags field indicates to the receiver the purpose of the frame. Figure 8.5 shows the six different control flag fields.

FIGURE 8.5

TCP uses control flags to indicate to the receiver how to process the data.

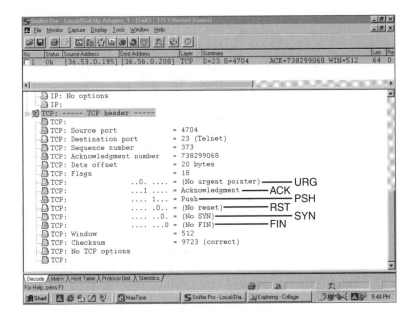

The following describes the functions of the six one-bit control flag fields:

- **URG (Urgent)** Set by sending host to indicate that data contained within this frame has high priority. When the sending host sets this bit, the Urgent Pointer, which appears under the URG bit, identifies (or points to) the next byte in the frame following the urgent data.

- **ACK (Acknowledgement)** The sending host sets this bit to indicate that this frame includes an acknowledgement of previously received data.

- **PSH (Push)** Each TCP session controls when data received is passed to upper-layer applications for processing. When the sending host sets this bit, the receiver must not wait; instead it must send the data (push) immediately to the upper-layer process. By setting this bit the sending TCP host forces the receiving TCP host to pass the data up without delay.

- **RST (Reset)**   Set when user aborts a session or an error occurs in a connection to indicate the session should be reset.

- **SYN (Synchronization)**   Establishes a session between ports/sockets by synchronizing sequence numbers.

- **FIN (Finish)**   Closes an established session and indicates that the sender has finished sending data.

Window

The amount of data that a host can receive varies, depending on the host's resources and how many transmissions that host is currently receiving. The two-byte window field defines the maximum amount of data in bytes that a TCP host can receive. A host uses this field for flow control. A window size of zero indicates that this host cannot receive data at this time. This typically indicates congestion or a lack of resources.

Checksum—2 Bytes

The two-byte checksum field is used to detect bit damage that might have occurred during transit. The checksum verifies the bits within the TCP header, a pseudo IP header, and the upper-layer data. The checksum is calculated by the sending host and compared to the receiving host for validity. If the checksum does not match, the receiving host trashes the frame and gives no notification to the sending host. The sending host assumes responsibility for detecting the lost frame and retransmits. TCP keeps track of information contained within the IP header, such as source and destination addresses, to assist in detecting problems such as improperly routed frames.

Urgent Pointer

The 2-byte Urgent Pointer field exists only when the urgent (URG) bit has been set. When the sending host sets the urgent bit, the Urgent Pointer identifies the byte in the frame that follows the urgent data to clearly identify where nonurgent data begins.

TCP Options—Variable Length

TCP options field can be variable lengths, depending on the options chosen by the sending host. For example, the sending host could choose maximum segment size, which indicates the largest segment size this TCP host will accept. Without this option, the host would accept any segment size. The maximum segment size (MSS) option is the most commonly used option. A complete discussion of options is well beyond the scope of this book.

TCP

The length field (which is a variable length field) identifies the total length of the TCP header and subsequent data, and does not include the TCP pseudo header information. Because the size of the TCP header and its subsequent data varies, this value also varies. Although TCP includes the TCP length field as part of its header, the TCP length field does not actually appear in the TCP header in a Sniffer (protocol analysis) detail output.

The TCP pseudo header provides error control on the IP header and detects misdirected frames. It ensures that the correct destination host receives a sent datagram. TCP does not include the information contained in the pseudo header. TCP stores this information in a TCP memory buffer called a *TCB (transmission control block)*. Figure 8.6 shows an example of a TCP pseudo header.

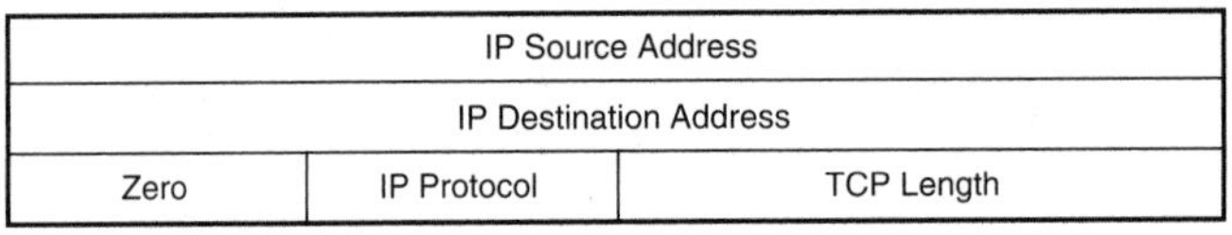

FIGURE 8.6
The TCP pseudo header allows TCP to double-check that the datagram has arrived at the correct destination.

IP Source Address		
IP Destination Address		
Zero	IP Protocol	TCP Length

Fundamentals of TCP Operation

TCP provides a bidirectional communication pipe between remote host processes, identified by ports. As described within RFC 793, TCP controls the communications between these processes by providing the following:

- Connection setup and teardown

- Multiplexing

- Data transfer

- Flow control

- Reliability

- Precedence and security

TCP can be thought of as the Fed-Ex of protocols, which boasts "When it absolutely, positively has to get there overnight!" In other words, it guarantees delivery of packets. TCP actually can boast a speedier delivery of packets than Fed-EX; however, TCP still remains slower than UDP (which provides no reliability).

Achieving such a high standard of delivery involves overhead in the form of establishing, maintaining, and terminating sessions between hosts. Unlike connectionless protocols, TCP does not rely on lower layers to track data. TCP does not limit itself by only identifying the sending and receiving host process, placing data on the wire, and hoping it arrives at its destination without any follow-up. TCP uses sequencing and acknowledgements to guarantee the delivery of packets.

Unlike its counterpart UDP, when TCP receives a stream of data (messages), it breaks the streams into segments and assigns sequence numbers to each byte prior to delivery by IP within a datagram. These sequence numbers require corresponding acknowledgements to be returned from the destination to ensure it has received from the sender each segment within the datagram. TCP maintains a copy of the segments contained within a buffer at the host, known as a TCB (transmission control block). If it does not receive an acknowledgement, it assumes the datagram has been lost and retransmits it. We discuss this in more detail later in this chapter.

Connection Setup and Teardown

To provide reliable data delivery between processes, TCP must make a connection before the upper-layer applications can exchange any meaningful data. To accomplish this, TCP establishes a connection known as a *logical circuit* between the remote host ports first. This connection links ports or processes running within each host. TCP maintains this connection throughout the entire conversation and tears down the connection when it is no longer needed.

Once IP learns the logical address of the destination host, TCP sets up a session that provides the reliable foundation for the upper-layer protocols to deliver data. When the user or one of the hosts requests to close a session, TCP tears the session down. We discuss the session setup and teardown procedures and exchanges in more detail later in this chapter.

Multiplexing

Multiplexing capability enables TCP to establish and maintain multiple communication paths between two hosts simultaneously. Multiplexing also allows a single host to distinguish and maintain sessions with many hosts simultaneously. Hosts need this capability because usually they run multiple applications or services such as Telnet, FTP (File Transfer Protocol), or other services. TCP has to distinguish one process from another, and manage and maintain the communications for these processes.

To accomplish this, TCP utilizes ports to differentiate communications and manage them (see RFC 1078 TCP port service Multiplexer TCPMUX). As mentioned in Chapter 6, "Routing Protocols," there are two main port types: server ports and client ports. Server ports identify major applications or services; for example, Telnet (port 23), SMTP (port 25), and FTP (ports 20, 21). Client ports vary; they are chosen on the fly and dynamically applied, ranging 1024–65536.

Each time a host starts a process it causes a port to open, allocating resources to that process. When the process no longer needs the port it closes the port, releasing the resources associated with that port for reallocation. TCP uses these ports to identify which process on the sending host should be linked to which process on the destination host. The port on the host, along with the Network layer (DoD Internet) logical IP address, identifies a unique process on a host, referred to as a *socket*. Once the established TCP connection between hosts links them together, these two sockets, referred to as a *socket pair* (see Figure 8.7), form a connection. This pairing enables a host to distinguish among multiple connections from the same host or different hosts.

FIGURE 8.7

Note that the client's IP address, client port, server's IP address and server port make up what is called a *socket pair.*

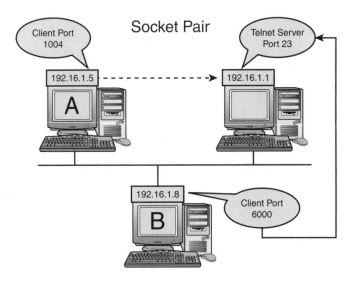

Data Transfer

TCP receives and organizes streams of data (messages) from upper-layer processes or applications as segments and passes them down to be formatted as datagrams by IP (Network layer) for addressing, packing, and delivery. When IP receives datagrams from a remote host, it inspects the protocol address within the IP header to determine whether to send the information through TCP or UDP for processing. Figure 8.8 shows an IP header referencing TCP as the upper-layer protocol.

FIGURE 8.8

TCP passes down segments to IP (Network layer) for conversion to datagrams.

```
Sniffer Pro - Local/Dial-Up Adapter_1 - [Snif3: 3/1 Ethernet frames]
File  Monitor  Capture  Display  Tools  Window  Help

IP: ----- IP Header -----
IP:
IP: Version = 4, header length = 20 bytes
IP: Type of service = 00
IP:     000. .... = routine
IP:     ...0 .... = normal delay
IP:     .... 0... = normal throughput
IP:     .... .0.. = normal reliability
IP: Total length    = 40 bytes
IP: Identification  = 742
IP: Flags           = 0X
IP:     .0.. .... = may fragment
IP:     ..0. .... = last fragment
IP: Fragment offset = 0 bytes
IP: Time to live    = 255 seconds/hops
IP: Protocol        = 6 (TCP)
IP: Header checksum = 6EEA (correct)
IP: Source address      = [36.53.0.195]
IP: Destination address = [36.56.0.208]
IP: No options
IP:
TCP: ----- TCP header -----
TCP:
TCP: Source port        = 4704
TCP: Destination port   = 23 (Telnet)

Decode  Matrix  Host Table  Protocol Dist.  Statistics
For Help, press F1
Start                MaxTime          Sniffer Pro - Local/Dia.   Exploring - Collage              5:49 PM
```

TCP runs on top of the Internet Protocol that provides Network Layer addressing and connectionless delivery of datagrams between hosts. The protocol type value 06 identifies TCP within the IP header. The protocol type value 17 identifies UDP within the IP header.

When TCP receives segments within datagrams from IP it reassembles them into organized data streams (messages), identifies the receiving client or server port, and passes them on to the appropriate (upper-layer) application for processing. The upper (applications) and lower (Internet Protocol) layers have a bidirectional relationship depending on the direction of the data flow. TCP provides the same fundamental services to all upper-layer protocols. This is a simplistic view of how TCP operates; we will discuss TCP operation in more detail later in this chapter.

Flow Control

TCP needs a method of controlling the inbound flow of data. Flow control guarantees that incoming traffic does not overwhelm a host's receive buffer and that the receiving host can adequately process and respond to the sending host's requests. The window mechanism identified within the TCP header provides this function. We will take a detailed look at flow control and the TCP header later in this chapter.

Each end host maintains its own window and advertises this window to the other side. When congestion occurs, a host reduces its window size and advertises it to the other side. In effect, the host asks the other side to slow down its transmissions.

When congestion no longer exists, a host can increase the size, alerting the other side that it can send more data. The capability to dynamically increase or decrease the window as needed is referred to as a *sliding window.* An administrator can configure the initial window size at the host. This configuration varies depending on the operating system used.

Reliability

Reliability comes from TCP's guaranteed delivery of packets. TCP requires the sequencing of each byte sent and a corresponding acknowledgement of each byte from the other side. This enables a host to detect whether information has been lost or sent out of order.

The receiving host does not send an ACK if datagrams become lost in transit. The transmitting (sending) host has the task of detecting lost or missing frames and retransmits if necessary. If the sending host does not receive an acknowledgement within a specified period of time, it retrieves a copy of the previously sent information from its TCB buffer and retransmits the lost data. The sending host uses a timer based on a round-trip delay calculation to detect a lost frame and retransmit. If a timer expires before receiving an acknowledgement of sent data, the sending host assumes the datagram is lost and retransmits.

TCP deals with damaged frames through a CRC field contained within the TCP header. The sending host performs a CRC calculation before transmitting. The receiving host performs a CRC check upon receipt to determine whether a datagram has been damaged while in transit.

If the receiving host detects a damaged datagram it simply trashes the frame without notifying the source host. Eventually, the source host realizes something has happened to this frame because it has not received a corresponding acknowledgement from the receiving host. At this point the TCP timer expires, causing this host to retransmit the data.

Precedence and Security

The DoD mandates that all protocols implemented within its networks support a multilevel security model and precedence levels. TCP can utilize the service and security options within IP to provide this level of service to upper-layer applications. Figure 8.9 shows the options available within the Type of Service field. TCP offers these types of services to upper-layer applications:

- Precedence
- Delay
- Throughput
- Reliability

The options within the Type of Service field of the IP header indicate how a datagram should be handled. When implemented, the Type of Service options, precedence delay, throughput, and reliability influence route selection when delivering datagrams. For example, if an application requires a datagram to be sent by a fast path when there is more than one path to a destination, it can request routers to send the frame over the path offering the lowest delay.

FIGURE 8.9
ToS bits influence how a datagram should be handled.

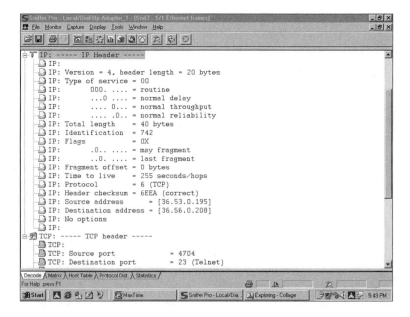

The first option, known as *precedence,* indicates whether this datagram carries routine or high-priority (precedence) information; the higher the precedence level, the higher the security level. A host with a mismatched or lower precedence (security level) cannot establish a connection to a process with another host having a higher security level. Thus a host rejects a connection request based on a multilevel security basis.

Although the IP header contains the Type of Service options, TCP can make use of these functions on a per-connection basis through bi-directional communication. TCP can store these options in its TCP memory buffer to provide increased security and more efficient delivery of application data.

Connection-oriented Characteristics

As we discussed in Chapter 6, protocols fall into one of two categories: connection-oriented or connectionless. As a connection-oriented protocol, TCP implements all six of these basic characteristics:

- Session setup

- Teardown

- Sequencing

- Acknowledgements

- Keepalives

- Flow control

The following sections detail how each of these basic characteristics work.

Session Setup

Before any data transmission can occur, a reliable connection-oriented logical circuit needs to be established between remote hosts communicating processes or applications. Session establishment remains the same regardless of the process. TCP identifies all upper-layer processes and applications using a port or socket address. TCP uses these port addresses to distinguish one process from another within the same host, which ensures proper delivery and processing.

For example, when a user wants to initiate a Telnet client session with a remote Telnet server, the user starts a local Telnet client process. This initiation causes the local host to open a source client port identifying this Telnet process using a variable port value within the range 1024–65,536. TCP uses this source port along with a destination port (well-known port 23 for Telnet), which indicates the intended recipient of this message. Using both the source port and the destination port enables TCP to keep track of a pair of communicating processes and know the processes between which it is opening a session.

If a user initiates a session with a remote host using a host name rather than an IP address, some type of name resolution must occur that maps the host name to a Network layer address of either the ultimate destination (if on the same subnet) or the gateway. After learning the Network layer address of the destination IP host, ARP resolves this address to a MAC address for local delivery.

Socket Pairing

Once the address resolution process has been completed, TCP has enough information to begin the session setup process. The source Network layer address, client port/socket, and destination Network layer address and server port/socket make up what is called a *socket pairing*. Because the same client or multiple clients connecting to the same remote server port/socket can request multiple TCP connections, socket pairing separates the different requests, uniquely identifying and handling the communication between pairs. Because of the potential multitude of connections, socket pairing remains critical to TCP's success.

Session setup begins by the TCP client setting a bit, known as the SYN bit, within the TCP header indicating a request for synchronization with the destination TCP process. The receiving host's TCP session must ACK the receipt of this SYN request and send its own SYN request. This SYN also must be acknowledged by the previous host.

Figures 8.10, 8.11, and 8.12 comprise an example of a session setup. The summary screen shows two hosts (192.42.252.20 and 192.42.252.1) in the process of establishing a TCP connection. The first frame indicates that host 192.42.252.20, using a client port of 2921, requests a TCP connection by sending the initial SYN to the Telnet server, indicated by port 23 and IP address 192.42.252.1.

FIGURE 8.10

The first part of a TCP session setup starts by the client sending the server a SYN. Notice this frame does not contain an ACK field because neither client nor server has sent any previous data to acknowledge.

Frame 1

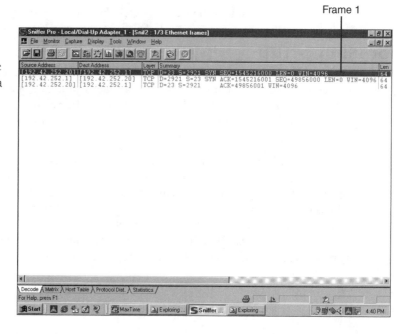

The Telnet server sends the second frame, which serves as an ACK of the previous SYN sent by the client and a new SYN request sent by this host. Notice this frame carries an ACK field, which acknowledges the initial SYN by the client. Because TCP can communicate in full-duplex mode, which means it can send and acknowledge receipt of data within the same frame instead of requiring a separate frame to perform this function, this host can include its SYN request within the same frame. This allows TCP to operate more efficiently

FIGURE 8.11

The second part of a TCP session setup is the server's acknowledgement (ACK) of the client's SYN and sending its own SYN request to the client.

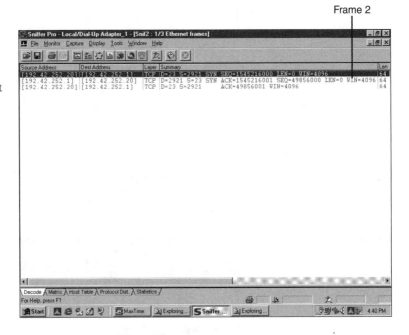

The client sends the third frame as an ACK of the previous SYN sent by the Telnet server. Now that the two hosts have established a TCP session they can transmit Telnet data. Note that no matter what type of upper-layer applications a host requests (Telnet, SMTP, FTP, and so forth), this three-frame exchange process always occurs.

The requests and acknowledgements found in the frame exchange are known as the *three-way handshake*. Because TCP has the capability of full-duplex communication, it needs only three frames instead of four to complete this process. When the destination receives the first SYN request from the sender, the destination responds by acknowledging the sender with its own SYN request within the same frame.

To complete the transaction, the sender sends its ACK that it has received the destination's SYN request in the next and final frame of the three-way handshake. Figures 8.13, 8.14, and 8.15 comprise a detailed example of a three-way handshake. As you can see within the TCP header, the host has set the SYN bit (indicated by a value of 1). In addition, the host has stated several starting parameters, such as its ISN (initial sequence number 1545216000), window size (4096 bytes), and maximum segment size (1024 bytes). We will discuss these values in more detail later in this chapter.

FIGURE 8.12

The third part of a TCP session setup is the client acknowledging (ACK) the server's SYN.

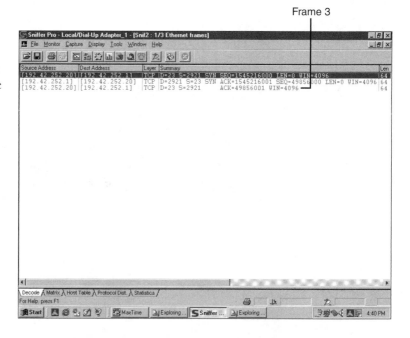

FIGURE 8.13

Note the SYN sent by the client in the first part of the three-way handshake.

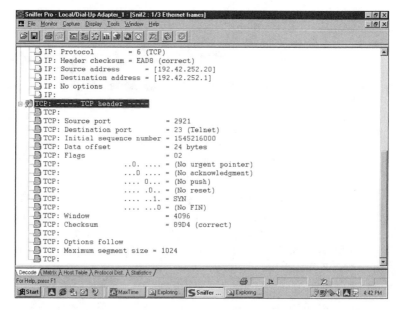

Figure 8.14 shows the response frame from the Telnet server (IP address 192.42.252.1, source port 23). Notice the server includes its ACK indicating that it has received the client's initial request (sequence number 1545216000). The acknowledgement states that this host next

expects sequence number 1545216001, which implies that it received all sequence numbers up to, but not including this value. You also can see the Telnet server's ISN of 49856000. The server has set the SYN bit indicating that it would like to synchronize with the client, setting its window size to 4096 bytes and maximum segment size to 1024 bytes.

FIGURE 8.14

Note the ACK and SYN sent by the server in the second part of the three-way handshake.

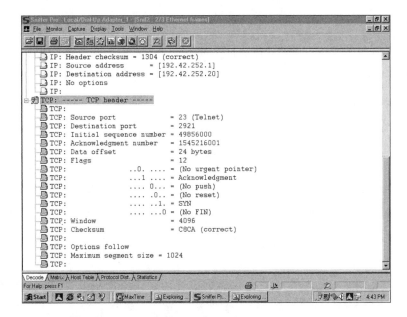

The client sends the last frame of the three-way handshake to acknowledge receipt of the server's previous SYN request. This host acknowledges receipt of the Telnet server's previously sent sequence number by indicating that it next expects to receive sequence number 49856001. Both hosts have synchronized and know each other's starting parameters.

Within the SYN request frames TCP includes starting parameters that must be agreed upon by both ends to successfully synchronize their sessions and begin the process of sending meaningful user data. These parameters include their receive buffer size (which is elastic), initial sequence number to be used when data transmission begins, and the optional maximum segment size this TCP host can accept. We will discuss these parameters in more detail later in this chapter.

Session Teardown

The user or TCP can request a session teardown. If a user no longer wishes or needs the services of the remote application, he or she can exit the local application, causing a session teardown request to be sent. The TCP session teardown process is similar to the session setup. It utilizes a three-frame exchange to close the session. Either side can request a teardown. Host 192.42.252.1, sequence number 49856607, sends the initial teardown request in the first frame, indicated by the FIN (Finish) request. Figures 8.16, 8.17, and 8.18 illustrate an example of a session teardown request.

FIGURE 8.15

Note the ACK sent by the client in the second part of the three-way handshake.

FIGURE 8.16

A FIN is sent as the first part of the session teardown.

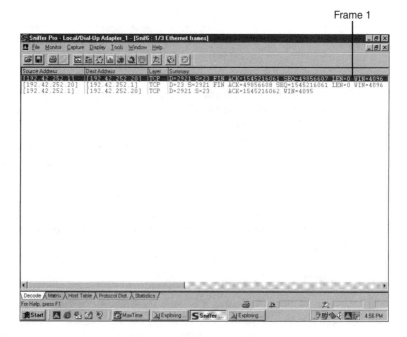

The recipient sends the second frame acknowledging the previous FIN request and expects to receive a subsequent sequence number 49856608. Additionally, this host sends its own FIN request with sequence number 1545216061. The host that initially requested the teardown sends the final frame, acknowledging the previous FIN. This closes the connection and the hosts cannot exchange upper-layer information until they establish a new TCP session.

FIGURE 8.17

As the second part of the session teardown, the host sends an ACK and its own FIN request.

Frame 2

FIGURE 8.18

As the third and final part of the session teardown, the host acknowledges (ACK) the other host's FIN request.

Frame 3

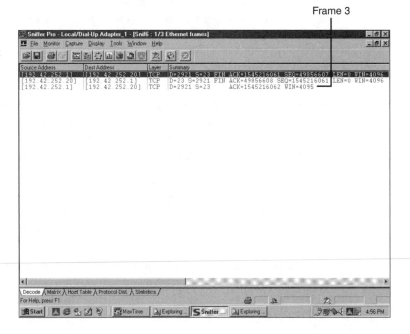

TCP sends a similar request when an unrecoverable error or denial of access occurs in a TCP session setup. When one of these problems occurs, it causes either the client or server TCP process to issue the teardown request. Whatever the reason for the teardown, it uses a three-way handshake to accomplish the session teardown. Just like the session setup sequence, the teardown process uses a three-frame sequence.

The host requesting session closure sets a FIN bit within the TCP header indicating a request to close the session; it then sends the FIN bit to the other side. The recipient must in turn acknowledge receipt of the initial FIN and send its own FIN, which then is acknowledged by the original host requesting to close the session. At this point both sides release the allocated resources and make them available for other processes.

Sequencing and Acknowledgements

The cornerstone of TCP's services is to provide the most reliable transmission of data. To guarantee the delivery of datagrams, TCP sequences each byte of data it sends. This might seem like overkill because many protocols sequence each datagram regardless of the byte size; however, this guarantees that all sent data is tracked. Tracking all the sent data can detect and correct lost data, duplicated data, and data delivered out of order.

Each time a host sends data, TCP assigns a sequence number to each byte and waits for a positive ACK of the assigned sequence numbers from the other side within a specific amount of time. (An algorithm, which we will discuss later in the chapter, calculates this time.) If the receiver does not respond within that specific amount of time, the sending host retransmits the data.

The receiver utilizes the same sequence numbers to acknowledge receipt of data to detect missing, sent out of order, or duplicated data sent by the other side. Once the receiver has the sequenced data it can reorder these segments into data streams (messages) to be passed to the upper-layer process or application for processing. The receiving host buffers incoming TCP segments before passing this information up to the application and uses sequence numbers to detect whether it has received data out of order.

Because datagrams might take very different paths before reaching their destinations, a significant delay can occur for some of these segments. The receiving host acknowledges data received in sequential order. For example, if a sending host sends sequence numbers 1, 2, 3, and 4 but the destination receives only 1, 2, and 4, the receiver acknowledges only segments 1 and 2 by sending ACK=3.

The receiver buffers segment 4 in hopes that segment 3 will appear shortly. If segment 3 does not arrive at the destination, the sending host has to retransmit the data. Hopefully, segment 3 arrives and the receiver puts the segments in order, acknowledging receipt of 3 and 4 and passing this information up for processing.

During the session setup process each end host's TCP session uses an algorithm to derive a starting sequence value to be used for data exchange. Within their initial SYN frames, each host advertises its own starting sequence value. Figure 8.19 shows an example of a TCP session setup with the initial sequence number and SYN bit set.

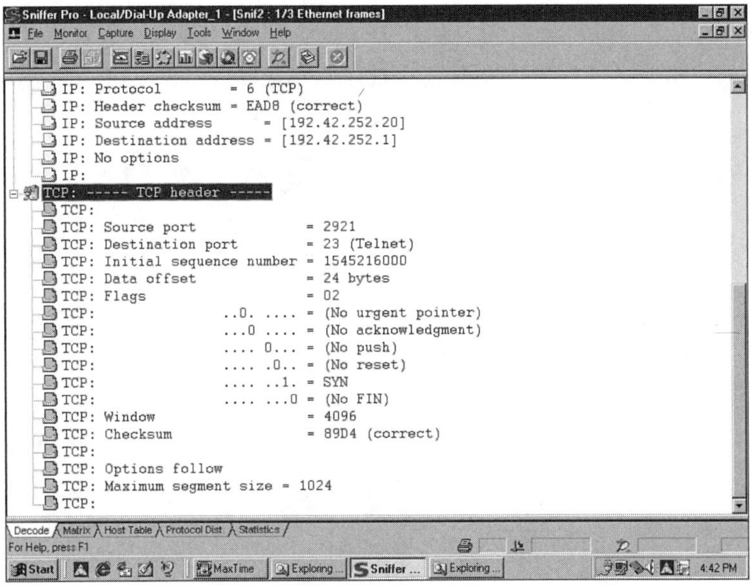

FIGURE 8.19

Note this host advertises an initial sequence value of 1545216000 during the SYN request exchange.

```
Sniffer Pro - Local/Dial-Up Adapter_1 - [Snif2 : 1/3 Ethernet frames]
File  Monitor  Capture  Display  Tools  Window  Help

    IP: Protocol        = 6 (TCP)
    IP: Header checksum = EAD8 (correct)
    IP: Source address      = [192.42.252.20]
    IP: Destination address = [192.42.252.1]
    IP: No options
    IP:
    TCP: ----- TCP header -----
    TCP:
    TCP: Source port        = 2921
    TCP: Destination port   = 23 (Telnet)
    TCP: Initial sequence number = 1545216000
    TCP: Data offset        = 24 bytes
    TCP: Flags              = 02
    TCP:              ..0. .... = (No urgent pointer)
    TCP:              ...0 .... = (No acknowledgment)
    TCP:              .... 0... = (No push)
    TCP:              .... .0.. = (No reset)
    TCP:              .... ..1. = SYN
    TCP:              .... ...0 = (No FIN)
    TCP: Window           = 4096
    TCP: Checksum         = 89D4 (correct)
    TCP:
    TCP: Options follow
    TCP: Maximum segment size = 1024
    TCP:

Decode  Matrix  Host Table  Protocol Dist  Statistics
For Help, press F1

Start    MaxTime   Exploring   Sniffer ...   Exploring      4:42 PM
```

Each side of the connection can send and acknowledge data within the same datagram. This datagram has a sequence field and an acknowledgement field. The sequence field indicates the starting sequence of the first byte of data being transmitted within this datagram. The acknowledgement field indicates the receipt of data from the other side up to, but not including the sequence number reflected, which represents the value expected in the next datagram sent.

Once both sides establish a session, the sender sequences each byte and the receiver acknowledges each byte. Every TCP header has a length field indicating in bytes how much data has been transmitted within this datagram. The destination adds this value to the starting sequence number sent by the source to determine what the acknowledgement value should be upon the return.

For example, if the sending host has a sequence number of 100, he sends 100 bytes of data (representing the length in bytes). The receiving host would then send in the response frame an ACK of 200, which represents the starting sequence number expected in the next datagram. To figure the formula during sequencing, the starting sequence number (in this case 100) plus length in bytes sent (in this case 100) equals acknowledgement (200). Apply this formula to the frames in Figures 8.20 and 8.21. Telnet provides a great example, as it typically sends data only one byte at a time, making it easy to understand how sequencing and acknowledgements work.

The first frame shows that host 192.42.252.20 has sent the one byte of Telnet data by looking at the Telnet header. You can see the character being transmitted as 1. Look at the end of the TCP header and note in brackets [1 byte(s) of data] is being transmitted. This is the length field. Also note the sequence number of this frame, 1545216045. Use the formula to anticipate what ACK value the recipient should respond with. Sequence number (1545216045) plus length (1) equals 1545216046. The second frame shows the response to the first frame. The Telnet server acknowledges receipt of the 1 (length field) sent by sending an ACK value of 1545216046, just as we expected.

FIGURE 8.20

TCP sequences every octet.

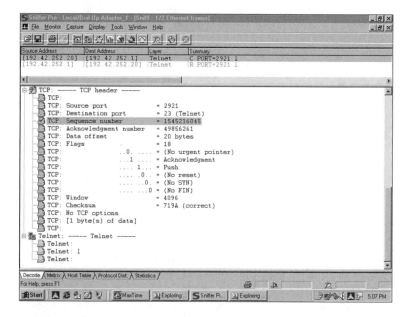

FIGURE 8.21

TCP acknowledges each octet.

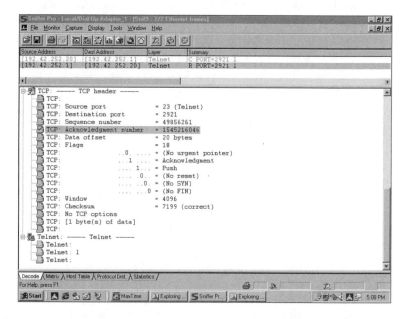

Retransmission

The sending host determines whether a datagram needs to be retransmitted. Because datagrams can take separate paths and might get lost, the sending device keeps a copy in case it needs to retransmit a datagram to a destination host. When the source host sends data it places a copy of the data into a retransmission queue in case this information needs to be resent and starts a timer. If the sending host receives a corresponding acknowledgement in response to the previously sent information, it deletes the copy from its queue. If the sending host does not receive a response, or if the timer expires, it assumes the datagram is lost in transit and retransmits the datagram from the queue.

Timers

An algorithm calculates the value of the retransmission timer based on the amount of time it takes between sent datagrams and receipt of the corresponding acknowledgements. This algorithm dynamically calculates the retransmission timer by evaluating the time between a transmitted datagram and its subsequent acknowledgement. It then uses this result to compute an SRTT (smooth round trip timer). The SRTT uses this value and a base value configured on the host to calculate an RTO (retransmit timeout) value used by the host. An administrator can change the base value to affect the RTO of a TCP host. The configuration of this parameter varies depending on the operating system in use.

It's not critical that you know the exact algorithm the host uses; only that this value controls how long a TCP host waits for an acknowledgement before it assumes a previously sent datagram has been lost and needs retransmission. Figure 8.22 shows an example of TCP's timeout and retransmission. In it host A sends sequence #11 and #12 to host B. Host B acknowledges receipt of those sequence numbers with ACK=12 and ACK=13. By sending ACK=13, host B next expects to receive sequence #13 from host A. Host A sends sequence #13 and a transmission error occurs somewhere in the path, causing the frame to be lost. Because host A does not receive an acknowledgement from host B, the transmit timer expires. At this point host A assumes that the frame was lost in transit and retransmits sequence #13.

FIGURE 8.22

If a host does not receive an acknowledgement, it retransmits the data.

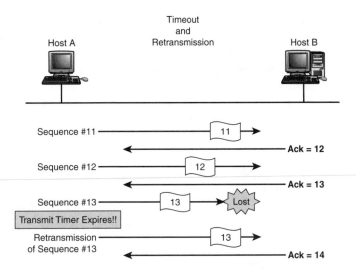

Because of the wide fluctuations in bandwidth and transmission speeds of networks, some-times the retransmission timer cannot keep up with the transmissions. This situation occurs when the base value on a host needs adjusting. If the retransmission timer is too low in value, a host might retransmit a datagram too quickly.

In this case, a destination host sends an acknowledgement for the previous frame but before the host actually receives it, the retransmission timer expires. The source host then assumes that the destination host did not receive previously sent frame and retransmits another copy. This scenario causes duplicate datagrams to be sent, adding more traffic and congestion (need-less traffic) to the network load. This type of needless traffic tends to be especially problematic on slow WAN links because resources are at a premium.

If the opposite is true (the base value of the timer is too high), it could slow so much that con-nections drop. If the sending host cannot detect and retransmit lost datagrams within a timely manner, applications might give up and close the connection.

Keepalives

Every connection-oriented protocol needs some way to maintain the logical circuit between communicating processes even when no data is being exchanged; TCP is no exception. To maintain the logical circuit TCP sends a datagram called a *keepalive* in which no upper-layer data is present. It uses these types of datagrams to keep the session alive; hence the name. Because the frame contains no data, the length field value is zero, which means the subsequent ACK number does not advance.

Congestion

TCP uses keepalives as a normal part of session maintenance; however, this adds overhead to the network. Depending on how many open TCP connections you have on your network, keepalives can cause a large amount of unnecessary overhead to an already congested link. Note that connections to remote hosts, if unused, should be released (closed) and opened only when needed.

Think about all the users you have on your network. Now think about all the shortcuts and mapped drive connections they have on their local computers that point to remote hosts. These shortcuts and mapped drives provide a quick and easy way for users to connect to remote hosts using their resources effortlessly. However, consider that for each of these quick references to exist each of these connections needs to be opened and maintained by TCP, even when they are not in use. Now go and disconnect them. Unmap drives that are not currently in use or after use. Limit the amount of desktop shortcut connections users can maintain. This cuts down on tons of needless TCP traffic and frees up critical bandwidth, especially on slower WAN links.

Flow Control

Flow control is a function of TCP's window feature. TCP uses flow control to manage the flow of data into a receiver's buffer to avoid overrunning the receiver. If a sending host transmits data faster than a receiver can process it, the receiver asks the sender to throttle back and send less data until the receiver can accept more.

Sometimes the receiver receives an overwhelming amount of data. If this occurs, it sends a choke packet to tell the sender to stop sending entirely. If the situation grows to a critical level, it might even close the TCP session.

The TCP header contains a field known as the *window* (see Figures 8.2 and 8.3 for an example within a TCP header). With each frame exchange, including the initial session setup (the SYN frame), each side of the conversation advertises to the other end the current size of its receive buffer. Figure 8.23 shows an example of a window advertisement.

FIGURE 8.23

Notice that both hosts advertise a window size of 4096, or WIN=4096.

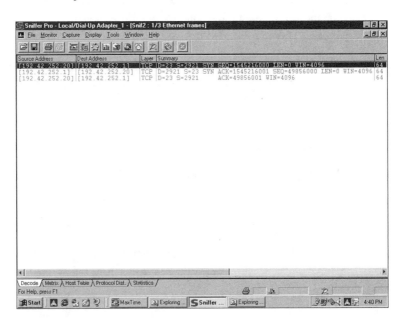

For example, if a host claims in its initial SYN frame that it can receive 4096 bytes of data by stating WIN=4096, the peer host cannot send more than 4096 bytes of data. Each host's window size becomes the peer host's send window, which means that a sender cannot send more than a receiver says it can receive. After the initial synchronization each frame carries the current host's receive window size, which is measured in bytes.

Hosts can adjust the window size within subsequent frames to indicate a smaller buffer when they have congestion or expand when congestion alleviates. For example, if a host attempts to maintain several client sessions, it could quickly find it is running out of resources and needs to control the flow of data by decreasing the TCP window size advertised on some of these connections. By doing this it allows the host to properly and efficiently process the data it receives from all hosts in a timely manner.

If TCP had no mechanism for congestion control, some sessions could monopolize the host's resources, causing other client sessions to time out and close. The window mechanism enables TCP to control the influx of traffic from a TCP session like a traffic cop. It increases the window size when it has plenty of resources to process requests (giving the green light to incoming traffic). It decreases the window size when it starts to experience congestion, asking sending hosts to slow down (giving the yellow light to incoming traffic). It stops traffic entirely when overloaded and advertises a window of zero, referred to as a *choke packet* (giving the red light to the sending host to stop transmitting entirely).

Figure 8.24 shows the various stages of windowing. Initially host B gives host A the green light, advertising that it can accept 4096 bytes as its window size. Host A responds by sending four frames containing 1024 bytes each. Host B, now experiencing congestion, advertises 1024 bytes as its window size, telling host A to slow down its transmissions (yellow light). Host A responds by sending the maximum window amount 1024 bytes of data. Host B, overwhelmed by the amount of transmissions it has received, responds by advertising a window of zero. By advertising Window=0, host B gives host A the red light, asking host A to stop sending data until it can accept more transmissions.

FIGURE 8.24

A host can control flow by telling the other the host to slow down, speed up or stop the transmission of frames.

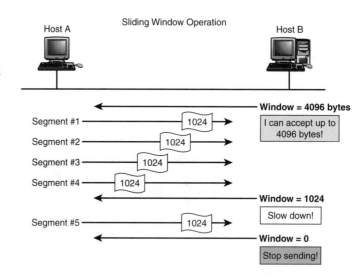

The sender uses the window as an indication of how much data it can send before the receiver must give it permission (by sending an ACK) to send more. If a zero window condition continues for a lengthy period of time without transitioning to a positive window size, eventually it forces the connection to close. Note that even if a zero window condition exists on a host, that host can still transmit data but can receive only critical frames such as ACKs and those carrying the RST (reset) or URG bits.

Figure 8.25 shows an example of a zero window condition. When a host advertises a zero window, it indicates to the sending host to stop sending data until it advertises a positive window size. When a host advertises a zero window, usually this indicates it has limited resources or is busy servicing other hosts and might be overwhelmed.

FIGURE 8.25

A host can stop the sending host from transmitting any more data with a choke packet.

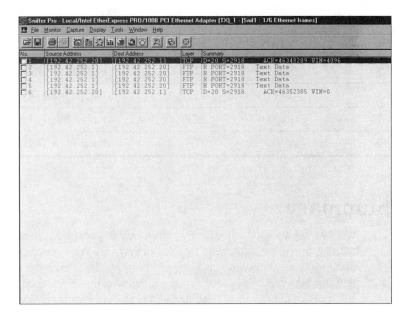

A zero window does not pose a problem unless it occurs frequently. When a host continuously advertises a zero window, this usually indicates that a host needs more memory, CPU power, or applications offloaded to other hosts. A zero window that persists for a lengthy period of time will cause connections to close.

TCP Ports

TCP uses well-known ports to establish a client-server relationship. TCP uses these ports at the Transport layer to identify which upper-layer processes have sent or should receive data streams. Table 8.1 lists many of the well-known TCP port numbers.

TABLE 8.1   Well-known TCP Port Numbers

Decimal	Keyword	Protocol(s)	Description
20	FTP-Data	TCP	File Transfer Protocol (Data)
21	FTP	TCP	File Transfer Protocol (Control)
23	Telnet	TCP	Telnet
25	SMTP	TCP	Simple Mail Transfer Protocol
49	LOGIN	TCP	Login Host Protocol

TABLE 8.1   Continued

Decimal	Keyword	Protocol(s)	Description
53	DNS	TCP/UDP	Domain Name Service
63	VIA-FTP	TCP	VIA-Systems-FTP
70	Gopher	TCP	Gopher File Service
80	WWW	TCP	World Wide Web Services

Summary

RFC 793 defines TCP. Since its invention, TCP has become a standard protocol used on the Internet, providing guaranteed delivery of data between hosts. It provides a bidirectional communication pipe between remote host processes, identified by ports. TCP controls the communications between these processes by providing connection setup and teardown, multiplexing, data transfer, flow control, reliability and precedence and security.

Because TCP guarantees delivery of data, it requires the sequencing of each byte sent and a corresponding acknowledgement of each byte from the other side. TCP accomplishes this in what is called a three-way handshake.

To manage the flow of data into a receiver's buffer, TCP utilizes flow control. Through the window mechanism contained in the TCP header, a receiver can ask the sender to slow down, speed up, or stop transmitting depending on how much data its buffer can accept. This process is called a sliding window, or windowing.

Review Questions

1. During TCP operation, what six fundamental functions does TCP use to control the communications between remote host process?

2. What must occur before upper-layer applications can exchange meaningful data?

3. What allows TCP the capability to establish and maintain multiple communication paths between two hosts simultaneously?

4. TCP receives _____ from upper-layer applications and organizes them into _____ to be passed down to the Network layer to become _____.

5. What mechanism controls the inbound flow of data?

6. How does TCP provide reliable delivery of packets?

7. What are the six basic characteristics of connection-oriented protocols?

8. What is socket pairing?

9. When does retransmission of data occur?

10. Name the different fields contained in a TCP header?

CHAPTER 9

USER DATAGRAM PROTOCOL (UDP)

You will learn about the following in this chapter:

- UDP Operation
- UDP Ports
- UDP Header

The User Datagram Protocol (UDP) as described in RFC 768 offers fast, unreliable delivery of messages between applications running on remote hosts. UDP maps to the OSI Transport and DoD Host-to-Host layers, and is an alternative to the slow but reliable TCP protocol. Figure 9.1 maps UDP to the OSI and DoD reference models.

FIGURE 9.1

Notice that UDP maps to the Transport layer of the OSI model and to the Host-to-Host layer of the DoD model.

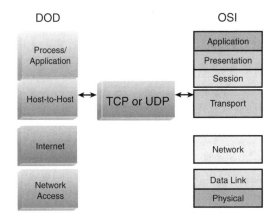

UDP Operation

Like TCP, UDP receives a stream of data (messages) from upper-layer applications or processes identified by ports. UDP at the Transport layer breaks down these streams of data into segments and hands them down to IP at the Network layer, packaging them as datagrams for delivery to the host across the internetwork. Protocol type 17 identifies UDP within the IP header. Figure 9.2 shows UDP identified in an IP header.

FIGURE 9.2

Notice that protocol type 17 identifies UDP within an IP header.

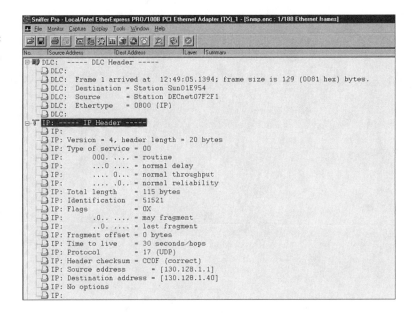

Unlike TCP, UDP does not set up sessions. As a connectionless protocol UDP does not sequence sent data or acknowledge received data. UDP assumes that some other protocol (usually an upper-layer protocol) will track whether the sent data has reached the destination. If the data does not reach its destination, UDP also assumes the upper-layer protocol will recognize this and request a retransmission of the data. Because UDP does not establish a connection, it has no logical circuit to establish before transmission. Because it has no logical connection between end hosts, it has no management responsibilities for maintaining a connection.

UDP does not fragment; it only identifies the source and destination port. Unlike TCP, which breaks upper-layer applications' bit streams into segments, UDP simply provides a bi-directional pipe between communicating devices. UDP relies on IP for fragmentation and reassembly.

UDP operates on a very simple basis—best effort delivery. Whereas TCP guarantees the delivery of data by sequencing and acknowledging every single byte sent or received, UDP offers only best effort delivery, relying on other layers to detect and recover lost or missing datagrams. However, despite not being able to guarantee delivery of packets, UDP has one advantage over TCP—speed. UDP's simplistic nature drastically reduces the overhead involved with transmitting data, making it a much faster, yet unreliable alternative to TCP.

UDP Applications

Application vendors can implement TCP or UDP at the Transport layer depending on the type of service the application requires. For example, most printing applications run on top of TCP because most users want to guarantee a successful print job, rather than hoping it prints. Two upper-layer protocols, FTP (File Transfer Protocol) and TFTP (Trivial File Transfer Protocol) provide similar functions but implement different Transport layer services. Both FTP and TFTP provide file transfer capabilities between hosts. FTP utilizes the services of TCP at the Transport layer to guarantee the successful completion of file transfers, detecting and correcting any lost, missing, or duplicated datagrams. FTP usually is used for the transfer of critical data.

TFTP provides the same file transfer services as FTP, except that it utilizes UDP for faster delivery and less overhead. This method of delivery has the drawback of being less reliable; however, as the name implies (Trivial File Transfer Protocol), TFTP is designed for quick delivery of small files (trivial files) between hosts. As you can see, vendors can choose which Transport layer protocol to implement depending on what type of service is more critical—speed or reliability. TFTP assumes the following:

- Stability of the network infrastructure

- Only trivial delivery errors (if any) may occur

We will discuss FTP in more detail in Chapter 12, "File Transfer Protocol (FTP)," and TFTP in Chapter 16, "Trivial File Transfer Protocol (TFTP)."

UDP Ports

As a connectionless protocol UDP does not sequence or acknowledge data. It simply identifies the sending (source) and receiving (destination) ports within the UDP header and relies on IP to package and deliver the information. Table 9.1 shows a list of common UDP ports (see Appendix C, "TCP/UDP Port Numbers," for a complete list of UDP Ports).

TABLE 9.1 UDP Ports

Decimal	Keyword	Protocol(s)	Description
53	DNS	TCP/UDP	Domain Name Service
67	BootPS	UDP	Bootstrap Protocol Server
68	BootPC	UDP	Bootstrap Protocol Client
69	TFTP	UDP	Trivial File Transfer Protocol
80	SNMP	UDP	Simple Network Management Protocol

UDP Header

In Chapter 7, "Transport/Host-to-Host Layer" we discussed the fields within the TCP header and their functions. TCP headers vary in length, depending on the TCP options in use, but always have a minimum of 20 bytes. However, the connectionless UDP contains minimal information in its header.

By comparison, UDP headers are only 8 bytes in length. Figure 9.3 gives an example of a UDP header as defined in RFC 768. Figure 9.4 shows a tangible UDP header as it actually appears during implementation.

Note

Like TCP, UDP must identify the source and destination ports. Unlike TCP, UDP does not include sequencing or acknowledgements. UDP uses a checksum in the header, which only detects damaged frames.

FIGURE 9.3
This figure merely shows the format of a UDP header. A UDP header contains 8 bytes.

Source Port	Destination Port
Length	Checksum
Data	

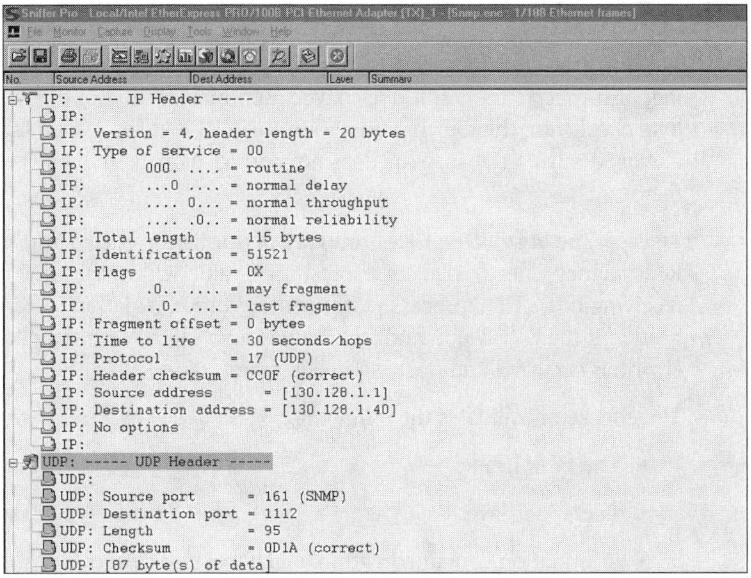

FIGURE 9.4

As you can see, a UDP header does not contain much information.

```
Sniffer Pro - Local/Intel EtherExpress PRO/100B PCI Ethernet Adapter (TX)_1 - [Snmp.enc : 1/188 Ethernet frames]
File  Monitor  Capture  Display  Tools  Window  Help

No.     Source Address          Dest Address          Layer   Summary
IP: ----- IP Header -----
    IP:
    IP: Version = 4, header length = 20 bytes
    IP: Type of service = 00
    IP:        000. .... = routine
    IP:        ...0 .... = normal delay
    IP:        .... 0... = normal throughput
    IP:        .... .0.. = normal reliability
    IP: Total length    = 115 bytes
    IP: Identification  = 51521
    IP: Flags           = 0X
    IP:        .0.. .... = may fragment
    IP:        ..0. .... = last fragment
    IP: Fragment offset = 0 bytes
    IP: Time to live    = 30 seconds/hops
    IP: Protocol        = 17 (UDP)
    IP: Header checksum = CCOF (correct)
    IP: Source address      = [130.128.1.1]
    IP: Destination address = [130.128.1.40]
    IP: No options
    IP:
UDP: ----- UDP Header -----
    UDP:
    UDP: Source port      = 161 (SNMP)
    UDP: Destination port = 1112
    UDP: Length           = 95
    UDP: Checksum         = 0D1A (correct)
    UDP: [87 byte(s) of data]
```

Source Port

The first field within the UDP header identifies the source port. This 2-byte field, similar to the TCP source port field, identifies the sending host's upper-layer application or process. The value of this port depends on whether the sending host is a client process or a server process. If it is a client process, the sending host chooses this port value within the range of 1,024 to 65,535. If this is a server process, such as a well-known application sending a request or responding to a client request, the value ranges between 1 and 1,023.

Destination Port

The second field in the UDP header, the destination port, has a 2-byte field. Similar to the TCP destination port field, it identifies the receiving host's upper-layer application or process. The value of this port depends on whether the receiving host is a client process or a server process. If it is a client process, this port value varies within the range of 1,024 to 65,535. If this is a server process, such as a well-known application, the value ranges between 1 and 1,023.

Length Field

The length field, the third field within the UDP header, specifies in bytes how much data is contained within this datagram. This value includes the UDP header and the data following (upper-layer protocols and information). The length field will be a minimum of 8 bytes, which is the total value of the fields within this header plus any upper-layer data and information.

Checksum

Although the connectionless UDP has no mechanism for detecting and correcting lost, missing, or duplicate frames, it does have a minimal method of detecting damaged frames. The 2-byte checksum, the fourth field within the UDP header, guarantees that the bits have not been damaged during transit. This does not correct damage frames; it simply detects and trashes them.

The sending host UDP process initially performs the checksum, known as a CRC (Cyclic Redundancy Check), placing the resulting value within the UDP header. At the destination, the receiving host's UDP process performs the same calculation to verify the contents of the header. If the CRC value finds the frames invalid, the receiving host assumes a transmission error has occurred and trashes the datagram.

The checksum validates the following:

- The UDP header

- The upper-layer data

- Information contained within a UDP pseudo header

The UDP pseudo header contains 12 bytes for the checksum computation within the UDP datagram. Note that the pseudo header contains certain fields from the IP header. However, the UDP pseudo header does not actually appear in the UDP header. UDP uses the pseudo header to ensure that data has arrived at the correct destination. Figure 9.5 shows an example of a UDP pseudo header.

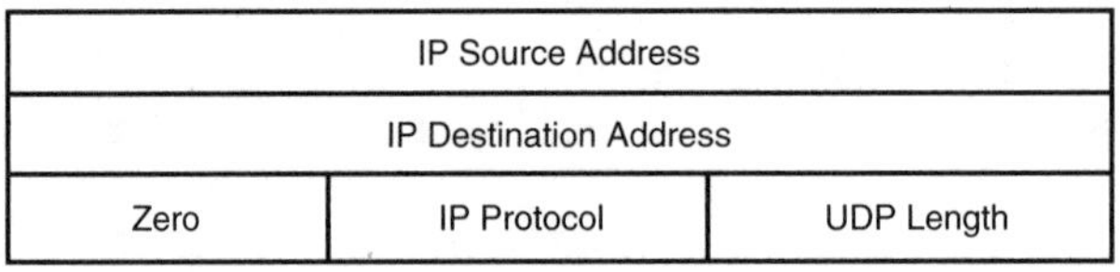

FIGURE 9.5
A UDP pseudo header enables UDP to make sure IP has not delivered or accepted a datagram to the wrong location, whether an incorrect host or upper layer.

IP Source Address		
IP Destination Address		
Zero	IP Protocol	UDP Length

The pseudo IP header contains the following information:

- Logical source address

- Destination network layer address

- Transport layer protocol type code

- UDP length

The UDP pseudo header has its name because UDP does not actually include this information within its header; instead it keeps track of this information to guard against misrouted datagrams. The host stores this information in its memory and UDP accesses it for reference purposes.

Summary

RFC 768 defines UDP. UDP offers fast, unreliable delivery of messages between applications running on remote hosts. UDP receives a stream of data (messages) from upper-layer applications or processes. UDP at the Transport layer breaks down these streams of data into segments and hands them down to IP at the Network layer, packaging them as datagrams for delivery to the host across the internetwork.

As a connectionless protocol UDP does not sequence sent data or acknowledge received data. UDP relies on other protocols to track whether sent data reaches its destination. Because UDP has no logical connection, this also means that it has no management responsibilities for maintaining a connection. UDP operates on a best effort delivery; although it cannot guarantee delivery of packets, the simplistic nature of UDP drastically reduces overhead and provides an alternative to the slower TCP. Application vendors can implement TCP or UDP at the Transport layer, depending on the type of service the application requires.

Review Questions

1. What RFC defines UDP?

2. What does UDP provide for applications running on remote hosts?

3. What protocol type identifies UDP in the IP header?

4. What relationship does UDP have with sequencing and acknowledging the receipt of sent data?

5. During UDP operation of transferring data, what does this protocol assume?

6. What management responsibilities does UDP have with maintaining a connection?

7. What does UDP offer that TCP doesn't?

8. What mechanism does UDP use to check only for damaged frames?

9. What three things does the checksum validate?

10. The UDP pseudo header contains what information?

CHAPTER 10

UPPER-LAYER PROTOCOLS

You will learn about the following in this chapter:

- Application Layer
- Presentation Layer

- Session Layer
- Upper-layer Protocols

Introduction to Upper-layer Protocols

The Process/Application layer of the DoD model considers the three upper-layer protocols of the OSI model—Application, Presentation, and Session—as one layer. At the Process/Application layer, you can interact with the host to perform these user functions:

- File transfer (FTP or TFTP)

- Client/Server file operations through Sun Microsystems (NFS)

- Remote access (Telnet)

- E-mail (SMTP)

- Network management (SNMP)

- Name resolution (DNS)

All the previously mentioned protocols have their own characteristics and reside at different layers of the OSI model, but sit on top of the DoD model as the single Process/Application layer. In this chapter we will discuss each layer in the OSI model, describe its function, and briefly describe each of the upper-layer protocols (ULPs). Figure 10.1 shows the different protocols that reside on the Process/Application layer and how it relates to the OSI model.

FIGURE 10.1

Note that the OSI model has three separate layers that reside in the Process/Application layer (the upper layer) of the DoD model.

ARPA Layer | **Protocol Implementation** | **OSI Layer**

ARPA Layer	Protocol Implementation								OSI Layer
	Hypertext Transfer	File Transfer	Electronic Mail	Terminal Emulation	Domain Names	File Transfer	Client / Server	Network Management	Application
Process / Application	Hypertext Transfer Protocol (HTTP) RFC 2068	File Transfer Protocol (FTP) MIL-STD-1780 RFC 959	Simple Mail Transfer Protocol (SMTP) MIL-STD-1781 RFC 821	TELNET Protocol MIL-STD-1782 RFC 854	Domain Name System (DNS) RFC 1034, 1035	Trivial File Transfer Protocol (TFTP) RFC 783	Sun Microsystems Network File System Protocols (NSF) RFCs 1014, 1057 and 1094	Simple Network Management Protocol (SNMP) v1: RFC 1157 v2: RFC1901-10 v3: RCF 2271-75	Presentation
									Session
Host-to-Host	Transmission Control Protocol (TCP) MIL-STD-1778 RFC 793						User Datagram Protocol (UDP) RFC 768		Transport
Internet	Address Resolution ARP RFC 826 RARP RFC 903			Internet Protocol (IP) MIL-STD-1777 RFC 791			Internet Control Message Protocol (ICMP) RFC 792		Network
Network Interface	Network Interface Cards: Ethernet, Token Ring, ARCNET, MAN and WAN RFC 894, RFC 1042, RFC 1201, and others								Data Link
	Transmission Media: Twisted Pair, Coax, Fiber Optics, Wireless Media, etc.								Physical

Unlike the other layers in the OSI and DoD models, the upper layers do not appear transparent to the end user. Users access the upper layer directly though the host's operating system. End users use the uppers layer to perform tasks like file transfer, network management, e-mail, and so on.

Application Layer

Many people confuse the *application layer* with *applications* such as Word, Excel, PowerPoint, and so on. Think of the Application layer as an open window that allows you access to the OSI model. The Application layer enables your applications to send data across the network. It simply allows access to the lower layers—a window to the OSI model.

For example, when you access your e-mail, you must specify the data you want to send. Of course, the Application prepares this data by adding header and control information for the peer layer before it passes it down to the next layer and eventually sends it out on the wire. The Application layer provides access to file and print services; for example, Microsoft's SMB-based *client redirector* and the *server responder,* which are implemented as file system drivers (RDR.sys and SRV.sys, respectively).

If you use Windows NT, your client redirector works as an Application-layer protocol. When you make a request for file and print services of a remote NT box, your redirector prepares that information for the next layer. The adjacent layer gets it ready to send over the wire. When it sends that information to the remote host, the receiving layer at the other end resides on the Application layer. This layer on the remote host corresponds with the server service; thus, the client requester piece and the server responder piece in Windows NT provide the requests and responses on behalf of an application (considered *Application layer services*).

Remember that the Application layer provides an interface to your protocol stack. Application layer services include the following:

- Applications with network and internetwork services
- File and print services
- E-mail
- Web access and HTTP
- Telnet access on a remote host
- File transfer (FTP and TFTP)

World Wide Web and HTTP (Hypertext Transfer Protocol)

Although almost everyone on the planet knows about the World Wide Web (WWW), most do not know that the protocol HTTP gives users access to the Web. The key mechanism for WWW communication, HTTP, enables you to transfer Web documents from server to a browser using TCP and a basic client/server architecture. Web pages consist of hypermedia documents. The prefix *hyper* means that a document can consist of links that refer to correlated documents; for example, links to Web pages that contain information about Picasso. The suffix *media* describes various items other than straight text, such as multimedia images.

When you want to access a Web page, you type in the URL (Uniform Resource Locator). The URL identifies a specific Web page and each Web page has an assigned unique name that identifies it. When you type in a request, or URL, it invokes a Web browser (the client) to access the server to obtain the Web page that you desire. HTTP allows for the communication between a browser and a Web server or between the intermediate machines, such as gateways and firewalls. We will discuss HTTP in greater detail in Chapter 15, "Hypertext Transfer Protocol (HTTP)."

E-mail and SMTP (Simple Mail Transfer Protocol)

Electronic mail (e-mail) enables you to send messages across the Internet using a standard client/server architecture. The client/server architecture enables both sides to send, store, and receive messages. SMTP dictates the standard for the exchange of e-mail between machines.

Mail systems use a technique called *spooling*. When you send a message to someone, the system stores the message (data) in a private area (called a *spool*) along with the delivery address (mailbox or e-mail address), sender's name, recipient's name and time the message was sent. The system then transfers the message to a remote machine (a background transfer). This enables the sender to continue using his or her machine after sending e-mail without waiting for the receiver to open the message.

The remote client machine uses the domain name system (DNS) to map to the receiver's IP address and forms a TCP connection to the mail server. When it succeeds, it transfers the copy of the message to the mail server, which stores it in its spool for the receiver to access. We will discuss SMTP in more detail in Chapter 13, "Simple Mail Transfer Protocol (SMTP)."

Telnet (Telecommunications Network)

It's three o'clock in the morning and you'd prefer to go back to sleep, but you need to check on a remote machine. Chances are you would want to use the Telnet protocol instead of driving all the way to work in your pajamas. Telnet enables you (the client) at a terminal to access a remote host (server). Using TCP, Telnet enables you to communicate directly from your keyboard as if connected to the remote machine. The path of data travels from your keyboard to your operating system (client) through a TCP connection to the remote operating system (server).

Telnet uses a network virtual terminal (NVT) to allow for a canonical (a standard) representation of data. Telnet also allows for client and server option negotiation. Additionally, Telnet provides symmetry in the negotiation syntax, which allows for either the client or server of the connection to request a specific option. We will discuss Telnet in more detail in Chapter 11, "Telnet."

File Transfer

Two protocols that provide file transfer service reside on the application layer: FTP (File Transfer Protocol) and TFTP (Trivial File Transfer Protocol). More people use FTP than TFTP; FTP accounts for a large portion of TCP/IP traffic. Both protocols enable you to transfer (read or write) files from your computer from a remote machine. Some companies have a file server in lieu of more expensive computers with local disk storage. Whichever protocol you employ, it dictates and enables the transfer of files between a client system and a server system.

FTP uses two TCP connections: one for data and one for control. This guarantees transfer of files, although it is slower. TFTP uses UDP, which does not guarantee delivery of the file but enables fast file transfer between machines. We will discuss FTP in more detail in Chapter 12, "File Transfer Protocol (FTP)," and TFTP in Chapter 16, "Trivial File Transfer Protocol (TFTP)."

Presentation Layer

The Presentation layer is layer 6 of the OSI model, just below the Application layer. At this layer data still appears in message format to be passed down to the Session layer. The Presentation layer primarily provides a common data format across different platforms. In other words, the Presentation layer translates information from the Application layer into a language that all the other layers can easily understand. The Presentation layer has the following responsibilities:

- Data conversion and translation

- Compression/decompression

- Encryption/decryption

- Multimedia and sound

Table 10.1 shows commonly used Presentation layer protocols.

TABLE 10.1 Commonly Used Protocols

Types	Protocols
Text- and data-related protocols	ASCII EBCDIC Encryption/decryption
Graphics or image-related protocols	TIFF
Presentation layer protocols	JPEG PICT GIF
Multimedia protocols	MIDI MPEG QuickTime

Several protocols existed before the introduction of the OSI model, but are still used today within the modern OSI model. This means that only a few true Presentation layer protocols exist, and that most ULPs do not map neatly to the OSI model. Most vendors implement protocols that span the entire upper three layers, skipping layers or performing functions on all three layers. Vendors decide which layer ULPs will perform on which level; thus some protocols may perform Presentation layer functions, but perform other ULP functions as well. In short, a true Presentation layer protocol is hard to find.

There is one true Presentation layer protocol: XDR (external data representation). Sun Microsystems utilizes XDR in its client/server-based Network File System (NFS) implementations. NFS uses this protocol, which is incorporated into the programming code to provide platform independence. We will discuss XDR and NFS in more detail in Chapter 18, "Open Network Computing Protocols."

Session Layer

The Session layer resides on layer 5 of the OSI Model, below the Presentation layer. At this layer data still appears in message format to be passed down to the Transport layer. This is the last layer in which user data remains in message format before the Transport layer changes them into segments.

Think of the Session layer as an activity coordinator. The Session layer coordinates dialog between two applications (an upper layer and lower layer). The Session layer then manages the communication activity of each side, monitoring the dialog and terminating the session when necessary.

The Session layer also controls the type and efficiency of conversation between the two applications. Applications can communicate in *full-duplex* or *half-duplex* mode. Half-duplex allows only one device to speak (transmit) at a time, like a one-way radio. Full-duplex allows either side to transmit simultaneously.

The Session layer includes the following protocols:

- NetBIOS
- SQL
- X Windows
- RPC

NetBIOS (Network Basic Input Output System)

Developed by IBM and Sytek, NetBIOS allows applications access to network devices. NetBIOS provides four main services: name service, session service, datagram service, and miscellaneous function. This book focuses on name service.

NetBIOS provides a simple way for users to access remote resources and service by using a name rather than an address. NetBIOS performs name resolution by transmitting a broadcast, querying the local segment for address resolution. Modifications to NetBIOS enable it to function at layer 3 by utilizing TCP/IP. We will discuss NetBIOS in more detail in Chapter 14, "Name Resolution."

NFS (Network File System) and ONC Protocols

Originally developed by Sun Microsystems, NFS enables a set of cooperating computers to share online files as if they were local. The file sharing appears nearly transparent to the user. Some companies also utilize NFS to interconnect their file systems.

NFS operates at the Application layer but requires two other protocols for functionality: XDR (eXternal Data Representation) and RPC (Remote Procedure Call). As the name suggests, XDR resides at the Presentation layer. RPC resides at the Session layer. The protocol group (XDR, NFS and RPC) is referred to as the ONC (Open Network Computing) protocols. Collectively, this family of protocols enables disparate systems to access files transparently, supporting PC-to-mainframe technologies.

A data representation language, XDR provides consistent data representation between different NFS implementations. A transport-independent messaging protocol, RPC enables transparent communication between a client and a server. We will discuss all the ONC protocol in more detail in Chapter 18.

Summary

The Process/Application layer of the DoD model considers the three upper-layer protocols of the OSI model to be one layer, referred to as upper-layer protocols. At this layer you can interact with the host to perform user functions. You can perform the following functions at this layer: file transfer, client/server file operations, remote access, e-mail, network management, and name resolution.

The three layers of the OSI Model that comprise the Process/Application layer of the DoD model are the Application, Presentation, and Session layers. The Application layer enables your applications to send data across the network. The Presentation layer primarily provides a common data format across different platforms. The Session layer coordinates dialogs between network devices.

Review Questions

1. What three OSI layers does the Process/Application layer of the DoD model consist of?

2. What is the primary function of the Process/Application layer?

3. What protocols reside at the Application layer?

4. What is the primary function of the Presentation layer?

5. What is the primary function of the Session layer?

6. What are the ONC protocols and on what layers do they reside?

CHAPTER 11

TELNET

You will learn about the following in this chapter:

- Telnet Client-server Relationship
- Telnet's Basic Services
- Network Virtual Terminal (NVT)
- Telnet Options

Remote Access

The Telnet (Telecommunications Network) protocol enables a user running a client terminal session to access a remote host (or Telnet server) across TCP/IP Internets. Telnet operates with TCP as the connection-oriented transport using well-known port 23 and enables the terminal and host to exchange 8-bit characters of data. Designed to work with any host and any terminal, Telnet establishes a TCP connection with a remote host; it then enables you to type commands from a keyboard as if attached to the remote machine's keyboard. With Telnet you can also read the remote host's output. The Telnet client-server relationship runs transparently, which means it gives the appearance that the keyboard and output display attaches directly to a remote host. Figure 11.1 shows the implementation of a Telnet client and server and illustrates a series of events that must happen to establish a Telnet session:

1. When you start the Telnet session, an application on the machine becomes the client.

2. The client establishes a TCP connection with a Telnet server (remote host) using the standard TCP three-way handshake as described in Chapter 8, "Transmission Control Protocol (TCP)."

3. The client communicates over the TCP connection from the keyboard and display as if connected directly to the remote host's terminal.

4. The server utilizes a pseudo terminal device. The pseudo terminal device describes the operating system entry point that allows a program such as Telnet to transfer data to another operating system as if coming from the same keyboard.

Telnet was developed in the 1970s when end devices were very expensive and dumb, typically relying on a remote host for processing. Dumb terminals would transmit each character one at a time to the remote server, which would echo the command issued by the client back to their screen. The clients needed this process because they had no place to store or process information. Today there are intelligent client devices that maintain their own resources and perform their own local processing if necessary, but they still must emulate the original model. Modern client devices now support transmission modes, such as line mode, making some Telnet implementations more efficient; however, not all implementations support this.

FIGURE 11.1
The data travels from the keyboard to the remote operating system.

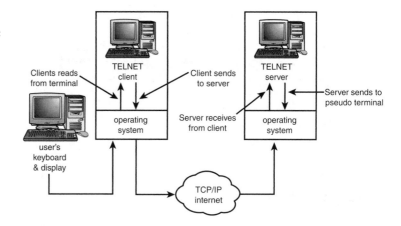

Transmission Modes

There are various transmission modes, including character and line mode. Character mode means one character, or one byte, is transmitted at a time—the least efficient method of transmission. Line mode allows an entire line to be transmitted in one chunk, allowing for a more efficient means of transmission.

Despite its lack of sophistication compared to other protocols, administrators widely use Telnet as a remote administration and troubleshooting tool. Usually, Telnet client software enables the user to attach to a remote machine by specifying its IP host name or IP address. When a Telnet client requests a session using an IP host name, the client first needs to resolve that name to a logical Network layer address and then to a local hardware address.

If a host attempts the connection using the Network layer address it only needs to perform the last two steps. Once the local host knows the local hardware address to use, it can address a datagram to the hardware address. TCP then can set up the connection between the hosts, making Telnet operational. We will describe name resolution in more detail in Chapter 14, "Name Resolution."

Telnet resides at the upper three layers (Application, Presentation, and Session) of the OSI model or the Process/Application layer of the DoD model (see Figure 10.1 in Chapter 10, "Upper-layer Protocols"). In the OSI model this arrangement has advantages and disadvantages. Telnet has the obvious advantage of an administrator making modifications to a device to which it is not directly attached. Additionally, the code is not embedded within the operating system, which makes it easier for an administrator to use.

However, Telnet is rather inefficient. Consider that each keystroke must travel

1. Through the operating system of the client.

2. From the client through the intranet or Internet to the server.

3. Through the server's operating system.

4. Back to the client, delivering the data to the application program the user is running.

Meanwhile, data in the form of output display has to travel back to the client over the same path. This requires a lot of overhead; thus it is an inefficient use of resources. In addition, this process occurs over a TCP session, which requires that each transmission be sequenced and acknowledgements returned, adding more overhead. With Telnet you trade overhead for reliability.

Basic Services

RFC 854 discusses Telnet's three basic services, and RFC 855 discusses the different Telnet options. We discuss the various Telnet options later in this chapter. Telnet offers three basics services:

1. Network Virtual Terminal (NVT), which provides a standard interface to remote systems

2. Capability for clients and servers to negotiate various options

3. Symmetric view of terminals and processes

We will discuss the basic services Telnet provides in the following sections.

Network Virtual Terminal

Telnet communicates by using TCP/IP protocols and bases its communication on a set of network standards (also called the canonical or standard form) known as Network Virtual Terminal (NVT). The NVT provides transparency and support for a minimum level of options between remote clients and servers being used by either side. By implementing a virtual terminal as a front end, this hides the differences between the communicating devices and provides a common set of commands and characteristics, in a sense creating all communicating devices "equal."

During Telnet, the user or client end is responsible for mapping incoming NVT codes to the actual codes required to operate the user's display device, making communication between disparate systems seamless. It also is responsible for converting keyboard sequences into NVT sequences. RFC 854 defines NVT as an imaginary device that forces the client operating system to map whatever type of terminal the user is on to the NVT, emulating a common terminal such as IBM 3270, VT100, VT200, and so on. The server then maps the NVT to whatever terminal type the server supports. When both ends convert their data into the canonical or standard form, they can communicate regardless of what kind of terminal each end has (for example, if one is DEC VT-100).

NVT ASCII

The defined NVT format uses a 7-bit ASCII code throughout the Internet protocol suite for characters and display devices. It transmits the 7-bit ASCII code in 8-bit octets with the most significant bit set to 0. The RFC defines the display device as a printer and requires it only to display the standard printing ASCII characters, the American Standard Code for Information Interchange, represented by 7-bit does and to recognize and process certain control codes.

ASCII
Many applications use ASCII code. Computers send messages in ASCII for you to read. These messages can range from error messages to status messages. ASCII represents both textual data (letters, numbers, and punctuation marks) and control characters, which are commands such as return and line feed.

This enables Telnet to operate between as many systems as possible because it accommodates the details of heterogeneous computers and operating systems. Some systems use different lines of text (for example, *carriage control* or *linefeed* character). To accommodate this Telnet defines how data and command sequences are sent across the Internet. Figure 11.2 shows the conversion process from the local host format to the NVT format.

FIGURE 11.2
NVT operation involves the conversion of user terminal and host format to and from NVT format.

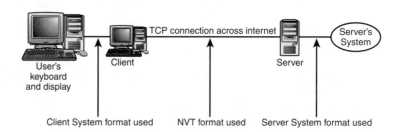

The NVT keyboard can generate all 128 ASCII codes by using keys, key combinations, or sequences, which include

- 95 characters that have printable graphics (letters, digits, punctuation marks) and share the same meaning

- 33 control codes

Table 11.1 shows the standard control codes that all Network Virtual Terminal implementations must understand.

TABLE 11.1   NVT Required Control Codes

Name	Code	Decimal Value	Function
NULL	NUL	0	No operation.
Line Feed	LF	10	Moves the printer to the next print line, keeping the same horizontal position.
Carriage Return	CR	13	Moves the printer to the left margin of the current line.

Table 11.2 shows optional control codes that still should have the indicated effect on the display whether understood by the NVT or not.

TABLE 11.2   Optional NVT Control Codes

Name	Code	Decimal Value	Function
BELL	BEL	7	Makes an audible or visible sign (does not move print head).
Back Space	BS	8	Moves print head one character position towards the left margin.
Horizontal Tab	HT	9	Moves the printer to the next horizontal tab stop. Remains unspecified how either end determines whether the location of tab stops.
Vertical Tab	VT	11	Moves the printer to the next vertical tab stop. How either end determines the location of the tab stops remains unspecified.
Form Feed	FF	12	Moves the printer to the top of the next page, keeping the same horizontal position. On visual displays this commonly clears the screen and moves the cursor to the top left corner.

Telnet Commands

Telnet NVT provides various commands that control interactions between the client and server and incorporates these commands into the data stream. The Telnet commands consist of a mandatory two-octet sequence and an optional third. Telnet uses the first octet to indicate that the information being sent is a command and should be interpreted as such, known as the "Interpret as command" (IAC) character. The second octet identifies the code for one of the commands listed in Table 11.3. The third octet further identifies the command's meaning when the previous command code is not enough. Table 11.4 shows the various TELNET options.

TABLE 11.3   Telnet Commands When Followed By IAC (255)

Command	Decimal Code	Meaning
EOF	236	End-of-file.
SUSP	237	Suspend current process (job control).
ABORT	238	Abort process.
EOR	239	End of record.
SE	240	End of subnegotiation parameters.
NOP	241	No operation.
DM	242	Data mark, portion of a Synch. Always accompanied with a TCP urgent notification.
BRK	243	Break; indicates the "break" signal.
IP	244	Suspend, interrupt or abort the process.
AO	245	Abort output. Allows the completion of the current process but does not send output to the user.
AYT	246	Are you there. Visible proof that the other end received the AYT.
EC	247	Erase character. The receiver should delete the last preceding undeleted character from the data stream.
EL	248	Erase line. Delete characters from the data stream back to but not including the previous CRLF.
GA	249	Go ahead. Tell other send that it can transmit.
SB	250	Subnegotiation of the indicated option follows.
WILL	251	Option negotiation. Indicates the desire to begin performing, or confirmation that you are now performing the indicated option.
WONT	252	Option negotiation. Indicates the refusal to perform, or continue performing the indicated option.
DO	253	Option negotiation. Indicates the request that the other party perform, or conformation that you expect the other party to perform the indicated option.
DONT	254	Option negotiation. Indicates the demand that the other party stop performing, or conformation that you no longer expect the other party to perform, the indicated option.
IAC	255	Interpret next octet as command.

Option Negotiation

Despite both sides assuming an NVT, Telnet's first exchange takes place with an option negotiation signal. Clients and servers use option negotiation to agree on features and options to be implemented during communication. Telnet treats both sides of the connection symmetrically—either side can request the use of an optional feature.

If the other side does not support the feature or is prohibited from using this feature, it rejects the request. Both sides agree upon and use the supported features and keep all other options at the minimum NVT standard. Once the client and server complete negotiation, they can begin to exchange data over the Telnet session.

Either side can send the following four requests:

- **WILL**—Sender wants to enable the option.

- **DO**—Sender wants the receiver to enable the option.

- **WONT**—Sender wants to disable the option.

- **DONT**—Senders wants the receiver to disable the option.

Figure 11.3 shows a Telnet session being set up by TCP using a three-way handshake. Figure 11.3 also shows negotiations between a client and a server as well as a client login. Notice TCP port 23 is the destination (D=23) port in the first frame.

FIGURE 11.3

Once the TCP session is set up (in frames 1, 2 and 3), the Telnet client and server negotiations begin, using WILL, DO, WONT and DONT exchanges.

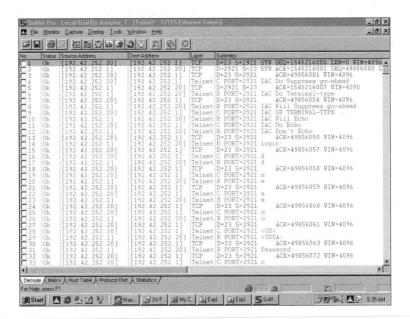

Telnet Options

A Telnet client and server can negotiate a variety of options using commands at any stage of the connection. This symmetry allows either the client or server to reconfigure its connection. The RFCs describe each one of these commands separately. Although more than 40 options exist, Table 11.4 shows the most important and widely used options.

TABLE 11.4   Telnet Options

Decimal Code	Name	RFC	Meaning
0	Binary transmission	856	Change transmission to 8-bit binary.
1	Echo	857	Permit one side to echo data it receives.
3	Suppress go ahead	858	No longer send go-ahead signal after data.
5	Status	859	Request for status of a TELNET option from a remote site.
6	Timing mark	860	Request the insertion of a timing mark in the return stream to synchronize the ends of a connection.
24	Terminal type	1091	Exchange information about the make and model of the terminal in use. This enables programs to alter output like cursor positioning sequences for the user's terminal.
25	End of record	885	Terminate data sent with EOR code.
31	Window size	1073	Convey window size to a Telnet server.
32	Terminal speed	1079	Exchange terminal speed information.
33	Remote flow control	1372	Enables, disables, and regulates flow control.
34	Linemode	1116	Use local editing and send complete lines; not single characters.
36	Environment variables	1408	Propagates configuration information.

The client and server agree on options through a process of negotiation that result in a common view of various extra capabilities that affect the interchange and operation of applications. Like most Telnet operations either end can enable or disable an option either locally or remotely. The initiator of the communication sends a 3-byte command:

IAC, (type of operation), (command)

The receiver responds in the same 3-byte form.

In addition, TELNET allows for either side to accept or reject a request to enable an option, but requires a side to always accept a request to disable. Table 11.5 shows an example of possible Telnet scenarios given these four option negotiations commands: WILL, DO, WONT and DONT.

TABLE 11.5   Various Possible Responses

Sender Sent	Receiver Responds	Implication
WILL	DO	Sender wants to enable an option if the receiver can handle it; receiver responds that it can. Option goes into effect.
WILL	DONT	Sender wants to enable an option if the receiver can handle it; receiver cannot support the option. Option does not go into effect.
DO	WILL	Sender wants the receiver to enable an option; receiver responds that it can. Option goes into effect.
DO	WONT	Sender wants the receiver to enable an option; the receiver responds that it can't. Option does not go into effect.
WONT	DONT	Sender wants to disable an option. Receiver can respond only with DONT, which confirms the sender's request.
DONT	WONT	Sender wants the receiver to disable an option. Receiver can respond only with WONT, which confirms that it will no longer perform this option.

For example, if the sender wants to the other end to echo, it sends the following byte sequence:

255 (IAC), 251 (WILL), 1 (ECHO)

The final byte of the three-byte sequence identifies the action. If the receiver can support the option, it will respond with

255 (IAC), 253 (DO), 1 (ECHO)

A Telnet client server exchange basically boils down to either side (a client or server) saying to the other, "I will *x*," which means "*Will you allow me to use option x?*" The receiver then responds either, "I DO *x*," or "I DONT *x*," which means either "*I do allow you to use option x*" or "*I don't allow you to use option x.*" Either way, both sides respond in symmetry for option processing—the receiving side responds with a positive or negative response to the sender's request.

Figures 11.4, 11.5, and 11.6 show the option negotiation process between client and server.

FIGURE 11.4

Note that the server (TCP port 23) is asking the client (TCP port 2921) to identify its terminal type (IAC Do Terminal-Type).

FIGURE 11.5

The client states its terminal type as Sun.

FIGURE 11.6

The server negotiates who will echo keystrokes and also includes the terminal type agreed upon as SunOS (Unix-based operating system).

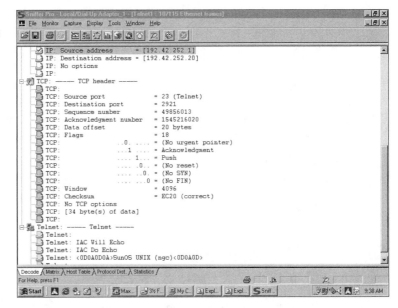

Suboption Negotiation

Some of the negotiable option values require more information once both sides have agreed on the support of the option (either disabled or enabled). Normally the client sends and the server responds with the initial 3-byte sequence. The client and server communicate values through an exchange of value query commands and responses in the following forms:

IAC (255), SB (250), (option code number), 1, IAC, SE

and

IAC (255), SB (250), (option code), 0, (value), IAC, SE

The suboption information includes the specific value to facilitate implementation of the agreed-upon feature.

Summary

Telnet establishes a TCP connection with a remote host; it then allows you to type commands from your keyboard as if attached to the remote machine's keyboard. With Telnet you can read the remote host's output as well. The Telnet client-server relationship runs transparently, which means it gives the appearance that your keyboard and output display attaches directly to a remote host.

Telnet offers three basics services: Network Virtual Terminal (NVT), client and server negotiation of various options, and a symmetric view of terminals and processes. The NVT provides transparency and support for a minimum level of options between remote clients and servers used by either side.

Telnet NVT provides various commands that control interactions between the client and server. Telnet incorporates these commands into the data stream. Telnet uses the first octet, known as the interpret as command (IAC) character, to indicate that the information being sent is a command.

Clients and servers use option negotiation to agree on features and options to be implemented during communication. Telnet treats both sides of the connection symmetrically—either side can request the use of an optional feature. Either side can request WILL, DO, WONT, or DONT.

Review Questions

1. What does Telnet enable a user to do?

2. What series of events have to occur to establish a Telnet session?

3. What are Telnet options used for?

4. Although there are more than 40 Telnet options, what are the 12 most important and widely used options?

5. What three basic services does Telnet offer?

6. What is the NVT and what function does it provide during Telnet operation?

7. What is the 7-bit ASCII code used for?

8. What does symmetrical connection mean?

9. What is the IAC character?

10. During option negotiation what four requests can either side ask for?

11. What six possible various responses can occur during option negotiation?

CHAPTER 12

FILE TRANSFER PROTOCOL (FTP)

You will learn about the following in this chapter:

- FTP Session
- Data Representation
- Data Structures

- Transmission Modes
- Commands
- Replies

Introduction to File Transfer

RFC 959 describes one of the most popular Process/Application protocols within TCP/IP applications, File Transfer Protocol (FTP). FTP accounts for most of the file transfer on the Internet and enables a remote or local client and server to efficiently transfer files or data using TCP's reliable transport. In other words, it enables the user to transfer files between two computers; usually through the Internet. Generally speaking, you have to have an account on the remote FTP server to access files (see anonymous FTP later in this chapter). Refer to Figure 10.1 in Chapter 10, "Upper-layer Protocols," to see how FTP maps to the OSI and DoD model.

FTP has four objectives:

- Promote sharing of files (computer programs or data)
- Encourage indirect or implicit use of remote computers
- Shield a user from variations in file storage systems among hosts
- Transfer data reliably and efficiently

FTP provides file transfer services between remote hosts. File transfer copies a complete file from system to system. With FTP you must identify yourself to the FTP server through a unique user or anonymous (if supported) account to log on and transfer files, which we explain later in this chapter. Like Telnet, FTP works between different hosts, which can run different operating systems using different file structures and even different character sets. Unlike Telnet, which uses the 7-bit ASCII NVT to achieve heterogeneity, FTP supports a limited number of file types and file structures.

The History of FTP

FTP's long evolution started in 1971 when Abhay Bhushan (RFC 114) developed the first transfer file mechanisms for implementation on hosts at MIT. Eric Harslem and John Heafner followed shortly thereafter with RFC 141, "Comments on RFC 114 (a File Transfer Protocol)." The rest of FTP's history unfolds as follows:

- **June 23, 1971**—Bhushan provides RFC 172, a user-level oriented protocol for file transfer between host computers (including terminal IMPs).
- **November 17, 1971**—Bhushan revises RFC 172 in RFC 265.
- **December 8, 1971**—Alex McKenzie suggests further changes in RFC 281.
- **January 25, 1972**—Bhushan proposes the use of "set data type" in RFC 294.
- **July 8, 1972**—Bhushan introduces RFC 354, which makes RFCs 264 and 265 obsolete. At this point Bhushan defines FTP as a protocol for file transfer between hosts on the ARPANET, with the main function of FTP to transfer files efficiently and reliably between hosts and to allow the convenient use of remote file storage capabilities.
- **February 16, 1973**—McKenzie publishes the first official FTP document in RFC 454.
- **July 12, 1973**—Nancy Neigus publishes the new official FTP document in RFC 542. Although the general structure remains the same, RFC 542 reflects the considerable changes from the previous versions of FTP.
- **1974**—A barrage of comments appears in RFCs 607, 614, and 624 (and countless others). This inspires RFC 686 entitled *Leaving Well Enough Alone*, by Brian Harvey on May 10, 1975.
- **June, 1980**—Motivated by the change from NCP to TCP, Jon Postel publishes RFC 765 as the specification of FTP for use on TCP.
- **October, 1985**—Postel and Joyce Reynolds publish the current specification of FTP, RFC 959. This RFC corrects some minor documentation errors, improves the explanation of some protocol features, and adds some commands.

FTP Session

Say you need to download a new driver for your Soundblaster. You initiate this by locally executing an FTP session through your Internet browser. Typically, an FTP session involves the interaction of five software elements:

- **User Interface**—Provides a user interface and drives the client protocol interpreter.
- **Client PI**—The client protocol interpreter. Issues commands to the remote server protocol interpreter and drives the client data transfer process.
- **Server PI**—The server protocol interpreter. Responds to commands from the Client PI and drives the server data transfer process.

- **Client DTP**—Client data transfer process. Communicates with the server data process and the local file system.

- **Server DTP**—Server data transfer process. Communicates with the client DTP and the remote file system.

The User-FTP includes

- User Interface (UI)

- Client Protocol Interpreter (PI)

- Client Data Transfer Process (DTP)

The Server-FTP includes

- Server Protocol Interpreter (PI) (control port)

- Server Data Transfer Process (DTP) (data port)

FTP differs from other protocols in that it utilizes two separate TCP port connections: one between the PIs, the control connection and one between the DTPs, the data connection. The client and server PIs use a TCP control connection to establish and manage the FTP communication between hosts. This TCP connection establishes itself through the normal client-server manner. This TCP connection must be established before either host can transfer data.

The server PI listens on well-known port number 21 for control connection requests and waits for a client communication. The client PI initiates the connection by sending a TCP SYN request (see Chapter 8, "Transmission Control Protocol (TCP)") in the form of a control message addressed to the destination TCP on well-known port 21. Once both sides have established a control connection, this connection stays active for the entire time the client communicates with the server. FTP uses the connection for commands from the client to the server and for the server's responses to the client.

The DTPs create a data connection every time a client and server transfer a file; this also can occur at other times (as shown later in this chapter). The client passes a data address to the well-known port 20 (designated FTP data port) on the server DTP. The client FTP side uses an internally assigned (variable) client port number. Thus, FTP uses two logical connection paths: one for control (port 21) and one for data (port 20). The control connection TCP port 21 must exist before any data exchange. When a user wants to transfer a file (send or retrieve), the user executes an FTP command to do so. This causes a second connection to open for data transfer (TCP port 20).

FTP can make use of the "minimize delay" ToS within the IP for the IP type of service because the user normally types in the commands, which is a slow process. TCP utilizes this information to set the push bit within its header, causing each host's session to send FTP messages up the protocol stack for processing without delay. This increases the processing time during client-server exchanges.

Note

Remember an application can use IP type of service to request a router to forward traffic along a specific path based on the level of service requested. For more about ToS, please refer to Chapter 3, "Network Layer/Internet Protocols."

The data connection also can use the "maximize throughput" ToS within the IP header to increase file transfer performance.

Implementations vary by vendor; however, the result of using the appropriate qualities of services for both control and data is increased performance, which speeds the client-server negotiation and file transfers. Figure 12.1 shows a general diagram of an FTP client server relationship. Figures 12.2 and 12.3 show the two different connections between client and server as seen through a Sniffer.

FIGURE 12.1
The protocol interpreter deals with the commands and replies. The user interface presents the type of interface used to the interactive user and converts these into FTP commands sent across the connection.

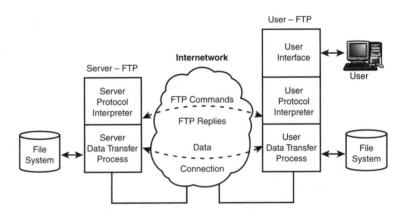

FIGURE 12.2

As you can see, the client (64.0.0.57) has a variable port 2001 (within the range 1024 through 65536). Note that the push bit is set to speed the processing of information.

FIGURE 12.3

An FTP data port opens each time a file transfer is requested using TCP port 20 (well-known TCP server port for FTP data). Note the data being sent within the FTP header.

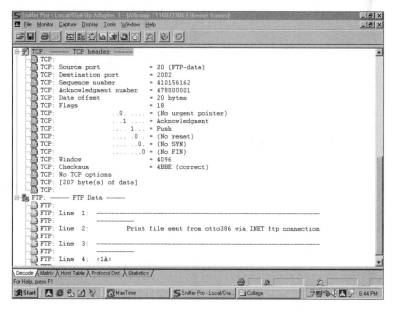

Data Representation

FTP has many options to resolve data representation and storage. Before data transmission between client and server, session negotiation must occur, with both sides agreeing on data representation parameters. Figure 12.4 shows a client and server negotiating the file type.

FIGURE 12.4
FTP clients and servers negotiate the file type being transferred. In this example the file type being sent is ASCII (seen in the FTP header).

There are three parameters FTP needs to decide on prior to transferring a file:

- **Data representation**—Identifies the type of data being sent
- **Data structure**—Specifies the format of the data being transferred
- **Transmission mode**—Specifies how the data transmits across the connection

FTP can represent data in one of four ways:

- ASCII (default)
- EBCDIC
- Image file type (also called binary)
- Local file type

In addition, ASCII and EBCDIC file types have the following format control options:

- Nonprint
- Telnet format command
- Fortran carriage control

FTP can use three types of data structure:

- File (default)
- Record
- Page

FTP has three types of transmission modes available:

- Stream (default)
- Block
- Compressed

The various combinations of these options add up to 72 different options. FTP's options for resolving representations and storage differences are to

- Provide support for *every* data and file type
- Convert files to a single network server file type
- Assume files share a few basic properties and support those properties

The designers of FTP could have chosen a *canonical* (a standard that both ends must convert to) file type such as Telnet's NVT; instead they assumed that they shared basic properties. Please refer to Chapter 11, "Telnet," for more information about NVT.

FTP Data Types

The file type specifies the format of the data being sent. FTP transfers the text file across the data connection in NVT ASCII. This means the sender has to convert the local text file into NVT ASCII, and the receiver has to convert NVT ASCII to the local text file. The end of each line indicates a CR/LF pair (carriage return/line feed, NVT ASCII representation), which means a receiver scans every byte looking for a CR/LF pair. Figures 12.5, 12.6, 12.7, and 12.8 show the four different data types that FTP can utilize: ASCII, EBCDIC, image, and local.

FIGURE 12.5

FTP uses ASCII (8-bit characters) as its default data type for text files.

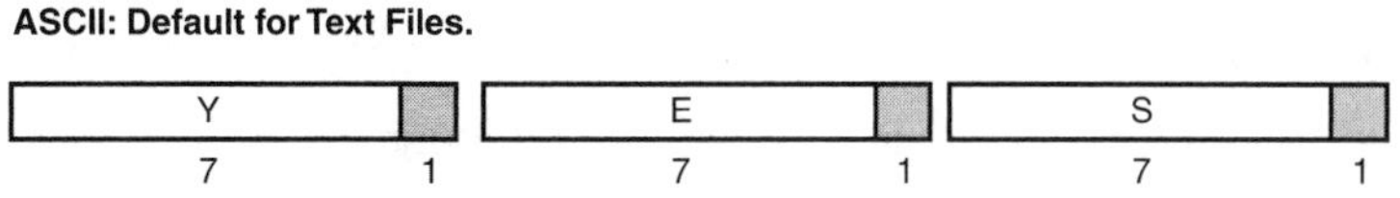

ASCII: Default for Text Files.

Y		E		S	
7	1	7	1	7	1

This conversion explains why Unix hosts always show more bytes transferred than the actual file size. Note that if one or both systems do not use ASCII text encoding, the data transfer processes assume the responsibility to convert between NVT ASCII and the local text file (encodings). Although FTP can utilize any of the four choices for FTP data type, you most likely encounter only ASCII and Image data types in the real world.

FIGURE 12.6

EBCDIC (8-bit characters), which are primarily used for IBM text files, provide an alternative method of transferring text files when both ends have EBCDIC systems.

EBCDIC: Used for IBM Text Files.

Y	E	S
8	8	8

FIGURE 12.7

Image file type (8-bit characters), which are normally used for exchanges between machines of the same type and to transfer binary files, uses a contiguous stream of bits to send data.

IMAGE: Used for exchanges between machines of the same type.

FIGURE 12.8

Local file type, which is used to transfer files between hosts with different byte sizes and where the data unit size must be preserved, uses a byte size defined by the local host.

LOCAL BYTE: Used for situations where the data Unit Size must be preserved.

Y	E	S
X	X	X

Format Control

The FTP data types also have options for format control. Usually you use the format control option when text files are being transferred to printing devices. The various formats control the various ways in which vertical format information can encode within a file, including indicating the start of a page. However, only ASCII and EBCDIC file types can utilize these options:

- **Nonprint (default)**—Contains no printing controls (no vertical printing information).

- **Telnet format control**—Controls characters as specified in the Telnet protocol (Telnet vertical format) for the printer to interpret.

- **Fortran carriage control**—Controls vertical spacing with the first character of each line (the Fortran format control character).

FTP Data Structures

Files can have internal structures. During transfer, the structure remains intact. The data transfer processes are responsible for mapping between transmitted structures and local structures. The different options enable FTP to work among hosts running different operating systems and using different data structures. FTP can use three different data structures: file structure, record structure and page structure.

Note

It is important to note that FTP data structures also are referred to as FTP file structures; however, in this book for clarity's sake, we refer to them as data structures.

The data structure has no internal structure and transfers in a stream of contiguous bytes. FTP uses the file structure by default. The record structure, which is used only with text files, uses a file made up of sequential records. The page structure uses files made up of independent, indexed pages and is provided by the TOPS-20 operating system. The page structure is used for discontinuous files in which a file descriptor or some other associated information with the data exists. Each page transmits with a page number, which allows the receiver to store the pages in any order. Figures 12.9, 12.10, and 12.11 show the different data structures.

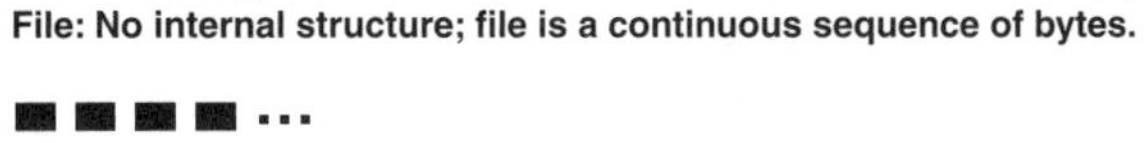

FIGURE 12.9
This figure shows the file structure.

File: No internal structure; file is a continuous sequence of bytes.

FIGURE 12.10
This figure shows the record structure.

Record: File made up of sequential records.

FIGURE 12.11
This figure shows the page structure.

Page: File made up of independent, indexed pages.

FTP Transmission Modes

The transmission mode determines how a file transmits across the data connection. There are three modes: stream, block, and compressed; although there are three transmission modes, you will most likely encounter stream mode in the real world. Stream mode, in which data is transmitted in a stream of bytes, is the default; it allows record structures. In stream mode the sender closes the data connection with an end of file for a file structure. In a record structure a special 2-byte sequence indicates the end of record and end of file.

Block mode terminals utilize block mode. Block mode transmits data as a series of data blocks preceded by one or more header bytes.

Compressed mode is rarely used and compression versions can vary among FTP versions. Compressed mode compresses filler (ASCII or EBCDIC files) and replicated data. It also compresses text and binary repeated values in the file (for example, a string of binary zeros). Additionally, compressed mode maximizes bandwidth. Compression varies depending on what type of file is being compressed. For example, if compress mode compresses an ASCII or EBCDIC filler, cccccccccc (10 bytes of data), into two bytes of data, there will be 2 bits to specify that it compressed the 10 bytes of replicated data; 6 bits for the binary code for 10 bytes of data (001010 = binary 10); and 8 bits for ASCII or EBCDIC files, indicated by c. For example, if compress mode compresses a binary file (space, space, space, space, or 4 bytes of data) into one byte, there will be 2 bits for specifying that it compressed the 2 bytes of filler data (bits equal 11) and 6 bits for a count filed (000100 equals binary four).

FTP Commands

The server and client protocol interpreters communicate commands and replies across the control connection as NVT ASCII (Telnet) strings. These Telnet strings start with three or four uppercase NVT ASCII characters with a CRLF at the end of each command. The client can send the server over 30 commands. These commands have three categories: access control, transfer parameter, and service. The access control commands determine which client can gain access to a specific file. Table 12.1 shows the different access control commands the server can invoke.

TABLE 12.1   HFTP Access Control Commands

String and Argument	Description
*ACCT[account-info]	Identifies user's account.
CDUP	Change to parent directory on remote system.
CWD[pathname]	Change to working directory on remote system.
PASS[password]	User's password. Use immediately after the USER command.

TABLE 12.1   Continued

String and Argument	Description
QUIT	Quit or break the connection.
*REIN	Reinitialize, logout without breaking the connection. Follow with new USER command for different user.
*SMNT[pathname]	Structure mount. Gives the remote system pathname of a file system structure.
USER[username]	Username on server.

Commands with an asterisk in front of them indicate commands that are rarely used.

FTP uses the transfer parameter commands to change the default parameters used to transfer data on a FTP connection. Table 12.2 shows the different transfer parameter commands.

TABLE 12.2   FTP Transfer Parameter Commands

String and Argument	Description
MODE[mode]	Transmission mode: Stream, block, or compress (parameters S, B or C).
*PASV	Tells the server DTP to listen on the data port for a connection.
PORT[host-port]	Specifies the client port number that the DTP should listen on for a connection request.
STRU[structure]	File structure: File, Record, or Page (parameters F, R, or P).
TYPE[type]	File type: ASCII, EBCDIC, image or local

Commands with an asterisk in front of them indicate commands that are rarely used.

FTP uses service commands when a user requests a file transfer or file operation. The FTP server's local rules govern the pathname argument. Table 12.3 shows the various FTP server commands.

TABLE 12.3   FTP Server Commands

String and Argument	Description
ABOR	Abort previous service command and any data transfer.
*ALLO[bytes]	Allocate space for file before sending. Parameters specify number of bytes.
*APPE[pathname]	Append file to existing file.

TABLE 12.3   Continued

String and Argument	Description
DELE[pathname]	Delete file on remote system.
HELP[string]	Retrieve help information from server; for example, a list of commands supported.
LIST[pathname]	Sends a list of files or text over the data connection on a remote system.
MKD[pathname]	Make directory.
NLST[pathname]	Name list. Sends an entire list of the current directory of the server via the data connection.
NOOP	No operation.
PWD	Print work directory. Shows current directory name on server.
*REST[marker]	Restart transfer from server marker.
RETR[pathname]	Retrieve file from server.
RMD[pathname]	Remove directory.
*RNFR[pathname]	Rename from. Specifies the old pathname of a file to be renamed. Follow with RNTO command.
*RNTO[pathname]	Rename to. Specifies the new pathname of a file. Used with the RNFR command.
*SITE[string]	Site parameters. Used by server to site specific server services.
*STAT[pathname]	Status.
STOR[filename]	Store files at the server.
*STOU	Store unique. Like the STOR command, except overwrites existing file.
*SYST	Reports operating system.

Commands with an asterisk in front of them indicate commands that are rarely used.

FTP commands use the Telnet protocol's requirements for all communications over the control connection. All commands with arguments have a space <SP> prior to the command. All commands end with a carriage return, line feed <CRLF> character. FTP commands that require access-control identifiers, data transfer parameters, or service request partition the commands between the <SP> and <CRLF> characters.

FTP Replies

FTP replies appear as three-digit numbers with an optional message in the form of text following the number string. The FTP reply format allows both the interactive user and the software to read the replies, providing information explaining the response. The software uses the three-digit numbers to determine what to do next and you can use the text, or optional message, to figure what the software intends to do next. This handy feature eliminates the need to memorize a tedious series of numerical reply strings.

FTP replies guarantee synchronization of requests and actions during file transfer and ensure the user always knows the state of the server. Each command issued must generate at least one reply. Commands can appear in sequential groups, in which case the reply will show an intermediate state while processing all the commands. If a failure occurs while executing any of the commands the entire command sequence needs to be repeated.

FTP replies appear with the three-digit numeric code followed by a space <SP>, the text message, and the standard end-of-line code <CRLF> to terminate the reply. Replies that exceed one line must be bracketed and a special format must be applied. For a complete explanation of multiline replies, please refer to RFC 959.

The three digits of each reply have a special meaning. The first digit denotes either a positive or negative outcome has occurred. The second digit shows approximately what kind of error has occurred. Affected by the second digit, the third digit gives a finer look into what kind of error has occurred. Table 12.4 reflects the meaning of the first digit, Table 12.5 reflects the second, and Table 12.6 reflects a sampling of the third digit.

TABLE 12.4   The Meaning of the First Digit of the Reply Code

Type	Description
1yz	Positive preliminary reply. Wait to send another command.
2yz	Positive completion reply.
3yz	Positive intermediate reply. Need to send another command.
4yz	Transient negative completion reply. Command did not complete; re-issue later.
5yz	Permanent negative completion reply. Cannot execute the command; do not retry.

The y represents the encoding for the second digit, the z represents the encoding for the third digit, and the x represents the encoding for the first digit.

TABLE 12.5   The Meaning of the Second Digit of the Reply Code

Digit	Description
x0z	Syntax error
x1z	Information
x2z	Connection status
x3z	Authentication and accounting
x4z	Unspecified
x5z	File system status

TABLE 12.6   Examples of the Third Digit of the Reply Code

Number	Description
125	Data connection open, transfer open
200	Command OK
211	System busy
212	Directory status
213	File status
214	Help messages for the human user
331	User name OK, password required
425	Unable to open data connection
452	Error writing file
500	Syntax error (did not recognize command)
501	Syntax error (invalid arguments)
502	Unimplemented MODE type

Table 12.6 gives a partial list of the reply codes for the third digit. For a complete list consult RFC 959.

FTP Operation and Examples

FTP operation starts with a human user's needs. Without a human at the helm—or in this case at the keyboard—none of these events can transpire. Using the Sniffer output in Figure 12.11

as an example, let's say you want to transfer a software program that your company has available on an FTP server:

1. You (FTP client 64.0.0.57) would execute the commands at the keyboard to set up a TCP control session with an FTP server (63.0.0.1). Note in Figure 12.11 the first three frames show the standard TCP three-way handshake with TCP port 21 as the destination.

2. Once both sides have established a connection, they exchange FTP messages. Note in frame four the server indicates it is ready to communicate.

3. The client and server go through the authentication process (frames five through eight).

4. In frame nine the client sends a RETR (retrieve) request, asking the server to get (download) a file (your software file).

5. The client's RETR command causes a TCP port 20 FTP data connection to set up (frames 10–12).

6. Once both sides set up the data connection, the file negotiation takes place.

7. When the server completes the download, the data port closes (frames 15, 17, and 18). The control port remains open during the duration of the entire session between client and server. At this point you could request another file. The data port closes upon completion of the data transfer.

8. In this case you need only that software file, so you execute the quit command, terminating the entire connection as indicated by the "goodbye" and followed by TCP port 21 teardown (frames 19–22).

FIGURE 12.12

FTP operation starts with a human's need. In this case FTP client 64.0.0.57 wants to get a file from FTP server 63.0.0.1.

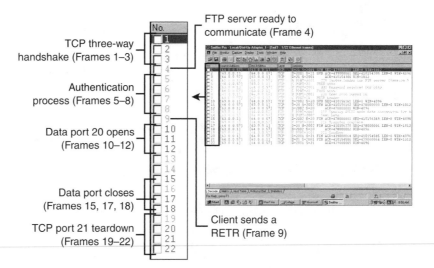

Anonymous FTP

Most of the time you must have a valid user account with the FTP server with which you want to transfer files. However, some machines offer the ability to transfer files through the Internet without having a specific user account through anonymous FTP. This means you do not have to be an official user of a particular system to gain access to the files that system offers.

If configured to support anonymous FTP users, servers offer an enormous amount of information to whomever wants it—from software to cooking recipes. However, the owners of these servers can pull the plug on it anytime they want, making it no longer available to everyone through the anonymous FTP account. This would require you to get an account with that particular server.

Many machines on the Internet offer Anonymous FTP. These machines allow you to log on using the user name "anonymous" or "ftp." When the server prompts you with a password you can type your e-mail address. Most providers of these services like to know who they deal with; however, not all require you enter a password. Once the server authenticates your password you can look around and retrieve whatever files you wish. Normally, you will find all the interesting files on a directory called a *pub*.

Providing anonymous access is a security breach and should be closely monitored. When implementing an FTP server make sure the anonymous account does not have access to sensitive company information or disable the account altogether; only allow specific user accounts with password access to the system. The last thing you want is somebody looking for a recipe for paella only to stumble upon and "accidentally" transfer the addresses and phone numbers of all the employees in your company or other sensitive information.

Summary

FTP allows you to transfer files between two computers usually through the Internet. FTP has four objectives: promote sharing of files, encourage indirect or implicit use of remote computers, shield a user from variations in file storage systems among hosts, and transfer data reliably and efficiently.

FTP has five software elements: user interface, client PI, server PI, client DTP, and server DTP. The user FTP consists of the user interface and the client PI and DTP. The server FTP consists of the server PI and DTP. FTP differs from other protocols in that it utilizes two separate TCP network connections: one for control and one for data.

FTP must decide on three parameters when transferring a file: data representation, data structure, and transmission mode. FTP represents data in one of four ways: ASCII, EBCDIC, image or local file types. FTP uses three types of data structure: file, record or page. FTP has three types of transmission modes available: stream, block, or compressed.

The server and client protocol interpreters communicate commands and replies across the control connection as NVT ASCII (Telnet) strings. These Telnet strings start with three or four uppercase NVT ASCII characters with a CR and LF at the end of each command.

FTP replies appear as three-digit numbers with an optional message in the form of text following the number string. This format allows both the user and the software to read the replies. Replies serve to guarantee both the synchronization of requests during file transfer and that user knows the state of the server.

Although some machines require that you have an account with a system to transfer files, some machines offer files through the Internet without an account through anonymous FTP.

Review Questions

1. What does FTP allow you to do and what are its four objectives?

2. What five software elements make up an FTP session?

3. What is the protocol interpreter's job during an FTP session?

4. What is the job of the data transfer process during an FTP session?

5. What two TCP network connections does FTP make, and for what is each connection used?

6. What three parameters do FTP utilities use to resolve data representation?

7. In what four ways can FTP represent data types?

8. In what three ways can FTP represent data structure?

9. What three transmission modes can FTP use?

10. What three format controls does FTP use, and what data types utilize these format controls?

11. What are the characteristics of stream mode and how does it work?

12. FTP commands come in what three categories, and what do the PIs use these commands for?

13. What do FTP replies guarantee and what format do they follow?

14. What is Anonymous FTP?

CHAPTER 13

SIMPLE MAIL TRANSFER PROTOCOL (SMTP)

You will learn about the following in this chapter:

- The X.400 Naming Model
- The SMTP Model and Format
- SMTP Commands and Replies
- Mail Retrieval Protocols
- MIME

You could say it was the protocol that inspired a movie—but even before the Tom Hanks and Meg Ryan movie *You've Got Mail*, almost everyone in the world knew what e-mail was. However, behind the scenes—not of a simplistic plotted movie but the magic of e-mail—lay the protocol that made it all work. Defined by RFC 821, Simple Mail Transfer Protocol (SMTP) provides the exchange of electronic mail (e-mail) between a sender (client) and receiver (server). RFC 821 works in conjunction with RFC 822, which addresses the format of these messages.

SMTP uses TCP to transport messages through well-known port 25. The connection-oriented TCP helps to provide dependable delivery of these messages, but SMTP in and of itself does not provide end-to-end reliability. Like every upper-layer application that runs on top of TCP, SMTP sets up the TCP session before the transmission of data between hosts.

As previously mentioned, SMTP uses a typical client/server relationship and provides a common communication channel (a TCP connection) for mail exchange between hosts. Mail exchange involves a series of request/response transactions between an SMTP client (sender) and a server (receiver). SMTP facilitates the delivery of mail messages (known as a message transfer agent or MTAs) between remote client and server mail applications (known as user agents or UAs). You don't interact with SMTP to create your e-mail. SMTP functions in the background provide mail delivery between remote hosts and require some type of front-end mail for you to interact with. Figure 13.1 illustrates the SMTP components.

FIGURE 13.1

The Mail Transfer
Protocol (SMTP) model.

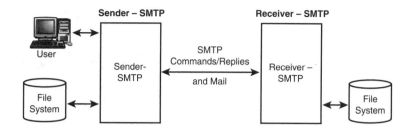

The sender communicates with the receiver through a series of SMTP requests and responses that control the delivery of messages. The protocol uses the "Mail from" (the sender) and "RCPT to" (identifying the recipient's) commands to exchange e-mail messages. For example, if you want to send your mother an e-mail

1. Open the mail application that links you to the SMTP client module, the UA (User Agent) on this host.

2. Compose a nice e-mail telling your mother how much you love her and so on.

3. Address it with a destination address (your mother's e-mail address). Your source address (your e-mail address) normally attaches itself to the message dynamically; if not, also enter that.

4. Press "send" to initiate the TCP session setup. The protocol now takes over.

5. The client opens a local TCP port for the UA and requests a TCP connection to the SMTP server (MTA).

6. Once a TCP connection is established between the UA and MTA, the receiver (Mom's e-mail account) responds with Opcode 220, which means "I'm ready for mail!"

7. The sender (your e-mail account) issues the hello command, including its name, "HELLO: Sender Name" to show that the mail message is beginning.

8. The server responds with Opcode 250, which means "OK," and the mail transaction begins.

9. The SMTP-client sends a "Mail From" command identifying the full name of the sender to the server.

10. The SMTP server verifies the "Mail From" contents for syntax and completeness and responds with an "OK."

11. The SMTP client then sends the RCPT To command identifying the intended recipient (Mom) of the mail message to the server.

12. If the SMTP-server can accept mail for that recipient, it responds with an OK reply. If not, it replies rejecting the recipient (but not the whole mail transaction).

13. The SMTP-client and SMTP-server may negotiate several recipients. After negotiation of the recipients, the SMTP-client sends the mail data.

14. Eventually, your mom opens the e-mail and smiles at the nice message you sent her.

Perhaps this is why the world loves e-mail so much. Not only did you make your mom happy by sending her such a nice e-mail; you did so without being on the phone for two hours. You also avoided all those nagging questions about when you plan to have children with quick, painless, easy communication—e-mail.

Let's take a look at how an SNMP session looks through a protocol analyzer. As shown in Figure 12.2 the source host, SMTP client Atlantis, identifies itself to the SMTP server (192.42.252.1) by saying "Hello." The server responds by saying "Pleased to meet you." The authentication process continues with the client identifying the sender (Mail From) and the server responds by positively acknowledging the sender (sender OK). The client specifies the recipient of the message (RCPT To:); then sends the data, ending it with a period (.). The SMTP server then delivers the mail.

FIGURE 13.2

The SMTP protocol must establish a TCP connection before any delivery of e-mail can occur.

X.400 Naming Model

To better understand how SMTP works you must examine the X.400 naming model, as SMTP follows its conventions. Figure 13.3 shows a basic X.400 model through an example of e-mail exchange using TCP/IP. The user agents and message transfer agents exchange electronic mail messages. The X.400 model consists of four main components: message transfer agents (MTAs), message stores (MSs), user agents (UAs), and access units (AUs).

The User Agent (UA) in the example is responsible for composing and analyzing RFC-822 message headers. Users have immediate interaction with the e-mail system through the UA. Through the UA the user composes, submits, and receives e-mail messages. The UA usually constructs the SMTP envelope at the originating site when it first queues the message for transmission by the Sender-SMTP program. Either information in the message header, supplied by the user interface (for example, to implement a carbon copy [cc]), or local configuration information (for example, mailing list) determine the envelope address. The MAIL and RCPT commands transmit the envelope separately from the message itself; we discuss SMTP commands later in this chapter.

FIGURE 13.3
The user agent enables you to write, send, and receive e-mail messages.

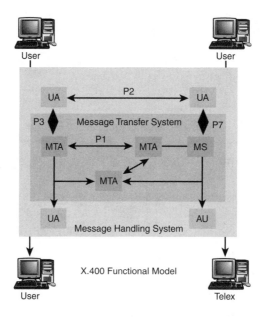

Message Transfer Agents (MTAs)

According to 1123 SMTP server programs have similarities to X.400 MTAs. MTAs execute mail exchange and are responsible for routing e-mail messages through internetworks. These message switches connect to form the Message Transfer System (MTS). MTAs have the following functions:

- Accept messages by the UA or other MTAs, routing the message to the appropriate recipient's UA or other MTAs en route to the ultimate destination.

- Analyze the recipient list in the message and perform routing decisions.

- Pass a message to the UA and create a delivery notification, if requested.

- Send messages to an MTA that indicate they need to be passed to another MTA.

- Generate an NDN, which is a non-delivery notification if the mail is undeliverable to a false or nonexistent address.

- Copy a message and delivering each copy to a different recipient for multi-addressed messages.

A committee of the International Telecommunications Union developed and implemented the X.400 model for the Telecommunication Unions X.400 standards CCITT (Consultative Committee for International Telegraphy and Telephony). It defines a range of protocols for addressing mail between e-mail servers including

- Multimedia messages (voice, graphics, fax, text)

- Interfacing unlike systems together

- Security of message transmission

- Reliable transport of messages

- Archive of messages

- Directory services for locating addresses

- Reporting delivery and receipt of messages

SMTP Format

The mail consists of the message, made up of a header and body, and "the envelope," which is the SMTP source and destination address. RFC 821 specifies the contents and interpretation of the envelope. The following example shows two SMTP commands (discussed later in the chapter) that specify the envelope:

- MAIL From:`<heather@itacademy.com>`

- RCPT To:`jason@itacademy.com`

RFC 822 states that the body of the message utilizes the American Standard Code for Information Interchange (ASCII) text. ASCII represents both textual data (letters, numbers, and punctuation marks) and control characters, which are commands such as return and line feed. As with other coding systems, ASCII converts information into standardized digital formats using seven-digit binary numbers. Binary numbers consist of various sequences of 0s and 1s. Computers communicate with each other, process and store data with these digital formats. NVT, using 7-bit codes for characters, transmits the 7-bit ASCII code into 8-bit octets with the most important bit set to 0.

The header consists of a series of lines of text known as *header fields*. The majority of header fields depend on the implementation of a particular system—few header fields are mandatory. A blank line divides the header from the body. The body of the message contains only ASCII text; the maximum line length must not exceed 1000 characters. The message also must not exceed a predefined maximum size. We will explain how to transcend these rules later in this chapter.

Most systems use a variation of the following mail format example below, provided by Appendix A of RFC 822. RFC describes its example of an SMTP format "as complex as you're going to get." It shows 11 fields in use, which is more than most mail systems.

Date	:	27 Aug 76 0932 PDT
From	:	Ken Davis <Kdavis@This-Host.This-net>
Subject	:	Re: The Syntax in the RFC
Sender	:	Ksecy@Other-Host
Reply-To :		Sam. Irving@Reg.Organization
To	:	George Jones <Group@Some-Reg.An-Org>,
		Al .Neuman@MAD.Publisher
CC	:	Important folk:
		Tom Softwood <Balsa@Tree.Root>,
		"Sam Irving'@Other-Host;,
		Standard Distribution:
		/mian/davis/people/standard@Other-Host,
		"<Jones>standard.dist.3"@Tops-20-Host>;
Comment :		Sam is away on business. He asked me to handle
		His mail for him. He'll be able to provide a more accurate
		explanation when he returns Next week.
In-Reply-To:		<some.string@DM.Group>, Georgeks message
X-Special-action:		This is a sample of the user-defined field-
		Names. There could also a be a field-name
		"Special-action", but its name might later be
		preempted
Message-ID :		4231.629.Xyzi-What@Other-Host

SMTP Commands

SMTP commands (RFC 821) classify the mail transaction or mail system function requested by the user. SMTP commands consist of a command code and an argument (see Table 13.1). SMTP commands have some basic rules:

- A command code and an argument make up each SMTP command.

- Four alphabetic characters in either upper- or lowercase comprise the command code.

- One or more space characters separate this code from the argument.

- Because each host can have a particular rule for mail addresses, reverse path and forward path arguments are case sensitive.

- The character sequence carriage return-line feed (<CRLF>) concludes the argument field.

- Square brackets enclose optional arguments.

Table 13.1 shows the standard command codes and arguments that SMTP uses.

TABLE 13.1   SMTP Command Codes

Command Code and Argument	What It Does
HELO <SP> <domain> <CRLF>	Identifies the sender-SMTP to receiver-SMTP.
MAIL <SP> FROM: <reverse path> <CRLF>	Delivers mail data to mailbox.
RCPT <SP> TO:<forward-path> <CRLF>	Identifies mail data recipient.
DATA <CRLF>	Sends the contents of the mail message.
RSET <CRLF>	Ends existing mail transaction, causing both ends to reset. This action junks any stored information about sender, recipients, or mail data.
SEND <SP> FROM:<reverse-path <CRLF>	Delivers mail to the terminals.
SOML <SP> FROM:<reverse-path <CRLF>	Sends or mails.
SAML <SP> FROM:<reverse-path <CRLF>	Sends or mails.
VRFY <SP> <string><CRLF>	Verifies that the argument identifies a user. This enables the client to ask the sender to verify a recipient address without sending mail to the recipient (usually used by a system administrator for debugging mail delivery problems).
EXPN <SP> <string> <CRLF>	Confirms that the argument identifies a mailing list. This expands the list.
HELP [<SP> <string> <CRLF>	Sends information.
NOOP <CRLF>	No operation.
QUIT <CRLF>	Sends OK reply; then closes channels.
TURN <CRLF>	Exchanges Sender/Receiver roles to send mail in the opposite direction without taking down the TCP connection and creating a new one. (Sendmail does not support this command).

<SP> represents a Space character. <CRLF> represents Carriage Return and Line Feed characters.

SMTP Replies

SMTP replies acknowledge receipt of SMTP datagrams and error notification. Replies include a three-digit number code (sent as three alphanumeric characters) followed by text. A three-digit code, <SP>, one line of text, and <CRLF> comprise a reply. The texts vary for each reply code and the various combinations indicate the purpose of the reply.

SMTP clients and servers use the three digits to communicate receipt of information and notify the other side when it has encountered an error. The three-digit number has a hierarchy. The first digit represents general information, and the second and third digits further define the reply, giving the receiving host enough information to determine whether an error has occurred so it can determine how to process the message.

The receiver does not need to look at the message text; it only looks at the reply digits to determine whether to trash the message if there is an error or pass it on to the user. Table 13.2 demonstrates the meanings of the first digit. Table 13.3 shows the meaning of the second digit. Table 13.4 shows a numeric order list of reply codes completed by the third digit.

TABLE 13.2   Meanings of the First Digit

First Digit	Meaning
1yz	Positive preliminary reply
2yz	Positive completion reply
3yz	Positive intermediate reply
4yz	Transient negative completion reply
5yz	Permanent negative completion reply

TABLE 13.3   Meanings of the Second Digit

Second Digit	Meaning
x0z	Syntax
x1z	Information
x2z	Connection
x3z	Unspecified as yet
x4z	Unspecified as yet
x5z	Mail system

TABLE 13.4   Numeric Order List of Reply Codes

Reply Code	Meaning
211	System status or system help reply.
214	Help message; used by the human user.

TABLE 13.4   Continued

Reply Code	Meaning
220 <domain>	Service ready.
221 <domain>	Service closing transmission channel.
250	Requested mail action okay, completed.
251	User not local—Will forward to <forward-path>.
354	Start mail input—End with <CRLF>.
421 <domain>	Service not available; closing transmission channel. Can be a reply to any command if the service knows it must shut down.
450	Requested mail action not taken—Mailbox unavailable (mailbox busy).
451	Requested action aborted—local error in processing.
452	Requested action not taken—insufficient system storage.
500	Syntax error, command unrecognized. This can include errors such as the command line being too long.
501	Syntax error in parameters or arguments.
502	Command not put into action.
503	Bad sequence of commands.
504	Command parameter not implemented.
550	Requested action not taken—mailbox unavailable (mailbox not found; no access).
551	User not local—please try <forward-path>.
552	Requested mail action aborted—exceeded storage allocation.
553	Requested action not taken—mailbox name not allowed.
554	Transaction failed.

MIME

Originating in the '80s, SMTP has always had a large user base because of its simplicity. In many cases, users have exceeded its ability, wanting to transmit messages other than text, such as a graphic, scanned photographic or video clip. SMTP simplicity causes the following restrictions:

- The message must contain only ASCII characters.

- The maximum line length must not exceed 1000 characters.

- The message must not exceed a predefined maximum size.

Multipurpose Internet Mail Extension (MIME) enhances the capabilities of standard Internet electronic mail and, more important, SMTP. Use of the MIME standard enables messages to contain additional types:

- Characters sets other than ASCII

- Multimedia: image, audio, and video messages

- Multiple objects in a single message

- Multi-font messages

- Messages of unlimited length

- Binary files

The Internet Engineering Task Force Working Group defined MIME in 1992 in RFC 1521 and 1522. MIME defines the method in which files are attached to the SMTP messages. It builds on the older standard by defining additional fields for the mail message header that describe new content types and a specific message body organization.

MIME extensions provide for transmissions of data previously unsupported in Internet mail by encoding the message into readable ASCII to create a standard e-mail message. Extension of SMTP protocol provides transport for new message types. RFC 1652 defines the extension for the transmission of unencoded 8-bit MIME messages. With this service extension the receiver SMTP can declare support for 8-bit body parts. The receiver also can request 8-bit transmission of a particular message. MIME resides in the 822 mail header.

Summary

Operating in the TCP/IP protocol suite, Simple Mail Transfer Protocol (SMTP) defines the format for e-mail servers to send and receive messages and for a client to send messages to a server. SMTP starts working after the client opens a TCP connection with the server on well-known port 25. The client and server then use SMTP as a communication channel. The client sends the mail to the server through a series of carefully defined command-response transactions.

The X.400 Model shows the interchange of electronic mail between User Agents and Message Transfer Agents. User Agents (UAs), also present in the SMTP Model, facilitate immediate user interaction. Through the UA the user creates, enters, and receives e-mail messages. Message Transfer Agents (MTAs), analogous to STMP programs, carry out mail exchange and communicate using NVT ASCII. X.400 defines a scope of protocols for addressing mail between e-mail servers.

In the SMTP format mail consists of a header, body, and envelope. The envelope consists of the SMTP source and destination address. The header consists of a series of lines of text, or fields. The header fields required depend on the conventions of a particular system. Although SMTP specifies that the body of the message should contain only limited amounts of ASCII text, Multipurpose Internet Mail Extension (MIME) transcends these rules to include non-ASCII documents, audio, video and images.

Review Questions

1. What is the main function of SMTP?

2. How do User Agents function in the SMTP model?

3. How does SMTP differ from UA?

4. Describe three of SMTP's limitations.

5. List three rules in SMTP command protocol.

6. Explain why replies are important to smooth mail transactions.

7. Why is the SMTP reply important to the user?

8. Explain how MIME functions with SMTP.

CHAPTER 14

NAME RESOLUTION

You will learn about the following in this chapter:

- Naming Computers
- Namespace
- DNS Delegation of Authority

- Caching
- Domain Server Message Format
- Internet Domain Names and Their Types

Why Do We Need Name Resolution?

Back in the Stone Age of networking, users could identify and specify machines only by using long, cumbersome numeric addresses. However, internetworking brought a hierarchical IP addressing scheme, which used classful addresses (Network layer), and protocol software (such as ARP) that could change addresses back into low-level addresses. Low-level addresses (MAC address) are unique numbers that machines understand and use to forward datagrams locally on a point-to-point basis. We discussed the Network layer in Chapter 3, "Network Layer/Internet Protocols," and Chapter 4, "Address Resolution," and Data Link layer is addressed in Chapter 1, "Overview of Industry Models and Standards."

Think of each computer as a telephone. A telephone can't understand your name because it consists of letters and describes a person; not another telephone's address. If your mom wants to call you on the telephone, she can't just shout out your name. A name is not enough to locate the destination or place the call.

She needs to know your phone number to call you. Telephone numbers consist of a hierarchical numbering scheme identifying the area, the city, and the house of the telephone. Telecommunication switches use this information within the public switched telephone network to locate the destination and complete the call.

Your computer also needs to know the Internet Protocol (IP) Address if you want it to call or reach a remote host or Web site. Like a telephone number, the IP Address (Network layer address) consists of numbers so that each computer can understand it and find the path to the destination.

Once the computer can identify the destination, the source and destination identify the lower-level address (MAC address) for point-to-point delivery through that path. Basically, the ability to use a name instead of an address is for our benefit; not the computer's. When a user attempts to locate a resource using a name, devices need to resolve that name to a logical Network layer address, which in turn must be resolved to a Data Link layer address when it reaches the destination network for delivery. All this must occur before any data transmission.

TCP/IP applications use DNS as a sort of telephone operator. Like a telephone operator, you can give DNS a name and get a number (IP address). This service eliminates the need for a namespace.

Namespace

Currently, the Internet consists of millions of hosts, each with its own IP address and name (if configured). To reach a host, you can use the name instead of the IP address. However, for the name to be resolved to an address you need one of two things: a DNS server (telephone operator) or a local table.

Domain Name Servers provide name-to—IP Address lookup services, much like a telephone operation. For instance, when you want to call Sergio's Pizza, you might know the name but not the number. You have two choices:

- Look in your local telephone book (local table)
- Call 411 and have an operator help you (DNS server)

Whatever method you use, you must resolve the name to the number before dialing, allowing you to complete the call and access the resource—PIZZA! How do you keep track of all these Universal and IP addresses? In the beginning, when only a few hundred hosts existed on the Internet, it was easy. A single list in the form of a text file called the *namespace* held all the information. The Network Information Center (NIC) kept track of the list and decided who was out or in, keeping out obscene names and names that might be confused with other names.

When you wanted to participate on the Internet, you had to contact NIC to receive a copy of this list and add it to all local Internet gateways that performed the necessary resolution. Each time a name or IP address changed (added or removed from the Internet), the list changed and you had to obtain a new one. Maintaining this list and keeping up with the changes, and the local resources necessary to keep such a large list proved highly impractical. Thus, DNS emerged to address the flat, static nature of name resolution. This enables a dynamic hierarchical service to handle resolution for hosts throughout the Internet.

Think of NIC's namespace as your address or telephone book. You decide who's in and who's out, and insert an extra initial (or other special indicator) in case you have people on the list who share the same name. For example, if you have two people named Katie, you might name one Kate and assign one a nickname such as Kat or perhaps file them under their last names, Stevens and Pollock. You could name them Katie1 and Katie2, depending on when you met them, or by the jobs they have. Regardless of what naming scheme you decide on, there are a lot of combinations.

Note

Note that the Domain Name System (DNS) eliminates the need for the namespace by making it possible for you to find the IP address for every domain name and vice versa.

Both the namespace and your address book share a problem, especially if someone else wants to use it: clarity and usability. Because only you use the list, you understand all the personal nicknames, strange symbols, or omissions of last names on the list. Most likely, other people could not use the same list to easily find telephone numbers. They wouldn't know that you filed Katie Stevens' number under just Kat and Katie Pollock under Katie. They might end up calling Katie Pollock when they wanted to call Katie Stevens. The older you get, the more people, numbers, nicknames, married couples, and business contacts get entered in the book, making the address book harder and harder for another user to differentiate telephone numbers by using just names.

The namespace's local host table had the same problem. Each name on the list consisted of a string of characters without any other structure. When NIC had a small list, the small number of Internet users could understand and use it. As that list and number of users grew, they could no longer use a namelist. A namelist has the following problems:

- It makes expansion difficult

- Work overload complicates the expansion problem

- It's inefficient and costly

Just as the number of people you know in your lifetime expands, so does the Internet. As the Internet world expanded, and new users increasingly registered computers and domain names, NIC found it impossible to keep out names that would conflict with existing names, just like an expanding address book.

The list of phone numbers you need to know and what they mean (business, friends, family, doctors, and so on) increases daily—entering and organizing them can be taxing. Imagine the strain on NIC trying to organize the Internet where thousands of sites come in every day, each with hundreds of individual computers and workstations. Each time someone connected a new personal computer, NIC had to approve it.

With the Internet going global and the seemingly infinite number of users, it would have been impossible, inefficient, and costly for NIC to continue to use a namelist. In the old Internet world, NIC would have had to create and maintain another list at each site every time it added a new computer name, wasting time and money.

DNS Delegation of Authority

If you had an expanding business with mounting responsibilities, you would delegate those responsibilities to other departments to ease the burden. The Domain Naming System (DNS) follows the same idea; it operates like a large, well-run corporation. When a corporation grows, executives divide the responsibilities among various departments to decrease workload and maintain functionality. Each executive can hire and fire, dish out responsibilities, and further designate authority.

DNS works the same way. It operates as a hierarchical tree in which the NIC governs the top-level domains and gives the rest of the responsibilities to names servers. Table 14.1 shows the DNS root or top-level domains.

TABLE 14.1   Top-level Domains

Domain	Purpose
MIL	U.S. Military
GOV	U.S. Government
EDU	Educational
COM	Commercial
NET	NICs and NOCs
ORG	Nonprofit organization
CON	Two-letter country code; for example, US represents United States, UK represents United Kingdom, and so on

Proposed Top-Level Names

The seven three-character top-level domains often are referred to as *generic* domains. The two-character top-level domains (or *CON* domain) are based on country codes. Other top-level names have been proposed, including .firm, .shop, .web, .arts, .rec, .info, .nom, .aero, .biz, .coop, .info, .museum, .name and .pro.

You may have heard about .tv, which is already a country code for the small pacific island Tuvalu. The .tv campaign has now been remarketed as a television domain by domain registrars. For more information visit `http://www.icann.org.tlds`.

Name servers provide *resource records* (*RRs*), which enable you to resolve, or find the IP address for a domain name and vice versa. Think of name servers as secretaries. If you want to make an appointment with your doctor you don't call your hospital's CEO; you talk directly to the receptionist. Name servers provide the same efficiency and ease. You can resolve a Domain Name without the wasted time and energy of moving through the entire DNS hierarchy. Figure 14.1 shows the hierarchical organization of DNS.

FIGURE 14.1

The hierarchical organization of DNS enables fur-
ther delegation of
addresses that are mean-
ingful to the user.

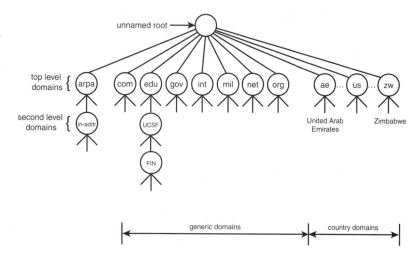

NIC, the chief executive, maintains the top portion of the hierarchical tree (the top-level
domains) *partitions* the Domain name that you type in to specific *zones,* self-governing sub-
trees of the DNS tree. These second-level zones also can divide into smaller zones. For example, if your site functions for a University, each zone could represent a department. If your site
operates for a business, each zone could represent a location, such as a branch office or a division of responsibility (the human resources department).

Using Figure 14.1 as an example, you'll note that the University of San Francisco has further
delegated its address to `ucsf.edu`. This differentiates it from the other educational sites; for
example, San Francisco State University (`sfsu.edu`). It could further subdivide that address by
department; for example, using `fin.ucsf.edu` to represent the financial aid department at the
University of San Francisco. We will look at this hierarchical division of Internet domain
names later in this chapter.

Just as each division of an office needs workers to run it, so does each zone. You need a primary name server for the zone and one or more secondary name servers. The primary name
server loads information from the disk files. The secondary server gets information from the
primary. Like any employee, these servers need to be independent and able to fix mistakes as
they happen so errors do not affect the name services for their zones.

To add a new host to a zone, enter the necessary information—or at least the name and IP
Address—to a disk file on the system where the primary server works. This action alerts the
primary and it starts rereading its configuration files. The secondary server asks the primary
server for new information about every three hours. If the secondary finds anything new, it
gets it from the primary with a zone transfer.

Still, these smooth-running servers don't always possess the information you request (when
this occurs, the server is not considered *authoritative* for that information). When this happens, the server gets hold of another name server. It refers the name resolution request to that

server in hopes that it might resolve the name and IP address or pass it on to a name server that does possess the information that you request (considered an *authoritative server*).

Name servers do not need to know how to reach every other name server. However, they must know the IP addresses of the root name servers. As in any office, you don't have to know every phone number to get information; you just need to know a few reliable sources. The root servers function as the phone book managers; they know the names and IP addresses of each authoritative server for all the second-level domains. After the server queries the root server, the root server tells the server to contact another authoritative server. This referral process enables a request to traverse the namespace tree until it finds a name server that knows the name (considered as authoritative for that name) and can resolve it, supplying the IP address to the requesting client.

Authoritative or Not Authoritative?

Name servers are considered authoritative when they possess the name and can resolve it. When they do not possess the name (not considered authoritative), they pass the request to another name server in hopes that it is authoritative.

DNS also can trace a domain name to a mail exchanger address and can store any kind of list of hierarchical names that you want during configuration. You can use this feature to match your business needs. For example, you can store a list of services along with the resolution from each name to the telephone number your customers would need to find out about the service. Alternatively, you could store a list of products along with the resolution of names and addresses of vendors who sell the products.

Internet Domain Names

When you look at a domain name, you first notice it consists of a series of abbreviations separated by periods. If you use the Internet heavily or if you run a site yourself, you know that the hierarchical order of these abbreviations did not come about by accident. The placement and abbreviations themselves have a purpose. Think of a 10-digit telephone number: You know the first three digits always function as the area code because the area code always comes first. If you don't put the area code first or omit it completely, you can't reach the person you are trying to call.

The DNS organized the hierarchy of names so that you can quickly connect to the server to find each Web site address you type in. Let's look at how DNS divides up each domain name. DNS breaks up each section of the Domain name that represents a site or group into a section called a *label* or a *domain;* for example, Fre.devry.edu.

DNS breaks up the Domain name into three domains. The lower the domain level, the more specific it gets. In this example, the lowest domain level is Fre.devry.edu, the domain name for the Fremont Campus of DeVry University. Devry.edu exists as the second-level domain, the domain name for DeVry University. Edu, the domain name educational institutions use, represents the top-level domain. If you have typed long, specific domain names, imagine these names uncompressed and written in their full names. DNS uses this order to compress domain names, making them easier for you to type and organize.

When you build a domain system you can choose labels for all parts of your domain name hierarchy because DNS specifies only the form of the name; not the value. However, like most of us, you just follow the labels used by the official Internet domain system. Although the system establishes order, it does so inclusively and flexibly. The system accepts all domains and lets you choose whether you want to have a geographical or an organizational naming hierarchy. Also, when you attach your TCP/IP installations to the global Internet you don't have to change names.

Queries and Mappings

DNS uses both mappings and queries to resolve the IP address from the domain name or vice versa. To help them resolve IP addresses or domain names, DNS servers keep their mapping information by saving it to disk or caching it into RAM. We discuss caching later in this chapter. You will need to understand the following terminology to understand any further discussion on DNS:

- *Mapping* and *resolving* both mean tracing an IP address from the domain name.

- *Inverse mappings* trace the domain name from the IP address.

- *Inverse queries* function as the commands you use to produce inverse mappings. Inverse queries usually require the server to search the entire set of servers, which is rarely used.

Caching

Like an efficient clerical worker, name servers store all of the information requests (mappings) by filing them away (saved to disk) or caching them (saved to RAM). This way, the server keeps up on the most recently requested data and has the newly requested name resolutions. Caching also lowers the cost of resolving nonlocal names because of its speed. Caching goes through different steps to resolve IP addresses:

1. When the server receives a request to resolve a name, it checks to see whether that name is part of its zone (this server is authoritative for that information).

2. If not, the server checks its cache, which holds information for about two days.

3. If it finds the information in the cache, it reports it to the client.

4. When the server gives the information to the client, it lets the client know that it got the information locally or from some other authority server (not its local table). It gives the domain name and the binding (the IP address mapped to the requested name).

5. The information could be out of date. If you want speed, just use what the server gave you. If you want accuracy, contact the authority server and verify your information.

Domain Server Message Format

If the server still cannot find the answer after checking its cache, it becomes a client (acting as a proxy for the source host) and uses a message format to ask multiple questions to the authoritative server in one message.

Each message contains three things:

- A domain name to be resolved

- The class, or protocol family the domain name uses

- The type of domain name

The queried server responds with answers to the questions (contained in variable fields in the message). If the server still doesn't have the answers, its reply contains information and the IP addresses for servers that might have the information. Figure 14.2 shows an example of a DNS message format. We explain each field in detail following the figure.

FIGURE 14.2
A DNS message has a fixed 12-byte header followed by four variable length fields.

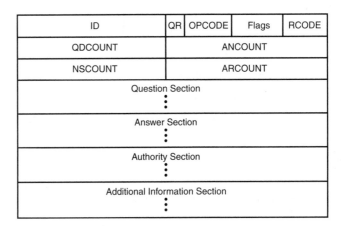

Identifier (ID)

The 16-bit identification field matches queries and responses. The client sets the identification; the server returns it.

QR

The 1-bit QR field identifies whether the message is a query or response. Zero (QR=0) means a query; one (QR=1) means response.

Opcode

The 4-bit Opcode field further defines the QR bit. Table 14.2 shows the various Opcodes and their meanings.

TABLE 14.2   Opcodes

Opcode	Meaning
0	Standard query (QUERY)
1	Inverse query (IQUERY)
2	Server status request (STATUS)
3-15	Reserved

Flags

The 7-bit flag field further describes the message. The flags field divides into five more sections (see Figure 14.3):

- **AA (authoritative answer)**—Bit 5. This 1-bit flag field stands for authoritative answer, which means the name server is authoritative for the particular domain in question.

- **TC (truncation)**—Bit 6. This 1-bit flag field stands for truncated, which means that the reply exceeded 512 bytes, returning only the first 512 bytes of the reply.

- **RD (recursion desired)**—Bit 7. This 1-bit flag field stands for recursion desired. Set in a query and returned in a reply, this flag (when set) indicates the name server to deal with the query itself—a recursive query. However, if flag does not have the bit set and the name server does not have an AA, the name server it requested returns a list of all other name servers that have the answer to the query—an *iterative query*.

- **RA (recursion available)**—Bit 8. This 1-bit flag field stands for recursion available. If the server supports recursion, field has a bit set to 1. Most name servers support recursion.

- **Zero**—Bits 9–11 are always set at zero (0).

Note that Figure 14.3 also shows the QR, Opcode and Rcode fields and their relationship to the flags field.

FIGURE 14.3
Note the relationship of the other fields to the divided flags field.

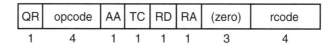

QR	opcode	AA	TC	RD	RA	(zero)	rcode
1	4	1	1	1	1	3	4

Rcode

This 4-bit field stands for response code and completes the parameters of the bits 0 through 11. Table 14.3 shows the different Rcode meanings.

TABLE 14.3   Rcodes

Field	Meaning
0	No error
1	Format error in query
2	Server failure
3	Name does not exist
4	Not implemented
5	Refused
6	Reserved for future use

The Rcode field completes the parameters that begin the QR field, bits 0–15. Table 14.4 is a quick reference of the different bits in the parameters fields. Use this table with Figure 14.2 (DNS Message Format).

TABLE 14.4   The Meaning of the Bits in the Parameter Field

Bit Placement	Meaning

0	Operation:
	    0 Query
	    1 Response

1–4	Query Type:
	    0 Standard Query
	    1 Inverse query
	    2 Server status
	    3–15 reserved

5	Set if authoritative answer (AA)
6	Set if message truncated (TC)
7	Set if recursion desired (RD)
8	Set if recursion available (RA)
9–11	Reserved (set to zero)

TABLE 14.4   Continued

Bit Placement	Meaning
12–15	Response Type: 0 No error 1 Format error in query 2 Server failure 3 Name does not exist 4 Not implemented 5 Refused 6–15 reserved

Answers and Questions Headers

The next four 16-bit fields specify the variable length of the remaining four sections. The four fields affect each other. Table 14.5 shows these fields and their meanings.

TABLE 14.5   Final Four Fields in a DNS Message

Field	Meaning
QDCOUNT	Number of Questions Entry
ANCOUNT	Number of Resource Records (RRs) in the Answer section
NSCOUNT	Number of Name Servers Resource Records (RRs) in the Authority section
ARCOUNT	Number of Resource Records (RRs) in the Additional Records section

The number of sections are self explanatory. The client writes in only the question section of the message format. Normally, the number of questions field is 1 and the other three counts are 0. The number of answers has a count of 1 whereas the remaining two counts are 0. Normally, the question section has just one question in the field. Figure 14.4 shows the message format.

FIGURE 14.4
This shows the message format of a DNS query message.

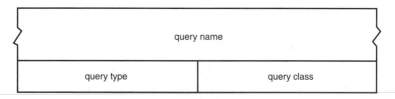

The question portion consists of three sections: query name, query type, and query class. Query name represents the query domain name. The query type encodes the type of question (a machine name or mail address). This generates a response (called a resource record, or RR). Each response has a type, which we will discuss later. The query class field allows for Internet names to be used. The server fills in the answers section. The answers, authority, and additional information sections all are made up of RRs illustrating domain names and resolutions. Each RR illustrates one name.

Domain Name Types

Once DNS puts your name in the system, it gives it a *type* to show if your Domain Name functions as the address of a machine, an e-mail box, another user, and so on. This way, even though DNS lumps all of the types together, your Web site visitors can find your address easily. Table 14.6 shows the DNS RR types.

TABLE 14.6   DNS RR Types

Name	Description	Contents
A	Host address	32-bit IP address
CNAME	Canonical name	Canonical domain name, used by some FTP sites as an alias for another system
HINFO	CPU and OS	Name of the CPU and the Operating System
MINFO	Mailbox information	Information about a mailbox or a mail list
MX	Mail exchange	The 16-bit preference and name of the host that works as a mail exchanger for the domain
NS	Name server record	Identifies authoritative name servers
PTR	Pointer record	The IP address shown as its domain name in backward form with "in-addr.arpa" after it
SOA	Start of authority	Fields defining which part of the naming hierarchy a servers uses
TXT	Vague text	Unintelligible string of ASCII text

DNS Examples

Let's take a look at some DNS examples as seen through a Sniffer. We will start with a host sending a query and follow this request until it is resolved. Figure 14.5 shows a host sending a query to resolve a name to an Internet address.

FIGURE 14.5
Note the UDP ports of the source (2798) and destination (53) indicating this request came from the DNS client going to the well-known DNS port.

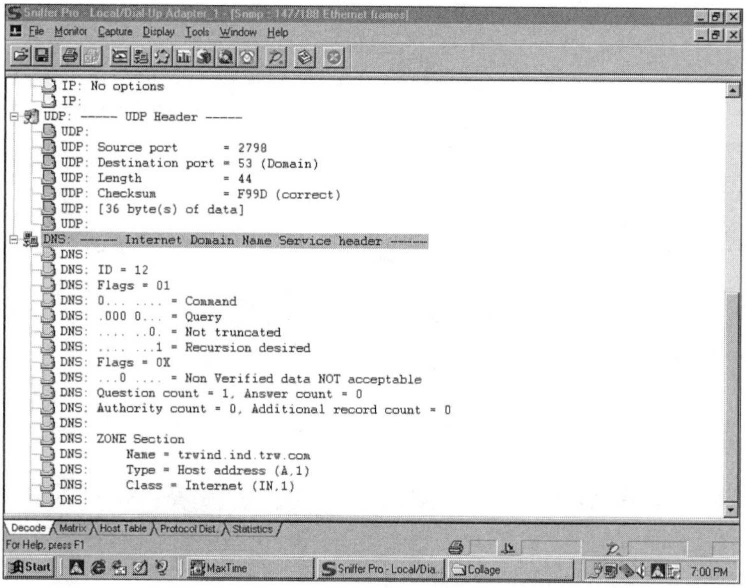

Using Figure 14.5 as an example, you can see in the DNS header this is a Query to resolve the name `trwind.ind.trw.com` to an Internet address for a host. The client has set the recursion bit, indicating to the receiving DNS server to forward this request on to another server if it is not authoritative for this domain and cannot successfully resolve this name with local information. Figure 14.6 shows a nonauthoritative server querying another server for a client.

FIGURE 14.6
Note the DNS UDP ports of the source and destination both are 53, which means that both sending and receiving hosts are DNS servers utilizing the well-known server port.

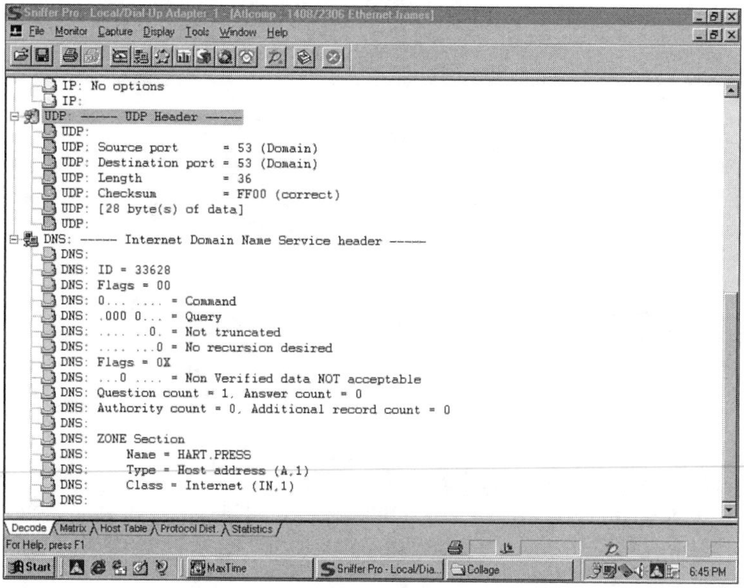

Using Figure 14.6 as an example, when both the source and destination host use the same DNS UDP ports, it means that both the sending and receiving hosts are DNS servers. This happens when one DNS server is not authoritative for the information being requested and must query another server for this information on behalf of a client.

The requesting server has included a unique ID number of 33628 to which the corresponding reply will match. Note that the question count is 1, which means this server has one question (piece of information). The answer count is 0 because no answer has been received yet. It also has set the authoritative bit, which means this server does not have the information necessary to answer the client query to resolve the name hart.press because it is not authoritative for the domain. This is why this server sends this query in the first place. It wants to resolve the name hart.press; the type of address it is looking to resolve to is a host address of the class type Internet.

Figure 14.7 shows a server sending an error code, offering no resolution.

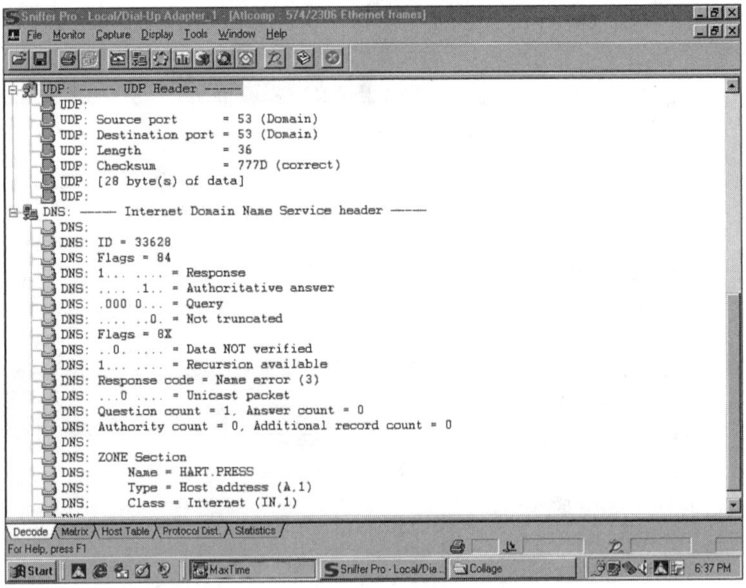

FIGURE 14.7

Note the ID number matches the previously sent ID within the query datagram in Figure 14.6.

Using Figures 14.6 and 14.7 as examples, note that the number IDs match in each figure. This shows DNSs correctly matching requests with responses. In Figure 4.17, note that this server is authoritative for the domain in question; however, it has no such name within the mapping table. Because it has no such name within the mapping table, the server sends an error indicated by response code 3, which offers no resolution.

Figure 14.8 shows a DNS server resolving a name and mapping it to an IP address. Note the TTL value of 43200, which means that the client can assume this information is valid, cache it, and continue to use it until the timer expires, at which time the client must query again for the same information.

FIGURE 14.8

This is an authoritative response from a DNS server resolving the name sushi.stanford.edu and mapping it to the IP address 36.8.0.53.

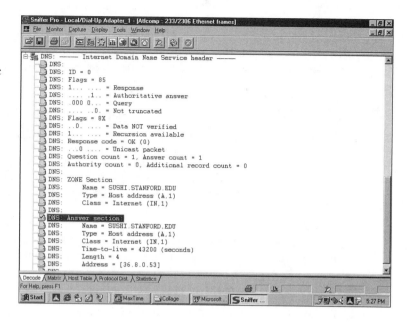

NetBios

NetBIOS (Network Basic Input Output System) is an extension of BIOS (Basic Input Output System), which represents a host's fundamental capability to access to its own local resources. IBM and Sytek extended this functionality to accessing information located on remote hosts and called it NetBIOS. Their objective was to provide a very simple way for users to access remote resources and services by using a name rather than an address.

Each NetBIOS device is given a unique 15-character name; services running within the host can also have names associated with them. These unique names enable a user to find a specific service running within a host by specifying the name. In the early days of networking when IBM and Sytek introduced this protocol, no routers existed. IBM's network architecture used a flat-bridged network with all hosts belonging to the same network. IBM originally implemented NetBIOS within a host's firmware, using a Layer 2 protocol for delivery known as NetBEUI (NetBIOS Basic Extended User Interface).

NetBEUI delivers Layer 2 NetBIOS datagrams between hosts relying on source and destination MAC addresses to identify communicating hosts. Because they had no routers, this proved a successful and easy way to locate resources. NetBIOS hosts would simply send out a broadcast to all hosts on the network querying to resolve the destination host's NetBIOS name to a MAC address. Because Layer 2 devices do not filter broadcasts, all hosts would receive this broadcast, and the host assigned this name would respond with a directed datagram to the originating source host with its MAC address. The host would complete the name resolution process once the source host had resolved the destination host's name to MAC address, enabling the two remote hosts to exchange data through directed datagrams.

NetBIOS hosts send the initial query as a broadcast. The hosts then communicate, including the response that resolved the name to a MAC address, directly between hosts. Once a querying host resolves a name through NetBIOS, it stores this information in cache and retains it for a period of time in case it needs the information for future communications.

NetBIOS and NetBEUI

Many people confuse NetBIOS and NetBEUI; that confusion is understandable because they are so closely intertwined within the firmware. NetBEUI is strictly a Layer 2 protocol implementation designed to carry NetBIOS datagrams over a flat-bridged network. NetBEUI has no Layer 3 information; therefore no Layer 3 logical addressing. Because NetBEUI carries no Layer 3 logical address, you cannot route it. As a Layer 2 protocol, it limits itself to Layer 2 information and addressing (MAC addresses).

NetBIOS originally ran directly on top of this Layer 2 protocol, functionally providing a broadcast name service to hosts on the same network. You cannot route NetBEUI; however, modifications to NetBIOS have enabled it to be carried over routable protocols such as IP and IPX. This allows it to be forwarded beyond a Layer 3 boundary (across a router).

NetBIOS does not limit itself to name resolution. It also manages sessions between hosts, deals with browser requests, and so on. However, for the purpose of this book, we will focus only on the name resolution functions of NetBIOS.

NetBIOS Over TCP/IP

As previously mentioned, IBM originally designed NetBIOS to run exclusively over NetBEUI in a flat-bridged network used with IBM's LAN Server and OS/2 operating systems. Microsoft adopted the protocol for use in its LAN Manager implementation, the predecessor to its popular Windows Operating system NT product line. In this earlier implementation, there were no modifications to NetBIOS or NetBEUI, making them unroutable, which limited clients to accessing only local resources.

By the mid-1990s Microsoft programmers extracted NetBIOS from NetBEUI, making it portable to other protocols such as IP and IPX. By separating NetBIOS from NetBEUI, they fashioned NetBIOS as true Session layer protocol with logical APIs (Application Programming Interfaces). The logical APIs allowed NetBIOS to run over various Transport and Network layer protocols, making it routable and still maintaining the user-friendly naming service.

If you have installed a Microsoft Windows client or server product, you might have noticed that you have a choice of protocols: IP, IPX, and/or NetBEUI. This choice reflects the current flexibility that allows NetBIOS to run over one or all of them simultaneously, depending on your network needs. Because this book focuses on the TCP/IP protocol suite, we will no longer discuss how NetBIOS functions over the other protocols and take a closer look at how it runs on top of TCP/IP.

The Session layer protocol NetBIOS has programming hooks that enable it to port to TCP/IP, a routable protocol. However, NetBIOS uses broadcast by nature, which means that routers do not forward it. This presents a problem because most networks do not exist as one flat-bridged network, but many networks separated by routers. To solve this problem, the modified NetBIOS allows it to be carried over TCP/IP well-known UDP and TCP ports 137, 138, and 139 (see Table 14.7). Although NetBIOS has other ports defined, it uses these ports primarily. RFCs 1001 and 1002 define NetBIOS over TCP/IP.

TABLE 14.7   NetBIOS TCP/IP Ports

Port Number	Description
137	NetBIOS name service (NBNS). Provides name resolution.
138	NetBIOS datagrams used for browser service. Enables hosts to announce and locate services by name.
139	NetBIOS datagrams used for persistent net use connections. Enables hosts to connect to remote resources.

Users can access a remote host's resources by using a UNC (universal naming convention), which consists of the computer name followed by a share name and references a path to the shared resources on a remote host. The following is an example of a UNC: \\HeathersPC\home.

The UNC also can be used to create a persistent connection to a remote host's file system, mapping a local host drive. For example, you can use the **net use** command to map a local drive, such as E: to *Heather's home directory* on *Heather's PC* by typing **net use d:\\HeatherPC\home\heather**. Once you use this command on a local host, you can access this path by simply typing **d:** as if it were a local path.

When you use a UNC to access a resource on a remote host, this name must be resolved to a logical Network layer IP address. Once the IP address of the destination host is discovered, this address must be resolved to a local MAC address for point-to-point delivery. (We discussed address resolution in Chapter 4.) Because we already know how Network layer address resolution works, we won't discuss it in this chapter. Instead, we will focus on how NetBIOS resolves names in a TCP/IP network.

Node Types

Remember that NetBIOS has and always will use broadcasts, and routers do not pass broadcasts. When a user issues a request to access a remote host using a name, depending on the client's configuration, NetBIOS might after checking its local cache, use the following methods to resolve the name to a Network layer address:

- **B-node (broadcast node type)**   Tries broadcast; then LMHosts file.
- **P-node (point-to-point node type)**   Tries NBNS server only.

- **M-node (mixed node type)**   Client tries b-node, p-node, then LMHosts file.
- **H-node (hybrid node type)**   Client tries p-node, b-node, then LMHosts file.

A host always looks in its local name cache first to see if it has recently resolved the requested name to an IP address. This saves bandwidth because a broadcast or directed query does not have to be sent out on the wire if one exists. If the host does not have an entry within the name cache and cannot find one by querying, it tries a node type depending on a client's configuration.

B-node

Clients check their caches first. If that fails to result in a resolution, it makes several attempts to broadcast a query out on the local segment. If it does not receive a response, as a last resort it checks (if configured) the local host's LMHost file (LM stands for LAN Manager, which is the original Microsoft operating system implementation for clients and servers). Created by an administrator or user, this simple, local text file contains NetBIOS name-to-IP address mappings, serving the identical function as an IP host table mentioned earlier in this chapter.

P-node

P-node hosts check their caches first and then try to resolve names by sending a directed datagram to a NBNS (WINS) server, Microsoft's name for a server managing name-to-IP address resolution. This node type does not generate any broadcast traffic. However, if this host has no entry in cache or in the WINS database, or the server is unavailable, the query fails. This is the most unforgiving method of resolution.

M-node

In mixed node, clients of course will try cache first. If that fails, clients will try b-node and p-node. Finally they will check the local LMHost file before giving up.

H-node

Most implementations use this as the default mode because it provides the most versatility. The order of resolution goes as follows:

1. Cache
2. P-node
3. B-node
4. LMHosts

Most prefer this method because it tries a P-node before broadcasting, which increases network performance by eliminating unnecessary broadcasts from the network. Only P-node supports NetBIOS name resolution across routers. Because p-node clients must know the IP address of the NBNS (WINS) server before sending a query, they have no need to send it as a broadcast. Because it uses a directed datagram instead of a broadcast, routers can forward it.

So how does a client learn this address? Either an administrator configures this address on the local host or it learns this address upon boot up from a DHCP server as one of the assigned parameters. An administrator generally assigns p-node clients a primary and secondary WINS server address so if the first server is unavailable, it can try the secondary server.

WINS (Windows Internet Name Server)

Microsoft's NBNS implementation is called WINS, which stands for Windows Internet Name Server. WINS basically provides dynamic NetBIOS name resolution for NetBIOS hosts, similar to a DNS server. WINS servers maintain a database of NetBIOS-to-IP address mappings. Administrators strategically place these WINS servers throughout an IP network to service name-to-address resolution requests sent by clients. An administrator can build this database manually or WINS servers can dynamically add learned names and addresses to this table.

When online and configured with the IP address of a WINS server, WINS clients will register their names and addresses with this server in case some host wants to resolve the name. Upon startup, hosts that do not know what their WINS servers are will broadcast their NetBIOS names announcing their existence on the network. When this happens, a local WINS server receives the broadcast, learns the name and addressing, and enters this in its database.

WINS Proxy Agent

Most Microsoft operating system products, and some routers support name resolution by functioning as a WINS *proxy agent* or server for local hosts that do not have p-node capability. Clients that do not have p-node capability can broadcast resolution requests only on the local segment, which prevents them from registering and resolving names through a remote WINS server.

A proxy agent is any host configured to intercept local resolution broadcast requests and relay them as directed datagrams to a remote WINS server for name resolution. When the response comes back, the relay agent caches the local request for future use and passes this information on to the source host. This enables backward compatibility with older implementations that support only b-node.

NetBIOS Examples

Let's take a look at some NetBIOS examples as seen through a Sniffer. Figure 14.9 shows a NetBIOS name service query; using it as an example, within the WINS header you can see the ID number used to match the query with the response, as shown in Figure 14.10. You might have noticed that this header and its fields are strikingly similar to the previously discussed DNS header; that is because their functions are the same. This is a query to resolve the name P60 to a WINS NetBIOS name to an Internet address.

FIGURE 14.9

In the UDP header note the NetBIOS name service port numbers identify the source and destination (port 137).

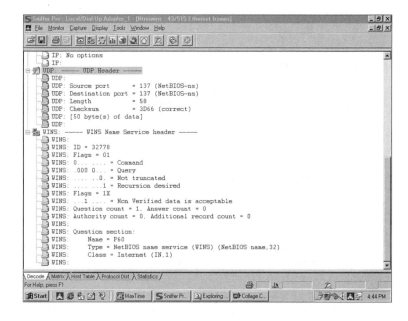

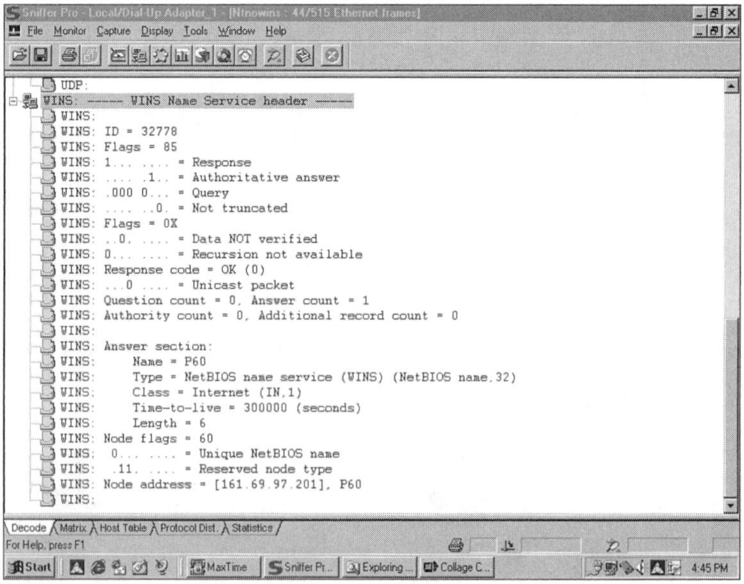

FIGURE 14.10

The server sends a directed datagram response to a query.

The server shown in Figure 14.10 is authoritative for the name being requested. The response has been sent as a directed datagram resolving the name to the address 161.69.97.201, verifying that this name is unique and that the client's node type is h-node (reserved node type). The requesting host will cache this information for later use. The TTL timer of 300000 seconds, indicated by the WINS servers, specifies how long the source host can consider this information valid without having to return for more updated information.

Summary

In the olden days, people had to use numeric addresses instead of names for their hardware and software. Computer innovations made it possible for users to name their computers according to their locations or functions. Internetworking brought domain names and protocol software that can change these domain names back into low-level addresses. Low-level addresses consist of numbers so the computers can understand them.

Before long, this simple list turned into a big burden consisting of three problems: usability, workload, and cost. The namespace was not detailed enough for new computer users to understand. The blossoming Internet caused a big headache for the NIC with thousands of new computers and workstations being connected every day. Finally, the NIC had to go around updating the namespace at each computer each time someone registered a new computer, wasting time and money.

The Domain Name System (DNS) eliminates the need for the namespace by making it possible for you to find the IP address for every domain name and vice versa. The DNS divides the responsibilities of knowing this information into zones. Primary and secondary servers work at each zone.

NetBIOS provides a simple way for users to access remote resources and services by using a name rather than an address. Each NetBIOS device has a unique 15-character name and services running within the host also might have names associated with them. These unique names enable a user to find a specific service running within a host by specifying the name.

Review Questions

1. Describe three problems with namespace.

2. Explain how primary servers differ from secondary servers.

3. Why can't computers understand a domain name?

4. Explain how DNS designates its authority.

5. Define the term "caching" and how servers use it for name resolution.

6. Why would a server use a message format?

7. List what each message must contain in a message format.

8. What is the difference between NetBIOS and NetBEUI?

9. How is NetBIOS able to do name resolution at Layer 3?

10. What are the three primary TCP/UDP ports used by NetBIOS and what are they used for?

11. What are the different NetBIOS node types? Briefly describe each.

12. What is a WINS proxy agent?

CHAPTER 15

HYPERTEXT TRANSFER PROTOCOL (HTTP)

You will learn about the following in this chapter:

- HTTP Qualities
- HTTP Components
- HTTP Sessions
- Message Formats
- Error Messages
- Status and Error Codes
- HTTP Connections and Lengths

HTTP and the World Wide Web

You are babysitting your eight-year-old cousin and he really wants to see the new Disney animation flick. You open your computer's home page and click the entertainment link. The entertainment Web page opens and you see the web address in the URL content window. Before the address, you notice *HTTP*, the first bit of the URL. You find the nearest theater showing the Disney movie and your cousin smiles joyfully when he finds out he'll be seeing today's show.

Every time you click a link or type in a query, you use the Hypertext Transfer Protocol (HTTP), the most widely used and recognizable protocol on the Internet. HTTP makes communication between your workstation's browser and a Web server happen. Your browser works as an application program and opens Web pages. Using HTTP's features, it travels and grabs information outside the host's operating system and hardware. Although HTTP started out helping only simple data transfer, it now supports complex data types such as the multiple graphic images you see every day on the Web.

Hyper

The term *hyper* in hypertext means that the document has links you can choose.

In this chapter we discuss the components that enable HTTP to make its journey and then go through the processes HTTP uses when you want to find a Web page. For all you computer nerds (like myself), we get into nitty-gritty detail by showing you how and why error messages occur, the various message formats, and what each part in the message means.

HTTP Features

Like a good employee, HTTP has specific qualities that set it apart. HTTP uses these qualities to make what has been commonly referred to as "surfing the web," a simple and painless process. HTTP's unique characteristics include the following:

- It works at the Application level, providing a communication link and message forwarding; it does not offer reliability or perform retransmission.

- The server does not keep a history of HTTP sessions or your HTTP requests.

- HTTP provides bidirectional transfer, meaning the server can transfer a copy of the requested Web page to the browser and the browser can transfer to the server.

- It uses *capability negotiation,* which means browsers and servers together can figure out details such as which character set they want to use for their requests and responses.

- It supports caching, which means to save time, your browser caches a copy of each Web page it retrieves for you. If you want the page again, HTTP has the browser ask the server whether the contents of the present page differ from the cached copy. We will discuss caching further in Chapter 14, "Name Resolution."

- HTTP enables support for intermediaries, which means any machine along the path between the browser and the server can be a proxy server. These proxy servers cache Web pages. They also use the cache to answer queries. We discuss proxy servers further in the following section.

HTTP Components

Just as the Beatles song says, "I get by with a little help from my friends," HTTP gets by with a little help from its friendly components. This section explores all the components HTTP uses when you want to find and open a Web page. Table 15.1 describes HTTP's components.

TABLE 15.1   HTTP Components

Components	Description
Browser	An independent front end existing as a Graphic User Interface (GUI) tool that changes your commands into HTTP requests and responses. The term *graphic* means you can see it.
Communication chains	Work as the requests and responses that servers and browsers send back and forth to each other. Response chains usually carry the requested information. You will see these communication chains at work later in this chapter.
Gateway	An intermediary HTTP host working as an HTTP-enabled server, transparently enabling you to get to resources and services on behalf of the origin server.
Origin server	An HTTP server. Gets its name by being the first place to have the resources you want; it hosts the information. (Consider this server "the hostess with the mostest.")
Proxy	Works as an intermediary HTTP host functioning as either an HTTP client or server so the UA and the origin server can exchange information. Proxy agents pass requests from clients to servers. Servers also respond to the request itself when the information you want is local.
User agents (UAs)	UAs start an HTTP session and request information for you. We will go into more detail about UAs in Chapter 13, "Simple Mail Transfer Protocol (SMTP)."
Resources	Also referred to as *method tokens*. Resources are the pieces of information you want and what HTTP sessions try to get.
Tunnel	Works as an intermediary software interface that gets transparent relay of HTTP sessions between two end host connections.

Transparent or Non-transparent Proxy Agents

You can configure proxy agents transparently or nontransparently depending on requirements. Transparent proxy agents can't change client requests or server responses unless the information they pass through allows for identification and authentication of clients. However, nontransparent agents can change HTTP requests and responses to support services, such as filtering or group identification if they need to.

HTTP Sessions

HTTP relies on TCP at the Transport layer to provide guaranteed delivery of data using well-known server port 80 for communication. Remember that the HTTP session begins with you, the user. An HTTP session follows these steps:

1. You open your browser and identify information or a resource you want.

2. An HTTP connection request goes out to start an HTTP session between the client (UA) and either an origin server or intermediary.

3. A Uniform Resource Identifier (URI) identifies this resource or service.

Note

HTTP may need to open several TCP sessions when receiving an HTML page, for example, for each object on the page and the HTML text itself.

When HTTP can identify a resource by name, it uses the Uniform Resource Name (URN) convention, more commonly known as the Uniform Resource Locater (URL). Here is a URL following the URN format:

`http://home-movies.excite.com/`

You can see that this first part of the URN identifies the protocol; in this case HTTP. The next part of the URN describes the host you are trying to reach on an origin server; for example, `www.home-movies.excite.com`. Additional path information follows and ends with the specific resource you request (entertainment).

The origin server can service the request the UA sends. Intermediary proxy agents pass this request on as it goes to an origin server. An HTTP gateway also can service this request directly. All methods remain transparent to you; the gateway services the request even though the origin server appears to have done the job. As far as the client knows, it successfully achieves communication with and gets the requested resource on that server. Figures 15.1, 15.2, and 15.3 show three communication chains that HTTP processes can take. Figure 15.1 shows UA-to-origin server communication chain.

Figure 15.2 shows a UA through an intermediary-to-origin server communication path. Note that on the way to the origin server, the request chain must go through any number of HTTP components, or intermediary devices. These devices act as communication links between the client and the server.

Figure 15.3 shows a UA-to-intermediary communication path. After the client sends its request chain to the origin server, the first intermediary device sends it out, and then the second intermediary device stops it and services it. This second intermediary has information the UA requested locally, so it sends a response chain to the client with the information.

FIGURE 15.1
Notice how the UA communicates directly with the origin server. No intermediary HTTP hosts are needed.

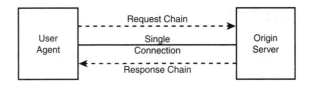

FIGURE 15.2
Proxy agents or intermediary devices pass requests from clients to servers.

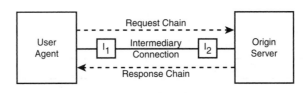

FIGURE 15.3
A request chain can include more than one intermediary device. In this case, the second intermediary device has the information.

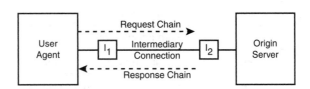

When an intermediary device handles requests, the origin server's processing time decreases, and performance and response to client requests increases. Some companies strategically place frequently requested information on intermediary devices and allow these devices to directly handle requests so that the origin servers have less work and responsibility. Intermediary devices also cache the information the client previously requested from an origin server and store this information in the hopes for a request for the same information.

HTTP Message Format

As in any protocol, the client and server communicate through a series of messages called *replies* and *responses*. We refer to HTTP messages that clients send as *request claims* and replies made by intermediaries or origin servers as *response chains*. Both message types follow a general format in this order:

- Generic start line, called a *request line* for request messages and a *stats line* for reply messages
- General header
- Message header
- One empty line
- Message body

Generic Start Line

A generic start line consists of either a request line or a status line. A UA sends a request line and an origin or gateway server indicating a response sends a status line. Generic start lines include the URI specifying the referenced resource. They function as operational indicators describing the action to be taken on the resource, and the HTTP protocol version being used, followed by a CR/LF (carriage return/line feed). Table 15.2 describes HTTP method tokens and their function.

TABLE 15.2   Method Tokens and Their Functions

Method Tokens	Functions
GET	Requests to get resource.
HEAD	Tests hypertext connections.
PUT	Requests to forward information.
OPTIONS	Finds the HTTP features and abilities for the UAs.
POST	Creates a new resource on the origin server, such as putting out a new message on the bulletin board.
DELETE	A client sends this command so the origin server will delete a resource.
Trace	Helps test and diagnose errors.
Connect	Proxy agents set up for tunneling use this command.

General Header

All message headers begin with the same general header. This applies to both request and response messages, but does not apply to the entity being transferred. HTTP's general header contains the following fields:

- Cache-control
- Connection
- Date
- Pragma
- Trailer
- Transfer-encoding
- Upgrade

- Via

- Warning

We will describe each field in the following sections.

Cache-Control

The cache-control passes the information through the request response path, controlling the caching operation of HTTP UAs, intermediaries, and origin servers. Cache control dictates:

- When to cache or store sent or received information

- How long the information should stay cached

- Whether the cached information remains public or private

Connection

The connection field shows HTTP clients which connection characteristic, such as persistence, it wishes to apply. These optional client connection characteristics might or might not require support from intermediary or origin servers. Proxy agents receiving client connection options can apply the characteristics to the connection or deny it, but will not pass this characteristic on to the next intermediary or origin server in the communication chain.

Date

The originator sets the date. The date field shows the date and time of the request or response.

Pragma

The pragma field defines which directions an optional set of vendors should include in the request or response chains.

Trailer

The trailer field value indicates a given set of header fields will be in the trailer of a message, encoded with chunked transfer coding.

Transfer-Encoding

The transfer-encoding field describes the method used to transfer and encode the message body—in short, what transformation has been applied to the message to ensure "safe transport" through the network. Transfer-coding differs from content-coding because transfer-coding is a property of the message, not of the entity.

Messages can be broken into chunks, each chunk containing its own length value, followed by an optional trailer containing entity-header fields. When users transfer large streams of information, it breaks into smaller, more manageable pieces called chunks, all belonging to the same stream. Each of these chunks must be identifiable as belonging to the stream and the length of the chunk by the recipient. Chunking allows dynamically produced material to be transferred along with the information necessary for the recipient to verify that it has received the message intact (by verifying its length value).

The chunked transfer-encoding method is an essential part of this field. If transfer-coding is applied to a message body, the transfer-coding must include chunked, or the connection terminates. The chunked transfer-coding must be the last transfer-coding applied to the message body and cannot be applied more than once to a message body.

Upgrade

The upgrade field settles protocol and version type to resolve compatibility issues between communicating devices.

Via

Intermediary devices such as gateways and proxies use this field. It enables these devices to keep track of forwarded messages and to identify various protocols and capabilities implemented by all devices involved in the request/reply chain.

Warning

The warning field gives an error notification.

Message Headers (Request, Response, or Entity)

The HTTP protocol operates as a request/response protocol. The client sends a request to the server and the server responds with a reply. This can generate one of three types of specific message headers: request, response, or entity.

Request Header

Within the first line a request message from a client to a server includes the method to be applied to the resource, the identifier of the resource, and the protocol version in use. A request header allows a client to send additional information about the request to the server not contained in that first line or the general header. The request header has information about the client that you are working on, the resource you ask for and the server. Table 15.3 describes what specific request headers mean.

TABLE 15.3   Request Headers and Their Meanings

Request Header	Meaning
Accept-Charset	Shows the character sets that are okay for the response
Accept-Encoding	Puts a limit on the content encoding values
Accept-Language	Puts a limit on the number of natural languages in the set
Authorization	Has the qualifications for a UA

TABLE 15.3   Continued

Request Header	Meaning
From	The e-mail address of whomever directs the requesting UA
Host	Internet host and port number of the requested resource
If-Modified-Since	Makes sure the cached info is up to date
If-None-Match	Used with a method to make it conditional
If-Range	Requests all or part of a unit
If-Unmodified-Since	Used with a method to make it conditional
Max-Forwards	Puts a limit on the amount of proxies or gateways that can put forward a request
Proxy-Authorization	Enables the client identify itself to a proxy
Range	Defines a resource piece
Referer	The URL address from which the Request-RI was obtained
UA	Has information about the UA that started the request

Response Header

Servers send a response header in response to UA requests; these messages consist of three-digit codes identifying the response type. We will discuss the response messages, three-digit status, and error codes later in this chapter.

Entity

Although optional, the entity header further defines information about the resource you request. Table 15.4 shows the meanings of the entity headers.

TABLE 15.4   Entity Headers and Their Meanings

Entity Header	Meaning
Allow	Shows which methods the resource supports
Content-Base	Defines the base URL
Content-Encoding	Adapts the media type
Content-Language	Explains the natural languages
Content-Length	Specifies the extent of the body of the message in octets
Content-Location	Gives the resource location for the unit

TABLE 15.4   Continued

Entity Header	Meaning
Content-MD5	Provides a complete message reliability check
Content-Range	Specifies where to insert a part of the body
Content-Type	Shows what type of media the body will have
ETag	States what the tags (described later in the chapter) will be for the related entity
Expires	Shows the date/time right before the response expires
Last-Modified	The last date/time the original resource underwent changes

Empty line (CRLF)

This empty line takes out the end of the preceding message header.

Message Body

The body (untransparent) is everything you can see. The header messages are for the browser to read.

HTTP Response Messages, Status, and Error Codes

As in any well-running protocol, the servers give out response messages in reply to requests. Response messages let the client know exactly what is going on through a specific format encompassing certain codes and phrases. Response messages have the following format:

- Status Line

- Headers

- CRLF

- Message body

The status line consists of a protocol version. The status code and the textual phrases that go with it follow the status line. HTTP status and error codes share the same three-digit format as FTP, as discussed in Chapter 12, "File Transfer Protocol (FTP)." These codes vary from informational to notification of a failed request. The first digit shows the general message category. The last two digits identify the message within the category. RFC 2616 states that the following message categories exist because of the last two digits:

- **1xx:**Informational   Request received, continuing process.
- **2xx:**Successful   The action was successfully received, understood and accepted.
- **3xx:**Redirection   Must take further action to complete request.
- **4xx:**Client-related error   Request contains bad syntax or cannot be fulfilled.
- **5xx:**Server-related error   Server failed to fulfill request.

Table 15.5 shows the specific meanings for each of the numeric status codes.

TABLE 15.5   HTTP Status Codes and Their Meanings

Status Code	What it Means
100	Continue
101	Switching protocols
200	Okay
201	Created
202	Accepted
203	Non-authoritative information
204	No content
205	Reset content
206	Partial content
300	Multiple choices
301	Moved permanently
302	Moved temporarily
303	See other
304	Not modified
305	Use proxy
400	Bad request
401	Unauthorized
402	Needs payment
403	Prohibited
404	Not found

TABLE 15.5   Continued

Status Code	What it Means
405	Method not allowed
406	Unacceptable
407	Needs proxy authentication
408	Requests time out
409	Conflict
410	Gone
411	Needs length
412	Precondition failed
413	Request entity too large
414	Request URL too large
415	Media type not supported
500	Internal server error
501	Unimplemented
502	Bad gateway
503	Unavailable service
504	Gateway time out
505	HTTP version unsupported

HTTP Error Messages

During a weekend of Web surfing you probably have seen this annoying message:

Bad Request

Your browser sent a request that this server could not understand.

After verbally stating your thoughts about this message to your computer, you might have sat back and wondered how and why this message came about. These irksome error messages appear when a Web server receives an illegal request. Usually, a browser sends this request and the browser tries unsuccessfully to show you whatever the server gives it. Therefore, the servers usually create error messages in Hypertext Markup Language (HTML).

HTML consists of text you can read along with embedded commands for the computer that give the rules for display. These commands, also called *tags,* come between less than and greater than symbols. If you do any programming, these tags should look familiar.

Here is how your error message would look in the HTML format:

```
<HTML>

  <HEAD><TITLE>400 Bad Request</TITLE>

  </HEAD>

  <BODY>

      <H1>Bad Request</H1> Your browser sent a request

      that this server could not understand.

      </BODY>

    </HTML>
```

Only the browser uses the head of the document—everything between <HEAD> and </HEAD>. You see only the body of the message.

Summary

Hypertext Transfer Protocol (HTTP) works as a communication link between your browser and a server when you want to find and open up Web pages. You browser works as an applications program, opening the Web pages for you. The Web page displays using Graphical User Interface (GUI) so you can see it.

HTTP has specific qualities. It does not offer reliability nor does it retransmission itself. The server doesn't file away a history of HTTP sessions or your HTTP requests. HTTP supports bidirectional transfer, meaning transfer from the server to the browser and from the browser to the server. HTTP lets the browsers and servers decide which details they want to use for their requests and responses. HTTP uses caching to save time and supports intermediaries so that any machine in the path can be a proxy server.

Proxy servers enable the user agent (UA) and the origin server to exchange information. The UAs request information for you; the origin server holds the information, called *resources,* that you want. The requests and information replies are called *communication chains.*

HTTP sessions start when you open your browser and request information. TCP at the transport layer ensures delivery of this data. The request goes to an origin server or intermediary. A Uniform Resource Identifier (URI) identifies the resource. The name of this resource the Uniform Resource Locator (URL) follows the Uniform Resource Name (URN) convention.

Review Questions

1. Why do you need to use HTTP?

2. What function does HTTP have with the browser and the server?

3. What is the browser's function?

4. At which level does HTTP work and how does this affect its capabilities?

5. List three more of HTTP's qualities.

6. Explain how HTTP's support of caching adds efficiency.

7. Explain what a proxy does.

8. Which HTTP components can be a proxy?

9. State the general HTTP message format.

10. Who can read the message body?

11. Who can read the headers?

12. Why do you receive error messages?

CHAPTER 16

TRIVIAL FILE TRANSFER PROTOCOL (TFTP)

> **You will learn about the following in this chapter:**
> - TFTP Packet Types
> - TFTP Operation
> - TFTP Extensions

Introduction to File Transfer Protocols

Although most people use FTP as their file transfer protocol in the TCP/IP suite (see Chapter 12, "File Transfer Protocol" (FTP)), not all applications need or can handle the complexity or the full functionality FTP provides. For example, FTP requires clients and servers to establish, maintain, and manage multiple TCP connections. For a PC that doesn't have a sophisticated operating system or one that has limited capacity, this might prove difficult if not impossible. In addition, FTP can be difficult to program.

The TCP/IP suite provides a solution: TFTP (Trivial File Transfer Protocol). TFTP provides a simple, unsophisticated, and inexpensive file transfer service between hosts. Defined by RFC 1350, TFTP reads or writes files for a client to or from a server. Each exchange begins with a client requesting to either read or write a file from a server. TFTP offers no services other than this simple, fast file transfer; it has the distinct advantage of remaining as simple as the Hula-Hoop.

Although initially designed to be embedded within Ethernet ROM chips of diskless clients, other data link architectures support TFTP's use. TFTP's original design transfers 512-byte blocks of data using UDP port 69, but current implementations support larger blocks. Unlike TCP and FTP, it provides no authentication and no guarantee of delivery. The sending side (TFTP client) opens a variable client UDP port (referred to as a TFTP or transfer ID), requests a file, and waits for the acknowledgement of each block before sending another block. In turn, the receiving side acknowledges each block when it receives the data.

TFTP does not require a ton of overhead like FTP, which uses two TCP connections (rather than connectionless UDP) to establish communication and transport data. However, because TFTP uses UDP for transport, it cannot guarantee the delivery of data. By utilizing UDP as for transport, it also makes implementing TFTP easier; hence its trivial nature and name. Because TFTP restricts itself to only simple file transfer it provides a smaller and much faster, yet reliable solution to FTP. Smaller applications can prove very important for diskless devices because TFTP can easily fit into read-only memory (ROM).

When a diskless workstation powers on, it can retrieve a boot image or configuration from memory on a remote server. This allows it to obtain necessary initialization parameters remotely. TFTP provides the advantage of allowing an operating system to utilize bootstrapping code stored on a TFTP server. For example, if you turn on your computer TFTP can enable you to bootstrap from a local or remote TFTP server.

TFTP Packet Types

Similar to the protocol, TFTP keeps its operation simple. The first packet sent (by the client) requests a file transfer (from the server) and establishes the communication between the variable client UDP port (known as TID) and well-known TFTP port 69 for the server. This packet specifies a file name and whether it requests to *read* (*RRQ*), meaning to transfer from the server to the client or *write* (*WRQ*), meaning to transfer from the client to the server.

TFTP accomplishes these tasks by transferring a continuous stream of datagrams in 512-byte data blocks (or larger if supported). The final block contains less than 512 bytes, or configured block size, which signifies the end of the stream. Any transmission error encountered kills the transfer. TFTP has five different packet types, described in Table 16.1; the Opcodes within the header distinguish each type.

TABLE 16.1   TFTP Packet Types

Opcode	Packet Type/Operation
1	Read Request (RRQ)
2	Write Request (WRQ)
3	Data (DATA)
4	Acknowledgement (ACK)
5	Error (ERROR)

Figure 16.1 shows the different TFTP packet formats.

FIGURE 16.1

The initial 2 bytes (Opcode) identify the TFTP message format. Note that RRQ and WRQ share the same packet format. The first packet sent by the client will be either an RRQ or WRQ.

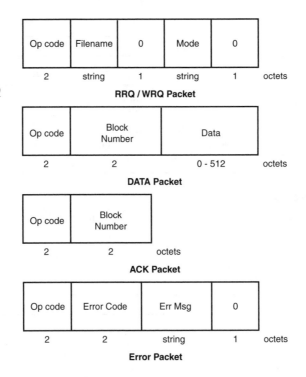

RRQ / WRQ Packet

DATA Packet

ACK Packet

Error Packet

RRQ and WRQ Packets

As previously mentioned, RRQ and WRQ packets have the same structure. These packets begin a request and determine what file needs to be transferred. Table 16.2 describes the fields contained within the RRQ or WRQ packet.

TABLE 16.2   RRQ/WRQ Packet Fields

Field	Octets	Description
Opcode	2	Identifies the packet type: • 1 = RRQ • 2 = WRQ
Filename	String	String of netascii, similar to ASCII, (8-bit code defined by ANSI X3.4-1968) characters that specify the filename. Computer sends these alphanumeric codes for human consumption.

TABLE 16.2   Continued

Field	Octets	Description
Zero (two fields)	1	Terminates the filename and mode fields.
Mode	String	Specifies transfer mode: • Netascii • Octet (raw 8-bit bytes) • Mail (netascii characters destined for the user instead of the host); obsolete.

Data Packets

The data packets, or Type 3 packets, transfer the requested data. Table 16.3 describes the fields contained within a data packet.

TABLE 16.3   Data Packet Fields

Field	Octets	Description
Opcode	2	Identifies the data packet with Opcode 3.
Block number	2	Identifies the particular fixed block of data.
Data	0-512	Carries the actual information to be transferred. Any block containing less than 512 or configured block size (up to a maximum of 65,464 bytes) marks the end of the data transfer. See RFC 2348 for block size extension options.

ACK Packet

The *ACK* packet acknowledges the receipt of each block (data packet) received during data transfer. TFTP utilizes the lock-step acknowledgement method, which means each data packet has to be acknowledged before transmission of another. Remember TFTP transmits data one at a time in blocks, with the first data block numbered one. Because TFTP operates over UDP, it does not provide for windowing. TFTP must acknowledge all packets except error packets. ACK or error packets acknowledge data and WRQ packets, whereas data and error packets acknowledge RRQ or ACK packets.

Table 16.4 describes the fields contained within an ACK packet.

TABLE 16.4 ACK Packet Fields

Field	Octets	Description
Opcode	2	Identifies the ACK packet with Opcode 4.
Block number	2	Corresponds to the block number of the data packet.

Error Packets

The error packet acknowledges any of the other packet types and signifies that an error has occurred. The error code appears as a number that indicates what type of error has occurred. These error messages appear for the human's benefit and appear in netascii. Most errors cause termination of the connection. Table 16.5 describes the fields contained within an error packet.

TABLE 16.5 Error Packet Fields

Field	Octets	Description
Opcode	2	Identifies the error packet type with Opcode 5.
Error code	2	Describes the problem using seven different error codes (see Table 16.6).
Error message	String	Netascii string.
Zero	1	Completes the packet.

When an error occurs the host sends an error packet, terminating the connection. Three events generate error packets:

- The host cannot satisfy a request (for example, cannot locate a file).

- The host receives a delayed or duplicated packet.

- When the host loses access to a resource such as a disk during the transfer.

The 2-octet error code field contains a value that describes what error has occurred. Table 16.6 describes each value and its meaning.

TABLE 16.6   Error Code Values

Value	Description
0	Not defined, see error message (if any)
1	Cannot find file
2	Access violation
3	Disk full or allocation exceeded
4	Illegal TFTP operation
5	Unknown transfer ID
6	File already exists
7	No such user

TFTP Operation

As previously mentioned, the TFTP client initiates the connection by requesting to read or write a file from or to the server. The client does this by opening up a variable port (TFTP TID) to the receiver's well-known TFTP server port 69. The client specifies the identification of the file name and data type within the initial request. Once the client sends the initial request, the TFTP server reassigns itself a new UDP port to use as its TID for the duration of this data transmission and the transfer begins. If the client makes a read request the server begins the transfer; if the client makes a write request the client begins the transmission.

TFTP implements UDP at the transport layer, identifying the source and destination TIDs as port identifiers. The sender calculates a UDP checksum covering the TFTP header and data before transmission. The receiver verifies the checksum to guarantee that the bits received were not damaged during transit. The transmission continues until the client or server transfers the entire file. Figures 16.2, 16.3, and 16.4 show a TFTP client sending a write request; we will describe the request frame by frame.

TFTP implements a simple sequence and acknowledgement scheme within its request/response exchange, allowing only one outstanding datagram at a time. Each time the sender transmits a datagram it holds a datagram locally for retransmission. If either side loses the datagram, the sender eventually detects this because it does not receive acknowledgement from the other side. It then times out and retransmits the buffered information.

FIGURE 16.2

Notice that TFTP client 128.1.0.2 (UDP port 1001 equals the TID) transmits a request to write the file junk.txt to TFTP server 128.1.0.1 (UDP port 69). The UDP header contains no sequencing information; just a simple checksum and length field.

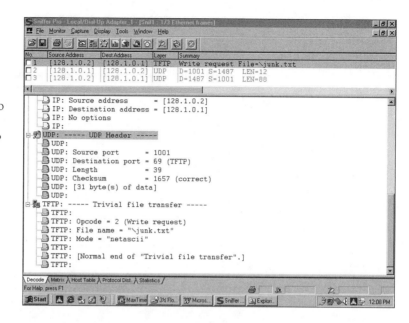

FIGURE 16.3

The second frame contains a connectionless acknowledgement from the TFTP server, indicating its reassigned UDP port number, which is chosen randomly. This server has a new UDP port/TID of s=1487.

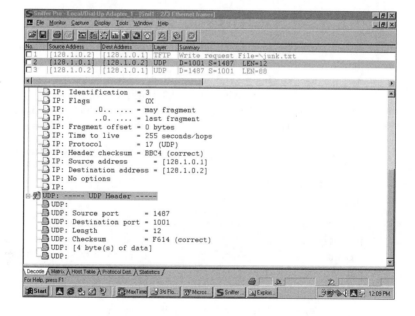

FIGURE 16.4

This frame shows the client sending the first data block within the stream.

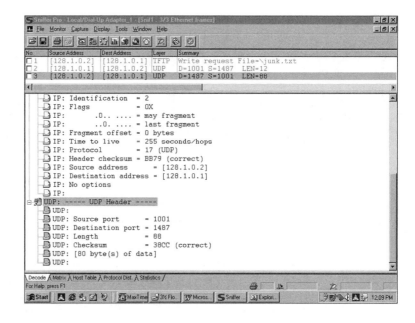

TFTP Extensions

The original TFTP specifications have been extended to allow for option negotiation between the client and the server. Only one specific option has been defined (blocksize); however, the specification remains general enough that vendors can implement their own options as necessary. A larger blocksize increases the file transfer performance between remote hosts. Older implementation might not support this extension, which limits the transfer to the original 512-byte standard.

The client side controls the option negotiation. The server side cannot request option negotiation; it can only respond to the client. If a client wishes to implement additional options beyond the normal TFTP specification, the client can append this information to its initial read or write request.

TFTP servers that support option negotiation have an option acknowledgement (OACK) packet to notify the client if it supports this option. When a server accepts the option, it includes it in the OACK packet. If it does not accept the option it simply ignores it, leaving it out of the OACK frame.

Clients implement only what servers allow. The client can request multiple options during the negotiation process by simply listing them within the read or write packet. The client appends the option request to the standard read or write request used to initialize the session between the client and server. For clients that support option negotiation, two additional frames appear in the header: *option,* which specifies the option requested, such as blocksize and *value,* which specifies the value for this option. For example, the expected value of blocksize ranges from 0 to 65464.

OACK Packet

The OACK packet uses an operation code of six. The server sends the OACK packet to reject or acknowledge options requested by the client. Table 16.7 describes the OACK packet fields. The option and value pair repeats depending on the number of options requested.

TABLE 16.7   OACK Packet Fields

Field	Octets	Description
Opcode	2	Identifies the OACK packet with Opcode 6.
Option1	2	Corresponds to the first option listed within the client's read or write request packet. Additional options list as option2, option3, and so on and correspond to the client's read or write request.
Value1	2	Corresponds to the first option listed within the client's read or write request packet. Additional values list as value2, value3 and so on and correspond to the client's read or write request packet.

Summary

TFTP provides a simple, fast, and inexpensive file transfer service between hosts. TFTP reads or writes files for a client to or from a server. Each exchange begins with a client requesting to either read or write a file from a server.

The first packet sent requests a file transfer from the server and establishes the communication between the variable client UDP port (known as TID) and well-known TFTP port 69 for the server. Original TFTP versions transfer files in 512-byte blocks although current implementations can transfer more. A block containing less than 512 bytes signifies the last block.

TFTP has five packet types: RRQ, WRQ, ACK, data, and error. The RRQ or WRQ specifies a file name and whether it requests to read (RRQ) or write (WRQ) the file. Data packets transfer the requested data. ACK packets acknowledge receipt of the blocks of data. Error packets signify when an error has occurred during the transfer of the blocks of data.

Review Questions

1. What are the differences between FTP and TFTP?

2. What are some of the benefits of using TFTP?

3. What type of service does TFTP provide?

4. How does each exchange begin?

5. What five packets does TFTP use and what functions do they serve?

6. What does a block of less than 512 bytes signify?

7. What is the lock-step acknowledgement method and how does TFTP utilize it?

8. What three events trigger an error packet?

9. What does it mean to read a file and write a file?

10. Briefly describe TFTP operation.

11. TFTP extensions allow for option negotiation between client and server. How does this affect blocksize?

12. How does TFTP option negotiation work?

13. What is an OACK packet?

CHAPTER 17

SNMP (SIMPLE NETWORK MANAGEMENT PROTOCOL)

You will learn about the following in this chapter:

- Network Management
- SNMP
- Managers, Agents, and Proxies
- SNMP Message Format

Introduction to Network Management

Actual network management might seem like a fantasy for many network managers. After all, when do they actually have time to manage their networks? Perhaps it is only after they solve all the immediate issues that threaten to make their networks toast.

What is network management exactly? Some think it means eliminating problems when they occur; others think it means anticipating network problems before they arise—or at least limiting the difficulties to only minor catastrophes. Whether you take a proactive or reactive approach to network management, one protocol has stood out to address both ways of thinking: SNMP (Simple Network Management Protocol).

RFC 1157 defines the original implementation of SNMP and is the main remote network management protocol in use today. Originally designed to facilitate the remote management of Internet hosts and gateways, SNMP, previously known as SGMP (Simple Gateway Management Protocol), has evolved to support a variety of end devices.

The IAB (Internet Activities Board) has a major hand in the development of a vendor-neutral management protocol for managing Internet systems. Internet committees formed in the mid to late 1980s to discuss potential management protocols; three protocols emerged:

- **HEMS**   High-level Entity Management Systems
- **SGMP**   Renamed as SNMP
- **ISO's CMIP**   Common Management Information Protocol

Note

The ISO (International Organization for Standardization) is an international body that sets specific standards for network protocols. The most popular is seven-layer OSI Reference Model.

After careful consideration they deemed SGMP the short-term protocol of choice, but planned to switch to the ISO standard CMIP management protocol in the future. As previously mentioned, SGMP, now renamed to SNMP, remains the most widely used management protocol within the industry and is the official standard.

SNMP provides a simple vendor-independent management solution. All of the mentioned protocols make use of management information RFCs 1065 and 1066, which describe how managed objects should be identified through the implementation of the *ASN.1* (*Abstract Syntax Notation 1*) method of representing managed objects through arbitrary data structures.

Within RFC 1156, the standard Internet *MIBs* (*Management Information Bases*), referred to as MIB I and II, identify well-known managed objects and define them within a hierarchical tree structure. All SNMP implementations must minimally support these MIBs. However, they can implement their own MIB sub-trees containing manageable objects as long as they follow the *SMI* (*Standard Management Information*) requirements defined in RFC 1156.

SNMP

SNMP runs on top of UDP, providing fast delivery of management requests and responses between hosts running SNMP-based applications, such as SunNetManager or HP's OpenView. These represent just a few of the many applications that make use of SNMP to remotely monitor and manage SNMP-enabled devices.

SNMP provides delivery services of management requests and responses on behalf of the applications. It runs independent of the applications specifics, lower-layer architecture, and upper-layer applications. This makes SNMP a simple and generic, yet powerful network management protocol portable to many different platforms, operating systems, and protocols. Although SNMP historically was carried over IP, because of its generic nature it can run over other protocol suites such as IPX.

SNMP has three main entities that make remote management possible:

- **Manager**   Command generators and notification receivers
- **Agent**   Command responders and notification originators
- **Proxy**   Forwarders

Software running within a device implements all three entities and provides SNMP messaging services to the Application level software.

SNMP Managers

As hosts, SNMP managers run management control software (such as OpenView) to remotely control and monitor SNMP agents. These hosts provide a central management point and user interface using SNMP to deliver commands to agents. This enables the operator to retrieve information, change configuration values, and even reboot a device. SNMP managers also receive unsolicited notification messages (known as *trap messages*) from agents informing them of some type of violation, such as a command received by an unauthorized SNMP manager to change a configuration value.

Two examples of requests are get requests, which are used to read information and set requests, which are used to modify parameters. SNMP managers direct their requests to the destination UDP port 161 running within an agent. Managers listen for trap messages from agents on UDP port 162.

SNMP Agents

As hosts, SNMP agents run SNMP responder and notification generation software. Agents listen for SNMP requests from managers through their receiving UDP port 161. SNMP managers query agents for information, which they store in a local database referred to as an *MIB* (*Management Information Base*). Because of its small size, the agent software fits in ROM chips, which generally are included in devices as part of their firmware, such as in a transceiver port for a router or switch interface. These agents keep track of the MIB database, structured as a hierarchical tree consisting of many objects to be managed and monitored.

For example, an Ethernet Interface would represent a managed object within the context of a specific agent such as a router. You could monitor this interface for specific information relating to traffic going across the interface, such as tracking the number of broadcasts, CRC error, collisions, and so on.

In addition to responding to manager queries to retrieve or modify specific information, you can configure agents to alert managers. Agents alert managers by sending an unsolicited trap message when problems occur or when something attempts to violate the agent, such as a request to modify a parameter coming from an unauthorized manager. Agents send trap messages to managers addressed to UDP port 162.

MIB View

Each agent stores its collection of locally managed objects within its MIB, also referred to as the *MIB view.* When managers request access to an object contained within the MIB view, they must specify the object name, represented as an ASN.1 notation. The ASN.1 notation specifically describes the location of the object within the information base and the *instance,* the unique occurrence of the object within the managed device.

A series of positive integers describing the path within the MIB tree represents the object name that identifies the location of the object. Vendors can register for their own sub-tree IDs, which enable them to extend the Internet tree to include their specific objects. IANA gives sub-tree IDs to organizations.

Proxy

SNMP proxies provide message forwarding between agents and managers. Proxies also act as an intermediary between agent hosts using different versions of SNMP, which enables compatibility between the hosts.

Community

SNMP agents must register with managers to start receiving requests and to know to whom and where to send notification messages. How agents identify and register with managers depends upon implementation. Agents and managers must belong to the same domain, known as a *community,* to facilitate the exchange of messages. There is one default domain, known as the *public domain;* however, you can define others on the manager and agents so that other managed communities can exist. By defining other communities, which you can name anything you like, you limit unauthorized access.

If someone wants to add his or her own management host to a network to maliciously gain access to agents, first he or she would have to guess the name of the community and configure his or her manager for the same name. Of course, just creating new communities and naming them something esoteric won't prevent a clever hacker from learning this information, so authentication and access control lists protecting managed objects remains a must. SNMP does not have a function for specific authentication and access control; however, the applications that use SNMP do.

If you have a proxy involved, it also must belong to the same community as the agents and manager and must register with both of them for message forwarding to begin. All entities must be locally configured with the appropriate community name and any necessary authentication and security information. Agents also need to know the Network layer address of the manager to send all responses and unsolicited notification messages.

SNMP Message Format

All SNMP messages follow the same basic structure, except the Trap message. Each request carries a version number, community name for minimal authentication, and one or more *PDUs* (*Protocols Data Units*) depending on the information being requested by the manager. Figure 17.1 shows the architecture of the SNMPv1 communication network. Figure 17.2 shows the basic format of SNMP messages.

FIGURE 17.1

Note that SNMP uses only five messages, part of the protocol's "simple" approach to network management.

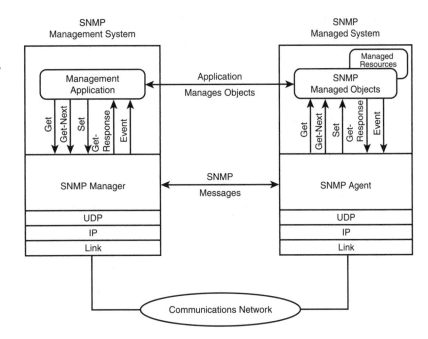

FIGURE 17.2

All SNMP messages (get request, get next request, get response and set request), except the trap message, use the same basic format.

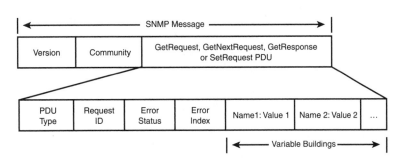

Version

The version field specifies the SNMP version type being used. Both manager and agent must use the same version or the request must go through a proxy, which can translate between the two.

Community Name

This field identifies the community name. You can achieve simple authentication between managers and agents by configuring them to belong to the same community. Administrators assign community names, which are simple plain text names used to group authorized managers with agents. Agents can belong to only one community at a time. Managers can belong to multiple communities, enabling them to associate with many different agents.

SNMP Protocol Data Units (PDUs)

These field identifies the type of PDU. SNMP has five mandatory PDU types:

- Get request
- Get next request
- Get response
- Set request
- Trap

All get and set PDUs contain the following same fields (see Table 17.1). The *Trap* PDU has a different message format and field, which we will discuss later in this chapter.

TABLE 17.1   General PDU Fields

Field	Description
Request ID	Each request carries a unique ID used to match with the corresponding response that the agent returns.
Error status	Used to indicate whether an error was encountered. This value will always be zero for requests. If some value other than zero appears, the PDU encountered one of the following errors: • 0=no error • 1=PDU too big • 2=no such name • 3=bad value • 4=read only • 5=general error
Error index	Specifies the type of error encountered, when error status value indicates there was an error.
Object ID and value	References specific object ID and value represented in ASN.1.

Trap PDUs

Trap PDUs use a different message format than the four get and set PDUs because it reports on occurrences rather than responding to a manager's query. Figure 17.3 shows the trap PDU structure; Table 17.2 describes its fields.

FIGURE 17.3

Note that a trap PDU uses
a different structure from
the other PDUs.

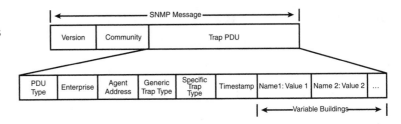

TABLE 17.2   Trap PDU fields

Field	Description
Enterprise	Identifies the object type that generated the trap.
Agent address	Specifies the Network layer address of the agent who originated the trap message.
Generic trap ID	Specifies the reason for the trap: • 0=cold start • 1=warm start • 2=link down • 3=link up • 4=authentication failure • 5=EGP neighbor loss • 6=enterprise specific
Specific trap ID	Identifies vendor-specific trap.
Time stamp	Indicates the time at which the agent generated the trap as a result of some event.
Object Id and value	Identifies the object ID and value for which the trap was generated.

Summary

In the mid- to late 1980s Internet committees discussed potential management protocols; from those talks three protocols emerged: HEMS, CMIP, and SGMP (later renamed SNMP, or Simple Network Management Protocol). SNMP was supposed to be a short-term solution for network management but has remained the primary protocol for network management.

SNMP provides delivery services of management requests and responses on behalf of the applications. It runs independent of the application's specifics, making it generic and portable to many different solutions. Its managers run management control software used to remotely control and monitor SNMP agents. Managers query agents for information. Agents run SNMP responder and notification generation software and listen for SNMP requests from managers.

Review Questions

1. What was SNMP previously known as?

2. What three main SNMP entities make remote management possible?

3. What are SNMP agents?

4. What are SNMP proxies?

5. What are SNMP managers?

6. What is a Trap PDU?

CHAPTER 18

OPEN NETWORK COMPUTING PROTOCOLS

You will learn about the following in this chapter:

- ONC Protocols
- NFS (Network File Systems)
- XDR (External Data Representation)
- RPC (Remote Procedure Calls)

Introduction to Open Network Computing Protocols

Sun Microsystems developed the distributed file system protocol known as *NFS* (*Network File System*) and released it in 1985 as part of its *ONC* (*Open Network Computing*) family of products. The term ONC collectively describes the many protocols and services offered by Sun as a platform and independent operating system. This independence enables disparate systems to access files transparently supporting PC-to-mainframe technologies.

Although NFS exists at the Application layer of the OSI model, it requires the implementation of two other protocols for functionality: *XDR* (*External Data Representation*) and *RPC* (*Remote Procedure Calls*). XDR provides Presentation layer functionality; RPC performs Session layer functionality. We will discuss all ONC protocol in more detail later this chapter.

All three protocols collectively provide transparent access to distributed file systems across LAN or WAN environments and map to the DoD's Application/Process layer of the model. We start our discussion with the uppermost protocol, NFS, and move down. Figure 18.1 shows how the ONC protocols map to the OSI model.

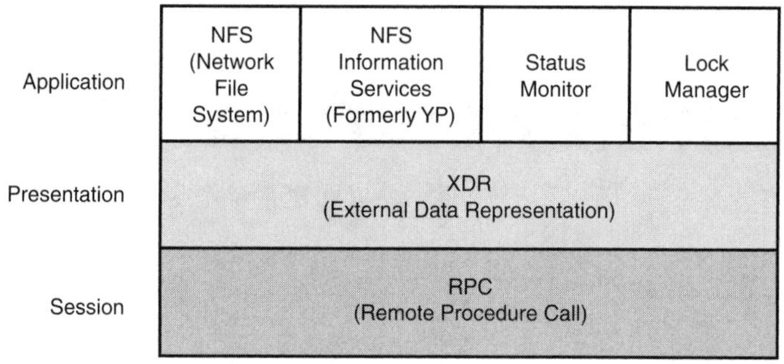

FIGURE 18.1

Collectively the ONC protocol family provides transparent access to distributed file systems across LAN or WAN environments.

Application	NFS (Network File System)	NFS Information Services (Formerly YP)	Status Monitor	Lock Manager
Presentation	XDR (External Data Representation)			
Session	RPC (Remote Procedure Call)			

NFS Features

As the name Network File System implies, NFS provides access to information through distributed file systems over any network architecture. NFS functions as a client/server-based protocol, enabling NFS clients to access globally distributed files by sending requests to remote NFS servers.

NFS supports many client operating systems (MS DOS, NetWare, Windows, NT, VMS, and so forth) and supports Data Link LAN and WAN architectures such as Ethernet, Token-Ring, X.25, Frame Relay and so on (see Table 18.2). Implementations involve client and server software programs (NFS); a data representation interpreter (XDR), which provides operating system independence; and a communication protocol (RPC), which provides the link between them passing requests and responses.

The current version, NFS version 3, has replaced version 2; Sun never released version 1. Sun originally developed NFS and its components to run on top of UDP at the Transport layer; however, NFS can run on top of TCP. Although NFS is strictly implemented over the TCP/IP protocol suite currently, it is not limited to the TCP/IP protocol suite and may be carried over any other protocol suite in the future. Table 18.1 lists the various NFS version 2 and 3 features.

TABLE 18.1   NFS Versions 2 and 3 Features

Feature	V2	V3	Benefit
Automatic mounting	Yes	Yes	Global file systems remain accessible and transparent to users.
Scalability	Yes	Yes	Network can easily grow as a company grows.
Centralized administration	Yes	Yes	Eliminates tedious administrative tasks.
Shared file system namespace	Yes	Yes	Users and application can move easily throughout the network.
Supports diskless, dataless, and autoclient configurations	Yes	Yes	Supports low-cost client system.

TABLE 18.1   Continued

Feature	V2	V3	Benefit
Flexible security architecture	Yes	Yes	Meets particular security needs by having a wide choice of security mechanisms.
Multiple authentication flavors	Yes	Yes	DES, Kerberos, "Unix Style."
Multiple authorization flavors	Yes	Yes	ACLS, "Unix Style"
Dual v1 and v2 support	N/A	N/A	N/A
NFS TCP	Yes	Yes	Provides efficient data transport over WAN/LAN.
Performance improvements	Yes	Yes	Fast access to remote files.
Local disk caching	Yes	Yes	Increases cache space, increases performance.
Asynchronous	No	Yes	Improves client write throughput.
Reduced attributes requests	No	Yes	Increases scalability and overall performance.
64 bit sizes and offset support	No	Yes	Can access multi-gigabyte files on NFS servers.
Read-only replica server support	Yes	Yes	Replica can replace a server if it goes down.
Highly available NFS server (optional)	Yes	Yes	Able to handle system or network failures.
Reduced requests for directory lookup information	No	Yes	Increased scalability and performance.

Table 18.2 shows a list of vendors and OS platforms.

TABLE 18.2   Multi-Vendor NFS Products

Vendor	OS Platform
Amdahl	UTS
Apple	A/UX
Beame and Whiteside	DOS, Windows
BSDI	Unix
Cray	UNICOS
DEC	Ultrix, VMS
Dell	SVR4
FTP Software	DOS, Windows, OS/2

TABLE 18.2   Continued

Vendor	OS Platform
Frontier Technology	DOS, Windows
Hewlett-Packard	HP-UX
IBM	AIX, MVS
Intel	Unix
ICL	Unix
Net Manage	DOS, Windows
Nixdorf	TOS 35
Novell	Netware
OSF	OSF1
Santa Cruz Operation	SCO Unix
Sunsoft	Solaris, DOS, Windows
Silicon Graphics	IRIX
Process Software	VMS
Sony	NeWs
Texas Instruments	TI SVR3.2
TGV	VMS

NFS Operation

At the center of the model are geographically distributed file servers (NFS servers), which provide client access to shared information (see Figure 18.2). NFS servers provide shared access to file systems through a process known as *exporting*. Shared server directories are known and referred to as *exported file systems*. Using the export command, server administrators must define which parts of the file system stored on the server are eligible for export to clients.

Once an administrator has defined the export areas, NFS clients can use the mount command to logically attach to the server's export area, linking the remote file system structure to a locally defined area on the client, known as the *mount point*. This process enables the user to access the remote file system as if it were local. Figure 18.2 shows an example of the basic components required to share and access files between clients and servers.

FIGURE 18.2

Use the mount command to tell the Unix kernel that a new filesystem should be attached to the file at a specified mount point.

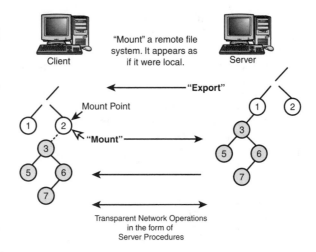

NFS Client

The software needed to participate in file sharing depends on the type of operating system and system architecture. Each client requires an NFS program to make *mounting* and *unmounting* requests. Mounting enables the remote shared export area to be incorporated into the local client's file system, referred to as the *client tree*. Unmounting, the opposite of mounting, enables a client to release a previously mounted file system, releasing the associated resources and detaching the export area from the local tree's mount point.

The mount point is the point within the client's local tree. It defines where the mounted file system attaches. An enhanced mount tool, referred to as the *automounter,* enables the automatic mounting and dismounting of exported file systems based on configured mapping information. The automounter works just like the manual mount command that links a remote export area to a point in the client's local file system (mount point). However, the process occurs dynamically based on predefined mappings.

The concept of mounting a remote file system and making it appear local is not new and should not seem foreign to you if you have worked with any other operating systems, such as NetWare or any Microsoft Windows product. With these operating systems you refer to mounting as *mapping*. To access a resource on a remote host, you simply use an unused local drive letter, such as E:, F:, and so on, and create a mapping to a directory within a remote host's file system. After you perform this task, simply access the remote area by typing in the letter you used to map to the remote resource. The drive letter represents our local mount point and the client subsequently uses it to refer to the remote area.

Think of mapping as a shortcut. If each time you needed to access a remote resource you had to build a complete path to the server and the subdirectory to gain access, it would consume an unbelievable amount of time, slowing down access to remote resources. By creating a map, you pave a direct path to the resources and simply refer to it each time you want to access it.

A user-friendly name can identify the local mount point such as: /home/heather. Or, it can simply use a local drive letter (E:, F:, and so on). The export area on the server to be mounted (exported file system) can lie anywhere within the server's file structure, containing multiple sublevel directories and files, such as NFSServ:/export/homedir/heather.

Once the client has performed a local mount, it links the remote file system structure to the local mount point. Collectively, mount points form a namespace. The user can now access any information stored within the exported file system simply by referring to the client name */home/heather* or the drive letter representing the remote area, such as f:. Figure 18.3 shows an example of the automounter maps and the NFS namespace.

FIGURE 18.3
NFS clients gain access to files from NFS servers by mounting the server's exported file system. NFS clients need a map to the server's file system.

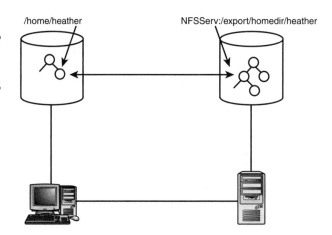

If you no longer need access to a resource, you can simply unmap (or unmount) the exported file system. To save time you can create local mapping configuration files, which the automounter will use to dynamically mount and unmount exported file systems when necessary, enabling you to tie up resources only when needed.

NFS Server

NFS servers contain distributed file systems that can be shared by defining export areas (exported file systems) through the export command within the share program. NFS servers respond to NFS client requests for shared information.

An administrator must create an export configuration file and define the following:

- What files you want to be shared
- Who can access the shared area
- Any restrictions relating to accessing this area and its information
- The complete pathname specifying the directories to be exported
- A list of NFS clients allowed to access the exported areas
- A list of specific restrictions relating to access the information within the area

When an NFS server initializes, its share program uses the information contained within the export configuration file to establish export capabilities and identify exportable file systems. Two operating system processes, *mount-d* and *nfs-d* (d means daemon) support clients' requests for access to the servers file system.

Automounter Components and Operation

As previously mentioned, the automounter is an enhanced mount tool. It enables the automatic mounting and dismounting of exported file systems based on configured mapping information. The automount process uses three main components:

- Automount command
- Automount-d (daemon)
- Autofs (automount virtual file system)

Autocommand

Upon system boot the autocommand initializes. After initialization, it opens and references the auto_master (configuration mapping file), which stores the local pathnames (mount points) to exported file system mappings. It uses this information to build a local mount table on the host.

Once it builds the local mount table, a user can access the file system by using the **cd** command. When a user attempts to access a local mount point, the autofs (auto file system), which represents the local placeholder (virtual file system) for the file system the client wishes to access, invokes the automount daemon to retrieve the requested file system and mount it.

The automount-d on the client sets up a communication path with the nfs-d on the server to export the remote file system. Once the client has mounted the remote file system, the automounter and its components have finished their responsibilities, and it is unnecessary to facilitate continual file access.

XDR

A component within NFS, XDR makes NFS portable across various operating system platforms. Developed by Sun Microsystems, the Internet has since adopted and included it in RFC 1014. Primarily XDR provides platform independence.

NFS client and server programs can run on drastically different operating systems and hardware, from Macintosh to Unix hosts, yet still share files transparently. XDR provides this capability by hiding the specific operating system internals from each side, translating machine-specific information before transmission or after reception.

XDR provides a standard library of programming routines written in C programming language, which enables vendors to implement it within their own environments representing data in a machine-independent fashion. Figure 18.4 show how XDR provides machine-independent functionality.

FIGURE 18.4
XDR translates and presents data so that two different operating systems can communicate with each other.

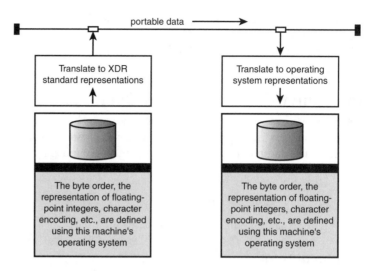

How data is stored—the specific byte order, memory addresses, and so on—is important only to the local host's XDR process. XDR has a bidirectional logical link between NFS and RPC. When the NFS program on a host generates information for transmission, it gives this to XDR for processing before passing it down to RPC for Session layer management.

In reception mode, XDR receives NFS messages from RPC, and interprets and translates this information into a format this host's operating system can understand. Remember the discussion regarding Presentation layer protocols in Chapters 1 and 10: The presentation layer's job is to present data in a format consistent with the host's operating system and machine-specific requirements, performing translation, encryption, decryption, conversion from ASCII to EBCDIC and reverse, and so on.

The Presentation layer's functions generally are included within the programming of most upper-layer protocols and not separately defined as is the case with XDR. Sun Microsystems defined a separate protocol within its suite to enable vendors to more efficiently and specifically alter the functionality within their XDR implementations. XDR facilitates communication with disparate hosts, enabling programmers to specifically tailor the protocols to their operating systems' needs, making portability to other operating systems easier. Although defined as a separate protocol, XDR performs an integral part of the upper-layer protocols' functionality and as such cannot be seen within the Sniffer output.

RPC

Sun Microsystems also developed RPC (Remote Procedure Calls); the Internet adopted it as RFC 1057. RPC offers a protocol and independent interface capable of providing a bidirectional communication link between remote communicating processes. It resides at the Session layer; thus it has the responsibility of setting up a session between two host processes, and maintaining and tracking the session. When the hosts no longer need the logical session, RPC tears down the session and releases local resources.

Remote Procedure Calls describes RPC's function. Think in terms of a local process running on a host and how it makes requests for information; this is a Local Procedure Call (LPC). Now consider the fact that the local host is requesting a procedure to be performed by a remote host and expects that host to process the request and send a response; this is a function of RPC. Figure 18.5 shows the relationship between LPC and RPC.

FIGURE 18.5
Hosts make procedure calls that look local when actually a remote machine executes them.

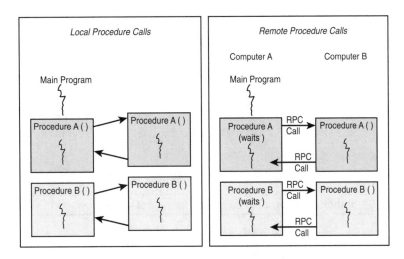

Hosts running RPC use it to send remote procedure calls such as read, write, print and so on to a destination host, which processes the request and responds through RPC with a positive or negative result. RPC remains unaware of the operating system running on the local host and remote host, and relies on upper layers such as XDR to interpret the machine-specific information carried within the message request or response.

Think of RPC as a facilitator that simply and generically carries the specific request from an upper-layer protocol, making sure it was sent and received. RPC typically runs on top of UDP for fast delivery; however, because of its generic nature it can run on top of TCP for additional reliability. RPC has such generic makeup in its operation that it has since been ported to other operating systems and protocol environments, such as Microsoft's NT platform.

Call Message

Each remote procedure has an active client side that sends a call message to the server, which returns a reply message. The network consists of one or more remote programs. The following sections describe the RPC header and fields within a call (request) message. An RPC call message has the following fields:

Transaction ID

The transmitter assigns an ID number. RPC uses this field to match calls and replies.

Type

The type field identifies the RPC message type as either a call or reply:

- 0 = Call
- 1 = Reply

Version

The version field identifies the RPC protocol version in use. The version number should always be 2.

Program

The program field identifies the upper-layer application program that is using RPC, such as NFS. Table 18.3 lists programs that have registered RPC values and can run on top of RPC.

TABLE 18.3   Registered RPC Programs

RPC Number	Program	Description
100000	PMAPPROG	Portmapper
100001	RSTATPROG	Remote stats
100002	RUSERSPROG	Remote users
100003	NFSPROG	NFS
100004	YPPROG	Yellow Pages
100005	MOUNTPROG	Mount daemon
100006	DBXPROG	Remote DBX
100007	YBINDPROG	YP binder
100008	WALLPROG	Shutdown message
100009	YPPASSWDPROG	YP Password password server
100010	ETHERSTATPROG	Ethernet Stats
100011	QQUOTAPROG	Disk quotas
100012	SPRAYPROG	Spray packets
100013	IBM3270PROG	3270 mapper
100014	IBMRJEPROG	RJE mapper

TABLE 18.3   Continued

RPC Number	Program	Description
100015	SELNSVCPROG	Selection service
100016	RDATABASEPROG	Remote database access
100017	REXECPROG	Remote execution
100018	ALICEPROG	Alice office automation
100019	SCHEDPROG	Scheduling service
100020	LOCKPROG	Local lock manager
100021	NETLOCKPROG	Network lock manager
100022	X.25PROG	X.25 INR Protocol
100023	STATMON1PROG	Status monitor 1
100024	STATMON2PROG	Status monitor 2
100025	SELNLIBROG	Selection library
100026	BOOTPARAMPROG	Boot parameters service
100027	MAZEPROG	Mazeware game
100028	YPUPDATEPROG	UP update
100029	KEYSERVEPROG	Key server
100030	SECURECMDPROG	Secure login
100031	NETFWDIPROG	NFS net forwarder init
100032	NETFWDTPROG	NFS net forwarder trans
100033	SUNLINKMAP_PROG	Sunlink MAP
100034	NETMONPROG	Network monitor
100035	DBASEPROG	Lightweight database
100036	PWDAUTHPROG	Password authentication
100037	TFSPROG	Translucent file service
100038	NSEPROG	NSE server
100039	NSE_ACTIVATE_PROG	NSE activate daemon
150001	PCNFSDPROG	PC password authorization
200000	PYRAMIDLOCKINGPROG	Pyramid-locking
200001	PYRAMIDSYS5	Pyramid-sys5

TABLE 18.3   Continued

RPC Number	Program	Description
200002	CADDS_IMAGE	CV cadds_image
300001	ADT_RFLOCKPROG	ADT file locking

Procedure

The field identifies the application-specific procedure number. This value varies depending on the procedure being requested and the application requesting the procedure. Consult your vendor documentation for specific procedure numbers. Table 18.4 lists the NFS server procedures.

TABLE 18.4   NFS Server Procedures

Procedure Number	Procedure Name	Procedure Functionality
0	Do nothing	Allows server response testing and timing
1	Get file attributes	Allows client to determine a server file's attributes
2	Set file attributes	Allows client to set (some of) a server file's attributes
3	Get filesystem root	Obsolete
4	Look up file name	Allows client to perform a directory look-up on a file
5	Read from symbolic link	Allows client to read data from a file pointed to by a symbolic link
6	Read from file	Allows client to read data from a file
7	Write to cache	Used with NFS Version 3 only.
8	Write to file	Allows client to write data in a server file
9	Create file	Allows client to create a new file on a server
10	Remove file	Allows client to remove a file from a server
11	Rename file	Allows client to rename a file on a server
12	Create link to file	Allows client to create a file that links to another file
13	Create symbolic link	Allows client to create a file that is a symbolic link

TABLE 18.4   Continued

Procedure Number	Procedure Name	Procedure Functionality
14	Create directory	Allows a client to create a directory on a server
15	Remove directory	Allows a client to remove a directory on a server
16	Read from directory	Allows client to read some entries in a server directory
17	Get filesystem attributes	Allows client to inspect the attributes of a server

Table 18.5 lists the mount server procedures.

TABLE 18.5   Mount Server Procedures

Procedure Number	Procedure Name	Procedure Functionality
0	Do nothing	Allows server response testing and timing
1	Add mount entry	Adds another filesystem to the list of remote filesystems a client has access to
2	Return mount entries	Allows a client to look at its list of mounted filesystems
3	Remove mount entry	Deletes a filesystem from the list of remote filesystems a client has access to
4	Remove all mount entries	Deletes all filesystems from the list of remote filesystems a client has access to
5	Return export list	Allows a client to look at the list of remote filesystems that a specific server offers

Authentication Type

The authentication type identifies the authentication indicator. This value specifies whether authentication is being requested and if so, which type:

- 0 = Null (none)
- 1 = Unix (Unix authentication)
- 2 = Short (Vendor-specific authentication)
- 3 = DES (data encryption standard)

Authentication Byte Size

The authentication byte size field identifies the number of bytes of authentication that will follow.

Authentication Data

The authentication data field has a variable length and includes authentication specific information.

Authentication Verification

The authentication verification field specifies the authentication method the receiver is expected to use to verify this call or reply. Communicating hosts must support the same authentication type:

- 0 = Null (None)

- 1 = Unix (Unix authentication)

- 2 = Short (vendor-specific authentication)

- 3 = DES (data encryption standard authentication)

Reply Message

As previously mentioned, each remote procedure call has an active client that sends a call to the server, which returns a reply. A call message can take on one of two forms: it can be either rejected or accepted. The following sections describe the RPC header and fields within a Reply (response) message. Only two fields within the reply differ from the call message:

- Status

- Accept status

Status

The status field identifies whether the server accepted or denied the previously sent call. Two values appear in this field:

- 0 = Accepted

- 1 = Denied

Accept Status

The accept status field further describes the meaning of the accepted or denied status indicator. The following accept status values exist:

- 0 = Success

- 1 = Program unavailable

- 2 = Program version mismatch

- 3 = Procedure unavailable

- 4 = Garbage arguments to procedure

NFS Examples

There are many different types of NFS procedures; therefore, each NFS header varies depending on the call or reply. Figure 18.6 shows a read a file request procedure (type 6). Note that the procedure type is 6 for read a file request. The file handle, which is the long numerical number following this field, identifies the specific file on the remote host.

FIGURE 18.6

Note that NFS uses a client/server paradigm where a local client that runs the application can have access to files from a server that manages the file or application program.

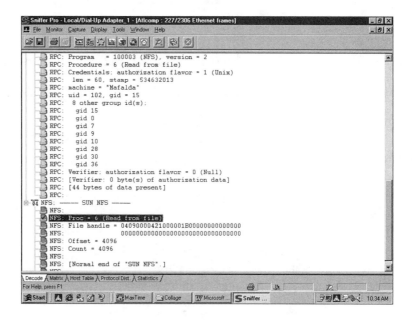

Note in Figure 18.6 that the offset value of 4096 bytes refers to the starting point within the requested file at which the read request should begin. This means the request should start reading at 4906 bytes within the file; count 4096 means read 4906 bytes total.

Figure 18.7 shows an NFS response to a previous read request, procedure type 6 (read a file). Notice the NFS server verifies the client's user ID and Group ID information, and permissions associated with each to ensure the user has the appropriate permission to perform the procedure requested. The user and group permissions allow rw (read and write) privileges.

Figure 18.8 shows an example of an RPC call. In this figure, first look at the UDP destination port identifying RPC as port 2049. Now look in the RPC header: RPC will use the transaction ID to match to a corresponding reply when it receives it. The type of RPC message being sent is a call. The registered program value for NFS is 100003; version type is 2. The authentication type is Unix. Note the machine name is being passed (Mafalda) along with the user IDs (UIDs) and group IDs (GIDs) to enable the receiver to authenticate and verify this request before processing.

FIGURE 18.7
With NFS a client, regardless of location of the client or server, can have transparent access to files.

Summary

NFS initiates a request or responds to a request to perform a read, write, copy, rename and so on. NFS prepares this request or response operation for transmission, and then it hands this procedural call or response to XDR for interpretation and encoding translation. XDR passes this information to RPC, which is responsible for setting up and maintaining a session between the two hosts.

Questions

1. What are the three protocols in the ONC family?

2. What is the primary function of NFS?

3. What is the primary function of XDR?

4. What is the primary function of RPC?

5. What company developed the ONC protocols?

APPENDIX A

RFCS ORGANIZED BY CHAPTER

Chapter 1: Overview of Industry Models and Standards

1095 CommonManagement Information Services and Protocol Over TCP/IP(CMOT). U.S. Warrier and L. Besaw. (April 1989) (Format: TXT=157506 bytes)

1180 TCP/IP Tutorial. T. J. Socolofsky and C. J. Kale. (January 1991) (Format: TXT=65494 bytes) (Status: INFORMATIONAL)

1195 Use of OSI IS-IS for Routing in TCP/IP and Dual Environments. R. W. Callon. (December 1990) (Format: TXT=187866, PS=362052 bytes) (Status: PROPOSED STANDARD)

Chapter 2: IP Addressing

1219 On the Assignment of Subnet Numbers. P. F. Tsuchiya. (April 1991) (Format: TXT=30609 bytes) (Status: INFORMATIONAL)

Chapter 3: Network Layer/Internet Protocols

760 Internet Protocol

777 Internet Control Message Protocol

781 Specification of the Internet Protocol (IP) Timestamp Option

791 Internet Protocol

792 Internet Control Message Protocol

815 IP Datagram Reassembly Algorithms

1011 Official Internet Protocols. J.K. Reynolds and J. Postel. (June 1987) (Format: TXT=129194 bytes) (Status: INFORMATIONAL) (Obsoletes RFC0991) (Status: UNKNOWN)

1016 Something a Host Could Do With Source Quench. The Source Quench Introduced Delay (SquID). W. Prue, J. Postel. (July 1987) (Format: TXT=47922 bytes) (Status: UNKNOWN)

1018 Some Comments on SquID. A.M. McKenzie. (August 1987) (Format: TXT=7931 bytes) (Status: UNKNOWN)

1025 TCP and IP Bake Off. J. Postel. (September 1987) (Format: TXT=21297 bytes) (Status: UNKNOWN)

1027 Using ARP to Implement Transparent Subnet Gateways. S. Carl-Mitchell and J. S. Quarterman. (October 1987) (Format: TXT=82440 bytes) (Status: HISTORIC)

1051 Standard for the Transmission of IP datagrams and ARP Packets Over ARCNET Networks. P. A. Prindville. Mar-01-1988. (Format: TXT=7779 bytes) (Obsoleted by RFC1201, std0046) (Status: UNKNOWN)

1054 Host Extensions for IP Multicasting. S. E. Deering. May-01-1988. (Format: TXT=45465 bytes) (Obsoletes RFC0988) (Obsoleted by RFC1112) (Status: UNKNOWN)

1055 Nonstandard for Transmission of IP Datagrams Over Series l Lines: SLIP. J.L. Romkey. Jun-01-1988. (Format: TXT=12911 bytes) (Status: STANDARD)

1063 Path MTU Discovery Options. J. C. Mogul, C. A. Kent, C. Partridge, and K. McCloghrie. Jul-01-1988. (Format: TXT=27121 bytes) (Obsoleted by RFC119) (Status: UNKNOWN)

1071 Computing the Internet Checksum. R. T. Braden, D. A. Borman, and C. Partridge. Sep-01-1988. (Format: TXT=54941 bytes) (Updated by RFC1141) (Status: UNKNOWN)

1077 Critical Issues in High-bandwidth Networking. B. M. Leiner. Nov-01-1988. (Format: TXT=116464 bytes) (Status: UNKNOWN)

1141 Computation of the Internet Checksum via Incremental Update. T. Mallory and A. Kullberg. Jan-01-1990. (Format: TXT=3587 bytes) (Updates RFC1071) (Updated by RFC1624) (Status: INFORMATIONAL)

1188 Proposed Standard for the Transmission of IP Datagrams Over FDDI Networks. D. Katz. Oct-01-1990. (Format: TXT=2242 bytes) (Obsoletes RFC1103) (Status: DRAFT STANDARD)

1191 Path MTU DiscOvery. J. C. Mogul, S. E. Deering. Nov-01-1990. (Format: TXT=47936 bytes) (Obsoletes RFC1063) (Status: DRAFT STANDARD)

1208 Glossary of Networking Terms. O. J. Jacobsen and D. C. Lynch. Mar-01-1991. (Format: TXT=41156 bytes) (Status: INFORMATIONAL)

1256 ICMP Router Discovery Messages. S. Deering. Sep-01-1991. (Format: TXT=43059 bytes) (Also RFC0792) (Status: PROPOSED STANDARD)

1413 Identification Protocol. M. St. Johns. January 1993. (Format: TXT=16291 bytes) (Obsoletes RFC931) (Status: PROPOSED STANDARD)

1624 Computation of the Internet Checksum via Incremental Update. A. Rijsinghani, Editor. May 1994. (Format: TXT=9836 bytes) (Updates RFC1141) (Status: INFORMATIONAL)

1788 ICMP Domain Name Messages. W. Simpson. April 1995. (Format: TXT=11722 bytes) (Status: EXPERIMENTAL)

2002 IP Mobility Support. C. Perkins. October 1996. (Format: TXT=193103 bytes) (Updated by RFC2290) (Status: PROPOSED STANDARD)

2005 Applicability Statement for IP Mobility Support. J.Solomon. October 1996. (Format: TXT=10509 bytes) (Status: PROPOSED STANDARD)

2041 Mobile Network Tracing. B. Noble, G. Nguyen, M. Satyanarayanan, and R. Katz. December 1996. (Format: TXT=64688 bytes) (Status: INFOMRATIONAL)

2058 Microsoft Vendor-specific RADIUS Attributes. C. Rigney, A. Rubens, W. Simpson, S. Willens. January 1997. (Format: TXT=118880 bytes) (Obsoleted by RFC2138) (Status: PROPOSED STANDARD)

2059 RADIUS Accounting. C. Rigney. January 1997. (Format: TXT=44237 bytes) (Obsoleted by RFC2139) (Status: INFORMATIONAL)

2113 IP Router Alert Option. D. Katz. February 1997. (Format: TXT=7924 bytes) (Status: PROPOSED STANDARD)

2138 Microsoft Vendor-specific RADIUS attributes. C. Rigney, A. Rubens, W. Simpson, S. Willens. April 1997. (Format: TXT=12407 bytes) (Obsoletes RFC2058) (Status: PROPOSED STANDARD)

2139 RADIUS Accounting. C. Rigney. April 1997. (Format: TXT=44919 bytes) (Obsoletes RFC2059) (Status: INFORMATIONAL)

2194 Review of Roaming Implementations. B. Aboba, J. Lu, J. Ding. W. Wang. September 1997. (Format: TXT=81533 bytes) (Status: INFORMATIONAL)

2290 Mobile-IPv4 Configuration Option for PPP IPCP. J. Solomon and S. Glass. February 1998. (Format: TXT=39421 bytes) (Updates RFC2002) (Status: PROPOSED STANDARD)

2344 Reverse Tunneling for Mobile IP. G. Montenegro. May 1998. (Format: TXT=39468 bytes) (Status: PROPOSED STANDARD)

2356 Sun's SKIP Firewall Traversal for Mobile IP. G. Montenegro and V. Gupta. June 1998. (Format: TXT=53198 bytes) (Status: INFORMATIONAL)

2477 Criteria for Evaluating Roaming Protocols. B. Aboba and G. Zorn. December 1998. (Format: TXT=23530 bytes) (Status: INFORMATIONAL)

2486 The Network Access Identifier. B. Aboba and M. Beadles. January 1999. (Format: TXT=14261 bytes) (Status: PROPOSED STANDARD)

2501 Mobile Ad hoc Networking (MANET): Routing Protocol Performance Issues and Evaluation Considerations. S. Corson and J. Macker. January 1999. (Format: TXT=28912 bytes) (Status: INFORMATIONAL)

2521 ICMP Security Failures Messages. P. Karn and W. Simpson. March 1999. (Format: TXT=14637 bytes) (Status: EXPERIMENTAL)

2548 Microsoft Vendor–specific RADIUS Attributes. G. Zorn. March 1999. (Format: TXT=80763 bytes) (Status: INFORMATIONAL)

2607 Proxy Chaining and Policy Implementation in Roaming

Chapter 4: Address Resolution

826 Ethernet Address Resolution Protocol: On Converting Network Protocol Addresses to 48-bit Ethernet Address for Transmission on Ethernet Hardware

903 Reverse Address Resolution Protocol

925 Multi-LAN Address Resolution

1027 Using ARP to Implement Transparent Subnet Gateways. S. Carl-Mitchell and J. S. Quarterman. Oct-01-1987. (Format: TXT=21297 bytes) (Status: UNKNOWN)

1029 More Fault-tolerant Approach to Address Resolution for a Multi-LAN System of Ethernets. G.Parr. May-01-1988. (Format: TXT=44019 bytes) (Status: UNKNOWN)

1107 Plan for Internet Directory Services. K. R. Sollins. Jul-01-1989. (Format: TXT=51773 bytes) (Status: INFORMATIONAL)

1112 Host Extensions for IP multicasting. S. E. Deering. Aug-01-1989. (Format: TXT=39904 bytes) (Obsoletes RFC0988, RFC1054) (Updated by RFC2236) (Status: STANDARD)

1293 Inverse Address Resolution Protocol. T. Bradley and C. Brown. January 1992. (Format: TXT=11368 bytes) (Obsoleted by RFC2390) (Status: PROPOSED STANDARD)

1329 Thoughts On Address Resolution for Dual MAC FDDI Networks. P. Kuehn. May 1992. (Format: TXT=58150 bytes) (Status: INFORMATIONAL)

1433 Directed ARP. J. Garrett, J. Hagen, and J. Wong. March 1993. (Format: TXT=41028 bytes) (Status: EXPERIMENTAL)

1868 ARP Extension-UNARP. G. Malkin. November 1995. (Format: TXT=7681 bytes) (Status: EXPERIMENTAL)

1931 Dynamic RARP Extensions for Automatic Network Address Acquisition. D. Brownell. April 1996. (Format: TXT=47005 bytes) (Status: PROPOSED STANDARD)

2390 Inverse Address Resolution Protocol. T. Bradley and C. Brown, A. Malis. August 1998. (Format: TXT=20849 bytes) (Obsoletes RFC1293) (Status: PROPOSED STANDARD)

Chapter 5: IP Routing

917 Toward An Internet Standard Scheme For Subnetting

932 Toward An Internet Standard Scheme For Subnetting

936 Toward An Internet Standard Scheme For Subnetting

940 Toward an Internet Standard Scheme For Subnetting

950 Internet Standard Subnetting Procedure

1042 Standard for Transmission of IP datagrams Over IEEE 802 Networks. J. Postel and J. K. Reynolds. Feb-01-1988. (Format: TXT=34359 bytes) (Obsoletes RFC0948) (Status: STANDARD)

1136 Administrative Domains and Routing Domains: A Model for Routing in the Internet. S. Hares and D. Katz. Dec-01-1989. (Format: TXT=22158 bytes) (Status: INFORMATIONAL)

1219 On the Assignment of Subnet Numbers. P. F. Tsuchiaya. Apr-01-1991. (Format: TXT=30609 bytes) (Status: INFORMATIONAL)

1234 Tunneling IPX Traffic Through IP Networks. D. Provan. Jun-01-1991. (Format: TXT=12333 bytes) (Status: PROPOSED STANDARD)

1335 A Two-tier Address Structure for the Internet: A Solution to the Problem of Address Space Exhaustion. Z. Wang and J. Crowcroft. May 1992. (Format: TXT=15418 bytes) (Status: INFORMATIONAL)

1347 TCP and UDP with Bigger Addresses (TUBA), A Simple Proposal for Internet Addressing and Routing. R. Callon. June 1992. (Format: TXT=26563, PS=42398 bytes) (Status: INFORMATIONAL)

1365 An IP Address Extension Proposal. K. Siyan. September 1992. (Format: TXT=12790 bytes) (Status: INFORMATIONAL)

1366 Guidelines for Management of IP Address Space. E. Gerich. October 1992. (Format: TXT=17793 bytes) (Obsoleted by RFC1466) (Status: INFORMATIONAL)

1375 Suggestion for New Classes of IP Addresses. P. Robinson. October 1992. (Format: TXT=16990 bytes) (Status: INFORMATIONAL)

1385 EIP: The Extended Internet Protocol. Z. Wang. November 1992. (Format: TXT=39123 bytes) (Status: INFORMATIONAL)

1454 Comparison of Proposals for the Next Version of IP. T. Dixon. May 1993. (Format: TXT=35064 bytes) (Status: INFORMATIONAL)

1466 Guidelines for Management of IP Address Space. E. Gerich. May 1993. (Format: TXT=22262 bytes) (Obsoletes RFC1366) (Status: INFORMATIONAL)

1475 TP/IX: The Next Internet. R. Ullmann. June 1993. (Format: TXT=77854 bytes) (Status: EXPERIMENTAL)

1526 Assignment of System Identifiers for TUBA/CLNP Hosts. D. Piscitello. September 1993. (Format: TXT=16848 bytes) (Status: INFORMATIONAL)

1550 IP: Next Generation (IPng) White Paper Solicitation. S. Bradner and A. Mankin. December 1993. (Format: TXT=12472 bytes) (Status: INFORMATIONAL)

1597 Address Allocation for Private Internets. Y. Rekhter, B. Moskowitz, D. Karrenberg, and G. de Groot. March 1994. (Format: TXT=17430 bytes) (Obsoleted by BCP0005, RFC1918) (Status: INFORMATIONAL)

1621 Pip Near-term Architecture. P. Francis. May 1994. (Format: TXT=128905 bytes) (Status: INFORMATIONAL)

1622 Pip Header Processing. P. Francis. May 1994. (Format: TXT=34837 bytes) (Status: INFORMATIONAL)

1627 Network 10 Considered Harmful (Some Practices Shouldn't be Codified). E. Lear, E. Fair, D. Crocker, and T. Kessler. June 1994. (Format: TXT=18823 bytes) (Obsoleted by BCP0005, RFC1918) (Status: INFORMATIONAL)

1667 Modeling and Simulation Requirements for IPng. S. Symington, D. Wood, and M. Pullen. August 1994. (Format: TXT=17291 bytes) (Status: INFORMATIONAL)

1668 Unified Routing Requirements for IPng. D. Estrin, T. Li, and Y. Rekhter. August 1994. (Format: TXT=5106 bytes) (Status: INFORMATIONAL)

1669 Market Viability as a IPng Criteria. J. Curran. August 1994. (Format: TXT=8099 bytes) (Status: INFORMATIONAL)

1670 Input to IPng Engineering Considerations. D. Heagerty. August 1994. (Format: TXT=5350 bytes) (Status: INFORMATIONAL)

1671 IPng White Paper on Transition and Other Considerations. B. Carpenter. August 1994. (Format: TXT=17631 bytes) (Status: INFORMATIONAL)

1672 Accounting Requirements for IPng. N. Brownlee. August 1994. (Format: TXT=6184 bytes) (Status: INFORMATIONAL)

1673 Electrical Power Research Institute Comments on IPng. R. Skelton. August 1994. (Format: TXT=7476 bytes) (Status: INFORMATIONAL)

1674 A Cellular Industry View of IPng. M. Taylor. August 1994. (Format: TXT=6157 bytes) (Status: INFORMATIONAL)

1675 Security Concerns for IPng. S. Bellovin. August 1994. (Format: TXT=8290 bytes) (Status: INFORMATIONAL)

1676 INFN Requirements for IPng. A Ghiselli, D. Salomoni, and C. Vistoli. August 1994. (Format: TXT=8493 bytes) (Status: INFORMATIONAL)

1677 Tactical Radio Frequency Communication Requirements for IPng. B. Adamson. August 1994. (Format: TXT=24065 bytes) (Status: INFORMATIONAL)

1678 IPng Requirements of Large Corporate Networks. E. Britton and J. Tavs. August 1994. (Format: TXT=18650 bytes) (Status: INFORMATIONAL)

1679 HPN Working Group Input to the IPng Requirements Solicitation. D. Green, P. Irey, D. Marlow, and K. O'Donoghue. August 1994. (Format: TXT=17846 bytes) (Status: INFORMATIONAL)

1680 IPng Support for ATM Services. C. Brazdziunas. August 1994. (Format: TXT=17846 bytes) (Status: INFORMATIONAL)

1681 On Many Addresses per Host. S. Bellovin. August 1994. (Format: TXT=11964 bytes) (Status: INFORMATIONAL)

1682 IPng BSD Host Implementation Analysis. J. Bound. August 1994. (Format: TXT=22295 bytes) (Status: INFORMATIONAL)

1683 Multiprotocol Interoperability In IPng. R. Clark, M. Ammar, and K. Calvert. August 1994. (Format: TXT=28201 bytes) (Status: INFORMATIONAL)

1686 IPng Requirements: A Cable Television Industry Viewpoint. M. Vecchi. August 1994. (Format: TXT=39052 bytes) (Status: INFORMATIONAL)

1687 A Large Corporate User's View of IPng. E. Fleischman. August 1994. (Format: TXT=34120 bytes) (Status: INFORMATIONAL)

1688 IPng Mobility Considerations. W. Simpson. August 1994. (Format: TXT=19151 bytes) (Status: INFORMATIONAL)

1705 Six Virtual Inches to the Left: The Problem With IPng. R. Carlson, and D. Ficarella. October 1994. (Format: TXT=65222 bytes) (Status: INFORMATIONAL)

1707 CATNIP: Common Architecture for the Internet. M. McGOvern and R. Ullmann. October 1994. (Format: TXT=37568 bytes) (Status: INFORMATIONAL)

1710 Simple Internet Protocol Plus White Paper. R. Hinden. October 1994. (Format: TXT=56910 bytes) (Status: INFORMATIONAL)

1715 The H Ratio for Addresses per Host. C. Huitema. November 1994. (Format: TXT=7392 bytes) (Status: INFORMATIONAL)

1719 A Direction for IPng. P. Gross. December 1994. (Format: TXT=11118 bytes) (Status: INFORMATIONAL)

1726 Technical Criteria for Choosing IP The Next Generation (IPng). C. Partridge and F. Kastenhoz. December 1994. (Format: TXT=74109 bytes) (Status: INFORMATIONAL)

1744 Observations on the Management of the Internet Address Space. G. Huston. December 1994. (Format: TXT=43675 bytes) (Status: PROPOSED STANDARD)

1752 The Recommendation for the IP Next Generation Protocol. S. Bradner and A. Mankin. January 1995. (Format: TXT=127784 bytes) (Status: PROPOSED STANDARD)

1753 IPng Technical Requirements Of the Nimrod Routing and Addressing Architecture. N. Chiappa. December 1994. (Format: TXT=46586 bytes) (Status: INFORMATIONAL)

1797 Class A Subnet Experiment. Internet Assigned Numbers Authority (IANA). April 1995. (Format: TXT=6779 bytes) (Status: EXPERIMENTAL)

1809 Using the Flow Label Field in IPv6. C. Partridge. June 1995. (Format: TXT=13591 bytes) (Status: INFORMATIONAL)

1814 Unique Addresses Are Good. E. Gerich. June 1995. (Format: TXT=5936 bytes) (Status: INFORMATIONAL)

1860 Variable Length Subnet Table for IPv4. T. Pummill and B. Manning. October 1995. (Format: TXT=5694 bytes) (Obsoleted by RFC1878) (Status: INFORMATIONAL)

1878 Variable Length Subnet Table for IPv4. T. Pummill and B. Manning. December 1995. (Format: TXT=19414 bytes) (Obsoletes RFC1860) (Status: INFORMATIONAL)

1879 Class A Subnet Experiment Results and Recommendations. B. Manning. January 1996. (Format: TXT=10589 bytes) (Status: INFORMATIONAL)

1880 IPv6 Address Allocation Management. IAB&IESG. December 1995. (Format: TXT=3215 bytes) (Status: INFORMATIONAL)

1883 Internet Protocol, Version 6 (IPv6) Specification. S. Deering and R. Hinden. December 1995. (Format: TXT82089 bytes) (Status: PROPOSED STANDARD)

1884 IP Version 6 Addressing Architecture. R. Hinden and S. Deering, Editors. December 1995. (Format: TXT=37860 bytes) (Obsoleted by RFC2373) (Status: PROPOSED STANDARD)

1885 Internet Control Message Protocol (ICMPv6) for the Internet Protocol Version 6 (IPv6). A. Contra and S. Deering. December 1995. (Format: TXT=32214 bytes) (Status: PROPOSED STANDARD)

1886 DNS Extensions to support IP version 6. S. Thomson and C. Huitema. December 1995. (Format: TXT=6424 bytes) (Status: PROPOSED STANDARD)

1887 An Architecture for IPv6 Unicast Address Allocation. Y. Rekhter and T. Li, Editors. December 1995. (Format: TXT=66066 bytes) (Status: INFORMATIONAL)

1888 OSI NSAPs and IPv6. J. Bound, B. Carpenter, D. Harrington, J. Houldsworth, and A. Lloyd. August 1996. (Format: TXT=36469 bytes) (Status: EXPERIMENTAL)

1897 IPv6 Testing Address Allocation. R. Hinden and J. Postel. January 1997. (Format: TXT=6643 bytes) (Status: EXPERIMENTAL)

1900 Renumbering Needs Work. B. Carpenter and Y. Rekhter. February 1996. (Format: TXT=9528 bytes) (Status: INFORMATIONAL)

1916 Enterprise Renumbering: Experience and Information Solicitations. H. Berkowitz, P. Ferguson, W. Leland, and P. Nesser. February 1996. (Format: TXT=16117 bytes) (Status: INFORMATIONAL)

1918 Address Allocation for Private Internets. Y. Rekhter, B. Moskowitz, D. Karrenberg, G. J. de Groot, and E. Lear. February 1996. (Format: TXT=22270 bytes) (Obsoletes RFC1627, RFC1597) (Also BCP0005) (Status: BEST CURRENT PRACTICES)

1933 Transition Mechanism for IPv6 Hosts and Routers. R. Gilligan and E. Nordmark. April 1996. (Format: TXT=47005 bytes) (Status: PROPOSED STANDARD)

1955 New Scheme for Internet Routing and Addressing (ENCAPS) for IPNG. R. Hinden. June 1996. (Format: TXT=10115 bytes) (Status: INFORMATIONAL)

1970 Neighbor Discovery for IP Version 6(IPv6). T. Narten, E. Nordmark, and W. Simpson. August 1996. (Format: TXT=197632 bytes) (Status: PROPOSED STANDARD)

1971 IPv6 Stateless Address Autoconfiguration. S. Thomson and T. Narten. August 1996. (Format: TXT=61210 bytes) (Obsoletes RFC1971) (Status: DRAFT STANDARD)

1972 Transmission of IPv6 Packets Over Ethernet Networks. M. Crawford. August 1996. (Format: TXT=6353 bytes) (Status: PROPOSED STANDARD)

1981 Path MTU DiscOvery for IP version 6. J. McCann, S. Deering, and J. Mogul. August 1996. (Format: TXT=56890 bytes) (Status: PROPOSED STANDARD)

2008 Implications of Various Address Allocation Policies for Internet Routing. Y. Rekhter and T. Li. October 1996. (Format: TXT=34717 bytes) (Also BCP0007) (Status: BEST CURRENT PRACTICES)

2019 Transmission of IPv6 Packets Over FDDI Networks. M. Crawford. October 1996. (Format: TXT=12344 bytes) (Status: PROPOSED STANDARD)

2023 IP Version 6 Over PPP. D. Haskin, E. Allen. October 1996. (Format: TXT=20275 bytes) (Status: PROPOSED STANDARD)

2036 Observations on the Use of Components of the Class A Address Space Within the Internet. G. Huston. October 1996. (Format: TXT=20743 bytes) (Status: INFORMA-TIONAL)

2071 Network Renumbering Overview: Why Would I Want It and What Is It Anyway? P. Ferguson and H. Berkowitz. January 1997. (Format: TXT=33218 bytes) (Status: INFORMATIONAL)

2072 Router Renumbering Guide. H. Berkowtiz. January 1997. (Format: TXT=110591 bytes) (Status: INFORMATIONAL)

2073 An IPv6 Provider-based Unicast Address Format. Y. Rekhter, Pl Lothberg, R. Hinden, S. Deering, and J. Postel. January 1997. (Format: TXT=15549 bytes) (Obsoleted by RFC2374) (Status: PROPOSED STANDARD)

2080 RIPng for IPv6. G. Malkin, R. Minnear. January 1997. (Format: TXT=47534 bytes) (Status: PROPOSED STANDARD)

2081 RIPng Protocol Applicability Statement. G. Malkin. January 1997. (Format: TXT=6821 bytes) (Status: INFORMATIONAL)

2101 IPv4 Address Behavior Today. B. Carpenter, J. Crowcroft, and Y. Rekhter. February 1997. (Format: TXT=31407 bytes) (Status: INFORMATIONAL)

2133 Basic Socket Interface Extensions for IPv6. R. Gilligan, S. Thomson, J. Bound, and W. Stevens. April 1997. (Format: TXT=69737 bytes) (Status: INFORMATIONAL)

2147 TCP and UDP Over IPv6 Jumbograms. D. Borman. May 1997. (Format: TXT=1883 bytes) (Status: PROPOSED STANDARD)

2185 Routing Aspects of IPv6 Transition. R. Callon and D. Haskin. September 1997. (Format: TXT=31281 bytes) (Status: INFORMATIONAL)

2292 Advanced Sockets API for IPv6. W. Stevens and M. Thomas. February 1998. (Format: TXT=152077 bytes) (Status: INFORMATIONAL)

2373 IP Version 6 Addressing Architecture. R. Hinden, S. Deering. July 1998. (Format: TXT=52526 bytes) (Obsoletes RFC1884) (Status: PROPOSED STANDARD)

2374 An IPv6 Aggregatable Global Unicast Address Format. R. Hinden, M. O'Dell, and S. Deering. July 1998. (Format: TXT=25068 bytes) (Obsoletes RFC2073) (Status: PROPOSED STANDARD)

2375 Address Assignments. R. Hinden and S. Deering. July 1998. (Format: TXT=14356 bytes) (Status: INFORMATIONAL)

2391 Load Sharing Using IP Network Address Translation (LSNAT). P. Srisuresh and D. Gan. August 1998. (Format: TXT=44884 bytes) (Status: INFORMATIONAL)

2450 Proposed TLA and NLA Assignment Rule. R. Hinden. December 1998. (Format: TXT=24486 bytes) (Status: INFORMATIONAL)

2452 IP Version 6 Management Information Base for the Transmission Control Protocol. M. Daniele. December 1998. (Format: TXT=19066 bytes) (Status: PROPOSED STANDARD)

2454 IP Version 6 Management Information Base for the User Datagram Protocol. M. Daniele. December 1998. (Format: TXT=15862 bytes) (Status: PROPOSED STANDARD)

2460 Internet Protocol, Version 6 (IPv6) Specification. S. Deering and R. Hinden. December 1998. (Format: TXT=85490 bytes) (Obsoletes RFC1883) (Status: DRAFT STANDARD)

2461 Neighbor DiscOvery for IP Version 6(IPv6). T. Narten, E. Nordmark, and W. Simpson. December 1998. (Format: TXT=222516 bytes) (Obsoletes RFC1970) (Status: DRAFT STANDARD)

2462 IPv6 Stateless Address Autoconfiguration. S. Thomson and T. Narten. December 1998. (Format: TXT=61210 bytes) (Obsoletes RFC1971) (Status: DRAFT STANDARD)

2463 Internet Control Message Protocol (ICMPv6) for the Internet Protocol Version 6 (IPv6) Specification. A. Contra and S. Deering. Decemer 1998. (Format: TXT=34190 bytes) (Obsoletes RFC1885) (Status: DRAFT STANDARD)

2464 Transmission of IPv6 Packets Over Ethernet Networks. M. Crawford. December 1998. (Format: TXT=12725 bytes) (Obsoletes RFC1972) (Status: PROPOSED STANDARD)

2465 Management Information Base for IP Version 6: Textual Conventions and General Group. D. Haskin and S. Onishi. December 1998. (Format: TXT=77339 bytes) (Status: PROPOSED STANDARD)

2466 Management Information Base for IP Version 6:ICMPv6 Group. D. Haskin and S. Onishi. December 1998. (Format: TXT=27547 bytes) (Status: PROPOSED STANDARD)

2467 Transmission of IPv6 Packets Over FDDI Networks. M. Crawford. December 1998. (Format: TXT=16028 bytes) (Obsoletes RFC2019) (Status: PROPOSED STANDARD)

2470 Transmission of IPv6 Packets Over Token Ring Networks. M. Crawford, T. Narten, and S. Thomas. December 1998. (Format: TXT=21677 bytes) (Status: PROPOSED STANDARD)

2471 IPv6 Testing Address Allocation. R. Hinden, R. Fink, and J. Postel. December 1998. (Format: TXT=8031 bytes) (Obsoletes RFC1897) (Status: EXPERIMENTAL)

2472 IP Version 6 Over PPP. D. Haskin, E. Allen. October 1996. (Format: TXT=20275 bytes) (Status: PROPOSED STANDARD)

2473 Generic Packet Tunneling in IPv6 Specification. A. Contra and S. Deering. December 1998. (Format: TXT=77956 bytes) (Status: PROPOSED STANDARD)

2491 IPv6 Over Non-broadcast Multiple Access (NBMA) networks. G. Armitage. P. Schulter, M. Jork, and G. Harter. January 1999. (Format: TXT=100782 bytes) (Status: PROPOSED STANDARD)

2492 IPv6 Over ATM Networks. G.Armitage, P. Schulter, M. Jork January 1999. (Format: TXT=21199 bytes) (Status: PROPOSED STANDARD)

2497 Transmission of IPv6 Packets Over ARCnet Networks. I. Souvatzis. January 1999. (Format: TXT=10304 bytes) (Also RFC1201) (Status: PROPOSED STANDARD)

2526 Reserved IPv6 Subnet Anycast Addresses. D. Johnson and S. Deering. March 1996. (Format: TXT=14555 bytes) (Status: PROPOSED STANDARD)

2529 Transmission of IPv6 Over IPv4 Domains Without Explicit Tunnels. B. Carpenter and C. Jung. March 1999. (Format: TXT=21049 bytes) (Status: PROPOSED STANDARD)

2545 Use of BGP-4 Multiprotocol Extensions for IPv6 Interdomain Routing. P. Marques and F. Dupont. March 1999. (Format: TXT=10209 bytes) (Status: PROPOSED STANDARD)

2546 6Bone Routing Practice. A. Durand and B. Buclin. March 1999. (Format: TXT=17844 bytes) (Status: PROPOSED STANDARD)

2553 Basic Socket Interface Extensions for IPv6. R. Gilligan, S. Thomson, J. Bound and S. Stevens. March 1999. (Format: TXT=89215 bytes) (Status: INFORMATIONAL)

2590 Transmission of IPv6 Packets Over Frame Relay

2675 IPv6 Jumbograms

2710 Multicast Listener DiscOvery (MLD) for IPv6

2711 IPv6 Router Alert Option

Chapter 6: Routing Protocols

823 DARPA Internet Gateway

827 Exterior Gateway Protocol Formal Specification

875 Gateways, Architectures, and Heffalumps

888 Exterior Gateway Protocol Formal Specification

890 Exterior Gateway Protocol Formal Specification

904 Exterior Gateway Protocol Formal Specification

911 EGP Gateway Under Berkeley UNIX 4.2

970 On Packet Switches With Infinite Storage

975 Autonomous Confederations

985 Requirements for Internet Gateways—Draft

1046 Queuing Algorithms to Provide Type-of-service for IP Links. W. Prue and J. Postel. Feb-01-1988. (Format: TXT=30106 bytes) (Status: UNKNOWN)

1058 Routing Information Protocol. C.I. Hedrick. Jun-01-1988. (Format: TXT=93285 bytes) (Updated by RFC1388,RFC1723) (Status: HISTORIC)

1074 NSFNET Backbone SPF-Based Interior Gateway Protocol. J. Rekhter. Oct-01-1988. (Format: TXT=36000 bytes) (Obsoleted by RFC1323) (Status: UNKNOWN)

1075 Distance Vector Multicast Routing Protocol. D. Waitzman, C. partridge, and S. E. Deering. Nov-01-1988. (Format: TXT=54731 bytes) (Status: EXPERIMENTAL)

1092 EGP and Policy-based Routing in the New NSFNET Backbone. J. Rekhter. Feb-01-1989. (Format: TXT=11865 bytes) (Status: UNKNOWN)

1093 NSFNET Routing Architecture. H. W. Braun. Feb-01-1989. (Format: TXT=20629 bytes) (Status: UNKNOWN)

1102 Policy Routing in Internet Protocols. D. D. Clark. May-01-1989. (Format: TXT=59664 bytes) (Status: UNKNOWN)

1104   Models of Policy-based Routing. H. W. Braun. Jun-01-1989. (Format: TXT=25468 bytes) (Status: UNKNOWN)

1105   Border Gateway Protocol (BGP). K. Loughheed and Y.Rekhter. Jun-01-1989. (Format: TXT=37644 bytes) (Obsoleted by RFC1163) (Status: EXPERIMENTAL)

1125   Policy Requirements for Interadministrative Domain Routing. D. Estrin. Nov-01-1989. (Format: TXT=55248, PS=282123 bytes) (Status: UNKNOWN)

1131   OSPF Specification. J. Moy. Oct-01-1989. (Format: TXT=268, PS=857280 bytes) (Obsoleted by RFC1247) (Status: PROPOSED STANDARD)

1133   Routing Between the NSFNET and the DDN. J. Y. Yu and H. W. Braun. Nov-01-1989. (Format: TXT=23169 bytes) (Status: INFORMATIONAL)

1136   Administrative Domains and Routing Domains: A Model for Routing in the Internet. S. Hares and D. Katz. Dec-01-1989. (Format: TXT=22158 bytes) (Status: INFORMATIONAL)

1142   OSI IS-IS Intradomain Routing Protocol. D.Oran. Feb-01-1990. (Format: TXT=425379, PS=1204297 bytes) (Status: INFORMATIONAL)

1163   Border Gateway Protocol (BGP). K. Lougheed and Y Rekhter. Jun-01-1990. (Format: TXT=69404 bytes) (Obsoletes RFC1105) (Obsoleted by RFC1267) (Status: HISTORIC)

1164   Application of the Border Gateway Protocol on the Internet. J. C. Honig, D. Katz, M. Mathis, Y. Rekhter and J. Y. Yu. Jun-01-1990. (Format: TXT=56278 bytes) (Obsoleted by RFC1268) (Status: HISTORIC)

1195   Use of OSI IS-IS for Routing in TCP/IP and Dual Environments. R. W. Callon. Dec-01-1990. (Format: TXT=187866, PS=362052 bytes) (Status: PROPOSED STANDARD)

1222   Advancing the NSFNET Routing Architecture. H. W. Braun and Y. Rekhter. May-01-1991. (Format: TXT=15067 bytes) (Status: INFORMATIONAL)

1245   OSPF Protocol Analysis. J. Moy. Jul-01-1991. (Format: TXT=26160, PS=33546 bytes) (Also RFC1247,RFC1246) (Status: INFORMATIONAL)

1246   Experience With OSPF Protocol. J. Moy. Jul-01-1991. (Format: TXT=70441, PS=141924 bytes) (Also RFC1247, RFC1245) (Status: INFORMATIONAL)

1247   OSPF Version 2. J. Moy. Jul-01-1991. (Format: TXT=433332,PS=989724 bytes) (Obsoletes RFC1131) (Obsoleted by RFC1252) (Status: PROPOSED STANDARD)

1252   OSPF Version 2 Management Information Base. F. Baker and R. Coltun. Aug-01-1991. (Format: TXT=74471 bytes) (Obsoletes RFC1248) (Obsoleted by RFC1253) (Also RFC1247,RFC1245) (Status: PROPOSED STANDARD)

1253   OSPF Version 2 Management Information Base. F. Baker and R. Coltun. Aug-01-1991. (Format: TXT=74453 bytes) (Obsoletes RFC1252) (Obsoleted by RFC1850) (Also RFC1247, RFC1245, RFC1246) (Status: PROPOSED STANDARD)

1254   Gateway Congestion Control Survey. A. Mankin and K. Ramakrishnan. Jul-01-1991. (Format: TXT=67609 bytes) (Status: INFORMATIONAL)

1264   Internet Engineering Task Force Internet Routing Protocol Standardization Criteria. R. M. Hinden. Oct-01-1991. (Format: TXT=17016 bytes) (Status: INFORMATIONAL)

1265   BGP Protocol Analysis. Y. Rekhter. Oct-01-1991. (Format: TXT=20728 bytes) (Status: INFORMATIONAL)

1266   Experience With the BGP Protocol. Y. Rekhter. Oct-01-1991. (Format: TXT=21928 bytes) (Status: INFORMATIONAL)

1267   Border Gateway Protocol 3(BGP-3). K. Lougheed and Y. Rekhter. Oct-01-1991. (Format: TXT=80724 bytes) (Obsoletes RFC1163) (Status: HISTORIC)

1268   Application of the Border Gateway Protocol in the Internet. Y. Rekhter and P. Gross. Oct-01-1991. (Format: TXT=31102 bytes) (Obsoletes RFC1164) (Obsoleted by RFC1655) (Status: HISTORIC)

1269   Definitions of Managed Objects for the Border Gateway Protocol: Version 3. S. Willis and J. W. Burruss. Oct-01-1991. (Format: TXT=25717 bytes) (Status: PROPOSED STANDARD)

1322   A Unified Approach to Interdomain Routing. D. Estrin, Y. Rekhter, and S. Hotz. May 1992. (Format: TXT=96934 byres) (Status: INFORMATIONAL)

1364   BGP OSPF Interaction. K. Varadhan. September 1992.

1370   Application Statement for the OSPF. Internet Architecture Board, L. Chapin. October 1992. (Format: TXT=4303 bytes) (Status: PROPOSED STANDARD)

1383   An Experience in DNS-based IP Routing

1387   RIP Version 2 Protocol Analysis. G. Malkin. January 1993. (Format: TXT=5998 bytes) (Obsoleted by RFC1721) (Status: INFORMATIONAL)

1388   RIP Version 2 Carrying Additional Information. G. Malkin. January 1993. (Format: TXT=16227 bytes) (Obsoleted by RFC17213) (Updates RFC1058) (Status: PROPOSED STANDARD)

1389   RIP Version 2 MIB Extensions. G. Malkin, F. Baker. January 1993, (Format: TXT=23569 bytes) (Obsoleted by RFC1724) (Status: PROPOSED STANDARD)

1397   Default Route Advertisement In BGP2 and BGP3 Version of The Border Gateway Protocol. D. Haskin. January 1993. (Format: TXT=4124 bytes) (Status: PROPOSED STANDARD)

1403   BGP OSPF Interaction. K. Varadhan. January 1993. (Format: TXT=36173 bytes) (Obsoletes RFC1290) (Also FY10010) (Status: INFORMATIONAL)

1465   Routing Coordination for X.400 MHS Services Within a Multi-Protocol/Multi-Network Environment Table Format V3 for Static Routing.

1477 IDPR as a Proposed Standard. M. Steenstrup. July 1993. (Format: TXT=77854 bytes) (Status: EXPERIMENTAL)

1478 An Architecture for Interdomain Policy Routing. M. Steenstrup. July 1993. (Format: TXT=275823 bytes) (Status: PROPOSED STANDARD)

1479 Inter-domain Policy Routing Protocol Specification: Version 1. M. Steenstrup. July 1993. (Format: TXT=275823 bytes) (Status: PROPOSED STANDARD)

1482 Aggregate Support in the NSFNET Policy-based Routing Database. Mark Knopper and Steven J. Richardson. July 1993. (Format: TXT=25330 bytes) (Status: INFORMATIONAL)

1504 Appletalk Update-based Routing Protocol: Enhanced Appletalk Routing. A. Oppenheimer. August 1993. (Format: TXT=201553 bytes) (Status: INFORMATIONAL)

1517 Applicability Statement for the Implementation of Classless Inter-Domain Routing (CIDR). Internet Engineering Steering Group, R. Hinden. September 1993. (Format: TXT=7357 bytes) (Status: PROPOSED STANDARD)

1519 Classless Interdomain Routing (CIDR): an Address Assignment and Aggregation Strategy. V. Fuller, T. Li, J. Yu, and K. Varadhan. September 1993. (Format: TXT=59998 bytes) (Obsoletes RFC1338) (Status: PROPOSED STANDARD)

1519 Exchanging Routing Information Across Provider Boundries in the CIDR Environment. Y. Rekhter and C. Topolcic. September 1993. (Format: TXT=20389 bytes) (Status: INFORMATIONAL)

1581 Protocol Analysis for Extensions to RIP to Support Demand Circuits. G. Meyer. February 1994. (Format: TXT=7536 bytes)

1582 Extensions to RIP to Support Demand Circuits. G. Meyer. February 1994. (Format: TXT=63271 bytes) (Status: PROPOSED STANDARD)

1583 OSPF Version 2. J. Moy. March 1994. (Format: TXT=532636, PS=990794 bytes) (Obsoletes RFC1247) (Obsoleted by RFC2178) (Status: DRAFT STANDARD)

1584 Multicast Extensions to OSPF. J. Moy. March 1994. (Format: TXT=262463, PS=426358 bytes) (Status: PROPOSED STANDARD)

1585 MOSPF: Analysis and Experience. J. Moy. March 1994. (Format: TXT=29754 bytes) (Status: INFORMATIONAL)

1586 Guidelines for Running OSPF Over Frame Relay Networks. O. deSouza and M. Rodrigues. March 1994. (Format: TXT=14968 bytes) (Status: INFORMATIONAL)

1587 The OSPF NSSA Option. R. Coltun and V. Fuller. March 1994. (Format: TXT=37412 bytes) (Status: PROPOSED STANDARD)

1654 A Border Gateway Protocol 4 (BGP-4). Y. Rekhter and T. Li, Editors. July 1994. (Format: TXT=130118 bytes) (Obsoleted by RFC1771) (Status: PROPOSED STANDARD)

1701   Generic Routing Encapsulation (GRE). S. Hanks, T. Li, D. Farinacci, and P. Traina. October 1994. (Format: TXT=15460 bytes) (Status: INFORMATIONAL)

1702   Generic Routing Encapsulation Over IPv4 Networks. S. Hanks, T. Li, D. Farinacci, and P. Traina. October 1994. (Format: TXT=7288 bytes) (Status: INFORMATIONAL)

1721   RIP Version 2 Protocol Analysis. G. Malkin. November 1994. (Format: TXT=6680 bytes) (Obsoletes RFC1387) (Status: INFORMATIONAL)

1722   RIP Version 2 Protocol Applicability Statement. G.Malkin. November 1994. (Format: TXT=10236 bytes) (Status: DRAFT STANDARD)

1723   RIP Version 2—Carrying Additional Information. G. Malkin. November 1994. (Format: TXT=18597 bytes) (Obsoletes RFC1388) (Updates RFC1058) (Status: DRAFT STANDARD)

1745   BGP4/IDRP for IP-OSPF Interaction. K.Varadhan, S. Hares, and Y. Rekhter. December 1994. (Format: TXT=43675 bytes) (Status: PROPOSED STANDARD)

1765   OSPF Database Overflow. J.Moy. March 1995. (Format: TXT=21613 bytes) (Status: EXPERIMENTAL)

1771   A Border Gateway Protocol 4 (BGP-4). Y. Rekhter and T. Li. March 1995. (Format: TXT=11606 bytes) (Status: INFORMATIONAL)

1772   Application of the Border Gateway Protocol in the Internet. Y. Rekhter & P. Gross. March 1995. (Format: TXT=43916 bytes) (Obsoletes RFC1655) (Status: DRAFT STANDARD)

1773   of the BGP-4 protocol. P. Traina. March 1995. (Format: TXT=19936 bytes) (Obsoletes RFC1656) (Status: INFORMATIONAL)

1774   BGP-4 Protocol Analysis. P. Traina, Editor. March 1995. (Format: TXT=23823 bytes) (Status: INFORMATIONAL)

1786   Representation of the IP Routing Policies in a Routing Registry (ripe-81++). T. Bates, E. Gerich, L. Joncheray, J. M. Jouanigot, D. Karrenberg, M. Terpstra, and J. Yu. March 1995. (Format: TXT=133643 bytes) (Status: INFORMATIONAL)

1787   Routing in a Multi-provider Internet. Y. Rekhter. April 1995. (Format: TXT=20754 bytes) (Status: INFORMATIONAL)

1793   Extending OSPF to Support Demand Circuits. J. Moy. April 1995. (Format: TXT=16389 bytes) (Status: EXPERIMENTAL)

1817   CIDR and Classful Routing. Y. Rekhter. August 1995. (Format: TXT=3416 bytes) (Status: INFORMATIONAL)

1863   A BGP/IDRP Route Server Alternative to Full Mesh Routing. D. Haskin. October 1995. (Format: TXT=37426 bytes) (Obsoletes RFC1645 bytes) (Status: EXPERIMENTAL)

1923   RIPv1 Applicability Statement for Historic Status. J. Halpern & S. Bradner. March 1996. (Format: TXT=5560 bytes) (Status: INFORMATIONAL)

1965 Autonomous System Confederations for BGP. P. Traina. June 1996. (Format: TXT=13575 bytes) (Status: EXPERIMENTAL)

1966 BGP Route Reflection: An alternative to Full Mesh IBGP. T. Bates and R. Chandrasekeran. June 1996. (Format: TXT=14320 bytes) (Status: EXPERIMENTAL)

1992 The Nimrod Routing Architecture. I. Casineyra, N. Chiappa, and M. Steestrup. August 1996. (Format: TXT=46255 bytes) (Status: INFORMATIONAL)

1997 BGP Communities Attribute. R. Chandra, P. Traina, and T. Li. August 1996. (Format: TXT=8275 bytes) (Status: PROPOSED STANDARD)

1998 An Application of the BGP Community Attribute in Multi-home Routing. E. Chen & T. Bates. August 1996. (Format: TXT=16953 bytes) (Status: INFORMATIONAL)

2009 GPS-based Addressing and Routing. T. Imielinski and J. Navas. November 1996. (Format: TXT=66229 bytes) (Status: EXPERIMENTAL)

2082 RIP-2 MD5 Authentication. F. Baker and R. Atkinson. January 1997. (Format: TXT=25436 bytes) (Status: PROPOSED STANDARD)

2091 Triggered Extensions to RIP to Support Demand Circuits. G. Meyer and S. Sherry. January 1997. (Format: TXT=44835 bytes) (Status: PROPOSED STANDARD)

2092 Protocol Analylsis for Triggered RIP. S. Sherry, G. Meyer. January 1997. (Format: TXT=10865 bytes) (Status: INFORMATIONAL)

2102 Multicast Support for Nimrod: Requirements and Solution Approaches. R. Ramanathan. February 1997. (Format: TXT=50963 bytes) (Status: INFORMATIONAL)

2103 Mobility Support for Nimrod: Challenges and Solution Approaches. R. Ramanathan. February 1997. (Format: TXT=41352 bytes) (Status: INFORMATIONAL)

2117 Protocol Independent Multicast-Sparse Mode (PIM- SM): Protocol Specification. D. Estrin, D. Farinacci, A. Helmy, D. Thaler, S. Deering, M. Handley, V. Jacobson, C. Liu, P. Sharma, and L. Wei. June 1997. (Format: TXT=151886 bytes) (Obsoleted by RFC2362) (Status: EXPERIMENTAL)

2154 OSPF with Digital Signatures. S. Murphy, M. Badger, B. Wellington. June 1997. (Format: TXT=72701 bytes) (Status: EXPERIMENTAL)

2178 OSPF Version 2. J. Moy. July 1997. (Format: TXT=495866 bytes) (Obsoletes RFC1583) (Obsoleted by RFC2328) (Status: DRAFT STANDARD)

2189 Core-based Trees (CBT Version 2) Multicast Routing. A. Balardie. September 1997. (Format: TXT=52043 bytes) (Status: EXPERIMENTAL)

2201 Core-based Trees (CBT) Multicast Routing Architecture. A. Ballardie. September 1997. (Format: TXT=38040 bytes) (Status: EXPERIMENTAL)

2260 2260 Scalable Support for Multi-homed Multi-provider Connectivity. T. Bates, Y. Rekhter. January 1998. (Format: TXT=28085 bytes) (Status: INFORMATIONAL)

2270 Using a Dedicated AS for Sites Homed to a Single Provider. J. Stewart, T. Bates, R. Chadra, and E. Chen. January 1998. (Format: TXT=12063 bytes) (Status: INFORMA-TIONAL)

2280 Routing Policy Specification Language (RSPL). C. Alaettinoglu, T. Bates, E. Gerich, D. Karrenberg, D. Meyer, M. Terpstra, and C. Villamizar. January 1998. (Format: TXT=114985 bytes) (Status: PROPOSED STANDARD)

2281 Cisco Hot Standby Router Protocol (HSRP). T. Li, B. Cole, P. Morton, D.Li. March 1998. (Format: TXT=35161 bytes) (Status: INFORMATIONAL)

2283 Multiprotocol Extensions for BGP-4. T. Bates, R. Chandra, D. Katz, Y. Rekhter. February 1998. (Format: TXT=18946 bytes) (Status: PROPOSED STANDARD)

2328 OSPF Version 2. J. Moy. April 1998. (Format: TXT=447367 bytes) (Obsoletes RFC2178) (Also STD0054) (Status: STANDARD)

2329 OSPF Standardization Report. J. Moy. April 1998. (Format: TXT=15130 bytes) (Status: INFORMATIONAL)

2338 Virtual Router Redundancy Protocol. S. Knight, D. Weaver, D. Whipple, R. Hinden, D. Mitzel, P. Hunt, P. Higginson, M. Shand, and A. Lindem. April 1998. (Format: TXT=59871 bytes) (Status: PROPOSED STANDARD)

2362 Protocol Independent Multicast-Sparse Mode (PIM-SM): Protocol Specification. D. Estrin, D. Farinacci, A. Helmy, D. Thaler, S. Deering, M. Handley, V. Jacobson, C. Liu, P. Sharma, and L. Wei. June 1998. (Format: TXT=159833 bytes) (Obsoletes RFC2117) (Status: EXPERIMENTAL)

2370 The OSPF Opaque LSA Option. R. Coltun. July 1998. (Format: TXT=33789 bytes) (Also RFC2328) (Status: PROPOSED STANDARD)

2385 Protection of BGP Sessions via the TCP MD5 Signature Option. A. Heffernan. August 1998. (Format: TXT=12315 bytes) (Status: PROPOSED STANDARD)

2439 BGP Route Flap Damping. C. Villamiar, R. Chandra, R. Grovindan. November 1998. (Format: TXT=86376 bytes) (Status: PROPOSED STANDARD)

2453 RIP Version 2. G. Malkin. November 1998. (Format: TXT=98462 bytes) (Obsoletes RFC1388, RFC1723) (Updates RFC1723, RFC1388) (Also STD0056) (Status: STANDARD)

2519 A Framework for Interdomain Route Aggregation. E. Chen, J. Stewart. February 1999. (Format: TXT=25394 bytes) (Status: INFORMATIONAL)

2622 Routing Policy Specification Language (RPSL)

2650 Using RPSL in Practice

2676 QoS Routing Mechanisms and OSPF Extensions

2715 Interoperability Rules for Multicast Routing Protocols

Chapter 7: Transport/Host-to-Host Layer

1162 Connectionless Network Protocol (ISO 8473) and End Systems to Intermediate System (ISO 9542) Management Information Base. G. Satz. Jun-01-1990. (Format: TXT=109893 bytes) (Obsoleted by RFC1238) (Status: EXPERIMENTAL)

Chapter 8: Transmission Control Protocol (TCP)

675 Transmission Control Protocol

700 Protocol Exerperiment

721 Out-of-Band Control Signals in a Host-to-Host Protocol

761 Transmission Control Protocol

793 Transmission Control Protocol

794 Pre-emption

813 Window and Acknowledgement Strategy in TCP

872 TCP-on-a-LAN

879 TCP Maximum Segment Size and Related Topics

889 Internet Delay Experiments

896 Congestion Control in IP/TCP Internetworks

962 TCP-4 Prime

964 Some Problems With the Specifications of the Military Standard Transmission Control Protocol

1006 ISO Transport Services On Top of TCP: Version 3. M.T. Rose and D.E. Cass. May-01-1987. (Format: TXT=31935 bytes) (Obsoletes RFC0983) (Status: STANDARD)

1072 TCP Extensions for Long-delay Paths. V. Jacobson and R.T. Braden. Oct-01-1988. (Format: TXT=36000 bytes) (Obsoleted by RFC1323) (Status: UNKNOWN)

1078 TCP port service Multiplexer (TCPMUX). M.Lottor.Nov-01-1988. (Format: TXT=3248 bytes) (Status: UNKNOWN)

1106 TCP Big Window and NAK Options. R. Fox. Jun-01-1989. (Format: TXT=37105 bytes) (Status: UNKNOWN)

1110 Problem With the TCP Big Window Option. A. M. McKenzie. Aug-01-1989. (Format: TXT=5778 bytes) (Status: UNKNOWN)

1144   Compressing TCP/IP Headers for Low-speed Serial Links. V. Jacobson. Feb-01-1990. (Format: TXT=120959, PS=534729 bytes) (Status: PROPOSED STANDARD)

1185   TCP Extensions for High-speed Paths. V. Jacobson, R. T. Braden, and L. Zhang. Oct-01-1990. (Format: TXT=49508 bytes) (Obsoleted by RFC1323) (Status: EXPERIMENTAL)

1263   TCP Extensions Considered Harmful. S. O'Malley and L. L. Peterson. Oct-01-1991. (Format: TXT=54078 bytes) (Status: INFORMATIONAL)

1323   TCP Extensions for High Performance. V. Jacobson, R. Braden, and D. Borman. May 1992. (Format: TXT=84558 bytes) (Obsoletes RFC1072, RFC1185) (Status: PROPOSED STANDARD)

1337   TIME-WAIT Assassination Hazards for TCP. R. Braden. May 1992. (Format: TXT=22887 bytes) (Status: INFORMATIONAL)

1379   Extending TCP for Transactions—Concepts. R. Braden. November 1992. (Format: TXT=91353 bytes) (Status: INFORMATIONAL)

1644   T/TCP—TCP Extensions for Transactions Functional Specifications. R. Braden. July 1994. (Format: TXT=87362 bytes) (Status: EXPERIMENTAL)

1693   An Extension of TCP: Partial Order Service. T. Connolly, P. Amer, and P. Conrad. November 1994. (Format: TXT=26163 bytes) (Status: PROPOSED STANDARD)

2001   TCP Slow Start, Congestion Avoidance, Fast Retransmit, and Fast Recovery Algorithms. W. Stevens. January 1997. (Format: TXT=12981 bytes) (Status: PROPOSED STANDARD)

2018   TCP Selective Acknowledgement Options. M. Mathis, J. Mahdavi, S. Floyd, A. Romanow. October 1996. (Format: TXT=25671 bytes) (Status: PROPOSED STANDARD)

2140   TCP Control Block Interdependence. J. Touch. April 1997. (Format: TXT=26032 bytes) (Status: INFORMATIONAL)

2398   Some Testing Tools for TCP Implementors. S. Parker, C. Schmechel. August 1998. (Format: TXT=24107 bytes) (Obsoletes NONE) (Updates NONE) (Also NONE) (Status: INFORMATIONAL)

2414   Increasing TCP's Initial Window. M. Allman, S. Floyd, and C. Partridge. September 1998. (Format: TXT=32019 bytes) (Status: EXPERIMENTAL)

2415   Simulating Studies of Increased Initial TCP Window Size. K. Poduri and K. Nichols. September 1998. (Format: TXT=24205 bytes) (Status: INFORMATIONAL)

2416   When TCP Starts Up With Four Packets Into Only Three Buffers. T. Shepard, C. Partridge. September 1998. (Format: TXT=12663 bytes) (Status: INFORMATIONAL)

2488 Enhancing TCP Over Satellite Channels using Standard Mechanisms. M. Allman, D. Glover, and L. Sanchez. January 1999. (Format: TXT=47857 bytes) (Also BCP0028) (Status: BEST CURRENT PRACTICE)

2525 Known TCP Implementation Problems. V. Paxson, M. Allman, S. Dawson, W. Fenner, J. Griner, I. Heavens, K. Lahey, H. Semke, and B. Volz. March 1999. (Format: TXT=137201 bytes) (Status: INFORMATIONAL)

2581 TCP Congestion Control. M. Allman, V. Paxson, W. Stevens. April 1999. (Format: TXT=31351 bytes) (Obsolets RFC2001) (Status: PROPOSED STANDARD)

2582 The NewReno Modification to TCP'S Fast Recovery Algorithm. S. Floyd, T. Henderson. April 1999. (Format: TXT=29393 bytes) (Status: EXPERIMENTAL)

Chapter 9: User Datagram Protocol (UDP)

768 User Diagram Protocol

Chapter 11: Telnet

91 Proposed User-User Protocol

97 First Cut at a Proposed Telnet Protcol

103 Implementation of Interrupt Keys

110 Response to NWG/RFC 110

114 File Transfer Protocol

135 Response to NWG/RFC 110

137 Telnet Protocol—a Proposed Document

139 Discussion of Telnet Protocol

158 Telnet Protocol: A Proposed Document

172 File Transfer Protocol

190 DEC PDP-10-IMLAC Communication System

205 NETCRT—a Character Display Protocol

206 User Telnet—a Description of Initial Implementation

215 NCP, ICP, and Telnet: The Terminal IMP Implementation

216 Telnet Access to UCSB'S Online System

265 File Transfer Protocol

318 Telnet Protocols

328 Suggested Telnet Protocol Changes

339 MLTNET: A "Multi Telnet" Subsystem for Tenex

340 Proposed Telnet Changes

346 Response to NWG/RFC 346

354 File Transfer Protocol

355 Response to NWG/RFC 346

357 Echoing Strategy for Satellite Links

377 Using TSO via ARPA Network Virtual Terminal

393 Comments on Telnet Protocol Changes

426 Reconnection Protocol

435 Telnet Issues

452 TELENET Command on Host LL

466 Telnet Logger/Server for Host LL-67

495 Telnet Protocol Specifications

513 Comments on New Telnet Specifications

529 Note on Protocol Synch Sequences

542 File Transfer Protocol

559 Comments on The New Telnet Protocol and its Implementation

560 Remote Controlled Transmission and Echoing Telnet Option

562 Modifications to the Telnet Specifications

563 Comments on the RCTE Telnet Option

570 Experimental Input Mapping Between NVT ASCII and UCSB Online System

576 Proposal and Identifying Linking

581 Corrections to RFC 560: Remote Controlled Transmission and Echoing Telnet Option

587 Announcing New Telnet Option

593 Telnet and FTP Implementation Schedule Change

594 Second Thoughts in Defense of Telnet Go-Ahead

600 Interfacing an Illinois Plasma Terminal to the ARPANET

651 Revised Telnet Status Option

652 Telnet Output Carriage-return Disposition Option

653 Telnet Output Horizontal Tabstops Option

654 Telnet Output Horizontal Tab Disposition Option

655 Telnet Output Formfeed Disposition Option

656 Telnet Output Vertical Tabstops Option

657 Telnet Output Vertical Tab Disposition Option

658 Telnet Output Linefeed Disposition

659 Announcing Additional Telnet Options

669 July, 1975 Survey of New-Protocol Telnet Servers

679 July, 1975 Survey of New-Protocol Telnet Servers

681 Network UNIX

688 Tentative Schedule for the New Telnet Implementation for the TIP

701 July, 1975 Survey of New-Protocol Telnet Servers

702 July, 1975 Survey of New-Protocol Telnet Servers

703 July, 1975 Survey of New-Protocol Telnet Servers

718 Comments on RCTE from the Tenex Implementation Experience

719 Discussion on RCTE

726 Remote Controlled Transmission and Echoing Telnet option

727 Telnet Logout Option

728 Minor Pitfall in the Telnet Protocol

729 Telnet Byte Macro Option

730 Telnet Data Entry Terminal Option

731 Telnet Data Entry Terminal Option

735 Revised Telnet Byte Macro Option

736 Telnet SUPDUP Option

746 SUPDUP Graphics Extension

747 Recent Extensions to the SUPDUP Protocol

748 Telnet SUPDUP-Output Option

764 Telnet Protocol Specifications

765 File Transfer Protocol

779   Telnet Send-Location Option

782   Virtual Terminal Management Protocol

818   Remote User Telnet Service

854   Telnet Protocol Specifications

855   Telnet Option Specifications

856   Telnet Binary Transmissions

857   Telnet Echo Option

858   Telnet Suppress Go-Ahead Option

859   Telnet Status Option

860   Telnet Timing Mark Option

861   Telnet Extended Options: List Option

884   Telnet Terminal Type Option

885   Telnet End of Record Option

927   TACACS User Identification Telnet Option

930   Telnet Terminal Type Option

946   Telnet Terminal Location Number Option

959   File Transfer Protocol

1041 Telnet 3270 Regime Option. Y. Rekhter. Jan-01-1988. (Format: TXT=11608 bytes) (Status: PROPOSED STANDARD)

1043 Telnet Data Entry Terminal option: DODIIS Implementation. A. Yasuda and T. Thompson. Feb-01-1988. (Format: TXT=59478 bytes) (Updates RFC0732) (Status: PROPOSED STANDARD)

1053 Telnet X.3 PAD Option. S. Levy and T. Jacobson. Apr-01-1988. (Format: TXT=48952 bytes) (Status: PROPOSED STANDARD)

1073 Telnet Window Size Option. D. Waitzman. Oct-01-1988. (Format: TXT=7639 bytes) (Status: PROPOSED STANDARD)

1079 Telnet Terminal Speed Option. C. L. Hedrick. Dec-01-1988. (Format: TXT=4942 bytes) (Status: PROPOSED STANDARD)

1080 Telnet Remote Flow Control Option. C. L. Hedrick. Nov-01-1099. (Format: TXT=6688 bytes) (Obsoleted by RFC1372) (Status: UNKNOWN)

1091 Telnet Terminal-type Option. J. VanBokkelen. Feb-01-1989. (Format: TXT=13439 bytes) (Obsoletes RFC0930) (Status: PROPOSED STANDARD)

1096   Telnet X Display Location Option. G. A. Marcy. Mar-01-1989. (Format: TXT=4634 bytes) (Status: PROPOSED STANDARD)

1097   Telnet Subliminal-Message option. B. Miller. Apr-01-1989. (Format: TXT=5490 bytes) (Status: UNKNOWN)

1116   Telnet Linemode Option. D. A. Borman. Aug-01-1989. (Format: TXT=47473 bytes) (Obsoleted by RFC1184) (Status: PROPOSED STANDARD)

1143   The Q Method of Implementing TELNET Option Negotiation. D. J. Bernstein. Feb-01-1990. (Format: TXT=23331 bytes) (Status: EXPERIMENTAL)

1184   Telnet Linemode Option. D. A. Borman. Oct-01-1990. (Format: TXT=53085 bytes) (Obsoletes RFC1116) (Status: DRAFT STANDARD)

1205   5250 Telnet Interface. P. Chmielewski. Feb-01-1991. (Format: TXT=27170 bytes) (Status: INFORMATIONAL)

1372   Telnet Remote Flow Control Option. C. Hedrick, D. Borman. October 1992. (Format: TXT=11098 bytes) (Obsoletes RFC1080) (Status: PROPOSED STANDARD)

1408   Telnet Environment Option. D. Borman, Editor. January 1993. (Format: TXT=13119 bytes) (Obsoleted by RFC1571) (Status: HISTORIC)

1409   Telnet Authentication Option. D. Borman, Editor. January 1993. (Format: TXT=13119 bytes) (Obsoleted by RFC1416) (Status: EXPERIMENTAL)

1411   Telnet Authentication: Kerberos Version 4. D. Borman, Editor. January 1993. (Format: TXT=7967 bytes) (Status: EXPERIMENTAL)

1412   Telnet Authentication: SPX.K. Alagappan. January 1993. (Format: TXT=6952 bytes) (Status: EXPERIMENTAL)

1416   Telnet Authentication Option. D. Borman, Editor. February 1993. (Format: TXT=13270 bytes) (Obsoletes RFC1409) (Status: EXPERIMENTAL)

1571   Telnet Environment Option Interoperability Issues. D. Borman. January 1994. (Format: TXT=8117 bytes) (Updates RFC1408) (Status: INFORMATIONAL)

1572   Telnet Environment Option. S. Alexander. January 1994. (Format: TXT=14676 bytes) (Status: PROPOSED STANDARD)

1576   TN3270 Current Practices. J. Penner. January 1994. (Format: TXT=24477 bytes) (Status: INFORMATIONAL)

1646   TN3270 Extensions for Luname and Printer Selection. C. Graves, T. Butts, and M. Angel. July 1994. (Format: TXT=27564 bytes) (Status: INFORMATIONAL)

1647   TN3270 Enhancements. B. Kelly. July 1994. (Format: TXT=84420bytes) (Obsoleted by RFC2355) (Status: PROPOSED STANDARD)

1921   TNVIP Protocol. J. Dujonc. March 1996. (Format: TXT=57475 bytes) (Status: INFORMATIONAL)

2066 TELNET CHARSET Option. R. Gellens. January 1997. (Format: TXT=26088 bytes) (Status: EXPERIMENTAL)

2217 Telnet Com Port Control Option. G. Clark. October 1997. (Format: TXT=31664 bytes) (Status: EXPERIMENTAL)

2355 TN3270 Enhancements. B. Kelly. June 1998. (Format: TXT=89394 bytes) (Obsoletes RFC1647) (Status: DRAFT STANDARD)

Chapter 12: File Transfer Protocol (FTP)

133 File Transfer and Recovery

141 Comments on RFC 114: A File Transfer Protocol

238 Comments on DTP and FTP Proposals

250 Some Thoughts on File Transfer

269 Some Experience with File Transfer

281 Suggested Addition to File Transfer Protocol

294 The Use of "Set Data Type" Transaction in File Transfer Protocol

310 Another Look at Data and File Transfer Protocols

385 Comments on the File Transfer Protocol

412 User FTP Documentation

413 File Transfer Protocol (FTP) Status and Further Comments

430 Comments on File Transfer Protocol

438 FTP Server-Server Interaction

448 Print Files in FTP

463 FTP Comments and Response to RFC 430

468 FTP Data Compression

478 FTP Server-Server Interaction—II

479 Use of the FTP by the NIC Journal

480 Host-dependent FTP Parameters

486 Data Transfer Revisited

487 Free File Transfer

501 Un-muddling "Free File Transfer"

505 Two Solutions to a File Transfer Access Problem

506 FTP Command Naming Problem

520 Memo to FTP Group: Proposal for File Access Protocol

532 UCSD-CC Server-FTP Facility

535 Comments on File Access Protocol

571 Tenex FTP Problem

607 Comments on the File Transfer Protocol

614 Response to RFC 607: "Comments on the File Transfer Protocol"

624 Comments on the File Transfer Protocol

630 FTP Error Code Usage for More Reliable Mail Service

640 Revised FTP Reply Codes

691 One More Try on the FTP

697 CWD Command of FTP

737 FTP Extension: XSEN

743 FTP Extension: XRSO/XRCP

775 Directory-oriented FTP Commands

949 FTP Unique-named Store Command

1415 FTP-FTAM Gateway Specification. J. Mindel and R. Slaski. January 1993. (Format: TXT=128261 bytes) (Status: PROPOSED STANDARD)

1440 SIFT/UFT: Sender-initiated/Unsolicited File Transfer. R. Troth. July 1993. (Format: TXT=17366 bytes) (Status: EXPERIMENTAL)

1545 FTP Operations Over Big Address Records (FOOBAR). D. Piscitello. November 1993. (Format: TXT=8985 bytes) (Obsoleted by RFC1639) (Status: EXPERIMENTAL)

1579 Firewall-friendly FTP. S. Bellovin. February 1994. (Format: TXT=8806 bytes) (Status: INFORMATIONAL)

1635 How to Use Anonymous FTP. P. Deutsch, A. Emtage, and A. Marine. May 1994. (Format: TXT=27259 bytes) (Also FYI0024) (Status: INFORMATIONAL)

1639 FTP Operations Over Big Address Records (FOOBAR). D. Piscitello. June 1994. (Format: TXT=10055 bytes) (Obsoletes RFC1545) (Status: EXPERIMENTAL)

2204 ODETTE File Transfer Protocol. D. Nash. September 1997. (Format: TXT=151857 bytes) (Status: INFORMATIONAL)

2228 FTP Security Extensions. M. Horowitz, S. Lunt. October 1997. (Format: TXT=58733 bytes) (Updates RFC0959) (Status: PROPOSED STANDARD)

2389 Feature Negotiation Mechanism for the File Transfer Protocol. P. Hethmon and R. Elz. August 1998. (Format: TXT=18536 bytes) (Also RFC0959) (Status: PROPOSED STANDARD)

2428 FTP Extensions for IPv6 and NATs. M. Allman, S. Ostermann, and C. Metz. September 1998. (Format: TXT=16028 bytes) (Status: PROPOSED STANDARD)

2577 FTP Security Considerations. M. Allman and S. Ostermann. May 1999. (Format: TXT=17870 bytes) (Status: INFORMATIONAL)

2640 Internationalization of File Transfer Protocol

Chapter 13: Simple Mail Transfer Protocol (SMTP)

196 Revision of the Mail Box Protocol

221 Revision of the Mail Box Protocol

224 Revision of the Mail Box Protocol

278 Revision of the Mail Box Protocol

333 Proposed Experiment with a Message Switching Protocol

458 Mail Retrieval via FTP

475 FTP and Network Mail System

491 What is "Free"?

498 On Mail Service to CCN

524 Thoughts on the Mail Protocol Proposed in RFC 524

539 Thoughts on the Mail Protocol Proposed in RFC 524

555 Responses to Critiques of the Proposed Mail Protocol

561 Standardized Network Mail Headers

574 Announcement of a Mail Facility at UCSB

577 Mail Priority

644 On the Problem of Signature Authentification for Network Mail

680 Message Transmission Protocol

706 On the Junk Mail Problem

720 Address Specification Syntax for Network Mail

724 Proposed Official Standard for the Format of ARPA Network Text Messages

732 Standard for the Format of ARPA Network Text Messages

744 MARS—a Message Archiving and Retrieval Service

751 Survey of FTP mail and MLFL

753 Internet Message Protocol

754 Out-of-net Host Addresses for Mail

757 Suggested Solution to the Naming, Addressing, and Delivery Problem for ARPANET Message System

763 Role Mailboxes

771 Mail Transition Plan

772 Mail Transfer Protocol

780 Mail Transfer Protocol

784 Mail Transfer Protocol: ISI TOPS20 Implementation

785 Mail Transfer Protocol: ISI TOPS20 File Definitions

786 Mail Transfer Protocol: ISI TOPS20 MTP-NIMAIL Interface

788 Simple Mail Transfer Protocol

806 Proposed Federal Information Processing Standard: Specification for Message Format for Computer-based Message Systems

821 Simple Mail Transfer Protocol

822 Standard for the Format of ARPA Internal Text Messages

841 Specification for Message Format for the Computer-based Message System

886 Proposed Standard for Message Header Munging

915 Network Mail Path Service

918 Post Office Protocol: Version 2

934 Proposed Standard for Message Encapsulation

937 Post Office Protocol: Version 2

974 Mail Routing and the Domain System

975 UUCP Mail Interchange Format Standard

976 Network News Transfer Protocol

984 PCMAIL: A Distributed Mail System for Personal Computers

987 Addendum to RFC 987: (Mapping Between X.400 and RFC-822)

993 PCMAIL: A Distributed Mail System for Personal Computers

1026 Addendum to RFC 987:(Mapping Between X.400 and RFC-822). S.E. Kille. Sep-01-1987. (Format: TXT=7117 bytes) (Obsoleted by RFC1327, RFC1495, RFC2156) (Updates RFC0987) (Updated by RFC1138, RFC1148) (Status: UNKNOWN)

1047 Duplicate Messages and SMTP. C. Partridge. Feb-01-1998. (Format: TXT=15423 bytes) (Obsoleted by RFC1084, RFC1395, RFC1497, RFC1533) (Status: UNKNOWN)

1049 Content-type Header Field for Internet Messages. M. A. Sirbu. Mar-01-1988. (Format: TXT=51540 bytes) (Obsoleted by RFC1057) (Status: HISTORIC)

1056 PCMAIL: A Distributed Mail System for Personal Computers. M. L. Lambert. Jun-01-1988. (Format: TXT=12911 bytes) (Status: STANDARD)

1064 Interactive Mail Access Protocol: Version 2. M. R. Crispin. Jul-01-1988. (Format: TXT=57813 bytes) (Obsoleted by RFC1176, RFC1203) (Status: UNKNOWN)

1081 Post Office Protocol: Version 3. M. T. Rose. Nov-01-1988. (Format: TXT=37009 bytes) (Obsoleted by RFC1225) (Status: UNKNOWN)

1082 Post Office Protocol: Version 3. Extended Service Offerings. M. T. Rose. Nov-01-1988. (Format: TXT=25423 bytes) (Obsoleted by RFC1225) (Status: UNKNOWN)

1090 SMTP on X.25. R. Ullmann. Feb-01-1989. (Format: TXT=6141 bytes) (Status: UNKNOWN)

1113 Privacy enhancement for Internet Electronic Mail: Part I—Message Encipherment and Authentication Procedures. J. Linn. Aug-01-1989. (Format: TXT=89293 bytes) (Obsoletes RFC0989, RFC1040) (Obsoleted by RFC1421) (Status: HISTORIC)

1114 Privacy Enhancement for Internet Electronic Mail: Part II Certificate–based Key management. S. T. Kent, J. Linn. Aug-01-1989. (Format: TXT=69661 bytes) (Obsoleted by RFC1422) (Status: HISTORIC)

1115 Privacy Enhancement for Internet electronic mail: Part III—Algorithms, Modes, and Identifiers. J. Linn. Aug-01-1989. (Format: TXT=18226 bytes) (Obsoleted by RFC1422) (Status: HISTORIC)

1137 Mapping Between Full RFC 822 and RFC 822 with Restricted Encoding. S. Kille. Dec-01-1989. (Format: TXT=6266 bytes) (Updates RFC0976) (Status: HISTORIC)

1138 Mapping Between X.400(1988)/ISO 10021 and RFC 822. S. E. Kille. Dec-01-1989. (Format: TXT=191029 bytes) (Obsoleted by RFC1327, RFC1495, RFC2156) (Updates RFC0822, RFC0987, RFC1026) (Updated by arfc1148) (Status: EXPERIMENTAL)

1148 Mapping Between X.400 (1988)/ISO 10021 and RFC 822. S.E. Kille.

1153 Digest Message Format. F. J. Wancho. Apr-01-1990. (Format: TXT=6632 bytes) (Status: EXPERIMENTAL)

1154 Encoding Header Message Field for Internet Messages. D. Robinson and R. Ullmann. Apr-01-1990. (Format: TXT=12214 bytes) (Obsoleted by RFC1505) (Status: EXPERIMENTAL)

1168 Intermail and Commercial Mail Relay Services. A. Westine, A. L. DeSchon, J. Postel, C. E. Ward. Jul-01-1990. (Format: TXT=149816 bytes) (Status: INFORMATIONAL)

1176 Interactive Mail Access Protocol: Version 2. M. R. Crispin. Aug-01-1990. (Format: TXT=67330 bytes) (Obsoletes RFC1064) (Status: EXPERIMENTAL)

1203 Interactive Mail Access Protocol: Version 3. J. Rice. Feb-01-1991. (Format: TXT=123325 bytes) (Obsoletes RFC1064) (Status: HISTORIC)

1204 Message Posting Protocol (MPP). S. Yeh, D. Lee. Feb-01-1991. (Format: TXT=11371 bytes) (Status: EXPERIMENTAL)

1211 Problems With Maintenance of Large Mailing Lists. A. Westine, J. Postel. Mar-01-1991. (Format: TXT96167 bytes) (Status: INFORMATIONAL)

1225 Post Office Protocol: Version 3. M. T. Rose. May-01-1991. (Format: TXT=37340 bytes) (Obsoleted RFC1081) (Obsoleted by RFC1460) (Status: DRAFT STANDARD)

1327 Mapping Between X.400(1988)/ISO 10021 and RFC 822. S. Hardcatle-Kile. May 1992. (Format: TXT=228598 bytes) (Obsoletes RFC987, RFC1026, RFC1138, RFC1148) (Obsoleted by RFC1495, RFC2156) (Updates RFC0822, rfc0822) (Status: PROPOSED STANDARD)

1339 Remote Mail Checking Protocol. S. Dorner and P. Resnick. June 1992. (Format: TXT=13115 bytes) (Status: EXPERIMENTAL)

1341 Multipurpose Internet Mail Extensions (MIME) Part One: Format of Internet Message Bodies. N. Borenstein and N. Freed. June 1992. (Format: TXT=211117, PS=347082 bytes) (Obsoleted by RFC1521) (Status: PROPOSED STANDARD)

1342 MIME (Multipurpose Internet Mail Extensions), Part Three. K. Moore. June 1992. (Format: TXT=15845 bytes) (Obsoleted by RFC1522) (Status: INFORMATIONAL)

1343 A User Agent Configuration Mechanism for Multimedia Mail Format Information. N. Borenstein. June 1992. (Format: TXT=29295, PS=59978 bytes) (Status: INFORMATIONAL)

1344 Implications of MIME for Internet Gateways. N. Borenstein. June 1992. (Format: TXT=25872, PS=51812 bytes) (Status: INFORMATIONAL)

1357 A Format for E-mailing Bibliographic Records. D. Cohen. July 1992. (Format: TXT=25021 bytes) (Obsoleted by RFC1807) (Status: INFORMATIONAL)

1405 Mapping Between X.400 (1984/1988) and Mail-11 (DECnet mail). C. Allocchio. January 1993. (Format: TXT=33885 bytes) (Obsoleted by RFC2162) (Status: EXPERIMENTAL)

1425 SMTP Service Extensions. J. Klensin, WG Chair, N. Freed, Editor, M. Rose, E. Stefferud & D. Crocker. February 1993. (Format: TXT=20932 bytes) (Obsoleted by RFC1651) (Status: PROPOSED STANDARD)

1426 SMTP Service Extension for 8bit-MIMEtransport. J. Klenisin; W. G. Chair; N. Freed, Editor; M. Rose; E. Stefferud; and D. Crocker. February 1993. (Format: TXT=1161 bytes) (Obsoleted by RFC1652) (Status: PROPOSED STANDARD)

1427 SMTP Service Extension for Message Size Declaration. J. Klensin; W. G. Chair; N. Freed, Editor; K. Moore. February 1993. (Format: TXT=17856 bytes) (Obsoleted by RFC1653) (Status: PROPOSED STANDARD)

1428 Transition of Internet Mail from Just-Send-8 to 8-bit SMTP/MIME. G. Vaudreuil. February 1993. (Format: TXT=12064 bytes)(Status: INFORMATIONAL)

1460 Post Office Protocol, Version 3. M. Rose. June 1993. (Format: TXT=38827 bytes) (Obsoletes RFC1225) (Obsoleted by RFC1725)

1494 Equivalences Between 1988 X.400 and RFC-822 Message Bodies. H. Alvestrand & S. Thompson. August 1993. (Format: TXT=37273 bytes) (Status: PROPOSED STANDARD)

1495 Mapping Between X.400 and RFC-822 Message Bodies. H. Alvestrand, S. Kille, R. Miles, M. Rose, and S. Thompson. August 1993. (Format: TXT=20071 bytes) (Obsoletes RFC987, RFC987, RFC1026, RFC1138, RFC1148, RFC1327) (Obsoleted by RFC2156) (Status: PROPOSED STANDARD)

1496 Rules for Downgrading Messages from X.400/88 to X.400/84 when MIME Content Types are Present in the Messages. H. Alvestrand, J. Romaguera, and K. Jordan. August 1993. (Format: TXT=8411 bytes) (Status: PROPOSED STANDARD)

1502 X.400 Use of Extended Character Sets. H. Alvestrand. August 1993. (Format: TXT=27976 bytes) (Status: PROPOSED STANDARD)

1505 Encoding Header Message Field for Internet Messages. A. Costanzo, D. Robinson, and R. Ullmann. August 1993. (Format: TXT=63796 bytes) (Obsoletes RFC1154) (Status: EXPERIMENTAL)

1506 A Tutorial on Gatewaying Between X.400 and Internet Mail. J. Houttuin. September 1993. (Format: TXT=85550 bytes) (Status: INFORMATIONAL)

1521 Multipurpose Internet Mail Extensions (MIME) Part One: Mechanisms for Specifying and Describing the Format of Internet Message Bodies. N. Borenstein and N. Freed. September 1993. (Format: TXT=187424, PS=393670 bytes) (Obsoletes RFC1341) (Obsoleted by RFC2045, RFC2046, RFC2047, RFC2048, RFC2049, BCP0013) (Updated by RFC1590) (Status: DRAFT STANDARD)

1522 MIME (Multipurpose Internet Mail Extensions), Part Two: Message Header Extensions for Non-ASCII Text. K. Moore. September 1993. (Format: TXT=22502 bytes) (Obsoletes RFC1342) (Obsoleted by RFC2045, RFC2046, RFC2047, RFC2048, RFC2049, BCP0013) (Status: DRAFT STANDARD)

1523 The Text-enriched MIME Content Type. N. Borenstein. September 1993. (Format: TXT=32691 bytes) (Obsoleted by RFC1563, RFC1896) (Status: INFORMATIONAL)

1524 A User Agent Configuration Mechanism for Multimedia Mail Format Information. N. Borenstein. September 1993. (Format: TXT=26464 bytes) (Status: INFORMATIONAL)

1544 The Content-MD5 Header Field. M. Rose. November 1993. (Format: TXT=6478 bytes) (Obsoleted by RFC1864) (Status: PROPOSED STANDARD)

1556 Handling of Bidirectional Texts in MIME. H. Nussbacher and Y. Bourvine. December 1993. (Format: TXT=9273 bytes) (Status: INFORMATIONAL)

1563 The Text-enriched MIME Content Type. N. Borenstein. January 1994. (Format: TXT=32913, PS=73543 bytes) (Obsoletes RFC1523) (Obsoleted by RFC1896) (Status: INFORMATIONAL)

1590 Media Type Registration Procedure. J. Postel. March 1994. (Format: TXT=13044 bytes) (Obsoleted by RFC2045, RFC2046, RFC2047, RFC2048, RFC2049, BCP0013) (Updates RFC1521) (Status: INFORMATIONAL)

1615 Migrating Form X.400(84)to X.400(88). J. Houttuin and J. Craigie. May 1994. (Format: TXT=39693 bytes) (Status: INFORMATIONAL)

1616 X.400(1988)for the Academic and Research Community in Europe. RARE WG-MSG Task Force 88. E. Huizer and J. Romaguera, Editors. May 1994. (Format: TXT=107432 bytes) (Status: INFORMATIONAL)

1641 Using Unicode With MIME. D. Goldsmith and M. Davis. July 1994. (Format: TXT=11258, PS=20451 bytes) (Status: EXPERIMENTAL)

1642 UTF-7 A Mail-safe Transformation Format of Unicode. D. Goldsmith and M. Davis. July 1994. (Format: TXT=27770, PS=50907 bytes) (Obsoleted by RFC2152) (Status: EXPERIMENTAL)

1648 Postmaster Convention for X.400 Operations. A. Cargille. July 1994. (Format: TXT=8761 bytes) (Status: PROPOSED STANDARD)

1649 Operational Requirements for X.400 Management Domain in the GO-MHS Community. R. Hagens and A. Hansen. July 1994. (Format: TXT=23138 bytes) (Status: INFORMA-TIONAL)

1651 SMTP Service Extensions. Klensin, N. Freed, M. Rose, E. Stefferud, and D. Crocker. July 1994. (Format: TXT=22153 bytes) (Obsoletes RFC1425) (Obsoleted by RFC1869, STD0010) (Status: DRAFT STANDARD)

1652 SMTP Service Extension for 8-bit MIME Transport. Klensin, N.Freed, M. Rose, E. Stefferud, and D. Crocker. July 1994. (Format: TXT=11842 bytes) (Obsoletes RFC1426) (Status: DRAFT STANDARD)

1653 SMTP Service Extension for Message Size Declaration. J. Klenisn, N. Freed, and K. Moore. July 1994. (Format: TXT=17883 bytes) (Obsoletes RFC1427) (Obsoleted by RFC1870, STD0011) (Also STD0011) (Status: DRAFT STANDARD)

1685 Writing X.400 O/R Names. H. Alvestrand. August 1994. (Format: TXT=21242 bytes) (Also RTR0012) (Status: INFORMATIONAL)

1711 Classifications in E-mail Routing. J. Houttuin. October 1994. (Format: TXT=47584 bytes) (Status: INFORMATIONAL)

1725 Post Office Protocol, Version 3. J. Meyers and M. Rose. November 1994. (Format: TXT=35058 bytes) (Obsoletes RFC1460) (Obsoleted by RFC1939, STD0053) (Status: DRAFT STANDARD)

1730 Internet Message Access Protocol, Version 4. M. Crispin. December 1994. (Format: TXT=156660 bytes) (Obsoleted by RFC2060, RFC2061) (Status: PROPOSED STAN-DARD)

1731 IMAP4 Authentication Mechanisms. J. Myers. December 1994. (Format: TXT=11433 bytes) (Status: PROPOSED STANDARD)

1732 IMAP4 COMPATABILITY WITH IMPAP2 AND IMPA2BIS. M. Crispin. December 1994. (Format: TXT=9276 bytes) (Status: INFORMATIONAL)

1733 DISTRIBUTED ELECTRONIC MAIL MODELS IN IMAP4. M. Crispin. December 1994. (Format: TXT=6205 bytes) (Status: INFORMATIONAL)

1734 POP3 Authentication command. J. Myers. December 1994. (Format: TXT=8499 bytes) (Status: PROPOSED STANDARD)

1740 MIME Encapsulation of Macintosh Files—MacMIME. P. Falstrom, D. Crocker, and E. Fair. December 1994. (Format: TXT=31297 bytes) (Status: PROPOSED STANDARD)

1741 MIME Content-type for BinHex Encoded Files. P. Faltstrom, D. Crocker, and E. Fair. December 1994. (Format: TXT=10155 bytes) (Status: INFORMATIONAL)

1767 MIME Encapsulation of EDI Objects. D. Crocker. March 1995. (Format: TXT=15293 bytes) (Status: PROPOSED STANDARD)

1806 Communicating Presentation Information in Internet Messages: The Content-Disposition Header. R. Troost and S. Dorner. June 1995. (Format: TXT=15548 bytes)

1807 A Format for Bibliographic Records. R. Lasher and D. Cohen. June 1995. (Format: TXT=29417 bytes) (Obsoletes RFC1357) (Status: INFORMATIONAL)

1820 Multimedia E-mail (MIME) User Agent Checklist. E. Huizer. August 1995. (Format: TXT=14672 bytes) (Obsoleted by RFC1844) (Status: INFORMATIONAL)

1830 SMTP Service Extensions for Transmission of Large and Binary MIME Messages. G. Vaudreuil. August 1995. (Format: TXT=16555 bytes) (Status: EXPERIMENTAL)

1838 Use of an X.500/LDAP Directory to Support Mapping Between X.400 and RFC 822 Addresses. S. Kille. August 1995. (Format: TXT=12216 bytes) (Obsoleted by RFC2164) (Status: EXPERIMENTAL)

1844 Multimedia E-mail (MIME) User Agent Checklist. E. Huizer. August 1995. (Format: TXT=15072 bytes) (Obsoletes RFC1820) (Status: INFORMATIONAL)

1845 SMTP Service Extension for Checkpoint/Restart. D. Crocker, N. Freed and A. Cargille. September 1995. (Format: TXT=15399 bytes) (Status: EXPERIMENTAL)

1846 SMTP 521 Reply Code. A. Durand and F. Dupont. September 1995. (Format: TXT=6558 bytes) (Status: EXPERIMENTAL)

1847 Security Multiparts for MIME: Multipart/Signed and Multipart/Encrypted. J. Galvin, S. Murphy, S. Crocker, and N. Freed. October 1995. (Format: TXT=23679 bytes) (Status: PROPOSED STANDARD)

1848 MIME Objects Security Services. S. Crocker, N. Freed, J. Galvin, and S. Murphy. October 1995. (Format: TXT=95010 bytes) (Status: PROPOSED STANDARD)

1854 SMTP Service Extension for Command Pipelining. N. Freed. October 1995. (Format: TXT=14097 bytes) (Obsoleted by RFC2197) (Status: PROPOSED STANDARD)

1864 The Content-MD5 Header Field. J. Myers and M. Rose. October 1995. (Format: TXT=7216 bytes)

1869 SMTP Service Extensions. J. Klensin, N. Freed, M. Rose, E. Stefferud, and D. Crocker. November 1995. (Format: TXT=23299 bytes) (Obsoleted by RFC1651) (Also STD0010) (Status: STANDARD)

1870 SMTP Service Extension for Message Size Declaration. J.Klensin, N. Freed, and K. Moore. November 1995. (Format: TXT=18226 bytes) (Obsoletes RFC1653) (Also STD0010) (Status: STANDARD)

1872 The MIME Multipart/Related Content-type. E. Levinson. December 1995. (Format: TXT=15565 bytes) (Obsoleted by RFC2112) (Status: EXPERIMENTAL)

1873 Message/External-Body Content-ID Access Type. E. Levinson. December 1995. (Format: TXT=5878 bytes) (Status: EXPERIMENTAL)

1891 SMTP Service Extension for Delivery Status Notifications. K. Moore. January 1996. (Format: TXT=65192 bytes) (Status: PROPOSED STANDARD)

1892 The Multipart/Report Content-type for the Reporting of Mail System Administrative Messages. G. Vaudreuil. January 1996. (Format: TXT=7800 bytes) (Status: PROPOSED STANDARD)

1893 Enhanced Mail System Status Codes. G. Vaudreuil. January 1996. (Format: TXT=28218 bytes) (Status: PROPOSED STANDARD)

1894 An Extensible Message Format for Delivery Status Notifications. K. Moore and G. Vaudreuil. January 1996. (Format: TXT=77462 bytes) (Status: PROPOSED STANDARD)

1895 The Application/CALS-1840 Content-type. E. Levinson. February 1996. (Format: TXT=10576 bytes) (Status: INFORMATIONAL)

1896 The text/enriched MIME Content-type. P. Resnick & A. Walker. February 1996. (Format: TXT=45926, PS=81217 bytes) (Obsoletes RFC1523, RFC1563) (Status: INFORMATIONAL)

1957 Some Observations on Implementations of the Post Office Protocol (POP3). R. Nelson. June 1996. (Format: TXT=2325 bytes) (Updates RFC1939) (Status: INFORMATIONAL)

1985 SMTP Service Extension for Remote Message Queue Starting. J. DeWinter. August 1996. (Format: TXT=14815 bytes) (Status: PROPOSED STANDARD)

2015 MIME Security with Pretty Good Privacy (PGP). M. Elkins. October 1996. (Format: TXT=14223 bytes) (Status: PROPOSED STANDARD)

2016 Uniform Resource Agents (URAs). L. Daigle, P. Deutsch, B. Heelan, C. Alpaugh, M. Maclachlan. October 1996. (Format: TXT=38355 bytes) (Status: EXPERIMENTAL)

2033 Local Mail Transfer Protocol. J. Myers. October 1996. (Format: TXT=14711 bytes) (Status: INFORMATIONAL)

2034 SMTP Service Extension for Returning Enhanced Error Codes. N. Freed. October 1996. (Format: TXT=10460 bytes) (Status: PROPOSED STANDARD)

2045 Multipurpose Internet Mail Extensions (MIME) Part One: Format of Internet Message Bodies. N.Freed & N. Borenstein. November 1996. (Format: TXT=72932 bytes) (Obsoletes RFC1521, RFC1522, RFC15900) (Updated by RFC2184, RFC2231) (Status: DRAFT STANDARD)

2046 Multipurpose Internet Mail Extensions (MIME), Part Two: Media Types. N. Freed and N. Borenstein. November 1996. (Format: TXT=105854 bytes) (Obsoletes RFC1521, RFC1522, RFC1590) (Status: DRAFT STANDARD)

2047 MIME (Multipurpose Internet Mail Extensions), Part Three: Message Header Extensions for Non-ASCII Text. K. Moore. November 1996. (Format: TXT=3326T2 bytes) (Obsoletes RFC1521, RFC1522, RFC1590) (Updated by RFC2184, RFC2231) (Status: DRAFT STANDARD)

2048 Multipurpose Internet Mail Extensions (MIME), Part Four: Registration Procedures. N.Freed, J. Klensin, and J. Postel. November 1996. (Format: TXT=45033 bytes) (Obsoletes RFC1521, RFC1522, RFC1590) (Also BCP0013) (Status: BEST CURRENT PRACTICE)

2049 Multipurpose Internet Mail Extensions (MIME), Part Five: Conformance Criteria and Examples. N. Freed & N. Borenstein. November 1996. (Format: TXT=51207 bytes) (Obsoletes RFC1521, RFC1522, RFC1590) (Status: DRAFT STANDARD)

2060 Internet Message Access Protocol, Version 4rev1. M. Crispin. December 1996. (Format: TXT=166513 bytes) (Obsoletes RFC1730) (Status: PROPOSED STANDARD)

2061 IMPA4 Compatibility With IMAP2BIS. M. Crispin. December 1996. (Format: TXT=5867 bytes) (Obsoletes RFC1730) (Status: INFORMATIONAL)

2062 Internet Message Access Protocol—Obsolete Syntax. M. Crispin. December 1996. (Format: TXT=14222 bytes) (Status: PROPOSED STANDARD)

2076 Common Internet Message Headers. J.Palme. February 1997. (Format: TXT=47639 bytes) (Status: INFORMATIONAL)

2077   The Model Primary Content-type for Multipurpose Internet Mail Extensions. S. Nelson, C. Parks, Mitra. January 1997. (Format: TXT=30158 bytes) (Status: PROPOSED STANDARD)

2086   IMAP4 ACL Extension. J. Myers. January 1997. (Format: TXT=13925 bytes) (Status: PROPOSED STANDARD)

2087   IMAP4 QUOTA Extension. J. Myers. January 1997. (Format: TXT=8524 bytes) (Status: PROPOSED STANDARD)

2088   IMAP4 Non-synchronizing literals. J. Myers. January 1997. (Format: TXT=4052 bytes) (Status: PROPOSED STANDARD)

2095   IMAP/POP Authorize Extension for Simple Challenge/Response. J. Klensin, R. Catoe, and P. Krumviede. January 1997. (Format: TXT=10446 bytes) (Obsoleted by RFC2195) (Status: PROPOSED STANDARD)

2110   MIME Encapsulation of Aggregate Documents Such As HTML (MHTML). J. Palme and A. Hopmann. March 1997. (Format: TXT=41961 bytes) (Status: PROPOSED STANDARD)

2112   The MIME Multipart/Related Content-type. E. Levinson. February 1997. (Format: TXT=17052 bytes) (Obsoletes RFC1872) (Obsoleted by RFC2387) (Status: PROPOSED STANDARD)

2142   Mailbox Names for Common Services, Roles, and Functions.D. Crocker. May 1997. (Format: TXT=12195 bytes) (Status: PROPOSED STANDARD)

2152   UTF-7 A Mail-Safe Transformation Format of Unicode. D. Goldsmith, M. Davis. May 1997. (Format: TXT=28065 bytes) (Obsoletes RFC1642) (Status: INFORMATIONAL)

2156   MIXER (Mime Internet X.400 Enhanced Relay): Mapping between X.400 and RFC 822/MIME. S. Kille. January 1998. (Format: TXT=280385 bytes) (Obsoletes RFC0987, RFC1026, RFC1138, RFC1148, RFC1327, RFC1495) (Updates RFC0822) (Status: PROPOSED STANDARDS)

2157   Mapping between X.400 and RFC-822/MIME Message Bodies. H. Alvestrand. January 1998. (Format: TXT=92554 bytes) (Status: PROPOSED STANDARD)

2158   X.400 Image Body Parts. H. Alvestrand. January 1998. (Format: TXT=5547 bytes) (Status: PROPOSED STANDARD)

2160   Carrying PostScript in X.400 and MIME. H. Alvestrand. January 1998. (Format: TXT=7059 bytes) (Status: PROPOSED STANDARD)

2161   A MIME Body Part for ODA. H. Alvestrand. January 1998. (Format: TXT=8009 bytes) (Status: EXPERIMENTAL)

2162   MaXIM-11—Mapping Between X.400/Internet Mail and Mail-11 Mail. C. Allocchio. January 1998. (Format: TXT=58553 bytes) (Obsoletes RFC1405) (Status: EXPERIMENTAL)

2163 Using the Internet DNS to Distribute MIXER Conformant Global Address Mapping (MCGAM). C. Allocchio. January 1998. (Format: TXT=58789 bytes) (Obsoletes RFC1664) (Status: PROPOSED STANDARD)

2164 Use of the X.500/LDAP Directory to Support MIXER Address Mapping. S. Kille. January 1998. (Format: TXT=16701 bytes) (Obsoletes RFC1838) (Status: PROPOSED STANDARD)

2177 IMAP4 IDLE command. B. Leiba. June 1997. (Format: TXT=6770 bytes) (Status: PROPOSED STANDARD)

2180 IMAP4 Multi-accessed Mailbox Practice. M.Gahrns. July 1997. (Format: TXT=24750 bytes) (Status: INFORMATIONAL)

2184 MIME Parameter Value and Encoded Word Extensions: Character Sets, Languages, and Continuations. N. Freed and K. Moore. August 1997. (Format:TXT=17635 bytes) (Obsoletes RFC2184) (Obsoleted by RFC2184, RFC2231) (Updates RFC2045, RFC2047, RFC2183) (Status: PROPOSED STANDARD)

2192 IMAP URL Scheme. C. Newman. September 1997. (Format: TXT=31426 bytes) (Status: PROPOSED STANDARD)

2193 IMAP4 Mailbox Referrals. M. Gahrns. September 1997. (Format: TXT=16248 bytes) (Status: PROPOSED STANDARD)

2195 IMAP/POP Authorize Extension for Simple Challenge/Response. J. Klensin, R. Catoe, P. Krumviede. September 1997. (Format: TXT=10468 bytes) (Obsoletes RFC2095) (Status: PROPOSED STANDARD)

2197 SMTP Service Extension for Command Pipelining. N. Freed. September 1997. (Format: TXT=15003 bytes) (Obsoletes RFC1854) (Status: DRAFT STANDARD)

2220 The Application/MARC Content-type. R. Guenther. October 1997. (Format: TXT=7025 bytes) (Status: INFORMATIONAL)

2221 IMAP4 Login Referrals. M. Gahrns. October 1997. (Format: TXT=9251 bytes) (Status: PROPOSED STANDARD)

2231 MIME Parameter Value and Encoded Word Extensions: Character Sets, Languages, and Continuations. N. Freed and K. Moore. November 1997. (Format: TXT=19280 bytes) (Obsoletes RFC2184) (Updates RFC2045, RFC2047 RFC2183) (Status: PROPOSED STANDARD)

2298 An Extensible Message Format for Message Disposition Notifications. R. Fajman. March 1998. (Format: TXT=62059 bytes) (Status: PROPOSED STANDARD)

2302 Tag Image File Format (TIFF)—Image/tiff MIME Sub-type Registration. G. Parsons, J. Rafferty, S. Zilles. March 1998. (Format: TXT=14375 bytes) (Status: PROPOSED STANDARD)

2311 S/MIME Version 2 Message Specification. S. Dusse, P. Hoffman, B. Ramsdell, L. Lundblade, L. Repka. March 1998. (Format: TXT=7091 bytes) (Status: INFORMATIONAL)

2312 S/MIME Version 2 Certification Handling. S. Dusse, P. Hofffman, B. Ramsdell, and J. Weinstein. March 1998. (Format: TXT=39829 bytes)

2318 The Text/CSS Media Type. H. Lie, B. Bos, and C. Lilley. March 1998. (Format: TXT=7819 bytes) (Status: INFORMATIONAL)

2342 IMAP4 Namespace. M. Gahrns and C. Newman. May 1998. (Format: TXT=19489 bytes) (Status: PROPOSED STANDARD)

2359 IMAP4 UIDPLUS Extension. J. Myers. June 1998. (Format: TXT=10862 bytes) (Status: PROPOSED STANDARD)

2384 POP URL Scheme. R. Gellens. August 1998. Format: TXT=13649 bytes) (Status: PROPOSED STANDARD)

2387 The MIME Multipart/Related Content-type. E. Levinson. August 1998. (Format: TXT=18864 bytes) (Obsoletes RFC2112) (Status: PROPOSED STANDARD)

2424 ContentDuration MIME Header Definition. G. Vaudreuil and G. Parsons. September 1998. (Format: TXT=7116 bytes) (Status: PROPOSED STANDARD)

2425 A MIME Content-type for Directory Information. T. Howes, M. Smith, and F. Dawson. September 1998. (Format: TXT=64478 bytes) (Status: PROPOSED STANDARD)

2426 vCard MIME Directory Profile. F. Dawson and T. Howes. September 1998. (Format: TXT=74746 bytes) (Status: PROPOSED STANDARD)

2442 The Batch SMTP Media Type. N. Freed, D. Newman, H. Belissen, and M. Hoy. November 1998. (Format: TXT=18384 bytes) (Status: INFORMATIONAL)

2449 POP3 Extension Mechanism. R. Gellens, C. Newman, and L. Lundblade. November 1998. (Format: TXT=36017 bytes) (Updates RFC1939) (Status: PROPOSED STANDARD)

2476 Message Submission. R. Gellens and H. Klensin. December 1998. (Format: TXT=30050 bytes) (Status: PROPOSED STANDARD)

2480 Gateways and MIME Security Multiparts. N. Freed. January 1999. (Format: TXT=11751 bytes) (Status: PROPOSED STANDARD)

2487 SMTP Service Extension for Secure SMTP Over TLS. P. Hoffman. January 1999. (Format: TXT=15120 bytes) (Status: PROPOSED STANDARD)

2503 MIME Types for Use with the ISO ILL Protocol. R. Moulton and M. Needleman. February 1999. (Format: TXT=9078 bytes) (Status: INFORMATIONAL)

2505 Anti-Spam Recommendations for SMTP MTAs. G.Lindberg. February 1999. (Format: TXT=53597 bytes) (Also BCP0030) (Status: BEST CURRENT PRACTICES)

2524 Neda's Efficient Mail Submission and Delivery (EMSD) Protocol Specification Version 1.3. M. Banan. February 1999. (Format: TXT=153171 bytes) (Status: INFORMA-TIONAL)

2554 SMTP Service Extension for Authentication. J. Meyers. March 1999. (Format: TXT=20534 bytes) (Status: PROPOSED STANDARD)

2557 MIME Encapsulation of Aggregate Documents Such As HTML (MHTML). J. Palme, A. Hopmann, and N. Shelness. March 1999. (Format: TXT=61854 bytes) (Obsoletes RFC2110) (Status: PROPOSED STANDARD)

2586 The Audio/L16 MIME

2595 Using TLS with IMAP, POP3, and ACAP

2632 S/MIME Version 3 Certificate Handling

2633 S/MIME Version 3 Message Specification

2634 Enhanced Security Service for S/MIME

2645 On-demand Mail Relay (ODMR) SMTP With Dynamic IP Addresses

2646 The Text/Plain Format Parameter

2683 IMAP4 Implementation Recommendations

Chapter 14: Name Resolution

752 Universal Host Table

756 NIC Name Server—a Datagram-based Information Utility

799 Internet Name Domains

811 Hostname Server

819 Domain Naming Convention for Internet User Applications

830 Distributed System for Internet Name Service

881 Domain Names Plan and Schedule

882 Domain Names: Concepts and Facilities

883 Domain Names: Implementation Specification

897 Domain Name System Implementation Schedule—Revised

920 Domain Requirements

921 Domain Name System Implementation Schedule—Revised

953 Hostname Server

973   Domain System Changes and Observations

1001 ProtocolStandard for a NetBIOS Service on a TCP/UDP Transport: Concepts and Methods. NetBIOS Working Group. Defense Advanced Research Projects Agency, Internet Activities Board, End-to-End Services Task Force. Mar-01-1987. (Format: TXT=158437 bytes) (Status: STANDARD)

1002 Protocol Standard for a NetBIOS Service on a TCP/UDP Transport: Detailed Specifications. NetBIOS Working Group. Defense Advanced Research Projects Agency, Internet Activities Board, End-to-End Services Task Force. Mar-01-1987. (Format: TXT=170262 bytes) (Status: STANDARD)

1031 MILNET Name Domain Transition. W. D. Lazear. Nov-01-1987. (Format: TXT=20137 bytes) (Status: UNKNOWN)

1032 Domain Administrators Guide. M. K. Stahl. Nov-01-1987. (Format: TXT=29454 bytes) (Status: UNKNOWN)

1033 Domain Administrators Operations Guide. M. Lottor. Nov-01-1987. (Format: TXT=37263 bytes) (Status: UNKNOWN)

1034 Domain Names—Concepts and Facilities. P. V. Mockapetris. Nov-01-1987. (Format: TXT=129180 bytes) (Obsoletes RFC0973, RFC0882, RFC0883) (Obsoleted by RFC1065, RFC2308) (Updated by RFC1101, RFC1183, RFC1348, RFC1876, RFC1982, RFC2065, RFC2181, RFC2308) (Status: STANDARD)

1035 Domain Administrators Guide. M. K. Stahl. Nov-01-1987.   (Format: TXT=29454 bytes) (Status: UNKNOWN)

1036 Domain Administrators Guide. M. Lottor. Nov-01-1987. (Format: TXT=37263 bytes) (Status: UNKNOWN)

1037 Domain Names—Concepts and Facilities. P. V. Mockapetris. Nov-01-1987. (Format: TXT=129180 bytes) (Obsoletes RFC0973, RFC0882, RFC0883) (Obsoleted by RFC1065, RFC2308) (Updated by RFC1101, RFC1183, RFC1348, RFC1876, RFC1982, RFC1995, RFC1996, RFC2065, RFC2181, RFC2136, RFC2137, RFC2308) (Status: STANDARD)

1038 Domain Names—Implementation and Specification. P. V. Mockapetris. Nov-01-1987. (Format: TXT=125626 bytes) (Obsoletes RFC0973, RFC0882, RFC0883) (Updated by RFC1101, RFC1183, RFC1348, RFC1876, RFC1982, RFC1995, RFC1996, RFC2065, RFC2181, RFC2136, RFC2137, RFC2308) (Status: STANDARD)

1101 DNS Encoding of Network Names and Other Types. P. V. Mockapetris. Apr-01-1989. (Format: TXT=28677 bytes) (Updates RFC1034, RFC1035) (Status: UNKNOWN)

1183 New DNS RR Definitions. C. F. Everhart, L. A. Mamakos, R. Ullmann, and P. V. Mockapetris. Oct-01-1990. (Format: TXT=23788 bytes) (Updates RFC1034,RFC1035) (Status: EXPERIMENTAL)

1348 DNS NSAP Resource Records. B. Manning. July 1992. (Format: TXT=6871 bytes) (Obsoleted by RFC1637) (Updates RFC1034, RFC1035) (Updated by RFC1637) (Status: EXPERIMENTAL)

1383 An Experiment in DNS-based IP Routing. C. Huitema. December 1992. (Format: TXT=32680 bytes) (Status: EXPERIMENTAL)

1386 The US Domain. A. Cooper and J. Postel. December 1992. (Format: TXT=62310 bytes) (Obsoleted by RFC1480) (Status: INFORMATIONAL)

1394 Relationship of Telex Answerback Codes to Internet Domains. P. Robinson. January 1993. (Format: TXT=43776 bytes) (Status: INFORMATIONAL)

1464 Using the Domain Name System to Store Arbitrary String Attributes. R. Rosenbaum. May 1993. (Format: TXT=7953 bytes) (Status: EXPERIMENTAL)

1480 The US Domain. A. Cooper and J. Postel. June 1993. (Format: TXT=100556 bytes) (Obsoletes RFC1386) (Status: INFORMATIONAL)

1535 A Security Problem and Proposed Correction With Widely Deployed DNS Software. E. Gavron. October 1993. (Format: TXT=9722 bytes) (Status: INFORMATIONAL)

1536 Common DNS Implementation Errors and Suggested Fixes. A.Kumar, J. Postel, C. Neuman, P. Danzig, and S. Miller. October 1993. (Format: TXT=25476 bytes) (Status: INFORMATIONAL)

1537 Common DNS Operational and Configuration Errors. P. Beertema. October 1993. (Format: TXT=19825 bytes) (Obsoleted by RFC1912) (Status: INFORMATIONAL)

1591 Domain Name System Structure and Delegation. J. Postel. March 1994. (Format: TXT=16481 bytes) (Status: INFORMATIONAL)

1637 DNSAP Resource Records. B. Manning and R. Colella. June 1994. (Format: TXT=21768 bytes) (Obsoletes RFC1348) (Obsoleted by RFC1706) (Updates RFC1348) (Status: EXPERIMENTAL)

1706 DNS NSAP Resource Records. B. Manning and R. Colella. October 1994. (Format: TXT=19721 bytes) (Obsoletes RFC1637) (Status: INFORMATIONAL)

1712 DNS Encoding of Graphical Location. C. Farrell, M. Schulze, S. Pleitner, and D. Baldoni. November 1994. (Format: TXT=13237)

1713 Tools for DNS Debugging. A. Romao. November 1994. (Format: TXT=33500 bytes) (Also FYI10027) (Status: INFORMATIONAL)

1794 DNS Support for Load Balancing. T. Brisco. April 1995. (Format: TXT=15494 bytes) (Status: INFORMATIONAL)

1876 A Means for Expressing Location Information in the Domain Name System. C. Davis, P. Vixie, T. Goodwin, and I. Dickinson. January 1996. (Format: TXT=29631 bytes) (Updates RFC1034, RFC1035) (Status: EXPERIMENTAL)

1912 Common DNS Operational and Configuration Errors. D. Barr. February 1996. (Format: TXT=38252 bytes) (Obsoletes RFC1537) (Status: INFORMATIONAL)

1982 Serial Number Arithmatic. R. Elz and R. Bush. August 1996. (Format: TXT=14440 bytes) (Updates RFC1034, RFC1035) (Status: PROPOSED STANDARD)

1995 Incremental Zone Transfer in DNS. M. Ohta. August 1996. (Format: TXT=16810 bytes) (Updates RFC1035) (Status: PROPOSED STANDARD)

1996 A Mechanism for Prompt Notification of Zone Changes (DNS NOTIFY). P. Vixie. August 1996. (Format: TXT=15247 bytes) (Updates RFC1035) (Status: PROPOSED STAN-DARD)

2010 Operational Criteria for Root Name Servers. B. Manning and P. Vixie. October 1996. (Format: TXT=14870 bytes) (Status: INFORMATIONAL)

2052 A DNS RR for Specifying the Location of Services (DNS SRV). A. Gulbrandensen, P. Vixie. October 1996. (Format: TXT19257 bytes) (Status: EXPERIMENTAL)

2065 Domain Name System Security Extensions. D. Eastlake, 3rd Edition. C. Kaufman. January 1997. (Format: TXT=97718 bytes) (Updates RFC1034, RFC1035) (Status: PROPOSED STANDARD)

2136 Dynamic Updates in the Domain Name System (DNS UPDATE). P. Vixie, Ed., S. Thomson, Y. Rekhter, J. Bound. April 1997. (Format: TXT=56354 bytes) (Updates RFC1035) (Status: PROPOSED STANDARD)

2137 Secure Domain Name System Dynamic Update. D. Eastlake. April 1997. (Format: TXT=24824 bytes) (Updates RFC1035) (Status: PROPOSED STANDARD)

2181 Clarification of DNS Specification. R. Elz and R. Bush. July 1997. (Format: TXT=36989 bytes) (Updates RFC1034, RFC1035, RFC1123) (Status: PROPOSED STANDARD)

2182 Selection and Operation for Secondary DNS Servers. R. Elz, R. Bush, S. Bradner, and M. Patton. July 1997. (Format: TXT=27456 bytes) (Also BCP0016) (Status: BEST CURRENT PRACTICE)

2219 Use of DNS Aliases for Network Services. M. Hamilton and R. Wright. October 1997. (Format: TXT=17858 bytes) (Also BCP0017) (Status: BEST CURRENT PRACTICE)

2230 Key Exchange Delegation Record for the DNS. R. Atkinson. October 1997. (Format: TXT=25563 bytes) (Status: INFORMATIONAL)

2240 A Legal Basis for Domain Name Allocation. O. Vaughan. November 1997. (Format: TXT=13602 bytes) (Obsoleted by RFC2352) (Status: INFORMATIONAL)

2308 Negative Caching of DNS Queries (DNS NCACHE). M. Andrews. March 1998. (Format: TXT=41428 bytes) (Obsoletes RFC1034) (Updates RFC1034, RFC1035) (Status: PRO-POSED STANDARD)

2317 Classless IN-ADDR.ARPA Delegation. H. Eidnes, G. de Groot, and P. Vixie. March 1998. (Format: TXT=17744 bytes) (Also BCP0020) (Status: BEST CURRENT PRACTICE)

2517 Building Directories from DNS: Experiences from WWWSeeker. R. Moats and R. Huber. February 1999. (Format: TXT=14001 bytes) (Status: INFORMATIONAL)

2535 Domain Name System Security Extensions. D. Eastlake. March 1999. (Format: TXT=110958 bytes) (Updates RFC2181, RFC1035, RFC1034) (Status: PROPOSED STANDARD)

2539 Storage of Diffie-Hellman Keys in the Domain Name System (DNS). D. Eastlake. March 1999. (Format: TXT=21049 bytes) (Status: PROPOSED STANDARD)

2540 Detached Domain Name System (DNS) Information. D. Eastlake. March 1999. (Format: TXT=12546 bytes) (Status: EXPERIMENTAL)

2541 DNS Security Operational Considerations. D. Eastlake. March 1999. (Format: TXT=14498 bytes) (Status: INFORMATIONAL)

2606 Reserved Top-level DNS Names

2671 Extension Mechanisms for DNS (EDNSO)

2672 Non-terminal DNS Name Redirection

2673 Binary Labels in the Domain Name System

Chapter 15: Hypertext Transfer Protocol (HTTP)

1009 Requirements for Internet Gateways. R. T. Braden and J. Postel. Jun-01-1987. (Format: TXT=128173 bytes) (Status: HISTORIC)

1945 Hypertext Transfer Protocol—HTTP/1.0. T. Berners-Lee, R. Fielding, and H. Frystuk. May 1996. (Format: TXT=137582 bytes) (Status: INFORMATIONAL)

2068 Hypertext Transfer Protocol—HTTP/1.1 R.Fielding, J. Gettys, J. Mogul, H. Frystyk, and T. Berners-Lee. January 1997. (Format: TXT=378114 bytes) (Status: PROPOSED STANDARD)

2069 HTTP Authentication: Basic and Digest Access Authentication. J.Franks, P.Hallam-Baker, J. Hostetler, P. Leach, A. Luotonen, E. Sink, L. Stewart. January 1997. (Format: TXT=41733 bytes) (Status: PROPOSED STANDARD)

2109 HTTP State Management Mechanism. D. Kristol and L.Montulli. February 1997. (Format: TXT=43469 bytes) (Obsoletes RFC1920) (Status: PROPOSED STANDARD)

2145 Use and Interpretation of HTTP Version Numbers. J. C. Mogul, R. Fielding, J. Gettys, and H. Frystuk. May 1997. (Format: TXT=13659 bytes) (Status: INFORMATIONAL)

2169 A Trivial Convention for using HTTP in URN Resolution. R. Daniel. June 1997. (Format: TXT=17763 bytes) (Status: EXPERIMENTAL)

2227 Simple Hit Metering and Usage Limiting for HTTP. J. Mogul and P. Leach. October 1997. (Format: TXT=85127 bytes) (Status: PROPOSED STANDARD)

2295 Transparent Content Negotiation in HTTP. K. Holtman and A. Mutz. March 1998. (Format: TXT=125130 bytes) (Status: EXPERIMENTAL)

2518 HTTP Extensions for Distributed Authoring—WEBDAV. Y. Goland, E. Whitehead, A. Faizi, S. Carter, and D. Jensen. February 1999. (Format: TXT=202829 bytes) (Status: PROPOSED STANDARD)

2616 Hypertext Transfer Protocol—HTTP/1.1

2660 The Secure Hypertsext Transfer Protocol

Chapter 16: Trivial File Transfer Protocol (TFTP)

906 Bootstrap Loading Using TFTP

1782 TFTP Option Extension. G. Malkin and A. Harkin. March 1995. (Format: TXT=11508 bytes) (Obsoleted by RFC2347) (Updates RFC1350)

1783 TFTP Blocksize Option. G. Malkin and A. Harkin. March 1995. (Format: TXT=7814 bytes) (Obsoleted by RFC2348) (Updates RFC1350) (Updated by RFC1350) (Status: PROPOSED STANDARD)

1784 TFTP Timeout Interval and Transfer Size Option. G. Malkin and A. Harkin. March 1995. (Format: TXT=6106 bytes) (Obsoleted by RFC2349) (Updates RFC1350) (Status: PROPOSED STANDARD)

1785 TFTP Option Negotiation Analysis. G. Malkin and A. Harkin. March 1995. (Format: TXT=3354 bytes) (Updates RFC1350) (Status: INFORMATIONAL)

2090 TFTP Multicast Option. A. Emberson. February 1997. (Format: TXT=11857 bytes) (Status: EXPERIMENTAL)

2347 TFTP Option Extension. G. Malkin and A. Harkin. May 1998. (Format: TXT=13060 bytes) (Obsoletes RFC 1782) (Updates RFC1350) (Status: DRAFT STANDARD)

2348 TFTP Blocksize Option. G. Malkin and A. Harkin. May 1998. (Format: TXT=9515 bytes) (Obsoletes RFC1783) (Updates RFC1350) (Status: DRAFT STANDARD)

2349 TFTP Timeout Interval and Transfer Size Option. G. Malkin and A. Harkin. May 1998. (Format: TXT=7848 bytes) (Obsoletes RFC1784) (Updates RFC1350) (Status: DRAFT STANDARD)

Chapter 17: Simple Network Management Protocol (SNMP)

1067 Simple Network Management Protocol (SNMP). J.D. Case, M. Fedor, M. L. Schoffstall, and J. Davin. Aug-01-1988. (Format: TXT=69592 bytes) (Obsoleted by RFC1098) (Status: UNKNOWN)

1089 SNMP Over Ethernet. M. L. Schoffstall, C. Davin, M. Fedor, and J. D. Case. Feb-01-1989. (Format: TXT=4458 bytes) (Status: UNKNOWN)

1098 Simple Layer Management Protocol (SNMP). J. D. Case, M. Fedor, M. L. Schoffstall, and C. Davin. Apr-01-1989. (Format: TXT=71563 bytes) (Obsoleted by RFC1157) (Status: UNKNOWN)

1157 Simple Network Management Protocol (SNMP). J. D. Case, M. Fedor, M. L. Schoffstall, and C. Davin. May-01-1990. (Format: TXT=74894 bytes) (Obsoletes RFC1066) (Status: HISTORIC)

1161 SNMP Over OSI. M. T. Rose. Jun-01-1990. (Format: TXT=16036 bytes) (Obsoletes by RFC1418) (Status: EXPERIMENTAL)

1187 Bulk Table Retrieval for the SNMP. M. T. Rose, K. McCloghrie, and J. R. Davin. Oct-01-1990. (Format: TXT=27220 bytes) (Status: EXPERIMENTAL)

1212 Concise MIB Definitions. M. T. Rose, K. McCloghrie. Mar-01-1991. (Format: TXT=43579 bytes) (Status: STANDARD)

1215 Convention for Defining Traps to Use With the SNMP. M. T. Rose. Mar-01-1991. (Format: TXT=19336 bytes) (Status: INFORMATIONAL)

1227 SNMP MUX Protocol and MIB. M. T. Rose. May-01-1991. (Format: TXT=25868 bytes) (Status: HISTORIC)

1228 SNMP-DPI: Simple Network Management Protocol Distributed Program Interface, Version 2.0. G. Carpenter and B. Wijnen. May-01-1991. (Format: TXT=96972 bytes) (Obsoleted by RFC1592) (Status: EXERIMENTAL)

1229 Extensions to the Generic-interface MIB. K. McCloghrie. May-01-1991. (Format: TXT=36022 bytes) (Obsoleted by RFC1573) (Updated by RFC1239) (Status: PROPOSED STANDARD)

1239 Reassignment of Experimental MIBs to Standard MIBs. J. K. Reynolds. Jun-01-1991. (Format: TXT=3656 bytes) (Updates RFC1229, RFC1230, RFC1231, RFC1232, RFC1233) (Status: PROPOSED STANDARD)

1270 SNMP Communication Services. F. Kastenholz. Oct-01-1991. (Format: TXT=26167 bytes) (Status: INFORMATIONAL)

1283 SNMP Over OSI. M. Rose. December 1991. (Format: TXT=16857 bytes) (Obsoleted by RFC1418) (Status: EXPERIMENTAL)

1298 SNMP Over IPX. R. Wormley, S. Bostock. February 1992. (Format: TXT=7878 bytes) (Obsoleted by RFC1420) (Status: INFORMATIONAL)

1303 A Convention for Describing SNMP-based Agents. K. McCloghrie and M. Rose. February 1992. (Format: TXT=22915 bytes) (Also RFC1155, RFC1212, RFC1213, RFC1157) (Status: INFORMATIONAL)

1351 SNMP Administrative Model. J. Davin, J. Galvin, and K. McCloghrie. July 1992. (Format: TXT=80721 bytes) (Status: PROPOSED STANDARD)

1352 SNMP Security Protocols. J. Galvin, K. McClghrie, and J. Davin. July 1992. (Format: TXT=80721 bytes) (Status: PROPOSED STANDARD)

1353 Definitions of Managed Objects for Administration of SNMP Parties. K. McCloghrie, J. Davin, and J. Galvin. July 1992. (Format: TXT=59556 bytes) (Status: PROPOSED STANDARD)

1369 Implementation Notes and Experience for the Internet Ethernet MIB. F. Kastenholz. October 1992. (Format: TXT=13921 bytes) (Status: PROPOSED STANDARD)

1418 SNMP Over OSI. M. Rose. March 1993. (Format: TXT=7721 bytes) (Obsoletes RFC1161, RFC1283) (Status: PROPOSED STANDARD)

1419 SNMP Over AppleTalk. G. Minshall and M. Ritter. March 1993. (Format: TXT=16470 bytes) (Status: PROPOSED STANDARD)

1420 SNMP Over IPX. S. Bostock. March 1993. (Format: TXT=6762 bytes) (Obsoletes RFC1298) (Status: PROPOSED STANDARD)

1441 Introduction to Version 2 of the Internet-standard Network Management Framework. J.Case, K. McCloghrie, M. Rose, and S. Waldbusser. April 1993. (Format: TXT=25386 bytes) (Status: PROPOSED STANDARD)

1442 Structure of Management Information for Version 2 of the Simple Network Management Protocol (SMIv2). J. Case, K. McCloghrie, M. Rose, and S. Waldbusser. April 1993. (Format: TXT=95779 bytes) (Obsoleted by RFC1902) (Status: PROPOSED STANDARD)

1443 Textual Conventions for Version 2 of the Simple Network Management Protocol (SMIv2). J. Case, K. McCloghrie, M. Rose, and S. Waldbusser. April 1993. (Format: TXT=60947 bytes) (Obsoleted by RFC1903) (Status: PROPOSED STANDARD)

1444 Conformance Statements for Version 2 of the Simple Network Management Protocol (SMIv2). J. Case, K. McCloghrie, M. Rose, and S. Waldbusser. April 1993. (Format: TXT=57744 bytes) (Obsoleted by RFC1904) (Status: PROPOSED STANDARD)

1445 Administrative Model for Version 2 of the Simple Network Management Protocol (SNMPv2)

1446 Security Protocols for Version 2 of the Simple Network Management Protocol (SNMPv2). J.Galvin and K. McCloghrie, M. Rose, and S. Waldbusser. April 1993. (Format: TXT=99443 bytes) (Status: HISTORIC)

1448   Protocol Operations for Version 2 of the Simple Network Management Protocol (SNMPv2). J. Case, K. McCloghrie, M. Rose, and S. Waldbusser. April 1993. (Format: TXT=74224 bytes) (Obsoleted by RFC1905) (Status: PROPOSED STANDARD)

1449   Transport Mappings for Version 2 of the Simple Network Management Protocol (SNMPv2). J. Case, K. McCloghrie, M. Rose, and S. Waldbusser. April 1993. (Format: TXT=41161 bytes) (Obsoleted by RFC1906) (Status: PROPOSED STANDARD)

1452   Coexistence Between Version 1 and Version 2 of the Internet-standard Network Management Framework. J. Case, K. McCloghrie, M. Rose, and S. Waldbusser. April 1993. (Format: TXT=32176 bytes) (Obsoleted by RFC1908) (Status: PROPOSED STANDARD)

1503   Algorithms for Automating Administration in SNMPv2 Managers. K. McCloghrie and M. Rose. August 1993. (Format: TXT=33542 bytes) (Status: INFORMATIONAL)

1856   The Opstat Client-Server Model for Statistical Retrieval. H. Clark. October 1995. (Format: TXT=29954 bytes)(Status: INFORMATIONAL)

1901   Introduction for Community-based SNMPv2. SNMPv2 Working Group, J.Case, K. McCloghrie, M. Rose, and S. Waldbusser. January 1996. (Format: TXT=15903 bytes) (Status: EXPERIMENTAL)

1902   Structure of Management Information for Version 2 of the Simple Network Management Protocol (SMIv2). SNMPv2 Working Group, J.Case, K. McCloghrie, M. Rose, and S. Waldbusser. January 1996. (Format: TXT=77453 bytes) (Obsoletes RFC1442) (Status: DRAFT STANDARD)

1903   Textual Conventions for Version 2 of the Simple Network Management Protocol (SMIv2). SNMPv2 Working Group, J. Case, K. McCloghrie, M. Rose, and S. Waldbusser. January 1996. (Format: TXT=52652 bytes) (Obsoletes RFC1443) (Status: DRAFT STANDARD)

1904   Conformance Statements for Version 2 of the Simple Network Management Protocol (SMIv2). SNMPv2 Working Group, J.Case, K. McCloghrie, M. Rose, and S. Waldbusser. January 1996. (Format: TXT=47083 bytes) (Obsoletes RFCE1444) (Status: DRAFT STANDARD)

1905   Protocol Operations for Version 2 of the Simple Network Management Protocol (SNMPv2). SNMPv2 Working Group, J.Case, K. McCloghrie, M. Rose, and S. Waldbusser. January 1996. (Format: TXT=55526 bytes) (Obsoletes RFC1448) (Status: DRAFT STANDARD)

1906   Transport Mappings for Version 2 of the Simple Network Management Protocol (SNMPv2). SNMPv2 Working Group, J.Case, K. McCloghrie, M. Rose, and S. Waldbusser. January 1996. (Format: TXT=27465 bytes) (Obsoletes RFC1449) (Status: DRAFT STANDARD)

1908 Coexistence between Version 1 and Version 2 of the Internet-standard Network Management Framework. SNMPv2 Working Group, J. Case, K. McCloghrie, M. Rose, and S. Waldbusser. January 1996. (Format: TXT=21463 bytes) (Obsoletes RFC1452) (Status: DRAFT STANDARD)

1909 An Administrative Infrastructure for SNMPv2. K. McCloghrie. February 1996. (Format: TXT=45773 bytes) (Status: EXPERIMENTAL)

1910 User-based Security Model for SNMPv2. G. Waters. February 1996. (Format: TXT=98252 bytes) (Status: EXPERIMENTAL)

2011 SNMPv2 Management Information Base for the Internet Protocol Using SMIv2. K. McCloghrie. November 1996. (Format: TXT=31168 bytes) (Updates RFC1213) (Status PROPOSED STANDARD)

2012 SNMPv2 Management Information Base for the Transmission Control Protocol using SMIv2. K. McCloghrie. November 1996. (Format: TXT=16792 bytes) (Updates RFC1213) (Status PROPOSED STANDARD)

2013 SNMPv2 Management Information Base for the User Datagram Protocol using SMIv2. K. McCloghrie. November 1996. (Format: TXT=9333 bytes) (Updates RFC1213) (Status PROPOSED STANDARD)

2039 Applicability for Standards Track MIBs to Management of World Wide Web Servers. C. Kalbfleisch. November 1996. (Format: TXT=31966 bytes) (Status: INFORMATIONAL)

2089 V2ToV1 Mapping SNMPv2 Onto SNMPv1 Within a Bilingual SNMP Agent. B. Winjnene, D. Levi. January 1997. (Format: TXT=23814 bytes)

2107 Ascend Tunnel Management Protocol—ATMP. K. Hamzeh. February 1997. (Format: TXT=44300 bytes) (Status: INFORMATIONAL)

2257 Agent Extensibility (AgentX) Protocol Version 1. M. Daniele, B. Wijnen, D. Francisco. January 1998. (Format: TXT=177452 bytes) (Status: PROPOSED STANDARD)

2261 An Architecture for Describing SNMP Management Frameworks. D. Harrington, R. Presuhn, B. Wijnen. January 1998. (Format: TXT=128036 bytes) (Obsoleted by RFC2271) (Status: PROPOSED STANDARD)

2262 Message Processing and Dispatching for the Simple Network Management Protocol (SNMP). J. Case, D. Harrington, R. Presuhn, B. Wijnen. January 1998. (Format: TXT=88254 bytes) (Obsoleted by RFC2272) (Status: PROPOSED STANDARD)

2263 SNMP Applications. D. Levi, P. Meyer, and B. Stewart. January 1998. (Format: TXT=143493 bytes) (Obsoleted by RFC2273) (Status: PROPOSED STANDARD)

2264 User-based Security Model (USM) for Version 3 of the Simple Network Management Protocol (SNMPv3). U. Blumenthal and B. Wijnen. January 1998. (Format: TXT=168759 bytes) (Obsoleted by RFC2274) (Status: PROPOSED STANDARD)

2265 View-based Access Control Model (VACM) for the Simple Network Management Protocol(SNMP). B. Wijnen, R. Presuhn, and K. McCloghrie. January 1998. (Format: TXT=77807 bytes) (Obsoleted by RFC2275) (Status: PROPOSED STANDARD)

2271 An Architecture for Describing SNMP Management Frameworks. D. Harrington, R. Preesuhn, and B. Wijnen. January 1998. (Format: TXT=128227 bytes) (Obsoletes RFC2261) (Status: PROPOSED STANDARD)

2272 Message Processing and Dispatching for the Simple Network Management Protocol (SNMP). J. Case, D. Harrington, R. Preesuhn, B. Wijnen. January 1998. (Format: TXT=88445 bytes) (Obsoletes RFC2262) (Status: PROPOSED STANDARD)

2273 SNMPv3 Applications. D.Levi, P. Meyer, and B. Stewart. January 1998. (Format: TXT=143754 bytes) (Obsoletes RFC2263) (Status: PROPOSED STANDARD)

2274 User-based Security Model (USM) for Version 3 of the Simple Network Management Protocol (SNMPv3). U. Blumenthal and B. Wijnen. January 1998. (Format: TXT=168950 bytes) (Obsoletes RFC2265) (Status: PROPOSED STANDARD)

2275 View-based Access Control Model (VACM) for the Simple Network Management Protocol(SNMP). B. Wijnen, R. Presuhn, and K. McCloghrie. January 1998. (Format: TXT=77998 bytes) (Obsoletes RFC2265) (Status: PROPOSED STANDARD)

2438 Advancement of MIB Specifications on the IETF Standards Track. M. O'Dell, H. Alvestrand, B. Wijens, and S. Bradner. October 1998. (Format: TXT=13633 bytes) (Also BCP0027) (Status: BEST CURRENT PRACTICE)

2493 Textual Conventions for MIB Modules Using Performance History Based on 15-minute Intervals. K. Tesink, Editor. January 1999. (Format: TXT=18749 bytes) (Status: PRO-POSED STANDARD)

2570 Introduction to Version 3 of the Internet-standard Network Management Framework. J. Case, R. Mundy, D. Partain, and B. Stewart. April 1999. (Format: TXT=50381 bytes) (Status: INFORMATIONAL)

2571 An Architecture for Describing SNMP Management Frameworks. B. Wijnen, D. Harrington, and R. Presuhn. April 1999. (Format: TXT=139260 bytes) (Obsoletes RFC2271) (Status: PROPOSED STANDARD)

2572 Message Processing and Dispatching for the Simple Network Management Protocol (SNMP). J. Case, D. Harrington, R. Presuhn, and B. Wijnen. April 1999. (Format: TXT=96035 bytes) (Obsoletes RFC2272) (Status: DRAFT STANDARD)

2573 SNMP Applications. D. Levi, P. Meyer, B. Stewart. April 1999. (Format: TXT=150427 bytes) (Obsoletes RFC2273) (Status: DRAFT STANDARD)

2574 User-based Security Model (USM) for Version 3 of the Simple Network Management Protocol (SNMPv3). U. Blumenthal, B. Wijnen. April 1999. (Format: TXT=190755 bytes) (Obsoletes RFC2274) (Status: DRAFT STANDARD)

2575 View-based Access Control Model (VACM) for the Simple Network Management Protocol(SNMP). B. Wijnen, R. Presuhn, and K. McCloghrie. April 1999. (Format: TXT=79642 bytes) (Obsoletes RFC22275) (Status: DRAFT STANDARD)

2578 Structure of Management Information Version 2 (SMIv2). K. McCloghrie, D. Perkins, J. Schoenwaelder. April 1999. (Format: TXT=89712 bytes) (Obsoletes RFC1902) (Also STD0058) (Status: STANDARD)

2579 Textual Conventions for SMIv2. K. McCloghrie, D. Perkins, J. Schoenwaelder. April 1999. (Format: TXT=59039 bytes) (Obsoletes RFC1903) (Also STD0058) (Status: STANDARD)

2580 Conformance Statements for SMIv2. K. McCloghrie, D. Perkins, J. Schoenwaelder. April 1999. (Format: TXT=54253 bytes) (Obsoletes RFC1904) (Also STD0058) (Status: STANDARD)

2593 Script MIB Extensibility Protocol Version 1.0

Chapter 18: Open Network Computing Protocols

1014 XDR: External Data Representation standard. Inc. Sun Microsystems. Jun-01-1987. (Format: TXT=39316 bytes) (Status: UNKNOWN)

1094 NFS: Network File System Protocol specification. Inc. Sun Microsystems. Mar-01-1989. (Format: TXT=51454 bytes) (Also RFC1813) (Status: INFORMATIONAL)

1813 NFS Version 3 Protocol Specification. B. Callaghan, B. Pawlowski & P. Staubach. June 1995. (Format: TXT=229793 bytes) (Also RFC1094) (Status: INFORMATIONAL)

2054 WebNFS Client Specification. B. Callaghan. October 1996. (Format: TXT=4128 bytes) (Status: INFORMATIONAL)

2055 WebNFS Server Specification. B. Callaghan. October 1996. (Format: TXT=20498 bytes) (Status: INFORMATIONAL)

2623 NFS Version 2 and Version 3 Security Issues and the NFS Protocol's Use of RPCSEC_GSS and Kerberos V5

2624 NFS Version 4 Design Considerations

APPENDIX B

ABBREVIATIONS AND ACRONYMS

A

ABR	area border router
ACK	acknowledgement
ANSI	American National Standards Institute
API	application program interface
ARP	Address Resolution Protocol
ARPANET	Advance Research Projects Agency network
AS	autonomous system
ASBR	autonomous system border router
ASCII	American Standard Code for Information Interchange
ASN.1	Abstract Syntax Notation One
ATM	Asynchronous Transfer Mode

B

BDR	backup designated router
BER	Basic Encoding Rules
BGP	Border Gateway Protocol
BIND	Berkeley Internet Name Domain
BootP	Bootstrap Protocol
BPF	Berkeley Packet Filter
BRI	Basic Rate Interface
BSD	Berkeley Software Distribution

C

CCITT	Consultative Committee for International Telegraphy and Telephony
CIDR	classless interdomain routing
CIX	Commercial Internet Exchange
CLNP	Connectionless Network Protocol
CPU	central processing unit
CSMA/CD	carrier sense multiple access collision detection
CRC	cyclic redundancy check
CSLIP	compressed SLIP
CSMA	carrier sense multiple access
CSU	channel service unit
CUT	Coordinated Universal Time

D

DARPA	Defense Advanced Research Projects Agency
DCE	Distributed Computing Environment
DDN	Defense Data Network
DDR	Dial-on-Demand Routing
DECNet	Digital Equipment Corporation Network
DEMUX	Demultiplexer
DF	don't fragment field (IP header)
DHCP	Dynamic Host Configuration Protocol
DLC	Data Link control
DLPI	Data Link Provider Interface
DNS	Domain Name System
DoD	Department of Defense (Reference Model)
DR	designated router

DSAP	Destination Service Access Point
DSU	data service unit
DTP	data transfer process
DTS	Distributed Time Service
DUAL	Diffusing Update Algorithm
DVMRP	Distance-vector Multicast Routing Protocol

E

EBGP	external BGP (router)
EBONE	European IP Backbone
EOL	end of option list
EGP	Exterior Gateway Protocol
EIGRP	Enhanced Interior Gateway Routing Protocol
EMI	electromagnetic interference

F

FCS	frame check sequence
FDDI	Fiber Distributed Data Interface
FIFO	first in, first out
FIN	finish flag, TCP header
FQDN	fully qualified domain name
FTP	File Transfer Protocol

G–H

HA	hardware address
HDLC	high-level data link control

I

IAB	Internet Architecture Board
IAC	interpret as command
IANA	Internet Assigned Number Authority
IBGP	internal BGP (router)
ICMP	Internet Control Message Protocol
IDRP	Interdomain Routing Protocol
IEEE	Institute of Electrical and Electronics Engineers
IESG	Internet Engineering Steering Group
IETF	Internet Engineering Task Force
IGMP	Internet Group Management Protocol
IGP	Interior Gateway Protocol
IGRP	Interior Gateway Routing Protocol
IP	Internet Protocol
IPNG	Internet Protocol Next Generation
IPX	Internetwork Packet Exchange
IRTF	Internet Research Task Force
ISDN	Integrated Services Digital Network
IS-IS	Intermediate System to Intermediate System Protocol
ISN	initial sequence number
ISO	International Organization for Standardization
ISOC	Internet Society

J–L

LAN	Local Area Network
LAPB	Link Access Procedure, Balanced
LAPD	Link Access Procedure, D channel
LBX	low bandwidth X
LCP	link control protocol

LFN	long fat network
LIFO	last in, first out
LLC	logical link control
LSA	Link-state advertisement
LSRR	loose source and record route

M

MAC	media access control
MBONE	multicast backbone
MIB	management information base
MILNET	Military Network
MIME	multipurpose Internet mail extensions
MS	message store
M/S	master/slave
MSL	maximum segment lifetime
MSAU	Multi-station Access Units
MSS	maximum segment size
MTA	maximum transfer agent
MTU	maximum transfer unit
MUX	Multiplexer

N

NAT	Network Address Translation
NBMA	non-broadcast multi-access
NCP	Network Control Protocol
NDN	non-delivery notification
NetBIOS	Network Basic Input Output System
NFS	Network File System
NIC	network interface card

NIT	network interface tap
NNTP	Network News Transfer Protocol
NOAO	National Optical Astronomy Observatories
NOP	no operation
NSFNET	National Science Foundation network
NSI	NASA Science Internet
NSSA	not so stubby area
NTP	Network Time Protocol
NVT	network virtual terminal

O

Opcode	Operation code
OSF	Open Software Foundation
OSI	Open Systems Interconnection (Reference Model)
OSPF	Open Shortest Path First

P

PA	protocol address
PDU	protocol data unit
PI	protocol interpreter
POSIX	Portable Operating System Interface
PPP	Point-to-Point Protocol
PRI	Primary Rate Interface
PSH	push flag (TCP header)

Q

QoS	Quality of Service

R

RARP	Reverse Address Resolution Protocol
RFC	Request for Comment
RFI	radio frequency interference
RIP	Routing Information Protocol
RPC	remote procedure call
RR	resource record
RRQ	read request
RST	reset flag, TCP header
RTO	retransmission timeout
RTT	round-trip time

S

SA	source address
SACK	Selective Acknowledgement
SAP	service access point
SDLC	Synchronous Data Link Control
SLIP	Serial Line Internet Protocol
SMI	structure of management information
SMTP	Simple Mail Transfer Protocol
SNA	System Network Architecture
SNAP	Subnetwork Access Protocol
SNMP	Simple Network Management Protocol
SQE	Signal Quality Error
SRRT	smooth round trip timer
SSAP	source service access point
SWS	silly window syndrome
SYN	synchronize sequence numbers flag, TCP header

T

TCP	Transmission Control Protocol
TFTP	Trivial File Transfer Protocol
TLI	Transport Layer Interface
ToS	type-of-service
TTL	time-to-live
TUBA	TCP and UDP with bigger addresses
Telnet	Telecommunication Network Protocol

U

UA	user agent
UDP	User Data Protocol
UI	user interface
URG	urgent pointer flag (TCP header)
UUCP	Unix-to-Unix Copy

V

VC	virtual circuit
VLAN	Virtual Local Area Network
VLSM	Variable Length Subnet Mask

W

WAN	Wide Area Network
WRQ	write request
WWW	World Wide Web

X–Z

XDR	external data representation
XID	exchange ID or transaction ID
XTI	X/Open Transport Layer Interface

APPENDIX C

TCP/UDP PORT NUMBERS

*T*able C.1 shows a list of TCP/UDP port numbers.

TABLE C.1   TCP/UDP Port Numbers

Decimal	Keyword	Protocol	Description
20	FTP-DATA	TCP	File Transfer (Default Data)
21	FTP	TCP	File Transfer (Control)
23	TELNET	TCP	Telnet
25	SMTP	TCP	Simple Mail Transfer Protocol
37	NTP	TCP	Time or Network Time Protocol
49	LOGIN	TCP	Login Host Protocol
53	DNS	TCP/UDP	Domain Name Service
63	VIA-FTP	TCP	VIA-Systems-FTP
67	BOOTPS	UDP	Bootstrap Protocol Server
68	BOOTPC	UDP	Bootstrap Protocol Client
69	TFTP	UDP	Trivial File Transfer
69	TFTP	TCP	Trivial File Transfer Protocol
70	Gopher	TCP	Gopher File Service
80	WWW	TCP	World Wide Web Services
137	NetBIOS-NS	TCP	NetBIOS Name Service
139	NetBIOS-DG	TCP	NetBIOS Datagram Service
161	SNMP	UDP	Simple Network Management Protocol
161	SNMP	TCP	Simple Network Management Protocol
179	BGP	TCP	Border Gateway Protocol

GLOSSARY

Numeric

1BASE5   Implements the IEEE 802.3 standard using 1Mbps transmission on a baseband medium with a maximum segment length of 500 meters.

10BASE2   Implements the IEEE 802.3 (Ethernet) standard using 10Mbps transmission on a baseband medium with a maximum segment length of 185 meters.

10BASE5   Implements the IEEE 802.3 (Ethernet) standard using 10Mbps transmission on a baseband medium with a maximum segment length of 500 meters.

10BASE-T   Implements the IEEE 802.3 (Ethernet) standard using 10Mbps transmission on a baseband medium. Using this standard you can attach AUI-compatible devices to 24-gauge, unshielded twisted pair cable, rather than the usual coaxial media.

100BASE-FX   Implements the IEEE 802.3 (Ethernet) standard using 100Mbps transmission on a baseband medium with multi-mode fiber-optic cable.

100BASE-T   Implements the IEEE 802.3 (Ethernet) standard using 100Mbps transmission on a baseband medium with UTP wiring.

100BASE-T4   Implements the IEEE 802.3 (Ethernet) standard using 100Mbps transmission on a baseband medium with four pairs of Category 3, 4, or 5 UTP wiring.

100BASE-TX   Implements the IEEE 802.3 (Ethernet) standard using 100Mbps transmission on a baseband medium. This standard enables the attachment of AUI-compatible devices to 24-gauge, unshielded twisted-pair cable, rather than the usual coaxial media.

100BASE-X   Fast Ethernet specification using 100Mbps transmission, which refers to the 100BASEFX and 100BASETX standards for Fast Ethernet over fiber-optic cabling.

100VG-AnyLAN   100Mbps Fast Ethernet and Token-Ring media technology that uses four pairs of Category 3, 4, or 5 UTP cabling.

A

ABR (area border router)   A router located on the border of one or more OSPF areas that connects those areas to the backbone network.

AC (access control)   DLC byte on the IEEE 802.5 Token-Ring network that contains the token indicator and frame priority information.

access list   List kept by routers to control access to or from the router for a number of services.

access method   The means by which network devices access the network.

access server   Processor connecting asynchronous devices to a LAN or WAN through emulation software.

ACK (Acknowledge)   Network packet that acknowledges the receipt of data.

acknowledgement   Notification sent from one network device to another acknowledging that a particular event has occurred.

active monitor   Computer on a Token-Ring acting as a controller for the ring. It regulates the token and other aspects of performance.

address   Data structure for identifying a unique entity.

address mapping   Technique for different protocols to interoperate by translating addresses from one format to another.

address resolution   Method for resolving differences between computer addressing schemes.

adjacency   The process of forming a neighbor relationship.

ADSP (AppleTalk Data-Stream Protocol)   Protocol that establishes and maintains full-duplex communication between two AppleTalk sockets.

advertising   The process by which a service makes its presence known on a network. Also used by routers to propagate route information.

agent   Software that processes queries and returns replies.

algorithm   A defined rule or process for arriving at a solution to a problem.

all-routes explorer packet   Explorer packet that travels the entire SRB network, following all possible paths to a destination.

AMI (alternative mark inversion)   (T1 lines) A pulse transmission T1 line coding scheme using alternate polarities in the pulse train.

ANSI (American National Standards Institute)   An industry-supported organization that helps to develop trade and communications standards.

API (applications program interface)   The programming interface that corresponds to the boundary between protocol layers. It specifies the functions and data used by one program module to access another.

AppleTalk   A series of communications protocols designed by Apple Computer, Inc.

application layer   Layer 7 of the OSI Reference Model, which provides services to application processes outside the OSI model. These can include e-mail, file transfer, and terminal emulation.

architecture   Refers to how a system is designed, and how its components connect and operate with each other.

ARCnet   Baseband token-passing network from the Datapoint Corporation. It can communicate among up to 255 stations at 2.5Mbps.

area   A set of network segments and their attached devices.

ARP (address resolution protocol)   Used within TCP/IP to find a node's DLC address from its IP address. Interpreted in the TCP/IP suite. It can also be interpreted in the Banyan VINES PI suite.

ARPANET (Advanced Research Projects Agency Network)   A packet-switching network established in 1969.

AS (autonomous system)   A collection of networks under a common administration. They share a common routing strategy.

ASBR (autonomous system boundary router)   An ABR located between an OSPF autonomous system and a non-OSPF network.

ASCII (American Standard Code for Information Interchange)   Provides mapping between numeric codes and graphical characters. Used universally for PC and non-IBM mainframe applications.

asynchronous transmission   Method of data transmission enabling characters to be sent at irregular intervals. This is done by preceding each character with a start bit and following it with a stop bit. One common application is to communicate with modems and printers.

AUI (attachment unit interface)   A drop cable for Ethernet between the station and transceiver.

AutoSPID (automatic service profile identifier)   A feature of a terminal adapter; it downloads SPID information from a compatible switch.

availability   The amount of time a network is operational.

B

B channel (Bearer channel)   A 64kbps channel that is end-user data.

backbone   The backbone is the part of the communications network that carries the heaviest traffic. It is the basis for the design of the whole network service.

background task   A secondary job that is performed while the user performs a primary task, such as a network server carrying out the duties of the network (controlling communications) while the users are running applications (such as word processors) in the foreground.

bandwidth   The amount of data that can be moved through a particular communications link.

bandwidth domain   All devices that share the same bandwidth.

bandwidth reservation   A process of assigning bandwidth to users and applications served by a given network. It gives priority to different traffic flows based on how critical and delay sensitive they are.

baseband   A transmission technique that sends data bits without using a higher carrier frequency. The entire bandwidth of the transmission medium is used by one signal.

baud rate   A measure of the signaling speed in data communications. It specifies the number of signal elements that can be transmitted each second. For most purposes, at slow speeds, a baud rate is the same as the speed in bits per second.

BDR (backup designated router)   In OSPF, a backup to the DR.

beacon   A Token-Ring packet that signals a serious failure on the ring.

BECN (Backward Explicit Congestion Notification)   Frame Relay. The sixth bit in the second octet of the Frame Relay header. It is used to inform a subscriber device of congestion in the backward direction.

BGP (Border Gateway protocol)   BGP, as defined in RFC 1771, enables the user to create loop-free, interdomain routing between autonomous systems.

binary   A numbering system using 1s and 0s (1=on; 0=off).

BIOS (basic input/output system)   A set of routines that work with the hardware to support the transfer of information between elements of the system. These include memory, disks, and the monitor.

bit   A binary digit used in the binary numbering system. It can be 0 or 1.

bit rate   The speed at which bits are transmitted, commonly expressed in bits per second (bps).

BNC (Bayonet Network Connector)   A standardized coaxial cable connector; used for ARC-NET networks and Thin Ethernet ("Cheapernet") cables.

BOOTP (Boot protocol)   A protocol within TCP/IP used for downloading initial programs into networked stations. Interpreted in the TCP/IP PI suite.

BPDU (Bridge protocol data unit)   A spanning-tree protocol packet sent out at configurable intervals to exchange information with bridges in the network.

bps (bits per second)   A measure of the rate of data transmission.

breakout box   A test device used to view the signals in an RS-232, a V.35, or other interface. The breakout box is used to diagnose problems with the interface.

bridge   A device used to connect two separate networks into one extended network. Bridges forward only packets that are meant for the other network.

broadband   A transmission technique that sends data bits encoded within a much higher radio-frequency carrier signal. The transmission medium can be shared by many simultaneous signals because each of them uses only a portion of the available bandwidth.

broadcast   (1) A message directed to all stations on a network or collection of networks. (2) A destination address that designates all stations.

buffer   A software program, storage space in RAM, or a separate device used to store data. For example, the Sniffer Network Analyzer's capture buffer serves as a temporary storage space for captured network data until it can be analyzed or saved to disk.

bursty traffic   Data communications term that refers to an uneven pattern of data transmission.

bus   A common physical signal path composed of wires or other media, across which signals can be sent from one part of a computer to another (also known as a highway).

bus topology   A linear LAN architecture in which transmissions from network stations propagate the link of the medium and are received by all other stations.

byte   A series of consecutive binary digits operated on as a unit.

C

CA (Certificate Authority)   A third party that validates identities and creates digital certificates.

caching   A form of replication in which information learned during the previous transaction is used to process later transactions.

capture   The process by which the Sniffer analysis application records network traffic for interpretation. Generally speaking, this interpretation takes place during the display. However, the Expert Sniffer analysis application can simultaneously capture and interpret network traffic.

category cabling   Consists of five grades of UTP cabling described in the EIA/TIA-586 standard.

CCITT (Consultative Committee for International Telegraphy and Telephony)   The former name of International Telecommunications Union (ITU) that is a specialized body within the United Nations. It sponsors a number of standards dealing with data communications networks, telephone switching standards, terminals, and digital systems.

channel   A communications path.

channel attached   Refers to the attachment of devices directly by data channels to a computer.

channelized E1   Access link operating at 2.048Mbps.

channelized T1   Access link operating at 1.544Mbps.

CHAP (challenge handshake authentication protocol)   Security feature supported on lines with PPP encapsulation that helps prevent unauthorized access.

chat script   A group of three chat strings (setup, listen, and disconnect) that controls communication parameters for an asynchronous device.

chat string   A UNIX-style command/response sequence of characters downloaded to a serial device to control the device.

CIDR (classless interdomain routing)   Multiple contiguous Class C addresses owned by ISPs and assigned to downstream customers are summarized into one or more advertised IP addresses.

CIR (committed information rate)   The largest number of bits per second that a frame relay network agrees to carry over a PVC. CIR is assigned at the time of subscription to the frame relay service.

circuit   A communications path between two or more points.

circuit switching   A switching system in which a dedicated physical circuit path must exist between sender and receiver for the duration of the call.

classful routing protocols   Routing protocols that do not transmit information about the prefix length.

classless routing protocols   Routing protocols that include prefix length with routing updates.

CLI (command-line interface)   An interface that enables the user to interact with the operating system by entering commands and optional arguments.

client   (1) A module that uses the services of another module—for example, the Session layer is a client of the Transport layer. (2) A PC or workstation that accesses services or applications from another server PC or workstation.

CODEC (coder-decoder)   A device that often uses PCM in transforming analog signals into a digital bit stream and digital signals into analog.

collision   In Ethernet, the result of two nodes transmitting simultaneously. The frames from each device collide and are damaged when they meet on the physical media.

collision domain   In Ethernet, the network area in which frames that have collided are propagated.

community   In SNMP, a logical group of managed devices and NMSs in the same administrative domain.

community string   A text string that acts as a password and is used to authenticate messages sent between a management station and a router containing an SNMP agent.

compression   The reduction of the bandwidth or bits necessary to encode information.

concentrator   A central point for connecting several individual stations to a network ring. Commonly found on FDDI networks.

connection-oriented   Data transfer that requires the establishment of a virtual circuit.

connectionless   Data transfer that occurs without the existence of a virtual circuit.

convergence   The speed and capability of a group of internetworking devices running a specific routing protocol to arrive at a consistent understanding of the topology of an internetwork after a change in that topology.

core layer   Layer in a hierarchical network that provides optimal transport between sites.

CPU (central processing unit)   The main processor in a device, such as a computer or router.

CRC (cyclic redundancy check)   A check-word, typically 2 or 4 bytes at the end of a frame, that is used to detect errors in the data portion of the frame.

CSMA/CA (Carrier Sense Multiple Access with Collision Avoidance)   Random access or contention-based control technique. The algorithm used in LocalTalk networks that controls transmission.

CSMA/CD   Carrier Sense Multiple Access with Collision Detection. Random access or contention-based control technique. The algorithm used by IEEE 802.3 and Ethernet networks that controls transmission.

CSU (channel service unit)   An interface to a common carrier's transmission facilities that ensures digital signals placed on the line are shaped and timed correctly. Often it is combined with a Data Service Unit (DSU).

custom queuing   A method of queuing used to guarantee bandwidth for traffic by assigning queue space based on port number, protocol, or other criteria.

cut-through packet switching   A packet switching approach that streams data through a switch so that the leading edge of the packet exits the switch at the output port before the packet finishes entering the input port.

D

D Channel   Data channel used for signaling between the switching equipment and the customer's equipment. This channel is not used for carrying user data.

DAC (dual attachment concentrator)   A concentrator offering two connections to the FDDI network, capable of accommodating the FDDI dual ring and other ports for the connection of other concentrators or FDDI stations.

DAS (dual attachment station)   An FDDI station offering two connections to the FDDI dual counter-rotating ring.

datagram   A logical grouping of information sensed as a Network layer unit over a transmission medium without prior establishment of a virtual circuit.

Data Link layer Layer 2 of the OSI Reference Model, which provides reliable transit of data across a physical link.

DB-9 A 9-pin standardized connector used in personal computers for a Token-Ring network connection (female), serial I/O port (male), and RGBI output (also used for LocalTalk).

DB-15 A 15-pin standardized connector used at the transceiver, the drop cable, and the station of IEEE 802.3 or Ethernet network components.

DB-25 A 25-pin standardized connector used in personal computers for parallel output ports (female connector on IBM PC chassis) or for serial I/O ports (male connector on 1BM PC chassis).

DCE (data circuit-terminating equipment) Also called data communications equipment. On a serial communications link, it is the device that connects the DTEs into the communication line or channel.

DDP (Datagram delivery protocol) Adds to the services of the underlying link access protocol by including an internetwork of interconnected AppleTalk networks, with a provision to address packets to sockets within a node. Interpreted in the AppleTalk PT suite.

DDR (dial-on-demand-routing) A technique in which a Cisco router can automatically initiate and close a circuit-switched session as transmitting stations demand.

DE (discard eligibility) The seventh bit of the second octet of the frame relay header. A value of 1 in the DE bit indicates that the frame is eligible for discard by a congested network.

decapsulation The unwrapping of data from a particular protocol header.

decryption The restoring of data to its original, unencrypted state.

dedicated LAN Network segment allocated to a single device.

dedicated line A line reserved for transmissions, rather than being switched as transmission is required.

default route A routing table entry used to direct packets for which the next hop is not explicitly listed in the routing table.

default router The router to which packets are directed when a next hop is not explicitly listed in the routing table.

delay The time between the beginning of the transaction by a sender and the first response received by the sender.

delay-sensitive traffic Traffic requiring timeliness of delivery and that varies its rate accordingly.

destination address The part of a message indicating for whom the message is intended.

DHCP (Dynamic Host Configuration Protocol) Enables IP addresses to be allocated dynamically so addresses can be reused after hosts no longer need them.

dial-up line   A communications circuit established by a switched-circuit connection using the telephone network.

DIP switch (dual inline package switch)   A switch attached to a printed circuit board; usually a small screwdriver is required to change it. There are two settings—on and off. Printed circuit boards usually have "banks" of multiple DIP switches that are used to configure the board in a semi-permanent way.

DISC   Disconnect. An LLC non-data frame indicating that the connection established by an earlier SABM or SABME is to be broken.

display   The process in which the Sniffer analyzer interprets the traffic recorded during capture. During display, the analyzer decodes the layers of protocol in the recorded frames and displays them as English abbreviations or summaries.

distance vector routing algorithm   Class of routing algorithms calling for each router to send some or all of its routing table to its neighbors.

Distribution layer   The layer in a hierarchical network that provides policy-based connectivity.

DLC (Data Link Control)   The lowest protocol layer within the transmitted network frame. Its fields typically include the source address, the destination address, and sometimes additional control information.

DLCI (Data Link connection identifier)   10-bit number used by the frame relay protocol that identifies a virtual circuit.

DM (Disconnected Mode)   An LLC message acknowledging that a previously established connection has been broken.

DNS (domain name service)   A protocol within TCP/IP used for discovering information about resources using a database distributed among different name servers. Interpreted in the TCP/IP suite.

DR (designated router)   An OSPF router generating LSAs for a multi-access network.

DS0 (digital signal level 0)   T1 lines. A single 64Kbps channel in a DS1 signal. See also *DS1* and *DS3*.

DS1 (digital signal level 1)   T1 lines. Basic digital signal for transmission over T1 facilities. The DS1 signal consists of 24 channels at 64Kbps (called DS0, or Digital signal level 0, channels), plus 8Kbps used for synchronization and signaling—for a total bandwidth of 1,544Kbps.

DS3 (digital signal level 3)   T3 lines. Specification for transmitting digital signals at 44.736Mbps.

DSAP (destination service access point)   The LLC SAP for the protocol expected to be used by the destination station for decoding the frame data.

DSL (Digital Subscriber Line)   Technology used between the customer premise and service provider using high-frequency ranges to enable higher bandwidth capacity over standard copper wires.

DSU (data service unit)   A device that connects terminal equipment to digital communications lines. See also *CSU*.

DTE (data terminal equipment)   A generic term used to describe the host or end user machine on a serial communications link.

DUAL (diffusing update algorithm)   A convergence algorithm used in enhanced IGRP, which provides loop-free operation throughout a route computation.

duplex   A characteristic of data transmission, either full- or half-duplex. Full-duplex permits simultaneous two-way communication. Half-duplex means only one side can talk at a time.

DVMRP (Distance Vector Multicast Routing Protocol)   A protocol for routing multicast datagrams through an internetwork.

dynamic routing   Routing that automatically adjusts the network topology or traffic changes.

E

E1   A digital transmission link with a capacity of 2.048Mbps (CCITT version of T1).

EBCDIC (Extended Binary Coded Decimal Interchange Code)   Mapping between numeric codes and graphical characters used for IBM mainframe computers and communications protocols defined by IBM.

Echo   (1) A request/response protocol within XNS used to verify the existence of a host. (2) A protocol within AppleTalk that enables any node to send a datagram to any other node and to receive an echoed copy of that packet in return to verify the existence of that node or to make round-trip delay measurements. Interpreted in the AppleTalk PI suite. (3) A protocol transmitted by a Net RPC frame in Banyan VINES.

EGP (Exterior Gateway Protocol)   A protocol within TCP/IP used in exchanging routing information among gateways belonging to either the same or different systems.

EIA (Electronic Industries Association)   A standard organization specializing in the electrical and functional characteristics of interface equipment.

EIGRP (Extended Interior Gateway Routing Protocol)   An enhanced version of IGRP and a suite of Cisco routing protocols used in TCP/IP and OSI internetworks.

ELAP   See *LAP*.

encapsulation   The wrapping of data in a particular protocol header.

encryption   Applying a specific algorithm to data to alter its appearance and make it incomprehensible to those who are not authorized to see the information.

Error   A protocol within XNS by which a station reports receiving and discarding a defective packet. Interpreted in the XNS PI suite.

error rate   In data transmission, the ratio of the number of incorrect elements transmitted to the total number of elements transmitted.

ESF (Extended Superframe Format)   T1. A modification of the DS1 format that uses the 193rd bit to signal line problems.

Ethernet   A CSMA/CD network standard originally developed by Xerox; similar to (and often used interchangeably with) the IFFE 802.3 standard.

Ethertype   A 2-byte protocol-type code in Ethernet frames used by several manufacturers but independent of the IEEE 802.3 standard.

event   A network message that indicates irregularities in operation of the physical elements of a network.

expansion   Running a compressed data set through an algorithm that restores the data set to its original size.

explorer packet   The packet generated by an end station trying to find its way through an SRB network.

exterior gateway protocol   An internetwork protocol used to change routing information between autonomous systems.

F

Fast Ethernet   Includes any number of 100Mbps Ethernet specifications, at a speed 10 times faster than the 10BaseT Ethernet specification.

FC (frame control)   On a Token-Ring network, the DLC byte that contains the frame's type.

FCS   See *frame check sequence.*

FDDI (Fiber distributed data interface)   An ANSI/ISO standard that defines a 100Mbps LAN over a fiber-optic medium using a timed token over a dual ring of trees.

FE (framing error)   An error that occurs because of incorrect framing of data units transmitted. In asynchronous transmission, this is usually due to a deviation in the stop bit cell.

FECN (forward explicit congestion notification)   (Frame relay) The fifth bit in the second octet of the frame relay header. Used to inform a subscriber device of congestion in the forward direction.

FEP (front-end processor)   Sits in front of a computer and is designed to handle the telecommunications burden so the computer can concentrate on handling the processing burden.

fiber-optic cable   A cable that conducts modulated light transmission.

filter   The Sniffer analysis application uses several varieties of filters, including capture filters that determine which arriving frames the analyzer discards and which it retains. The Sniffer also uses display filters that determine which frames in the capture buffer will be displayed. Eliminating a frame from a display with a display filter does not remove the frame from memory.

firewall   An access server or router designated as a buffer between any connections from public networks to a given private network. A firewall router ensures the security of the private network.

flash update   A routing update sent asynchronously in response to a change in the network topology.

floating static route   A static route that has a higher administrative distance than a dynamically learned route, so that it can be overridden by dynamically learned routing information.

flooding   A technique used by bridges and switches in which traffic received on an interface is sent out from all the interfaces of the device, except the interface from which the information was originally received.

flow control   Hardware or software mechanisms used in data communications to turn off transmission when the receiving workstation is incapable of storing the data it is receiving. Refers to various methods of regulating the flow of data during a conversation. Buffers are an example of flow control.

fragmentation   The process of breaking a packet into smaller units when transmitting over a network that can't support a packet of the original size.

frame   The multi-byte unit of data transmitted at one time by a station on the network. It is synonymous with the term packet.

frame check sequence (FCS)   In bit-oriented protocols, a 16-bit field added to the end of a frame that contains transmission error-checking information.

Frame Relay   A streamlined access protocol commonly used for LAN interconnectivity.

FRMR (frame reject)   An LLC command or response indicating that a previous frame had a bad format and is being rejected. The FRMR frame contains five bytes of data that explain why the previous frame was bad.

Front-end processor   See *FEP.*

FS (frame status)   A byte appended to a Token-Ring network frame following the CRC. It contains the Address Recognized and Frame Copied bits.

FTP (file transfer protocol)   (1) A protocol based on TCP/IP for reliable file transfer. Interpreted in the TCP/IP PI suite. (2) A protocol transmitted by a Net RPC frame in Banyan VINES.

full-duplex   The capability to have simultaneous data transmission between a sending and receiving station.

full mesh   A network in which devices have been organized in a mesh topology, with each network node having a virtual or physical circuit connecting to every other network node.

functional address   A limited broadcast destination address for IEEE 802.5 Token-Ring networks. Individual bits in the address specify attributes that stations eligible to receive the frame should have. Similar to multicast address.

G

gateway   A computer that connects two different networks. Usually, this means two different kinds of networks. However, in TCP/IP terminology a gateway connects two separately administered subnetworks, which might or might not be running the same networking protocols.

GNS (Get Nearest Server)   Request packet sent by a client on an IPX network to locate the nearest active server of a particular type.

GUI (graphical user interface)   Pronounced "goo-ey." An operating system or environment that displays options onscreen as icons or picture symbols.

H

handshaking   The electrical exchange of predetermined signals when a connection is made between two devices carrying data. Computers must *handshake* through a procedure of *greeting* the opposite device.

HDLC (high-level data link control)   A standard bit-oriented protocol developed by the International Standards Organization (ISO). In HDLC, control information is always placed in the same position. Specific bit patterns used for control differ dramatically from those used to represent data, minimizing errors. Many internetworking companies (such as Cisco and Vitalink) have developed proprietary versions of HDLC that the Sniffer Internetwork analysis application can decode.

header   The beginning portion of a message that contains the destination address, source address, message-numbering, and other information. The header helps direct the message along its journey. Different protocols implement headers in different ways.

heartbeat   On Ethernet, the SQE signal generated by the transceiver at the end of a transmitted frame to check the SQE circuitry. See *SQE TEST*.

hop   A term used in routing. A hop is one data link. A path to the final destination on a net is a series of hops away from the origin. Each hop has a cost associated with it, enabling the calculation of a least-cost path.

hop count   A routing metric used to measure the distance between a source and its destination.

host   A computer system on a network.

host number   The part of an IP address that designates which node on the subnetwork is being addressed.

hub   A concentrator and repeater for the network. Generally speaking, a hub is a central point for wiring or computing in a network.

I

IARP (Inverse Address Resolution Protocol)   IARP enables a frame relay station to discover the protocol address corresponding to a given hardware address.

ICMP (Internet Control Message Protocol)   A protocol within TCP/IP mainly used to report errors in datagram transmission. Interpreted in the TCP/IP suite.

ID   Identification.

IEEE (Institute of Electrical and Electronics Engineers, Inc.)   A standards body that focuses primarily on the Physical and Data Link layers and extends to LAN management. Standards documents are available from them at 345 East 47th Street, New York, NY 10017.

IETF (Internet Engineering Taskforce)   A taskforce of more than 80 groups responsible for developing Internet standards.

I-Frame (information frame)   An LLC, HDLC, or SDLC frame type used to send sequenced data that must be acknowledged.

IGMP (Internet Group Management Protocol)   Used to keep neighboring multicast routers informed of the host group memberships present on a particular local network.

IGP (Interior Gateway Protocol)   Internet protocol used to exchange routing information within an autonomous system.

IGRP (Interior Gateway Routing Protocol)   Cisco routing protocol designed for campus-wide use, as opposed to wide-area use.

Interface   (1) A connection between two devices or systems. (2) A network connection in routing terminology. (3) A shared boundary in telephony. (4) The boundary between adjacent layers of the OSI model.

Internet   The largest global internetwork, connecting thousands of networks worldwide.

internet   Short for internetwork, and not to be confused with Internet.

internetwork   A collection of one or more networks with different protocols and connecting devices.

Intranet   A network that is internal to an organization, based on Web technology.

I/O (Input/Output)   The part of a computer system or the activity that is primarily dedicated to the passing of information into or out of the central processing unit or memory.

IP (Internet Protocol)   The lowest-layer protocol under TCP/IP that is responsible for end-to-end forwarding and long packet fragmentation control. Interpreted in the TCP/IP PI suite. A similar protocol is interpreted in the Banyan VINES PI. See also *IPX* and *ISO*.

IP address   32-bit address assigned to hosts using TCP/IP. Sometimes called an Internet address.

IP multicast   Routing technique enabling IP traffic to be sent from one source to several destinations, or from many sources to many destinations.

IPX   Internet packet exchange. Novell's implementation of Xerox Internet Datagram Protocol. Interpreted in the Novell NetWare PI suite.

ISDN (Integrated Services Digital Network)   A digital telephone technology that combines voice and data services on a single circuit.

ISL (inter-switch link)   Cisco protocol maintaining VLAN information as traffic flows between switches and routers.

ISO (International Standards Organization)   (1) A consortium that is establishing a set of networking protocols. (2) The protocols standardized by that group.

ISP (Internet service provider)   Provides Internet access to a company or individual.

ITU-T (International Telecommunications Union Telecommunication Standardization Sector)   International body that sets worldwide standards for telecommunications technologies.

J–K

Kbps (Kilobits per second)   A measure of the rate of data transmission.

keepalive interval   The time between each keepalive message sent by a network device.

keepalive message   Message sent by one network to another informing it that the circuit between the two is still alive.

L

LAN (local area network)   The hardware and software used to connect computers in a limited geographical area.

LANE (LAN emulation)   Enables an ATM network to function as a LAN backbone.

LAP (Link Access Protocol)   The logical-layer protocol for AppleTalk. It exists in two variants: ELAP (for Ethernet) and LLAP (for LocalTalk networks). Interpreted in the AppleTalk PI.

LAPB (Link Access Protocol Balanced)   A subset of HDLC.

LAPD (Link Access Protocol-D)   A link control protocol based on HDLC that is related to ISDN.

LAT (Local Area Transport)   The DECnet protocol that handles multiplexed terminal (keyboard and screen) traffic to and from timesharing hosts. Interpreted in the DECnet PI suite.

latency   (1) The delay between the time a device requests access to a network and the time it is allowed to transmit. (2) Also called insertion delay, the delay between the time a device receives a frame and the time the frame can be forwarded out the destination port.

leased line   A telephone line rented for exclusive, continuous use. Commonly used to connect remote LANs. The same as a leased circuit, dedicated circuit, or leased channel.

link   Network communications channel consisting of a transmission or circuit path and all the related equipment between a sender and a receiver. Often used in reference to a WAN connection.

link protocol   The set of rules by which a logical data link is set up and by which data transfers across the link. Includes formatting of the data.

Link state routing protocol   Also known as Shortest Path First Algorithm. Examples of Link state protocols are NLSP and OSPF. Link state routing protocols maintain topology maps, offer faster convergence, and send updates only when changes occur on the network.

LLAP   See *LAP.*

LLC (Logical Link Control)   A protocol that provides connection control and multiplexing to subsequent embedded protocols; standardized as IEEE 802.2 and ISO/DIS 8802/2.

LMI (Local Management Interface)   An access signaling protocol defined for frame relay circuits. LMI carries information on the status of permanent virtual circuits between the network and a subscriber device. Additions to LMI can include multicasting, global addressing, and flow control.

load balancing   The capability of a router to distribute traffic over all its network ports. This helps increase effective network bandwidth.

local explorer packet   A packet generated by an end system in an SRB network to find a host connected to the local ring.

LOOP (Loopback)   A protocol under Ethernet for sending diagnostic probe messages.

LSB (least significant bit)   The lowest-order (usually rightmost) bit of a binary number.

M

MAC (Medium Access Control)   The protocol layer that describes network management frames sent on the 802.5 Token-Ring. Most MAC frames are handled transparently by the network adapter.

MAC address   Standardized Data Link layer address required of every device or port connected to a LAN. Also known as a MAC layer address, hardware address, or physical address.

MAN (metropolitan-area network)   A network spanning a metropolitan area.

managed device   A network device that can be managed by a network management protocol.

Manchester encoding   A data encoding technique that uses a transition at the middle of each bit period that serves as a clock and also as data.

MAU (multiple access unit)   (Also known as a medium attachment unit.) The wiring concentrator or transceiver used for attaching stations connected to the network.

MB (megabyte)   A measure of the rate of data transmission.

MBps (megabytes per second)   A measure of the rate of data transmission.

mesh   A network topology in which devices are organized in a segmented manner with many interconnections placed between network nodes.

MIC (media interface connector)   An optical fiber connector pair that links the fiber media to the FDDI node or another cable.

mirroring   Synchronizing two disks on a file server.

modem   A contraction of modulate and demodulate. A conversion device installed in pairs at each end of an analog communications line. The modulator part of the modem codes digital information onto an analog signal by varying the frequency of the carrier signal. The demodulator part extracts digital information from a modulated carrier signal.

MOP (Maintenance Operations Protocol)   A protocol under DECnet for remote testing and problem diagnosis.

MSB (most significant bit)   The highest-order bit of a binary number, not including the sign bit.

MTBF (mean time between failure)   The average time between failures of a device.

MTU (maximum transmission unit)   The maximum packet size, in bytes, that a particular interface can handle.

MTU Discovery   A function enabling software to discover and use the largest frame size that will travel over the network without requiring fragmentation.

multicast   (1) A message directed to a group of stations on a network or collection of networks (contrast with broadcast). (2) A destination address that designates such a subset.

multiplexing   Sending several signals over a single line and separating them at the other end.

N

NAK (negative acknowledgment)   A response from the recipient of data to the sender of that data that indicates the transmission was unsuccessful (that is, the data was corrupted by transmission errors).

NBMA (non-broadcast multi-access)   A multi-access network that either does not support broadcasting or in which broadcasting is not feasible.

NCP (NetWare Core Protocol)   Novell's Application layer protocol for the exchange of commands and data between file servers and workstations. Interpreted in the Novell NetWare PI suite.

NDS (Network Directory Services)   NDS is a Novell application that operates with NCP to manage network resources.

NetBEUI (NetBIOS Basic Extended User Interface)   A programming specification for NetBIOS.

NetBIOS (Network Basic Input/Output System)   (1) A protocol implemented by the PC LAN program to support symbolically named stations and the exchange of arbitrary data. (2) The programming interface (API) used to send and receive NetBIOS messages. Several different and incompatible implementations of NetBIOS exist, each with a separate API; for example, in the IBM and Novell suites.

NetWare   The networking system designed by Novell, Inc. and the protocols used therein.

network   A collection of computers, printers, switches, routers, and other devices that are capable of communicating with each other over a transmission medium.

network address   A Network layer address referring to a logical network device; also known as a protocol address.

network layer   Layer 3 of the OSI Reference Model. It provides connectivity and path selection between two end systems.

network management   Systems that help maintain or troubleshoot a network.

network management protocol   The protocol that management entities within NMSs use to communicate with agents in managed devices.

network topology   The geography of a network. Examples of network topologies include ring, bus, and star.

NFS (network file system)   A protocol developed by Sun Microsystems for requests and responses to a networked file server.

NLM (NetWare Loadable Module)   An individual program that can be loaded into memory and function as part of the NetWare NOS.

NLSP (NetWare Link Services Protocol)   A Link state protocol that improves the performance, reliability, scalability, and manageability of IPX traffic in large-scale LAN-WAN internetworks.

nodes   Points on a network where service is provided or used, or where communications channels are interconnected. "Node" sometimes is used interchangeably with the term "workstation."

non-local traffic   Traffic needing to travel to different network segments.

NOS (network operating system)   A term used to refer to distributed filesystems.

N(R) (receive sequence number)   An LLC or HDLC field for information frames indicating the sequence number of the next frame expected; all frames before N(R) are thus implicitly acknowledged.

N(S) (send sequence number)   An LLC or HDLC field for information frames that indicates the sequence number of the current frame within the connection.

NT1 (Network Termination 1)   In ISDN, a device providing the interface between customer premises equipment and central office switching equipment.

NTP/SNTP (Network Time Protocol/Simple Network Time Protocol)   NTP or SNTP provides the mechanisms to synchronize time distribution in the Internet.

Null modem   Cross-pinned cable used for DTE to DTE.

NVRAM (non-volatile RAM)   RAM that retains its contents when a unit is powered off.

O

octet   String of eight bits; synonymous with byte.

ODI (Open Data-Link Interface)   A Novell specification providing a standardized interface for NICs (network interface cards), enabling multiple protocols to use a single NIC.

OSI (open systems interconnection)   A generalized model of layered architecture for the interconnection of systems.

OSPF (Open Shortest Path First)   A Link state IGP routing algorithm proposed to succeed RIP on the Internet.

Overhead   Information that provides support for computing processes but is not an intrinsic part of the data or operation.

P

packet   Multi-byte unit of data transmitted one unit, or packet, at a time by a station on the network. Synonymous with the term "datagram."

packet switching   Method for sending data in packets through a network to a remote location. Data is subdivided into individual packets, each with its own identification and carrying the destination address. Packets then can be sent by different routes and reassembled in sequence by the packet ID.

PAD (packet assembler disassembler)   Computer on an X.25 network that enables asynchronous terminals to use the synchronous X.25 network by packaging asynchronous traffic into packets.

parallel interface   An interface that permits parallel transmission (or simultaneous transmission of the bits making up a character or byte) over separate channels or on different carrier frequencies of the same channel.

parity bit   A binary bit appended to an array of bits to make the sum of the bits always odd or always even. Used with a parity check for detecting errors in transmitted binary data.

parity check   A process for detecting whether bits of data have been altered during transmission of that data.

partial mesh   A network in which devices are organized in a mesh topology, with some network nodes organized in a full mesh, but with others that are connected to only one or two other nodes in the network.

PAT (port address translation)   Cisco feature that enables the translation of private addresses into registered IP addresses by using port numbers.

patch panel   A device in which temporary connections can be made between incoming and outgoing lines. Used for modifying or reconfiguring a communications system or for connecting test instruments (such as the Sniffer Network Analyzer) to specific lines.

path control layer   Layer 3 in the SNA architectural model. Performs sequencing services related to proper data reassembly.

payload   The portion of a frame that contains the upper-layer information (data).

PC (personal computer)   Common abbreviation for a personal computer.

PDU (protocol data unit)   The data delivered as a single unit between peer processes on different computers. An OSI term for information at any layer in the OSI model.

PDV (path delay value)   The total round-trip propagation delay in an Ethernet network.

Physical layer   Layer 1 of the OSI Reference Model. Concerned with the mechanical and electrical aspects of maintaining links between end systems.

pilot   A pilot of a network is a scaled-down prototype used to demonstrate basic functions; used most often for smaller networks.

Ping   A TCP/IP tool supplied with TCP/IP Distributed Sniffer System. Ping is a diagnostic utility that sends ICMP Echo Request messages to a specific IP address on the network.

policy routing   A routing scheme that forwards packets to specific interfaces based on user-configured policies.

port   The physical access point to a computer, multiplexer, device, or network where signals can be sent or received.

PPP (Point-to-Point Protocol)   RFC 1331. PPP is a link-level protocol that bypasses X.25 for communication between systems that are directly connected, running any of a variety of protocols directly over HDLC.

pps (packets per second)   A measurement of throughput and performance of networks and networking devices.

preamble   A fixed data pattern transmitted before each frame to allow receiver synchronization and recognition of the start of a frame.

Presentation layer   The sixth layer of the OSI model (ISO 8823). It controls the formats of screens and files. Control codes, special graphics, and character sets work in this layer.

PRI (primary rate interface)   ISDN interface to primary rate access.

priority queuing   A method of queuing used to guarantee bandwidth for traffic by assigning space based on protocol, port number, or other criteria. Priority queuing has four levels: low, normal, medium, and high. The high queue is emptied first.

private addresses   Reserved IP addresses to be used internally only. They include: 10.0.0.0–10.255.255.255, 172.16.0.0–172.31.255.255, and 192.168.0.0–192.168.255.255.

process switching   An operation that provides full write evaluation and per-packet load balancing across parallel WAN links. It involves the transmission of entire frames to the route for CPU, where they are repackaged for delivery to or from a WAN interface, with the router making a route selection for each packet.

protocol   A specific set of rules, procedures, or conventions governing the format and timing of data transmission between two devices.

protocol stack   A set of related communications protocols that operate together and address communication at the seven layers of the OSI Reference Model.

prototype   A prototype of a network involves implementing a portion of the network to prove that its design meets the requirements used for larger networks.

provisioning   Defining the type of WAN, including the specifications and options.

proxy   An entity that stands in for another entity in the interest of efficiency.

proxy ARP (Proxy Address Resolution Protocol)   A variation of the ARP protocol in which an intermediate device sends an ARP response on behalf of an end node to the requesting host.

PUP (PARC Universal Packet)   A type of Ethernet packet formerly used at the Xerox Corporation's Palo Alto Research Center. Interpreted in the XNS/MS-Net and the TCP/IP PIs but not included in their protocol diagrams because it's no longer in regular use.

PVC (permanent virtual circuit)   A unique, predefined logical path between two endpoints of a network. Used by frame relay.

Q

query   A message inquiring about the value of a variable or set of variables.

queue   (1) A list of elements, in order, waiting to be processed. (2) In routing, a backlog of packets waiting to be forwarded.

QoS (quality of service)   A measure of performance for a transmission system that reflects its transmission quality.

R

RAM (random access memory)   Memory that can be read and written by a microprocessor.

RARP (Reverse Address Resolution Protocol)   A protocol within TCP/IP used for finding a node's IP address, given its DLC address. Interpreted in the TCP/IP PI suite.

Rate-sensitive traffic   Traffic that is willing to give up timeliness for guaranteed rate.

reassembly   Putting an IP datagram together again at its destination, after it has been fragmented.

redistribution   Distributing routing information discovered through one routing protocol in the update messages of another routing protocol.

redundancy   Duplication of devices, connections, or services, so that in case of failure, these can perform the work of the ones that failed.

REJ (Reject)   An LLC frame type that requests retransmission of previously sent frames.

reliability   The ratio of expected to received keepalives from a link. If this is a high ratio, the line is reliable.

REM (ring error monitor)   A station on the 802.5 Token-Ring network that collects MAC layer error messages from the other stations.

repeater   A device inserted at intervals along a circuit to boost, amplify, and regenerate the signal being transmitted.

response time   The amount of time to receive a response to a request for a service from the network system.

RFC (Request For Comment)   Designation used in DoD/TCP protocol research and development.

RG-58   The designation for 50-ohm coaxial cables used by Cheapernet (thin Ethernet).

RG-59   The designation for 75-ohm coaxial cables used by PC Network (broadband).

RG-62   The designation for 93-ohm coaxial cables used by ARCNET.

RII (routing information indicator)   If the first bit in the source address field of a Token-Ring frame is 1, the data field begins with routing information. Interpreted by the Token-Ring or Ethernet Sniffer analysis application independent of other PIs.

ring   A connection of two or more stations in a logically circular topology. Information is passed sequentially between active stations.

ring topology   A network topology that consists of a series of repeaters connected to one another by unidirectional transmission links to form a single closed loop. Each station on the network connects to the network at a repeater. Ring topologies are most often organized in a closed-loop star.

RIP (Routing Information Protocol)   A protocol within the XNS and TCP/IP families used to exchange routing information among gateways. Interpreted in the XNS PT suite and TCP/IP PI suite.

RISC (reduced instruction set computer)   A type of microprocessor design that focuses on rapid and efficient processing of a relatively small set of instructions.

RJ-45   The designation for the 8-wire modular connectors used in 10BASE-T networks. It is similar to, but wider than, the standard (RJ-11) telephone modular connectors.

rlogin (remote login)   A terminal emulation program offered in most UNIX implementations.

RMON (Remote Monitoring)   Management Information Base (MIB). Uses SNMP and standard MIB design to provide multi-vendor interoperability between monitoring products and management stations.

RNR (Receive Not Ready)   An LLC and HDLC command or response indicating that transmission is blocked.

ROM (read-only memory)   Memory that can be read by the microprocessor but not written.

route   A path through an internetwork.

route summarization   The consolidation of the advertised addresses in a routing table. This reduces the number of routes in the routing table, the routing update traffic, and the overall or router overhead.

routed protocol   A protocol that can be routed by a router. A routed protocol contains enough Network layer addressing information for user traffic to be directed from one network to another network. Routed protocols define the format and use of the fields within a packet.

router   An internet linking device operating at the Network layer (ISO layer 3).

routing   The process of finding a path to a destination host. Routing can be complex in larger networks because of the many potential intermediate destinations that a packet might travel through before reaching its destination host.

routing domain   A group of end systems and intermediate systems operating under the same set of administrative rules.

routing metric   A standard of measurement, such as a path length, that is used by routing algorithms to determine the optimal path to the destination. This information is stored in routing tables. Metrics include communication cost, bandwidth, hop count, delay, path cost, MTU, and reliability.

routing protocol   A routing protocol supports a routed protocol by providing mechanisms for sharing routing information. Routing protocol messages move between the routers. A routing protocol enables the routers to communicate with other routers to update and maintain routing tables. Routing protocol messages do not carry end-user traffic from network to network. A routing protocol uses the routed protocol to pass information between routers.

routing table   A table stored in a router or some other internetworking device that keeps track of routes to particular network destinations and metrics associated with those routes.

routing update   A message sent from a router to indicate network reachability and associated cost of information. Typically sent at regular intervals after a change occurs in the network topology.

RPC (Remote Procedure Call)   A protocol for activating functions on a remote station and retrieving the results. Interpreted in the Sun PI suite. A similar protocol exists in Xerox XNS.

RPL (Remote Program Load)   A protocol used by IBM on the IEEE 802.5 Token-Ring network to download initial programs into networked stations. Interpreted in the IBM PI suite.

RPS (ring parameter server)   A station on a Token-Ring network that maintains MAC layer information about the LAN configuration, such as ring numbers and physical location identifiers.

RR (receive ready)   An LLC non-data frame indicating readiness to receive data from the other station.

RS232 or RS232C (Recommended Standard 232)   EIA standard defining electrical characteristics of the signals in the cables that connect a DTE and a DCE.

RTMP (Routing Table Maintenance Protocol)   Used in AppleTalk networks to enable internetwork routers to dynamically discover routes to the various networks of an internet. A node that is not a router uses a subset of RTMP (the RTMP stub) to determine the number of the network to which it is connected and the node IDs of routers on its network. Interpreted in the AppleTalk protocol interpreter.

S

S or S Frame (Supervisory Frame)   An LLC, HDLC, or SDLC frame type used for control functions.

SABM (set asynchronous balanced mode)   An LLC non-data frame requesting the establishment of a connection over which numbered information frames can be sent.

SABME (set asynchronous balanced mode [extended])   SABM with two more bytes in the control field. Used in LAPB.

SAC   Single attachment concentrator. A concentrator that offers one S port for attachment to the FDDI network and M ports for the attachment of stations or other concentrators.

SAP (service access point)   (1) A small number used by convention, or established by a standards group, that defines the format of subsequent LLC data; a means of demultiplexing alternative protocols supported by LLC. (2) (Service Advertising Protocol) Used by NetWare servers to broadcast the names and locations of servers and to send a specific response to any station that queries it.

SDLC (Synchronous Data Link Control)   An older serial communications protocol that was the model for LLC and with which it shares many features.

security management   One of five categories of network management defined by ISO for management of the OSI networks. Subsystems within these control access to various network services.

segment   (1) A section of any network that is bounded by routers, bridges, or switches. (2) In a LAN using a bus topology, a continuous electrical circuit often connected to other segments with repeaters. (3) In the TCP specification, a single Transport layer unit of information.

serial interface   An interface that requires serial transmission, or the transfer of information in which the bits composing a character are sent sequentially. Implies only a single transmission channel.

server   A node or software program that provides services to clients.

Session   Name for the Session layer protocol in the ISO series, interpreted in the ISO PI suite.

Session layer   Layer 5 of the OSI Reference Model. This layer establishes, manages, and terminates sessions between applications, and manages data exchange between Presentation layer entities.

shielded cable   A cable that has a layer of shielded insulation to reduce electromagnetic interference.

silicon switching   A type of switching in which an incoming packet matches an entry in the silicon switching cache located in the SSE of the SSP module.

simplex   The capability for data transmission in only one direction between a sending station and a receiving station.

single-route packet   A packet in an SRB network that follows only one specific path to its destination.

sliding window flow control   A method of flow control in which a receiver gives a transmitter permission to transmit data until a window is full. When the window is full, the transmitter must stop transmitting until the receiver advertises a larger window.

SLIP (Serial Line Internet Protocol)   Standard protocol for point-to-point serial connections using a variation of TCP/IP.

SMB (server message block)   A message type used by the IBM PC LAN program to make requests from a user station to a server and receive replies. Many of the functions are similar to those made by an application program to DOS or to OS/2 running on a single computer.

SMDS (switched multi-megabit data service)   A packet-switched, datagram-based WAN networking technology.

SMT (station management)   Provides ring management, connection management, and frame services for an FDDI ring.

SMTP (Simple Mail Transfer Protocol)   A protocol within TCP/IP for reliable exchange of electronic mail messages. Interpreted in the TCP/IP PI suite.

SNA   (1) (Systems Network Architecture) A set of protocols used by IBM for network communications, particularly with mainframe computers. Interpreted in the IBM PI suite. (2) (Sniffer Network Analyzer). Network General's network analyzer that attaches to a network to monitor, record, analyze, and interpret network transmissions. Monitoring and analysis functions are separate, menu-driven activities that provide high-level analysis and troubleshooting for complex local and wide-area network installations.

SNAP (Subnetwork Access Protocol)   Sometimes called Subnetwork Access Convergence Protocol. An extension to IEEE 802.2 LLC that permits a station to have multiple Network layer protocols. The protocol specifies that DSAP and SSAP addresses must be AA hex. A field subsequent to SSAP identifies one specific protocol. Interpreted in the TCP/IP PI suite and the AppleTalk PI suite.

SNMP (Simple Network Management Protocol)   Interpreted in the TCP/IP suite.

SNRM (set normal response mode)   Places a secondary station in a mode that precludes it from sending unsolicited frames. The primary station controls all message flow. Used in SDLC.

SNRME (set normal response mode [extended])   SNRM with two more bytes in the control field. Used in SDLC.

socket   A logically addressable entity or service within a node, serving as a more precise identification of sender or recipient.

source address   The part of a message that indicates from whom the message came.

spanning tree   A method of creating a loop-free logical topology on an extended LAN. Formation of a spanning tree topology for transmission of messages across bridges is based on the industry-standard spanning tree algorithm defined in IEEE 802.id.

spanning-tree algorithm   An algorithm used to create a spanning tree.

spanning-tree protocol   A bridge protocol that utilizes the spanning-tree algorithm. This enables a learning bridge to dynamically work around the loops in a network topology by creating a spanning tree. Bridges exchange BPDU messages with other bridges to detect loops. They then remove loops by shutting down selected bridge interfaces.

SPF (shortest path first)   A routing algorithm that iterates on length of a path to determine the shortest path spanning tree.

SPID (service profile identifier)   A number that some service providers use to define the services to which an ISDN device subscribes.

split horizon   A routing rule that states a router can't send routing information about a network out of the same interface from which it learned that information.

SPX (Sequential Packet Exchange)   Novell's version of the Xerox protocol called SPP. Interpreted in the Novell NetWare PI suite.

SQE (signal quality error)   The 802.3/Ethernet collision signal from the transceiver.

SQE Test   The SQE signal generated by the transceiver at the end of a transmitted frame to check the SQE circuitry, (also known as heartbeat in Ethernet).

SQL (Structured Query Language)   Used to access databases.

SQL server   A server that understands Structured Query Language.

SR/TLB (source-route translational bridging)   A method of bridging in which source route stations can communicate with two transparent bridge stations with the help of an intermediate bridge that translates between the two bridge protocols.

SSAP (source service access point)   The LLC SAP for the protocol used by the originating station.

SSE (silicon switching engine)   A routing and switching mechanism that compares the Data Link or Network layer header of an incoming packet to a silicon switching cache, determines the appropriate action, and forwards the packet to the proper interface. It can perform switching independent of the system processor.

SSP   (1) (silicon switch processor) A high-performance silicon switch for Cisco 7000 series routers that provides distributed processing and control for interface processors. (2) (switch-to-switch protocol) A protocol specified in the DLSw standard that routers used to establish DLSw connections, forward data, locate resources, and handle flow control and error recovery.

S/T Interface   In ISDN, the connection between a BRI interface and an NT1 device.

static route   Route that is explicitly configured and entered into the routing table.

store and forward packet switching   A packet switching technique in which frames are fully buffered and processed before being forwarded out the appropriate port. This includes calculating the CRC and checking the destination address. Bridges and switches using this method verify the frame prior to forwarding it. If a frame has been damaged, that frame is not forwarded. Store and forward devices isolate collision domains.

STP (shielded twisted pair)   A two-pair wiring medium used in a variety of network implementations. See also *Spanning-Tree protocol*.

stub area   An OSPF area that carries a default route, intra-area routes, and inter-area routes, but does not carry external routes.

stub network   A part of an internetwork that can be reached by only one path.

SUA (stored upstream address)   The network address of a Token-Ring station's nearest upstream neighbor. Texas Instruments calls this the UNA.

subinterface   One of a number of virtual interfaces on a single physical interface.

subnet   A term used to denote any networking technology that makes all nodes connected to it appear to be one hop away. In other words, the user of the subnet can communicate directly to all other nodes on the subnet. A collection of subnets together with a routing or network layer combine to form a network.

subnet address   A portion of an IP address that is specified as the subnetwork by the subnet mask.

subnet mask   A 32-bit number associated with an IP address; each bit in the subnet mask indicates how to interpret the corresponding bit in the IP address.

SVC (switched virtual circuit)   A virtual circuit set up on demand, as in the case of a dial-up telephone line or an X.25 call.

switch   (1) A network device that filters, forwards, and floods frames based on the destination address of each frame. (2) An electronic or mechanical device that enables a connection to be established as necessary and terminated when there is no longer a session to support.

symptom   An abnormal or unusual network event indicative of a possible network problem.

SYN (synchronized)   (1) The synchronized bit in a TCP segment used to indicate that the segment is a SYN segment. (2) The first segment sent by the TCP protocol; used to synchronize the two ends of a connection in preparation for opening a connection.

synchronous transmission   A method of data transfer in which information is transmitted in blocks (frames) of bits separated by equal time intervals.

Syslog   A service that receives messages from applications on the local host or from remote hosts that have been configured to forward messages.

T

T1   A digital transmission link with a capacity of 1.544Mbps.

T3   A digital transmission link with a capacity of 44.736Mbps.

TA (terminal adapter)   An external connection to a PC or another device.

TACACS (Terminal Access Controller Access Control System)   An authentication protocol that provides remote access authentication and related services such as event logging. Uses user passwords.

TCP (Transmission Control Protocol)   The connection-oriented byte-stream protocol within TCP/IP that provides reliable end-to-end communication by using sequenced data sent by IP. Interpreted in the TCP/IP PI suite.

TCP/IP (Transmission Control Protocol/Internet Program)   A suite of networking protocols originally developed by the U.S. government for ARPANET and now used by several LAN manufacturers. The individual TCP/IP protocols are listed separately in this glossary.

Telnet   Protocol for transmitting character-oriented terminal (keyboard and screen) data. Interpreted in the TCP/IP suite.

terminal   A simple device, such as a computer, at which data can be entered or retrieved from the network.

terminator   A resistive connector used to terminate the end of a cable or an unused tap into its characteristic impedance. The terminator prevents interference-causing signal reflections from the ends of the cable.

TFTP (Trivial File Transfer Protocol)   A protocol within TCP/IP used to exchange files between networked stations. Interpreted in the TCP/IP PI suite.

throughput   The quantity of data successfully transferred between nodes per unit of time, usually seconds.

THT (token holding timer)   The maximum length of time a station holding the token can initiate asynchronous transmissions. The THT is initialized with the value corresponding to the difference between the arrival of the token and the TTRT (FDDI).

token   A small message used in some networks to represent the permission to transmit; it is passed from station to station in a predefined sequence.

token bus   A type of LAN in which all stations can hear what any station transmits and in which permission to transmit is represented by a token sent from station to station.

Token-Ring   A ring-shaped LAN in which each station can directly hear transmissions from only its immediate neighbor. Permission to transmit is granted by a token that circulates around the ring.

topology   The physical arrangement of network nodes and media within an enterprise networking structure.

ToS (type of service)   A field in an IP datagram that indicates how the datagram should be handled.

traffic shaping   The use of queues to limit traffic congestion on a network. Data is buffered and then sent into the network in regulated amounts, ensuring that traffic will fit within the promised traffic envelope for the particular connection.

transparent bridging   A bridging scheme in which bridges pass frames one hop at a time based on tables associating end nodes with bridge ports. Often used in the Ethernet network.

Transport layer   Layer 4 of the OSI Reference Model. The Transport layer is responsible for reliable network communication between end nodes. It implements flow and error control and often uses virtual circuits to ensure reliable data delivery.

trap   A message sent by an SNMP agent to an NMS, console, or terminal indicating the occurrence of a significant event.

tree topology   A LAN topology similar to a bus topology. Tree networks contain branches with multiple nodes.

TSR (Terminate and Stay Resident)   A DOS program that, once loaded into RAM, remains there in the background until unloaded or power is shut off.

TTL (time to live)   A field in an IP header that indicates how long a packet is considered valid.

tunneling   An architecture that provides a virtual data link connection between two similar networks through a foreign network.

twisted pair   A relatively low-speed transmission medium consisting of two insulated wires arranged in a regular spiral pattern. The wires can be shielded or unshielded.

U

UA (unnumbered acknowledgment)   An LLC frame that acknowledges a previous SABME or DISC request.

UDP (User Datagram Protocol)   A protocol within TCP/IP for sending unsequenced data frames not otherwise interpreted by TCP/IP.

UI (unnumbered information)   An LLC, HDLC, or SDLC frame type used to send data without sequence numbers.

U Interface   The connection between an NT1 device and the ISD network.

UNA (upstream neighbor address)   The network address of a Token-Ring station's nearest upstream neighbor. IBM calls this the SUA.

UNI (User-to-Network interface)   An ATM forum specification defining an interoperability standard for the interface between ATM-based products located in a private network and ATM switches located in the public carrier networks.

unicast   A message sent to a single network destination.

unicast address   An address that specifies a single network device.

UNIX   A popular portable operating system written by AT&T.

utilization   The percentage of the total capacity of a network segment.

UTP (unshielded twisted pair)   A four-pair wire medium used in a variety of networks. UTP does not require a fixed spacing between connections.

V

V.24   An ITU-T standard for Physical layer interfaces between DTE and DCE.

V.25bis   An ITU specification that describes procedures for call setup and teardown over the DTE-DCE interface in a PSDN.

V.32   An ITU-T standard serial-line protocol for bi-directional data transmission.

V.32bis   An ITU-T standard that extends V.32 to speeds of up to 14.4Kbps.

V.34   An ITU-T standard that specifies a serial-line protocol.

V.35   A CCITT wideband interface recommendation for WANs.

VC (virtual circuit)   A logical circuit created to ensure reliable communication between two network devices. A virtual circuit can be either permanent or switched and is used in frame relay and X.25. In ATM virtual circuits are called virtual channels.

VINES (Virtual Network Software)   The networking operating system developed by Banyan Systems, Inc. and the protocols used therein. Notable components are StreetTalk and Net RPC.

virtual circuit   A communications link that appears to be a dedicated point-to-point circuit.

VLAN (Virtual LAN)   A logical, rather than physical, grouping of devices. Devices are grouped using switch management software so that they can communicate as if they were attached to the same wire, when in fact they might be located on a number of different physical LAN segments.

VLSM (variable length subnet mask)   The capability to specify a different subnet mask for the same network number on different subnets. VLSM can help optimize available address space.

VPN (virtual private network)   Enables IP traffic to travel securely over a public TCP/IP network by encrypting all traffic from one network to another. A VPN uses tunneling to encrypt all information at the IP level.

VT (virtual terminal)   An entity that is part of the Application layer protocol and enables an application to interact with a terminal in a consistent manner independent of the terminal characteristics.

W

WAN (wide area network)   A collection of LANs, or stations and hosts, extending over a wide area that can be connected through common carrier or private lines. Typically, transmission speeds are lower on a WAN than on a LAN.

WFQ (weighted fair queuing)   A method of queuing that prioritizes low-volume traffic over high-volume traffic to ensure satisfactory response time for common user applications.

wildcard mask   A 32-bit quantity used in conjunction with an IP address to determine which bits in an IP address should be ignored when comparing that address with another IP address. A wildcard mask is specified when setting up access lists.

window   The number of data segments the sender is allowed to have outstanding without receiving an acknowledgment.

windowing   A method to control the amount of information transferred end to end, using different window sizes.

WINS (Windows Internet Naming Service)   Enables clients on different IP subnets to register dynamically and browse the network without sending broadcasts.

workgroup   A collection of workstations and servers on a LAN designed to communicate and exchange data with one another.

WWW (World Wide Web)   A large network of Internet servers providing hypertext and other services to terminals running client applications.

WWW browser   A GUI-based hypertext client application, used to access hypertext documents and other services located on remote servers throughout the WWW and Internet.

X–Y

X.25   A CCITT recommendation that defines the standard communications interface for access to packet-switched networks.

XID (exchange identification)   An LLC unnumbered frame type used to negotiate which LLC services will be used during a connection.

XNS (Xerox Network Systems)   A family of protocols standardized by Xerox; particularly the Internet Transport Protocols.

X Window   Protocol for the management of high-resolution color windows at workstations. Originated by MIT, DEC, and IBM, and subsequently transferred to a consortium of vendors and developers.

Z

ZIP (Zone Information Protocol)   Used in AppleTalk to maintain an Internet-wide mapping of networks to zone names. ZIP is used by the Name Binding Protocol (NBP) to determine which networks belong to a given zone. Interpreted in the AppleTalk PI suite.

Zone   In AppleTalk networks, a set of one or more nodes within an internet.

ANSWERS

Chapter 1

1. The major objective of the OSI model is to define a vendor-neutral framework for communication. This allows coexistent communication between similar and dissimilar protocols, hardware, operating systems and network architectures.

2. Session layer.

3. Although the Transport layer usually is described by these characteristics it really depends on what protocol is used at this layer. For instance, if TCP is used, the question is absolutely true. If UDP is used, no part of the question is true.

4. Layer two of the OSI model, the Data Link, is where switches and bridges exist. Switches and bridges use layer two (MAC addresses) to make forwarding decisions.

5. Network layer.

6. Process/Application, Host-to-Host, Internet, network access.

7. CRC calculation and verification, and media access are two examples.

8. UDP.

Chapter 2

1. Class A (1-127), Class B (128-191), Class C (192-223), Class D (224-239), Class E (240-247).

2. Subnet masks determine whether a destination is local, which tells the source host whether it can deliver the datagram itself or send it to a gateway for forwarding. The subnet mask of the source host is compared to the destination host's IP address using bitwise ANDing to determine what portion of the address defines the network.

3. Network layer addresses are logical and represent the Layer 3 4-byte IP address of the host. These addresses are assigned either manually or dynamically.

4. 255.255.255.255 signifies a networkwide message sent to all nodes and all networks. Used for broadcast purposes, 0.0.0.0 is an unknown network or host that typically is used to define a default gateway or last resort. 127.0.0.1 is used for internal loopback

testing. The following private addresses are used within a company's network typically to facilitate better IP addressing implementation. These addresses may not be used out on the Internet. Companies implementing these addresses must use NAT to allow for translation to a registered address that may be used out on the Internet: 10.0.0.0–10.255.255.255, 172.16.0.0–172.31.255.255, 192.168.0.0–192.168.255.255.

5. 8 bits.

6. 14 subnetworks and 14 hosts.

7. 255.255.255.224.

8. 126 subnets and 510 hosts.

9. 5 bits, which would allow up to 30 hosts.

10. 10 bits, which would allow 1022 hosts.

11. 182 (128+32+16+4+2+1)

12. 11001001 (128+64+8+1)

The Binary equivalent of 201 is 11001001 be it a decimal or a subnet mask.

Chapter 3

1. IP.

2. ICMP echo (type 8) and reply (type 0).

3. It packages it as datagrams, including the source and destination Network layer IP addresses.

4. An IP header has a minimum of 20 bytes unless options are present. The IP header fields within that 20 bytes are version, header length, type of service, total length, identification, flags, fragment offset, time to live, protocol, checksum, source address and destination address. Other headers include options and data. The question asks which fields are in that header. I assume this is the protocol type field with 0800, but you may want to mention what field it is.

5. It is used by applications to specify a level of routing service it would like a router to use when it forwards datagrams.

6. The identification and fragment offset fields.

7. ICMP type 3 is a destination unreachable. If this message is received it means the requested destination network, host, or port is either too far or not available.

8. A type 3 ICMP message is Destination Unreachable. A type 3 ICMP message with an error code of 4 signifies that a fragmentation is needed, but don't-fragment bit set error has occurred.

9. This means the requested host is unreachable.

10. Type 11; this means the TTL timer has expired (reached a value of 0).

Chapter 4

1. ARP performs logical Network layer-to-Data Link hardware address resolution. ARP resolution is broadcast based.

2. RARP performs Data Link hardware address to logical Network layer address resolution. RARP is used by end devices to retrieve their IP addresses and configuration parameters from a RARP server. Requests and responses are broadcast based.

3. BootP replaced RARP. The main difference between BootP and RARP is that gateways or relay agents cannot forward RARP requests and responses.

4. The main difference between DHCP and BootP is that DHCP does not use a static mapping table. DHCP can support static and dynamic address mappings.

5. Depending on implementation, hosts can use these three mechanisms to remove old or invalid entries from the ARP table: timeout, unicast poll, and Link layer or higher layer device.

6. Proxy ARP allows a device, such as a gateway, to respond to ARP requests on behalf of a remote host.

7. The Opcode field defines the type of ARP or RARP operation being performed. An Opcode value of 1 equals a ARP request, 2 equals an ARP reply, 3 equals a RARP request, and 4 equals a RARP reply.

8. When a host wants to communicate with a remote device it compares the destination host's IP address to the source host's local subnet mask to determine whether the remote host resides on the local segment. If the source host determines the destination resides on the same subnet, it might "shout" (send a local ARP). If not, it must "route" (send a local ARP to resolve the gateway's hardware address) to forward future datagrams.

9. DHCP has seven message types: discover, offer, request, ACK, NAK, decline, and inform.

10. The four DHCP message types that accomplish the initial four-phase configuration process between client and server are discover, offer, request, and ACK.

Chapter 5

1. Directly connected interface, static, default, or dynamic.

2. Manual entry of each route in the route table by an administrator, no route update traffic, ideal for point-to-point WAN links or dial-up networks, can use as backup when primary link fails, impractical to have entire network static, disadvantage of extreme administrative overhead, better to implement on small networks.

3. Broadcast, classful routing (updates do not include the subnet mask), timers control updates, the entire table is always sent regardless of a change, subject to routing loops, best used in small to medium networks, maximum distance defines the diameter of the network, uses hops as its sole metric.

4. You would want to use static routing in small networks or point-to-point links. If you want to entirely eliminate route update traffic, use static routing. You would use dynamic routing if you want your routers to automatically detect and adjust around failed links or routers.

5. Default routing provides a route to be used as a last resort, when no other route to a destination exists.

6. IGP and EGP.

7. IP RIPv1, IP RIP v2, IGRP, EIGRP, and OSPF.

8. IP RIPv1, IP RIP v2, and IGRP.

9. Hops; IP RIP has a maximum hop count of 15. IGRP has a maximum hop count of 255.

10. Count to infinity, holddowns, split horizon, poison reverse.

11. Split horizon prevents routing loops by preventing routing information from being advertised out the same interface on which it was received.

12. Bandwidth, delay, reliability, load, and mtu.

13. OSPF.

Chapter 6

1. RIP is considered to be an IGP and a distance vector routing protocol.

2. RIP has the following characteristics: broadcast based, IGP, works best on small-sized networks, and distance-vector routing protocol.

3. RIP uses shortest distance, measured in hops.

4. Routers broadcast their entire routing table every 30 seconds.

5. 25

6. 15

7. Multicast, authentication, VLSMs (classless routing).

8. Version 2 is backwards compatible to Version 1 and Link State protocols are more proficient.

9. RIPv1 has the following disadvantages: broadcast based, sends out the entire table even when no changes occur, slow convergence due to periodic timers, maximum distance

limitation of 15 hops, prone to routing loops and classful routing protocol (does not support VLSM).

10. RIP uses count to infinity, holddowns, split horizon and poison reverse.

11. RIP employs holddown, invalid and periodic update.

12. OSPF is considered to be an IGP and link state routing protocol.

13. Link capacity, load, MTU, reliability and delay.

14. OSPF has the following advantages over RIP: ability to configure hierarchical routing domains, ability to adapt quickly to internet changes, only sends topology changes in updates when changes occur, supports large networks, supports load balancing, authentication of routing tables exchanges, supports VLSMs and uses multicasting.

15. OSPF has the following features: multicasting, fast convergence, triggered updates, classless routing, ToS or QoS, authentication, equal and unequal cost routes and can implement single or multiple areas.

16. Adjacency (neighbor table), link state (topology table), and forwarding (route table).

17. It is a router's neighbor table. If a router has not formed an adjacency with their neighbor, they cannot exchange routing information.

18. It is a complete map of the internetwork topology.

19. A forwarding database is a local route table that has a table of the "best route" to forward traffic.

20. OSPF uses LSAs to form their link state database and to communicate within an area or out of an area.

21. An OSPF Intra-Area Advertisement are only sent by routers to other routers within a specific area and an Inter-Area Advertisement are sent by ABR routers to other routers in directly connected areas.

22. Down, Init, Exstart, Exchange, Loading, and Full.

23. Internal, Backbone, ABR, ASBR.

24. Type 0.

25. Hello, database description, link state request, link state update and link state acknowledgement.

26. Hello packets establish and maintain adjacencies.

27. An OSPF Database Description packet summarizes database content.

28. IGRP can use a combination of metrics including: bandwidth, internetwork delay time, reliability and load.

29. A maximum hop count of 255 allows for support of larger networks.

30. Update, invalid, holddown, flush timer.

31. EIGRP has the following features: faster convergence through triggered updates, VLSMs, supports multiprotocol, keeps backup paths in route table, supports ToS or QoS, uses cost-based metrics like IGRP and multicast or unicast.

32. EIGRP is considered a balanced hybrid protocol.

33. It has the advantage of allowing a company to run multiple protocols but maintain one routing table, but has the disadvantage of limiting you to Cisco equipment.

34. The best route is consider the successor and the backup is considered a feasible route.

35. Hello/ACKs, updates, queries, replies, and requests.

36. An EGP connects independent ASs together while an IGP connects an independent AS.

37. VLSMs, route aggregation, and CIDR.

38. You would want to implement BGP in the following situations: if you have multiple exit points connecting to a single ISP, if you have multiple paths to different ISPs and would like to dictate traffic, you need intelligent path selection and specific criteria, or your network's infrastructure is used as a transit area for other organizations' traffic.

39. A *full-mesh* topology requires separate logical TCP connections between all BGP routers within the same AS, allowing gateways to quickly determine whether a loop exists and pruning it. A *partial mesh* topology does not require all routers to maintain logical connections with one another.

40. BGP speakers, peers, internal peers and external peers.

41. Route information received, route information to be advertised, their local BGP table.

42. TCP.

43. Open, update, keepalive, notification.

44. The open message initiates a BGP peer relationship between internal or external peers.

45. Notification messages (message type 3) occur when BGP routers encounter an error. These messages cause the TCP session to be torn down.

46. Path attributes.

47. Well-known mandatory, well-known discretionary, optional transitive, optional nontransitive.

48. When multiple paths exist to route traffic outside of this AS, routers within an AS may set the local preference value higher for one path, indicating the preferred route.

49. BGPv4 supports VLSMs, summarization and local preference while BGPv3 does not. In addition, BGPv4 supports both full and partial mesh while v3 supports only full.

Chapter 7

1. Controls end-to-end communication between two processes running on different hosts, provides connection-oriented or connectionless services to upper layers, uses client and server port address to identify processes running within a host, segments data for upper-layer applications.

2. All connection-oriented protocols exhibit these characteristics: session setup, session teardown, acknowledgements, sequencing, flow control, keepalives, reliable/guarantee delivery, slower delivery of data, tons of overhead, error recovery and retransmission of data.

3. Well-known server ports define well-known programs used in the industry that have become the official standard for addressing such programs. They have a range of 0-255.

4. Lesser-known server ports are reserved ports that vendors can implement on an as-needed basis and have a range of 256-1023.

5. Client ports are variable (or ethereal) ports made up on the fly each time a client process begins and opens a new port and have a range of 1024-65536.

6. The client and server ports clearly identify the process communicating on each box. By linking the sending host's address and port to the destination host's address and port, TCP or UDP can manage the communication between these hosts and their processes, and distinguish them from other virtual connections to the same hosts.

7. UDP offers fast, unreliable delivery of messages between applications running on remote hosts. TCP offers slower but guaranteed delivery of data.

8. It is an alert to the sending host to slow down transmission or stop altogether.

9. They have to choose between speed (UDP) and reliability (TCP).

10. TCP utilizes acknowledgements and sequencing to help keep track of data and guarantee delivery.

Chapter 8

1. During TCP operation, TCP uses connection setup and teardown, multiplexing, data transfer, flow control, reliability, and precedence and security to control the communications between remote host process.

2. TCP must establish a logical circuit or session between communicating ports before upper-layer applications can exchange meaningful data.

3. Multiplexing enables TCP to establish and maintain multiple communication paths between two hosts simultaneously.

4. TCP receives datastreams (messages) from upper-layer applications and organizes them into segments to be passed down to the Network layer to become a datagram.

5. Windowing controls the inbound flow of data.

6. TCP provides reliable delivery of packets through sequencing and acknowledgements.

7. Connection-oriented protocols have six basic characteristics: session setup, sequencing, acknowledgements, keepalives, session teardown, and flow control.

8. Socket pairing is the combination of the source and destination hosts' Network layer IP addresses and Transport layer port addresses.

9. Retransmission occurs after a logical circuit (TCP connection) is established between remote host processes.

10. The TCP header contains source port, destination port, acknowledgement number, data offset, reserved, control flags, window, checksum, urgent point and TCP options fields.

Chapter 9

1. RFC 768 defines UDP.

2. UDP provides connectionless, unreliable, fast delivery of data for applications running on remote hosts.

3. Protocol type 17 identifies UDP in the IP header.

4. UDP does not utilize sequencing and acknowledgements to guarantee delivery of data. It relies on other protocols to perform this function. It simply identifies the source and destination ports, sends the data, and hopes it arrives at the destination.

5. During UDP operation of transferring data, UDP assumes that there is a stable and reliable network infrastructure supporting the transmission of data. It relies on other protocols to detect and correct errors.

6. UDP has no management responsibilities for maintaining a connection. UDP does not establish a connection between hosts; therefore, it does not need to maintain a connection.

7. UDP offers speedier delivery of packets and less overhead than TCP.

8. UDP uses CRC (Cyclic Redundancy Check), which checks for damaged frames in the UDP header, upper-layer data and pseudo IP header.

9. The checksum validates the UDP header, upper-layer data, and pseudo IP header.

10. The pseudo IP header contains the source and destination Network layer addresses, Transport layer protocol type code, and UDP length value.

Chapter 10

1. Application, Presentation, and Session.

2. To provide access to resources and services on remote hosts, file transfer (FTP or TFTP), file and print operations, e-mail.

3. FTP and TFTP.

4. Providing a common data format across different platforms.

5. Coordinates dialogs between two applications.

6. NFS (application layer), XDR (presentation), and RPC (session).

Chapter 11

1. Enables a user running a client terminal session to access a remote host (or Telnet server) across TCP/IP Internets.

2. When the user starts the Telnet session, an application on the user's machine becomes the client. The client establishes a TCP connection with a Telnet server (remote host) using the standard TCP three-way handshake as described in Chapter 8, "Transmission Control Protocol (TCP)." The client communicates over the TCP connection from the user's keyboard and display as if connected directly to the remote host's terminal. The server utilizes a pseudo terminal device. The pseudo terminal device describes the operating system entry point that enables a program like Telnet to transfer data to another operating system as if coming from the same keyboard.

3. Used for negotiating parameters between clients and servers.

4. Binary transmission, echo, suppress go ahead, status, timing mark, terminal type, end of record, window size, terminal speed, remote flow control, line mode, environment variables.

5. Network Virtual Terminal (NVT)—Provides a standard interface to remote systems, allows clients and servers to negotiate various options and symmetric view of terminals and processes.

6. The NVT provides transparency and support for a minimum level of options between remote clients and servers being used by either side. By implementing a virtual terminal as a front end, this hides the differences between the communicating devices and provides a common set of commands and characteristics.

7. Characters and display device.

8. Either side can request the use of an optional feature. If the other side does not support the feature or is prohibited from allowing this feature to be used, it rejects the request. Both sides agree upon and use the supported features, and keep all other options at the minimum NVT standard.

9. Interpret As Command.

10. WILL—Sender wants to enable the option, DO—Sender wants the receiver to enable the option, WONT—Sender wants to disable the option, DONT—Senders wants the receiver to disable the option.

11. WILL/DO, WILL/DON'T, DO/WILL, DO/WONT, WONT/DONT, and DON'T/WONT.

Chapter 12

1. FTP allows a remote or local client and server to efficiently transfer files or data using TCP's reliable transport: promote sharing of files (computer programs or data), encourage indirect or implicit use of remote computers, shield a user from variations in file storage systems among hosts, and transfer data reliably and efficiently.

2. User Interface—Provides a user interface and drives the client protocol interpreter.

    Client PI—The client protocol interpreter. Issues commands to the remote server protocol interpreter and drives the client data transfer process.

    Server PI—The server protocol interpreter. Responds to commands from the Client PI and drives the server data transfer process.

    Client DTP—Client data transfer process. Communicates with server data process and local file system.

    Server DTP—Server data transfer process. Communicates with client DTP and the remote file system.

3. Protocol interpreter deals with the commands and replies.

4. The server PI listens on well-known port number 21 for control connection requests and waits for a client communication. The client PI initiates the connection by sending a TCP SYN request in the form of a control message addressed to the destination TCP on well-known port 21.

5. Ports 20 (data) and 21 (control).

6. Data representation—Identifies the type of data being sent.

    Data structure—Specifies the format of the data being transferred.

    Transmission mode—Specifies how the data transmits across the connection.

7. ASCII (default), EBCDIC, Image file type (also called *binary*), Local file type.

8. FTP can use three types of data structure: File (default), Record, Page.

9. Stream (default), Block, Compressed.

10. Nonprint, Telnet format command, Fortran carriage control.

11. Stream mode as the following characteristics: default mode, data transmitted in a stream of bytes, and allows record structures.

12. The server and client protocol interpreters communicate commands and replies across the control connection as NVT ASCII (Telnet) strings. FTP commands come in the following three categories: access control, transfer parameter and service.

13. FTP replies appear as three-digit numbers with an optional message in the form of text following the number string. The FTP reply format enables both the interactive user and the software to read the replies, providing information explaining the response. FTP replies guarantee synchronization of requests and actions during file transfer and that the user always knows the state of the server.

14. Transfer files through the Internet without having a specific user account through anonymous FTP. This means you do not have to be an official user of a particular system to gain access to files that system offers.

Chapter 13

1. Simple Mail Transfer Protocol (SMTP) provides the exchange of electronic mail (e-mail) between a sender (client) and receiver (server).

2. Users have immediate interaction with the e-mail system through the UA. Through the UA the user composes, submits, and receives e-mail messages.

3. SMTP facilitates the delivery of mail messages (known as a Message Transfer Agent or MTA) between remote client and server mail applications (known as User Agents).

4. SMTP has the following limitations: the message must contain only ASCII characters, the maximum line length must not exceed 1000 characters, and the message must not exceed a predefined maximum size.

5. SMTP has the following rules: a command code and an argument make up each SMTP command, four alphabetic characters in either upper- or lowercase comprise the command code, one or more space characters separate this code from the argument, path arguments are case sensitive, CRLF concludes argument field and square brackets enclose optional arguments.

6. SMTP clients and servers use the three digits to communicate receipt of information and notify the other side when it has encountered an error.

7. SMTP replies include a three-digit number code meant for the computer and text for the user. The user can then use this information to determine the status of his or her request.

8. MIME extensions provide for transmissions of data previously unsupported in Internet mail by encoding the message into readable ASCII to create a standard e-mail message.

Chapter 14

1. The namespace has the following problems: It makes expansion difficult, work overload complicates the expansion problem, and it is both inefficient and costly.

2. The primary name server loads information from the disk files. The secondary server gets information from the primary.

3. Because computers use numbers (for example, IP addresses and MAC addresses) for addressing, not a name, a method, such as DNS, needs to exist for name resolution.

4. It uses a hierarchical system starting with top-level domain names, then breaking it up into lower-level domains that are more specific.

5. Caching means to store information in RAM. Name servers store all of the information requests (mappings) by filing them away (saving to disk) or caching them (saving to RAM). This way, it keeps up on the most recently requested data and has the newly requested name resolutions. Caching also lowers the cost of resolving nonlocal names because of its speed.

6. If the server still cannot find the answer after checking its cache, it becomes a client (acting as a proxy for the source host) and uses a message format to ask multiple questions to the authoritative server in one message.

7. Each message contains three things:

    - A domain name to be resolved

    - The class, or protocol family the domain name uses

    - The type of the domain name

8. NetBEUI is strictly a Layer 2 protocol implementation designed to carry NetBIOS datagrams over a flat-bridged network. NetBIOS is a datagram and naming service.

9. Modifications to NetBIOS allow it function at layer three by utilizing TCP/IP.

10. 37,138 and 139

11. NetBIOS has the following node types:

    - **B-node** (broadcast node type)—Tries broadcast, then LMHosts file.

    - **P-node** (point-to-point node type)—Tries NBNS server only.

    - **M-node** (mixed node type)—Client tries b-node, p-node, then LMHosts file.

    - **H-node** (hybrid node type)—Client tries p-node, b-node, then LMHosts file.

12. Intercept local resolution broadcast requests and relay them as directed datagrams to a remote WINS server for name resolution.

Chapter 15

1. You need to use the HTTP protocol to find a Web page that you want. You can visibly see HTTP in the first part of the URL.

2. HTTP makes communication between your workstation's browser and a Web server happen.

3. Your browser works as an application program and opens Web pages.

4. HTTP works at the application level focusing on providing a communication link and message forward. It does not offer reliability or perform retransmission.

5. HTTP has the following qualities: bi-directional transfer, capability negotiation, support for intermediaries, supports caching, does not keep a history of HTTP sessions or your HTTP requests, and works at application level to provide a communication link and message forward.

6. HTTP supports caching. This means that to save time, your browser caches a copy of each Web page it retrieves for you. If you want this page again, HTTP has the browser ask the server whether the contents of the present page differ from the cached copy.

7. Works as an intermediary HTTP host functioning as either an HTTP client or server so the UA and the Origin server can exchange information. Proxy agents pass requests from clients to servers. Servers also respond to the request itself when the information you want is local.

8. Any machine along the path between the browser and the server can be a proxy server.

9. HTTP has the following general message format: a generic start line, called a *request line* for request messages and a *stats line* for reply messages, a general header, a message header, one empty line and the message body.

10. The message body is for you to read.

11. The header messages are for the browser to read.

12. Error messages give you an indication as to what type of error was encountered and what went wrong with the delivery.

Chapter 16

1. FTP runs on top of TCP making it connection oriented; TFTP runs on top of UDP making it connectionless.

2. It is a simple and fast file transfer protocol with little overhead.

3. Fast, unreliable connectionless file transfer.

4. The sending side (TFTP client) opens a variable client UDP port (referred to as a TFTP or transfer ID), requests a file, and waits for the acknowledgement of each block before

sending another block. In turn, the receiving side acknowledges each block when it receives the data.

5. HTTP uses the following five packets: read request, write request, data, acknowledgement, and error. Read request and write request files begin a request and determine what file needs to be transferred. Data packets transfer the requested data. The *ACK* packet acknowledges the receipt of each block (data packet) received during data transfer. The error packet acknowledges any of the other packet types and signifies that an error has occurred.

6. The end of a file transfer.

7. TFTP utilizes the lock-step acknowledgement method, which means that each data packet has to be acknowledged before transmission of another. Remember TFTP transmits data in blocks one at a time with the first data block numbered one.

8. The following three things trigger an error packet: the host cannot satisfy a request, the host receives a delayed or duplicated packet, and when the host loses access to a resource.

9. If the client makes a read request, the server begins the transfer. If the client makes a write request, the client begins the transmission.

10. The TFTP client initiates the connection by requesting to read or write a file from or to the server. The client does this by opening a variable port (TFTP TID) to the receiver's well-known TFTP server port 69. The client specifies the identification of the file name and data type within the initial request. Once the client sends the initial request, the TFTP server reassigns itself a new UDP port to use as its TID for the duration of this data transmission and the transfer begins.

11. The blocksize option allows for larger datagrams to be exchanged. A larger blocksize increase the file transfer performance between remote hosts.

12. Servers that support option negotiation have an option acknowledgement (OACK) packet to notify the client if it supports this option. When a server accepts the option, it includes it in the OACK packet. If it does not accept the option it simply ignores it, leaving it out of the OACK frame. Clients implement only what servers allow. The client might request multiple options during the negotiation process by simply listing them within the read or write packet. The client appends the option request to the standard read or write request used to initialize the session between the client and server.

13. The OACK packet is an option acknowledgment of a negotiated option.

Chapter 17

1. SGMP.

2. Agents, managers, and proxies.

3. SNMP agents run SNMP responder and notification generation software.

4. SNMP proxies provide message forwarding between agents and managers. Proxies also act as an intermediary between agent hosts using different versions of SNMP, which allow compatibility between the hosts.

5. As hosts, SNMP managers run management control software used to remotely control and monitor SNMP agents. These hosts provide a central management point and user interface using SNMP to deliver commands to agents. Managers are known as command generators and notification receivers.

6. A trap PDU is an unsolicited message sent by an Agent to an SNMP manager because of a triggered event such as authentication failure.

Chapter 18

1. NFS, RPC, and XDR.

2. NFS provides access to information through distributed file systems over any network architecture.

3. XDR translates and presents data so that two different operating systems can communicate with each other. XDR provides platform independence.

4. RPC provides a protocol and independent interface capable of providing a bidirectional communication link between remote communicating processes. RPC resides at a Session layer, thus it has the responsibility of setting up a session between two host processes, and then maintaining and tracking the session.

5. Sun Microsystems.

INDEX

Symbols

* (asterisk) FTP server commands, 279

Numbers

1 command (RIP), 142

1 hello packets, 174

1 ID value (LSAs), 161

1 link state type (LSAs), 157-158

1—Origin type code (well-known mandatory attribute), 195

2—AS_path type code (well-known mandatory attribute), 195

2-byte checksum or Urgent Pointer, 217

2 command (RIP), 143

2 database description packets, 174

2 ID value (LSAs), 161

2 link state type (LSAs), 157-158

3-byte signal circles (Token-Ring), 24

3 command (RIP), 143

3 ID value (LSAs), 161

3 link state request packets, 174

3 link state type (LSAs), 157-159

3—Next_Hop type code (well-known mandatory attribute), 196

4 command (RIP), 143

4 ID value (LSAs), 161

4 link state type (LSAs), 157-159

4 link state update packets, 174

4—Multi-Exit-Disc type code (optional nontransitive attribute), 196-197

5 command (RIP), 143

5 ID value (LSAs), 161

5 link state acknowledgement packets, 174

5 link state type (LSAs), 157-160

5—Local Pref type code (well-known discretionary attribute), 196-198

6—Atomic_Aggregate type code (well-known discretionary attribute), 197

6-bit control flags, 216-217

7—Aggregator type code (optional transitive attribute), 197

7 link state type (LSAs), 157-160

8 total bits (IP headers), 64

9 command (RIP), 143

9 (request) packet, 150

10 command (RIP), 143

10 (response) packet, 150

10Base2 (Slow Ethernet specification), 21

10Base5 (Slow Ethernet specification), 21

10BaseT (Slow Ethernet specification), 21

11 (acknowledgement) packet, 150

11 command (RIP), 143

100BaseFX standard, 22

100BaseT4 standard, 22

100BaseTX standard, 22

100BaseX standards, Fast Ethernet, 22

A

A (RR type), 310

AA (authoritative answer) flag, 307

ABOR command, 279

ABRs

    LSAs, 3 and 4 link state types, 159

    routers, 167

Abstract Syntax Notation 1 (ASN.1), 346

Accept-Charset request headers, 328

Accept-Encoding request headers, 328

Accept-Language request headers, 328

accessing files by NFS clients, 358

ACCT [account-info] command, 278

ACK (acknowledgement)
  control flag, 216, 224-229
  11 packet, 150
  hosts, 233
  implied, 214
  messages, 112
  numbers, 214-215
  packets, 338
  values, 212-214
address classes (IP addressing), 35-40
address family identifier field, RIPv1 headers, 143
Address Mask Reply Type 18, 86
Address Mask Request Type 17, 86
address resolution, 89
Address Resolution Protocol. *See* ARP
addresses
  agent address (trap PDU field), 351
  broadcast, host bits, 52
  Class C, route summarization, 53-55
  client hardware, 108, 121-122
  Data Link layer, 13
  destination, IP headers, 73
  gateway IPs, 108, 121
  hardware, 91, 98, 103
  IP, 108, 121, 144, 305
  logical, 12
  low-level, 299
  node, 35
  protocols, 98-103
  reserved, 39
  sender's hardware, 99, 104
  server IPs, 108, 121
  subnet masks, bitwise ANDing, 40-43
  subnetting, 44-55
  target hardware, 99, 104

adjacency databases, 155, 164
advertisements
  external, 159-160
  inter-area, 158-159
  intra-area, 157-158
  LSAs (link state advertisements), 156-160
  RIP (Routing Information Protocol), 144
advertising router field, 161, 180
agents
  address (trap PDU field), 351
  MTAs (message transfer agents), 291
  proxy, 324
  SNMP (Simple Network Management Protocol), 347
  UAs (user agents), 287-290
aggregation, 52-53
algorithms
  Bellman-Ford, 138
  CRC, 13
  cyclical redundancy check (CRC), 9
  DUAL (Diffusing Update Algorithm), 184
  FCS, 13
  frame check sequence (FCS), 9
  LSA (Link State Algorithm), 152
  timers, 233-234
allocating configuration information (DHCP), 111
Allow entity headers, 329
ALLO [bytes] command, 279
Aloha Net, 14
American National Standards Institute (ANSI). 25
American Registry for Internet Numbers (ARIN), 35

American Standard Code for Information Interchange (ASCII), 260, 275
ANCOUNT domain server message format, 309
ANSI (American National Standards Institute), 25
ANSI X3T9.5 specification, FDDI (Fiber Distributed Data Interface), 25
answer headers, domain server message format, 309
APIs (Application Programming Interfaces), 314
APPE [pathname] command, 279
Application layer (OSI Reference model), 9-10, 251-253
Application Programming Interfaces (APIs), 314
applications
  Data Link architecture, 14
  UDP (User Datagram Protocol), 243
architectures, Data Link, 14-25, 167
ARCOUNT domain server message format, 309
Area 0, 171-173
area ID field, 174
areas
  backbone (Area 0), 170
  multiple area implementation, 169-170
  NSSAs (not so stubby areas), 159
  standard (Area 0), 170-171
  stub, 171-172
  types of, 170
  virtual links, 172-173
ARIN (American Registry for Internet Numbers), 35
ARP (Address Resolution Protocol), 40, 89

broadcast based, 92

cache mechanisms, 94

hardware addresses, 91

headers, 96

hosts, 92-94

Network layer, 89

operation, 91-94

Proxy ARP, 95-96

and RARP (Reverse Address Resolution Protocol), comparing, 101-102

AS (autonomous systems), 138, 169-170

ASBRs, 159-160, 167

ASCII (American Standard Code for Information Interchange), 260, 275

ASN.1 (Abstract Syntax Notation 1), 346

asterisk (*), FTP server commands, 279

ATM (Asynchronous Transfer Mode) protocol, 30

attributes, path, 191, 194-198

authentication field, 175

authoritative name servers, 304

authority, delegation of, 301-304

Authorization request headers, 328

auto file systems (autofs), 359

autocommands, 359

autofs (auto file system), 359

automatic allocation of configuration information (DHCP), 111

automounter, NFS (Network File System) servers, 359

autonomous systems (AS), 138, 169-170

B

backbone areas (Area 0), 170

backbone routers, 167

backup designated router field, 178

bad request error messages, 332-333

balanced hybrid protocols, 184

balanced signaling, 15

balancing loads, 155, 184

Bandwidth metric, 181

Bellman-Ford algorithm, 138

best paths, 129

BGP (Border Gateway Protocol), 137, 187

    BGPv3 and BGPv4, comparing, 198

    datagrams, 191

    external peer routers, 189

    full-mesh topology, 189

    headers, 191-194

    identifier field, 192

    IGPs (Interior Gateway Protocols) and EGPs (Exterior Gateway Protocols), comparing, 188-189

    internal peer routers, 189

    neighbor routers, 189

    operation, 190-191

    partial-mesh topology, 189

    path attributes, 191, 194-198

    peer routers, 189

    routers, 189-190

    speaker routers, 189

BGPv3 and BGPv4, comparing, 198

Bhushan, Abhay, 270

bidirectional transfers, 322

binary numbering system, 33

binary numbers, converting to decimal numbers, 33-34

bits, 13

    bit 3, IP headers, 65

    bit 4, IP headers, 65

    bit 5, IP headers, 65

    bit 6, IP headers, 66-67

    bit 7, IP headers, 66-67

    bits 0–2 (precedence bits), IP headers, 64-65

    determining number of, 45-46

    E (options field), 177

    hosts in broadcast addresses, 52

    parameter field, 308-309

    repeating, 23

    T (options field), 177

    ToS bits (8 total bits), IP headers, 64

bitwise ANDing, 40-43

block transmission mode, 278

boot file names, 109, 122

BOOTP (Bootstrap Protocol), 89, 104-109

Border Gateway Protocol. *See* BGP

breaking up networks, 44

broadcast addresses, host bits, 52

broadcast-based LAN networks, 168

broadcasts

    ARP (Address Resolution Protocol), 92

    NBMA (nonbroadcast multi-access) networks, 168-169

    RARP (Reverse Address Resoution Protocol), 100

browsers (Web), HTTP (Hypertext Transfer Protocol), 323

C

cache mechanisms, ARP (Address Resolution Protocol), 94

cache-control field, 327

caching

    HTTP (Hypertext Transfer Protocol), 322

    IP addresses, resolving, 305

calculations

host ranges, 48-51

subnet ranges, 47

call messages, RPC (Remote Procedure Calls), 361-365

capability negotiations, 322

carriage control text, 260

carriage returns, FTP (File Transfer Protocol) commands, 280

Carrier Sense Multiple Access with Collision Detection (CSMA/CD), 16

catchall messages, 85

CD command, 359

CDUP command, 278

Cerf, Vinton, TCP (Transmission Control Protocol), 211

chains, 323-324

channel access methods, 16-17, 24-25

character mode, 258

checksum

CRC (Cyclic Redundancy Check), 246

field, 174

ICMP (Internet Control Message Protocol) header or message formats, 76

IP headers, 72-73

LS checksum field, 162

2 bytes, 217

UDP (User Datagram Protocol), 246-247

choke packets, 236

chunking messages, 327

CIDR (class interdomain routing), 52-55

circuit-switched connections, 26-28

circuits

demand, 148-150

logical, 219

Cisco

EIGRP (Enhanced Interior Gateway Routing Protocol), 133

Snapshot routing, 149

Class A (Slash 8) addresses, 35-40

Class B (Slash 16) addresses, 35-40

Class B networks

host range, calculating, 50-51

subnets, 44, 49

Class C addresses, 53-55

Class C (Slash 24) addresses, 35-40

Class D addresses, 36, 39

Class E addresses, 36, 39

class interdomain routing (CIDR), 52-55

class routing, 132

classes, address (IP addressing), 35-40

classful routing, 132, 147

clients

DHCP (Dynamic Host Configuration Protocol), 112-119

DTP (data transfer process), 271

dumb terminals, 257

FTP, connections, 272

hardware addresses, 108, 122

IP addresses, 108, 121

NFS (Network File System), 357-358

PI (protocol interpreter), 270-271

proxy agents, 324

redirectors, 251

SMTP (Simple Mail Transfer Protocol), 287

Telnet, 257-258

trees, 357

CMIP (Common Management Information Protocol), 345

CNAME (RR type), 310

code

ASCII (American Standard Code for Information Interchange), 260

error, response messages, 330

ICMP (Internet Control Message Protocol) header or message formats, 75-76

Op (operation code), 107

Op (operation code 1 byte), 119

Opcode (operation code), 99, 103, 306

status, response messages, 330-332

three-digit number code, SMTP e-mail replies, 293-294

three-digit numeric code (FTP), 281

code values, 339

collisions, 17

COM domain, 302

commands

1 (RIP), 142

2 (RIP), 143

3 (RIP), 143

4 (RIP), 143

5 (RIP), 143

9 (RIP), 143

10 (RIP), 143

11 (RIP), 143

ABOR, 279

ACCT [account-info], 278

ALLO [bytes], 279

APPE [pathname], 279

autocommands, 359

cd, 359

CDUP, 278

command field, RIPv1 headers, 142-143

command messages, RIP (Routing Information Protocol), 142

CWD [pathname], 278

DATA, 293

DELE [pathname], 280

EXPN, 293

FTP (File Transfer Protocol), 278-280

HELO, 293

HELP, 293

HELP [string], 280

HFTP, 278-279

LIST [pathname], 280

MAIL FROM, 293

MKD [pathname], 280

MODE [mode], 279

mount, 356

NLST [pathname], 280

NOOP, 280, 293

PASS [password], 278

PASV, 279

PORT [host-port], 279

PWD, 280

QUIT, 279, 293

RCPT TO, 293

REIN, 279

REST [marker], 280

RETR [pathname], 280

RMD [pathname], 280

RNFR [pathname], 280

RNTO [pathname], 280

RSET, 293

SAML FROM, 293

SEND FROM, 293

SITE [string], 280

SMNT [pathname], 279

SMTP (Simple Mail Transfer Protocol), 292-293

SOML FROM, 293

STAT [pathname], 280

STOR [filename], 280

STOU, 280

STRU [structure], 279

SYST, 280

TURN, 293

TYPE [type], 279

USER [username], 279

VRFY, 293

comments, RFCs (Request for Comments), 30-31

Common Management Information Protocol (CMIP), 345

communication chains, HTTP (Hypertext Transfer Protocol), 323

community, SNMP, 348-349

companies, operating systems developed, 3

comparing

    ARP (Address Resolution Protocol) and RARP (Reverse Address Resolution Protocol), 101-102

    BGPv3 and BGPv4, 198

    connection-oriented and connectionless protocols, 206-207

    Ethernet frame types, 18

    Fast and Slow Ethernet, 21

    IGPs (Interior Gateway Protocols) and EGPs (Exterior Gateway Protocols), 188-189

    Internet and intranets, 31

    NetBIOS and NetBEUI, 314

    OSPF (Open Shortest Path First) and Distance-vector routing protocols, 153

    RIPv1 and RIPv2, 151-152

    UDP (User Datagram Protocol) and TCP (Transmission Control Protocol), 244

compatibility, RIPv1 and RIPv2, 152

complexity of networking, reducing, 7

components, HTTP (Hypertext Transfer Protocol), 322-323

compressed transmission mode, 278

CON domain, 302

conceptual frameworks, OSI Reference Model, 4

configuration information (DHCP), allocating, 111

congestion, connection-oriented protocols, 234

Connect method tokens, 326

connection field, 327

connection-oriented protocols, 223

    and connectionless protocols, comparing, 206-207

    flow control, 234-237

    keepalives, 234

    sequences, 230-234

    session setups, 223-227

    session teardowns, 227-230

    socket pairing, 224-227

    TCP (Transmission Control Protocol), 204-206

connectionless protocols, TCP (Transmission Control Protocol), 206

connections, 168, 219, 272

Content-Base entity headers, 329

Content-Encoding entity headers, 329

Content-Language entity headers, 329

Content-Length entity headers, 329

Content-Location entity headers, 329

Content-MD5 entity headers, 330

Content-Range entity headers, 330

Content-Type entity headers, 330

control codes, NVT (Network Virtual Terminal), 260

control flags, 216-217, 224-230

controlling flow, 221

controls, route update traffic, 148

converting binary numbers to decimal numbers, 33-34

core-distribution-access model, static routes, 126

count to infinity (maximum hop count), 130-131

CRC (Cyclic Redundancy Check), 9, 13, 246

CSMA/CD (Carrier Sense Multiple Access with Collision Detection), 16

CWD [pathname] command, 278

Cyclic Redundancy Check (CRC), 9, 13, 246

D

DARPA (Department of Defense Advanced Research Projects Agency), 5

data
  storing, 360
  transferring, 220-221

DATA command, 293

data field, 194

Data Link architecture, 167
  applications, 14
  Ethernet, 14-22
  FDDI (Fiber Distributed Data Interface), 25
  standards, 14
  Token-Ring, 22-24

Data Link layer (OSI Reference Model), 12-13

data offset, 215

data packets, 338

data representation FTP (File Transfer Protocol), 274-275

data structures, FTP (File Transfer Protocol), 274-277

data transfer process (DTP), clients or servers, 271

data types, 275-276

database description packet type, 174

Database Description packets, 178-179

databases, 155, 164

datagrams
  BGP (Border Gateway Protocol), 191
  Distance-vector routing protocols, 146
  IP headers, 62-73
  sending by Host A, 43
  ToS (Type of Service), 222
  user, routing purpose, 125

date field, 327

DDR (dial-on-demand routing), 28

dead interval field, 177-178

decimal numbering system, 33

decimal numbers, binary numbers, converting to, 33-34

decline messages, 112

dedicated (leased) lines, 26-27

dedicated leased-line connections (point-to-point connections), 168

default gateways, 127

default routes, 127

definitions
  graphic, 323
  hyper, 321
  routing, 40
  shouting, 40

Delay Time metric, 181

delays, propagation, 17

delegation of authority, DNS (Domain Naming System), 301-304

DELETE method tokens, 326

deleting headers or trailers, 9

DELE [pathname] command, 280

demand circuits, 148-150

Department of Defense Advanced Research Projects Agency (DARPA), 5

Department of Defense. See DoD (Department of Defense) Model

designated router field, 178

destination addresses, IP headers, 73

destination ports, 213, 245

Destination Unreachable Type 3, 78-82

DHCP (Dynamic Host Configuration Protocol), 89, 110-122

dial-on-demand routing (DDR), 28

Diffusing Update Algorithm (DUAL), 184

directly connected interfaces, 126

discover messages, 112

Distance-vector routing protocols
  datagrams, 146
  IGRP (Interior Gateway Routing Protocol), 129-131, 181-184
  OSPF (Open Shortest Path First), comparing, 153

DIX (Ethernet_II) (Ethernet frame type), 17

DLC (Data Link Control) headers, Ethernet value, 63

DNS (Domain Name System), 252, 301-312

DoD (Department of Defense) Model
  layers, 5-6

TCP/IP, 3

   Host-to-Host layer, 203, 211, 241

   Process/Application layer, 249

   Telnet, 258

   TCP (Transmission Control Protocol), 211

Domain Name System (DNS), 252, 301-312

domain servers, message formats, 306-310

domains, 348, 252, 302-303

DTP (data transfer process), clients or servers, 271

DUAL (Diffusing Update Algorithm), 184

dumb terminals, 257

duplexes, full-duplex or half-duplex communication modes, 10

dynamic allocation of configuration information, 111

Dynamic Host Configuration Protocol (DHCP), 89, 110-122

dynamic NATs (network address translations), 57-58

dynamic routes, 128

E

E bit (OSPF options field), 177

e-mail, 252, 287-294

early token release, 25

EBCDIC file types, FTP (File Transfer Protocol), 276

echo replies, 74

Echo Reply Type 0, 77-78

Echo Request Type 8, 77-78

echo requests, 74

EDU domain, 302

EGP (Exterior Gateway Protocols), 128, 137, 188-189

EIGRP (Enhanced Interior Gateway Routing Protocol), 128, 133, 184-187

empty line (CRLF), 330

encapsulation protocols, WAN (Wide Area Network) technologies, 29-30

Enhanced Interior Gateway Routing Protocol (EIGRP), 128, 133, 184-187

enterprise (trap PDU field), 351

entity headers, 329-330

error codes

   field, 194

   response messages, 330

   values, 339

error index (PDU field), 350

error messages, 79-82, 332-333

error packets, 339

error status (PDU field), 350

error subcode field, 194

ETag entity headers, 330

Ethernet

   AlohaNet, 14

   channel access methods, 16-17

   collisions, 17

   Data Link architecture, 14-22

   Fast and Slow Ethernet, comparing, 21

   Fast Ethernet, 21-22

   Frame Type Quick Reference, 21

   frames, 17-21

   Gigabit Ethernet, 22

   hardware failure, 17

   IEEE 802.3 specification, 14-16

   name mapping, 17

   propagation delay, 17

   Slow Ethernet, 21

SNAP, IEEE's 802.3 SNAP frame, 20

values, DLC (Data Link Control) headers, 63

versions, 14-15

Ethernet_802.2, IEEE's 802.3 frames, 20

Ethernet_802.3 (Novell proprietary) (Ethernet frame type), 17

Ethernet_802.3 frames, 20

Ethernet_II (DIX) (Ethernet frame type), 17

Ethernet_II frames, 19

Exchange state (routers), 165-166

Expires entity headers, 330

EXPN command, 293

Exstart state (routers), 164-165

extensions, TFTP (Trivial File Transfer Protocol), 342

Exterior Gateway Protocols (EGP), 128, 137, 188-189

external advertisements, 159-160

eXternal Data Representation (XDR) protocol, 10, 353, 359-360

external peer routers, 189

F

failures, hardware, 17

Fast Ethernet, 21-22

FCS (frame check sequence) algorithm, 9, 13

FDDI (Fiber Distributed Data Interface), 25

feasible successor routes, 185-186

fields

   ACK packets, 338

   address family identifier, RIPv1 headers, 143

   advertising router, 161, 180

   agent address (trap PDU), 351

   area ID, 174

authentication, 175

backup designated router, 178

BGP (Border Gateway Protocols), 191-194

BGP identifier, 192

cache-control, 327

checksum, 174

command, RIPv1 headers, 142-143

connection, 327

data, 194

data packets, 338

Database Description packets, 178-179

date, 327

dead interval, 177-178

designated router, 178

enterprise (trap PDU), 351

error code, 194

error index (PDU), 350

error packets, 339

error status (PDU), 350

error subcode, 194

generic trap ID (trap PDU), 351

headers, SMTP (Simple Mail Transfer Protocol), 291

hello interval, 177

Hello packets, 175-178

hold time, 192

IP address, RIPv1 headers, 144

length, 162, 191, 245

Link State Request packets, 161, 179-180

Link State Update packets, 180

LS age, 161

LS checksum, 162

LS sequence number, 162

LS type, 161

LSA (link state advertisement) header, 179

marker, 191

metric, RIPv1 headers, 144

my autonomous system, 192

neighbor, 178

network layer reachability information, 193

network mask, 176

Notification messages, 193-194

number of advertisements, 180

OACK packet, 343

object ID and value, 350-351

open messages, 191-192

Open Messages, 192

optional parameters, 192

options, 161, 177-179

OSPF (Open Shortest Path First), 173-175

packet length, 174

packet type, 173-174

parameter, bits, 308-309

path attributes, 193

PDUs (Protocol Data Units), 350-351

pragma, 327

request ID (PDU), 350

router ID, 174

router priority, 177

RRQ packets, 337-338

sequence number, 179

specific trap ID (trap PDU), 351

time stamp (trap PDU), 351

total length, IP headers, 67

total path attribute length, 193

trailer, 327

transfer-encoding, 327-328

type, 191

unfeasible routes length, 193

unused, RIPv1 headers, 143

Update messages, 192-193

upgrade, 328

version, 143, 192

version number, 174

via, 328

warning, 328

withdrawn routes, 193

WRQ packets, 337-338

File Transfer Protocol (FTP), 243, 253, 269-280, 335

    TFTP (Trivial File Transfer Protocol), 243, 253, 335-343

files

    accessing by NFS clients, 358

    boot file names, 109, 122

    EBCDIC file types, 276

    FTP structure, 277

    image file types, 276

    local file types, 276

    requests, redirectors, 5

    RRQ (request to read), 336

    transfer protocols, 335

    transferring, 253

    WRQ (request to write), 336

filesystems, mount command, 356

filtering, ICMP message errors, 82

FIN (finish) control flag, 217, 227-229

flags

    AA (authoritative answer), 307

    ACK (acknowledgement) control, 216, 224-229

    domain server message format, 307

    FIN (finish) control, 217, 227-229

    IP headers, 67-68

    PSH (push) control, 216

RA (recursion available), 307

RD (recursion desired), 307

RST (reset) control, 217

6 bits, control, 216-217

SYN (synchronization) control, 217, 224-230

TC (truncation), 307

2 bytes, DHCP (Dynamic Host Configuration Protocol) protocol headers, 121

URG (urgent) control, 216

Zero, 307

flow control, 206, 221, 234-237

Flush timers, 183

Ford-Fulkerson (Bellman-Ford algorithm), 138

formats

control, FTP data types, 276

Fortran carriage control, 276

ICMP (Internet Control Message Protocol) headers, 75-76

messages, 306-310, 325-330

nonprint (default) format control, 276

response messages, 330

SMTP (Simple Mail Transfer Protocol), 291-292

SNMP messages, 348-351

Telnet format control, 276

Fortran carriage control, 276

forwarding databases (OSPF), 155

fragment offset, IP headers, 68-71

fragmentation, ICMP message errors, 80-81

frame check sequence (FCS) algorithm, 9

Frame Relay protocol, 29

Frame Type Quick Reference, 21

frames

Ethernet, 17-21

IEEE's 802.3, 20

Token-Ring, 24

frameworks, conceptual, 4

framing packets, 12

From request headers, 329

FTP (File Transfer Protocol), 243, 253, 269-280, 335

TFTP (Trivial File Transfer Protocol), 243, 253, 335-343

Full state (routers), 166

full-duplex communication mode, 10

full-mesh topology, 189

functions

method tokens, 326

OSI Reference Model layers, 3, 6

G

gateways, 41, 139-140

checksum, 76

codes, 75-76, 84-86

default, 127

EGP (Exterior Gateway Protocols), 128

EIGRP (Enhanced Interior Gateway Routing Protocol), 133

HTTP (Hypertext Transfer Protocol), 323

ICMP (Internet Control Message Protocol), 73-82

IGP (Interior Gateway Protocols), 128

IP addresses, 108, 121

OSPF (Open Shortest Path First), 176

split horizon rule, 130

static routes, 126

general headers, 327-328

generic domains, 302

generic start lines, HTTP message formats, 326

generic trap ID (trap PDU field), 351

GET method tokens, 326

Gigabit Ethernet, Data Link architecture, 22

GOV domain, 302

governing groups, Internet technology, 31

Graphic User Interface (GUI), 323

graphic, defined, 323

groups, governing Internet technology, 31

GUI (Graphic User Interface), 323

H

half-duplex communication mode, Session layer (OSI Reference Model), 10

handshakes, three-way, 225-227

hardware

addresses, 91

ARP (Address Resolution Protocol) headers, 98

clients, 108, 122

RARP (Reverse Address Resolution Protocol) headers, 103

failure, 17

Htype (hardware type), 107

Htype (hardware type 1 byte), 120

sender's hardware addresses, 99, 104

target hardware addresses, 99, 104

types

ARP (Address Resolution Protocol) headers, 97

RARP (Reverse Address Resolution Protocol) headers, 103

Harslem, Eric, 270

Harvey, Brian (*Leaving Well Enough Alone*), 270

HDLC (High-Level Data Link Control), 29-30

HEAD method tokens, 326

headers

answer, domain server message format, 309

ARP (Address Resolution Protocol), 96-99

BGP (Border Gateway Protocols), 191-194

BOOTP (Boot Parameter) protocol, 105-109

DHCP (Dynamic Host Configuration Protocol) protocol, 106, 119-122

empty line (CRLF), 330

entity, 329-330

fields, SMTP (Simple Mail Transfer Protocol), 291

general, 326-328

HTTP message formats, 328-330

ICMP (Internet Control Message Protocol) formats, 75-76

IP (Internet Protocol), 62-73, 220

LSAs (link state advertisements), 160-162

OSPF (Open Shortest Path First), 175-180

pseudo, 218

pseudo IP, 246

question, domain server message format, 309-310

RARP (Reverse Address Resolution Protocol), 103-104

removing, 9

request, 328-329

response, 329

RIPv1, 142-144

TCP (Transmission Control Protocol), 212-218, 235

UDP (User Datagram Protocol), 244-247

Heafner, John, 270

hello interval field, 177

Hello messages, adjacency databases, 164

hello packet type, 174

Hello packets, 175-178

Hello/ACKs packets, 187

HELO command, 293

help, Frame Type Quick Reference, 21

HELP command, 293

HELP [string] command, 280

HEMS (High-level Entity Management), 345

HFTP access control commands, 278-279

high-layer, ARP cache mechanism, 94

High-Level Data Link Control (HDLC), 29-30

High-level Entity Management (HEMS), 345

HINFO (RR type), 310

history, FTP (File Transfer Protocol), 270

Hlen (hardware length), 107

Hlen (hardware length 1 byte), 120

hold down, 130-131

hold time field, 192

Holddown timers, 183

hops

BOOTP (Boot Parameter) protocol headers, 107

counts, maximum, 130-131

number of, 141

1 byte, 120

horizons, split horizon rule, 130

Host A and Host B, sending and receiving datagrams, 43

Host request headers, 329

Host-to-Host (DoD model), 203, 211, 241

hosts

acknowledgements, 233

ARP (Address Resolution Protocol), 92-94

bits, 45-46, 52

choke packets, 236

default routes, 127

dynamic routes, 128

flow control, 206, 236

headers and trailers, removing, 9

ICMP (Internet Control Message Protocol), 73-86

keepalives, 206

multiplexing, 219

ranges, calculating, 48-51

remote, 5, 257

routing, 125

server host names, 108, 122

sliding window control mechanisms, 206

static routes, 126-127

subnets, 42-43

window sizes, 235

HTTP (Hypertext Transfer Protocol), 251-252, 321-332

Htype (hardware type), 107

Htype (hardware type 1 byte), 120

hybrid protocols, 133, 184, 199

hyper (prefix), 252

hyper, definition, 321

Hypertext Transfer Protocol (HTTP), 251-252, 321-332

I-J

I (Init) or (More) Database Description packet option, 179

IAB (Internet Activities Board), 345

IAB (Internet Architecture Board), 31

ICMP (Internet Control Message Protocol), 73-86

ID (identifier), domain server message format, 306

identification, IP headers, 67

identifiers

    address family identifier field, 143

    checksum, 76

IDs

    1 ID value (LSAs), 161

    2 ID value (LSAs), 161

    3 ID value (LSAs), 161

    4 ID value (LSAs), 161

    5 ID value (LSAs), 161

    area ID field, 174

    generic trap ID (trap PDU field), 351

    link state ID field, 161, 180

    numbers, 312

    object ID and value, 350-351

    request ID (PDU field), 350

    router ID field, 174

    specific trap ID (trap PDU field), 351

    transactions, 107, 120, 362

IEEE 802.3 specification, 14-21, 24

IEEE 802.5 specification, 22-24

IETF (Internet Engineering Task Force), 31, 153

If-Modified-Since request headers, 329

If-None-Match request headers, 329

If-Range request headers, 329

If-Unmodified-Since request headers, 329

IGPs (Interior Gateway Protocols), 128, 137, 188-189

IGRP (Interior Gateway Routing Protocol), 128-129, 181-184

image file types, FTP (File Transfer Protocol), 276

implied acknowledgements, 214

inform messages, 112

Information Reply Type 16, 86

Information Request Type 15, 86

Init state (routers), 162-163

instances, 347

Integrated Services Digital Network (ISDN), 29

inter-area advertisements, 158-159

interfaces

    APIs (Application Programming Interfaces), 314

    directly connected, 126

    FDDI (Fiber Distributed Data Interface), 25

    GUI (Graphic User Interface), 323

    user, FTP (File Transfer Protocol), 270

Interior Gateway Protocols (IGPs), 128, 137, 188-189

Interior Gateway Routing Protocol (IGRP), 128-129, 181-184

internal peer routers, 189

internal routers, 167

International Organization for Standardization (ISO), 345-346

International Telecommunications Union, X.400 naming model (SMTP), 291

Internet

    ARIN (American Registry for Internet Numbers), 35

    domain names, 304-305

IAB (Internet Activities Board), 345

intranets, comparing, 31

routing tables, Web sites, 188

technology, governing groups, 31

Internet Activities Board (IAB), 345

Internet Architecture Board (IAB), 31

Internet Control Message Protocol (ICMP), 73-86

Internet Engineering Task Force (IETF), 31, 153

Internet Protocol. See IP

Internet Research Task Force (IRTF), 31

Internet Service Providers (ISPs), 53

Internet Society (ISOC), 31

interpreters, FTP (File Transfer Protocol), 270-271

intra-area advertisements, 157-158

intranets and Internet, comparing, 31

Invalid timers, 183

inverse mappings or queries, IP addresses, 305

IP (Internet Protocol), 61, 138

    address resolution, 89

    addresses, 108, 121, 144, 305

    addressing, 35-45, 53-58

    best paths, 129

    default routes, 127

    directly connected interfaces, 126

    distance-vector routing protocols, 129-131

    DLC (Data Link Control) headers, Ethernet value, 63

    dynamic routes, 128

    EIGRP (Enhanced Interior Gateway Routing Protocol), 133

    headers, 62-73, 220, 242, 246

hybrid routing protocols, 133

link state routing protocols, 132

RFC 791, 62

routing protocols, 129-133

static routes, 126-127

total length field, 64, 67, 71-73

IRTF (Internet Research Task Force), 31

ISDN (Integrated Services Digital Network), 29

ISO (International Organization for Standardization), 345-346

ISOC (Internet Society), 31

ISPs (Internet Service Providers), 53

K

Kahn, Robert, TCP (Transmission Control Protocol), 211

Keepalive messages, 194

keepalives, 206, 234

kernels (Unix), mount command, 356

keyboards, Telnet, 257

keystrokes, Telnet, 259

L

LANs (Local Area Networks), 168, 353-354

LAPB (Link Access Procedure, Balanced) (X.25) protocol, 30

Last-Modified entity headers, 330

late collisions, 17

layer 2 addresses, 13

layers

Application (OSI Reference model), 9-10, 251-253

Data Link (OSI Reference Model), 12-13

DoD (Department of Defense) Model, 5-6

high-layer, ARP cache mechanism, 94

Host-to-Host (DoD model), 203, 211, 241

Link, ARP cache mechanism, 94

Network (OSI Reference Model)

ARP (Address Resolution Protocol), 89-99

BOOTP (Bootstrap Protocol), 89

DHCP (Dynamic Host Configuration Protocol), 89

ICMP (Internet Control Message Protocol), 73-86

IP addressing, 35-53

IP (Internet Protocol), headers, 61-73

node addresses, 35

protocols, 12

RARP (Reverse Address Resolution Protocol), 89, 99-104

reachability information field, 193

RIP (Routing Information Protocol), 138

TCP (Transmission Control Protocol), 211

OSI Reference Model, 3-13, 249

Physical (OSI Reference Model), 13

Presentation (OSI Reference Model), 10, 253

Process/Application (DoD model), 249

Session (OSI Reference Model), 10-11

Transport (OSI Reference Model), 11-12

BOOTP (Boot Parameter) protocol, 104-105

DHCP (Dynamic Host Configuration Protocol), 110-122

hosts, 206

OSI Reference model, 203

ports, 207-209

protocols, 203-204

sockets, 207-209

TCP (Transmission Control Protocol), 203-207

UDP (User Datagram Protocol), 105-109, 203, 241

ULPs (upper layer protocols), 249, 251

lease duration, DHCP message exchanges, 119

leased (dedicated) lines, 26-27

Leaving Well Enough Alone, 270

length field, 162, 191, 245

lengths

Hlen (hardware length), 107

Hlen (hardware length 1 byte), 120

IP headers, 64, 67

line mode, 258

linefeed character text, 260

lines, 325-326, 330

Link layer, ARP cache mechanism, 94

link state acknowledgement packet type, 174

Link State Acknowledgement packets, 180-181

link state advertisements. *See* LSAs

Link State Algorithm (LSA), 152

link state databases (OSPF), 155

link state ID field, 161, 180

link state request packet type, 174

Link State Request packets, 179-180

link state routing protocols, 132

link state type field, 179

link state update packet type, 174

Link State Update packets, 180

links, virtual, 172-173

LIST [pathname] command, 280

load balancing, 155

Load metric, 182

Loading state (routers), 166

loads, IGRP networks, balancing and sharing, 184

local file types, FTP (File Transfer Protocol), 276

logical addressing, 12

logical circuits, 219

logical protocol addresses, 100-101

low-level addresses, 299

LS age field, 161

LS checksum field, 162

LS sequence number field, 162

LS type field, 161

LSA (Link State Algorithm), 152

LSAs (link state advertisements), 156

   1 ID value, 161

   1 link state type, 157-158

   2 ID value, 161

   2 link state type, 157-158

   3 ID value, 161

   3 link state type, 157-159

   4 ID value, 161

   4 link state type, 157-159

   5 ID value, 161

   5 link state type, 157-160

   7 link state type, 157-160

   areas, 170-173

   external advertisements, 159-160

   headers, 160-162

   inter-area advertisements, 158-159

   intra-area advertisements, 157-158

   link state advertisement field, 179-180

low-level addresses, 299

M

MAC (Media Access Control), 12

MAC address, low-level addresses, 299

MAIL FROM command, 293

Management Information Bases (MIBs), 346

managers, SNMP (Simple Network Management Protocol), 347

manual allocation of configuration information (DHCP), 111

mapping

   IP addresses, 305

   name resolution, 305

   names, Ethernet, 17

   NFS (Network File System), 357

   private addresses, 57

   TCP (Transmission Control Protocol), 203

   UDP (User Datagram Protocol), 203, 241

marker field, 191

masks

   subnet, 46-48

   VLSMs (variable length subnet masks), 44

Max-Forwards request headers, 329

maximum hop count, 130-131

McKenzie, Alex, 270

media (suffix), 252

Media Access Control (MAC), 12

message body (untransparent), 330

message formats

   domain servers, 306-310

   empty line (CRLF), 330

   entity headers, 329-330

   general headers, 326-328

   generic start lines, 326

   headers, 328

   HTTP (Hypertext Transfer Protocol), 325

   message body (untransparent), 330

   request headers, 328-329

   response headers, 329

   RIPv1, headers, 142-144

Message Transfer System (MTS), 290

messages

   ACK (acknowledgement), 112

   call, 361-365

   catchall, 85

   chunking, 327

   command, RIP (Routing Information Protocol), 142

   decline, 112

   DHCP (Dynamic Host Configuration Protocol), 111-112

   discover, 112

   error, 332-333

   exchanging, 112-119

   ICMP (Internet Control Message Protocol)

      0 (network unreachable), 79

1 (host unreachable), 79

2 (protocol unreachable), 79

3 (port unreachable), 79

4 (fragmentation needed), 80-81

5 (source route failed), 81

6 (destination network unknown), 81

7 (destination host unknown), 81

8 (source host isolated), 81

9 (destination network administratively prohibited), 81

10 (destination host administratively prohibited), 82

11 (network unreachable for ToS), 82

12 (host unreachable for ToS), 82

13 (communication administratively prohibited by filtering), 82

14 (host precedence violation), 82

15 (precedence cutoff in effect), 82

formats, 75-76

types, 77-86

inform, 112

Keepalive messages, 194

keepalives, 206

NAK, 112

Notification messages fields, 193-194

offer, 112

Open Messages fields, 191-192

release, 112

reply, stats lines, 325

request, 112, 325

response, 330-332

route pairs, 144

SNMP formats, 348-351

trap, 347

Update messages fields, 192-193

method tokens, 323, 326

metric field, RIPv1 headers, 144

methods, channel access, 16-17, 24-25

metrics, 181-182

MIBs (Management Information Bases), 346-347

MIL domain, 302

MINFO (RR type), 310

MKD [pathname] command, 280

models. *See also* DoD (Department of Defense) Model; OSI Reference Model

core-distribution-access, static routes, 126

X.400 naming model (SMTP), 289-290

modes

block transmission, 278

character, 258

compressed transmission, 278

line, 258

reception in XDR (External Data Representation), 360

stream transmission, 278

transmission, 258, 274-275, 278

MODE [mode] command, 279

mound command, 356

mount server procedures, RPC call messages, 365

MS (Master/Slave) (Database Description packet option), 179

MTAs (message transfer agents), 291

MTS (Message Transfer System), 290

multipath routing, 183

multiple area implementation, 169-170

Multiplexer/Demultiplexer (MUX/DEMUX), 28

multiplexing hosts, 219

MUX/DEMUX (Multiplexer/Demultiplexer), 28

MX (RR type), 310

my autonomous system field, 192

N

NAK messages, 112

name mapping, Ethernet, 17

name resolution, 299

DNS (Domain Naming System), 301-312

IP addresses, resolving, 305

namespace, 300-301

NetBEUI (NetBIOS Basic Extended User Interface), 313

NetBIOS (Network Basic Input Output System), 313-315

NIC (Network Information Center), 300

name servers, 302-304

names

boot files, 109, 122

community, SNMP message formats, 349

DNS (domain name system), 252

domains, 304-305

server hosts, 108, 122

URN (Uniform Resource Name), 324

X.400 naming model (SMTP), 289-290

namespace, 300-301

NAT (network address translation), 55-58

NBMA (nonbroadcast multiaccess) networks, 168-169

negotiations, capability, 322

neighbor field, 178

neighbor routers, 189

Neigus, Nancy, 270

NET domain, 302

NetBEUI (NetBIOS Basic Extended User Interface), 313-314

NetBIOS (Network Basic Input Output System), 11, 313-315

network address translation (NAT), 55-58

Network Basic Input Output System (NetBIOS), 11, 313-315

Network File System. *See* NFS

Network Information Center (NIC), 300

Network layer (OSI Reference Model)

ARP (Address Resolution Protocol), 89-99

BOOTP (Bootstrap Protocol), 89

DHCP (Dynamic Host Configuration Protocol), 89

ICMP (Internet Control Message Protocol), 73-86

IP addressing, 35-53

IP (Internet Protocol), headers, 61-73

node addresses, 35

protocols, 12

RARP (Reverse Address Resolution Protocol), 89, 99-104

reachability information field, 193

RIP (Routing Information Protocol), 138

TCP (Transmission Control Protocol), 211

network mask field, 176

network virtual terminal (NVT), 252, 259-260

networking complexity, OSI Reference Model layers, reducing, 7

networks. *See also* Telnet

areas, 170-173

AS (autonomous systems), 138

breaking up, 44

broadcast-based LAN, 168

Class B, 44, 49-51

default routes, 127

dynamic routes, 128

echo replies, 74

echo requests, 74

ICMP message errors, 79-82

IGRP (Interior Gateway Routing Protocol), 182-184

multiple area implementation, 169-170

NAT (network address translation), 55-58

NBMA (nonbroadcast multiaccess), 168-169

point-to-point connections, 168

SNMP (Simple Network Management Protocol), 345-351

static routes, 126-127

subnet masks, 40-43

subnetting, 44-55

traffic, routing or shouting, 40

WAN (Wide Area Network) technologies, 25-30

NFS (Network File System), 10

cd command, 359

clients, 357-358

features, 354

mapping, 357

multi-vendor products, 355-356

operation, 356

RPC (Remote Procedure Calls), 353

server procedures, RPC call messages, 364-365

servers, 358-359

users, autofs (auto file system), 359

version 2 or version 3 features, 354-355

XDR (External Data Representation), 353

NIC (Network Information Center), 300

NLST [pathname] command, 280

node addresses, 35

non-transparent proxy agents, 323

nonbroadcast multiaccess (NBMA), 168-169

nonprint (default) format control, 276

NOOP command, 280, 293

not authoritative name servers, 304

not so stubby areas (NSSAs), 159, 171-172

Notification messages fields, 193-194

NS (RR type), 310

NSCOUNT, domain server message format, 309

NSSAs (not so stubby areas), 159, 171-172

number of advertisements field, 180

numbering systems, binary or decimal, 33

numbers
acknowledgement, 214-215
ARIN (American Registry for Internet Numbers), 35
binary, converting to decimal numbers, 33-34
checksum sequence, 76
IDs, 312
LS sequence number field, 162
sequence, 214
sequence number field, 179
TCP (Transmission Control Protocol) ports, 237-238
TCP and UDP ports, 431
three-digit number code, SMTP e-mail replies, 293-294
version number field, 174

numeric code, three-digit (FTP), 281
NVT (Network Virtual Terminal), 252, 259-260

O

OACK (option acknowledgement) packet, 342-343
object ID and value, 350-351
objectives, FTP (File Transfer Protocol), 269
objects, instances, 347
octets, TCP (Transmission Control Protocol), 232
offer messages, 112
offsets
data, 215
fragment, IP headers, 68-71
on position, binary numbers, converting to decimal numbers, 34
ONC (Open Network Computing), 353-354

Op (operation code), 107
Op (operation code 1 byte), 119
Opcode (operation code), 99, 103, 306
Open Messages fields, 191-192
Open Network Computing (ONC), 353-354
Open Shortest Path First. *See* OSPF
operating systems, company developed, 3
operation code (Op), 107
operation code 1 byte (Op), 119
operation code. *See* OP; Opcode
operations
ARP (Address Resolution Protocol), 91-94
BGP (Border Gateway Protocols), 190-191
EIGRP (Enhanced Interior Gateway Routing Protocol), 184-186
NFS (Network File System), 356-359
OSPF (Open Shortest Path First), 156-162
Proxy ARP (Address Resolution Protocol), 95-96
RARP (Reverse Address Resolution Protocol), 100-101
logical protocol addresses, 100-102
TCP (Transmission Control Protocol), 218-222
TFTP (Trivial File Transfer Protocol), 340
UDP (User Datagram Protocol), 242-244
option acknowledgement (OACK) packets, 342
optional nontransitive attribute (4—Multi-Exit-Disc type code), 196-197

optional nontransitive category (path attributes), 195-196
optional parameters field, 192
optional parameters length field, 192
optional transitive attribute (7—Aggregator type code), 197
optional transitive category (path attributes), 195-197
options
field, 161, 177-179
IP headers, 73
variable lengths, 122, 217-218
OPTIONS method tokens, 326
ORG domain, 302
origin servers, HTTP (Hypertext Transfer Protocol), 323
OSI Reference Model
Application layer, 9-10, 251-253
conceptual frameworks, 4
Data Link layer, 12-13
ISO (International Organization for Standardization), 346
layers, 3-13, 249
mapping to WAN protocols, 26
Network layer
ARP (Address Resolution Protocol), 89-99
BOOTP (Bootstrap Protocol), 89
DHCP (Dynamic Host Configuration Protocol), 89
ICMP (Internet Control Message Protocol), 73-86
IP addressing, 35-53
IP (Internet Protocol), headers, 61-73

node addresses, 35

protocols, 12

RARP (Reverse Address Resolution Protocol), 89, 99-104

reachability information field, 193

RIP (Routing Information Protocol), 138

TCP (Transmission Control Protocol), 211

Physical layer, 13

Presentation layer, 10, 253

protocols, 4

redirectors, 5

remote hosts, 5

Session layer, 10-11

TCP (Transmission Control Protocol), 211

Telnet, 258

Transport layer, 11-12

BOOTP (Boot Parameter) protocol, 104-105

DHCP (Dynamic Host Configuration Protocol), 110-122

hosts, 206

OSI Reference model, 203

ports, 207-209

protocols, 203-204

sockets, 207-209

TCP (Transmission Control Protocol), 203-207

UDP (User Datagram Protocol), 105-109, 203, 241

when to use, 5

OSPF (Open Shortest Path First), 128, 132

ABR routers, 167

area ID field, 174

areas, 170-173

ASBR routers, 167

authentication field, 175

backbone routers, 167

broadcast-based LAN networks, 168

characteristics, 154-155

checksum field, 174

data link architectures, 167

database description packet type, 174

Database Description packets, 178-179

databases, 155

and Distance-vector routing protocols, comparing, 153

external advertisements, 159-160

fields, 173-175

gateways, 176

headers, 175

Hello messages, adjacency databases, 164

hello packet type, 174

Hello packets, 175-178

inter-area advertisements, 158-159

internal routers, 167

intra-area advertisements, 157-158

link state acknowledgement packet type, 174

Link State Acknowledgement packets, 180-181

link state request packet type, 174

Link State Request packets, 179-180

link state update packet type, 174

Link State Update packets, fields, 180

load balancing, 155

LSA (Link State Algorithm), 152

LSAs (link state advertisements), 156, 160-162

multiple area implementation, 169-170

NBMA (nonbroadcast multiaccess) networks, 168-169

operation, 156-157

options field, E bit or T bit, 177

packet length field, 174

packet type field, 173-174

point-to-point connections, 168

router ID field, 174

router states, 162-166

router types, 167

version 1, 153

version 2, 153

version number field, 174

P

packet length field, 174

packet type field, 173-174

packet-switched connections, 26-28

packets

9 (request) packet, 150

10 (response) packet, 150

11 (acknowledgement) packet, 150

ACK (acknowledgement), 338

choke, 236

data, 338

Database Description, 178-179

database description type, 174

delivering, 221-222

demand circuit, 150

error, 339

framing, 12

Hello, 175-178

hello type, 174

Hello/ACKs, 187

Link State Acknowledgement, 180-181

link state acknowledgement type, 174

Link State Request, fields, 179-180

link state request type, 174

Link State Update, fields, 180

link state update type, 174

OACK (option acknowledgement), 343

queries, 187

replies, 187

requests, 187

RRQ (request to read), 337-338

switching, 12

TFTP (Trivial File Transfer Protocol), 336-338

types, 149-150, 187

updates, 187

WRQ, 337-338

padding IP headers, 73

pages, FTP structure, 277

pairing sockets, 11, 219, 224-227

parameter field, bits, 308-309

Parameter Problem Type 12, 85

parameters, FTP (File Transfer Protocol), 274

partial-mesh topology, 189

partitions (domains), zones, 303

PASS [password] command, 278

PASV command, 279

path attributes

BGP (Border Gateway Protocol), 191, 194-198

field, 193

optional nontransitive attribute, 196-197

optional transitive attribute, 197

well-known discretionary attribute, 196-198

well-known mandatory attribute, 195-196

paths

hops, number of, 141

multipath routing, 183

selecting, 140-141

PDUs (Protocol Data Units), 348-351

peer routers, 189-190

Physical layer (OSI Reference Model), 13

Ping, 85

echo replies or requests, 74

Echo Reply Type 0, 77-78

point-to-point leased lines, 26

point-to-point connections, 168

Point-to-Point Protocol (PPP), 30

poison reverse, 130, 146

polls, unicast, ARP cache mechanism, 94

port 23 (Telnet), 257

ports, 11

destination, 213, 245

ICMP message error, 3 (port unreachable), 79

NetBIOS TCP/IP, 315

source, 213, 245

TCP (Transmission Control Protocol)

FTP (File Transfer Protocol), 271

numbers, 237-238

and UDP, numbers, 431

Telnet, 208

Transport layer, 207-209

UDP (User Datagram Protocol), 244, 311-312

PORT [host-port] command, 279

POST method tokens, 326

Postel, Joh, 270

PPP (Point-to-Point Protocol), 30

pragma field, 327

precedence

bits (bits 0–2), 64-65

ICMP message errors, 15 (precedence cutoff in effect), 82

security, 222-223

prefixes, hyper, 252

Presentation layer (OSI Reference Model), 10, 253

print services, requests, redirectors, 5

private addresses, mapping, 57

procedures, servers, RPC call messages, 364-365

Process/Application (DoD model), 249

products (NFS), multi-vendors, 355-356

program (RPC call messages), registered, 362-364

propagation delay, 17

Protocol Data Units (PDUs), 348-351

protocols. See also ARP; BGP; IP;

NFS; OSI; OSPF; TCP; Telnet; UDP

ATM (Asynchronous Transfer Mode), 30

balanced hybrid protocols, 184

comparing
    header fields, 191
    IGPs (Interior Gateway Protocols) and EGPs (Exterior Gateway Protocols), comparing, 188-189
    Keepalive messages, 194
    length field, 191
    marker field, 191
    Notification messages fields, 193-194
    open messages fields, 191-192
    Open Messages fields, 192
    operation, 190-191
    path attributes, 194-198
    routers, 189-190
    type field, 191
    Update messages fields, 192-193

BOOTP (Bootstrap Protocol), 89, 104-109

class routing, 132

classful routing, 132, 147

client PI (protocol interpreter), 270-271

CMIP (Common Management Information Protocol), 345

connection-oriented, 204-207, 223-237

connectionless, 206-207

DHCP (Dynamic Host Configuration Protocol), 89, 110-122

distance-vector, 129-131, 184

Distance-vector routing protocols, 146, 153

EGPs (Exterior Gateway Protocols), 128, 137

EIGRP (Enhanced Interior Gateway Routing Protocol), 128, 133, 184-186

encapsulation, WAN (Wide Area Network) technologies, 29-30

Frame Relay protocol, 29

FTP (File Transfer Protocol), 243, 269-272, 335

HDLC (High-Level Data Link Control), 29-30

HEMS (High-level Entity Management), 345

Host-to-Host layer, protocols, 203

HTTP (Hypertext Transfer Protocol), 251-252 321-332

hybrid, 133, 199

IAB (Internet Activities Board), 345

ICMP (Internet Control Message Protocol), 73-86

IGPs (Interior Gateway Protocols), 128, 137

IGRP (Interior Gateway Routing Protocol), 181-184

ISDN (Integrated Services Digital Network), 29

ISO (International Organization for Standardization), 346

link state routing, 132

Network layer (OSI Reference Model), 12

PDUs (Protocol Data Units), 348-351

PPP (Point-to-Point Protocol), 30

Presentation layer (OSI Reference model), 253

RARP (Reverse Address Resolution Protocol), 89, 99-104

RIP (Routing Information Protocol), 128, 138

RIPv1, 128

RIPv2, 128

routing, 129-133, 137

RPC (Remote Procedure Calls), 353

SDLC (Synchronous Data Link Control), 29

sender's protocol addresses, 99, 104

server PI (protocol interpreter), 271

single-routing-protocols, 184

SLIP (Serial Line Internet Protocol), 30

SMTP (Simple Mail Transfer Protocol), 252, 287-294

SNMP (Simple Network Management Protocol), 345-351

SubNetwork Access Protocol (IEEE 802.3) (Ethernet frame type), 17

target protocol addresses, 99, 104

TFTP (Trivial File Transfer Protocol), 243, 253, 335-343

Transport layer, 203-209

ULPs (upperlayer protocols), 249-251

WAN (Wide Area Network), mapping OSI Reference Model, 26

X.25 LAPB (Link Access Procedure, Balanced) protocol, 30

XDR (eXternal Data Representation), 10, 353

proxies

    agents, 323-324

    HTTP (Hypertext Transfer Protocol), 323

    servers, 322

    SNMP (Simple Network Management Protocol), 348

Proxy ARP (Address Resolution Protocol), 95-96

Proxy-Authorization request headers, 329

pseudo headers, 218, 246-247

PSH (push) control flag, 216

PTR (RR type), 310

public domains, 348

push (PSH) control flag, 216

PUT method tokens, 326

PWD command, 280

Q

QDCOUNT, domain server message format, 309

QR (query or response), domain server message format, 306

queries, 305

queries packets, 187

query or response (QR), domain server message format, 306

question headers, domain server message format, 309-310

QUIT command, 279, 293

R

RA (recursion available) flag, 307

rames, Ethernet_802.3, 20

Range request headers, 329

ranges, calculating

    hosts, 48-51

    subnets, 47

RARP (Reverse Address Resolution Protocol), 89, 99-104

Rcode, domain server message format, 307-309

RCPT TO command, 293

RD (recursion desired) flag, 307

records

    FTP structure, 277

    RRs (Resource Records), 309-310

Redirect Type 5, 83

redirectors

    clients, 251

    OSI Reference Model, 5

reference models. *See* OSI Reference Model

references, Frame Type Quick Reference, 21

Referer request headers, 329

registered programs (RPC call messages), 362-364

REIN command, 279

release messages, 112

reliability (guaranteed packet delivery), 221-222

Reliability metric, 182

remote hosts

    OSI Reference Model, 5

    Telnet, 257

Remote Procedure Calls (RPCs), 11, 353, 360-365

removing headers or trailers, 9

repeating, bit repeating, 23

replies

    BOOTP (Boot Parameter) protocol, 109

    echo, 74

    FTP (File Transfer Protocol), 281

    SMTP (Simple Mail Transfer Protocol), 293-294

replies packets, 187

reply messages, stats lines, 325

Request for Comments (RFCs), 30-31, 35

request ID (PDU field), 350

request to read (RRQ), 336

request to write (WRQ), 336

requests

    bad request error messages, 332-333

    BOOTP (Boot Parameter) protocol, 109

    chains, 324

    echo, 74

    file or print, redirectors, 5

    headers, 328-329

    HTTP (Hypertext Transfer Protocol), 322

    lines (request messages), 325

    messages, 112, 325

    mounting or unmounting, NFS clients, 357

    9 (request) packet, 150

    packets, 187

Requests for Comments. *See* RFCs

reserved TCP headers, 216

reserved addresses, 39

reset (RST) control flag, 217

resolution of addresses, 89

resolution of names. *See* name resolution

resolving IP addresses, 305

resource records (RRs), 302, 309-310

resources, HTTP (Hypertext Transfer Protocol), 323

responders, servers, 251

response headers, 329

response messages, 330-332

responses, 10 (response) packet, 150

REST [marker] command, 280

retransmissions, 233

RETR [pathname] command, 280

returns, carriage, FTP (File Transfer Protocol) commands, 280

Reverse Address Resolution Protocol (RARP), 89, 99-104

Reynolds, Joyce, 270

RFC 791, 62

RFC 821, SMTP (Simple Mail Transfer Protocol), 287

RFC 822, SMTP (Simple Mail Transfer Protocol), 289

RFC 1123, SMTP (Simple Mail Transfer Protocol), 290

RFCs (Requests for Comments), 30

  Address Resolution, 374

  FTP (File Transfer Protocol), 396-398

  HTTP (Hypertext Transfer Protocol), 414-415

  Industry Models and Standards, 371

  IP Addressing, 371

  IP Routing, 375-382

  Name Resolution, 410-414

  Network Layer/Internet Protocols, 371-374

  Open Network Computing Protocols, 421

  Routing Protocols, 382-388

  SMTP (Simple Mail Transfer Protocol), 398-410

  SNMP (Simple Network Management Protocol), 416-421

  TCP (Transmission Control Protocol), 389-391

  Telnet, 391-396

  TFTP (Trivial File Transfer Protocol), 415

  Transport/Host-to-Host Layer, 389

  UDP (User Data Protocol), 391

  Web site, 31

RIP (Routing Information Protocol), 128

  1 command, 142

  2 command, 143

  3 command, 143

  4 command, 143

  5 command, 143

  9 command, 143

  10 command, 143

  11 command, 143

  advertisements, 144

  AS (autonomous systems), 138

  Bellman-Ford algorithm, 138

  classful routing protocols, subnetting, 147

  command messages, 142

  demand circuits, 148-150

  gateways, 139-140

  messages, route pairs, 144

  Network layer protocol, 138

  paths, hops, number of, 141

  RIPv1 (version 1), 138-147, 151-152

  RIPv2 (version 2), 138, 150-152

  routers, 146

  timers, 147-148

  triggered updates, 149

RIPv1 (distance-vector routing protocol), 128-129

  disadvantages, 144-145, 147

  headers, 142-144

  message formats, headers, 142

  path selection, 140-141

  RFC 1058, 138

  RIPv2, comparing, 151-152

RIPv2 (distance-vector routing protocol), 128-129

  RFC 2453, 138

  RIPv1, comparing, 151-152

RMD [pathname] command, 280

RNFR [pathname] command, 280

RNTO [pathname] command, 280

route pairs, RIP messages, 144

route summarization, Class C addresses, 53-55

route update traffic control, 148

Router Advertisement Type 9, 84

router ID field, 174

router priority field, 177

Router Solicitation Type 10, 84

routers

  ABR, 167

  advertising router field, 161

  areas, 170-173

  ASBR, 167

  backbone, 167

  best paths, 129

  BGP (Border Gateway Protocols), 189-190

  broadcast-based LAN networks, 168

  EIGRP (Enhanced Interior Gateway Routing Protocol), 186

  Exchange state, 165-166

  Exstart state, 164-165

  external advertisements, 159-160

  external peer, 189

  Full state, 166

  ICMP (Internet Control Message Protocol), 73-86

  Init state, 162-163

  inter-area advertisements, 158-159

  internal, 167, 189

  intra-area advertisements, 157-158

  Loading state, 166

  multiple area implementation, 169-170

NBMA (nonbroadcast multiaccess) networks, 168-169

neighbor, 189

OSPF Hello messages, adjacency databases, 164

packet switching, 12

peers, 189-190

point-to-point connections, 168

poison reverse, 146

private addresses, mapping, 57

RIP, 146

routing protocols, 137

speaker, 189

states of, 162-166

Two-Way state, 163

types of, 167

routes

best paths, 129

default, 127

directly connected interfaces, 126

dynamic, 128

feasible successor, 185-186

ICMP message errors, 5 (source route failed), 81

static, 126-127

successor, 185-186

routing

CIDR (class interdomain routing), 52-55

classfulless, 132

classless, 132

DDR (dial-on-demand), 28

definition, 40

hosts, 125

multipath, 183

purpose, 125

Snapshot, 149

Routing Information Protocol. *See* RIP

routing protocols, 129, 137

classful, subnetting, 147

distance-vector, 129-131

EIGRP (Enhanced Interior Gateway Routing Protocol), 133

hybrid, 133

link state, 132

routing tables, Web sites, 188

RPCs (Remote Procedure Calls), 11, 353, 360-365

RRQ (request to read) packets, 336-338

RRs (resource records), 302, 309-310

RSET command, 293

RST (reset) control flag, 217

rules, split horizon, 130

S

SA (source address field), 24

SAML FROM command, 293

SDLC (Synchronous Data Link Control), 29

seconds, protocol headers, 107, 121

security

authentication field, 175

precedence, 222-223

SEND FROM command, 293

sender's hardware or protocol addresses, 99, 104

sequence number field, 179

sequence numbers, 76, 214

sequences, connection-oriented protocols, 230-234

Serial Line Internet Protocol (SLIP), 30

servers

DHCP (Dynamic Host Configuration Protocol), 112-119

domains, message formats, 306-310

DTP (data transfer process), 271

FTP (File Transfer Protocol)

connections, 272

server commands, 279-280

host names, protocol headers, 108, 122

HTTP (Hypertext Transfer Protocol), 322-323

IP addresses, protocol headers, 108, 121

mount procedures, RPC call messages, 365

names

authoritative or not authoritative, 304

RRs (resource records), 302

NFS (Network File System), 358-359, 364-365

PI (protocol interpreter), 271

proxy agents, 324

responders, 251

SMTP (Simple Mail Transfer Protocol), 287

Telnet, 257

Session layer (OSI Reference Model), 10-11

sessions

connection-oriented protocols223-230

FTP (File Transfer Protocol), 270-272

HTTP (Hypertext Transfer Protocol), 322-325

Telnet, starting, 257

SGMP (Simple Gateway Management Protocol), SNMP (Simple Network Management Protocol), 345-351

sharing IGRP network loads, 184

shouting, definition, 40

signaling, balanced or unbalanced, 15

Simple Gateway Management Protocol (SGMP), SNMP (Simple Network Management Protocol), 345-351

Simple Mail Transfer Protocol (SMTP), 252, 287-294

Simple Network Management Protocol (SNMP), 345-351

single-routing-protocols, 184

sites, Web
RFCs (Request for Comments), 31
routing tables, 188

SITE [string] command, 280

Slash 8 (Class A) addresses, 35-40

Slash 16 (Class B) addresses, 35-40

Slash 24 (Class C) addresses 35-40

sliding window control mechanisms, 206

SLIP (Serial Line Internet Protocol), 30

Slow Ethernet, 21

SMI (Standard Management Information), 346

SMNT [pathname] command, 279

SMTP (Simple Mail Transfer Protocol), 252, 287-294

SNA (Systems Network Architecture), 29

SNAP frames, IEEE's 802.3, 20

Snapshot routing, 149

Sniffer, acknowledgement numbers, 215

SNMP (Simple Network Management Protocol), 345-351

SOA (RR type), 310

sockets
pairing, 11, 219, 224-227
Transport layer, 207-209

Solderblum, Olaf (Token-Ring LAN standard), 22

SOML FROM command, 293

source address field (SA), 24

source ports, 213, 245

Source Quench Type 4, 82

spaces, FTP (File Transfer Protocol) commands, 280

speaker routers, 189

specialization (OSI Reference Model layers), promoting, 7

specific trap ID (trap PDU field), 351

specifications
ANSI X3T9.5, 25
IEEE 802.3, 14-21, 24
IEEE 802.5, 22-24
Slow Ethernet, 21

split horizon rule, 130

spooling, 252

stability of IGRP networks, 183

standard areas (Area 0), 170-171

Standard Management Information (SMI), 346

standard stub areas, 171

standards
100BaseFX, 22
100BaseT4, 22
100BaseTX, 22
100BaseX, 22
Data Link architecture, 14

states
link state routing protocols, 132
of routers, 162-166

static NATs (network address translations), 57

static routes, 126-127

stats lines (reply messages, 325

status codes, response messages, 330-332

status lines (response messages), 330

STAT [pathname] command, 280

STOR [filename] command, 280

STOU command, 280

stream transmission mode, 278

structures
FTP (File Transfer Protocol) data, 274-277
Token-Ring, 24

STRU [structure] command, 279

stub areas, 171-172

stubs, NSSAs (not so stubby areas), 159

subnets
bits, determining number of, 45-46
broadcast addresses, 52
Class B network, 49-51
host ranges, calculating, 50-51
hosts, 42-43
masks, 40-43, 46-48
ranges, calculating, 47

subnetting
Class B networks, 44
classful routing protocols, 147
IP addressing, 44-55

SubNetwork Access Protocol (IEEE 802.3) (Ethernet frame type), 17

successor routes, 185-186

suffixes, media, 252

summarization, 52-55

Sun Microsystems, 353

supernetting, 52-53

switching circuits, 27-28

switching packets, 12, 27-28

SYN (synchronization) control flag, 217, 224-230

Synchronous Data Link Control (SDLC), 29

SYST command, 280

systems

autonomous, multiple area implementation, 169-170

operating, company developed, 3

Systems Network Architecture (SNA), 29

T

T bit (OSPF options field), 177

tables (routing), Web sites, 188

target hardware or protocol addresses, 99, 104

TC (truncation) flag, 307

TCB (transmission control block), 218

TCP (Transmission Control Protocol), 11

ACK (acknowledgement) control flag, 224-229

values, 212-214

Cerf, Vinton, 211

connection-orientated protocol, 205-207, 223-237

connectionless protocols, 206

connections, setting up and tearing down, 219

data transfers, 220-221

FIN (finish) control flag, 227-229

flow control, 221

headers, 212-218, 235

Host-to-Host layer, 203, 211

implied acknowledgements, 214

IP headers, 220

Kahn, Robert, 211

logical circuits, 219

multiplexing, 219

Network layer, 211

octets, 232

operation, 218-219

OSI Reference model, 211

ports, 208, 237-238, 271

precedence and security, 222-223

reliability (guaranteed packet delivery), 221-222

SYN (synchronization) control flag, 224-227, 230

TCB (transmission control block), 218

three-way handshakes, 225-227

Transport layer, mapping to, 203

UDP (User Datagram Protocol), 244, 431

variable-length options, 217-218

windowing, stages, 236

zero windows, 236-237

TCP/IP (Transmission Control Protocol/Internet Protocol), 3, 314-315

tearing down connections, 219

technologies

Internet, governing groups, 31

WAN (Wide Area Network), 25-30

Telnet (Telecommunications network)

Application layer (OSI Reference model), 252

ASCII (American Standard Code for Information Interchange), 260

carriage control text, 260

clients, 257-258

DoD model, 258

dumb terminals, 257

format control, 276

keyboards, 257

keystroke travel, 259

linefeed character text, 260

NVT (Network Virtual Terminal), 252, 259-260

OSI model, 258

port 23, 257

remote hosts, 257

servers, 257

services, 259-260

sessions, starting, 257

TCP ports, 208

terminals

dumb, 257

NVT (Network Virtual Terminal), 259-260

text, carriage control ir linefeed character, 260

TFTP (Trivial File Transfer Protocol), 243, 253, 335-343

FTP (File Transfer Protocol), 243, 253, 269-280, 335

three-digit number code, 281, 293-294

three-way handshakes, 225-227

time, Delay Time metric, 181

Time Exceeded Type 11, 84-85

time stamp (trap PDU field), 351

time to live (TTL), IP headers, 71-72

timeout, ARP cache mechanism, 94

timers, 147-148, 183-184, 233-234

Timestamp Reply Type 14, 86

Timestamp Request Type 13, 86

Token-Ring, 22-25

tokens, 25, 323, 326

top-level domains, 302

topologies, full-mesh or partial-mesh, 189

ToS (Type of Service)

bits (8 total bits), IP headers, 64

datagrams, 222

FTP (File Transfer Protocol), 272

ICMP message errors, 82

total length field, IP headers, 67

total path attribute length field, 193

Trace method tokens, 326

traceroute utility, 85

traffic, 40, 148

trailer field, 327

trailers, removing, 9

transaction IDs, 107, 120, 362

transfer-encoding field, 327-328

transferring

data, 220-221

files, 253

transfers, bidirectional, 322

transmission control block (TCB), 218

Transmission Control Protocol. *See* TCP

transmission modes, 258, 274-278

transmissions, retransmissions, 233

transparent proxy agents, 323

Transport layer (OSI Reference Model), 11-12

BOOTP (Boot Parameter) protocol, 104-105

DHCP (Dynamic Host Configuration Protocol), 110-122

hosts, 206

OSI Reference model, 203

ports, 207-209

protocols, 203-204

sockets, 207-209

TCP (Transmission Control Protocol), 203-207

UDP (User Datagram Protocol), 105-109, 203, 241

trap messages, 347

trap PDUs (Protocol Data Units), 350-351

triggered updates, 149

Trivial File Transfer Protocol (TFTP), 243, 253, 335-343

FTP (File Transfer Protocol), 243, 253, 269-280, 335

TTL (time to live), IP headers, 71-72

tunnels, HTTP (Hypertext Transfer Protocol), 323

TURN command, 293

Two-Way state (routers), 163

TXT (RR type), 310

Type 0 (Echo Reply), 77-78

Type 3 (Destination Unreachable), 78-82

Type 4 (Source Quench), 82

Type 5 (Redirect), 83

Type 8 (Echo Request), 77-78

Type 9 (Router Advertisement), 84

Type 10 (Router Solicitation), 84

Type 11 (Time Exceeded), 84-85

Type 12 (Parameter Problem), 85

Type 13 (Timestamp Request), 86

Type 14 (Timestamp Reply), 86

Type 15 (Information Request), 86

Type 16 (Information Reply), 86

Type 17 (Address Mask Request), 86

Type 18 (Address Mask Reply), 86

type field, 191

Type of Service (ToS), datagrams, 222

types, RPC call messages, 362

types of messages, ICMP (Internet Control Message Protocol), 73-86

TYPE [type] command, 279

U

UAs (user agents), 287-290, 324

HTTP (Hypertext Transfer Protocol), 323

request headers, 329

UDP (User Datagram Protocol), 11, 138

applications, 243

BOOTP (Boot Paramater) protocol, 105

CRC (Cyclic Redundancy Check), 246

headers, 244-247

Host-to-Host layer, 203, 241

IP headers, 242

operations, 242-243

ports, 244, 311-312

pseudo IP headers, 246

TCP (Transmission Control Protocol), 244, 431

Transport layer, mapping to, 203, 241

ULPs (upper layer protocols), 249-253

unbalanced signaling, 15

unfeasible routes length field, 193

unicast poll, ARP cache mechanism, 94

Uniform Resource Identifiers (URIs), 324

Uniform Resource Name (URN), 324

Unix kernel, mount command, 356

untransparent message body, 330

unused, BOOTP (Boot Parameter) protocol headers, 107

unused field, RIPv1 headers, 143

Update messages fields, 192-193

update packets, 187

Update timers, 183

updates, triggered, 149

upgrade field, 328

upper layer protocols (ULPs),
249-253

URG (urgent) control flag, 216

Urgent Pointer (2 bytes), 217

URIs (Uniform Resource
Identifiers), 324

URN (Uniform Resource Name),
324

user agents. *See* UAs

User Datagram Protocol. *See* UDP

user datagrams, routing purpose,
125

user interfaces, FTP (File Transfer
Protocol), 270

users, NFS, autofs (auto file
system), 359

USER [username] command, 279

utilities

    Ping, 85

        echo replies or requests,
74

        Echo Reply Type 0,
77-78

    traceroute, 85

V

values

    ACK (acknowledgement),
212-214

    object ID and value, 350-351

variable length subnet masks
(VLSMs), 44

variable-length options, TCP
headers, 217-218

vectors, distance-vector routing
protocols, 129-131

vendors

    BOOTP (Boot Parameter)
protocol headers, 109

    NFS products, 355-356

    OSI Reference Model layers, 7

version 2 (NFS) features, 354-355

version 3 (NFS) features, 354-355

version 4 (IP), 64

version field, 143, 192

version number field, 174

versions

    Ethernet, 14-15

    RPC call messages, 362

    SNMP (Simple Network
Management Protocol), 349

via field, 328

views, MIB (Management
Information Bases), 347

virtual links, 172-173

VLSMs (variable length subnet
masks), 44, 132

voltage, balanced or unbalanced
signaling, 15

VRFY command, 293

W

WAN (Wide Area Network), 25-30,
353-354

warning field, 328

Web browsers, HTTP (Hypertext
Transfer Protocol), 323

Web sites

    RFCs (Request for
Comments), 31

    routing tables, 188

well-known discretionary attribute,
196-198

well-known discretionary category
(path attributes), 195-197

well-known mandatory attribute,
195-196

well-known mandatory category
(path attributes),
195-196

Wide Area Network (WAN), 25-30,
353-354

windowing, stages, 236

windows

    TCP headers, 217, 235

    zero, 236-237

withdrawn routes field, 193

WRQ (request to write), 336-338

WWW (World Wide Web),
251-252, 321

X-Z

X.25 LAPB (Link Access Procedure,
Balanced) protocol, 30

X.400 naming model (SMTP),
289-291

XDR (eXternal Data
Representation) protocol, 10,
353, 359-360

Zero flag, 307

zero windows, 236-237

zones, domain partitions, 303